OPERATION HUSKY

THE CANADIAN INVASION OF SICILY,

JULY 10—AUGUST 7, 1943

MARK ZUEHLKE

OPERATION HUSKY

DOUGLAS & McINTYRE

VANCOUVER/TORONTO/BERKELEY

Douglas & McIntyre Ltd.
2323 Quebec Street, Suite 201
Vancouver, British Columbia
Canada v5T 4s7
www.douglas-mcintyre.com

Library and Archives Canada Cataloguing in Publication
Zuehlke, Mark

Operation Husky : the Canadian invasion of Sicily,
July 10–August 7, 1943 / Mark Zuehlke.

Includes bibliographical references and index.

ISBN 978-1-55365-324-0

1. Operation Husky, 1943.
2. Canada. Canadian Army. Canadian Infantry Division, 1st—History.
3. Canada. Canadian Army. Canadian Tank Brigade, 1st—History.
4. World War, 1939-1945-Campaigns—Italy—Sicily.
5. Canada. Canadian Army—History—World War, 1939–1945. I. Title.
D763.S5Z83 2008   940.54'2158   C2008-905370-2

Editing by Kathy Vanderlinden
Jacket design by Naomi MacDougall
Interior design by Peter Cocking
Typeset by Ingrid Paulson
Maps by C. Stuart Daniel/Starshell Maps
Jacket photographs by Alexander M. Stirton/Canada Dept. of
National Defence/Library and Archives Canada/PA-115031
Printed and bound in Canada by Friesens
Printed on forest-friendly paper
Distributed in the U.S. by Publishers Group West

We gratefully acknowledge the financial support of the Canada
Council for the Arts, the British Columbia Arts Council, the Province
of British Columbia through the Book Publishing Tax Credit,
and the Government of Canada through the Book Publishing Industry
Development Program (BPIDP) for our publishing activities.

4/5 July 1943
Dear Family:

   I am very proud and happy in the knowledge that I am going to lead a Company of so fine a Regiment in an Assault Landing such as we are going to do in the early morning of next Saturday. I talk to them in their mess deck, telling them of the specific jobs, etc. and I am a lucky man indeed to have such a good lot of lads under my command. The average age is 24, although there are a number who, claiming 20, look about 18. In their shorts and open-necked, rolled-up sleeved shirts they look like a bunch of Boy Scouts. It is hard to believe that these Western Ontario school boys of 1939, and in some cases later, are the "tough assault troops" which will be the newspapers' probable description of them.

   They all have fighting spirit, but are school boyish in their enthusiasm; it seems a shame that so many of these splendid fellows will be dead or wounded before this week is out.

                 —Captain Strome Galloway, Royal Canadian Regiment

[CONTENTS]

WITH THE 1999 publication of *Ortona: Canada's Epic World War II Battle*, I unwittingly committed myself to a series of books chronicling the Canadian Army's World War II experience. I say unwittingly, because during the research and writing of *Ortona*, no thought had been given to its being the first in a series. There was no way of telling whether the book could attract a readership sufficient to convince a publisher of the value of more such titles. Happily, *Ortona* was well received in Canada and even beyond the nation's borders. It continues to be so still today.

Ortona's success encouraged me to embark on a series wherein each book would provide an exhaustive account of a specific battle or campaign of pivotal importance to Canada's involvement in the war. The first outing consisted of two more books on the Italian Campaign—*The Liri Valley* and *The Gothic Line*—which, together with *Ortona*, became known as the Italian trilogy. Next, *Juno Beach* and *Holding Juno* detailed the invasion of Normandy—the former covering, as Cornelius Ryan called it, "the longest day" of June 6, 1944, and the latter, the six following days, when it remained in the balance whether the Allies would be able to retain their hold on the beachhead.

To this point the books had followed a loosely chronological order, except that *The Gothic Line*, which concluded the Italian campaign, recounted events that occurred after the Normandy invasion. This was logical, as it took the trilogy through to completion.

Thereafter, however, I decided to depart from chronological faithfulness and, instead of relating the story of the bitter July and August battles in Normandy, jump forward to write *Terrible Victory,* an account of the gruelling campaign First Canadian Army fought between September 13 and November 6, 1944, to open the Scheldt Estuary and the Belgian city of Antwerp to Allied shipping. I did this because the Scheldt Campaign—the Canadian Army's most costly of World War II—had been sadly shunted into obscurity. It seemed time to put the campaign back into the spotlight of national remembrance.

Foregoing a chronological approach to the series freed me to repair an inadvertent oversight. Starting with *Ortona* had excluded the Canadian Army's divisional-scale combat debut from the apparent boundaries of my work. Or so it had earlier seemed. But if I could jump forward in time, it was equally possible to travel back to earlier events.

Which brings us to *Operation Husky*—the book you are currently reading.

The Canadian role in Operation Husky, the invasion of Sicily, is yet another story that has been ill told. No Canadian work dedicated solely to this campaign has previously been published. Yet the Sicily campaign was of critical importance to the Canadian Army. Because it represented the first divisional-scale combat operation in World War II, Sicily was where many officers and men—who would form the backbone of First Canadian Army in future campaigns and battles—began their transformation from trained neophytes into combat veterans.

I was puzzled: why had no book about this experience been written before? My fear was that, rather than being pure coincidence or oversight, the cause might be a lack of source material. As it turned out, nothing could have been further from the truth. For a campaign involving one division and one tank brigade, engaged in a relatively short, twenty-eight-day period of combat, the amount of paper produced chronicling it was incredible. Many regimental war diaries were full of battle accounts written by company commanders and even platoon commanders. Stuffed away in files at Library and Archives Canada and in the vaults at the Directorate of History and Heritage, Department of National Defence, were hundreds of pages of detailed reports on various aspects and moments of the fighting. I was blessed with so many riches that the book could have grown almost exponentially in size, something that would guarantee publisher apoplexy.

As has been my wont in the other books, I have told the story by mixing personal accounts of veterans in with the material drawn from official records, regimental histories, and many other sources in order to give the reader a "you are there" experience. Still, every attempt has been made to ensure that events are portrayed accurately. In many cases it was possible to rationalize differing accounts through painstaking cross-referencing. This proved particularly necessary with regard to dates. For some reason, in Sicily more than anywhere I have seen before, the war diarists often seemed confused about what day of the month they were recording. I agree with the suspicion of the Canadian Army official historian that the cause of this was that some war diaries were not being updated daily but, rather, whenever was convenient. Surprisingly, however, this did not result in great inaccuracies regarding the facts of events beyond the attribution of incorrect dates.

I was also happy to find little discrepancy between the official record of how events played out and what veteran memory reported. This was surprising given the confusion natural to an amphibious landing, the incredibly complex and rugged Sicilian landscape, and the rapid pace at which the Canadians advanced across the battleground. Where there was disagreement, I followed my standard practice of consulting every source I could find and then drawing a reasonable conclusion.

It should be noted that with each book, the number of veterans able to give interviews diminishes. Passage of time is taking its toll on our veterans, and the rate of their passing increases each year. For some still with us, memories are dimming, even fading to black. There is still time, but not much, before the last veteran of a war that can now be thought of as occurring long ago is gone. If you have a relative or acquaintance who is a veteran, please consider sitting down and recording what memories remain. Such material is of inestimable value to historians of World War II. Whether you use a tape recorder, digital recorder, or video camera or simply write their memories out longhand, consider donating this record to an archive, museum, or other depository where it can be preserved and made available to researchers.

The men and women who fought in World War II were indelibly marked by that experience. What they did and what they believed after peace returned them home was influenced by surviving a war. If we are to understand that generation that became our parents or grandparents or even great-grandparents, it is necessary to comprehend the reality endured when they were soldiers and young.

ACKNOWLEDGEMENTS

FIRST OFF, SPECIAL thanks must go to several veterans who assisted in different ways. Sheridan "Sherry" Atkinson kindly provided written accounts of his experiences as a young Royal Canadian Regiment (RCR) lieutenant during Operation Husky. Syd Frost, despite being seriously ill, offered advice for finding the monument to Canadians that stands near Ispica. Another RCR officer, Strome Galloway, through the years discussed the Sicily and Italian campaigns many times with me over dinner, lunch, or a drink when I was able to visit him in Ottawa. He's gone now, but his friendship is not forgotten. The same holds true for John Dougan, who passed away in October 2006. My understanding of World War II combat was much enhanced by the memories and opinions these two fine men offered. Non-veterans also helped with providing the personal stories of soldiers. Ken MacLeod, now living in Courtenay, B.C., again made his interviews with veterans available and this book is the richer for it.

My good friend Alex MacQuarrie, an Ottawa translator, spent many hours translating French-language documents relevant to the Royal 22e Régiment and also made sense of some German material.

Fortune shone on me when Marilyn Minnes asked that I accompany her 2007 Legacy Battlefield Tour of the Italian Campaign as

5

the historian. This provided the perfect opportunity to visit the Sicily battlefields once again. Thanks to the tour group as well for being so good about understanding the difficulty I and the other drivers—yes, I drove a nine-person van around Sicily and Italy—had negotiating Sicilian highways and byways. Those other drivers, Richard Gimblett and Jim Pengelly, did a great job, and I enjoyed our dinnertime talks. Richard's map-reading skills saved the day countless times.

Dr. Steve Harris, at the Directorate of History and Heritage, Department of National Defence, and other staff there were exceedingly helpful to my efforts in tracking down various documents important to understanding the campaign. This was also the case with staff at Library and Archives Canada. At the Canadian War Museum, Carol Reid and Jane Naisbitt once again ensured that I saw everything in that institution's archive and library, respectively, that pertained to Operation Husky. As always, staff at University of Victoria Special Collections greatly assisted my consulting of Dr. Reginald Roy's papers and the oral history collection there. Chris Case in Ottawa dug into his files for the master's thesis he is writing and came up with some solid nuggets of information I was unable to get hands on otherwise. Major Michael Boire of Royal Military College provided a copy of the never-published regimental history of the Three Rivers Tank Regiment, which saved the day on several occasions. Casting way out to Newark, New Jersey, I found David H. Lippman, who offered many suggestions on where to look for valuable accounts relevant to the U.S. Seventh Army's operations in Sicily and even provided a copy of the U.S. official history of the campaign.

Special thanks to my agent, Carolyn Swayze, for helping to ensure that the financial and career considerations stayed on track, freeing me to focus on the writing.

I am fortunate to have the support of Scott McIntyre, my publisher at Douglas & McIntyre, who continually shows his belief in the value of this series. This time, my long-standing editor, Elizabeth McLean, was unable to take on the daunting task of editing such a complex work. Kathy Vanderlinden took over and did a fine job. C. Stuart Daniel of Starshell Maps once again drew the essential maps to help readers navigate the battlefields as described in the text.

In 2000, my partner Frances Backhouse and I travelled by train, bus, and foot around much of Sicily. By design, we stayed in Agira's single small hotel in order to descend on foot from that mountaintop town to the valley below so that someone could mark Remembrance Day in the Agira Canadian Cemetery. Her enthusiasm for this idea was typical, but most appreciated. Through the years, she has always been willing to trek across one more battlefield, offered support when I'm racing to beat the clock of another crazy-tight deadline, and lent a patient ear to endless comments on war and the relating of veteran stories. Thanks, love.

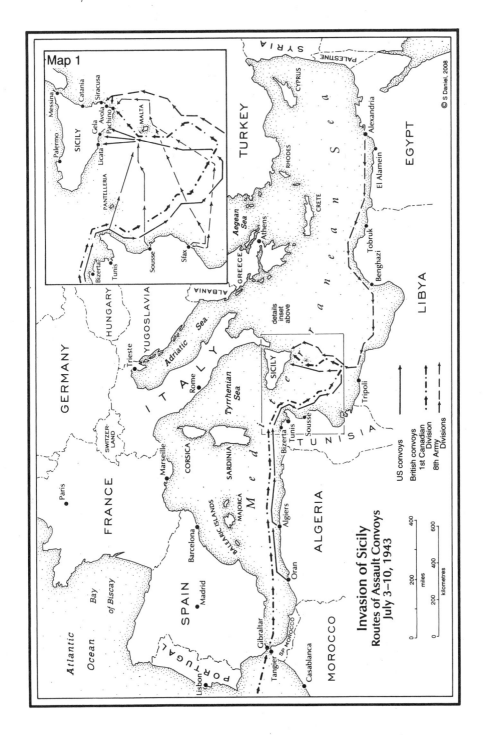

Map 1

Invasion of Sicily
Routes of Assault Convoys
July 3–10, 1943

US convoys
British convoys
1st Canadian Division
8th Army Divisions

© S Daniel, 2008

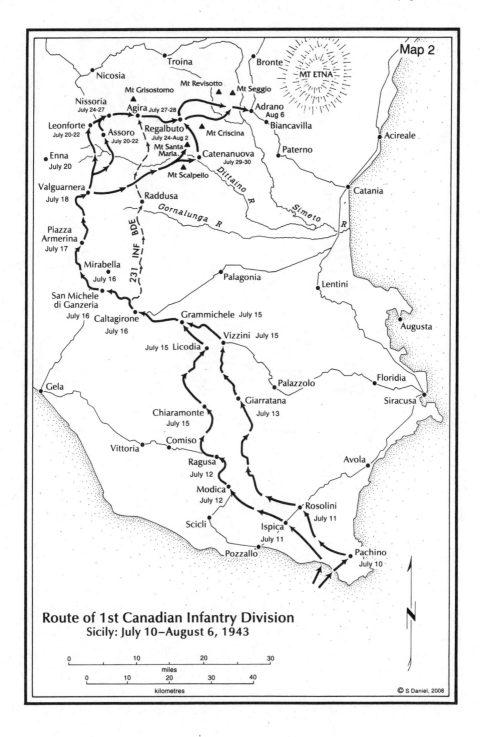

Map 2

Route of 1st Canadian Infantry Division
Sicily: July 10–August 6, 1943

© S Daniel, 2008

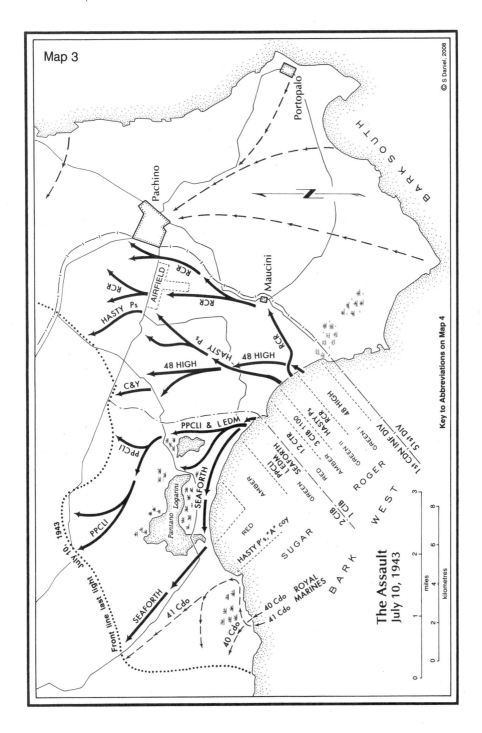

Map 3

© S Daniel, 2008

Key to Abbreviations on Map 4

The Assault
July 10, 1943

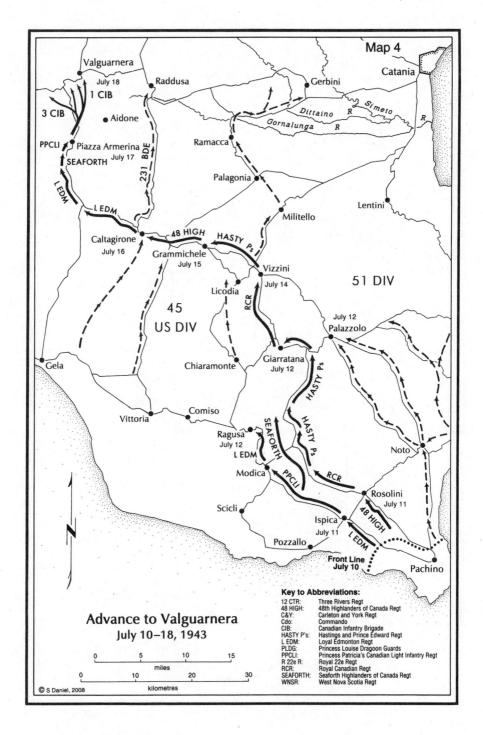

Map 4

Valguarnera
July 18
1 CIB
3 CIB
Aidone
Raddusa
Gerbini
Catania

PPCLI   Piazza Armerina
SEAFORTH   July 17
231 BDE
L EDM
L EDM
Ramacca
Palagonia
Dittaino R
Gornalunga R
Simeto R

Caltagirone
July 16
48 HIGH
Grammichele
July 15
HASTY Ps
Militello
Lentini

Vizzini
July 14
Licodia
RCR
51 DIV

45
US DIV
July 12
Palazzolo

Gela
Chiaramonte
Giarratana
July 12
HASTY Ps
HASTY Ps

Comiso
Vittoria
Ragusa
July 12
SEAFORTH
L EDM
RCR
Noto

Modica
PPCLI
Scicli
Rosolini
July 11
48 HIGH
Ispica
July 11
L EDM
Pozzallo
Front Line
July 10
Pachino

Advance to Valguarnera
July 10–18, 1943

N

0   5   10   15
miles

0   10   20   30
kilometres

© S Daniel, 2008

Key to Abbreviations:

12 CTR:	Three Rivers Regt
48 HIGH:	48th Highlanders of Canada Regt
C&Y:	Carleton and York Regt
Cdo:	Commando
CIB:	Canadian Infantry Brigade
HASTY P's:	Hastings and Prince Edward Regt
L EDM:	Loyal Edmonton Regt
PLDG:	Princess Louise Dragoon Guards
PPCLI:	Princess Patricia's Canadian Light Infantry Regt
R 22e R:	Royal 22e Regt
RCR:	Royal Canadian Regt
SEAFORTH:	Seaforth Highlanders of Canada Regt
WNSR:	West Nova Scotia Regt

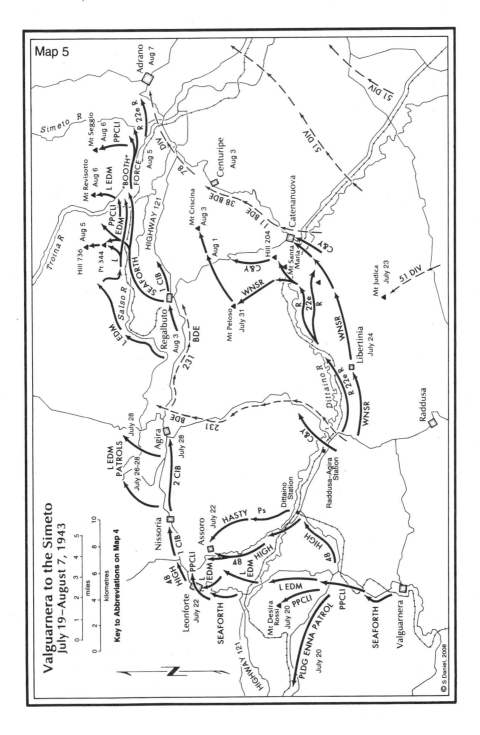

Map 5

Valguarnera to the Simeto
July 19–August 7, 1943

Key to Abbreviations on Map 4

© S Daniel, 2008

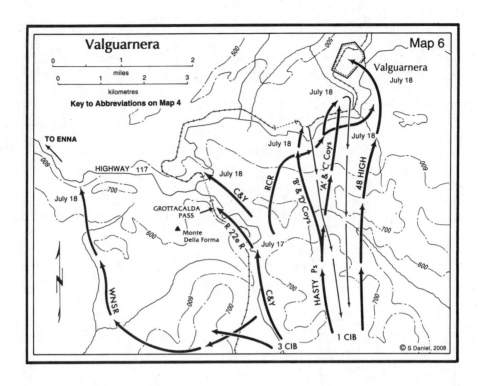

Map 6

Valguarnera

0 — 1 — 2 miles
0 — 1 — 2 — 3 kilometres

Key to Abbreviations on Map 4

Valguarnera
July 18

TO ENNA

HIGHWAY 117

July 18

July 18

July 18

July 18

July 18

July 18

GROTTACALDA PASS

RCR 22e R

Monte Della Forma

C&Y

RCR

'B' & 'D' Coy's

'A' & 'C' Coys

48 HIGH

July 17

WNSR

C&Y

HASTY Ps

3 CIB

1 CIB

© S Daniel, 2008

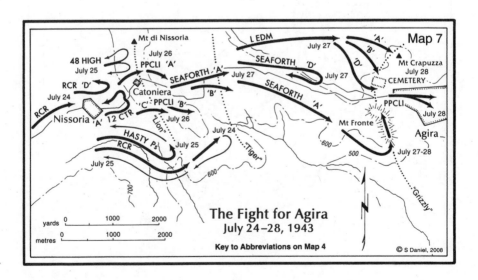

Map 7

Mt di Nissoria

L EDM

'A'

'B'

July 27

48 HIGH
July 25

July 26

PPCLI 'A'

SEAFORTH 'A'

SEAFORTH 'D'

July 27

'D'

Mt Crapuzza
July 28

RCR 'D'

July 24

Catoniera

'B'

SEAFORTH 'A'

July 27

CEMETERY

RCR

Nissoria

'A'

12 CTR

'C' PPCLI 'B'

July 26

"Lion"

July 24

PPCLI

July 28

Agira

HASTY Ps

RCR

July 25

"Tiger"

Mt Fronte

July 27-28

"Grizzly"

yards 0 — 1000 — 2000
metres 0 — 1000 — 2000

The Fight for Agira
July 24–28, 1943

Key to Abbreviations on Map 4

© S Daniel, 2008

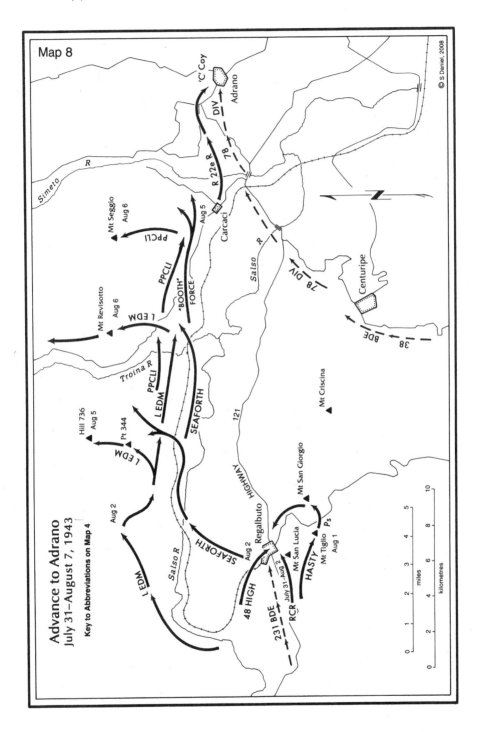

Map 8

Advance to Adrano
July 31–August 7, 1943
Key to Abbreviations on Map 4

© S Daniel, 2008

The Supreme Tragedy

CANADA COULD HAVE avoided invading Sicily. Indeed, it required the intercession of senior generals and the minister of national defence, Colonel John Ralston, as well as a personal plea by Prime Minister Mackenzie King to Sir Winston Churchill before Britain reluctantly invited Canadian troops to join the venture. From the British perspective, there was little to recommend diverting forces from First Canadian Army in England for service in the Mediterranean theatre.

Ever since the first flight of 1st Canadian Infantry Division had disembarked in Greenoch, Scotland, on December 16, 1939—just ninety-eight days after Canada declared war on the Axis powers in response to the assault on Poland—the British had resisted committing this increasingly potent force to combat operations. By April 6, 1942, when First Canadian Army headquarters opened for business at Headley Court, it had under command about 170,000 men organized into five divisions, two tank brigades, and various supporting arms. This was, however, an army still in a formative phase. Every Canadian soldier overseas had volunteered for combat duty, but only a relatively small number had any militia service and, because it had been so depleted during the interwar years, even fewer came from the regular army. The Imperial General Staff had immediately recognized that the Canadians—particularly the officers—needed a great deal more training before the army could be considered combat effective. With planning already begun for an eventual cross-channel invasion of northwest Europe, First Canadian Army was tapped to play an important role. Its strength was to be nurtured.

This sentiment perfectly suited First Canadian Army's commander, Lieutenant General Andrew McNaughton. Meeting with U.S. president Franklin D. Roosevelt on March 9, McNaughton had explained his army's purpose as being, first, to ensure the security of the United Kingdom and, second, to maintain "our foothold for an eventual attack on the Continent of Europe...There could be no question but that the war could only be ended by the defeat of Hitler and the only way of doing so was to attack him from the West." McNaughton emphasized that he "had never lost sight of this object and...had always been convinced that an offensive would sooner or later have to be launched from the United Kingdom across the narrow seas." The general assured Roosevelt that the Canadian government had "accepted" this view the previous week during an Ottawa meeting.[1]

The fifty-five-year-old McNaughton had served as an artillery officer in Lieutenant General Arthur Currie's 1 Canadian Corps during the Great War, rising in 1918 to command the heavy artillery unit. During the latter phase of the war, McNaughton duly noted Currie's refusal during the great German spring offensive to allow Canadian divisions to be severed from the corps to fill endangered sections of the British Expeditionary Force front. Currie had been adamant that the Canadians fight as one or not at all. McNaughton felt the same about First Canadian Army.

His position was unpopular with some subordinate senior officers and even with many of the troops idling the months away in southern England while battles raged in distant lands. Lieutenant General Harry Crerar, who in 1942 commanded one of McNaughton's corps, was the most vocal advocate for sending Canadian soldiers into harm's way at any opportunity. As Canada's chief of staff in 1941, Crerar had convinced a reluctant Mackenzie King to accede to a British call for men to reinforce Hong Kong's weak garrison against Japanese attack. When the colony surrendered on Christmas Day, 1941, all 1,975 men of the Royal Rifles of Canada and the Winnipeg Grenadiers were lost. In the winter of 1942, illness had forced McNaughton to return to Canada and temporarily relinquish command to Crerar. Believing army morale was poor due to lack of action and that people at home were impatient for their soldiers to fight, Crerar hectored the British chiefs of staff for a role in cross-channel raids. When McNaughton returned from sick leave that spring, the decision was already made that 2nd Canadian Infantry Division would star in a raid on Dieppe. On August 19, 1942, the raid ended in disaster, with 907 men killed and another 1,946 lost as prisoners.

Crerar never faltered, constantly undermining McNaughton's determination to keep First Canadian Army together. Although he was McNaughton's subordinate, Crerar had greater political clout and better contacts within Canada and Britain's military hierarchy. The chief of imperial general staff, General Sir Alan Brooke, and Crerar had been cronies during the Great War. Brooke considered McNaughton "devoid of any strategic outlook, and [that he] would sooner have risked losing the war than agree to splitting Canadian forces."[2] Crerar also had Canadian defence minister Ralston's ear and that of the Canadian chief of staff, Lieutenant General Kenneth Stuart. Both agreed the time was nigh for some element of First Canadian Army to fight—where mattered little.

Taking advantage of an October 1942 meeting with Churchill, Ralston urged that "active employment should be found for the Canadian Army at the first opportunity." There were no strings attached; it could "be used in whole or in part." Fighting a rearguard action, McNaughton conceded that the army should be employed where it could make "the maximum possible contribution," and that this might mean its fragmentation. But, he countered, "there was no reason to doubt that morale could be maintained even if we had to remain in England on guard for another year; that was therefore no reason in itself for advocating active operations for their own sake; that anything we undertook should be strictly related to military needs and objectives." And what could be more important than keeping the army together so it could eventually participate in the cross-channel invasion?[3]

Even Prime Minister King, who shared McNaughton's belief in a unified Canadian army overseas, was wavering by New Year's Day, 1943. In his national broadcast, King announced that "all our armed forces" would be fighting before the year was out. With the Royal Canadian Air Force and Royal Canadian Navy long engaged in combat operations, the reference could only pertain to the army.[4]

Concerns about First Canadian Army morale were unwarranted. Certainly there were cases of men not returning on schedule from leaves, but outright desertions were rare. Open insubordination was equally absent. Not that the men were angels. They chased women, drank too much, gambled fiercely, and brawled at the slightest provocation. For an army of young men on an overseas posting, this was just normal behaviour.

Occasionally a company or even a battalion lost its edge. The Seaforth Highlanders of Canada, its men growing increasingly restless in early 1943, showed a decline in efficiency that did not go unrecognized by 2nd Canadian Infantry Brigade's commander Brigadier Chris Vokes. Fortunately, the Seaforths had just gained a new commander. Lieutenant Colonel Bert Hoffmeister, known as "Hoffy" in the regiment, had been a Seaforth since he was a boy cadet in Vancouver. Hoffmeister had just completed several months' instruction at the Canadian Junior War Staff College. Although he had risen from the ranks to command, Hoffmeister was a businesslike, hard-working soldier who expected the best of officers and men alike. He mixed easily with the troops and was often informal, even casual in their company. But he brooked no nonsense. When Vokes pronounced his opinion of the Seaforth's current state, Hoffmeister set the matter right with a will.[5]

A major issue for most 1st Division battalions was that many of their officers and non-commissioned officers (NCOS) were too old for combat soldiering. The commander Hoffmeister replaced, Lieutenant Colonel J.M.S. Tait, had been a Seaforth officer throughout the 1920s and 1930s. Age and the long years of training in Britain had taken their toll on these men. Private Richard Latimer, a soldier with a predilection for mischief, noted that it "was only because of the lassitude and indifference of the officers and NCOS (most of whom, after all, had been overseas for over three years themselves) that we were able to stay out of serious trouble."[6]

Hoffmeister quickly rid the battalion of many old-guard officers and NCOs by arranging transfers back to Canada or to other, less demanding duties in Britain. As "a result of the new, firm hands which now controlled the Seaforths," the regimental historian later wrote, "a steady improvement in the morale of the unit was noticeable. Hoffmeister demanded a lot from all ranks, and not only did they respond to the challenge but their confidence in Hoffmeister grew weekly."[7]

The most pervasive problem was boredom, particularly among the men of 1st Canadian Infantry Division, rather than abnormal rates of ill discipline or decline in soldierly skills. Most 1st Division men had been in Britain for more than three years. Syd Frost, arriving from Canada in April 1943 as a freshly minted lieutenant and assigned to command a platoon in the Princess Patricia's Canadian Light Infantry (PPCLI), noted that "the officers and men had been soldiering in England since 1940 and were a highly skilled team. All the young NCOs and men had been brought up during the Depression; many had been unemployed. When the call went out for recruits in September 1939, they were the first to join. They could take care of themselves in any situation and were tremendous fighters in action.

"The men in my platoon were a tough bunch. They knew all the tricks of the professional soldier and were not at all impressed with my two pips and neatly pressed service dress. Luckily, my platoon sergeant understood my problem and came to my rescue with helpful hints on how to deal with this bunch of desperados. He told me, quite frankly, that the men were over-trained and would not brook any nonsense from a young officer out of the Officer Training School; they would take their time to assess me and, until they were satisfied I knew what I was doing, I would have a pretty rough time."[8]

At first the Canadians had felt a sense of purpose as defenders of the British Isles against possible German invasion. By 1942—with the Germans heavily engaged in Russia—that danger had passed. "Soldiering in Britain had become humdrum," observed Captain Strome Galloway of another 1st Division Permanent Force battalion, the Royal

Canadian Regiment. "With the Battle of Britain long over and the prospect of action against the enemy none too promising for some time at least, most of the adventure of soldiering had faded before our eyes. Our Army Commander, General Andy McNaughton, said that the Canadian Army was a 'dagger pointed at the heart of Berlin.' Most of us thought he was living in a dream world. Possibly we would never fight at all. The Russians would beat the Germans and Canada's overseas army would return home unblooded." Offered the chance in early 1943 to gain battle experience as one of 348 Canadian officers and NCOs posted to British units in Tunisia, Galloway jumped at it.

Given command of a company in 2nd Battalion, London Irish Rifles, Galloway saw some tough fighting that culminated in the capture of Bizerte and Tunis and the surrender of 240,000 enemy troops—about 125,000 from Germany's Afrika Korps. During the three-month posting, four officers and four NCOs were killed, another sixteen wounded, and one lost as a prisoner. But Galloway believed the survivors gained "a splendid introduction to the realities of our wartime career" that "gave us the edge over our stay-in-England comrades."[9]

Back in England, the training increasingly concentrated on combined operations involving amphibious landings against contested shores—a clear indication, everyone hoped, that the Canadians were being readied for an offensive operation. "We'll never be readier," Lieutenant Farley Mowat of the Hastings and Prince Edward Regiment wrote in his journal. "God knows…" The disappointment was palpable throughout the regiment's ranks when one training scheme ended in early January 1943 only to be followed by more interminable waiting. "Wet, cold and dreary, our spirits sank from day to day as we wallowed in the mindless ritual of barrack life. The real war was becoming increasingly chimerical…something to read about or hear described on the BBC."[10]

VARIOUS CANADIAN NEWSPAPER correspondents observing from the sidelines were quick to lament the fact that—with the exception of one bloody day at Dieppe—the nation's army had yet to see action. Lionel Shapiro reported in the Montreal *Gazette* that the troops considered themselves no more than "a sort of adjunct to the British Home Guard" and were regarded by Britons as "the country constabulary in the English countryside."

At home, newspaper editors, old soldiers, and politicians ever more loudly demanded the troops be deployed. Speaking to the Canadian Corps Association in Vancouver, Great War veteran Colonel J.A. Clark thundered: "It strikes me as one of the supreme tragedies of this war that the United States, following one year in the struggle, has already placed men in battle engagements in Africa while Canadian soldiers are sitting idle in England. This constitutes the greatest disgrace of the present war."

Government conspiracy was behind it, suggested the *Ottawa Citizen*. "All other Empire troops have had battle experience in this war... The British have been everywhere. Only Canadians, among the Allied combatants have not been tried...

"This, we confess, seems strange. To a great many it is disturbing."

In the House of Commons, opposition member R.B. Hanson complained that it was regrettable Canada's soldiers overseas should "have it thrown in their faces that while Australia and New Zealand are fighting gallantly on the sands of Africa personnel of the Canadian Army are not there."

From Toronto, R.B. Bennett, the former Conservative prime minister whom Mackenzie King's Liberals had swept from power in 1935, chided that he saw no reason the Canadian Army should see another Christmas without having fired a shot.

Such criticisms prompted Assistant Under-Secretary for External Affairs Hume Wrong to warn King that Canada was likely to "become the object of taunts similar to that which Henri Quatre addressed to a tardy supporter who arrived too late for the battle: 'Go hang yourself, brave Crillon, for we fought at Arques and you were not there!'"[11]

Assailed from without and equally from within his cabinet, King abandoned McNaughton on March 17, 1943, in a personal telegram to Churchill asking that he intervene to ensure that the Imperial General Staff consider "employment of Canadian troops in North Africa." The following day, Lieutenant General Stuart signalled McNaughton that, unless the cross-channel invasion occurred in summer 1943, "we should urge re-examination for one and perhaps two divisions going as early as possible to an active theatre."

McNaughton doggedly resisted. "I do not recommend that we should press for employment merely to satisfy a desire for activity or for representation in particular theatres however much I myself and all here may desire this from our narrow point of view."

Responding to King, Churchill advised that plans were under way to move a division from Britain to North Africa. But it would be British, for the selected division was well into training for a mission where plans were too far advanced for a substitution by Canadians. King pressed his case with British foreign secretary Anthony Eden, who asked Churchill to reconsider. What words passed between the two men went unrecorded, but in the late afternoon of April 23, General Brooke advised McNaughton that Churchill had instructed that any forthcoming operation should include Canadian troops. Brooke told McNaughton to determine whether his government would accept such an invitation. Without waiting for a response from Ottawa, Brooke informed Allied commanders in the Mediterranean theatre that Canadian troops would join the invasion of Sicily. "Both political and military grounds make it essential that Canadian forces should be brought into action this year. It had been hoped to employ them in operations across the channel from U.K. but likelihood of such operations has now become extremely remote owing to recent addition to Husky of practically all remaining craft.

"It has therefore been decided that 1 Canadian Division and a tank brigade similarly organized to 3 [British] Division and its tank brigade will replace latter in the Eastern Task Force for the Husky operation subject to confirmation from the Canadian Government which we hope will be immediately forthcoming.

"I very much regret this last minute change. We have been very carefully into its implications and consider it quite practicable. The Canadian Division is in a more advanced state of combined training than 3 Division and the Canadian planning staff have already started work with full assistance of 3 Division so no time is being lost."[12]

On April 25, McNaughton advised Brooke that the Canadian government had accepted the invitation. But there was one proviso:

McNaughton must be allowed to study the operation's general plan. If the plan looked likely to produce another Dieppe, the Canadians would bow out. McNaughton quickly got down to studying Operation Husky, as the invasion of Sicily was code-named. In the early morning of April 26, he cabled Lieutenant General Stuart in Ottawa. "I have satisfied myself that these plans represent a practical operation of war," he said. "I therefore recommend your approval of Canadian participation."[13]

Approval was granted the following day. The long wait was over. In less than three months, about 26,000 Canadian soldiers would join in the largest amphibious invasion in history.

PART ONE

TOWARDS AN INVASION

If the Army Can't Agree

O N APRIL 23, less than twenty-four hours after federal government approval was given, Eighth Army commander General
Bernard Law Montgomery signalled Lieutenant General Andrew
McNaughton: "Am delighted Canadian Division will come under me
for Husky."[1] Classic Monty hyperbole, still there might have been
some kernel of truth contained therein. For Montgomery knew
something of 1st Canadian Infantry Division. In 1941, as commander
of Britain's South Eastern Command, he had taken a personal interest in transforming the amateurish Canadians into professional
soldiers. Deeming their senior officers too old and inept, Montgomery
had imposed rigorous training schedules and schemes. He dis-
dained McNaughton, advising chief of imperial general staff, General
Sir Alan Brooke, that the Canadian was unfit for army field command.
One training exercise had followed another through 1941 and into
early 1942. Fox, Dog, Waterloo, Bumper, Beaver II, Beaver III, and
Tiger hammered the troops into shape and instilled skills required to
survive and even perhaps win battles. When Montgomery departed
Britain for the deserts of Africa in the summer of 1942, he had pronounced the Canadians professional enough.[2]

The immediate problem was that the Canadians had to hit the
ground running to meet the rapidly closing invasion deadline. As

Brooke had acknowledged in his signal to Mediterranean theatre commanders, this was a last-minute change. Most under the gun was 1st Canadian Infantry Division's commander, Major General Harry Salmon, and his General Staff officers. They had to quickly acquaint themselves with an invasion plan still in flux, identify potential problems, and seek solutions while also preparing the division for operations in a completely new theatre.

The forty-eight-year-old Salmon had won a Military Cross during the Great War and was considered one of Canada's best generals—particularly with regard to training. General staff officer (1) Lieutenant Colonel George Kitching, who acted as Salmon's chief of staff, found him an unceasing "stickler for detail." Tall, with "a good physique and a clipped moustache on a square and rugged face," Salmon exuded confidence. But he was also enigmatic. Kitching later judged him as "one of the most unusual men I...ever served under and I do not think many people, even his close friends, really knew the inner workings of his mind."[3]

Fortunately, Salmon and Kitching had the benefit of planning already undertaken by 3rd British Division headquarters staff. Within hours of McNaughton's notification, Salmon moved his people to Norfolk House on St. James's Square in London, which the British used as a top-secret headquarters for combined operations planning. Here, the British officers briefed them in detail. As soon as their counterparts departed, the Canadians got to work. They numbered just fifty senior officers—drawn from 1st Division's headquarters, its three infantry brigades, and the 1st Canadian Army Tank Brigade—which would provide the armoured contingent. Excepting McNaughton and a couple of his staff, nobody in First Canadian Army was yet privy to operational details. Norfolk House was locked down; heavy security ensured that nobody entered without a pass or removed any secret papers. Almost every document was labelled "Most Secret."

Salmon and his team checked into the Mayfair Hotel, about a mile from their new headquarters, but with discussion of the invasion forbidden beyond the walls of Norfolk House, the men spent most waking hours there. Kitching considered the discussion prohibition a blessing in disguise. Unexpectedly, Salmon, a workaholic who normally maintained a demeanour of stony reserve even over dinner and drinks, now "became cheerful and lively [at dinner] and thoroughly enjoyed his meals in restaurants when we had time to get them. He would stay up at night and have a drink with us even though we might have been working for 14 hours that day. He was a different man and I thoroughly enjoyed his company."[4]

The first five days passed in a hectic whirl. On April 27, barely forty-eight hours after being advised of their new assignment, Salmon presented his staff with a ten-page appreciation that assessed intelligence estimates of enemy dispositions and strengths relative to their own, topographical details of the identified beaches and defences, and allotment of ships; in the document Salmon also drew conclusions about whether the division could win a toehold. He warned that the planned heavy preliminary bombing of Sicily, well before the invasion convoy formed up off Malta, made gaining "strategical surprise impossible." But he was heartened by how thoroughly unsuited the designated beaches were for amphibious landings. There were two, lying on either side of the small fishing village of Scoglitti on Sicily's southern coast. Steep banks rose behind each, so that getting tanks and other vehicles off the beach would be extremely difficult. "I may achieve a certain measure of tactical surprise owing to unsuitability of beaches," Salmon explained. But the enemy, expected to be "at a high state of readiness," would undoubtedly block the division's push inland. Right now, however, enemy forces were reportedly weak enough that, even "if tactical surprise is lost, this should not preclude a successful landing unless enemy defences are considerably strengthened prior to D Day."[5]

Nothing was simple. Wherever the officers turned, more complications were revealed. When everyone was unexpectedly summoned to the War Office, they were surprised to find Montgomery waiting for them in a room adorned with large wall maps of Sicily. He had flown from North Africa to deliver a detailed briefing. Now the Canadians learned the full scope of the enterprise. They would be under Montgomery's command and folded into the Eighth Army, which was carrying off the British side of the invasion. Landing simultaneously would be another army, the American Seventh, under General

George S. Patton. Delivering two armies in a single day onto Sicilian beaches meant the invasion was the largest in history. There were not enough men in Northern Africa, so the Canadians would be sailing from Britain, while a large contingent of American troops came direct from the United States. "It can be appreciated," noted 1st Canadian Infantry Brigade commander Brigadier Howard Graham, "that the sailor boys had a tough task on their hands to co-ordinate the movement of convoys from North America, Great Britain, North Africa, and Malta so that all would arrive at their proper places at the proper time."[6]

A major headache was that Eighth Army's supply stores were so strained that nothing would be available from North Africa for the Canadians. They must bring their own supplies, sufficient to last forty-two days. This meant there would be ninety-two ships, excluding escorts, carrying the division. Instead of everyone sailing together, they would move in three convoys, the two main ones designated the Slow Assault Convoy and the other the Fast Assault Convoy. The slow one would assemble in Liverpool and sail on June 25, while the fast convoy would depart harbours in the River Clyde three days later. Aboard the slow convoy would be packed vehicles, equipment, and supplies not required to immediately support the assaulting troops during the first days of the invasion. The fast convoy would carry the assault troops and their weaponry. Movement of these convoys was to be so precise that they would marry up at a "release point" seven miles off Sicily on the night before the invasion. Following a few days behind these two convoys, a third carrying reinforcements, field hospitals, replacement equipment, and supplies would proceed to a staging area in North Africa, from which matériel and men would be transferred to Sicily as needed.[7]

Montgomery departed, leaving instructions that Salmon and some key staff officers should fly to Cairo in a few days for a meeting with the corps commander under whom the Canadians would serve, Lieutenant General Oliver Leese. The most worrisome aspect of the plans so far presented was that they were not finalized and were subject to minor or major change at a moment's notice. As had been the case since the decision to invade Sicily was agreed on at the Casablanca

Conference, Montgomery, his superiors, and the staff at the various headquarters were still arguing many key aspects fundamental to Husky.

EARLIER THAT YEAR, in January, the combined chiefs of staff had met Prime Minister Sir Winston Churchill and President Franklin D. Roosevelt in French Morocco, at Anfa Camp on the outskirts of Casablanca. Their purpose was to hammer out basic strategy for the year. With North Africa all but won, the pressing issue was how next to employ Commonwealth and American forces against Germany and her European allies. It was a heady time. German and Italian forces were cornered in Tunisia, the last Axis stronghold in North Africa. In Russia, the Germans had been forced onto the defensive in the aftermath of Sixth Army's destruction at Stalingrad. The Japanese tide had been stemmed in New Guinea and on Guadalcanal. Churchill cautiously mused that in the dawn of 1943 they were seeing, "perhaps, the end of the beginning."[8]

The Americans, particularly the Chief of Staff of the United States Army, General George C. Marshall, preferred an immediate invasion of Western Europe from Britain or, alternatively, landings in southern France. But the three-pronged invasion on November 8, 1942, of Morocco and Algiers and subsequent operations in North Africa— with heavy demands on shipping and supplies—had forced them to recognize that a cross-channel assault would be impossible until 1944. The British countered that Allied landings in southern France would preclude any chance of a cross-channel invasion. There was no way to limit the scope of such an operation. Any landings there would require such a vast commitment of manpower, shipping, and supplies that this would become the invasion of continental Europe, which the Allies were not yet ready to carry out. On the other hand, Churchill warned, the Allies "would be a laughing stock if in the spring and early summer no British or American soldiers were firing at any German or Italian soldiers."[9] So where to shoot?

Churchill and his chief of imperial general staff, General Sir Alan Brooke, knew the precise spot. The British arrived in Casablanca with a strategy to win agreement to an invasion of Sicily by patiently wearing down American resistance "like the dripping of water on a stone." Yet Churchill knew that any Mediterranean invasion point he put forward would be initially resisted by the Americans, who saw in every British strategical suggestion a veiled attempt to regain or expand their empire. This "atmosphere of veiled antipathy and mistrust" had clouded every conference since the war's outbreak.[10]

Casablanca proved no exception. This time, however, Churchill and Brooke were able to build a compelling case for invading Sicily. Benito Mussolini's Italy was on the verge of collapse, and Sicily would provide a perfect springboard onto the peninsula. An invasion there would force Italian surrender. With Italy broken, the British held, the Germans would not move to defend it. The Allies could gain a solid footing on the European mainland at little cost in blood—penetrating Hitler's Fortress Europe through its soft underbelly, as Churchill was fond of putting it. The British went on to predict that Turkey would join the Allied side and the Germans be forced to divert divisions that would otherwise have been deployed to Russia in order to shore up defences in southern Europe.[11]

General Dwight D. Eisenhower, the Commander-in-Chief of the Allied Expeditionary Force in North Africa, thought that invading Sicily made sense only if the motivation was to remove the island and her seaports as a threat to Allied shipping in the Mediterranean. The other Americans concurred, refusing to discuss further what might follow Sicily's capture out of a fear that British ambitions in the Mediterranean could indefinitely forestall a cross-channel invasion for lack of men and ships. Striking a conciliatory posture, Churchill and Brooke chose not to press the point. They could afford to leave in abeyance the idea of continuing on to mainland Italy. Instead, they forecast that Sicily's loss might suffice to bring about an Italian surrender and avoided speculating further as to whether the Germans would occupy and tenaciously defend the country.[12]

Neither delegation left Casablanca triumphant. But the British had succeeded on a number of levels that gave cause for satisfaction. Sicily would be invaded, and Italy might well follow. Another coup that left Brooke almost giddy with pleasure was that the Americans had been neatly outfoxed, leaving operational control of the invasion in

British hands. In a communiqué issued on January 23, Eisenhower was declared the "supreme commander." This technically gave him overall authority for Husky's planning and conduct, but the document went on to appoint General Harold Alexander his deputy commander-in-chief, charging him personally with "the detailed planning and preparation and for the execution of the actual operation when launched." Further, Admiral of the Fleet Andrew Cunningham would be the naval commander and Air Chief Marshal Arthur Tedder, the air commander. All three men were British.[13]

"Eisenhower," Brooke declared, "had neither the tactical [nor] strategical experience required for such a task." Making him senior "could not help flattering and pleasing the Americans in so far as we were placing our senior and most experienced commander to function under their commander who had no war experience." Eisenhower was effectively pushed "up into the stratosphere and rarefied atmosphere of a Supreme Commander, where he would be free to devote his time to the political and interallied problems."[14] Eisenhower was little fooled by this ruse, but there was nothing he could do about it. "I ceased to concern myself directly with the details of the Sicilian operations," he wrote.[15] Churchill emphasized in follow-up correspondence with Roosevelt "that the British should at least be equal partners with our Allies. The proportions of the armies available [for] July were: British, eight divisions; United States, six. Air: the United States, 55 per cent; British, 45 per cent. Naval, 80 per cent British...It did not seem too much in these circumstances that we should have at least an equal share of the High Command." Rather unctuously he would later claim "this was willingly conceded by our loyal comrades. We were moreover given the direct conduct of the fighting."[16]

THE MAN RESPONSIBLE for planning the invasion, however, was unable to turn his mind to the task. General Harold Alexander was already commander-in-chief for Tunisia, where battles still raged that required his daily attention. All he could do was hastily examine the tentative plan submitted to the Casablanca Conference by the Joint Planning Staff in London and agree it provided the framework for the Sicily invasion.[17]

Unable to release any senior officers to invasion planning, Alexander borrowed Major General Charles H. Gairdner from British headquarters in India. Gairdner opened Operation Husky's headquarters on February 12 in Bouzarea, a small town outside of Algiers. Gairdner temporarily had full responsibility for the invasion force, designated as 15th Army Group but cloaked in such secrecy that it was referred to only as Force 141. The two armies that composed it were also masked, with Eighth Army being alternately referred to as Force 545 or Eastern Task Force and Seventh Army as Force 343 or Western Task Force.

Although British officers constituted the brunt of Gairdner's staff, several Americans assumed key postings. Major General Clarence R. Huebner became his deputy and senior American representative, while Brigadier General Arthur S. Nevins served as Brigadier, General Staff (Plans). The senior naval and air force officers that gave Force 141 its interservice character were, however, all British.

At the same time that Force 141 opened shop, Force 545 took over office space in Cairo and Force 343 situated itself in Rabat, Morocco. These last two headquarters were inter-service in structure but not inter-Allied, as one concerned itself with Eighth Army and the other, Seventh Army. Since forces would also have to be sent from Britain and the United States, smaller offices were established in London and Washington to oversee planning at those ends. In London, the headquarters was at Norfolk House and was staffed by officers from 3rd British Division until they were replaced by 1st Canadian Infantry Division staff at the end of April.

Even accounting for air travel, these headquarters were badly scattered, so bringing everyone together was impossible. But each was tidily linked by cable. On paper the command chain seemed clear, but each headquarters tended to operate quasi-independently while emanating volumes of cables full of discussion, suggestions, and analyses of options. The mixture of physical separation and near-instantaneous communication, as Britain's official historian later wrote, fostered an atmosphere favouring "debate instead of hastening decisions."[18]

Because Eighth Army remained engaged in Tunisia, one of its corps commanders, Lieutenant General Miles Dempsey, took the helm in Cairo. This left General Bernard Montgomery and his chief of staff, Major General Francis "Freddie" de Guingand, free to concentrate on the continuing campaign.[19] Although Seventh Army's General George S. Patton initially took charge of Force 343, he quickly left planning details to his staff in order to take personal control over his army's II Corps on March 6. This formation was so badly disorganized it was deemed not battle worthy. As II Corps was supposed to provide Seventh Army's fighting teeth, whipping it into shape was his first priority. Patton was soon running around on a beach screaming at a squad of men from II Corps' 1st Division during a botched practice landing, "And just where in hell are your goddamned bayonets?"[20]

While all the senior commanders assigned to the invasion initially paid scant attention to its planning, Gairdner was clearly in over his head. In the early war years, Gairdner had commanded two armoured divisions before being assigned to India. He had no combat experience and little background in operational planning. Polite and well intentioned, he lacked the fortitude required to exert authority over a high command headquarters where personalities and egos were generally strong. Deputy chief of staff Huebner was the opposite—outspoken, rude, and ultimately unfit for senior staff duty. Alexander would declare Huebner "a square peg in a round hole" and fire him in July. The officers serving under these two men were also inexperienced in planning and executing combined operations.[21]

Hesitantly, with Joint Planning Staff's tentative plan in hand, Force 141 set to work. Despite the urgency of the invasion deadline—only 137 days remained until the "favourable July moon" date set by the combined chiefs of staff in their January 23 communiqué—the planners sluggishly studied the proposal. There was no sense that time was short—the British held that a division could be fully prepared and launched into battle by amphibious landing in sixty-eight days. Yet this estimate failed to take into account that Operation Husky entailed preparing two complete armies whose divisions had to be assembled, readied for battle, and delivered to the beaches from various parts of the world.[22]

The Joint Planning Staff had presented three options: an assault on either of two Sicilian port cities—Palermo or Catania—or possibly both simultaneously. Current Allied amphibious warfare doctrine maintained that a major port must fall into their hands shortly after the first beach landings to facilitate putting ashore follow-on supplies and reinforcements. The beaches could only serve as temporary landing facilities. Sicily had three port cities: Palermo on the northwestern flank, Messina at its northeastern tip, and Catania centred on the eastern coast. Messina had been eliminated at the outset. This port stood in the Straits of Messina, a turbulent passage churned by a six-knot current. At its narrowest, the strait was two miles wide, its opposite shore being the toe of mainland Italy's boot. Messina was believed to be heavily defended, sailing a large naval force into the strait seemed extremely risky, and the city lay beyond the range of Allied air forces operating out of bases in Tunisia—still to be captured—and Malta.

Lying as it did within range of Allied air cover, Catania presented a better prospect. But its port was smaller, judged capable of maintaining only four divisions in the first month of an invasion and six thereafter. Not enough, the planners decided, for subduing the enemy guarding Sicily. Palermo could meet an invasion force's needs, but a sole assault there left Catania and Messina in Axis hands for reinforcing their garrison on the island. Also, the majority of enemy airfields in Sicily were in the eastern and southeastern regions. If these were not seized quickly, German and Italian air forces would be able to strike the invasion force relentlessly because of the short turnaround times they would enjoy. Any Allied invasion of Sicily must have as its ultimate goal the closing of the Straits of Messina, preferably trapping a great number of enemy forces on the island that could then be eliminated at leisure. To advance only from Palermo towards Messina—while Catania and the eastern airfields remained unscathed—would ensure a tough, costly slog.

Force 141 planners decided the only solution was to launch simultaneous operations. Force 545 (British) would land on the island's southeastern tip at four points: Avola, Pachino, Pozzallo, and Gela. Three infantry divisions supported by two tank battalions would strike from the sea, and four parachute battalions would drop on prime airfields. Meanwhile, Force 343 (American) would simultaneously land one infantry division backed by a tank battalion at Sciacca and Marinella in Sicily's southwestern corner to capture airfields that would by the second day be capable of use by Allied air forces to cover a second phase of landings immediately east of Palermo. Two infantry divisions and two tank battalions would carry out this assignment. D plus 3 would see the British landing an infantry division supported by a brigade group on beaches close to Catania, to secure the port, and an airborne division on the Catania plain, to seize a clutch of airports there.

At the end of February, Alexander dropped in briefly on Gairdner for another quick consideration of what he termed "the London plan," since it was almost entirely the work of the British Joint Planning Staff. After taking issue with a few minor points, Alexander pondered whether, to simplify matters, the multipronged invasion idea should be abandoned and both task forces concentrated for a mass landing in the southeastern corner. Intelligence estimates showed the island was defended by two German and eight Italian mobile divisions, supported by five Italian coastal divisions. Gairdner's staff had calculated that ten Allied divisions would be required to defeat them, and even then the two opponents would be roughly equally matched. The port facilities in the southeastern corner, he insisted, were insufficient to support such a large force. Both Palermo and Catania must be won at the outset.[23]

Plans kept diverging, even about which divisions would compose the invasion force. Divisions assigned to Force 545 were particularly in flux. Initially, five British divisions—the 5th, 56th, and 78th deployed in North Africa and the 1st and 4th in Britain—were placed on the order of battle. But the 78th was fighting in Tunisia, and soon the 56th was also committed. Then the 1st and 4th divisions were transferred to North Africa and joined the fray. Not until the end of April, when 1st Canadian Division was swapped for the 3rd British Division, was the order of battle declared firm. There remained just seventy days to "complete a vast amount of detailed work." The invasion plan remained undecided and was the source of rancorous debate.[24]

On March 13, Dempsey and his naval counterpart at Force 545, Admiral Bertram Ramsay, had dropped in on Montgomery at his field headquarters in Tripoli while en route to a meeting with Gairdner in Algiers. Although Montgomery was focussed on the endgame in North Africa, he gave the Husky plan a cursory study before they arrived. Montgomery handed Dempsey a letter for Alexander that provided more detailed analysis, but after the two officers departed, he fired off a terse cable headlining his concerns. "In my opinion the operation planned in LONDON breaks every common sense rule of practical battle fighting and is completely theoretical. It has no hope of success and should be completely recast."[25]

When able to put their minds to Husky, Alexander, Air Chief Marshal Arthur Tedder, and Admiral Andrew Cunningham continued to see one problem after another. As March gave way to April, Alexander tinkered with the plan, taking a division from here and adding it there, but the two-pronged approach remained intact. He was increasingly anxious that this dispersal of strength presented great dangers. What if the enemy defending the island proved stronger and of higher quality than intelligence reports indicated? The invading forces, divided by design, could be destroyed one by one.[26]

Montgomery agreed and didn't mince words. "There is some pretty wooly thinking going on—tactically and administratively," he signalled Alexander on April 3. "I do not know who the best planner is, but I do suggest he comes to see me very soon, and before the thing gets too far. I have no intention of doing some of the things they suggest. We must get the initial stage-management right before we go into details."[27]

Aware that time was critical, Montgomery diverted his attention from the ongoing fighting to suggest that he and Alexander meet Eisenhower in Algiers to discuss Operation Husky. They met on April 19 and the Eighth Army commander presented a précis complete with suggestions for bringing order to a chaotic situation. "Detailed planning is being carried out by Staff Officers who are not in touch with battle requirements," he stated. "There is no responsible senior commander thoroughly versed in what happens in battle who is devoting *his sole attention* to the Husky operation. If we go on in this way much longer we may have a disaster. The preparations for the operation must be gripped firmly, and be handled in a sensible way." He recommended that Freddie de Guingand go to Cairo to represent Eighth Army in Force 545 planning. Eisenhower and Alexander consented.[28]

Four days later, Montgomery flew to Cairo to finally study the plan in detail. "They want me to operate in little [brigade groups] all over the place. I refuse," he declared in a signal to General Sir Alan Brooke. "They say there will only be slight resistance. I say that here in Tunisia the Italian is fighting desperately; he has never done so before; but he is doing so now. To operate dispersed, means disaster. We cannot go on in this way. Unless we have a good and firm plan *at once;* on which we can all work *there will be no Husky in July.* I hope that this is realized your end."[29]

IF BROOKE WAS not yet ready to concede the point, Alexander was. The fifty-one-year-old general was ready to let Montgomery recast Husky to his own design. In many ways Alexander was Montgomery's polar opposite. *New York Times* columnist Frank L. Kluchohn described him as having an "athlete's figure and Grecian profile." His moustache was close cropped and in "his favourite field uniform of breeches, high boots, jacket with red facings and cap with red band, this Irishman reminds one of a deadly poised rapier. His outstanding feature, cold blue eyes, capable of freezing under stress, point to the steel in his character.

"He has a fine smile, but when those eyes turn really cold his subordinates feel the inherent authority he possesses, then it becomes clipped and brittle. A champion athlete who has always kept in tip-top shape, he moves with a light rhythm and balance that point to another facet of his character. Alexander never allows himself to be upset.

"He does not have that extraordinary power to inspire troops possessed by Montgomery and Patton, but he knows men, how to pick and handle them. He knows what they are capable of doing. This is the mark of all successful commanders. Once he has picked a man for the job, he backs him to the limit."[30]

Montgomery had none of Alexander's physical presence. Five-foot-seven, weighing barely 147 pounds, and possessed of a sharp nose and pointed ears that seemed oversized for his head, Montgomery was casual in dress. Chukka boots, corduroy trousers or sagging khaki shorts (the latter worn with knee-length tan socks), khaki shirt with sleeves rolled, and the trademark armoured corps black beret that concealed his thinning hair. Montgomery's voice was high-pitched, meaning it carried well during open-air speeches to his troops. A teetotaller, this fifty-five-year-old general had a monkish air about him that his seemingly humourless nature reinforced. His eyes were striking blue-grey and piercing, icily intelligent, hinting at ruthlessness. Montgomery was charismatic. And he was a winner—the Hero of Alamein. In the bitter fall of 1942, Montgomery had led Eighth Army into an attack, advancing on October 23 behind a four-hour artillery barrage that dwarfed anything the British had fired in this war. Two weeks of blistering combat broke Rommel's Afrika Korps and sent it reeling. About fifty thousand men were left behind, nearly thirty thousand of them taken prisoner. British casualties numbered 13,560. Montgomery had won more than a victory—it was the turning point for the Western Allied war with Germany. Thereafter the Germans were on the defensive, giving ground rather than gaining it. The British press never forgot, and Montgomery, a deft self-promoter, played to the growing myth that he and *his* Eighth Army were invincible. Churchill, seldom one to be accused of false modesty, declared that Montgomery was "indomitable in retreat, invincible in advance, insufferable in victory!"[31]

Montgomery and Alexander had one great thing in common. Both had fought as young lieutenants in the Great War. They had gone over the top at the head of troops and saw what each believed had been needless slaughter brought about by poor leadership and dated tactics. Montgomery had been shot in the chest by a sniper at First Ypres, won the Distinguished Service Order (DSO), and survived the Somme. The "so-called 'good fighting generals' of the war appeared to me to be those who had a complete disregard for human life," Montgomery later wrote.[32] Equally appalled, Alexander guiltily confessed to finding in war "something terribly fascinating."[33] Despite being twice wounded, he considered it a "terrific adventure." Alexander was said to have gone over the top thirty times, a feat considered so remarkable that Irish Guardsmen under his command tried to follow precisely in his footsteps to stay safe during that long rush across No Man's Land.[34] He ended the war a lieutenant colonel. At Dunkirk, as commander of 1 Corps, Alexander was reportedly the last British soldier to step off the sand onto a rescue boat. By 1943, he and Montgomery had seen more than their share of war and each recognized that it was the "poor bloody infantry" that always had to win the ground. Now, separately and sometimes together, these two men looked at the Husky plan and their maps of Sicily and feared it would end in tragedy.

Alexander decided to bring all the senior parties together for a conference in Algiers on April 29, where Montgomery's suggested revisions would be discussed. Bedridden by illness, Montgomery sent de Guingand in his stead. En route, de Guingand's plane crashed. Although nobody was seriously hurt, de Guingand suffered a concussion. The British xxx Corps commander, Lieutenant General Oliver Leese, then rushed to Algiers. When nobody met him at the airport, Leese hitchhiked to Force 141 headquarters. He burst into the room to find all the senior officers "very well and correctly dressed" while he wore his "usual shirt and shorts and no medal ribbons." Gamely, Leese attempted to explain the plan, only to be rebuffed. Alexander's attempts to referee the meeting failed miserably, and it collapsed into a series of recriminations and backbiting.[35]

Montgomery's revisions made Eighth Army's landings on the southeastern coast the major push but retained a weakened second prong aimed at Palermo by Patton's Seventh Army. Tedder complained this left too many airfields in enemy hands. Axis airfields in Sicily were clustered on the island's three small areas of relatively level terrain: the Catania–Gerbini area on the east coast's Catania plain, inland from Gela on the south coast, and between Trapani and Palermo in the northwestern corner. The assault, Tedder argued, would fall too far south of the most important Catania–Gerbini cluster to bring these into Allied hands quickly enough. Cunningham, meanwhile, argued that gathering most of the invasion fleet off Siracusa invited disaster, because amphibious landings were best mounted across broad beach fronts as the original plan had envisioned. Patton, who until now had shown little more than passing interest in the invasion planning, allowed that "while I might get ashore, I won't live long."[36]

For three hours, one officer after another pitched in and several arguments broke out among the British army representatives. Exasperated, Cunningham sniffed, "Well, if the Army can't agree, let them do the show alone. I wish they would." The meeting was deadlocked. "It was one hell of a performance," Patton wrote in his diary. "War by committee." He blamed the impasse on Alexander, who "cut a sorry figure at times. He is a fence walker."[37]

But Alexander was fed up. Clearly, Tedder and Cunningham would not willingly consent to implementing Montgomery's plan. Yet the original plan could not be bent to satisfy either his or Montgomery's concerns. When a May 2 meeting, which Alexander missed, resolved nothing, he decided to implement most of what Montgomery had proposed. Rather than take the "operational" risk of dispersing his forces, Alexander opted for what he considered an "administrative" gamble. Gone was the objective of seizing major ports. Instead, Seventh Army would strike the southern corner of the island, while Eighth Army came ashore on the eastern flank. The only ports to be taken quickly would be the small one at Siracusa and the naval anchorage at Augusta, with Catania, it was hoped, falling soon thereafter. Patton's Seventh Army would supply itself from the beaches until D plus 14, when Alexander believed supplies could begin flowing from Siracusa to the Americans.

Alexander thought he possessed a trump card that made beach supply practicable. A few days earlier he had seen a demonstration of a remarkable vehicle, the DUKW. An American-made two-and-a-half-ton amphibious truck with six wheels that was capable of six knots in water, the DUKW struck him as "ingenious" and sure to revolutionize beach maintenance practices. With the July weather predicted to be mild and the seas calm, Alexander imagined hundreds of DUKWs shunting back and forth from freighters to the beach and the Americans being as fully supplied as if they had a port.

He fretted about one aspect of the new plan—the Americans carried all the risk of a supply breakdown if delivery over the beaches failed. There would be no glorious race for Messina by Patton and

his troops. Instead, they would cover Montgomery's left flank by liberating unknown little towns such as Gela, Licata, and Scoglitti,
while Montgomery's men captured Siracusa, Catania, and likely the
final objective of Messina. While the plan struck Alexander as the
only sound one, he feared Patton's resentment at having to dance to a
new tune played by a superior and British officer. But when Alexander cautiously presented the revised plan to Patton, the American
accepted it without any show of emotion.[38] In a letter to his wife,
Patton wrote, "The new set up is better in many ways than the old."
Partly, Patton cared less about where he was to fight than how he was
to fight. Once the target was clear, he was ready to go at it with all
the skill and strength he could muster. "Execution is the thing, that
and leadership," he believed.[39]

Finally, after several months of letting others move the invasion
planning along, Alexander had stepped to the plate in a manner that
Patton approved. On May 13, Alexander presented the plan to the Combined Chiefs of Staff and received their formal blessing. The same day,
the last remnants of German and Italian resistance in Tunisia ended
in a full surrender. Operation Husky could now receive everyone's
undivided attention. But the clock was ticking. Just fifty-eight days
until the landing craft launched.

[2]

Finally, the Final Plan

WHILE THE DEBATE over Operation Husky's general strategy had raged between the three headquarters in North Africa, Canadian planners in London strove to shape their role in the invasion. Until mid-May, when General Alexander finalized where the British Eighth Army and U.S. Seventh Army would go ashore, they had understood that 1st Canadian Infantry Division would land at Scoglitti in the Gela Gulf, with a British parachute battalion dropping ten miles inland on the nearby airfield at Comiso. Intelligence reported a battalion of Italian infantry garrisoned at Comiso, and Major General Harry Salmon hoped that by capturing the "airfield at the same time as I assault the beaches I should succeed in making [it] look both ways." If he could also quickly cut the road running east from Comiso to larger Ragusa it would be difficult, given the rugged countryside, for the stronger Italian force there to counterattack either airfield or beaches.[1]

Intelligence assessments of beach conditions and known defences at Scoglitti enabled Salmon and his staff to develop a detailed invasion plan by April 28. He expected stiff resistance from the pillboxes and machine-gun posts shown on aerial photos, but believed these defences too weak to prevent assault troops from securing the beach. Thereafter, Salmon planned to have 13,890 men ashore within twelve hours and 1,310 vehicles landed within eighteen hours. An

44

elaborate schedule, based on beach capacity, was prepared for transferring troops and vehicles ashore.[2]

Salmon convened a long session that afternoon with his general
staff officer (GSO), Lieutenant Colonel George Kitching; divisional
artillery commander, Brigadier Bruce Matthews; division chief engineer, Lieutenant Colonel Geoff Walsh; the division's three brigade
commanders, and other senior staff members. He confessed to being
worried that Eighth Army had yet to indicate that the operational
plan was finalized. With the deadline for completion of loading ships
assigned to the slow convoy set for mid-June—just six weeks away—
Salmon considered sealing matters of the greatest urgency. He would,
the general said, emphasize this point during his forthcoming meeting with Lieutenant General Oliver Leese in Cairo.

Discussion turned to who should accompany Salmon on the
morning's flight. Initially he wanted Kitching, but then decided on
the GSO's counterpart in the British 3rd Division, who had been
involved in the initial planning. That left Kitching free to advance the
plan in Salmon's absence. Walsh was dropped when it was learned
the plane would be a modified Hudson bomber, which had limited
load-carrying capacity. Every passenger pound eliminated could be
replaced by fuel to ensure sufficient range to fly from Britain to
Gibraltar for a refuelling stop and then on to Cairo.

After the meeting, Kitching went to Salmon's room and continued discussions while the general packed his bags and organized the
personal papers he would take. At 1900 hours, Salmon said he was
ready. Kitching thought Salmon was "in great form and in a happier
mood than I had ever seen him before." He was pleasantly surprised
when the general suggested dinner, for usually Salmon ate alone. "I
had never seen him let his hair down in the way he did that night,"
Kitching recalled. "He was full of fun ... He was assured and positive
and I was delighted to experience the change in the man." The two
lingered over drinks and did not return to the hotel until 0200.
Salmon turned at his hotel door and told Kitching "he hadn't enjoyed
himself so much for a long time." Kitching readily agreed.

Shortly after 0700, Kitching rode with Salmon and Walsh in a staff
car to Hendon Airport outside London. Accompanying Salmon on the

flight were Rear Admiral P.J. Mack—the naval officer assigned to command the Canadian support ships, 3rd Division's GSO, Lieutenant Colonel G.G.H. Wilson, the newly appointed 1st Division assistant adjutant and quartermaster general, Lieutenant Colonel C.J. "Chuck" Finlay, and Mack's naval assistant, Captain T.L. Beevor. The five men boarded the plane, while the other officers "saluted and waved, wishing them luck and God's speed." After watching the converted two-engine bomber lumber off the runway at about 0900, Kitching and Walsh returned to the Mayfair Hotel for a late breakfast.[3]

A couple of hours later, Kitching arrived at Norfolk House and was immediately called over by Brigadier Howard Graham, who was manning the army's top-secret phone line. Kitching noted that Graham was "pale and drawn."

"George," Graham said, "I'm sorry to tell you that Harry Salmon and all his party were killed when their Hudson crashed somewhere in Devon." Kitching felt the colour drain from his face. "Now what do we do?"

Quickly recovering, the two men sent signals alerting everyone to the tragedy. Kitching also ordered his chief staff officer (11), Major Dick Danby, to proceed immediately to the crash site and secure any documents. Danby found the plane so badly burned that none of the bodies were recognizable. But he found Salmon's briefcase. Amid the charred papers inside were the remnants of a personnel folder that read: "Recommended for promotion to Brigadiers: Lt.-Cols. Kitching and Walsh." With their sponsor dead, the recommendations were now meaningless, but Salmon's confidence "meant a great deal" to Kitching.[4]

The lieutenant colonel told General Andrew McNaughton of the crash via a scrambled phone call. The army commander wasted not a second filling the gaps created by Salmon's death. First, he reorganized a second flight due to depart on April 30 for Cairo, so that Kitching and 2nd Canadian Infantry Brigade commander Brigadier Chris Vokes—who had been pinch-hitting as the division's deputy commander—were added to the manifest. The two officers would begin discussions with Leese. McNaughton next called Major General Guy Simonds at 2nd Canadian Infantry Division headquarters.

Simonds was instructed to take over 1st Division and "put himself in the picture in regard to the forthcoming operations as quickly as possible."[5]

ON APRIL 20, just three days before his fortieth birthday, Simonds had been promoted from brigadier to major general and given command of 2nd Division. Now Simonds would lead Canadians into their first divisional-scale campaign. Tall, lean, and bronzed by the North African sun after an extended tour at Eighth Army headquarters, Simonds had grey-blue eyes that were as steady and unnerving as Montgomery's. His jet-black hair was set off by a little wave at the temples, his moustache thin and turned up at the ends. Simonds never rambled. Each sentence was clipped and precise. A *Winnipeg Free Press* reporter commented: "He's a marvelously keen observer who can put the picture into words without any need to write a long report about it. That's the Montgomery style."[6]

Hardly surprising, for Simonds had deliberately modelled himself after the Eighth Army commander—even to the point of favouring a black tanker's beret. The two men were alike in having quick, incisive minds, being arrogantly self-confident, and being impatient with perceived failings in others. Montgomery had taken an early interest in Simonds and still acted as an occasional mentor to one of the few Canadian officers he considered possessed of any talent.

Simonds lacked one Montgomery quality, that charismatic ability to win the confidence and admiration of the common soldier. Naturally aloof, Simonds had embraced the ramrod-straight persona of the Royal Military College (RMC) graduate and Permanent Force officer. He seemed incapable of relaxing. Old acquaintances were often taken aback. In the mid-1920s, working as a reporter with the Regina *Leader–Post,* Richard Malone had roomed with Simonds—then an artillery captain on the local district staff. With the war, Malone had joined the army and been posted to Britain as Defence Minister Colonel John Ralston's staff secretary during an extended mission in 1940. Here, he eventually crossed paths with then-brigadier Simonds. "Far from any friendly or relaxed greeting from an old friend of our rowdy bachelor days, I was accorded the strictly formal, frozen

Permanent Force treatment with the clipped sentences and raised eyebrows. Thank heaven I remembered to salute him, as I was, still, only a mere captain."[7]

Upon learning Simonds had been given command of 1st Division, Ralston studied a report on the new major general written by a senior officer. A "most outstanding officer but not a leader of the type that will secure the devotion of his followers...Temperamentally suited to serve as a high Staff Officer...Has undoubted ability and will fight his Division and make few mistakes," it concluded.[8]

Brigadier Chris Vokes, who commanded 2nd Canadian Infantry Brigade (2 CIB), was pleased by Simonds's appointment. They had been RMC classmates and as close to friends as Simonds would allow. Vokes "had every confidence that Guy would be an outstanding leader. I had a very high opinion of his military ability and of his leadership. I hoped... that the confidence was mutual. I knew, however, I would be judged on my performance and what my brigade did in action and, that if I didn't measure up, or if the brigade didn't, I would be fired by Guy, old friendship notwithstanding."[9]

This was the man who strode into Norfolk House two hours after his reassignment and demanded a detailed briefing. Although many papers had been lost in the plane crash, Kitching had a copy of Salmon's operational plan and quickly summarized it. Two of the division's three brigades would land on beaches close to Scoglitti, while a parachute battalion dropped near Comiso and seized the airfield there. Overlooking the beaches was a sharp-edged ridge from which the Italians could bring down artillery fire. This would be the division's first objective. The troops would then cut the Comiso–Ragusa road and link up with the paratroops. A major problem the engineers had to solve was that each beach was backed by dunes and high banks. Only one beach had a narrow track cut through. Until the engineers bulldozed gaps in these obstacles, little motorized traffic—including tanks and artillery tractors—could advance to support the infantry.

When Kitching finished, Simonds asked for the administrative and quartermaster plans, only to learn that the single copy had been in Lieutenant Colonel Chuck Finlay's briefcase. Simonds turned to Finlay's deputy, Major Ab Knight, and asked if he remembered enough details to rewrite the plan. Blessed with a photographic mem-ory, Knight assured the general he could not only rewrite it verbatim but also recall the questions Finlay had intended to raise in Cairo.[10]

Satisfied, Simonds turned to the individual brigade plans. As 1st Brigade would land on the division's right, Brigadier Howard Gra-ham led off, laying out a plan that adhered to accepted beach-landing doctrine. His troops would first secure a bridgehead and then advance on a nearby small airfield. Once these two tasks were com-pleted, the brigade would pursue the enemy. Simonds scowled, and snapped that securing the bridgehead was a "waste of time." There was the "necessity of getting on with the job of beating up the enemy." Graham was taken aback at being dressed down in front of his col-leagues simply for confirming Salmon's judgement that securing a bridgehead "was a wise and proper operation to minimize the risk of being driven back into the sea by an immediate counterattack."

When Simonds turned to Vokes, whose 2 CIB would land on the left, he skipped all mention of securing bridgeheads. Instead, Vokes would chase "the bloody Hun" or "the Ities" all the way to Messina. As his 3rd Brigade was in reserve, Brigadier Howard "Pen" Penhale refrained from offering any plan until it was clear how the advance brigades were "prospering." Unlike Simonds and the other two brig-adiers, Graham was not an RMC graduate. A militia-trained officer, he suspected this was the reason that Simonds made a point from then on of addressing him by last name while the other two were Chris and Pen.[11]

BY LATE AFTERNOON, the most pressing unresolved problem was that a plane had not been found to replace the one that had crashed. Upon learning of the crash and the lack of an immediately available plane capable of making the long journey to Cairo, Prime Minister Churchill offered his personal Liberator bomber. Early on the morn-ing of April 30, Kitching, Vokes, the division's chief signals officer, Lieutenant Colonel Jake Eaman, First Canadian Army's deputy chief of general staff, Brigadier Warwick Beament, and Lieutenant Colonel Don Tow boarded Churchill's plane at a Royal Air Force (RAF) airfield on Salisbury Plain. On the drive from London, Kitching and Vokes had speculated about Churchill's Liberator. "Comfortable beds? Arm-chairs? A dining room with attractive WAAFS to serve us? We got a rude shock as we climbed into the main bay of the converted bomber. It was completely open and the only furniture of any kind was about a dozen mattresses scattered around the floor. We found that these were to be our beds for the next twenty-four hours and our food would be haversack rations. It was a bit of a let-down but we found the mattresses were comfortable and that there were a number of clean pillows to enable us to prop up our heads to read or recline in the Roman fashion."[12]

The journey was long, Not until 1900 hours on May 1 did the Liberator set down at an air base outside Cairo. The officers were whisked by car into the city and checked into the famous Shepheard Hotel, declared a British bastion for the duration. Simonds was also en route to Cairo, his party having departed Britain that morning and due to arrive late the following day. Aboard Simonds's plane was Rear Admiral Philip L. Vian—replacing Rear Admiral P.J. Mack—as well as Lieutenant Colonel Geoff Walsh and Major Ab Knight.

Kitching and Vokes held preliminary discussions with xxx Corps planning staff, who indicated that the plan was undergoing major changes. Just before he left London, Simonds had been warned that a change in the Husky plan was "contemplated." During a refuelling stop in Gibraltar, he met a British general who "said that the change of Plan was still to the fore but that it was still not firm." From Gibraltar, his plane flew to an airfield near Algiers, where it was grounded by a sandstorm. Simonds seized the opportunity to visit Force 141 head-quarters. He carried away a "new Plan...that...was still not the final Plan." At 1700 hours on May 4, the plane touched down in Cairo, and the following morning, at precisely 0630, Simonds reported to Force 545 headquarters.[13]

Finally the final plan was final, he learned. Gone was the Canadian assault on Scoglitti. They would strike to the east on the right flank of Pachino peninsula. This was Sicily's southernmost feature and formed the island's southeastern corner. Simonds took the radical change in stride, sitting down to study intelligence summaries regarding enemy defences on the new beaches. Then Simonds walked into the model room and considered the three-dimensional displays of the island. Here, Simonds wrote, he "decided how...to carry out my share of the task allotted."

Rear Admiral Vian had been doing his own assessments. Vian told Simonds "he did not like the beaches, and considered them unsuitable for assault craft; but we decided and agreed that in spite of the difficulties the assault was feasible, and we could carry it out." At noon, Simonds met Lieutenant General Oliver Leese, who approved the division's operational outline. Simonds later wrote, "I pointed out to him that the enemy coastal defences on the right and left flanks of our sector required special attention and he agreed that 51st (Highland) Division would clear the defences on the right flank, and concurred on the inter-divisional boundary [as proposed by Simonds]. He agreed also to leave the Royal Marine Commandos with me (it had been decided to use them elsewhere) to pinch out the defences on the left flank."[14] Simonds was greatly relieved to keep the commandos. Without them, his left flank would have hung in the air because there was a yawning gap of about twenty miles between 1st Canadian Division and the nearest U.S. Seventh Army division that would be landing west of Eighth Army. Intelligence showed enemy coastal guns positioned there could fire on the Canadian beaches unless silenced. The commandos would do this.[15]

"I pointed out to General Leese that time was short as far as we were concerned, and that I had to get back to England within two weeks at the outside. I told him I had to put forward a firm plan, and leave Cairo with the clear understanding that whatever Plan I took back with me could not change as the loading of the ships was soon about to start and this could not be delayed.

"In the afternoon I made a further study of the map and model, and put the Plan down on paper and cabled it home that night. The plan was cabled to England within 24 hours of my arrival in Cairo and was never changed." It was the kind of decisive work Montgomery would have approved of and was typical of Simonds in action.

Over the next few days, Simonds and the other Canadian officers entered into a whirl of meetings with British counterparts. There was the need to ensure that Simonds and the 51st Division commander were clear on the boundaries they would maintain during the advance, so that neither strayed into the other's gunsights or allowed a gap to develop. Simonds and Vian agreed intelligence on the beaches was woefully inadequate and demanded photo reconnaissance be carried out by submarine. When Simonds attempted to get two small infantry assault ships added to his roster of ships in order to land the commandos an hour before the rest went in, Leese refused. That was about the only thing Simonds wanted that he failed to get.[16]

Vokes and Kitching, meanwhile, had been discussing weaponry. Some Canadian equipment was outdated or not used by the British in the Mediterranean. With its light armour and armament, the Canadian-made Ram would have to be replaced by the more robust American-built Sherman, which was emerging as the ubiquitous Western Allied tank. The Canadian anti-tank gunners would exchange their ineffectual 2-pound anti-tank guns for the more powerful 6-pound and 17-pound models. There would, the British officers warned, be other equipment changes and precious little time for retraining. Vokes and Kitching assured them that the Canadians were fast learners.[17]

Within five days of Simonds arriving in Cairo, the Canadians were ready to go home. Because of the risk of plane crashes, they split into two groups with Simonds leading one and Kitching the other. Not everyone would immediately return. Vian and his staff officer stayed behind. Everyone but Kitching and Vokes flew back to Britain aboard a RAF bomber. As the flight approached British shores, the pilot announced that Plymouth was dead ahead and they would land there. Glancing out a window, Simonds asked Major Knight whether he thought they were looking at Plymouth. "No," Knight said. Simonds ducked into the cockpit, and seconds later the plane's engines roared as it clawed back altitude. "I thought that wasn't Plymouth," Simonds told Knight. "The bearing of the sun was all wrong. It was Cork." Had the plane landed in neutral Eire, it was likely everyone aboard would have been interned.[18] "Our navigator had almost lost me somewhere over Eire," Simonds reported.[19]

Kitching and Vokes had a somewhat less dramatic though curious return. Dressed as civilians, the two officers boarded a British

Overseas Airways Corporation commercial liner. Shortly after take-off, the plane was forced to land at El Adem, near Tobruk, to fix a landing gear. Then it stopped at Algiers for engine work. After crossing the Mediterranean, an emergency landing in Lisbon led to its being pronounced unserviceable. Two Canadian officers, both looking precisely like soldiers in civilian garb, wandered about the Lisbon terminal in neutral but Fascist-inclined Portugal. Finally, they booked passage on a Dutch Airways flight for London, but were informed in whispered tones that the takeoff time was indefinite because the ticket agents for Lufthansa and Italy's Regia Aeronautica were spies. They would immediately alert the Luftwaffe in southern France whenever a flight by an Allied commercial carrier took off. Several such planes had been intercepted and shot down. Finally, in the middle of the night, the passengers were hustled aboard and the plane raced into the dark. Despite extreme turbulence that rendered almost everyone aboard airsick, the passage was made at low altitude to avoid detection by German radar.[20]

WITH THE OFFICERS back from Cairo and less than sixty days until Canadian troops were expected to splash ashore on Sicilian beaches, preparations quickened. Previously, hardly anyone in 1st Canadian Infantry Division aside from the approximately fifty officers at Norfolk House had possessed an inkling that their long wait in Britain would soon end. Now the sudden announcement that the division and 1st Canadian Army Tank Brigade would move from "Sussex by the Sea" to Scotland signalled that something was up, and the nature of the training, with its emphasis on amphibious landings, indicated the task ahead. But there were still no hints as to the division's ultimate destination.

In early May, the three rifle brigades started training at Inveraray for "an opposed landing" and "subsequent land operations including mountainous countryside." First, eight days of route marches, cross-country runs, cliff scaling, rope climbing, and tumbling down scramble nets, all while burdened with full packs. Next, the brigades boarded ships for a series of landings on "hostile" beaches defended by squads of Royal Marine commandos posing as the enemy.[21]

During one such landing, Lieutenant Colonel Bert Hoffmeister led his Seaforth Highlanders of Canada off landing craft into icy three- to four-foot-deep water. "We struggled ashore, weapons all full of sand and everything else, and we had to rush up to the positions we were to occupy and strip our weapons down. With rifles it wasn't quite so bad, they could force the actions, but my Tommy gun wouldn't work. I couldn't pull the bolt back, it was just full of sand, my pouches were full of sand and the revolver wouldn't work, although it was protected a little better with the holster…[We] got into our positions and dug ourselves in. It's a wonder we didn't lose half the battalion from pneumonia because every staff officer in the British Army had to come around and look at our positions. We crouched down there while we were just freezing in a high wind, low temperature and soaking wet in this cold water, but it certainly gave us a good idea of what is involved in getting down scrambling nets over a ship's side with all your equipment, while the craft is bobbing up and down and so on. This was a very fortuitous exercise for us to have done."[22]

Hoffmeister's .45-calibre Thompson submachine gun was one of a variety of new weapons and equipment supplied to accord with that of Eighth Army's other divisions. Despite its tendency to jam when exposed to sand, the gun's terrific stopping power made it a hit with the troops, particularly when compared to the lighter 9-millimetre Sten they had been using. With its easily disengaged safety catch, the Sten had been notorious for accidentally discharging and was more jam-prone than the Thompson.

"No. 1 novelty," as the weapon was designated on a top-secret British ordnance list to mask its true purpose, was the newly developed Projector Infantry Anti-Tank (PIAT) gun. Weighing thirty-two pounds and firing a 2.5-pound hollow-charge explosive bomb, the PIAT provided Commonwealth troops with a hand-held weapon capable of disabling tanks.[23] Difficult to load, prone to mechanical failure, and complicated to operate, it was more often cursed than praised by the soldiers assigned to use it. That its bomb was too light to penetrate anything but the thin side and rear armour of German tanks was another bone of contention the soldiers raised after trying it out during training exercises. They were told it was the PIAT or nothing.

Not only were new weapons introduced, but some battalions faced major reorganization. The Saskatoon Light Infantry (MG) Regiment, which numbered about five hundred men, was completely reorganized into three Brigade Support Groups. One group retained the Vickers .303 Machine Gun, Mark 1, that the entire battalion used to provide heavy machine-gun support to the infantry brigades. The second group received 4.2-inch mortars to give the division heavy mortar support, and the third was issued single-barrelled 20-millimetre Oerlikon anti-aircraft guns for air defence.

The SLI commander, Major Thomas de Faye, figured the men assigned to the Oerlikons could take the adjustment in stride, one fast-firing heavy gun not being that dissimilar from another. But for the two platoons each equipped with four mortars, which were mounted in fifteen-hundredweight trucks, there was a steep learning curve. Few had any previous mortar training. The officers and NCOs attended a rush course and then turned to training their men. There was nothing precise about the heavy mortar. With a range of 4,500 yards, its 19.5-pound bomb, de Faye quickly realized, was never going to be deliberately dropped "into somebody's back pocket. They were strictly an area weapon, but a very dangerous, very effective weapon for catching infantry in the open." With time short, de Faye knew his men would be "barely trained on these new equipments by the time we went into action with them."[24]

A welcome addition to the Canadian inventory were 100 DUKWS reportedly en route directly from the United States. But when the delivery date passed with no sign of the vehicles, it was feared they would not arrive before the invasion force departed. With only two of the amphibious trucks that had so impressed General Harold Alexander available in Britain, the driver-mechanics tasked with operating this missing fleet had to queue for days to clock even a few minutes of operational and maintenance time. Finally, in early June, the trucks appeared.[25]

Captain Howard Mitchell and his SLI mortar platoon managed one trial DUKW landing before a general order was issued for all the vehicles to be loaded on transport ships. Instead of being directed to a dockyard, Mitchell's group found itself driving onto a stretch of sand where an embarkation officer was busily issuing orders to an array of soldiers boarding either DUKWs or small landing craft. "See that ship out there?" the officer said to Mitchell. "Well, that is your ship. Good luck."

To Mitchell's untrained eye the vessel appeared to be standing at anchor about two miles offshore. "Actually," he soon realized, "it was about six miles out. And our DUKW's only carried enough gasoline for about 8 to 10 miles of sea travel. There was an odd wave but then land lubbers expected to see waves on the ocean. We struck out to our ship. The further out we got the rougher the waters seemed to get. We bobbed about like corks. Finally we reached our ship. The captain was furious. What kind of God Damned fools were we? Didn't we know that the water was too rough for him to pick us up with the davits? He had to pick us up. We didn't have gas enough to get us ashore again.

"Finally he agreed to take us aboard. I never realized what a tricky business it was. We got close and scrambled up rope ladders. With both the ship and the DUKW bobbing up and down, even getting started up that ladder was something. Getting the DUKW's hooked on was terrible. When they were finally aboard most of the davits had suffered and one was bent horribly. The skipper held me personally responsible for the damage to his fine ship."

It didn't help the naval captain's mood to realize the DUKWs he had loaded were actually on the manifest of a different ship, one tasked to carry SLI troops supporting the 2nd Canadian Infantry Brigade. He had been expecting troops from 3rd Canadian Infantry Brigade. With the damaged davits, nothing could be done to sort out the mess, so Mitchell and his men would travel to Sicily as part of 3 CIB.[26]

MISTAKES LIKE THE one that put Mitchell's DUKWs on the wrong ship proved remarkably rare as the complex loading proceeded through early June. The planners at Norfolk House had been meticulous. Major Robert Kingstone worked closely with a British combined operations officer, who was an expert in amphibious landings, to devise the loading plan for 1st Canadian Infantry Brigade's troops and equipment. "The landing tables alone were several hundred pages because you had both the assault convoys and the follow-up convoys to deal with and you had the sizes of vehicles and the capacity of ship holds to take various heights...It was a fascinating time actually."[27]

It was a near-Herculean task. To transport a total strength of 1,851 officers and 24,835 other ranks, complete with all their equipment and 30,000 tons of supplies, a distance of more than 2,000 miles would require 125 transport and escort vessels. Throughout the first three weeks of June, "long motor convoys began to arrive at ports up and down the west coast of Great Britain—in the Bristol Channel, on the Mersey, and along Clydeside—bringing heavily laden unit transport from the training areas. At the docks a vast assortment of stores gathered from ordnance depots all over the country found its way into the holds of waiting ships. Loading was done tactically...in such a way that vehicles and cargoes could be discharged in order of priority governed by the demands of the tactical plan and by the facilities for unloading that would be available on the beaches. Since it was essential that the vehicles, stores, supplies and ammunition necessary to maintain the assault should be landed as quickly as possible from the waiting convoys, the ships carrying the motor transport and the general cargo vessels had to be so grouped that their arrival at the 'Release Position' would immediately follow upon the landing of the assaulting waves. As the vessels in the English ports completed loading their respective quotas of vehicles and stores, they sailed up the west coast into the Clyde and anchored in their convoy assembly areas."[28]

What long after the invasion seemed so orderly to the Canadian Army's official historian in fact often bordered on the calamitous, and there was more on-the-spot innovation than the planners ever knew. In a number of cases, the cabs of trucks proved too high to fit inside low-ceilinged holds. Removing the cab, slicing a few inches off it with a torch, and then fitting it back together solved the problem and nobody cared if that meant its driver had to hunker down for lack of headroom.

Captain Jim Stone had reluctantly drawn duty as a ship's storage officer. Having enlisted in the Loyal Edmonton Regiment as a private in 1939, Stone had had pre-war experience in the British militia before emigrating to Canada. This put him on a promotional fast track to the rank of company sergeant major and, after two years' service in the ranks, on to officer training. By the spring of 1943, he was a Loyal Edmonton captain, hoping to lead one of the battalion's rifle companies into combat. Instead, he was sent on several transportation management courses to learn how to organize the movement of stores and equipment on an invasion beach, shuttle supplies and men about on trains, and finally stow things aboard ships according to a tactical plan. Upon learning he was to be detailed to precisely that last task instead of being given a rifle company, Stone railed at Lieutenant Colonel Jim Jefferson: "I'm going to take my Edmonton flashes off." Jefferson shook his head. "Don't. You'll be back." Stone groused, "I don't know. You get caught up in these staff things and you never know what will happen."

So it was that in early June, Stone stood aboard the freighter *Orestes IV* in a Birkenhead dock near Liverpool. The *Orestes* was to join the slow convoy, its holds to be filled with vehicles. Stone had been warned that the merchantmen would want to mess with the tactical loading plan and his job was to stand fast. Reporting to the ship's captain, Stone was directed to work out the loading details with the first mate. "I have the stowage plan here, Mr. Kay," Stone told the first mate. "This is the way the ship must be stowed."

Kay studied the plan for two long minutes. "That is the way the ship will not be stowed," he said.

"It's got to be stowed that way."

"It can't be stowed that way," an exasperated Kay replied. "We've got no heavy lifting gear forward, you see. So those heavy vehicles are going to have to go aft...the people who set the stowage plan in London had a complete plan of the decks of the ship but no knowledge of the lifting equipment on deck. It's not like going into the dock where you can pick things up from the dock. All the equipment has to be lifted out of the holds and put over the side. And so it's only what the lifting gear on the ship can manage."

Stone thought this over and realized "it was just nonsense to argue with people who knew what they were doing." So he said, "Look, I've got to get these vehicles off in this order."

Kay rubbed his chin thoughtfully. "Okay, you sit down and tell me right now what you consider is a priority." The two men assigned each vehicle a number that indicated priority in line. There were about forty heavier vehicles that had to be reassigned to the bottom of the list because they were to be stowed in the lowest hold, but otherwise Stone got everything the way he wanted it. Knowing there would be a flap if he reported varying the sacred loading plan, Stone said nothing.[29]

There were a lot of things not talked about for security reasons. Lavish amounts of special equipment to enable the Canadians to operate in a subtropical, mountainous environment were secreted away in ship holds for distribution once the convoy was at sea or even after the invasion was ashore. Khaki tropical uniforms that included shorts and puttees, rope-soled shoes, and tinted eye shields and glasses were to be broken out after sailing. Special camouflage paint would be used to repaint all the vehicles in desert colours. Other gear included: 100 sets of pack saddlery in case mules were pressed into service for off-road mountain transport, hundreds of Yukon and Everest packs to enable soldiers to carry large amounts of supplies if the mules were lacking, and many crates of fly swatters. Insects caused the planners great concern, particularly malaria-carrying mosquitoes. To ward them off, 45,000 mosquito nets and a similar number of bush nets were packed alongside vast stores of anti-malarial drugs, both as a preventive and for treatment after infection.[30]

Once the convoy sailed, the Canadians would take daily doses of the anti-malarial drug mepacrine, a synthetic substitute for quinine—the natural alkaloid extracted from the bark of the cinchona tree. Although the cinchona tree was native to South America, Dutch entrepreneurs had transplanted it to Java in the mid-nineteenth century and it came to dominate the world supply of quinine. With Java's invasion by the Japanese Imperial Army on February 28, 1942, and surrender nine days later, the Allies had lost access to quinine and so had turned to synthetic drugs that duplicated its effects. Mepacrine had several side effects—it turned skin jaundicelike yellow and similarly coloured urine. The latter prompted an official slogan intended to promote mepacrine use: "If you pee a golden stream it means you've taken your mepacrine." But rumours also abounded that the drug caused sterility, so attempts to avoid taking it were widespread.[31]

By the time the last supply container had been lowered into the holds of the transport ships, officers at the War Office in London boasted with satisfaction to Simonds that his was "to be the best found expedition which ever left the United Kingdom."[32] The ships were not yet quite ready to sail. Although the fast convoy was gathered in the Clyde, and although the men, having been granted and returned from a five-day embarkation leave, were now confined aboard, there remained one final training exercise to run. Designed as a dress rehearsal for Husky, Operation Stymie was to be a large-scale combined operation, with the infantry brigades landing on a section of Ayrshire coast that bore close physical resemblance to the Sicilian beaches for which they were bound. For security purposes, however, the soldiers were told the coastline actually resembled a part of German-occupied France. On June 17, twelve transports carrying 1st and 2nd brigades sailed out of the Clyde and, in the early hours of the following day, began lowering them, despite a heaving sea, into landing craft. Shortly after the small vessels cast away from the transports, rising winds and worsening wave action led to the landing force's hurried recovery. Four days later the bad weather had not abated, and Operation Stymie, true to its namesake, was cancelled.[33]

The cancellation came on June 21. Two days earlier, elements of the slow convoy, bearing the equipment and soldiers not designated to the initial assault force, had slipped their lines and left the Clyde. Over the next few days more ships departed, often at night, under a shroud of secrecy. On June 28, the Fast Assault Convoy steamed out of Greenoch and disappeared into the gathering darkness. The infantry battalions had been crowded aboard eight merchantmen recently converted into Landing Ship, Infantry (Large) vessels. One of these—the *Circassia*—served as 2 CIB's headquarters ship and also carried the entire battalion complement of more than eight hundred Seaforth Highlanders. Quarters were terribly cramped, and the first night at sea the Seaforths grumbled as they struggled to learn the difficult task of slinging the hammocks that would serve each night as their beds.[34]

Aboard the divisional command ship *Hilary*, the division's recently and reluctantly appointed historical officer, Captain A.T. "Gus" Sesia, realized at 0243 hours that the ship had slipped its cable and was under way only because the buoy to which the telephone cable providing a link to shore was drifting away. "For most of the first hour and a half of sailing," Sesia wrote in his diary, "I surveyed Greenock [Greenoch] and Gourock through our binoculars and watched bathers, lovers, passers-by, soldiers, sailors, airmen and civilians going about their devious ways. It was hard to realize that the day had come when we were actually on the way to participate in battle."[35]

3

Everyone Knowing His Job

CAPTAIN GUS SESIA was one of the few soldiers aboard the Canadian convoys apprised of their true destination. Although the rumour mill worked overtime, most everyone remained in the dark. When the tropical kit was broken out, speculation turned to Burma, but that just seemed too distant. Lieutenant Colonel Bert Hoffmeister and some other Seaforth Highlander officers "had Greece as one thought in mind, Crete, and we figured we were going into the Mediterranean. We didn't know where else we'd be going wearing clothes like that."[1]

One doggedly persistent rumour held that the tropical gear was an elaborate ruse to deceive German spies that might be aboard. In reality, the Canadians were bound to invade or raid Norway.[2] When the ships rounded the northern coast of Ireland and steamed south through the Atlantic in order to give the u-boat and e-boat infested Bay of Biscay a wide berth, proponents of the Norwegian caper reluctantly conceded its improbability.

The suspense was palpable during those first days at sea, just as it had been when they were embarked and awaiting the order to sail. During the time they had waited for the ships to cast their lines, many a senior officer had looked at the sealed collection of top-secret envelopes and boxes containing his briefing materials and considered taking an illicit peek. But the orders were firm: nothing to be opened until they were at sea and Major General Guy Simonds granted permission. The temptation remained, however, and Lieutenant Colonel Leslie Booth, commander of the Three Rivers Tank Regiment, succumbed to it. Breaking open the covering envelope, he gleaned from its contents that they were to invade Sicily. Unfortunately for the thirty-seven-year-old officer, it was precisely at that moment that Simonds happened to board the Landing Ship, Tank (LST)—one of six carrying the tankers and their Shermans—to personally wish Booth "good fortune and to see if there were any problems arising from our enforced confinement to the ships." Catching Booth red-handed, Simonds was rendered almost speechless with anger. He curtly ordered the officer to report to him aboard *Hilary* in two hours and stormed off the boat. Simonds fumed to his general staff officer, Lieutenant Colonel George Kitching, that he intended not only to severely reprimand Booth but to return him to Canada. Booth's second-in-command would take over the tank regiment. Considering the notion of replacing a regimental commander this late in the game ill conceived, Kitching countered that if Booth were fired, he would end up wandering around either Britain or Canada with the invasion secrets in his head for twelve days before the landings occurred. Better to keep him aboard.

Kitching had never met Booth and was struck when he came up the gangway by the fact that the tanker was barely five feet tall. He was also "shaking like a leaf." Kitching escorted Booth into Simonds's office and took up position behind the tanker. "I had never seen Guy Simonds in a cold rage before. Everything was ice. For five minutes he told Booth exactly what he thought of his conduct." Kitching worried that he "would have to support him physically as he wilted from the blast." When Simonds finally released Booth, Kitching helped him into the small motor launch that would take him back to the LST. Booth allowed that "his five minutes with Simonds...made him all the more determined that he and his regiment would do well."[3]

The intense secrecy cloaking 1st Canadian Infantry Division's destination reflected a grave concern that the landings would be thrown back into the sea if the Germans and Italians discovered that

Sicily was the invasion target. Currently, Sicily was not heavily defended, but if reinforced in strength—particularly by German divisions—the island could be rendered impenetrable. "Anybody but a bloody fool would *know* it is Sicily," Prime Minister Winston Churchill snorted even as he approved an arcane deception plan intended to throw the Germans off the scent.[4] Operation Mincemeat entailed dressing a corpse in a Royal Marine officer's uniform and planting on it papers that identified the body as Major William Martin, currently serving at Combined Operations Headquarters in London, but lost at sea in a fictitious air crash off Gibraltar. British intelligence ensured that the body washed up on a Spanish beach, where the contents of a dispatch case chained to his waist were discovered by local authorities and quickly turned over to the German consulate. The briefcase contained documents that hinted at where the Allies would strike after the campaign in Tunisia concluded. On one hand, the papers told German intelligence analysts that the Allies planned to invade Sicily, but only after first capturing Sardinia. Considered from a different angle, however, the documents suggested an invasion of Greece and sowed the seeds of suspicion that perhaps the Allies wanted the Germans to think Sicily was the target, which then logically meant it "can't be the real target."

Operation Mincemeat succeeded beyond all possible expectation. On May 11, German naval staff concluded it was impossible to judge the authenticity of the papers found on Martin's body. The same day, Adolf Hitler and Grand Admiral Karl Dönitz agreed that Sardinia's garrison should be kept at current strength and that an invasion of Sicily seemed unlikely. Two days later, the naval staff declared the documents authentic and a mock attack on Sicily would precede an invasion of Sardinia.[5]

Axis confusion was furthered by Hitler's penchant for thinking himself one step ahead of both his general staff and the Allies. Hitler decided the deception documents confirmed that the main Allied thrust would be directed at the Balkans. An invasion there, he said, was "more dangerous than the problem of Italy which, if the worst comes to the worst, we can always seal off somewhere."[6] Hitler's assessment that an invasion in the Balkans posed more danger to

Germany was correct, for it was from southeastern Europe that many vital raw materials, such as grain, timber, oil, and minerals, were drawn. As the American official historian later argued, "Hitler expected the Allies to land in Greece or the Balkans, and his reasoning was sound. Both areas were more important to the German economy than Italy. The populations were friendly to the Allies. An Allied invasion would supplement pressure, force the dispersal of Axis troops over widely separated areas, and forestall a Russian occupation of the Balkans."[7]

The German Armed Forces High Command, meanwhile, had also been closely examining the documents found on the dead courier. According to their analysis, an operation code-named "Husky" would land two British infantry divisions in Greece with another operation in the western Mediterranean against an unspecified target. But this landing would be supported by a "feint attack against Sicily." Sardinia and Corsica were deemed at risk and it was recommended that because the "report directs *special attention* on *Sardinia* and the *southwestern Greek ports*...the importance of increased preparedness in these sectors" was imperative.[8]

Tenth Army commander Generalfeldmarschall Albert Kesselring, who was responsible for German operations in southern Italy, was less convinced. While recognizing that "landings in the south of France or in the Balkans... might be assessed as a preliminary to operations with far-reaching strategic and political aims," Kesselring believed the Allies more likely sought to defeat Italy. Sicily provided a logical stepping stone onto the mainland, but so too did Sardinia or Corsica. And, like the other German analysts, Kesselring could not discount the possibility of Allied invasions in the Balkans, or southern France, or anywhere else in the Mediterranean for that matter. The Allied options seemed limitless. Yet whenever he looked at the map and saw Sicily sitting there so temptingly below the toe of Italy's boot, and considered what its possession would provide the Allied air and naval forces in terms of an operational base, it was hard to believe the invasion would not fall there.[9]

And the Axis forces were ill prepared to defend it. Although Italy's armed forces numbered two million men, about 1.2 million of these were serving abroad on fronts such as Russia and the Balkans. These troops were the country's best trained and equipped. The forces that remained in the homeland were of generally poor quality. Badly equipped and inadequately supplied, they were seriously demoralized by May 1943. News that Italy's very best divisions had surrendered—those that had shown such tenacity in the final stages of fighting in Tunisia—sent their spirits tumbling to even lower depths. The Tunisian defeat dealt a fatal blow not just to military morale, but to that of the entire population, which was shaken by the loss of this last remaining colony. A war that had never been popular became much less so. His Excellency Cavalier Benito Mussolini's prestige nosedived, and general war weariness began to manifest as open defeatism. When King Victor Emmanuel III suggested to Il Duce that Italy should "consider very seriously the possibility" of breaking with Nazi Germany to negotiate a separate peace, he only echoed popular opinion.[10] Mussolini rejected the suggestion.

Il Duce was woefully ignorant of both the general mood in Italy and the pathetic condition of his homeland army. He pronounced that Italians would defend their native soil to the bitter end, that any Allied attack "on our mainland" would be heroically defeated.[11] Yet Mussolini realized the first attack on Italian soil would more likely be directed either at Sardinia or Sicily. Whereas his army commanders favoured Sardinia, Mussolini suspected Sicily because its possession would give the Allies control of the Mediterranean Sea. None of the Italians were fooled by Operation Mincemeat into thinking the Allies would strike anywhere but Italy. Still, neither Mussolini nor the army command undertook any major effort to bolster Sicily's defences.

The commander-in-chief of Italy's Sixth Army technically commanded all Axis troops in Sicily. In 1943, Generale di Corpo Mario Roatta held this post from February to the beginning of June. Roatta recognized the danger to the island and worked feverishly to bolster Sicily's fortifications. But lacking necessary resources, he achieved minimal results. Roatta's request for cement to construct fixed defences typified the problems faced. Instead of the 160,000 tons he sought, Roatta was sent only 7,000 and told to share this amount with the naval and air commands on the island.[12]

The Axis chain of command on Sicily was chaotic. While all army units and some naval and air formations fell under Roatta's authority, those naval forces deemed to be in the three "fortress areas" of Messina–Reggio, Trapani, and Augusta–Siracusa were commanded by admirals who reported to a naval headquarters—Comando Militare Marittimo Autonomo della Sicilia—which was independent of Sixth Army. Anti-aircraft units were distinct again and under a commander who reported directly to the Ministry of War in Rome. The German army and air force ground crews technically fell under Roatta's command for political reasons, but Hitler had quietly arranged for General der Panzertruppen Fridolin von Senger und Etterlin to be posted as German liaison to Sixth Army's headquarters. His orders were to keep German troops under his administrative control.[13]

By the end of May, Roatta's morale was dipping perilously close to the same dismal level as that of the average soldier serving in Sicily. When German foreign minister Konstantin von Neurath toured Sicily to prepare a report on the defences for Hitler, Roatta said bluntly that he had little "confidence in the possibility of defending Sicily. He claimed he was too weak and that his troops were not properly equipped." Since the beginning of May, the Royal Air Force had been subjecting the island to severe bombing raids and strafing runs. Ferry traffic from the mainland to Messina had been brought to a near standstill. The Sicilian populace despised the Germans and believed that only liberation by the English would bring peace. Roatta divulged his woes in long, tedious detail that von Neurath delivered almost verbatim to Hitler. Asked his personal opinion of Roatta, von Neurath observed, "I wouldn't trust him further than I could kick him," and speculated that the general was plotting something.[14]

Perhaps he had been, for on May 30, Roatta was unexpectedly appointed Chief of the General Staff of the Army. His replacement in Sicily was Generale d'Armata Alfredo Guzzoni, a sixty-six-year-old called back to service after two years in retirement, who had never been to the island. His first inspection left the new general shocked and dismayed. At first glance, the command—numbering some 200,000 Italian troops backed up by another 32,000 German soldiers and 30,000 German Luftwaffe ground crews—should have been impressive. About half the Italian troops comprised four divisions and his army headquarters troops, while the rest were assigned to coastal defence divisions or various support services. Everything Guzzoni saw only convinced him that his Italian forces were "mediocre," with poor morale, equipment, and training to boot. A large number of the troops were Sicilians, who shared the civilian population's disillusion with the government and the war. Food shortages and the unrelenting Allied bombing increased their misery.[15] Just to feed the civilians and soldiers on the island required nearly eight thousand tons of supplies daily, but only about fifteen hundred to two thousand tons made it across the Straits of Messina. So everyone went hungry.[16]

The coastal defence divisions were badly understrength, and many of their troops were elderly. Defending a ninety-mile front from Siracusa to Cape Scaramia—which was precisely where Eighth Army planned to land—the 206th Coastal Division had just fifty-six outdated field guns, thirty-four mortars, and six hundred and ninety light and medium machine guns. On average, there was one anti-tank gun for every five miles of coastline. The much-touted Mobile Groups were equipped with obsolescent tanks and a smattering of self-propelled 47-millimetre guns, light artillery, and anti-tank weapons.[17] Even the four mobile infantry divisions were poor. The 28th (Aosta) and 54th (Napoli) were undermanned, short on equipment, and ill trained. Enjoying only slightly better morale, but otherwise equivalent to these two divisions, was the 26th (Assietta). More recently deployed to Sicily from Rome, the 4th (Livorno) Assault and Landing Division had better training and, rather than relying almost completely on horse-drawn transportation, was two-thirds motorized. It also had a good number of light tanks.[18]

Not only was the quality of troops poor, but the coastal defences were also a shambles and lacked a continuous system of fortification. In many sections, there were no minefields, obstacles, anti-tank ditches, pillboxes, or dugouts at all. Elsewhere, such defensive works were badly separated or sited, so that one position provided no support to another. Back of the beaches, little attempt had been made to construct defensive positions to provide in-depth strength.

Prior to retirement, Guzzoni had reputedly been one of Italy's more competent generals, which he soon proved was still the case. Despite the seemingly hopeless situation, the general did not despair. In a personal effort to turn the situation around, he logged seventeen-hour days. Given the lamentable condition of both defences and his Italian troops, Guzzoni realized that Sicily's salvation might depend on the two German divisions garrisoned there.[19]

Both were good. The Hermann Göring Panzer Division—a Luftwaffe unit originally formed to serve as the supreme air force commander's personal bodyguard but later released for combat duty—deployed to Sicily on June 20 at Kesselring's direct order. The best of its troops had been sent to Tunisia and had surrendered there, so it was capable of fielding only two full infantry battalions rather than its mandated two Panzer Grenadier regiments.[20] It also had lost a third of its artillery strength, a portion of its flak regiment, and about half of its supply and support units. However, the division was strong in terms of armour, with two tank battalions fielding ninety-nine tanks. About thirty-five of these, however, were outdated Mark IIIs that were more lightly armoured than the Allied Shermans. Mounting either a long-barrelled 50-millimetre or short-barrelled low-velocity 75-millimetre gun, they were barely a match for the Sherman's 76-millimetre gun. A roughly equal number of German tanks were Mark IVs armed with a 75-millimetre long-barrelled gun that could go head to head with a Sherman. A third armoured battalion was equipped with self-propelled guns. The division also had an attached army tank company, the 2nd Company of the 504th Heavy Panzer Battalion, recently supplied with seventeen Tiger I tanks. Weighing fifty-six tons, the Tiger mounted an 88-millimetre gun that greatly outmatched the Sherman's 76-millimetre. Its heavy armour rendered it almost impervious to anything but the luckiest of hits on a weak point. The Tiger, however, was new technology and prone to breakdown.[21] Generalmajor Paul Conrath commanded the Hermann Göring Division. A former Berlin State Police officer, Conrath had joined the Luftwaffe in 1935 and seen extensive service on the Russian front at the head of what had originally been formed as a regiment, then expanded to a brigade, and finally became the division he still led.

The other German division in Sicily had been cobbled together from troops drawn from bits and pieces of units scattered all over Italy, but most had either been serving in anti-aircraft units on the island or waiting there as reinforcements bound for Tunisia. Although designated the 15th Panzer Grenadier Division, its structure did not adhere to conventional form because of its ad hoc construction. At its core, however, were two Panzer Grenadier regiments—the 129th and 104th. The former was composed largely of men who had seen hard service on the Russian front fighting in Panzer divisions, while the latter was made up of wounded veterans of the Afrika Korps.[22]

As was the norm for Panzer Grenadier regiments, each battalion was better equipped with automatic weapons, anti-tank guns, and mortars than were regular German infantry regiments. Each battalion was armed with fifty-nine light and twelve heavy machine guns, three 75-millimetre anti-tank guns, six 8-centimetre mortars, and four 12-centimetre mortars. The mass of machine guns gave these battalions a weight of firepower far superior to any comparable Commonwealth unit. The division's tank regiment also fielded about sixty Mark III and Mark IV tanks, while another unit was armed with thirty-six multibarrelled rocket launchers, called *Nebelwerfers*. German artillery field pieces on the island numbered 104. Added to this was a plethora of anti-aircraft guns ranging from light-calibre weapons up to the deadly 88-millimetres that could equally serve an anti-tank or general artillery role.[23]

Assembly of this division had begun in April under the hand of Oberst Ernst-Günther Baade, an eccentric but brilliant officer. On June 9, however, Generalmajor Eberhard Rodt had taken over the division. Rodt had performed capably in a variety of command slots on the Russian front. Although the new commander had little knowledge of Sicily, the division's other officers had at least a few months' experience on the island and most of the troops also shared a good sense of the ground. Not as mechanized as the Hermann Göring Division, the 15th was still sufficiently mobile to enable its rapid deployment to wherever required.[24]

The mobility and strength of the German divisions prompted Guzzoni to position both of them inland from the southeastern coast as a reserve to the Napoli and two coastal divisions assigned to that area's defence. He also concentrated his best Italian division—the Livorno—here as an inland reserve in the expectation that the Allies would land on beaches in Sicily's southeastern corner. Guzzoni's plan called for the coastal divisions to fight a delaying action rather than try to immediately repel the invasion. He would then counterattack with the Livorno and German divisions and drive the Allied forces into the sea. Given his resources, Guzzoni's plan was sound, and he had correctly divined where the Allies would strike.[25]

But during a visit to the island on June 26, Generalfeldmarschall Kesselring questioned the plan. At Guzzoni's headquarters in Enna, Kesselring worried that the Italian was overconfident about where the Allied landing would fall. He insisted that the majority of the 15th Panzer Grenadier Division should be deployed in the western part of Sicily to protect Palermo and that one of its regimental groups be detached to directly defend Catania on the east coast. Only the Hermann Göring Division would be kept in the southeastern reserve. Kesselring's plan not only scattered one German division into packets but robbed Guzzoni of the concentrated punch he could have delivered by sending both divisions into battle side by side.

"Smiling Albert," as Kesselring's detractors had nicknamed him, had a sound reputation as a strategist and tactician. Now fifty-seven, Kesselring had transferred from the army to the Luftwaffe during the interwar years but always considered himself "a soldier heart and soul."[26] It was the role he now served, despite still wearing Luftwaffe insignia. Cheerful and optimistic to a fault, Kesselring also had an iron will and was always persuasive. In leaving it to the Luftwaffe Generalfeldmarschall to determine how German forces would be used in the defence of Sicily, Hitler had said, ruefully, that "Kesselring is no end of an optimist and we must be careful that in his optimism he doesn't fail to see the moment when optimism must be a thing of the past and severity take its place."[27] Yet on June 26, Kesselring behaved more as Hitler appeared to wish. He was forceful and convincing in presenting his argument, which suddenly had the Germans preparing to defend the island in every direction feasible. Despite the fact that Rodt and Guzzoni both disagreed, Kesselring refused to be swayed, and the Italian general reluctantly agreed to change his dispositions. Von Senger approved of the dispersal of a

German division to guard against a western invasion force that might cut off the Straits of Messina and trap their forces in Sicily. But he wished Kesselring had selected the weaker Hermann Göring for scattering and kept the 15th concentrated in the southeast.[28]

In a final private briefing with the German divisional commanders before he returned to Rome, Kesselring cautioned them: "It makes no difference whether or not you get orders from the Italian army at Enna. You must go into immediate action against the enemy the moment you ascertain the objective of the invasion fleet."

Conrath growled, "If you mean to go for them...then I'm your man." Kesselring allowed afterward that he returned home "feeling pretty confident" that an Allied invasion force striking Sicily could be repelled.[29]

FROM VARIOUS POINTS of the compass, the Allied invasion fleet closed on Sicily during the last days of June. On July 1, Major General Guy Simonds ordered the senior officer aboard each ship in the fast convoy to open the bags containing the plans for Operation Husky. The troops were then divided into two groups and, as each was brought up on deck, the officer made a brief announcement to "put them in the picture." On *Hilary*, Lieutenant Colonel George Kitching opened by saying, "We are on the largest combined operation ever mounted...and...our next stop is the southeastern peninsula of Sicily which we will assault and capture."[30] Upon being told that the division would join General Montgomery's Eighth Army, the men "cheered heartily."[31]

The bulging bags yielded a treasure trove of information. Bales of maps, air photos, operation orders, and intelligence pamphlets were unwrapped for study. One cabin on each ship was transformed into a briefing room equipped with "large scale models of the beaches and hinterland where the division was to assault."[32]

Aboard 2nd Canadian Infantry Brigade's headquarters ship *Circassia*, Captain Frederick Norman Pope gave the briefings. The brigade's intelligence officer, Pope lamented that "while the fellows upstairs were sunning themselves on the decks, I was down in the bowels of the ship taking in officers and men, a group at a time, and saying this is where they would be landing, and there were photo-

graphs taken from airplanes flying in so you had a landing view of
the coastline as you were coming into it. This is where you'll be landing, this is where your first objective is, and that's your second
objective. These people will be on your left flank, and, on the right,
you'll have so and so. And I was doing this all day, every day, for it
took all that time for everyone on board to go through...They were
all suntanned and I was still as white as white could be."[33]

An astonishing mass of detailed documents had been prepared.
The operational plan itself ran to more than two hundred pages—
the last document of that size ever produced by 1st Division.[34] While
Pope walked people through the briefing room, other officers lec-
tured the men on various aspects of the operation. Map-reading,
signals procedures, first aid, sanitation issues, and treatment of prisoners and civilians were singled out for special emphasis. Simonds
was determined that when 1st Division hit the Sicilian beaches, it
would "become known not only as a fighting division but as one possessing every good military quality." In a directive on training aboard
the ship, Simonds stressed that "good fighting must be associated
with smartness of turn out and keenness in all those things which
go to make a good soldier." The division, he said, would "go ashore
physically fit, with everyone knowing his job and what is required of
him, and with a definite urge to kill."[35]

Each man was issued a handbook entitled *Soldier's Guide to Italy*,
which "contained a description of the geography, the history, the government, the church, [and] the principal towns and industries of Italy
and told the soldier what his assignment was in the country and what
his relations were to be with civilians. It also gave him information
regarding various Italian customs, currency, weights and measures
and a list of useful Italian words and phrases."[36]

Almost all of Sicily, they learned, was "occupied by mountains and
hills, which fall either directly to the sea or to restricted coastal plains
or terraces...In Central and Southern Sicily the bare treeless ridges
and rolling hills composed in large part [of] clays and soft rocks form
difficult country, slopes are unstable and landslides probable."

Looming over the surrounding landscape on the island's eastern
coast was massive Mount Etna, the almost eleven-thousand-foot-high

active volcano that sprawled across more than six hundred square miles and had a base circumference of about ninety-three miles. Catania, the port city that was one of Eighth Army's major objectives, lay on the lower slopes of the volcano's southeastern corner. Its summit often wreathed by a mixture of smoke and cloud, Etna's last major eruption had been on June 30, 1942. It remained intensely active, spewing forth highly porous lava from a side vent on the southwest flank about two thousand feet below the summit.

Sicily's climate in summer was hot and dry "with conditions very constant, the temperatures mounting by day and falling by night with monotonous regularity." There existed three classes of roads, but on "nearly all routes there is a succession of ups and downs, and curves, owing to the mountainous nature of the Island." While state roads were well constructed, the provincial and communal roads, which were largely what 1st Division would be relying on, generally followed "a narrow and torturous course."

About 3.9 million Sicilians called the island home, and because the countryside was pestilent with malarial mosquitoes, the residents concentrated in towns. The guidebook described the people as "temperamental and hot headed, but lacking single-heartedness and constancy for a cause. The large mass of the population is politically apathetic partly owing to poverty. Life is harsh; the great majority of the population is engaged in agriculture, and except in a few favoured spots, their life is a constant struggle for existence. Big estates, absentee landlords, malaria and the great shortage of water in a country where there is no rain from May to October have kept the standard of living very low. The standard of education and literacy is also very low, some 40 per cent of the population being unable to read or write... The Sicilian peasant commonly lives in a small town perched on a hill and often approached by a track so steep and rough that even the Sicilian carts cannot mount it. This isolation has helped the survival of many old customs and habits of thought." Soldiers were advised that such was the state of apathy that the civilian population would take no active part in military operations, but would "greet the invading forces with sullen indifference, whether they are British, Canadian or American."[37]

Aboard the converted Dutch ship *Marnix van St. Aldegonde*, Captain Strome Galloway and several other Royal Canadian Regiment officers gathered around the model of the landing beaches. "The first thing that struck us all...was that the practice landings we had recently done on the Ayrshire coast had been on a section of beach and hinterland that was remarkably similar to where the Sicilian landing was to take place. The road exits from the beach were almost identical. The distances to the exercise objectives the same as to the actual objectives—an airfield and a coastal battery in Sicily. In fact, in our Scottish exercise those exact objectives had been simulated. The beaches were sandy as well. The only real differences, it seemed, were that tall vineyards had to be crossed in Sicily once we cleared the beach, and that our enemies would be real, waiting for us behind minefields, barbed wire and blazing weapons."[38]

Their sandy beach was code-named "Bark West." Measuring 8,300 yards long by 86 to 145 feet deep, the beach had a gentle grade running from the water to where it butted up against a steep limestone ridge varying in height from ten to fifteen feet and fronted by a system of low dunes. Behind the ridge lay several salt marshes and ponds that might or might not have dried up under the summer sun. The ground free of the marshes and ponds was taken up by an assortment of vineyards, closely planted citrus orchards, and grazing pastures. Several dried-up streambeds cut sharp paths down the gentle slope to gain the sea.

At first glance the beach appeared ideal for amphibious landings, until closer examination of the models revealed that standing out to sea from the "real" beach were several "false beaches or sandbars." Between the sandbars and Bark West the water was believed to be as deep as five feet, but nobody knew for sure. All that was known was "that if landing craft were going to ground on the sandbars then it was essential that the water inside the bars be not too deep for wading or driving motor vehicles."

These sandbars had been the subject of much discussion and concern at Norfolk House. On May 12, the Canadian staff officers there had concluded that the depth of water behind the sandbars would restrict the initial landings to just infantry "and that the casualties would...be very high." No intelligence gathered since had changed their thinking.

The fact was, if Bark West was fiercely defended, the Canadians were heading into a slaughter. Stretched along Bark West were fifteen known pillboxes and twenty machine-gun positions, with more such defensive works extending three miles inland to Pachino airfield. This airfield, northeast of the beach, was the first day's main objective. Pachino, population about 22,000, lay next to the airfield. Roughly midway between Bark West and Pachino, a coastal defence battery had been erected next to the hamlet of Maucini. The battery's four medium guns, set on a height of ground about one hundred feet above sea level, enjoyed an all-round field of fire and could range freely on every inch of Bark West. This battery was hidden in an orchard alongside a farmhouse and was surrounded by wire. Covering the approach to the airfield and also capable of ranging on the beach was another field-gun battery positioned immediately north of Pachino.

Predictions were that as the landing craft approached the beaches, they could come under fire from between eight and twelve artillery pieces and far more machine guns. The planners had postulated a grim scenario of what would happen if "the enemy put everything into their defence" and the infantry had to be dumped into the water to wade slowly ashore from landing craft stuck on the sandbars. Even on "reaching the beaches there would be wire entanglements and perhaps mines and booby traps to clear while under fire from enemy M.G. [machine gun] posts and pillboxes."[39]

In the end, all hopes had been pinned on the premise that the defences would prove lightly manned by inferior troops. xxx Corps commander Lieutenant General Oliver Leese had assured Simonds that he believed the beaches would be held only by Italians. And he had little regard for the Italian troops. "Once we have closed with him, he gives up," Leese said. "The great point about the Italian is that he does not hang on and fight, once the leading troops have by-passed him."[40]

Even if everything did go sour, the division should be able to win the sand and carry its objectives through sheer force of numbers. Two of the three brigades would be in the leading wave, and as long as a brigade managed to get the equivalent strength of even one of its battalions ashore, it would strike out for the inland objectives. If, however, "a whole Brigade were destroyed, the action of the Brigade which had been lost would be carried out by the Reserve Brigade."[41]

Nobody aboard the ships, except the officers who had been involved in preparing the operational plan at Norfolk House, was made privy to the full extent of their worries. But the dangers were clear to see. Hoffmeister understood that the Germans would stiffen the Italian backbone by sifting a number of their men in among the troops defending the beaches. "We were prepared for, maybe not a heavily opposed landing, but an opposed landing. We expected that we would have to fight our way across the beaches."[42]

On June 30, matters became even more complicated when a message from xxx Corps reported that a reconnaissance team had been slipped ashore at Bark West on the night of June 25–26. This commando team of scuba divers confirmed the existence of a sandbar that was about twenty yards wide and submerged under eighteen inches of water on the southern flank of Bark West. Although about six hundred yards of the bar lay outside the Canadian landing zone, eighty yards of its length protruded into the right flank of the beach— the portion of Bark West where 1st Canadian Infantry Brigade was slated to land. While the sandbar's existence was little surprise, the commandos had been taken aback to discover that on the shoreward side it fell away sharply to a depth of nine feet. Working their way north, the team had confirmed the existence of another sandbar off the section of the road where 2nd Canadian Infantry Brigade would land to the left of 1 CIB. Lying under about thirty inches of water and falling away shoreward to a depth of only five feet, this bar presented less of an obstacle.

After mulling over this information, Simonds ordered 1 CIB's Brigadier Howard Graham to change his landing plan. No longer would the brigade's assault battalions use the small Landing Craft, Assaults to gain the beach. Instead, they would go in on three larger Landing Craft, Tanks to the sandbar. From here they would launch aboard DUKW amphibious trucks, which would roll over the obstacle and carry them through to the beach. The fact that 1st Division had too few DUKWs to make this plan feasible was quickly remedied by xxx Corps headquarters rushing twenty-four extra DUKWs aboard three LCTs and sending them to join the convoy.[43]

The presence of the sandbars was common knowledge throughout the division and added to the general belief that just gaining the beach was going to be daunting. Corporal Felix Carriere, a Princess Patricia's Canadian Light Infantry runner, expected "we would be savaged reaching the beach." Yet he remained in good spirits, as did the men around him. "Morale was high," he said later. The twenty-two-year-old from a farm south of Winnipeg had, after more than three years of hard training in Britain, been honed into a "muscular 129-pound" soldier who "could run up and down ropes like crazy" and do anything else required of him with skill and daring.

Carriere spent little time thinking about the fighting ahead. What intrigued him about the *Soldier's Guide* was the information on the Italian people and their customs. His thoughts were those of a tourist bound for an exotic foreign country. *"Come si chiama? Questo?"* he repeated over and over again. "What is it called? This?" And Carriere would point at some object on the ship, practising for the day ahead when he got to make such a query to a real live Sicilian.[44]

On board *Circassia*, Lieutenant Robert L. McDougall sat on the deck writing a letter home to his mother and "enjoying the sunlight on this incredibly beautiful and peaceful evening. Here on the port side, except for a watchful ship of war guarding our flank, I can see only one limitless expanse of blue sea. Fine weather for a cruise—and what an extraordinary cruise this is. I find it all still a bit unreal... My pad is resting on a large map board which I have propped against my knees. On this map board are the maps of this enemy land which we are to invade and the whole operation I have marked out on the talc. As I say, it's all rather unreal. I look at that map-board in a detached sort of way and I study it and memorize names and roads and such-like, following the unfolding of the plan phase by phase; but I have gone through precisely the same motions on the large number of schemes we have done in the past few months and it is difficult to bring home a realization that this is the real thing...There is amazingly little feeling of tension amongst us—perhaps it's because even up to this late date we have had virtually nothing in the way of opposition. What human hands can do has been done; the rest is with God."[45]

4

Going to Be Some Party

E VERY DAY, MAJOR General Guy Simonds and Lieutenant Colonel George Kitching performed the same macabre ritual. Kitching would take a hat filled with equal-sized chits of paper on which the names of every ship bearing Canadian personnel and equipment was written and hold it out to the divisional commander. Simonds drew three chits and those ships were declared lost, victims of torpedoes from a German u-boat—the scenario at times being that about one thousand men aboard the fast convoy had drowned and burned in oil-drenched seas, or hundreds of trucks, tanks, guns, radios, and other equipment in the slow convoy had plummeted to the bottom of the Mediterranean. All lost, gone. Kitching and his staff would then sit down and coldly "examine the effect the loss of these three ships would have on our projected plans."

On July 3, Simonds pulled from the hat chits for three ships travelling in the Slow Assault Convoy—*City of Venice, St. Essylt,* and *Devis.* The coincidence was chilling, for it was aboard these vessels that equal portions of the divisional headquarters equipment—including all the trucks, Jeeps, radio sets, and a panoply of other gear that kept a division functioning—had been distributed. Were one or even, God forbid, two of these ships sunk, the headquarters could function almost as normal. But lose the three and the division was crippled.

Kitching considered the "chance of all three ships being sunk was a million to one." Deciding there was no point in studying the implications of such a wildly remote possibility, he asked Simonds to draw another three names from the hat, which the general did.[1]

As Simonds and Kitching were drawing lots, the slow convoy had passed the Straits of Gibraltar and started making its way along the North African coast between Oran and Algiers at a leisurely eight knots. Aboard *St. Essylt,* a dispirited and frustrated Major Cameron Ware brooded about the fate that put him on this ship rather than with the rest of the Princess Patricia's Canadian Light Infantry, sailing in the fast convoy aboard *Llangibby Castle.* The twenty-nine-year-old major could hardly believe his bad luck—declared Left Out of Battle and hence barred from being with the battalion during its combat debut. Left Out of Battle, a perfectly sensible precautionary measure, required every battalion to hold back a small number of officers and men to provide an experienced core around which to rebuild should the unit be decimated in the forthcoming assault. Soldiering was Ware's lifeblood. He had joined the militia as a boy soldier in 1927, entered Royal Military College in 1931, and been posted as a lieutenant to the Permanent Force PPCLI upon graduation. Nobody was a more faithful servant to the regiment and army than Ware—it had even been his boyhood dream that one day this regiment would be his to command. And now he was repaid by being bloody LOB when the PPCLI needed him most.

Ware should have seen it coming when he was made the battalion's second-in-command, but he had simply forgotten about the practice, which had been introduced during the Great War. The rules were clear. If the battalion commander was leading his men into a fight, the second-in-command became LOB. Same with the individual rifle companies and on down the chain, sometimes as far as individual sections within platoons. Perhaps Ware could have accepted it all more gracefully if he had been with the battalion on *Llangibby Castle,* but no, it was decided that he needed to be on a different ship in case the one with his commander, Lieutenant Colonel R.A. "Bob" Lindsay, was sunk. No good having the LOB men go down with the same ship as the rest of the battalion.[2]

So the PPCLI soldiers designated LOB were on this freighter, which was filled to bursting with 320 troops from a variety of units. In the lower holds were about one hundred vehicles and large quantities of ammunition that taken together amounted to a gross weight of nine hundred tons of matériel.[3] Ware was the senior army officer aboard so technically commanded the soldiers and was responsible for the stores. But there had been precious little to do except sit in the ever warmer sunshine until the order to break open the operational instruction bags had been received on July 1. For the past four days, he had been walking the men aboard through the instructions and now considered "everybody briefed and puffed up about what they were going to be doing" when they finally landed in Sicily days behind the assault battalions.

After dinner on the evening of July 4, Ware went up on deck wearing only his khaki shorts because of the heat and stood chatting with the ship's captain, Master Stephen Diggins. The two men leaned casually against one of the stacks, reviewing an earlier incident that had seemed to the soldier to be a great display of Royal Navy efficiency. There had been a u-boat alert, and the nine naval ships protecting the convoy had responded immediately. The single destroyer and one of the six corvettes raced with black flags raised—to alert the convoy ships to the u-boat danger—and unloaded dozens of depth charges on its suspected location. Whether the ships sank the German submarine or not, Ware was glad they were so vigilant and said so to the ship's captain.

"Don't worry, my boy," the captain said with a tired smile. "Whenever you see a black flag, don't worry about it. When you get torpedoed, you won't see any black flag. It'll be a complete surprise to everybody. Anyway, it's a nice quiet 4th of July."[4]

Precisely at this moment a huge explosion shook the converted passenger liner *City of Venice*, a short distance from *St. Essylt*. Dead in the water, the ship coasted to a halt. *St. Essylt* and the rest of the merchantmen kept steaming forward, rigidly adhering to Allied convoy protocol whereby the valuable cargo ships kept going while the naval escorts would provide what assistance they could. In this case, the naval rescue tug HMST *Restive* raced to the stricken ship and took it under tow while three corvettes began offloading personnel. Algiers was ninety miles to the west and the cutter made for the port. But when its crew proved unable to seal the holed hull, *City of Venice* was declared a loss and released.[5] Including its crew, the ship had 482 men aboard. Its master, 10 crew, and 10 Canadian soldiers were lost.[6]

From *St. Essylt,* Ware had watched *City of Venice* fade from sight and was just "waiting to get torpedoed." With each passing minute his conviction that the U-boat had them in its sights kept growing. All the soldiers had been called up on deck in readiness to abandon ship, if necessary. "It was a very nervous half hour because you were convinced you were going to get torpedoed and you wondered what would happen," he later said. "It was a relief when we got hit, but when we got hit, you sure knew you had been hit by something. There was a great sheet of flame from the forward end of the boat." In seconds, the forward holds, where the ammunition was stored, were ablaze. Ware expected the entire ship to simply go up in one massive blast of exploding artillery rounds. Instead, each shell exploded singly, sounding like fireworks from hell.

The crew put lifeboats over the side, and many of the soldiers pitched in to cast away inflatable rafts and life rings. Soon only a few crew and Ware remained aboard. Much of the ship was on fire and it was heeling badly, as Ware looked about to ensure that all the soldiers were off. He would have liked to have retrieved some clothes from his cabin, but one glance revealed that fires had spread throughout the ship's interior. He and Master Diggins shook hands and wished each other luck before clambering down ropes and dropping into the Mediterranean. Ware had "visions of the North Atlantic and being frozen to death...but the sea was like a nice warm bath." Losing sight of Diggins, Ware swam to a nearby raft and clung to the ropes running around its sides. He had no life jacket, had lost his shoes, and wore only his shorts. As with the *City of Venice,* the convoy "sailed majestically ahead. That's one of my saddest moments...floundering around in the water, watching the convoy sail on into the sunset." *St. Essylt* continued to burn, bathing the survivors in an eerie light as it settled slowly beneath the surface. Ware thought of all the secret operational documents aboard and how they should be burning safely, so there was no likelihood of their being captured by the enemy. They drifted through the night and then at dawn a corvette steamed up and began hauling men out of the water.[7] Despite the initial explosion and ensuing fires, only one crewman and one soldier from *St. Essylt* failed to be rescued.[8]

This was not the end of the slow convoy's ordeal. On the following afternoon, at 1545 hours, the merchantman *Devis* was struck by a torpedo "just aft of amidships. The explosion was immediately below the...Mess Decks, and blew the body of one man up on the bridge, and two more on the boat deck, as well as the rear end of a truck... Fire broke out immediately and within 3 to 4 minutes the fore part of the ship was cut off from the aft part. Explosions of ammunition were continuous. The men, with two exceptions, behaved extremely well. They took their boat stations in an orderly manner, and did not throw over the rafts or jump overboard until the order to abandon ship was given. In the meantime, they collected wounded and burned men, and took them overboard with them when they went." So wrote Major Douglas Harkness, the Canadian artillery officer in command of the soldiers aboard.[9]

The thirty-six-year-old officer had been in his cabin when the torpedo struck. He had attempted to organize rescue parties to go after men trapped below, but the fires were too hot. There were not enough lifeboats and rafts for everyone, so Harkness and many others were left to drift in the sea. The naval vessels raced about around them, dropping depth charges. With each explosion he felt his "insides being squeezed out." Some men who had been alive earlier disappeared, and Harkness was left with the lingering belief that these explosions "killed quite a few of our people that were in the water." Eventually a corvette picked up the survivors.[10] Fifty-two Canadian soldiers* perished while all the crew survived.[11]

---

* There is some discrepancy regarding Canadian casualties. The Canadian official history gives a total of five other ranks and one officer reported missing and presumed drowned from *City of Venice* and *St. Essylt*, while the usually reliable Uboat.net Web site cites ten Canadians as lost on *City of Venice* and one on *St. Essylt*. Both sources agree on a loss of fifty-two Canadians aboard *Devis*. In another discrepancy, all Canadian sources—particularly the eye-witness account by Cameron Ware and a report in 1st Canadian Infantry Division's War Diary of signals received giving the approximate times of each sinking—maintain there was a thirty-minute to one-hour delay between the torpedoing of *City of Venice* and *St. Essylt*. Uboat.net states that at 2140 hours the U-375 fired four torpedoes in a single spread at the convoy and reported sinking one freighter, but later was credited with sinking both vessels. Was there a second U-boat stalking the convoy that evening, which struck after U-375's attack? No records exist to confirm or deny this. Because the Uboat.net casualty figures included losses of merchant crewmen, I have used those in the text.

The survivors were carried by the corvettes to Algiers and unloaded on the docks. Barefoot, wearing only salt-grimed shorts, Ware walked up to a British officer and reported that he and his men were all off *St. Essylt*. The officer told Ware that he understood the Canadian troops were part of an operation, but he had no information on what it was about. Ware pointed at the soldiers. "These guys are all briefed. You better clap them somewhere where they can't be got at." The British officer did precisely that, ordering them all loaded into trucks and taken immediately to a prisoner-of-war camp. Ware was ill pleased at being locked up, but understood the rationale. "We were certainly in a safe place behind barbed wire. But we had to be, for D-Day was on July 10, and this was the 5th of July when we were incarcerated." The British offered up a clothing issue that consisted of two pairs of shorts and underwear, two shirts, a couple of pairs of socks, and a pair of boots.

As each day passed and the invasion drew closer, Ware kept insisting on meeting with the British officer. He was desperate to be released and get passage on a ship bound to join the invasion convoys off the coast of Sicily. Ware was supposed to be LOB, which meant on a freighter sitting off the coast for the invasion, not stuck in a concentration camp in Algiers. "Nothing we can do, old boy," was the routine reply.

WHILE THE LOSS of lives aboard the three torpedoed slow convoy ships was relatively small, the amount and nature of equipment and stores sent to the bottom of the Mediterranean was serious. A total of 562 vehicles were lost, leaving 1st Canadian Infantry Division facing a major transportation shortage. Also lost were fourteen 25-pounders, eight 17-pounders, and ten 6-pounder anti-tank guns that would significantly reduce the division's artillery support.[12] "In addition to the above," the divisional historical officer, Captain Gus Sesia, noted in his diary, "we lost great quantities of engineers' stores and much valuable signals equipment."[13] The biggest immediate blow was the loss of all divisional headquarters vehicles and equipment, including many precious wireless sets—precisely the nightmare scenario forecast and rejected by Kitching as infeasible when Simonds had drawn these ships by lot a few days earlier.

Equally serious was the loss in equipment and lives suffered by the Royal Canadian Army Medical Corps personnel attached to the division. Due to a loading error, instead of No. 9 Field Ambulance's vehicles being distributed among several ships, fifteen out of eighteen were on *Devis*.[14] Accompanying the vehicles was a medical officer and nineteen other ranks and medical orderlies.[15] Four of the other ranks were among the fifty-two Canadian troops killed and another four suffered injuries.[16] The other field ambulance, field dressing station, and field surgery units assigned to the division were largely unaffected. No. 5 Field Ambulance's vehicles had been distributed correctly, so only two of them and a ton of medical supplies went down with *St. Essylt*. *City of Venice* had just one medical officer, Captain K.E. Perfect, aboard and he escaped uninjured. But Perfect was overseeing safe passage of nine tons of stretchers and blankets, which all went to the bottom.[17]

Aboard *Hilary* in the Fast Assault Convoy, divisional staff through the evening of July 4 and all of July 5 scrambled to clarify what had happened to the three ships. Initial Royal Navy signals were disjointed, some indicating all ships lost, others that one vessel or another was under tow and might yet be saved. At one point on July 5, a Royal Air Force signal reported that a plane had spotted *Devis* still afloat. Excited officers quickly consulted a map, Sesia reported, and were disgusted to see the coordinates placed the ship "somewhere in the Sahara Desert!"[18]

A full accounting of the losses would not be completed for days. Even on July 7, reports were still coming in that *City of Venice* remained under tow and bound for Algiers. Finally, at 1900 hours on that day, its sinking was confirmed. The report also stated that most of the surviving Canadian troops had been loaded on a Landing Craft, Infantry in Algiers and were en route for Malta. From there, they would eventually rejoin the division.[19]

Compounding the loss of so many vehicles was the fact that the division had left Britain with a smaller than mandated number due to lack of shipping capacity. Once the seriousness of the situation was appreciated, Lieutenant Colonel D.G.J. Farquharson, the division's assistant director of ordnance services, and his staff "tried to make [the losses] good ... by emergency measures, improvising and obtaining what could be obtained buckshee from the Middle East." They soon had commitments for some vehicles, but these would not be available until after the initial landings. The fact that every vehicle to be found locally was a Dodge posed "a considerable ordnance problem, because what spare parts we had were based on Ford and Chevrolet makes." Improvisation would be the order of the day.[20]

All the time these assessments and response plans were being made, the Canadian convoys had continued steaming towards Sicily. After July 5, German submarine alarms became daily fare, particularly for the fast convoy. To make it more difficult for the u-boats, the ships maintained a fast pace and zigzagged to avoid being easily tracked. To ensure arrival off Sicily on schedule, each convoy's course had been meticulously charted to bring it to a specific waypoint at a precise hour. On July 6, the fast convoy was scheduled to pass Algiers at 2130 hours. Realizing the convoy would overshoot this waypoint by about four hours at its current speed, Rear Admiral Sir Philip Vian ordered the convoy "to kill time [by] zig-zagging to starboard and port." The Royal Navy headquarters at Algiers, meanwhile, was also tracking the convoy's pace and signalled for Vian to cut his speed dramatically and not pass Algiers until 0030 hours the morning of July 7. To avoid having the ships sitting virtually still for almost four hours, Vian ordered the convoy turned sharply about at 1325 hours with the intention of steaming for ninety minutes back the way they had come before returning to their assigned course.[21]

Captain Sesia had just stepped out on *Hilary*'s deck for some air and noticed "we were veering completely about. At the same time, two of the escorting destroyers on our starboard side high-tailed it ahead of us and dropped depth charges. The Black Pennant was run up on all ships and hooters hooted. All the ships in the convoy seemed to be turning in mad circles, and I never saw such frantic signalling by lights and flags both from the *Hilary* and the other vessels. Then came 'action stations.' There was no panic—all personnel proceeded to their stations adjusting their lifebelts and blowing them up. Undoubtedly, quite a number of us were thinking of the *Devis* and the other two vessels which had been torpedoed ... but ... we did not show it except that perhaps our expressions were a little grimmer than usual."[22]

After forty-five minutes, "stand down" was signalled. Sesia subsequently learned that the destroyer screen had spotted a u-boat travelling on the surface off to one side of the convoy as it came about. Two Royal Navy destroyers, *Whimbrel* and *Cygnet*, charged the u-boat but ended coming at it from opposite angles so that neither could open fire with guns for fear of hitting the other. *Whimbrel* attempted to ram the sub, but it managed to dive clear. The destroyers then alternated depth-charge runs. After *Cygnet*'s fourth attack, bubbles were spotted coming to the surface. *Whimbrel* immediately dropped charges on the bubbles and both destroyers reported hearing what sounded like a ballast tank blowing. More bubbles, now mixed with oil, rose on either side of *Cygnet* as she crossed the same marker. Each destroyer dropped another pattern of charges, but no further indication of the u-boat was seen. Both ships rejoined the convoy a few minutes after 1500 hours and the u-boat was claimed sunk (though no German records report a u-boat lost in the Mediterranean during this time period). In the action, *Whimbrel* dropped sixty-eight charges and *Cygnet*, fifty-nine.[23]

Because of the u-boat incident, the following day the fast convoy's destroyer escort was increased to a dozen ships. The *Delhi*, an anti-aircraft cruiser, which was also equipped with five 5-inch guns, joined the convoy because it was now deemed to be within range of German bombers stationed at airfields in Italy and Sicily. The Mediterranean was increasingly crowded with Allied ships. At 1200 hours, an American convoy consisting of two cruisers, six destroyers, and twenty merchantmen was spotted off to one flank. Three hours later, the fast-moving Canadian convoy passed another American convoy plodding eastward at a slower pace. In *Hilary*'s "naval operations room, convoys are plotted on the map (with one pin denoting not a ship, but each convoy) and from Gibraltar to Bizerta there are so many pins that one can hardly see the map. This is going to be some party!" the division's war diarist wrote. "While the sea thronged with Allied ships, the sky overhead was equally cluttered with Allied bombers and fighters. The former were bound for targets in southern Europe while the latter prowled above the convoys in order to intercept any Axis aircraft that might threaten the precious ships. On July 8, forty-one Mitchell bombers 'passed over our convoy on their way to bomb Sicily. According to the news broadcasts, Sicily is getting a non-stop pasting. We are now proceeding along the eastern coast of the Bone Peninsula. Tunisian villages with their mosques and minarets are plainly visible. So far no enemy aircraft have appeared, though the sea is filled with shipping as far as the eye can see. Mussolini's Lake, indeed!' "[24]

As the Canadian and American convoys streamed past Gibraltar into the Mediterranean during the first nine days of July, Northwest African Coast Air Force was there to meet them—flying a total of 1,426 sorties. Over a forty-eight-hour period starting the morning of July 7, fighters from this command carried out a record 574 sorties. The British convoys coming west from Egypt or through the Suez Canal were greeted by fighters from Air Headquarters, Air Defences Eastern Mediterranean, who sortied 1,421 times between July 1 and July 9. The Royal Navy weighed in with 600 sorties off ships and aircraft carriers engaged in anti-submarine hunts. Those convoys closing to within sixty miles of Malta in the last days before the invasion were further protected by fighters flying off the island's airfields.[25] One Canadian Spitfire squadron—417 (City of Windsor)—was operating in the Mediterranean during this time, and it was slated to move to Sicily as soon as airfields were captured and ready for use.

Given the formidability of the Italian navy, the invasion planners had feared its warships would venture forth from their sheltered harbours. None did so. In large part this was due to implementation in mid-May of intensive bombing raids on Italy's airfields, ports, and submarine bases. Over six successive weeks, 2,292 sorties by bombers and fighter bombers struck airfields in Sicily, Sardinia, and Southern Italy, while another 2,638 sorties were launched against other strategic targets in the region.[26] Between July 3 and the July 10 invasion date, Allied air forces concentrated their efforts on disabling, in the words of the British official historian, "whatever hostile air forces were likely to oppose the landings, and to assail the enemy's land, sea, and air communications within Sicily. The principal targets were airfield bases of the German Air Force, and the attack would, it was hoped bring his fighters to battle and cause them heavy losses. Day and night attacks upon communications would swell to maximum as D-Day approached. Beach defences were to be left alone so that surprise might not be prejudiced, but radar installations in Sicily and Sardinia were to be attacked. Just before the landings, specially-equipped aircraft would try to baffle the radar stations within whose scrutiny the areas of assault happened to be."[27]

Pitching into this effort with night raids were the Wellington bombers of Royal Canadian Air Force 331 Wing made up of three squadrons—420 (City of London), 424 (City of Hamilton), and 425 (Alouette). Most of their raids were concentrated against targets on either side of the Straits of Messina. This wing began operations from an air base in Malta on June 15 with plans to move it to Sicily as soon as possible.[28] The Canadian squadrons, along with twelve American Liberator squadrons, had been loaned to Northwest African Strategic Air Force from their commands in the United Kingdom to support the invasion.

Altogether, the Allied air presence in the Mediterranean heavily outnumbered that of the Axis forces. The Allies had 3,462 aircraft, of which about 2,510 were operational, opposing 1,750 enemy planes stationed in Sardinia, Sicily, and mainland Italy. Of the Axis aircraft, 960 were German. Hoodwinked into suspecting that either Greece or Crete was more likely to be invaded than Sicily, the Germans had diverted a larger number of aircraft to that region. Furthermore, only half the Luftwaffe bombers in Italy were stationed within effective range of Sicily—the rest were positioned to defend Sardinia, Corsica, and southern France. As the immediate countdown to the invasion began in early July, just 775 Luftwaffe aircraft could range on Sicily and 289 of these planes were on the island itself, only 143 of them operational. Also in Sicily were 145 Italian aircraft, of which only 63 were serviceable. Three-quarters of all these planes were either fighters or fighter bombers.

With each passing day, the number of serviceable Luftwaffe and Italian aircraft diminished as the Allies intensified their bombing of Sicilian airfields. One after the other, most of the island's airfields were so damaged that soon only two were considered fully operational.

By July 9, 323 German aircraft were declared destroyed in the Italian theatre, along with 105 Italian. The Allies, flying a total of 42,227 sorties between mid-May and the invasion, lost 250 aircraft—mostly brought down by anti-aircraft fire while operating over hostile territory.

Not only Sicilian airfields but also transportation hubs in cities and towns back of the invasion beaches were heavily bombed. There was little in the way of surgical precision about the bombing raids, many being carried out at night against blacked-out targets. Although massive strategic destruction was inflicted, it came at the price of many civilian casualties. Palermo was badly damaged, its rail and road transportation networks all but destroyed.[29] Similar punishment was meted out to Catania, and it soon became an almost deserted city, its streets torn up and blocked with debris from destroyed buildings. The sewage system ceased functioning entirely, and water and electrical supply was regularly disrupted for long periods. Little in the way of food was able to reach the city because the island's rail system had been smashed. There were too few trucks to move supplies on roads that were increasingly hazardous to travel on because of marauding Allied fighters and fighter bombers. Incompetence by the Fascist authorities exacerbated matters. An insufficient number of air-raid shelters had been constructed, and many of these were structurally unsound. As the bombings intensified, attempts to force civilians to clear roads to enable the movement of military transport only drove people into hiding. Before the invasion date, most of Catania's citizens had fled up the slopes of Mount Etna to find refuge in caves or woods. Catania's suffering was not unusual. In Siracusa, those who opted not to flee crowded into the ancient Christian catacombs of San Giovanni.[30]

While brutally executed, the Allied bombing yielded the desired effect. By July 9, the Luftwaffe and Italian air forces were largely paralyzed. The Italian navy cowered in its badly damaged ports. And the defenders on Sicily were desperately short of supplies and denied full freedom of movement along the island's interior roads and rail systems, most of which had been badly hammered. Military and civilian morale was desperately low.

By midday, the Canadian Fast Assault Convoy stood seventy miles south of Malta. Aboard *Hilary,* Captain Sesia looked about at "a veritable armada of warships, merchantmen and transports of every description and size."[31] Even to the east of his position the sea teemed with ships, for the British convoy coming from that direction had hugged the African coast until it stood just off Tripoli before heading directly towards Sicily. By noon, this convoy carrying the British 5th and 50th Divisions plus the 231st Infantry Brigade joined the others in "converging as if along the supporting strands of some huge spider's web upon Malta."[32]

Sailing in this convoy were four of Canada's Landing Craft Flotillas—the 55th and 61st Landing Craft, Assault (LCA) and the 80th and 88th Landing Craft, Mechanized (LCM). The LCA flotillas were equipped with the forty-one-foot-long wooden boats capable of carrying thirty men to a beach and unloading them off the front by dropping a ramp that the troops then stormed down. The LCM flotillas, meanwhile, were outfitted with vessels also mounting a landing ramp on the bow, but their fifty-foot steel hulls were better designed for carrying vehicles and equipment than men.[33] By 1943, LCMs were rarely used for landing troops. Instead, they each generally carried a single tank. Aboard the four flotillas were twenty-four officers and 376 ratings, all Canadians. Most were seasoned veterans of combined operations, having landed assault troops at Bruneval, St-Nazaire, Dieppe, North Africa, and in various commando cross-channel raids. The two LCA flotillas were tasked with landing the 231st Infantry Brigade's assault waves, while the two LCM flotillas would ferry vehicles and supplies on to British-captured beaches near Siracusa.[34]

The eastern convoy that these Canadian vessels were part of—code-named "Force A"—had come alongside the fast convoy at noon. Steaming well ahead of *Hilary,* but being quickly overtaken by the fast-running ships, was the Canadian slow convoy. As these convoys came together, Sesia saw the naval escorts that had guarded them during the voyage pull away, to be immediately replaced by four cruisers and six destroyers tasked with providing close support during the landings. As the fast convoy bore past the slow convoy, five ships from the latter sped up to join it. Had *St. Essylt* and *City of Venice* not been lost, they would also have contributed their vital stores, vehicles, and troops to the strength of the initial landing force. The rest of the slow convoy, which would remain well back until the stores and men aboard were required, quickly faded from view.[35]

Force A soon began drawing away from the fast convoy, as it veered back on a more easterly course to pass Malta on that flank while the Canadians went around to the west of the island. Then both began converging again, joined by two convoys composed of Landing Ship, Infantry (Medium) (LSI); Landing Craft, Tank (LCT); and Landing Ship, Tank (LST) vessels that had sailed out of Sfax on the Tunisian coast with the rest of British Eighth Army's divisions aboard. These vessels came up the middle between Force A and the fast convoy. As the Canadians cut close by the island of Gozo, the three convoys carrying the U.S. Seventh Army came alongside on the left. The American ships arrowed straight for their beaches, while the Canadians turned to the right and made for the western side of Pachino peninsula.[36]

Soon after this course change, the fast convoy and all the other Allied ships sailed into an unexpected gale whose large waves pitched smaller craft such as the LCMS, LSIS, LCTS, and LSTS badly about. But the pace of the ships never slackened. "From now on anything may happen to us," Sesia wrote. "The Italian fleet is still in Taranto and as far as we know shows no sign of moving. Can anyone imagine a similar threat against Britain without so much as a trawler coming out to intercept it? We are well within aircraft range, yet there has been little indication that the enemy suspects our presence, let alone intends to come out and attack us."[37]

On *Hilary*'s bridge, Rear Admiral Vian was unconcerned about the threat of Italian navy or Axis aircraft. Instead he stared at an intelligence signal reporting that a highly placed source inside the Italian military had leaked information that the anchor point for the Canadian convoy was "the centre of an extensive minefield which could be detonated electrically by the Headquarters of the enemy forces in the [Sicilian] capital city of Enna." Intelligence analysts warned that the source was generally regarded as unreliable.

Still, Vian faced a conundrum: should he sail into the middle of a possible minefield that, if detonated, could destroy the Canadian invasion force before it even reached the beach? Deciding he could not make this decision alone, Vian asked Simonds to come up from the operations room for a conference. Simonds sent Kitching instead, who carried the intelligence message back to the operations room. "Sir," Kitching said, "the Admiral asks what you think we should do." Simonds read the message and handed it back to Kitching. "Tell the Admiral that if I were he I would pay no attention to it." Vian smiled at this news. "Please give my compliments to General Simonds," he told Kitching, "and tell him from me that he would make an excellent admiral."[38]

If Simonds and Vian were prepared to gamble against the existence of an Italian minefield, they were less willing to defy Mother Nature. As the seas continued to roughen, signals passed back and forth among the Allied ships and headquarters in North Africa about the possibility that the landings would have to be delayed while the fleet waited out the storm. Sesia saw Simonds standing on the deck "gazing anxiously at the sky and the sea. He was alone and seemed extremely thoughtful." But at 2100 hours, the waves and wind subsided somewhat and word spread that the strike was on. "This is the final lap," Sesia thought. "At 0245 hours the . . . 1st [Canadian Division] will take part in the greatest combined operation yet mounted, and we shall invade Sicily."[39]

PART TWO

FIRST BLOODING

5

The Actuality of War

AT 1630 HOURS on July 9, the three battalions of 2nd Canadian Infantry Brigade assembled at assigned boat stations aboard their respective transport ships to hear Brigadier Chris Vokes's Order of the Day. "Actions speak louder than words! Go in and get the bastards," it read. "The words were typical of our [brigadier]," the Princess Patricia's Canadian Light Infantry war diarist recorded, adding that "a roaring cheer greeted them."[1]

The thirty-nine-year-old Vokes had a reputation as a rough-talking hard charger. His temper was as fiery as the red of his hair and walrus-style moustache. Major Thomas de Faye, whose Saskatoon Light Infantry company provided 2 CIB's heavy weapons support, considered him a "tough old bird, great boxer, tall, wide, and built like a bulldog, which also summed up his personality."[2]

Vokes believed a commander's duty to his troops was "to inspire their confidence and get the best out of them."[3] Lieutenant Colonel Bert Hoffmeister, who had taken over the Seaforths from Vokes, believed the brigadier was both competent and able to win the trust of soldiers. Using coarse, direct language when talking to the men was a key ingredient in his command style, but he was equally blunt with officers.[4]

On June 28, just before the fast convoy sailed from Britain, Vokes had gone to each of the brigade's three ships to deliver the same

97

rousing speech. The gist, so far as Seaforth Highlander of Canada's Padre Roy Durnford could discern, was that the brigade was expected to be the best there was and that any Germans met were to be "dealt with harshly."[5] Durnford realized that the brigadier's words were "designed to instill a certain fearsomeness into the character of his men. It was intensely blood-thirsty in its sentiment, and doubtless, from a military point of view, a much needed injection. For such a man as myself the speech was welcomed only for its brevity," the padre confided to his diary. "I find something repulsive in this business of teaching men to hate their fellows, and in rousing blood-lust in them. I maintain that a man can fight without bitterness. In any case it seems a poor sort of business to have to inculcate hatred by artificial means."[6]

Vokes would have vehemently disagreed. Soldiers needed to be bloodthirsty, and it was an attribute he sought to instill at every possible opportunity. On the morning of July 4, Vokes had circulated a personal message through the brigade. It read:

1. On the eve of our baptism by fire, for which we have all trained so hard and so long, I wish to issue the creed which will govern all of us throughout this and any subsequent campaign.

Firstly—We are free men fighting for a just cause. Therefore, we are invincible.

Secondly—We will seek out and destroy the enemy wherever he may be found.

Thirdly—We must be hard and ruthless; we must never relax or relent until the victory is ours.

Fourthly—We must never ask for quarter. Therefore, it will be our prerogative to grant it.

Fifthly—Only cowards surrender.

2. I am presenting each Unit of the Bde, herewith, a copy of the 2nd Bde Pennant to be known as the "GEORGE BAKER." We will carry them with us through ITALY and GERMANY.

3. And, finally, good luck—and good scalping—to you, one and all.[7]

While Vokes had time to rally his troops before the invasion, his counterpart at 1st Canadian Infantry Brigade, Brigadier Howard Graham, was largely preoccupied with the change forced upon his landing plans by the decision to use DUKW amphibious trucks to move three of his four assault companies from the sandbar to the beach. Graham disliked the idea. The DUKW had no armour to protect the troops. That the men would have to first transfer from the transports to LCTs and then clamber into vehicles they had never even seen before ensured the brigade would be late heading for the beach. This meant that 2 CIB on the left and the British 231st Brigade on the right would land without his brigade in the middle, leaving both of these units exposed to the possibility of deadly flanking fire and counterattacks. During a meeting held aboard *Hilary*, Graham urged Major General Guy Simonds and Rear Admiral Sir Philip Vian to scrap the DUKW scheme and instead allow the three companies of his brigade that would fetch up on the sandbar to go in behind 2 CIB. Once his companies passed the sandbar, their LCAs could turn sharply and race to line up with their assigned beach sectors. While that would still mean a delay in 1 CIB hitting the beach, it would be less than if they went with the DUKW plan.

Graham had devised this idea in concert with the captain of his headquarters' ship, Captain Andrew Gray of *Glengyle*, and both men pressed their respective superiors hard for agreement. Vian conceded that every objection raised was valid and their alternative plan was better. But it had been XXX Corps staff who instructed the use of the DUKWs, and there was neither the time nor the means to go about getting their approval to scrap the scheme. Graham kept waiting for Simonds to come to his aid, but the divisional commander offered no comment. DUKWs it would be, Vian finally declared, and there was nothing further that Graham and Gray could do. As the meeting broke up, Graham waited for Simonds to come over and offer commiseration, but "there was not a word of sympathy or support."

Back aboard *Glengyle*, Graham holed up in his cabin and started producing a concise précis that could be sent by lamp to Royal Canadian Regiment's Lieutenant Colonel Ralph Crowe aboard *Marnix van St. Aldegonde* to notify him that the battalion's two assault companies would land on DUKWs. The other assaulting battalion, the Hastings and Prince Edward Regiment, was aboard *Glengyle*. So he was able to brief its Lieutenant Colonel Bruce Sutcliffe personally on the change that affected only one of his assault companies—the other being able to skirt past the sandbar for an unimpeded run to the beach. Neither man questioned the order, but Graham chalked that up to the fact that the three of them knew each other well. Before his promotion to brigadier, Graham had commanded the Hasty Ps—Crowe had been one of Graham's company commanders and Sutcliffe his second-in-command.[8]

AS NIGHT DESCENDED around the Canadian Fast Assault Convoy, thousands of soldiers faced the prospect that this might be their last night on earth. Yet there seemed little visible apprehension. The gale had little effect on the infantrymen aboard most of the large transports. In *Llangibby Castle,* the men were fed a hot meal and then many went up on deck to await the order to get ready. Captain Donald Brain, whose 'B' Company would be one of the two in the battalion's leading wave, saw that the "night was beautifully clear and one could make out quite clearly the other ships of the convoy in the moonlight. From the decks we could watch bombing on shore and the sparks as A.A. shells burst above the target areas...fully half the men were out watching the display, while on the mess-decks men were making final adjustments to the fit and comfort of their equipment. All were confident and cheerful and I can honestly say that I did not meet one man who showed conscious signs of nerves. In one corner, the inevitable 'crap' game was in full swing."[9]

Also in full swing was a songfest in another corner, with Corporal Felix Carriere and a few other men providing musical accompaniment. "I played a guitar until my fingers were bleeding and we sang songs until silence was demanded."[10] The PPCLI officers had also got into the swing of things, gathering in the dining saloon for coffee and sandwiches at about 2300 hours and launching into a "sing-song...Every song in the repertoire—clean and unclean—was sung, and even college yells were hooted out. Then came the time to break up and dress for the occasion. From that time on, everything functioned as smoothly as any drill parade."[11]

At 0048 hours on July 10, *Hilary* dropped anchor about seven miles off the Sicilian coast. Around her the other ships followed suit.

This was the release point from which the assault craft would head for the beach. There was no sign of the reported minefield. But the seas had worsened again, the gale returning to fierce life. Even as the anchor chains rattled down, the LCAS aboard the big transports, such as *Circassia* and *Llangibby Castle,* were being loaded with the first assault wave.[12]

The time for planning was over, the time for execution imminent. On paper, British Eighth Army's landings were straightforward. Lieutenant Colonel George Kitching, 1st Canadian Division's general staff officer, had summarized everything clearly in a surprisingly brief operational order at the beginning of June, and none of the overarching details had changed. On the far right, the XIII Corps, under Lieutenant General Miles Dempsey, would land on several beaches along a ten-mile stretch of coast south of Siracusa that extended to the village of Avola. The amphibious assault would be preceded by glider-borne paratroops of 1st Airlanding Brigade from 1st Airborne Division, making night landings inland to block enemy attempts to reinforce the coastal defence forces. The initial primary objective of XIII Corps was to seize Siracusa port, which was small but vital to Allied plans. XXX Corps, including 1st Division, would at the same time be assaulting Pachino peninsula, while to the left of Eighth Army, the U.S. II Corps of Seventh Army would land on a long swath of south coastal beaches concentrated on Gela. The immediate American task was to seize airfields at Gela, Biscari, and Comiso. Helping in this task would be American paratroops from 82nd Airborne Division, which were to drop several miles inland of the coastal Gela directly in front of the village of Ponte Olivo. Here they would establish blocking positions.

XXX Corps would strike the peninsula from both flanks and head-on, with 231st Infantry Brigade Group landing on the eastern coast, 51st Highland Division the tip, and 1st Canadian Infantry Division the western coast. Because a gap of about twenty-five miles separated the Canadians from the Americans, Nos. 40 and 41 commandos of the British Special Service Brigade would land on the far western side of the bay, in which Bark West lay, to knock out coastal defence batteries there and then move to meet the Canadians advancing from the beach.

The Canadians had four objectives for July 10—to secure Bark West, protect the left flank of xxx Corps, capture Pachino airfield and make it operational for Allied aircraft, and begin advancing towards a road that cut along a sharp southwest-to-northeast axis from the coastal village of Pozzallo inland to Rosolini. This would enable them to conform to, and continue protecting, the western flank of 51st Highland Division as it pushed inland.

Phase One, seizing Bark West, would be kicked off by the commandos landing ahead of the Canadians. To their right, 2nd Canadian Infantry Brigade would land on a stretch of beach code-named "Sugar," while 1st Canadian Infantry Brigade would set down on "Roger," farther to the right yet. Each Canadian brigade would have two battalions forward and one in reserve. The Seaforth Highlanders would be on the left of 2 CIB's front and the Princess Patricia's Canadian Light Infantry on the right, with 1 CIB's Hastings and Prince Edward Regiment on that brigade's left and the Royal Canadian Regiment on the right. Each battalion would have two companies leading and two landing close behind as reserve. The Loyal Edmonton Regiment would be in brigade reserve for 2 CIB, and the 48th Highlanders of Canada would do identical duty for 1 CIB. The 3rd Canadian Infantry Brigade's Royal 22e Régiment (Van Doos), Carleton and York Regiment, and West Nova Scotia Regiment would wait offshore in reserve until the beach was secure.

After Bark West was secured, 2 CIB's immediate task was to strike westward to destroy enemy beach defences and link up with the commandos. Securing Pachino airfield would be 1 CIB's major objective, but they were also to eliminate the gun battery at Maucini to the south of the airfield. As the two lead brigades pushed towards their respective objectives, the rest of the division would be landing according to a phased schedule and establishing supporting operations. Included in these landings would be gun batteries from the 1st Canadian Field Regiment (Royal Canadian Horse Artillery) and the Shermans of the Three Rivers Tank Regiment from 1st Canadian Army Tank Brigade.[13]

Much attention had been paid in Kitching's orders to the problem of recognition signals and passwords because the initial part of the operation was expected to be carried out in darkness. So worried were Eighth Army planners of the prospect of friendly fire incidents that a single password sequence had been established for all troops. During the convoy the Canadians had gleefully practised the sequence until it was second nature. The challenge: "Desert Rats." Answer: "Kill Italians."[14]

IT WAS THE kind of challenge that tickled RCR second-in-command Major John Henry William "Billy" Pope's sense of humour. On *Marnix van St. Aldegonde,* he and a group of old friends had eaten during the late night of July 9 "off snowy white linen what many of us thought might be our last meal." There were five others: Lieutenant John Praysner and Captains Ron "Slim" Liddell, Strome Galloway, Ian Hodson, and Sam Lerner. As usual, Pope dominated the conversation. Not that the others minded—everyone liked Billy "of the close-cropped head, round as a cannon ball, with china-white teeth under a Zorro moustache." Throughout the voyage, Pope had repeatedly taken aside one or another of the battalion's lieutenants. "Have you seen much of death in the sun—in the morning?" he would ask. Before the apprehensive young man could reply, Pope flashed a grin, twitching the scar that curved down his cheek, and said, "Well, you will." Pope's explanation of the scar's origin typified the man. A sabre cut suffered in a student duel at university, he told strangers. Galloway and his friends knew the truth—the result of a motorcycle accident.[15]

Over coffee, Pope suddenly turned serious and broke the news that the assault companies would use DUKWS. Liddell was just explaining how this meant junking all his plans for loading 'A' Company, when Pope produced some fresh aerial reconnaissance overlays that made matters worse. Visible directly behind 'A' Company's stretch of sand were more machine-gun positions than had been earlier identified. Liddell scowled when a fellow captain quipped that the added guns improved his odds of winning a Distinguished Service Order or Military Cross.

Adjourning to the ship's lounge, the officers listened as a soldier drafted for the occasion pounded away on the piano until Padre Rusty Wilkes arrived to lead the Protestant officers in a divine service. In a smaller venue, Billy Pope acted as lay priest for the Catholic officers. After the services, the officers shook each other's hands. "See you in Sicily, old boy," several told Galloway. Before going to his cabin, Galloway checked into 'B' Company's mess deck. The men "were in fine fettle. In the dim lights the air was smoky and close. Corporal [Joseph Ernest] Norton was slitting his web belt and stuffing the slits with .303 ammunition in cowboy style. Burgoone, a Bren gunner, was trying out a can of self-heating soup—a gadget with a tiny spirit stove built in. A fuel pellet is lit and the soup in the upper section is heated in a few minutes."[16]

By the time Galloway reached the cabin he shared with Captain Liddell, the latter officer was already getting ready and the space was too cramped for two men to move about. Galloway reclined on a bunk. Throughout the voyage, their friendship had been strained by a competition that Lieutenant Colonel Crowe had imposed. The RCR had only two majors on strength—Billy Pope and 'D' Company's commander, Major Tom "Pappy" Powers—while each battalion was allowed three. It was a close call, Crowe had allowed, whether Galloway or Liddell should be awarded major's crowns. On one hand, Galloway was senior in service time and had three months' battle experience under his belt. But Liddell was a Permanent Force officer who was older and married. If Liddell died a captain, his wife would receive less of a pension. Galloway was unmarried. Unable to decide, Crowe promoted neither. The rank instead would go to whomever he felt performed better in the forthcoming battle. Both Liddell and Galloway disliked this idea, but Crowe was adamant. Trusting the odds lay with him, Galloway had secreted two sets of brass crowns in his battle pack to have at hand when he won the promotion.[17]

Stripped to the waist, Liddell lit a match to his copy of Crowe's battalion operation order, "then crushed the blackened paper in the wash basin and made a filthy paste out of it. Scooping this mess up, he smeared his face until it was as black as any end-man in a Dixie show! Slim maintained that this personal camouflage would conceal him from observation. He had ordered all his men to black their faces too." Galloway refused to follow suit. Liddell shrugged, pulled on his heavily laden web gear, picked up a Thompson submachine gun, and headed for his company's mess deck.

There was no rush, so Galloway checked on one of Liddell's lieutenants in the cabin next door. As instructed, Len Carline was just finishing blacking his face. "Then he draped himself with his webbing, moaning loudly about its weight. With Tommy-gun, eight loaded magazines, grenades, entrenching tool, 48-hour ration and personal kit piled on him he could hardly stand up. Len is a slight fellow. He said that to his dying day he'd always pity a pack mule!

"Harry Keene, one of my own subalterns, was in the next cabin. In there his batman, an 18-year-old youngster whom we call 'the innocent child,' was almost at the point of exasperation as he struggled manfully to shove Harry into the unyielding web equipment. While young Horton stuffed and tugged to gird his officer for battle, Harry amused himself by discussing his fat belly and munching a biscuit. We were issued with so much hardtack we had nowhere to carry it, so Harry was solving his problem by eating some of it then and there."

Soon kitted up, Galloway joined his company. Not one of the two assault companies, 'B' Company had been divided into serials that were each assigned to a specific LCA. The "men filed out from between their mess tables, a long khaki serpent of infantrymen, each grasping the bayonet scabbard of the man ahead to keep the line intact. We moved at a snail's pace along the corridors and up the companionways to the boat decks. As we ascended the stairs, the bright lights of below-decks receded and dim, blue lights became our only guide."

Stepping onto the outer deck, Galloway passed Lieutenant Gray of the War Graves Commission. "His face looked pale and eerie in the dim blue light. 'I'll be seein' you,' he remarked, with all good intentions."

"Not me, I hope," Galloway whispered back.[18]

"Attention, please. Attention, please," the public address systems on each infantry transport sounded. Then the number of a serial would be called to proceed to its boat position. Aboard *Circassia*, the Seaforth Highlanders waited their turns in mess decks that had been plunged into total darkness to prevent any light escaping through the doors opening to the boat deck. When their turn came, the men proceeded "very slowly in…one single line…and up the gangways they would go, along the dim corridors, up again to decks still higher till finally they reached the promenade or boat deck. Stumbling over the high sills of the ship's door-ways they would issue out into the open air and the moonlight. Out of the oppressively hot atmosphere of their close confinement below where little if any ventilation seemed to exist and into the cool night air. Silently—for the whole ship was bound in silence—they would creep forward till the leader had found his boat station and then, one by one, each man would file past him into the Landing Craft as it swung from its davits at the side of the ship. Here they would kneel on one knee with their rifles vertical in their hands until the craft had its full complement aboard in three rows—the officer being the last to enter as he was to be the first out on landing. There was always a slight hesitancy about taking the step from the ship into the swinging Landing Craft for the gap between revealed a long, long drop into the watery depths below.

"Thus they would kneel or half squat in tightly packed lines until... every section had found similar positions. In this way these boys would soon be lowered with other Landing Craft swinging below them from the Promenade deck into the sea and away to a hostile shore. The intense silence and darkness gave the whole procedure a weird and ghostly atmosphere."[19] Padre Durnford had walked with the men and watched them load into the LCAs. He wondered what "intensity of prayer existed among these lads who were about to face the ugly realities of war."[20]

While darkness cloaked the Canadian ships, Sicily burned. Ninety minutes before the convoy had reached the release point, flights of medium bombers had started raining bombs on the defences immediately inland. Pachino, Maucini, and Ispica all were badly bombed. Pachino airfield and its defensive works were struck. "A dull red glow suffused the sky to the north of us and we knew the small town of Pachino was ablaze," Durnford wrote.[21]

Aboard an LCA, Seaforth Sergeant Jock Gibson could scarcely believe that the invasion was on. The waves were tossing the flat-bottomed LCAs about like corks. The vessel's crew was throwing up over the sides; every soldier—except Gibson—was puking on the deck. Having spent years on West Coast tugboats, he possessed an iron stomach. "The sea didn't bother me a bit," he said later. But how the hell the men around him were going to fight when they got ashore, Gibson had no idea.[22]

Things were equally bad aboard the LCA carrying PPCLI's Corporal Felix Carriere. A lot of men were seasick, but Carriere was too keyed up to be affected. He and the others who felt okay whispered back and forth over the thumping roar of the two diesel engines that drove the LCAS. They had been told to stay quiet, that they were trying to surprise the enemy guarding the beaches.[23] Ahead, bombs were exploding. The Italians were madly lighting up the sky with flares, and anti-aircraft tracers stabbed towards the bombers. As the first wave of 2 CIB's LCAS cast off and wallowed towards the beach, HMS *Roberts*—a British monitor ship hovering nearby—belched fire from her heavy 15-inch guns, and shells screamed towards Pachino airfield's defences.[24] Aboard his lurching and bucking LCA, Lieutenant Farley Mowat of the Hastings and Prince Edward's 'A' Company watched in awe as four "incandescent spheres burst from her suddenly revealed grey bulk—four suns...that seemed to ignite the whole arc of the southern horizon in flickering red and yellow lightning." Other naval vessels weighed in and "cataclysmic thunder overwhelmed our world."[25]

IT WAS ABOUT 0130 hours when the first flight of 2 CIB's two assault battalions headed for shore. Twenty-four minutes earlier, the first troops from Nos. 40 and 41 commando units of the British Special Service Brigade had cast off.[26] The commandos headed towards the westerly outer curve of the bay to destroy the two coastal defence batteries that could bear on the main Canadian invasion force.[27] Leading the Seaforth's assault was 'A' Company under Captain Sydney Thomson on the right flank and Major J.W. "Jim" Blair's 'C' Company on the left. The LCAS were in a box formation. Aboard one of the craft, a man unaffected by the rolling seas sang "Heading for the Last Roundup" at the top of his lungs.[28] Right of the Seaforths, the PPCLI was also running for shore with Captain Don Brain's 'B' Company and Major A.E.T. Paquet's 'D' Company leading.[29] The reserve companies were not far behind, and aboard one of 'C' Company's LCAS

Lieutenant Colin McDougall noted the men in his platoon "were weighted down with extra loads of grenades, mortar bombs, SAA [small-arms ammunition] bandoliers, Bren magazines. During the past hour they had helped each other dress, like athletes or actors backstage. They carried more on their bodies than could have been expended in the most desperate firefight, but they did not know this yet because they did not know the actuality of war."[30]

While 2 CIB was away, its LCAS cutting through the darkness, 1 CIB's assault battalions anxiously awaited arrival of the LCTS bearing the DUKWS that three of the four companies were to board. These ships were lost, blindly groping through the blacked-out convoy in search of the ships bearing the Hasty Ps and RCR. Lowered on schedule aboard LCAS, the Hasty Ps in 'A' and 'C' companies were tossed about in the heaving hell of the storm. 'C' Company was to assault the beach to the west of 'B' Company—which was to land in DUKWS— while 'A' Company would stand off as a floating reserve until needed or the way was clear for the rest of the battalion to land.[31] The crews manning each LCA had cast away from *Glengyle* for fear of being thrown against her steel hulk and crushed. "The sea...played with the landing craft as if they were chips caught in a spring spate," the regimental historian later wrote. Nausea gripped almost the entire company, even the tall, broad-shouldered Captain Alex Campbell. The thirty-three-year-old company commander "was a fire-eating hulk of a man who had lost his father in one war with the Germans, and who had lost his brother in this one. Now in an interval between retchings he turned and voiced the battle slogan of his company. *'Nil carborundum illegitimo'*—'Don't let the bastards grind you down!'"[32]

The RCR had already lowered the second flight of troops in their LCAS on schedule so these craft would be clear of the transport ship when the LCTS arrived. As the LCA bearing Captain Galloway and a section of 'B' Company had been lowered, "it bumped against the side of the ship and pitched forwards and backwards as the davits dropped us. Halfway down we banged up against a bilge outlet and we all got drenched with the foul water, a lot of it getting into our mouths. Choking and spluttering, we eventually hit the sea and swung back and forth until we were cast loose."

For the next two hours the LCAs that 1 CIB had set loose motored around, trying to maintain their company formations in the inky darkness. The pilot of Galloway's craft seemed to be blundering blind, the LCA continuously banging into other craft. Galloway and the other men aboard hardly cared, as they "were hanging over the sides of the craft, puking into mare nostrum."[33]

Two and a half hours late, the LCTs finally appeared. Their lateness hardly surprised 1 CIB's Brigadier Howard Graham and his naval counterpart, Captain Andrew Gray, on *Glengyle*. They had predicted the LCTs would be "slow, very slow, to find us in the darkness and the great concourse of some two thousand ships. Once found, the problem was to tie up to us with great heaving seas bashing about and, once tied up, to get the men down scrambling nets with all their gear and into the bucking LCTs." He and Gray were in an "utter fury" of frustration, trying to implement a plan they opposed. It little helped their moods when at 0315 *Hilary*'s signal lamp flashed a message from Rear Admiral Vian. "Will your assault ever start?" the admiral demanded.[34]

That was the last straw for Graham. A minute later, he ordered the Hasty Ps in 'B' and 'A' companies to immediately head their LCAs for the sand. Thirty minutes later the rest of the brigade was still struggling aboard the LCTs when the division's assistant adjutant and quartermaster general, Lieutenant Colonel Preston Gilbride, came alongside in Vian's personal barge and delivered a terse signal from Simonds. "You must get your assaults away either in L.C.T.s or L.C.A.s," it read. By this time, of course, Graham had done all he could. The RCR assault companies and the Hasty Ps in 'B' Company were finally aboard the LCTs and crammed into the seven DUKWs tied down on their respective vessel's deck. The LCTs cast off at 0400 hours and started towards shore.

BY THE TIME 1 CIB was finally under way, 2 CIB's assault companies were already on the sand. Since they had entered the bay at about 0230 hours, the seas had moderated. Overhead, bombers still droned in to bomb Pachino. The fires burning in the town were supposed to act like beacons to help the LCA pilots steer to the assigned landing points, but the shoreline was so blacked out that many became disoriented.[35] Groping through the dark, anxiously consulting the compasses in the binnacles by their sides, the pilots aboard the Seaforth's LCAs blundered in a collective flotilla behind those bearing the PPCLI and ended up on that battalion's right flank, rather than, as planned, to the left.[36] The PPCLI fared better, the majority of the two companies staying on course and only a few LCAs straying off to land elsewhere.[37]

PPCLI captain Don Brain, leading 'B' Company, had his eyes fixed forward as the LCAs neared shore. "Flares could be seen being put up by an enemy even more uncertain than ourselves as to what to expect. Machine-gun tracer made very attractive patterns against the sky in the distance while on the shore every once in a while would appear a bright flash followed by a loud report as though someone were tossing grenades about."[38]

The flash was coming from a small artillery piece firing blindly out to sea. One lucky shot punched a hole in a PPCLI landing craft.[39] Its occupants were pulled off before it sank by the LCA carrying Corporal Felix Carriere.[40] Suddenly, the LCAs started shuddering to a halt as they grinded up on sand. The landing ramp dropped in front of Brain. He and his men "disembarked into water well above their waist." Off to one side, the captain saw other men had landed "in water six feet deep and had to abandon weapons and equipment and swim for it."[41] Private Chester Hendricks was one of these. He stepped off the ramp, carrying a Bren gun, and disappeared, only to bob up and start swimming shoreward without the light machine gun.[42]

"From the craft," Brain later related, "we made our way up a very sandy beach until we encountered wire which held us up for some time. In the meanwhile the enemy were tossing grenades amongst us. Fortunately the effect was almost entirely blast and no one came to grief, while a couple [Type] 36 grenades tossed at the enemy succeeded in killing them. Finally the wire was cut and we made our way to find an M.G. post with two sentries whom we wiped out. A search of the huts near the post brought to light another Italian obviously just awakened by the noise as he had not yet had time to put on his uniform."[43] 'D' Company's LCAs had stranded on a sandspit offshore, and the men "splashed through the shallows, climbed the first dune, stepped over the tripwires and saw before them the white floor of a dried salt lagoon—exactly where it ought to be."[44]

In 2 CIB's area, the sandbars were sporadically placed, so some LCAS managed to go right onto the beach while others became stranded off-shore. This was particularly true for the Seaforths. When the LCA carrying Lieutenant E.J.M. Church and his platoon dropped its ramp, a machine gun fired a burst right through the open gap. One of the navy personnel fell dead and several Seaforths went down wounded. "Bullets hammered on another craft but it had slewed around between the sandbar and the beach and had hit the beach backward. This saved more lives, for had the ramp been lowered directly on the beach more casualties would have been inevitable. Lieutenant J.J. Conway's pla-toon on the far right landed waist deep in water and were fired on and returned the fire as they waded in to the beach."[45]

The LCA with Sergeant Jock Gibson aboard hung up on a sandbar about one hundred yards from the beach. On the run in, he had been awed by how "the guns from the [Roberts] firing overhead, sounded like freight trains." Now, as the ramp came down, he and the other men lunged into the water. They wore Mae West life jackets, "which held us up, and [we] struggled towards where we could get our feet on the ground."[46]

Private George A. "Speed" Reid of 'C' Company was aboard an LCA with Private Ernest "Smokey" Smith, whose pilot "ran us up and down the beach until we told him to either land the goddamned boat or we would land it for him...The ramp went down, and we walked into water five-feet deep. Smokey Smith was in front of me, although he was supposed to be behind me. Well, we hit the water, and Smokey was going under, so I picked him up by the collar and held him up. I was six to ten inches taller than Smokey. Thank God I was able to grab him, because he made a hell of a lot better soldier than I did; later on, he won the Victoria Cross," Reid subsequently wrote.[47]

The Seaforths dashed ashore and up to the wire in full flight. Pri-vate Harry Rankin rushed the wire with a bangalore torpedo—a long pipe filled with explosive that when thrust deep into tangles of barbed wire could be detonated to rip a hole open through which the infantry could pass—only to find the obstacle barely existed. "You could walk over it, so I slammed my goddamned bangalore down and left. The job was to get in as quickly as you could. The guy next to me, his job was also to blow that wire and he was about fifteen feet away and he nearly blew me up. His job was to do that one thing, and I guess he couldn't think beyond that. Technically, I should have done that too, but I'd have had to lift the wire just to put the bangalore under it."[48]

When Sergeant Jock Gibson's platoon started up the sand they saw "a bunch of land mines lying exposed all over the place and there was concertina wire behind them. We just wondered how many more weren't uncovered. So we looked down the beach and there was a boat of some sort. Looked like a fishing boat, so we went down to it and then up through a barbed wire gap that had been left for the fishermen to go back and forth. Then some firing started and one of my fellows got killed. There wasn't a lot of fire, but it was nerve-wracking."[49]

Where 'A' Company's Captain Syd Thomson came to the barbed wire, it was so tightly strung that the men simply stepped on the top strand and walked over. Once over the wire, the company hugged the ground and took up a defensive position. Moments later, Thomson heard a rifleman say, "My bolt is stuck," and another say, "So is mine."

"It became evident that the extremely fine sand in the area was adhering to the slight film of oil on the rifle bolts and jamming them. We passed the word quickly, bolts were to be cleaned and weapons kept off the ground. We would have been in a sorry position had there been a proper defence."[50]

But the Seaforths were on the beach, and there was no longer any resistance. Thomson considered the assault companies had achieved their first objective, even if they were in the wrong place, and fired a flare signalling success. It was the first signal from the Canadians on Bark West to those waiting offshore.[51]

6

Which Direction Do We Take?

CAPTAIN SYD THOMSON fired his flare at about 0300 hours. The 1st Canadian Infantry Brigade had still not begun the run towards Roger—its section of Bark West—but a few minutes later, the Hastings and Prince Edward's 'A' and 'C' companies moved towards shore in their LCAS. Company 'B' was still going through the awkward process of boarding the LCT, as were the two Royal Canadian Regiment assault companies. Following British army organizational structures, each regiment mustered four rifle companies designated alphabetically from 'A' to 'D,' so the brigade radio net bristled with confused signals that this or that company from the Hasty Ps or RCR were away. Captain Ian Hodson, commanding the RCR's 'C' Company, jumped onto his LCT expecting to get all his men headed shoreward in a few minutes only to learn that just five of its seven DUKWS were operational. While he chewed on this unwelcome news, his men were trying to descend on a scramble net strung from the transport down to the LCT. "As the LCT rose, the net swung loose. When the LCT fell, the net tightened like a bow string. Picture some of the soldiers carrying awkward equipment like Bren guns, mortars, PIATS, bangalore torpedoes, 18 sets, climbing down this obstacle, in the dark. We lost no equipment, we lost no men, but we did lose time."

When everyone was finally loaded, Hodson and the other officers started directing the men into the DUKWS. "Confusion! Shouts! Somehow we packed them all in, 27 men to a vehicle." This rendered the amphibious trucks "grossly overloaded," but there was nothing the captain could do about that.[1] Finally, at 0400 hours, the LCTS cast away. The sky to the east was already glowing with a pre-dawn light.[2]

While in the heart of the bay the sea was calm, closer to the transports the waves still seethed. The LCAS carrying the Hasty Ps in 'A' and 'C' companies had been making slow progress shoreward and so were not that far ahead of the LCTS, despite their earlier start. In the blackness, 'A' Company had lost sight of 'C' Company, and the pilot in Lieutenant Farley Mowat's boat, charged with leading 'A' Company to Roger Beach, had unwittingly become turned about. With the other LCAS following right along, Mowat's craft chugged westward straight through the second wave of Seaforth Highlanders and Princess Patricia's Canadian Light Infantry battalions heading for Sugar. 'C' Company, meanwhile, stayed on track for the objective.[3] In the darkness, none of the men aboard the 2 CIB landing craft noticed the little 'A' Company boats pass by and carry on unimpeded towards a section of beach near where the British commandos had earlier landed.

Corporal John "Johnnie" Cromb was on one Seaforth craft carrying 'B' Company towards Sugar. The sky was rapidly brightening, and Cromb could see the beach more clearly with every passing minute. Cromb felt like a sitting duck out on the sea with daylight imminent and just wanted to get onto the sand, but the navy pilot kept "going from right to left, left to right and so on." Each time the LCA passed another vessel, the man would "holler in his English accent, 'I say, can you direct me to Sugar Amber. [Each beach had been subdivided into sections designated from left to right as Red, Amber, and Green.] My compass is on the blink.'" Finally the company commander, Captain Cyrus "Freddie" Middleton, growled at him. "Look, buster, just head for the beach and hit her anywhere, if you can find the island." Shrugging, the pilot headed in, hung up on the sandbar about one hundred yards short of the beach, dropped the ramp, and the Seaforths waded shoreward.[4]

It was broad daylight when the Hasty Ps and RCR companies finally reached the beach. The former's two companies both wandered astray with 'B' Company riding in on the DUKWs to land unopposed on Roger Green Beach instead of Roger Amber Beach. "Some wire obstacles were encountered and blown," wrote the Hasty Ps' war diarist. "The only enemy in this area were one or two snipers who were killed." 'C' Company also had an "uneventful approach and made an unopposed landing a mile to the east of their correct beach. Minor wire obstacles were encountered and blown allowing the company to penetrate inland and consolidate on the dunes." Once everyone was sorted out, 'C' Company started moving westward through the dunes towards their assigned landing point. They met no opposition.[5]

Aboard their LCTs, the RCR's 'C' and 'D' companies had come under sporadic shelling from the Italian coastal battery at Maucini. Because of the delay in getting under way, 'A' and 'B' companies in LCAs were following close behind. In one of the LCAs, Captain 'Slim' Liddell of 'A' Company noticed the shellfire, but the Italian rounds were failing to "come very close." He thought "daylight presented a weird spectacle, the horizon of the sea and sky could literally NOT be seen for ships of all sizes and shapes (all with their [anti-aircraft] balloons well up). Level with us were strings of LCAs wallowing along in line ahead with the monitor H.M.S. *Roberts* sitting in the middle of the small stuff having a few shots at something inland."[6]

Roberts's target was the Maucini coastal battery, and after it lobbed a few massive 15-inch shells in that direction, the Italian guns fell silent.[7] When the monitor ship started firing, the LCTs had just finished dispatching 'C' and 'D' companies aboard their DUKWs. Captain Ian Hodson "could follow the shells going inland. The noise was tremendous and the blast made our DUKWs settle in the water and then surge forward. Somewhat frightening!

"We headed for the beach. We saw no sign of the sand bar. We drove up on the sand and landed dry shod. I found myself beside a large hole in the sand in which were two photographs and piles of films. When and how did they get there? There were no signs of enemy, no shots had been fired. We organized ourselves and headed for the Pachino airstrip." Hodson's company was on the extreme right flank or "right of the line" for the entire Canadian invasion. "To one side was a miserable farmhouse surrounded by patches of cactus (eaten fried in olive oil by many Sicilians). From the farmhouse emerged the farmer, who it turned out had spent 17 years in Toronto, had made his pile and returned to his homeland to buy his dream house. Greetings and reminiscences caused some delay."[8]

WHILE THE INFANTRY companies that landed on Roger Beach had met little or no resistance, the Hasty Ps in 'A' Company met the stiffest opposition the Italians offered the Canadians. As the three LCAS carrying the company approached the western flank of Bark West, Lieutenant Mowat stared at the "formless strip of land with agonized intensity, desperately hoping to recognize some landmark. Nothing looked familiar." Astern of his LCA, Mowat could see Captain Alex Campbell standing in the bow of one LCA with his "bull head thrust forward under his ridiculously small steel helmet. He was cradling a Bren and firing brief bursts toward the shore."

Streams of red tracer arched out from a red-roofed building standing on a slight rise behind the beach, and the water between the two LCAS sprouted little waterspouts. Mowat ducked below the ramp, "revolver clenched in sweating palm." A second later a great spout of water rose alongside, hung overhead for a second, and then crashed down to drench everyone aboard with warm, salty water.

Suddenly the ramp dropped, and Mowat and the other Hasty Ps stood looking at a stretch of sea between them and the beach. The LCAS had struck a sandbar. Mowat waved his revolver, shouted for the men to follow, stepped off the ramp, and promptly sank feet first to the bottom in water well over his head. The lieutenant was so weighted down with equipment there was no way he could swim to the surface, so Mowat simply started walking, and shortly his head emerged. Looking over his shoulder, Mowat saw Company Sergeant Major Charles Frederick Rupert Nutley on the ramp. Holding his rifle in one hand, the fingers of the other pinching his nose, Nutley jumped into the water and the rest of the men followed suit. When Mowat burst from the sea, bullets started spitting up bits of sand nearby. He threw himself down, only to be tumbled by a breaking wave. Scrabbling beyond the surf line, Mowat looked seaward and saw the rest of the company stumbling out of the water.

The Italians had done a good job on their defences here. A thick tangle of wire cut across the breadth of the beach, and several over-looking farmhouses had been fortified. Heavy small-arms fire was coming from these positions. Nutley dropped beside Mowat and screamed for the men with the bangalores to blow the wire, but it was Campbell who barged past them and shoved one of the explosive pipes in and ignited it. 'A' Company rallied, and charged through the gap behind their captain.[9]

Picking their way around tall stands of bamboo, the Hasty Ps moved across a series of dunes. They had been going for several min-utes when someone realized Nutley was missing. A quick search found him lying on the beach, shot dead. Nutley should not have been there. Although nobody—including the army—knew his true age, he was clearly too old for combat. Having spent twenty years in the militia between the wars, Nutley had pulled in every marker owed him within the Hasty Ps to avoid being sent home before the regiment fought its first battle. Otherwise, he had said, his army career would have been a mockery. Instead, Nutley had been the first Hasty P to die.[10]

Had the company landed in its designated sector of Roger Beach, it would have come off the sand to head for pre-designated inland objectives. But Campbell knew what his men should do in this alien country. There were Italians firing from a white farmhouse dead ahead. He raised his arm and pointed at it. "Get on, you silly bas-tards! Get on with it," Campbell shouted, even as a bullet tore into one side of the muscle in his upper arm and out the other.[11] A thick stream of blood spouted out of the holes until a stretcher-bearer staunched the wound with a shell dressing.[12]

Campbell never faltered. He kept yelling orders, directing the com-pany into a manoeuvre that had Nos. 8 and 9 platoons providing covering fire from the sand dunes while Mowat's No. 7 Platoon "car-ried out a flank attack."[13] One man set up the company's 2-inch mortar and fired off almost all his smoke rounds in a matter of seconds to screen the platoon's attack. Mowat led his men up the slope towards the house in a charge with guns blazing. They came to a row of wire.

Tumbling over it, shorts, shirts, and skin torn by barbs, No. 7 Platoon barrelled on. "Hold your fire, you clods!" someone yelled from ahead. "Fix bayonets!" Mowat shouted. Steel hissed as the men yanked bayonets free of their scabbards and rammed them onto the Lee-Enfields' fitting. Coming onto the crest immediately in front of the house, No. 7 Platoon suddenly found itself facing a large party of commandos who had attacked the position from the rear moments earlier. Some of the men were firing through windows. "You chaps *did* look loverly!" said one commando. "Just like the light brigade. Never seen nothin' like it 'cept in that flick with Errol Flynn."

Mowat was trying to come up with some pithy retort when Campbell stomped up and yelled at him to push on to their objective. The lieutenant pointed out that he had no clue as to where they were or where they should be heading. An officer from one of the commando units showed the two Canadians their position on a map, and 'A' Company finally knew how far it had strayed.[14] While the two officers were getting their bearings, the rest of the Hasty Ps had been helping the commandos pull about twenty prisoners from the house.[15] Four machine guns were discovered inside—all covering the route taken by No. 7 Platoon's charge. Had the commandos not struck the building from the rear moments earlier, Mowat's men might well have been slaughtered.

At 0300 hours, the Special Service Brigade's Nos. 40 and 41 commandos had also landed off course—but only a little far to the left. Until they attacked the house, the commandos had met little opposition and were now planning to head inland on a northeasterly line of advance that would intersect with the Seaforths.[16]

'A' Company could have tagged along and been trending towards the rest of the regiment, but Campbell had no patience with that idea. He wanted to close with the enemy and the nearest would likely be directly north of the beach. So he ordered the men to saddle up and led them inland, "apparently intent on driving straight north to the Italian mainland."[17]

ACROSS THE BREADTH of Bark West the assault troops were moving off the beach towards assigned inland objectives, while the reserve companies poured ashore. Also arriving were the brigade's reserve battalions—2 CIB's Loyal Edmonton Regiment and 3 CIB's 48th Highlanders of Canada. There was little opposition on the beach; the Italians assigned to defend it were mostly already either dead, taken prisoner, or put to flight. The biggest hindrance to the speed of the buildup ashore remained the sandbars and problems transferring men and equipment from the transports into landing craft.

Loyal Edmonton Private Sam Lenko jumped off an LCA ramp into nine feet of water carrying three hundred rounds of Bren gun ammunition, two days' worth of rations, three grenades, his Lee-Enfield rifle, and a huge amount of bullets for it. He went right to the bottom, floundered to the surface, and would have drowned had a Royal Marine sergeant not dragged him to where a line had been strung from an LCI to the shore. Staggering onto the beach, Lenko saw an Italian soldier ahead. Shouldering his rifle, Lenko drew a bead. The Italian's uniform was ragged and he wore no shoes. His rifle was a great long antique-looking thing. "He's just a kid," Lenko thought. "Shoot him, Sam," a man next to him hissed. The boy's eyes were wide with fright, the knuckles of his hands white. "Shoot him, Sam," the man urged again. Lenko lowered his rifle. "Look, he ain't even got any shoes for Christ sake. I can't shoot him." He waved an arm at the boy. "*Vi!*" Lenko shouted—which his study of an Italian handbook aboard ship had taught him meant "Go!" Taking the hint, the boy chucked his rifle aside and sprinted inland.[18]

When the RCR's 'B' Company landed, Captain Strome Galloway plunged into water up to his waist and waded ashore. One of his platoon commanders, Lieutenant Freddie Syms, was already there. "No mines, keep going," he shouted to Galloway. The men trotted to a vineyard. "Here we stripped off our 'Mae Wests' and reorganized for our belated attack on the [Maucini] battery. BHQ [battalion headquarters] landed beside us, under a forest of aerials. I never saw so many wireless sets in my life," Galloway later wrote.[19]

Over in the Seaforth's sector, Lieutenant Colonel Bert Hoffmeister had also landed with his battalion headquarters. It had been an inglorious moment. The ramp at the front of the craft jammed, but when Hoffmeister tried to climb over, his weight caused it to release. The battalion commander plunged headfirst into four feet of water "and came up spluttering." After wading ashore, Hoffmeister realized he "hadn't a clue" where they were. "I was standing up there trying to see something that looked familiar." Only after Major Henry "Budge" Bell-Irving took a patrol forward for a short reconnaissance did Hoffmeister learn that the Seaforths had landed left of the PPCLI and were on the wrong section of Sugar Beach. The battalion's two reserve companies and the headquarters support platoons were all landing around Hoffmeister. There was nothing he could do but start organizing his men to move west past the PPCLI and then to their objectives. The two assault companies were already doing precisely that, their commanders thinking along the same lines and recognizing that they had to get back into the right position before heading for the inland objectives. Hoffmeister's biggest worry was that in pulling off this manoeuvre, the PPCLI and Seaforths would end up "shooting each other up." Thankfully, there was little interference from the Italians, for "had we been under heavy fire and in the full confusion of our first battle it could have been a very costly and disastrous thing for 2nd Brigade."[20]

SOME OF THE Seaforths had arrived at the beach aboard an LCI. From its deck, Corporal Bob Hackett "could make out the figures of men running to and fro. Everything seems under control, and in our hands, with the exception of a stretch of beach to the right," he later wrote in a letter to his family. "There we could see smoke screens, and could hear the firing of automatic weapons, so that we concluded close hand fighting had been encountered. Soon we touched down, and rubber boats we had brought with us for the purpose of ferrying [mortar] bombs to the shore proved useless on account of the big swell running. It was then decided to get the men off first by letting them wade in. The first batch to go in were... English Pioneers, and of the whole lot two could swim. As you jumped from the boat the water rose to your hips, but as you advanced toward the shore it became deeper, and with the swell behind you, and handicapped by equipment, it was all the sturdiest individual could do to make shore." Hackett was among these stronger men. He and Company Sergeant Major Joe Duddle dumped their equipment. Driving a bayonet into the sand to serve as an anchor and attaching a rope to it, they then spooled the line back out to the LCI for those men who were not strong swimmers to hang onto and pull themselves shoreward.

Hackett went out in the water to help however he could. The British pioneers—engineers who were to help with preparing the beach for heavy vehicle landings—were mostly Londoners who acted as if the only water they had ever seen before was in a bathtub. "It was a tough job as many panicked," Hackett wrote, "and I am sure would never have made it had we not been there to help them. One poor fellow near me...went under a dozen times before I reached him. I grabbed him, pulling him to the rope, and at the same time he clutched frantically, dragging me under with him. Finally I had to knock him out and dragged him by the feet with his head under water to the shore. He was absolutely purple, so I administered artificial respiration until he came around. I was pleased I had gone to this trouble as his face revealed such gratitude. Finally, after two hours in the water I got cramps and had to give up. I went back on board, and the navy were marvelous. They wrapped me in blankets and gave me tea, which brought me around in nothing flat."[21]

Seaforth Sergeant Bill Worton credited the rope with saving his life. A member of the battalion mortar platoon, he went into the water carrying his regular equipment and a 3-inch mortar's heavy base plate. Unable to swim a stroke, Worton would surely have drowned had he not flailed out and caught hold of the rope. Still clutching the base plate, the sergeant was able to drag himself ashore.[22]

For the Seaforths, very little seemed to be going smoothly. Their transport vehicles, particularly those of the Bren carrier platoon, had been loaded on a ship called *Alcinous* and were being offloaded onto the deck of a Landing Craft, Mechanized. Private Angus Harris, a Bren carrier driver, watched his carrier rising in slings above the ship as he started down a scrambling net to board the LCM. Suddenly, "someone screamed a warning. My carrier dangled, one end down, from its sling. One crewman had been slow in casting off the sling and the roll of the ship had jerked it into the air like a fish on the line. The landing craft, rising and falling like giant swoops on the waves, was twenty feet away. The carrier, four tons of armour plate, and loaded with high explosive, swung out and then in with a crash against the ship's side. I shot up the scrambling net like a cork out of a bottle and watched the proceedings from the safety of a higher deck. The crewmen winched up the carrier until it cleared the deck again, where it swung like a huge pendulum, brushing everything in its path in wild crashing sweeps.

"For some moments the carrier dominated our part of the invasion. But finally the crew of the landing craft brought it around to the other side of the ship where there seemed to be more protection, and finally coerced the maverick down and subdued it. The other carrier and the crews, myself included, followed, and we put off for Sicily."[23]

Over in 3 CIB's sector, the LCI carrying 'A' and 'B' companies and the battalion headquarters of the 48th Highlanders had repeatedly struck the sandbar while trying to get to the beach. Unable to find a route around it, the crew finally grounded the craft on the bar and left it to the infantry to get ashore on their own.[24] "We were beyond cursing," Lieutenant Bob Moncur later said. "We just stood there in a group and stared hopelessly at each other." The beach lay about two hundred yards away and a swimmer sent to test the depth returned with news that, shoreward of the sandbar, the water was about nine feet deep and stayed beyond wading depth until just before the waterline. Company Sergeant Major Gordon Keeler and some men swam in with a rope in tow. They planned to use the same "rope trick" that had well served the Seaforths. 'A' Company's Major Ken Whyte was the first out of the boat, loaded down with his gear and weapon, trying to simultaneously swim and pull himself along the rope one-handed. All he accomplished was a dislocated shoulder. The two men behind him nearly drowned, and all three were pulled back aboard the LCI.[25] When the rope drifted on the current to foul in the props of two LCMS broken down near the beach, the venture was abandoned.

Lieutenant Colonel Ian Johnston had, meanwhile, swum in and was stalking up and down the beach looking for a way to rescue his battalion. Finally he noticed the DUKWS, which had landed the two RCR and one Hasty P assault companies, milling around in the surf with no apparent purpose. Johnston pressed them into service and soon DUKWS were ferrying the men ashore.[26] Bailing out of their DUKW, the battalion's pipers strode up to the top of the beach, skirling away in full spate.[27]

AT 0645 HOURS, Major General Guy Simonds was confident the Canadians were solidly ashore and reported to xxx Corps commander Lieutenant General Oliver Leese that all the first objectives had been captured. The goal now was to land the rest of the division, expand the bridgehead, and, most importantly, seize Pachino airfield.[28]

Shortly after 0700 hours, the brigade headquarters sections of 1 CIB and 2 CIB began the run in. Brigadier Howard Graham had divided his section between two LCAs so that he would lead one ashore and Robert Kingstone, his brigade major, the other. But as Graham's LCA was being lowered, a heavy swell struck it, smashed the stern against the side of *Glengyle,* and damaged both propeller and engine. When the other LCA was safely lowered, the entire brigade headquarters descended the scramble nets and squeezed aboard.

The young naval petty officer commanding the LCA turned to Graham. "Which direction do we take, sir?" He had been told to follow the first LCA to the beach. Hiding his consternation, Graham patted the anxious-looking youth on the shoulder and said, "Okay, Admiral, steer for the shore and when you see a water tower, as you should in a few minutes, just steer for it and we'll all be happy. It's at the edge of an airfield near Pachino and that's where I'm bound for." Sure enough, the water tower soon came into sight about three miles inland from the beach. Unable to navigate around the sandbar, the LCA grounded on it. A DUKW came alongside and everyone piled in. The amphibious truck quickly deposited the men on the beach, and Graham stepped on the sand of Sicily without getting his feet wet.[29]

No vehicles had been landed in 3 CIB's sector yet, and all those of the brigade headquarters had been lost anyway aboard the sunken ships. One of the brigade's wireless sets was a heavy No. 22 that required three men to carry it in the absence of any vehicle. But Brigade Major Kingstone and a couple of men quickly solved the problem by commandeering a donkey and cart from a Sicilian farmer. When they mounted the wireless, the cart tipped back on its two wheels so far that the little donkey was lifted up off its feet. Only when a man on either side of the donkey leaned on the shafts to which it was tethered were its feet brought back on the ground and it could then go forward. With donkey and cart trailing behind, inexpertly driven by one of Graham's men, the brigade headquarters moved along the beach until it reached its originally agreed rally point. Graham said they would stay there until the RCR silenced the Maucini battery, after which brigade headquarters would move to a nearby position.[30]

While Graham and his team had been getting ashore, Brigadier Chris Vokes and his brigade headquarters had arrived on Sugar Beach aboard LCAS. The Edmontons had already landed and the beach was fully secure. When the ramp went down, Vokes turned and shouted, "Follow me, men." The brigade's intelligence officer, Captain Norman Pope, was unable to disguise a smile, but Vokes appeared not to notice. Vokes was carrying a riding crop and his revolver, having loaded Pope down with everything else. Pope "had his map. I had his binoculars, I had my own stuff... I was like a ruddy Christmas tree... I was carrying a big map board which I was hoping to keep records on of where units had got to as their reports came in. When I stepped off the ramp, we stepped... into about three-and-a-half feet of water and my knees buckled because the sand gave way underneath me and I went face flat forward into the water. Anyway, it was a beautiful sunny day, stinking hot." Pope figured he would dry out in no time.[31]

Bark West hummed with activity. At 0900, Landing Ship, Tank 321 pulled up 180 feet off Roger Beach's Red sector and the first tanks from the Three Rivers Tank Regiment growled off the front ramp into six feet of water and clawed their way ashore. By 1015, 'C' Squadron had removed the waterproofing kit from its Shermans and reported being available for service.[32]

Landing craft plied back and forth between the shore and transports. Teams of engineers equipped with bulldozers were carving a path through the dunes to enable vehicles to exit the beach. Engineers also blasted a gap in the sandbar off Sugar Amber to enable boat traffic to more easily come and go. Royal Canadian Army Service Corps personnel were also on the beach supervising the landing of equipment and establishing a vehicle concentration area for offloading supplies. Provost marshals, in their red caps, directed traffic and imposed order. Except for the exotic location, Bark West was taking on the appearance of an amphibious landing training beach in Britain.[33]

Aboard *Hilary,* however, Simonds and his staff were anxious. Despite his confident message to xxx Corps that the first objectives had been taken, the divisional commander worried that the delay landing 1 CIB had thrown the operational plan badly behind schedule. Because divisional headquarters had lost all its vehicles, Simonds decided that for now the operations staff would remain on *Hilary.* Only he and a small group that could fit into a single Jeep would go ashore, equipped with a wireless set that could link through the more powerful communications equipment on *Hilary* to the brigade and battalion headquarters.[34]

THE DIFFICULTIES IST Canadian Infantry Division faced in the landings were not unique. Elsewhere the Allies had encountered similar problems. On Eighth Army's far right, 5th British Division of XIII Corps either was delayed in getting its brigades ashore or landed them in the wrong place. Still, by evening its 17th Brigade entered and secured the town of Siracusa. This was the primary objective for the corps to win on D-Day. At Avola, twenty miles to the south, 50th Division had been thrown into confusion by the storm, many of its troops being landed in scattered groups. Although the assault battalions sorted themselves out quickly enough and pushed through to most of their objectives, the follow-on forces and buildup "from the sea was unpunctual and confused: equipment and stores went astray or arrived in the wrong order; by nightfall only nine field-guns were in action," the British official historian recorded.[35]

The Canadian 80th and 81st Landing Craft, Mechanized flotillas were in the thick of this jumble, but Norm Bowen, a coxswain on one of the LCMs, considered it far more organized than any other amphibious operation he had been on. Dieppe had been bad; North Africa "a disaster." Compared to those, "Sicily was a little more controlled." But it was still a madhouse with landing craft jostling for position and narrowly avoiding collisions, the coxswains yelling and hollering at each other to make way. Out to sea, the warships were blasting away and shells screamed continuously overhead. It was always the same, Bowen thought. "The noise goes right through you until you are shaking right through to your inner core and, boy, sometimes you are on queer street for a couple days after." Bowen was getting increasingly edgy and nervous, the product of having been in one too many amphibious operations. In addition to the big ones, such as Dieppe and North Africa, he had served in a dozen commando raids. So far, however, he was holding up fine on this job and the lack of opposition from the beach helped a lot.[36]

Well to the left of the beach where Bowen's LCM was operating, things had gone extremely well for 231st Brigade, landing as the right-flank unit of XXX Corps. The LCAS of the Canadian 55th and 61st flotillas were among those tasked with getting this brigade onto its beach. Pilots aboard motor launches had originally been assigned to guide the LCAS to their correct landing spots, but owing to the rough seas only one of these managed to marry up with the flotillas. One group of the 55th Flotilla finally "struck off on its own for the beaches." A single LCA, commanded by Lieutenant H.E. Trenholme, Royal Canadian Navy Volunteer Reserve, headed for its beach with a team of engineers aboard who were to land after the assault troops signalled it was secure. When Trenholme pulled into the beach, however, he came under Italian fire and quickly backed away. "Believing they had gone to the wrong beach, they struck off again, finally returning to this beach at 0452 when the breakwater, mined by the enemy, was blown up on their approach."[37] The 51st Highland Division, landing in the centre of the corps, had some difficulty locating the correct beaches and most of the brigades were slightly delayed in getting ashore. But the resistance from the Italians defending the beaches was so negligible that they were easily secured and the buildup was soon on schedule.

Forty miles west of the Canadians, the 45th U.S. Division had landed as the right-hand formation of II Corps. Rough seas, sandbars, and rocks all conspired to create chaos. The 157th Combat Team lost twenty-seven men, drowned when landing craft broached. Left of this unit, the 180th Combat Team became completely disorganized. Problems kept piling up as the buildup proceeded through the day, but still the division managed to secure its beachhead and advance to Vittoria.

Facing Gela, the 1st U.S. Division landed in the right place, at the right time, and met little resistance. By 0800 hours, the town was secure and the division was moving inland. But it soon faced some stiff counterattacks from the Livorno Division's 33rd Regiment, which delayed progress. The fleet landing this division was also struck by several German air raids, which sank the U.S. destroyer *Maddox* and caused heavy loss of life. Strong surf conditions and sandbars off the beaches also delayed the landings of tanks, which put the division at a considerable disadvantage when two battle groups of Hermann Göring Division counterattacked it.

More exposed to the storm than any other Allied division, 3rd U.S. Division off Licata had difficulty launching its assault craft, and landings were about ninety minutes behind schedule. Despite some initial stiff resistance, however, the division quickly secured the beach. By day's end, the Americans were all in solid positions after achieving advances ranging between one to two miles inland. Each beachhead, however, was significantly separated from the others, so that the divisions were operating virtually as independent forces.[38]

While the amphibious landings had gone off relatively well, the airborne assaults that preceded them had been a fiasco. Hundreds of transport aircraft and gliders had carried about five thousand airborne troops from airfields in Tunisia in the largest such operation to that time. The inexperience of aircrews became evident when poor navigation resulted in many planes drifting off course. High winds contributed to the problem, and unexpectedly heavy anti-aircraft fire as the planes approached the Sicilian coast caused pilots to take evasive action that scattered the aircraft every which way. The British 1st Airlanding Brigade was released aboard gliders while too far out to sea. Sixty-nine of the gliders crashed in the water, and 252 men of the 2,057-strong unit drowned. Only twelve gliders made it to the assigned landing zone, the rest being strewn across twenty-five miles of countryside. With the brigade plan in ruin, it fell to small groups of airborne troops to repair the wreckage, and they did so with typical élan. A vital bridge at Ponte Grande was taken by a handful of men, and elsewhere small teams managed to secure other key objectives.[39]

On the American side, the 82nd Airborne Division dropping by parachute was also scattered over a fifty-mile-wide area extending from Licata clear over to Eighth Army's operational sector at Noto.

Again, individual initiative saved the day as small groups either made their way to assigned objectives or simply attacked any enemy strong-point encountered. The confusion sown by the paratroops, combined with the often ad hoc blocking positions they threw into place inland and then fiercely defended, were credited by some German senior officers with saving the American divisions from being driven by the Hermann Göring Division "back into the sea."[40]

By midmorning, the Allied high command realized Operation Husky had succeeded in its essential first step. The two armies were ashore and the beachheads so firmly established there was little chance of being repelled. But, as the British official historian later wrote, "the margin between success and failure was narrow. One can only speculate whether the assault would have succeeded if the enemy had resisted more determinedly, and had used the forces which he actually had with greater skill, speed, and concentration. For the Allies had simply not had the means of providing sufficient reserves to overcome anything greater than a slight set-back."[41]

In a blustery speech before a crowd of thousands in Palermo on August 20, 1937, Benito Mussolini had declared Sicily impregnable. "You have seen grow before your eyes the state of military prepared-ness on land, sea and in the air which protects the island," he had thundered. "Only the greatest folly could lead one to contemplate an invasion. No one will ever land here, not even a single soldier!" But six years later, on July 10, the folly had been realized, and by sunup thousands of Allied soldiers stood on Sicilian soil.

7

Call This a Fight?

FROM BARK WEST, 1st Canadian Infantry Division's inland advance in the early morning hours of July 10 proceeded rapidly. On the division's right flank, Royal Canadian Regiment captain Slim Liddell's 'A' Company made a beeline cross-country towards Maucini. Although it showed on the maps as a village, the place consisted only of a large house with a few nearby outbuildings. Captain Strome Galloway's 'B' Company was a little slower getting off the mark but was soon headed for the coastal gun battery positioned a little way from Maucini. The advance had gone only about fifty yards when a bullet zipped over Corporal Anson Moore's head. Moore, a section leader in one of Galloway's platoons, thought the fire came from a small farmhouse. He had the section's Bren gunner fire a burst through the open door. Immediately a Sicilian farmer danced out waving a white sheet. Galloway ordered his men to keep moving.

A few minutes later, an "old and gnarled Sicilian accompanied by a youth" ran towards them. "The old man threw his arms about me, and thrust his stubbled cheek against mine, kissed me vigorously." Galloway pushed the old man gently aside while his men stood around laughing. Ahead, Galloway could see Liddell's company gaining distance and decided he'd better catch up. Ploughing into a drought-stricken and stunted vineyard, the captain "tripped over some barbed wire and fell flat on my face, gashing my left thigh and bleeding like a stuck pig." This was not the kind of glorious dash into the face of the enemy that Galloway had been reckoning on.[1]

By the time 'B' Company emerged from the vineyard, Liddell's men had closed on Maucini. "It turned out to be a huge building alright, a lot dirtier than the air photos indicated and garrisoned by a toothless old woman (very dirty) and three small kids (also dirty)," Liddell wrote. "The odd rifle and set of pouches indicated the hurried departure of Italian troops." 'A' Company then "stood grimly by waiting to shed their life's blood trying to blow a way through the wire if 'B' Company should find their job a bit too large and call for help."[2]

As Galloway's lead platoon approached the coastal battery, a machine gun ripped off a burst and then fell silent. Seconds later, several 15-inch rounds from *Roberts* crashed down around the battery. No way was Galloway sending his men forward with the monitor targeting his objective, so he ordered them to ground while a runner dashed back to battalion headquarters. Lieutenant Colonel Ralph Crowe and his headquarters outfit were just starting to move off the beach when the runner arrived with a request that the attached naval gunner officer call off the monitor. Back on the transport, Galloway and every man in the company had studied the plan for taking the battery. He could see now that everyone had remembered his job. Lieutenant Allan "Abe" Pettem and his platoon crawled over a stone wall to a spot of cover from which they would mount the frontal assault. Lieutenant Harry Keene swung out on one flank, so his platoon could cut off any attempt by the Italians to withdraw. The third platoon would provide Pettem's men with covering fire.

Some of Pettem's men were packing bangalores to blast a hole in what they expected to be a wire tangle several feet high. The real thing was just eighteen inches tall and consisted of a few strands. The men ditched the heavy explosives and, with Pettem leading the charge, hurdle-jumped the wire. Inside the perimeter, the four guns had been abandoned. There was not an Italian to be found. A lance corporal ducked into a house beside the gun lines and reported it empty. There was food on the table and some bedding was still warm.

Sergeant Jean Bougard, meanwhile, had spotted a nearby dugout and gone to investigate it. Staring into the darkness, he heard faint talking. Shouldering his Lee-Enfield, Bougard fired a shot into the dugout and out poured a herd of Italians babbling, *"Buono italiano,"* over and over. One of them had his lower lip torn away and blood was pouring out of the gaping wound.[3] The sergeant had bagged one captain, two lieutenants, and thirty-five artillerymen—the entire battery's garrison.[4] Near the dugout an abandoned machine-gun emplacement had a pool of blood on its concrete floor. Galloway looked at the blood, then the mouth wound, and decided it was probable that shrapnel from a shell off *Roberts* had caused it rather than Bougard's bullet.

A few minutes later, Lieutenant G.N.C. "Geoff" Campbell walked into the battery position with his platoon of pioneers in tow. The men stuffed explosives into the breeches of the four howitzers and blew them. While the pioneers were spiking the guns, Galloway's men relieved the prisoners of "pistols, other souvenirs, and stacks of Italian bank notes. Italian money, we figured, was going to come in handy." Sending the prisoners to the beach under the guard of a couple of men, Galloway led the rest of the company towards Pachino airfield.[5]

The advance by 'C' Company, which was to lead the airfield attack, "was not carried out in any prescribed military fashion" that its commander, Captain Ian Hodson, recognized. When one lieutenant spotted suspicious movement about one thousand yards away from the line of advance, he wandered off alone into the vineyards and olive groves to investigate without bothering to inform Hodson or his platoon sergeant. Once it dawned on the sergeant, whom Hodson considered "not the brightest," that he was now in charge of the platoon, the man had no idea what to do and stopped moving. Hodson stomped over and used "some strong language to straighten him out." When the wayward lieutenant reappeared from his solo sortie, Hodson dressed him down as well.

By the time he got this platoon ready to move, the rest of the company had gathered "like flies" around the corpse of an Italian soldier. Some men were "cutting off buttons, epaulettes, belt buckle." Hodson bellowed at his platoon commanders "to get busy and command their platoons" and, in some semblance of formation, 'C' Company finally headed for its objective.

Hodson was hanging back, keeping a watchful eye on the wandering lieutenant and his men. Consequently, he arrived at the airfield a few minutes behind the point platoon. He was "horrified" to see them "sitting in a circle in the middle of the landing strip, having a rest and a cigarette." Shouting and waving his arms, Hodson got them heading east across the airfield towards the water tower.[6]

LIEUTENANT COLONEL CROWE was watching 'C' Company's advance from a low rise about two hundred yards south of the airfield, after establishing his battalion headquarters, at about 1030 hours, inside a small gravel pit tucked into the south slope. The Italians, it appeared, had ploughed up the landing strip to render it useless and then withdrawn. Standing next to Crowe, Major Billy Pope, "who had 'overlooked' the fact that he was technically LOB," agreed. Pope had just driven up aboard one of the battalion's Bren carriers, the first RCR vehicle put ashore. The two men watched 'C' Company progress across the airfield while 'A' Company moved towards a cluster of barracks buildings in the northwest corner. Suddenly, artillery shells started exploding around the two companies, the telltale flashes of guns betraying the location of a coastal battery about one thousand yards north of the airfield.[7]

Hodson's 'C' Company ignored the fire and kept moving east of the airfield. 'A' Company, meanwhile, had established contact with 'D' Company of the Hastings and Prince Edward Regiment immediately west of its position. Its commander, Major A.A. "Bert" Kennedy, hurried over and told Liddell "to stop shooting at his lads whenever they moved forward."[8] Kennedy, the scion of an Owen Sound ship-propeller manufacturing firm, had commandeered the tiller of his LCA and confidently guided it ashore, with the other LCAS carrying his company and the battalion headquarters following behind. Accordingly, 'D' Company and Lieutenant Colonel Bruce Sutcliffe's headquarters unit had been the only Hasty Ps to land in the right spot. This had given Kennedy's men a head start inland, so it was now operating independently—although the Hasty Ps in 'A' Company were not far behind on the left flank.[9] When Liddell pointed out that none of his men were shooting at anything, the two officers realized "the local enemy must be getting active." 'A' Company was still being stalked by the coastal battery, the rounds falling around it being mistaken by Liddell for mortar bombs because they exploded with a "very loud bang" and "a lot of black smoke" but did no noticeable damage.

Kennedy pointed to a hill in front of his company, which had suddenly come alive with Italian troops firing from a concealed fortification, and said he was going to assault it. Liddell got his men throwing out supporting fire from the flank, while the Hasty Ps went right at the hill.[10] The fortified hill was quickly overrun, and Kennedy's men captured three medium machine guns and two 75-millimetre field guns. A few minutes later there was a sharp rattle of gunfire from left of the hill, and then some men from the Hasty Ps in 'A' Company appeared with seven prisoners. Word passed over the wireless that they had captured an Italian field gun and the tractor that had been towing it off.[11]

While Liddell had been helping the Hasty Ps take the hill, Crowe kept pestering him over the wireless to "get cracking" and finish clearing up the airfield.[12] A little after 1100 hours, Liddell led his men down the slope towards the barracks and into the face of fire coming from several machine guns and rifles. Suddenly, what had seemed a stroll under a hot sun turned deadly. Between 'A' Company and the Italian positions was a serious wire obstacle. It "was necessary to crawl under it looking for mines, holding up the wire so it wouldn't catch on equipment...and hope that whoever was doing the shooting wouldn't suddenly improve and get a hit." Once they broke through the wire and gained the open airfield, 'A' Company shook out into a perfectly extended line and quick-marched forward, shooting several snipers along the way to the barracks while the machine-gun fire continued to fly harmlessly overhead. The barracks proved abandoned, all clean and tidy, with neatly made beds. Enemy machine-gun fire kept coming at the company, but Liddell was unable to spot its source. What he still thought were mortars also kept firing on the company, their rounds exploding noisily and releasing black smoke clouds. To the northeast on the other side of a vineyard, Liddell spotted a well-camouflaged house and decided it was probably concealing the machine guns. As 'A' Company crawled into the intervening vineyard it came up against more thick tangles of wire. A standoff ensued, with both Italians and Canadians pouring out fire.[13]

The impasse was broken when a section composed of five privates managed to force their way over the wire and close on the two concrete machine-gun emplacements protecting the house. Thirty-one-year-old Private James Milford Butler of Chatham, Ontario, was killed in the attack. But Joe Grigas and Jack Gardner flanked one of the positions and killed its crew. This prompted the commanding Italian officer to order his men to lay down their arms, despite the fact that the fortification remained formidable. For their bravery, Grigas received the Distinguished Conduct Medal and Gardner, a Military Medal.

Everywhere 'A' Company looked Italians started coming out of holes, as the entire garrison surrendered. Nobody could manage an accurate count of how many prisoners were sent back to the beach. The battalion war diarist estimated 130.[14] Liddell was sure he counted 253.[15]

The fighting wound down at about 1300 hours. Lieutenant Colonel Crowe arrived a few minutes later and expressed his pleasure at the discovery that the fortification had housed four 6-inch coastal guns that were now silenced. There was also a truck standing in the yard filled with Italian light machine guns. Crowe told Liddell that 'D' Company was coming up on his left flank and would be moving to the north of it.[16]

'C' Company, meanwhile, was well northeast of the airfield, with the town of Pachino to its right. Neither Hodson nor his men were feeling alert. The after-effects of seasickness were setting in and the heat of the day was proving insufferable, with the temperature hovering between ninety and ninety-five degrees Fahrenheit. When word came over the wireless for the company to hold up, Hodson stopped his men in the shade of a long row of ten-foot-high cactus plants. "The troops were tired and there was dead silence. Suddenly, from nowhere, appeared an Italian soldier leading a mule on which was a very large wireless set. The Italian had not seen us and plodded along parallel to our line of recumbent soldiers, about 50 feet in front of us. No shots were fired, no sentries were calling out to their superiors to point out this soldier. Finally I got to my feet and shouted 'Platoon commanders, for God's sake, somebody, do something.' There were a few shouts, followed by some sporadic rifle fire. The Italian kept plodding along. Finally a soldier ran after him, knelt down and shot him. Not a very auspicious occasion."[17]

In the distance Hodson spotted tanks moving and felt a shiver of fear. He rummaged around in his tired memory to recall the enemy armour silhouette cards he had studied in training. Nothing looked right. Finally, as they rumbled closer, the tanks materialized into Shermans, and behind them plodded some veteran Desert Rats of the 51st Highland Division. They looked more like prospectors than soldiers, picks and shovels over their shoulders and wearing thick flannel shirts instead of the rather well-turned-out bush shirts that the Canadians had been issued. Some of Hodson's men sniggered at the British soldiers' appearance. In time, however, they would realize that the flannel absorbed sweat during the day and provided some warmth during cold nights. They would also learn that picks and shovels beat "fingernails and the edge of a steel helmet [for] digging weapon pits."[18]

Left of 'C' Company, Liddell's 'A' Company became involved in another exchange of fire. While the gun battle with unseen opponents raged, an officer from the 51st Highland's Devonshire Regiment ducked out of Pachino to brief Liddell on a plan to squeeze a suspected Italian battle group between the British troops and the RCR from both flanks. As the two officers discussed how to go about this, they realized their men were firing on each other and the Italian force was non-existent. Nobody on either side had been hit during the twenty-minute exchange.[19]

The RCR by now was on all its assigned objectives and, despite the delayed landing, was several hours ahead of schedule. 'D' Company had the battalion's last scrap of the day at about 1400 hours, running into a "gauntlet of some of the fiercest M.G. fire that the Italians had thrown at us," as the war diarist put it. Lieutenant Walter Roy's platoon had been well ahead of the rest of the company when the Italians opened up. Without waiting for the other platoons, Roy led his platoon into an attack only to be severely shot in the shoulder. Several other men were wounded before the company managed to overrun the enemy position and take forty prisoners.

By 1700 hours, the battalion was digging in for the night and also "into their 48-hour rations, and seldom was a mess tin of tea more enjoyed." The RCR, the war diarist proudly noted, "was the first to capture an enemy airfield in Sicily, they have done a good day's work and they know it."[20]

Hodson thought they had been mercifully lucky. They had "gained some experience (some of it admittedly not very good) but we were intact and ready for the next operation. Men had learned for themselves that in this heat we could not carry all the equipment issued to us. Without instructions or authority, on that very first day and during the next few days, we stripped down to the very basic necessities to become mobile and to conserve energy. We all recognized that we had a great deal to learn, but we had taken a first step toward becoming good soldiers."[21]

BY 1800 HOURS, the Hasty Ps had consolidated a defensive position on high ground left of the airfield. Except for 'A' Company, which had landed far to the west, and 'D' Company's skirmish at the fortified hill, the battalion had met little opposition.[22] As for 'A' Company, Captain Alex Campbell had marched the company up a road bordered by cactuses, "raising clouds of white dust as it went," until the leading platoon turned a corner and found itself facing a horse-drawn Italian artillery battery. Two teams of horses, each pulling a field gun, stared balefully at the Canadians. Immediately in front of the horses, a broken-down lorry blocked the road. The infantry had guns at the ready, the Italians milling around the truck did not, and a flurry of shots left three of the artillerymen bleeding to death in the ditch. Seven other gunners surrendered.[23]

Campbell's initial delight in this capture quickly turned to disgust. A bullet through the radiator had rendered the truck useless. The field guns were wooden-wheeled relics from the Great War that lacked even aiming sights. When a section returned from patrolling farther up the road with a report that they could hear tanks in the distance,

Campbell realized his little sojourn was perhaps ill advised. Leaving the guns and truck behind, 'A' Company marched with prisoners and horses in tow eastward to link up with the rest of the battalion.

Lost more than not, Campbell led his men along one winding track after another. With each passing hour the day grew hotter and the troops wearier, thirstier, and hungrier. Finally, at 1400 hours, they stumbled into the battalion perimeter to find their mates comfortably resting in the shade of olive groves. Campbell reluctantly went to the beach to get his bullet wound tended and returned a little later with his arm in a sling. The battalion medical officer, the captain said, had wanted to evacuate him to a hospital ship. Campbell had threatened to punch the doctor if he insisted on this course.[24]

About the time 'A' Company came into the perimeter, so did the Hasty Ps' second-in-command, Major John Buchan, 2nd Baron Tweedsmuir. Lord Tweedsmuir's father had been Canada's governor general from 1935 to his death in 1940 at age sixty-five. The thirty-one-year-old major had been assigned to the Hasty Ps shortly before they sailed from Britain, when the battalion's second-in-command, Major O'Connor Fenton, was injured in a motorcycle accident. Brigadier Howard Graham and the Hasty Ps' Lieutenant Colonel Bruce Sutcliffe had been preparing to promote one of the battalion's more than capable officers when they were suddenly informed by army headquarters that a British lord would be foisted on them. So far as Graham knew, "John Tweedsmuir, as he liked to be called, had never commanded anything, had never seen the [Hasty Ps], nor had I or anyone else in the brigade ever set eyes on him." Whether he would prove competent remained to be seen.[25] Tall, lanky, and very intense, he was soon nicknamed "Long John" or "Tweedie" by the troops.[26]

Tweedsmuir had been LOB during the initial landings but had organized a carrying party to bring supplies up to the battalion. He had found Lieutenant Colonel Sutcliffe and his battalion headquarters "in a vineyard full of olive and almond trees beside a deep cool well." The two officers discussed how well the day had developed and agreed the men were "all in good heart."[27]

On his way forward, Tweedsmuir had passed through the 48th Highlanders of Canada. This battalion had been left with little to do because 1 CIB's leading battalions had met such light resistance. Instead of closing with a determined enemy, the Highlanders fended off children begging for chocolates and cigarettes. They also ran afoul of the old Sicilian farmer from Toronto, who volunteered that he had owned a fruit store on Elizabeth Street behind the regiment's armoury. He had recognized their pipers.[28]

The Highlanders set up on three small hills about a mile inland and midway between the salt marshes behind the beach and Pachino airfield.[29] They had not fired a shot and so "spent time collecting tomatoes and fruit of all types." Their positions offered little shade and the men "found the heat oppressive. This part of Sicily all vineyards, dry and flat," bemoaned the battalion war diarist.[30]

Half a mile inland of the Highlanders, Brigadier Howard Graham had established his headquarters in a sandy orchard. Graham was exhausted, the stress of executing the landing of most of his assault force by LCMS and DUKWS having taken its toll on the fifty-four-year-old. As the sun went down, he noted that the heat of the day quickly dissipated. Rolling up in his greatcoat on the sand with a mosquito net draped over him, Graham fell into a deep sleep.[31]

WHILE 1 CIB had faced some semblance of organized resistance, particularly at Pachino airfield, 2nd Canadian Infantry Brigade met next to none. Once on the sand, its biggest problem arose from the Seaforth Highlanders of Canada having landed east of the Princess Patricia's Canadian Light Infantry rather than to their west. Before sunup, the Seaforths had completed the nearly three-thousand-yard trek across the beach and were busy raking in prisoners. Their first objective had been a causeway, where, after firing a few shots, they watched a sizable number of Italians come out "with their hands up. They were a sorry looking lot, no socks on their feet, shoes almost off their feet—and their uniforms were of the poorest quality." A Seaforth, wounded in the landing, escorted them to a prisoner cage set up on the beach and then reported to the nearby Regimental Aid Post for treatment.[32]

Lieutenant Colonel Bert Hoffmeister ordered a pause at the causeway to clear the sand out of weapons and eat some of the forty-eight-hour rations.[33] The battalion was soon on the move again, heading west towards its next objective—a height of ground beyond a saltwater lake that overlooked the beach. They reached this rise at about noon. Soon thereafter, contact was established with the Special Service Brigade commandos on the Seaforth's left. At times, as the battalion crossed over higher ground, Ispica was visible in the distance. It was on top of a hill about seven miles to the northwest, and intelligence reports predicted the Italians would make a stand there. This was hard to believe, given that so far they had been surrendering in droves.[34] Following Hoffmeister, like a loyal spaniel, was a young naval gunnery officer named Montgomery from *Roberts*. The lad was desperate for a target against which to direct the monitor's guns. "Sir, now?" he would ask whenever something that looked remotely worth shooting at appeared. But Hoffmeister, who had a good understanding "of the size of the shell and the shocking effect of a shell that size" kept demurring, "Monty, there's absolutely no target."

"Sir, I've never fired this son of a gun close to extreme range," Montgomery would sigh.

"Well, I'm not prepared to waste ammunition if there's no target and, of course, there's always the danger of a round falling short," the lieutenant colonel retorted.[35]

Coming onto another bit of high ground, the Seaforths were suddenly startled to see a group of Italians on horseback galloping along with some mortars mounted on limbers. The mortar crews rode into the grounds of a cemetery next to a large walled château to the left of the Seaforths, unlimbered their mortars, and immediately lobbed some bombs towards the Canadians.[36] "Monty, there's your target."

The lad grinned and started calling in coordinates. "The first round he fired just a little short," Hoffmeister later recalled, "and you could see the shell coming through the air in a great big blur. But the next one went right on the button and anything that was left that you could carry came streaming out of that château."[37]

After that the Seaforths just kept advancing, even pressing on after dark to a point about four miles south of Ispica in order to attack it the next day. While they were on the move, the town was continually subjected to heavy naval bombardment. The night portion of their march was a tough one. It "was pitch dark, and moving through vineyards, orchards and similar obstacles the heavily laden Seaforths gained their first experience at stumbling through an unfamiliar countryside in enemy territory." Dawn of July 11 found them on the low ridges that had been their destination—an inland march of some four miles—and the men collapsed for a few hours of welcome sleep.[38]

The PPCLI had covered even more ground after heading north from Bark West. Most of the rifle companies logged about seven miles in aggressive patrols aimed at cutting the roads running from Pachino to Ispica. Except for the Bren carrier platoon, whose LCT crew had become so disoriented they ended up at dawn standing off the 51st Highland Division's beach and had to turn about for Bark West, the entire battalion had been ashore by first light and ready to move. Lieutenant Colonel Bob Lindsay had sent the men due north towards their Phase One objective astride a road running on a northeasterly arc from the beach to intersect with a road and railway that ran in tandem northwest from Pachino.

Very little opposition was met during this phase, and the men had time to take a close look at the countryside. Most decided this coastal belt had little to recommend it. "The land, sloping very gradually to the sea," one officer wrote, "was terribly poor. Rock beds covered most of the surface and towards the sea the soil became almost pure sand. The vines were of a dwarf variety and provided little obstacle to the drift of the sand. To protect the young grain in the windswept soil the peasants had erected long rows of screens made of bamboos and rushes. Between these—which are six to ten feet apart—they grew their grain." Beyond the plain, they could see low, brown hills. It was these they marched towards, knowing their task in this invasion was to serve as "outriders," winning control of the high ground in order to protect Eighth Army's left flank during its drive up the coastal plain to Catania.[39]

By 1000 hours, the PPCLI had reached the road. Lindsay ordered three rifle companies to fan out to strike the Pachino–Ispica road in different places. The company-sized patrols were soon engaged in "several minor clashes, with few casualties. Many Italian prisoners were taken without their offering any fight...The natives were very friendly and appeared happy to have their country invaded by Allied forces," the PPCLI war diarist recorded.[40]

Those Italians who decided to make a stand did so in small groups usually quickly eliminated by the rifle company engaged. But there were exceptions. One section of 'D' Company sent to check a farmhouse approached so incautiously that it was ambushed and captured to a man by a party of Italian troops. When the section's platoon commander, Lieutenant G.S. Lynch, went looking for them, he was fired on as he walked up to the house. Returning fire with his pistol, Lynch was badly wounded as he escaped into a nearby vineyard. It took the officer several hours to drag himself back to 'D' Company's lines. In the meantime, the Italians at the farmhouse had decided to flee and let the platoon's section go.[41]

To the west, 'C' Company had been moving towards a point where maps showed a bridge crossing a narrow gully. Lieutenant Colin McDougall's platoon led, its sections arrayed in an H-shaped formation with the men in each section advancing in single file. The platoon walked "past vineyards and olive groves, through gardens of aloe and cypress," McDougall wrote. "Their boots crushed and released the scent of rosemary and thyme. There were flowering almond trees, distant orange groves—but no sign of enemy.

"The platoon was climbing on the road beside a lone poplar tree when there was a sharp, black explosion. Bits of dirt and gravel showered over them. Two men fell wounded. The others pushed on through a wooded parkland where they were again fired upon." McDougall led his men in a charge on some farmhouses that dominated the road, only to find them empty. There was no sign of the mortar or artillery piece that had fired and which had fallen silent after loosing the single round.

Hearing voices in the distance, McDougall signalled his men to be quiet and then crept out beyond the houses to look down the opposite slope into a low draw. About five hundred yards away, an officer had formed up a group of fifty Italians under the shade cast by a giant oak and was giving them a heated address. Using hand signals, McDougall spread his platoon swiftly into a firing line along the hillcrest. Men checked their sights. The lieutenant estimated the range and had it passed the length of the line by each man whispering it to the next. When everyone was ready, McDougall yelled, "Fire!" About thirty rifles and three Bren guns fired as one. "The knots of soldiers around the oak tree seemed to disintegrate. Some of the green-clad figures escaped to nearby bushes or defilades of ground, but most of them remained sprawled around the base of the tree."[42]

This action took place at about 1800 hours. Three hours earlier, another PPCLI patrol had carried out a brief reconnaissance to Burgio, a village standing on the road about five thousand yards due west of Pachino. Detecting some enemy movement, the patrol did not enter the village and withdrew without alerting the Italians to their presence. Nobody wanted to give the troops in the village cause to go on the alert, for in a few hours Burgio was scheduled to be attacked by 3rd Canadian Infantry Brigade's Carleton and York Regiment. At 2130 hours, the PPCLI's 'A' Company was at the head of the battalion "when it came under fire...An attack was put in and resulted in the surrender of the enemy and capture of 4 Italian guns intact. During this advance the sky was aglow with flak and tracer as enemy planes carried out an attack on our ships which were still unloading on the beaches."[43]

The four guns had been horse-drawn, and the PPCLI happily pressed forty large draft animals into service.[44] By 0045 hours, the battalion was out on 2 CIB's point and about five miles southeast of Ispica, which the brigade was to overrun come dawn.

FOR ITS PART, 3 CIB had begun landing on Bark West at about noon. The Carleton and York Regiment, supported by a squadron of Three Rivers Tank Regiment, headed immediately for Burgio. The combined arms force entered the village at 2000 hours and reported "no opposition or casualties."[45] This was typical fare for the division's reserve brigade on July 10. Most of the troops had got soaked in the landing, and there was a general feeling of letdown at the lack of any fighting. The brigade's transport officer, Captain D.H. Cunningham, watched sympathetically as the "troops, heavily laden with full marching order and some of them very wet—pushed up an ankle-deep sandy slope behind the beach toward [their assembly area]. The day was very hot and the men had been aboard ship for nearly four weeks—two factors that made the short trip to the assembly area a disagreeable one. However, the location was finally reached and the Brigade settled down to the task of assembling the boatloads into units again. Traffic control was established, signs were erected and the various headquarters, working at top speed, were soon organized and functioning smoothly. There was, however, one serious problem: the shortage of transport was acute. Some of the battalions had lots of transport, but so far as the Brigade headquarters was concerned, apart from two vehicles due to be landed later, all transport was at the bottom of the Mediterranean."[46]

Major General Guy Simonds had landed with a lead element of his divisional headquarters at 1100 hours. They stepped off LCAs into four feet of water and "waded ashore carrying equipment and documents on their heads." The only suitable place they could find for a headquarters close to the beach was "a civilian hovel, 12×16, inhabited by an old woman, 11 guinea pigs, 4 dogs, a goat and 4 [gallons] of wine all of which were quickly cleared out." Lost at sea, along with their vehicles, was much equipment that kept a divisional headquarters running. They had "no office supplies except those carried aboard the *Hilary* by clerks," few typewriters, and a severe shortage of wireless sets.

With nightfall, the sudden onslaught of a series of raids on the beaches by German fighters and bombers was met by heavy volleys of anti-aircraft fire from guns on both the ships and the beach. The planes attacking Bark West caused no real damage and failed to score any hits on the ships standing offshore, but there were reports of ships sunk elsewhere. During the night, divisional headquarters gathered a tally of Canadian casualties for the day, and there was much surprise at how light these proved to be. Seven other ranks were killed and three officers and twenty-two other ranks wounded. The Special Service Brigade commandos had faced a couple of stiff fights that left them with six dead and nineteen wounded.[47]

From his hovel, Simonds sent a wire to General Andrew McNaughton, who was monitoring the invasion from 15th Army Group's Advanced Headquarters in North Africa. "Landings effected with very little opposition and by 1200 hrs today all objectives for phase one were in my hands. Ineffective counter attacks in afternoon were repulsed. Casualties very light and first reports indicate do not exceed seventy-five killed and wounded including 40 and 41 Marine Commandos. We took over 700 prisoners and some material. Morale high and troops very confident of themselves. Details will follow. Success mainly due to excellent co-operation Royal Navy and RAF."

McNaughton quickly responded, "Canada will be very pleased at your achievement."[48]

Out on the firing line that the PPCLI had set up in the darkness, Lieutenant Colonel Bob Lindsay felt wary about how easily the day had gone. "In these early stages success came easily and swiftly," he pointed out to the company commanders, and he warned them against "any relaxation of the small points that make for the success of an operation."[49] It was a hard message to sell to the troops, who had seen scores of enemy surrender without a fight. This was especially the case as the monitor *Roberts* and other warships offshore hammered Ispica with intermittent bombardments throughout the night. In the Hasty Ps' perimeter, one soldier spoke for many that evening. "Call this a fight?" he asked. "Why, this is only fun and games. I wonder if it's all like this?"[50]

8

These Men Have Surrendered

THE ALLIED AMPHIBIOUS landings in Sicily had achieved a stunning tactical surprise. Only on July 9 had Tenth Army commander and Commander-in-Chief (South) Generalfeldmarschall Albert Kesselring and his staff in Rome discovered through aerial reconnaissance reports that the many ships recently spotted in the Mediterranean were all vectoring towards the southeastern corner of the island. Until then, Kesselring had not been certain whether the obviously massing invasion fleet was bound for Sardinia or Sicily, although the heavy bombing of the latter island made it the likely target.[1]

Peculiarly, in the week preceding the invasion, both Kesselring and Adolf Hitler had become dangerously complacent about the threat to Sicily, embracing notions that the Italians could be trusted to vigorously defend it. Hitler assured General der Artillerie Walter Warlimont, deputy chief of the Wehrmacht Operations Staff, that the "ordinary Italian soldier and the young officer reared in the school of Fascism, when called upon to defend their Motherland, would perhaps give proof of soldierly qualities surprising both to friend and foe." Warlimont considered this an "idealistic estimate based on airy-fairy ideas" that obscured "the military realities, the most important of which was that there was a fatal gap between the level of equipment of Italian forces and those of the Allies."[2]

Kesselring had more realistically come to the conclusion that Germany's partnership with Italy "was simply riding for a fall. There were often times when I reflected that it would be far easier to fight alone with inadequate forces than to have to accept so bewildering a responsibility for the Italian people's aversion to the war and our ally's lack of fighting ability and dubious loyalty."[3] On June 30, this frank assessment had led him to comment that, despite adequate strength of forces and supply to enable Sicily's defence from enemy attack, the "deciding factor" would be "the low spirit of the Italian troops." Deployment of the Hermann Göring Division to the island, he hoped, would "improve the morale of the Italians," but if "the island defences and the Italian soldiers fail, then the loss of the island must be expected sooner or later. German forces alone will not be able to defend Sicily for any length of time."[4] Yet to the puzzlement of his subordinates, instead of riding herd on the Italians to strengthen their martial ardour, Kesselring "deliberately retired into the wings, seeing that the defence of their native soil was pre-eminently the Italians' business."[5]

At 1630 hours on July 9, however, evidence that the invasion was imminent led Kesselring's headquarters to issue an alert to "all troops in Sicily."[6] While this alert might have reached the German divisions in a timely fashion, it only slowly trickled down the Italian chain of command. Not until 2220 hours did 206th Italian Coastal Division commander Generale di Brigata Achille d'Havet, responsible for defending the coast from Siracusa to Gela, learn that an invasion force was closing on his shores. With a gale rising off the coast, his naval adviser "assured him it was much too rough for a landing."[7] Consequently, his troops were allowed to "relax their vigil" in the belief that so long as the storm raged they were safe from attack.[8] When Eighth Army's assault battalions came ashore that night, this division was entirely surprised and "turned out to be very ineffective."[9]

This was despite the fact that Generale d'Armata Alfredo Guzzoni, who technically commanded all Axis forces in Sicily, had learned that Allied airborne troops were landing on the island at 0015 hours. Forty-five minutes later, Guzzoni ordered all Italian and German formations into action. "The enemy has started landing operations in Sicily," he announced. "I have the confidence that the very Italian population of this island will give the troops, who are to defend it, its material and spiritual support. Joined by one will, citizens and soldiers will oppose the invader with a united front, which will break his action and hold for us this precious part of Italy." By 0130 hours, troops of 206th Division had succeeded in dynamiting piers at Gela and Licata that the Americans had hoped to use for unloading supplies. Guzzoni also had directed Generale di Corpo Carlo Rossi's xvi Army Corps to move towards these two towns, while at 0145 hours the Italian xii Corps was similarly ordered to head for Siracusa.[10] But it was all too little and much too late to prevent the Allies getting ashore.

Communications between Guzzoni and the German commanders on the island were confused, and only one of the two divisions was situated to be of use. The decision, at Kesselring's insistence, to send most of 15th Panzer Grenadier Division to the Palermo area put it out of the action. Guzzoni issued instructions attaching the Hermann Göring Division to xvi Corps so that it could launch a counterattack in concert with the 4th (Livorno) Assault and Landing Division, but Generalmajor Paul Conrath never received them. Instead, the German divisional commander independently decided to split the division into two *Kampfgruppen* (battle groups), each having the strength of a reinforced regiment. One was predominantly infantry, the other armoured. Conrath planned to unleash them in simultaneous assaults against the American 1st and 45th divisions. By 0400, these two forces were heading for the Americans, who were simultaneously advancing on Caltagirone from the beaches.

Also closing on the Americans was xvi Corps's Mobile Group E, consisting largely of the Livorno Division. Advancing in two separate columns, the Italians had reacted more quickly than the Germans. Detected early by aerial reconnaissance, the Italians were dogged by naval bombardments from the cruiser *Boise* and other American warships. After hours of punishment that threw it into disorganization, Mobile Group E withdrew into the foothills northeast of Gela. The German *Kampfgruppen* proved equally incapable of making any significant gains against the Americans.[11]

As one negative report after another poured in, Kesselring realized only decisive action by the Germans could save the situation. "The Italian coastal divisions were an utter failure." Unaware that the Livorno Division had attempted a counterattack, he dismissed the Italian forces as entirely incompetent. The 54th Napoli Division "in the southwest corner of the island had melted into thin air."[12] At 0340 hours on July 11, Kesselring sent a terse report to Berlin that he had ordered Hermann Göring Division "to destroy the enemy who has advanced to Caltagirone." The third component of 15th Panzer Division—an infantry battalion with two artillery batteries—which had been left in the eastern sector of the island and designated Battle Group Schmalz after its commander, Oberst Wilhelm Schmalz, had been directed to recapture Siracusa.[13] Within minutes of sending this report, Kesselring was making arrangements to fly to Sicily because of the "impossibility of remedying the confusion in the command by my telephoned directives."[14] When Kesselring's report came in to the headquarters in Berlin, Warlimont saw that the "blanket of self-deception and wishful thinking was rent to pieces."[15]

ON JULY 11, little comprehending the magnitude of Axis disorganization, the Allies expected to face stiffening resistance and counterattacks aimed at pushing them back to the sea. The threat of counterattack led 1st Canadian Infantry Division to assume a generally defensive posture throughout the morning, which also provided time for the leading brigades to reorganize and set plans for a concerted push inland. As the morning wore on, it became evident the counterattack was not to materialize, so at noon the infantry units began to move.[16]

Major General Guy Simonds decided the division would advance in two separate columns, with 1st Canadian Infantry Brigade on the right and 2nd Canadian Infantry Brigade to the left. This left 3rd Canadian Infantry Brigade in reserve, as had been the case on July 10. Also, as on the previous day, the Canadians were guarding the left flank of Eighth Army's xxx Corps.[17] The road followed by 2 CIB, which ran through Ispica, Modica, and Ragusa, and the parallel road through Rosolini, taken by 1 CIB both proved to be "rocky trails rather than the good highways suggested by the maps."[18] This posed particular problems for the artillery regiments trying to follow behind the infantry, as their trucks were almost too wide for the tracks. Even seeing the road was difficult, as "huge clouds of dust rolled up wherever a vehicle moved."[19] Forced to creep carefully along through this blinding, self-generated dust cloud, the gunners were seldom within range of the rapidly advancing infantry and so could offer no support.

Following the route taken by 2 CIB, the 3rd Field Regiment suffered its first fatal casualty just a short way inland from the beach when the 19th Battery's clerk was knocked off a truck by a wire running across the road and crushed by the wheels of the gun the vehicle was towing. Forty-eight-year-old Lance Sergeant George John Jack died before the regiment's medical officer reached the scene.[20]

Meanwhile, at Pachino airfield, 1st Field Company, Royal Canadian Engineers was rendering the landing strips serviceable. In addition to ploughing up the strips, the Italians had sown many mines in the area and blocked nearby crossroads with large concrete obstacles. No. 1 Platoon cleared the mines while No. 2 Platoon, having found a dump of Italian box mines, detonated these under the concrete blocks and smashed them into easily movable chunks. By early afternoon, the approaches to the airfield were cleared sufficiently to allow the engineers to roll their heavy equipment, particularly bulldozers, onto the airfield and start levelling the landing strips.[21]

It also fell to the engineers and rear-area personnel, particularly soldiers in the Royal Canadian Army Service Corps (RCASC) either missing their trucks or not yet called upon to move supplies forward, to clean up the detritus of battle in the beachhead area. Some troops from the RCASC were ordered to bury the remains of an Italian artillery battery next to the road running from Pachino airfield to Burgio. The battery, one participant in the group wrote, "had come into pin-point range of our [naval] guns. The remains of the battery, animals and personnel...[give] one an impression of the deadliness of our...fire."[22]

Much of that deadly fire had been concentrated throughout the morning on Ispica, which 2 CIB's Loyal Edmonton Regiment was teeing up to attack in the early afternoon. Intelligence reports issued before the invasion had predicted this town would be a tough nut to crack. Perched on top of "a rock cliff towering sheer to a height of

150 feet and heavily defended by extensive barbed wire fields," Ispica was an ideal defensible position. The town itself was built upon a series of "stepped-up terraces well up on the crest of the rocky cliff. Towering above all is the town church in the early Renaissance style of architecture."[23]

It was a six-mile march through intense heat from their start point to Ispica. Ranging ahead of the battalion was a patrol of brigade scouts. When it probed the town's outskirts, some shots were fired from a house and a couple of grenades were pitched out at them. The patrol quickly fell back and sent a message that the Eddies should expect "street fighting."[24]

Lieutenant Colonel Jim Jefferson, the quiet, shy Great War veteran who commanded the Edmonton regiment, was never one to unnecessarily put men at risk. Instead of barging into a possible shootout in the streets, he had the artillery forward observation officer (FOO) travelling with the battalion send a message back to the British cruiser, HMS *Delhi*, to drop a salvo on the town with its five 5-inch guns.[25] Before the smoke cleared, Jefferson sent an Italian civilian into the town with an ultimatum for the garrison to surrender. At 1450 hours, the leading company cautiously crept up the road into the town and took its surrender. "The only difficulties encountered," wrote the regiment's war diarist, "were enthusiastic greetings of the civilian population and the frantic endeavours of the military population to surrender." Initially, about two hundred Italian troops laid down their arms, and many more were rounded up in the ensuing hours. Once Ispica was considered pacified, the Edmontons moved two miles northwest of it and established a defensive position astride the highway leading to Modica.[26]

This cleared Ispica's narrow main street for the Princess Patricia's Canadian Light Infantry and the main body of the Seaforth Highlanders to pass through between 1715 and 1730 hours. Both battalions had orders to move north of the village and set up defensive positions. "Many natives stood in the streets waving and clapping their hands at us," the latter battalion's war diarist recorded. "Wine and fruit were passed out to the troops, the hatred of Mussolini and the Germans being expressed time and again."[27]

Before the PPCLI and Seaforths advanced through Ispica, both battalions had been aggressively patrolling the countryside between the village and the coast. One PPCLI patrol, mounted on horses captured from artillery batteries the day before, was able to range quite far afield.[28] Every patrol sent forth met troops from the Italian 206th Coastal Defence Division, who were often "bedraggled and frightened," barefoot or wearing "cracked shoes," and eager to surrender despite seeming to expect "any moment to be shot."[29]

Captain Freddie Middleton of the Seaforth's 'B' Company was approached by a civilian. The civilian spoke a little English; Corporal John Cromb, a little Italian. This enabled Cromb to ascertain that "a captain and some of his compatriots were in a cave just off the road up on a hillside. It was felt, therefore, that my section and myself could take care of them. We left the company, climbed the steep hillside and took up positions outside. The Italian went inside to bring out the captain and his companions. The first individual to appear was a batman. He had a large valise under each arm and one in his hand and came out bowing very politely. Then followed two lieutenants, then the captain, then his companions—123 of them!" Cromb's section of ten men formed the Italians up and marched them down the hill to Middleton, who was at a loss as to how he could spare sufficient men to escort such a large party back to the beach. Finally, he simply wrote on a slip of paper: "These men have surrendered." Handing the slip to the Italian captain, Middleton told him to march his troops back unaccompanied.[30]

The Seaforth's 'C' Company, meanwhile, had been diverted southwest of Ispica to secure the little coastal village of Pozzallo. During the morning, the navy had dropped 160 shells on either flank of the place and then at 1315 hours sent a shore party in that accepted the surrender of two officers and ninety-six troops. When Major Jim Blair and his men arrived about an hour later, they relieved the naval personnel and were soon approached by ten officers and another 250 men anxious to give up. The village's Fascist mayor had fled and the citizens seemed close to starvation. Blair discussed things in pidgin Italian with the local Catholic priest and village postmaster, after which the Canadian troops "broke open a granary and organized the distribution of grain, bread and macaroni."[31]

By 1800 hours, 2 CIB's battalions were all north of Ispica setting up defensive positions for the night when, because "the enemy were ·

on the run, further orders were issued for the advance to continue and follow the retreating enemy to the high ground east of Modica. This advance was carried out under very hot and dusty conditions and the troops, though tired from the previous activities, carried on magnificently," the PPCLI war diarist reported.[32]

Ranging well ahead of the main columns on July 11, the artillery FOOS attached to each battalion hunted enemy positions to target for naval bombardment in order to eliminate them before they could delay the advance. Each FOO was normally accompanied by one of his regiment's soldiers, who helped carry and operate the heavy No. 18 wireless set. To provide the FOOS with mobility, each battalion had supplied their assigned gunner with a Bren carrier and four men from the carrier platoon.

Captain George "Duff" Mitchell of the 1st Field Regiment (Royal Canadian Horse Artillery) was acting as the naval FOO for the PPCLI with HMS Delhi on call. He and the carrier team were about halfway between Ispica and Modica and well out front of the marching infantry when Mitchell spotted a roadblock of "wire and mines, covered by two anti-tank guns" ahead. Calmly, Mitchell dismounted from the carrier and approached the Italians manning the roadblock. In the carrier, two men had a Bren gun apiece aimed at the enemy troops. The authority of these weapons, combined with his commanding manner, enabled Mitchell to force "the detachment of some 20 Italians to surrender and to dismantle the obstacle. This exploit, and the efficient way in which he maintained communication with his bombarding ship in calling down supporting fire, brought Captain Mitchell the first Military Cross to be awarded a Canadian in the Italian campaign," the army's official artillery historian later wrote.[33]

Late in the afternoon, 3rd Field Regiment received welcome news that 2 CIB had overrun a battery of Italian guns. As its 92nd Battery had lost its 25-pounders aboard one of the sunken ships, the decision was made to equip it with the captured weapons. The guns being horse-drawn, a call was issued for men with experience handling horses. A truck soon rushed to the scene "with a motley group of Westerners aboard—cooks, signallers, despatch riders and gunners, but all self-professed horsemen—under command of Lieutenant

M.H. "Mel" Watson and Regimental Sergeant Major Bill "The Whip" Adams, a horse artilleryman of Permanent Force days. They found the guns on the road to Ispica. They were 105-mm Howitzers, and sat in action just as they had been when overrun. There were four guns, four limbers, two wagons...and all the technical equipment, stores, signal equipment and gadgets necessary to fire the troop, as well as a plentiful supply of ammunition and some food.

"The first difficulty was with the horses. Several had already been taken by passing soldiers, the rest were wandering about the fields." It soon became evident that the horses, not understanding English, were incapable of responding to the commands issued with such authority by Regimental Sergeant Major (RSM) Adams. Finally, how-ever, the guns were hooked up and the battery moved off in pursuit of the infantry, only to be quickly forced into the ditch by a passing squadron of tanks. Plodding on until nightfall, the gunners made camp on the side of the road with hopes running high that the bat-tery would soon be able to put the Italian guns into action.[34]

AT MIDNIGHT, THE PPCLI was still on the march, "having met little opposition."[35] The battalion pushed through the night "and by 0500 hours next morning had completed a hot, dusty and exhausting march of 22 miles. At dawn they seized the high ground overlooking Modica, a town of 40,000 inhabitants which lies on the floor and slopes of the valley which carried the river of the same name."[36]

The PPCLI was not alone in covering significant ground during July 11 and the ensuing night. To 2 CIB's left, 1 CIB had been on the move, although its battalions had less ground to cover. At 1100 hours, with the "sun at its blazing peak," the 48th Highlanders marched three miles to Burgio and then awaited further orders. While the troops vied for spots in the shade, brigade and battalion officers sorted out the day's line of advance and objectives. So quickly had the Italian opposition collapsed that the schedule for progressing inland was outpaced. Lieutenant General Oliver Leese soon arrived at the 48th's headquarters with a gaggle of war correspondents in tow. He announced that the 51st Highland Division was far ahead of 1 CIB and the Canadians should immediately advance to Rosolini to protect the British division's exposed left flank. Brigadier Howard Graham put the 48th Highlanders out front with orders to force march the entire way.[37]

Rosolini was ten miles distant, and the hard pace soon had the "men suffering intensely from the heat."[38] The 48th Highlanders were followed in order by the Royal Canadian Regiment and the Hastings and Prince Edward Regiment—a long snaking line of soldiers raising clouds of dust with their passing that worsened conditions for those farther back. Men covered their mouths with handkerchiefs to ward off the dust. But the steel helmets began to bake their brains, and a handkerchief turned into a bonnet reduced the heat. Draped loosely, the handkerchiefs also served to protect exposed necks from sunburn. So intense was the glaring sun that some men closed their eyes for six steps, blinked them open for a brief, orienting glance, and then shut them again.[39]

Near their rest position the Hasty Ps had discovered "a lot of fruit—mulberries and peaches, and we were well dug in when the order came to move," Major Tweedsmuir wrote in his diary. "We started to march, we continued to march, we got on to a large main road, and on and on we went. Water bottles grew empty, feet got sore, and at every halt everyone lay down and got the maximum rest."[40]

In the centre of the line, the RCR battalion commander and company commanders marched together, forming a mobile Orders Group that could instantly respond to any enemy threat. Expectations ran high that the brigade would trip an ambush, but as the day progressed, no Italian or German troops were encountered. Only the heat remained—an implacable, unrelenting opponent. At one point, Captain Strome Galloway realized the RCR soldiers were seeing British troops from the 51st Highland Division's 7th Black Watch emerge like a mirage out of the dust and shimmering heat waves. "They looked lean and hard, and leathery brown cheeks could be seen under the white Sicilian dust. Compared to them we looked raw indeed." Soon these troops turned at a junction and vanished back into the haze.[41]

As the afternoon ground on, two carrier troops from the Three Rivers Tank Regiment jockeyed the marching infantry to the side of the road in their rush towards Rosolini. The troopers aboard the

Bren carriers were responding to orders from Brigadier Graham to hasten the Canadian advance in order to relieve a 51st Highland Division carrier troop that had accepted Rosolini's surrender at 1130 hours. Graham had realized that the tankers supporting his infantry had the only viable transport for quick movement. Cracking along at close to their top speed of thirty miles an hour, the carriers under command of Lieutenant R.W. "Pete" Ryckman soon cruised into the village. Half of it had been reduced to a smouldering ruin by naval shelling, but the villagers still turned out to greet the Canadians "with smiles, handshakes and shouts of welcome."

The British officers said the civilians claimed some three hundred Germans had pulled out shortly before their arrival. A single British soldier stood guard over about 150 Italians lined up alongside their stacked weapons. The village mayor assured Ryckman that he could maintain civil authority.[42] By the time the 48th Highlanders broke into Rosolini, with three companies carrying out a textbook assault from different angles of approach, order had been completely restored. No longer needed, Ryckman headed back to where the Three Rivers had established a tank laager and the infantry took over.[43] Here the battalion would spend what its commander Lieutenant Colonel Ian Johnston recorded as "a very uncomfortable night... due to the town being on fire in many places coupled with a horrible stench which seemed to pervade everywhere and on top of this it had turned quite cold."[44]

The RCR passed through the village after nightfall. Galloway thought it looked like "a City of the Dead. Not a light to be seen, and the stench of putrefying refuse, including human excreta was overpowering. Sweat poured off our bodies as we trudged through the maze of streets." The battalion moved about three miles beyond and concentrated around a large farmhouse while Lieutenant Colonel Ralph Crowe went by carrier to confer with Brigadier Graham. Having returned from a divisional briefing, Graham reported they were to advance towards Modica and Ragusa—which meant that 2 CIB and his brigade were closing on the same objectives. This was primarily to give the 51st Highland Division room to manoeuvre on the right. Meanwhile, the Seventh U.S. Army's 45th Division was making good progress on the left and contact with the Americans was expected to occur around Ragusa. The task at hand was to keep the advance cracking.

To that end, the RCR was ordered to immediately renew the advance, but riding on transport. As the RCR had only a small number of vehicles, a squadron of Three Rivers Tank Regiment Shermans was called forth. At 0100 hours on July 12, the battalion mounted up. Crowe was at the head of the column in a Bren carrier, using moonlight to read the map on his lap. The company commanders were crowded into a captured staff car, with Major Billy Pope at the wheel. After such a hot day, the temperature had dropped dramatically. Everyone in the car, except Pope, who had somehow kept a navy parka handy, had gas capes wrapped around their bodies. Pope kept nodding off and had to be prodded awake before he drifted into a ditch. The road snaked crazily across the black countryside, and Galloway expected them to roll into the middle of an ambush at any second. But nothing happened, and shortly after dawn Crowe brought the battalion precisely to its assigned concentration point four miles east of Ragusa. Galloway had never realized Crowe was such a fine map reader. His respect for the man increased.[45]

SHORTLY AFTER THE RCR jumped off the transport, they discovered part of the battalion was missing. The impromptu departure after midnight had gone unnoticed by thirteen exhausted men, all from the battalion headquarters company. The missing soldiers consisted of a section from the anti-tank platoon and several men from the 3-inch mortar platoon. Lieutenant Sheridan "Sherry" Atkinson was the senior officer in this number. When he and the others awakened to find the battalion gone, they had no idea where it had headed. Curiously, these troops all had Bren carriers to pull or carry their heavy weapons and yet they had been the ones left behind. Nobody could figure it. They just knew it was vital to catch up fast.

Taking directions from a military policeman directing traffic at an intersection, the small group headed up a road. "The further we proceeded," Atkinson and Lance Sergeant Harold Ghent later wrote, "the more it became apparent that we were in enemy territory as we encountered no Canadian troops, and the countryside was ominously quiet." They picked up other stragglers—a despatch rider with his motorcycle, a section from another regiment riding on a Bren carrier. Whenever they happened upon civilians, they cautiously sought directions and information. One group of Sicilians warned that the enemy was close by, and soon "a pillar of black smoke just to the right of a 'T' intersection" was spotted. The Canadians dismounted and approached on foot. Next to the intersection, a soldier stood by a wall with raised rifle. He fired, and a bullet snapped past Atkinson. The lieutenant's return fire also missed and the soldier ducked out of sight. At the side of the road, a three-ton Canadian truck was burning and next to its cab lay a corpse. Realizing they might be in the middle of a friendly fire situation, Atkinson and several men slowly moved forward. They identified the dead soldier as a member of the Seaforth Highlanders just as a machine gun opened up. The men hit the ground and one shouted, "Desert Rats!" Instead of "Kill Italians," the only reply was another machine gun burst. The men beat a hasty retreat.

Through his binoculars, Atkinson examined a well-fortified position in front of a church at the next intersection. He could see men moving behind the barricade. Retrieving a Bren gun from one of the carriers, Atkinson lay flat behind a stone gate pillar and fired at the position. Next thing, "I felt a strong blast of air close to my face which I found very puzzling. After firing a few more rounds from the Bren gun, I felt a further strong blast, and decided to have another look at the apparent source. This time, I discovered that the enemy had an artillery weapon aimed down the street, over open sights, and the blasts that I had felt were caused by heavy AP [armoured piercing] shells that were being aimed directly at me, and were just missing me by inches! I decided that the odds were in their favour."

Deciding to meet gun for gun, the Canadians brought up their 6-pounder anti-tank gun. But each time they poked its barrel out to draw a bead on the enemy artillery piece they drew mortar fire, forcing them to pull it back to safety. Stumped, Atkinson was pondering what to do next when a motorcycle roared up behind his position. Atkinson was frantically trying to wave down the driver to prevent his boring right into the enemy kill zone when a machine-gun burst prompted the rider to roll off his motorcycle into a ditch alongside the lieutenant. It took a second before he realized the man on the dirt beside him was 2 CIB's Brigadier Chris Vokes. Vokes growled that he had been told the road was clear. Worse, Major General Guy Simonds and his headquarters unit were not far behind. He wanted that road-block eliminated without delay. Could Atkinson's men wipe out the barrier if they were supported by three self-propelled 25-pounder field guns? Atkinson said he thought so. Vokes handed him his Thompson submachine gun to bolster the group's firepower, righted the motorcycle, and went hunting for the guns.

In short order a British FOO arrived with a wireless set. He was from the Royal Devon Yeomanry, which had a battery of 25-pound-ers that had been mechanized by mounting each gun on the chassis of an antiquated Valentine tank. This self-propelled regiment was on loan to the Canadian division because none of its inherent artil-lery, which was all towed, could match the infantry's pace of advance. The FOO promised a barrage behind which the thirteen soldiers could close on the blockade. Atkinson split his men into two groups. One, under a sergeant, would attack from the left while Atkinson struck from the right.

Advancing behind the barrage, the two groups closed quickly on the barricade without drawing much fire. As they broached the defences, Atkinson realized the position had been abandoned. The bombardment had set several nearby buildings alight. Knowing the enemy troops could not have gone far, the thirteen Canadians began warily searching the church and houses. When two men went behind one building, a machine gun crackled. Atkinson dashed around the corner to find one of them had shot a turkey dead. From the other side of the church came more gunfire. This time when Atkinson arrived on the scene, he found that the sergeant and his men had killed an Italian, which had prompted the rest of the garrison to sur-render. They numbered one officer and seventy-eight other ranks. The Italians had been armed with seven artillery pieces, one anti-tank gun, five machine guns, and several new Fiat trucks bursting with supplies. Atkinson's group had suffered not a single casualty.

The Canadians were in the process of searching the Italians for hidden weapons when a man wearing a "white uniform, gold epaulets on his shoulders, a chest of medals on his left breast and... a very fancy hat" appeared. Atkinson thought the Italian must be a naval officer but discovered he was in fact the mayor of Modica "and that he wanted to surrender the town to us!" Modica was visible about half a mile to the west. Deciding the opportunity was too good to pass up, Atkinson climbed on his motorcycle and Lance Corporal Verne Mitchell hopped behind. As they motored towards Modica, the immaculately dressed mayor jogged along beside, "holding on to his medals with one hand and his hat with the other. He was a sorry sight and lost all semblance of the dignity of his office.

"The entrance to the town was down a long winding hill with most of the houses on the left side of the road. Many houses had balconies on the second floor, and white surrender sheets had been strung over the rails. The population lined the streets and filled the balconies, cheering and waving at L/Cpl. Mitchell and Lieut. Atkinson as they made their grand entrance with the Mayor still jogging along beside them—now completely exhausted and perspiring heavily."

In the town square, the two Canadians were confronted by "a large body of Italian troops all lined up in three ranks with their rifles neatly stacked in piles in front of them! Later, when we counted the soldiers they totaled almost 900... We were dumbfounded and for a moment almost turned tail, thinking we had been led into an ambush. It readily became apparent, however, that the war was over for them, and that all they wanted was someone to accept their surrender." Mitchell nervously asked Atkinson what they should do. The lieutenant answered that he was going to bring up the rest of the men and Mitchell should keep the Italians under guard. Aghast at the idea, Mitchell accepted his orders with a lot of mumbling. Atkinson had equally "grave doubts" about this decision but no idea of what else to do. He kicked the motorcycle to life and went to get his tiny occupation force.[46]

[9]

On Shank's Mare

HOURS BEFORE THE RCR's Lieutenant Sherry Atkinson and his gaggle of troops had eliminated the Italian roadblock and then liberated Modica, the FOO travelling with the Princess Patricia's Canadian Light Infantry had also given the town its freedom. Late on the evening of July 11, Royal Canadian Horse Artillery captain George Mitchell, in his Bren carrier, had ranged far ahead of the marching infantry column in search of worthwhile targets for the naval ships offshore. This quest finally brought him to Modica's southern outskirts. Dismounting from the carrier, Mitchell and a couple of PPCLI men acting as guards for him had cautiously crept a short distance into the town. They met several civilians, who said there were no Germans there and that the town wanted to surrender. Anxious because the place was teeming with Italian troops that seemed to be just milling around and lacking any leadership, the Canadians withdrew to the heights overlooking the town.

Unlike most Sicilian towns, Modica lay in the bottom of a deep gully. When the entire battalion joined Mitchell on the heights at dawn, he and Lieutenant Colonel Bob Lindsay agreed Modica's poor strategic position made it unlikely the enemy would try defending the town. But because of the large number of Italian troops Mitchell had seen, they called down a short artillery bombardment before sending a strong fighting patrol in that gathered up a "considerable number of prisoners."[1]

The situation in Modica was confused by the sheer number of Italian soldiers—all anxious to surrender—and the fact that the PPCLI had lost cohesion by sending in a number of patrols with no means of contacting each other. One battalion support company patrol under Sergeant N.L.G. McGowan entered a building and discovered an Italian general and his headquarters staff inside. They were willing to surrender but insisted it be to another general.[2] There not being any Canadian divisional generals in the neighbourhood, the sergeant withdrew and reported their find to battalion headquarters—which concluded the general must be the commander of the 54th Napoli Division.[3]

With Lindsay intent on getting his battalion marching north towards the next objective, the PPCLI made little effort to round up all these potential prisoners. Instead, Lindsay ordered the battalion to pass through Modica and make for Ragusa, where it was to await motor transport for the next phase of advance. Consequently, the elegantly dressed mayor never managed to formally surrender to anyone, and the Italian general continued to wait for the arrival of a Canadian general. Later that morning, when sounds of fighting were heard east of the town, the mayor ventured forth and met Atkinson—to whom he was finally able to formally, if not very grandly, surrender Modica. After Atkinson went back for the rest of his men, Lance Corporal Verne Mitchell was left warily eyeing the hundreds of Italian troops standing about. They could turn him into cut bait in a moment, he knew. Mitchell noticed, however, that a few men wore different uniforms than the soldiers and realized these were national paramilitary police—the Carabiniere. Using his limited Italian, he inveigled them into mounting guard on the Italian troops in order to ensure the soldiers did not mix with the civilians and attempt to get lost in the gathering crowd. This was no easy task, as many of the women were wives or girlfriends of the soldiers. These women kept trying to break through the police lines to join their men.

When Atkinson arrived with his eleven men, everything appeared in hand. But he was still worried. The roadblock fight suggested there might still be Italian troops willing to counterattack, and what if all these hundreds in town decided to renege on their surrender? Everywhere he looked were neat stacks of rifles and machine guns. Lance Sergeant Harold Ghent had the solution. Revving up a Bren carrier, he crushed the weapons under its tracks, eliciting frenzied cheers from the citizenry and more than a few from the soldiers. "We had great difficulty rationalizing this strange situation with our known concepts of warfare," Atkinson and Ghent later related.

Things only got more surreal. At noon, the Canadians were invited to join the Caribiniere at their barracks. After watching carefully to ensure their hosts ate first from the communal serving pot, they tucked into pasta laced with goat's cheese and washed down with ice-cold lemonade. Lunch finished, Atkinson was approached by a senior ranking Italian army officer. He identified himself as Generale di Brigata Achille d'Havet and, presumably having abandoned his earlier demand for someone of equal rank, offered to surrender to any Canadian with a rank of major or above. Noting that the general was wearing the British Military Cross, which he had received during the Great War from none other than the Duke of Connaught, Atkinson allowed d'Havet the courtesy of retaining his pistol. He then had the man locked up in the Carabiniere's jail. Lacking a wireless set, Atkinson had no way of rustling up a senior officer on demand. The surrender would just have to wait.

Several hours later, a troop of Shermans from the Three Rivers Regiment rolled into town. Using the troop commander's wireless, Atkinson notified 2 CIB headquarters that a general in Modica wished to surrender.[4] Eventually, a Jeep arrived with 2 CIB's Brigade Major Richard S. "Dick" Malone and his driver aboard. After concluding a stint as staff secretary to the minister of national defence, Malone's army career had blossomed. He had returned to Canada to attend the Canadian War Staff College, been posted back to England, where he served briefly in the Queen's Own Rifles before being assigned as a staff captain in the 5th Canadian Armoured Division, and then had been promoted to brigade major in the fall of 1942. A soldier whose experience was confined to staff appointments, Malone was nonplussed to find himself virtually alone in the midst of hundreds of

Italian troops, most of whom had either a "small bundle or shabby suitcase of personal belongings" at their feet. He was approached by an Italian naval aide, who spoke English and who took him to the Italian headquarters to meet the general—the latter having been released from jail for the surrender. For awhile Malone was left idling in a waiting room, growing more anxious by the minute as he imagined the general and his staff burning and destroying vital intelligence papers. Finally, he burst into the office waving his pistol and shouting in broken Italian that he demanded an unconditional surrender. This was duly offered. Leaving his driver armed with a Bren gun to ensure no papers were destroyed, Malone, the general, and several Italian officers crowded into a Fiat staff car and drove off to find Simonds, because d'Havet was once again insisting he would turn over his pistol to none other than an equal. Before the car departed, Malone took the precaution of removing the general's pennant from the flag staff mounted atop the radiator and replacing it with his rather soiled white handkerchief.

On the town's outskirts, Malone met Lieutenant Colonel Leslie Booth, who was leading more of his Three Rivers Regiment Shermans towards Modica. Malone had neglected to even notice Atkinson, his small party, or the tank troop, so he told the tanker the only Canadian in the town was his driver, and that reinforcement would be appreciated. Booth promised to get there immediately. Next, to his astonishment, Malone encountered a car carrying Lieutenant General Oliver Leese. The xxx Corps commander had no interest in wasting time taking d'Havet's surrender. He told Malone to get Simonds to do this and also tell him to get his men cracking past Modica. This dithering around the town was taking far too long.[5]

Near divisional headquarters, the Italian staff car was spotted by a motley crew of war correspondents crammed so tightly into a Jeep that two army cameramen were sitting on the hood. There were five men aboard, all burdened by the gear correspondents carried—still and movie cameras, cartons of film, portable typewriters, their personal kit. The men were Canadian Press war correspondent Ross Munro, Canadian Broadcasting Corporation reporter Peter Stursberg (who had neither a microphone nor any sound recording equipment and so was reduced to filing paper copy), two army photographers, and Captain Dave Maclellan, whose job was to keep them all out of mischief. Like the good ambulance chasers they were by instinct, the correspondents set off in hot pursuit of the staff car.

Malone found divisional headquarters in an olive grove. Simonds, donning his beret as he walked, came towards the car. Stursberg thought the two generals a study in contrasts—the Italian old and portly, the Canadian lean and vigorous. His pistol still holstered at his side, d'Havet insisted he should not have to relinquish it because his coastal division had consisted of only nine battalions and had been facing an entire Allied army. Deciding not to argue military protocol, Simonds just ensured the gun had no ammunition. Stursberg suspected the Canadian general probably rued losing what would have been a wonderful souvenir.[6]

Less interested in the surrender proceedings than in the Italian staff car, Malone was trying to slip away in it before anyone noticed. Simonds, however, caught up and, after returning Malone's salute, circled the car in a slow inspection. "Finally, he paused in front of the hood. Then, without a trace of a smile, he slowly unscrewed the little silver flag staff from the radiator cap.

"'I think I can use this,' he said. That was all. The car was mine, and I lost no time sorting out the gears and driving off to dangle my prize before old Chris [Vokes]." Malone still had d'Havet's general's pennant wadded in his pocket and he kept it as a personal memento.[7]

Having seen the surrender through, the war correspondents headed north. Their hope was to catch up with the rapidly advancing brigades on divisional point. They rolled up the highway that Atkinson and his lost RCR troops had taken, driving past where the Seaforth truck had been ambushed. The body of the driver still lay beside it, but was now covered by a white tarpaulin upon which some civilian had rested a bouquet of flowers. Long lines of Italian troops marching towards the beaches clogged the road and impeded their progress. Many, seeing the correspondents and their cameras, waved and made Churchill's famous V-for-victory sign in hopes of being immortalized on film. By the time the correspondents passed through Modica it was late in the day, and the infantry brigades were long gone.[8]

WHILE RCR LIEUTENANT Sherry Atkinson and his group were carrying out their exploits around Modica, the rest of the battalion had spent the early morning of July 12 capturing Ragusa. This they achieved by the simple expedient of having a battery of the Royal Devon Yeomanry fire a salvo into the town—which, like Modica, was tucked into a valley rather than perched on a hilltop. Lieutenant Colonel Ralph Crowe then sent Captain Dick Dillon and his carrier section from the Support Company, under the protection of a white flag, to accept the Italian garrison's expected surrender. Dillon returned to report that the town had already been occupied by a company from the 45th U.S. (Thunderbird) Division and he had decided against sticking around to see how they felt about being shelled.[9]

The American presence in Ragusa meant there was no further need to have the Canadians advancing westward, for Seventh Army was already there. So Simonds swung both the 1st and 2nd brigades northward towards Giarratana. This was a classic Sicilian hilltop village about fifteen miles away by road. With the 45th Division so close on the left and the 51st Highland Division coming up on the right towards Palazzolo—a village just three miles east of Giarratana—the Canadians were being squeezed out by these faster advancing divisions. The Americans were highly motorized—so much so that the RCR groused that it seemed they all whizzed about, with their distinctive shoulder patches featuring a yellow eagle over a red square, in Jeeps each mounted with a small-calibre gun, "while ninety percent of our moves take place on shank's mare."[10] The British on the left were less of an irritant, but they still had landed in Sicily with all their transport and so were not reduced to marching everywhere.[11]

Reliant on boot power, the division's advance became increasingly ragged during the morning, and by afternoon a pause was needed to bring the two leading brigades into alignment. There were also several villages along their route that had to be swept for enemy troops. The Loyal Edmonton Regiment took responsibility for ensuring that Modica was completely secured. Lieutenant Colonel Jim Jefferson also sent 'B' Company with a troop of tanks to Scicli, midway between Modica and the coast. Applying the now standard ploy, the tanks fired three shots into Scicli and the infantry advanced to accept the predictable surrender—this time bagging 1,100 troops. Fortunately, the Italians had their own transport and so were loaded into trucks and driven back to a prisoner-of-war cage that had been erected in Ispica. The rest of the battalion, meanwhile, travelled aboard tanks and various Canadian and captured light transport to Ragusa, which lay within Eighth Army's assigned zone of responsibility. Finding the Americans still ensconced here, the Edmontons established a defensive position on the northern outskirts. The PPCLI arrived soon after and set up on some high ground east of the town.

Both the PPCLI and the Edmontons had enjoyed the advantage of advancing on the relatively good road running through Modica and on to Ragusa without being seriously challenged. Not so the Seaforth Highlanders. Advancing east of Modica, with Captain Syd Thomson's 'A' Company leading, the battalion had come upon a truck parked crossways in the road. Drawing his revolver, Thomson started walking with a couple of men towards the vehicle. With his first step the captain realized "the revolver marked me as an officer. Several shots were fired from the side of the road and I got one on the inside fleshy part of my right thigh which just missed providing me with the voice of a tenor. Fortunately the bullet went clear through. We were wearing shorts with two very small belt buckles, difficult enough at the best of times, but quite impossible for my shaking fingers. I could not drop my shorts for an examination. However, by putting a hand up one leg I was reasonably satisfied that I was not to become a eunuch." While the battalion pressed on, Thomson was put in the manger of a large barn after having his wound dressed by the medical officer, Captain W.K. "Ken" MacDonald. Doped up on morphine, he fell asleep only to be suddenly awakened by sounds. Approaching were two Sicilian farmers carrying pitchforks. Fearing they planned on running him through, Thomson raised his covering blanket so they could see the revolver in his hand. The two men backed off carefully and then proceeded to fork hay into a manger containing two oxen. Later, two Seaforth stretcher-bearers arrived, bundled the captain into a donkey cart, and evacuated him to hospital.[12]

While Thomson had been lying in the manger, the Seaforth rifle companies had veered off the road onto a mule track. They were strung out in one long snaking file through "a continuous cloud of fine white dust which when mixed with the perspiration of the body made a white layer of dust over each man. It seemed to work into every nook and cranny, into our boots and up to the hair on our heads," the war diarist recorded.[13] Shortly before midnight, the Seaforths entered Ragusa en route to their assigned concentration point two miles northwest of the town. In the past twenty-four hours they had covered about thirty miles on foot.[14]

Padre Roy Durnford had been on the march with the troops as they descended into Ragusa. "We came upon it in the moonlight, the pale green light of the moon gave the city a ghostly appearance. Not a sound was about as we entered, marching at well-spaced intervals in single file. The streets were empty and the houses were all shuttered. Churches looked vast as they towered above us in black silhouettes against the sky. The business part of this strange city was impressive... Through the winding streets of Ragusa we went till we came to a gorge separating the business section of the city from the unbelievably fascinating part of the 'residential' area. On the steep slopes of the gorges abounding in all directions houses huddled precariously. Some were cave dwellings cut into the sheer sides of sandstone walls. In odd designs and weird flourishes these houses in their hundreds resembled nothing quite so much as a dream—a dream of a lost city, of ancient days and strange people. One could almost feel for certain that through the latticed shutters in a hundred windows, the eyes of unfriendly, not to say menacing, people were staring down at us as we descended into first this gorge and then that."

After the Seaforths passed through the town and ascended out of the valley, Durnford looked back and realized Ragusa "was quite hidden from the plains above it...The empty streets, the shuttered windows and the silence broken by the hollow sound of marching feet had made us all feel that we had intruded upon forbidden places." Reaching their destination in the late evening of July 12, the Seaforths fell out in an orange grove and happily dug into rations before collapsing into sleep.[15]

MIDNIGHT ON THE night of July 12–13 had brought no such release from the march for I CIB's battalions. The Hastings and Prince Edward Regiment and 48th Highlanders had made a gruelling effort that day to catch up with the RCR near Ragusa. The 48th's 'A' Company had led the way, and one of its soldiers later scribbled down some fragmented memories. "It was soon terrifically hot. We marched and marched. It grew terrifically dusty. It was dust, dust, dust. We marched. I was thirsty, thirsty, thirsty—and there was no water. We marched and marched. Our tin hats would fry eggs. We marched. Men collapsed from heat exhaustion. We marched, counting one, two, three, four. Some were crying (literally) from blistered feet. We marched. Some had dysentery. We marched, one, two, three, four. We stopped for one hour for lunch. There was no lunch but a biscuit. We marched. There were terrible sun blisters. We marched. About 1400 hours we fell out. We were to rest. We did, but we marched in the heat in our sleep."[16]

During the lunch and short break at 1400 hours, many of the men who had earlier fallen out of line due to sunstroke were able to catch up. In the late afternoon, the 48th Highlanders formed ranks again and punched out another two and a half miles to come alongside the RCR.[17] The Hasty Ps, too, had men felled by the "terrific heat." But most of these managed to catch up when the battalion reached the brigade rendezvous point. There both battalions collapsed.[18] Men "lay in the ditches, stupefied, and simply waiting. In two and a half days they had fought a battle and then marched almost fifty miles. It was not credible that they could do more," wrote the Hasty Ps' regimental historian.[19]

What was credible and what was demanded by generals were two different things. As soon as darkness fell, weary officers and sergeants moved among their men, ordering them to their feet. As 1 CIB was now well in the division's van it fell to it to actualize Leese's instruction that the Canadians get cracking. Taking point from the RCR, the Hasty Ps mounted three companies on tanks and every other available piece of wheeled transport, which included artillery tractors, Jeeps, motorcycles, and only a handful of trucks. These companies set off on what they considered "heavenly chariots," while luckless 'C' Company resorted to footslogging.[20] They headed into country that became "increasingly rugged as the sprawling ridges of the Iblei Hills climb towards their junction with the Erei Mountains."[21] They were bound for Giarratana, and it was expected that the enemy—finally, Germans—would try to get there beforehand.[22] It was a race, for perhaps the Hasty Ps could get to the village first and there would be no need to wrest it from a determined enemy's hands. With the Hasty Ps at the head, followed by the 48th Highlanders and then the RCR, 1st Brigade staggered forward. At 2130 hours, the companies aboard vehicles entered Giarratana without having encountered any opposition. The Canadians had won the race. As the crow flies, 1 CIB was roughly thirty miles inland from the beach, but it had been more than fifty miles over rough roads. The advance had now stretched the division's supply lines to the maximum for the small number of available vehicles. The troops—having covered most of this ground on foot and not yet being acclimatized to Sicily's subtropical heat—were clearly exhausted.

In the early morning of July 13, General Montgomery ordered a halt on his extreme left flank and said the Canadians should advance no farther than Giarratana for thirty-six hours. This would allow the division to regain its strength and reorganize for the next leg of the advance. Behind the leading brigades, the situation was becoming increasingly chaotic. The beach was a mess of supply dumps vulnerable to sporadic but destructive Luftwaffe air raids. Inland, the artillery regiments were struggling on inadequate roads to catch up to the infantry and being occasionally strafed by German aircraft.

The 92nd Battery from 3rd Canadian Field Regiment, which had equipped itself with a captured horse-drawn artillery battery, was attacked by nine German fighter planes in quick succession on the late morning of July 12. Lacking maps, the battery had only shortly before wandered astray after leaving the area of Ispica. It was just passing a DUKW carrying a number of officers and men from the divisional artillery headquarters when the enemy fighters struck. The German fighters tore into the DUKW with machine-gun fire that wounded Brigade Major R.S. Dyer and five gunners. Dyer's badly mangled leg had to be amputated.[23]

Only three 92nd men were wounded in the wild seconds of the strafing run, despite there not having "been the slightest warning of the attack and none had even had time to get off the road. But the greatest damage was to the horses and guns. Sixteen of the twenty-four animals were killed or wounded and had to be destroyed and the guns and wagons were so badly damaged that they were useless. And that was the sudden end of the history of the 92nd Battery (Horsed)," the 3rd Field Regiment's official historian lamented. Turning the rest of the horses loose and abandoning the guns in a field by the road, the disheartened gunners trudged to Modica, where in the late afternoon their spirits rose as they took the surrender of about two hundred Italian troops on the town's outskirts. By the end of the day, the 92nd Battery had linked up with the rest of the field regiment. Its gun lines now established four miles east of Ragusa, the regiment had yet to fire a shot during the invasion.[24]

THE LUFTWAFFE AIR attack that surprised the artillerymen was one of many on July 12. Despite the massive weight of anti-aircraft guns positioned on the beaches and aboard the ships standing offshore, a number of German fighters risked destruction to carry out strafing and bombing runs. While these caused little damage on the British or Canadian beaches, they were still unnerving for the naval personnel. Coxswain Norm Bowen was aboard one of the Landing Craft, Mechanized vessels of the Canadian 80th and 81st flotillas working off the British beaches near Siracusa. He had just pulled up alongside the hospital ship *Talamba* with a full load of wounded Tommies when several German Stukas screamed out of the sun to attack a monitor and cruiser standing close by. "The stuff was coming down," he recalled, "and water was coming in [to the boat from damage to its bottom] and we started slinging the wounded aboard." Bowen was up in his chair behind the wheel so was level with the lowest deck of the hospital ship. Suddenly he heard this very cultured voice ask, "Would you like a cup of tea?" He turned to face an older, impeccably dressed nursing sister. Thinking he would like something a lot stronger than tea, Bowen replied, "Yes, Sister." When she returned with the tea, Bowen hurriedly said, "Just the cup, not the saucer." His hands were shaking so badly cup and saucer would just go flying. Gripping the cup in both hands, he drank its contents in one long chug. "It's not much fun, is it?" the woman asked. "No, Sister, it's not." The nursing sister reached out and touched his cheek gently. "God bless you," she said and was gone.

Bowen's LCM made for shore. At night, or when the LCMs were not needed for immediate runs, the Canadian sailors crowded into a cave just off the sand. There were about eighty naval personnel living in this dark, filthy warren. Craving a shower, Bowen had managed to hitch a ride out to the merchant ship on which a navy gunner he knew was posted. The gunner handed him a towel and soap and "was that shower ever good." Bowen had just dressed and was coming out on deck when a German bomb slammed into the side of the ship and blew him over backwards. "They don't go boom, they go bam," he said when some men picked him up. Bowen had not a scratch, but blood was coming out of his nose and ears. Getting dropped back on the beach, he staggered into the cave. His commander saw that Bowen was stumbling about strangely. "What the hell's the matter with you?" he demanded. "I dunno, don't know," the coxswain replied. "The bomb landed. I'm queer." He was told to get his head down for a bit. Bowen's headache was fierce and unabating.

Sometime later he learned the hospital ship had been sunk with some loss of life. Bowen wondered about the nurse and hoped she was safe. His headaches were a constant torment. A couple of days later, bodies from the hospital ship drifted ashore. Bowen stood on the beach watching an LCA towing in the corpse of a nursing sister. An officer yelled to him, "Bowen, bring your knife." He walked reluctantly to the surf line. The body was badly swollen and distorted. The skin was so swollen around either a watch or identity bracelet that nobody could tell which it was. "Norm," the officer said, "you cut down and see if we can get an ID."

"Sure," Bowen answered. Then he bent down and saw the woman's grey hair and knew it was the nursing sister who had wished God to bless him. "I just had to go away by myself," he later recalled. A few days afterward, Bowen saw a medical officer about his still terrific headaches. The doctor looked him over. "Boy, you had one hell of a concussion. I can't do anything about it now, it's too late." The doctor grinned. "Tell you what, don't get involved in very loud noises."

"Jesus," Bowen shot back, "tell that to the Germans."[25]

MONTGOMERY'S THIRTY-SIX-HOUR STAND-DOWN order for the Canadians not only allowed the exhausted infantry brigades time to reorganize and rest, but also enabled the supply chain to catch up. While 1 CIB spent the time concentrated around Giarratana, 2 CIB was situated between Modica and Ragusa. The reserve brigade, 3 CIB, took up positions south of Giarratana, with the Three Rivers Tank Regiment laagering in the same area. On July 13, Major General Simonds established divisional headquarters eight miles north of Modica.

Behind this leading edge of the Canadian division, the Royal Canadian Army Service Corps worked round the clock to get supplies in order for the advance into the heart of Sicily. "The vehicles are never empty," the RCASC war diarist wrote on July 13. "Rations and supplies are brought forward and prisoners and salvage sent back. Transport is on the move 24 hours a day . . . It had been impossible to give the vehicles any maintenance at all, and the personnel have been able recently to snatch only the barest of rest. Their health seems not to have suffered in any way. In all their dirt and grime, they seem very happy and willing to work themselves to the limit. The run from this point back to the beach is approximately 40 kilometres over the worst possible dirt roads and tracks. It speaks very highly for the driving personnel that they have been able to keep their vehicles on the road continuously without accident and practically without the slightest breakdown. Any breakdowns have been immediately attended by vehicles of the workshops sections which have been stationed at strategic points along the route with instructions to help all and sundry."

A shuttle service established refuelling points along the route and supply transfer stations so one convoy could hand off supplies to another working closer to the front and then go back for another load. By the morning of July 14, the division had gone from always being short of everything to having a reserve consisting of 8,400 rations, 3,840 gallons of fuel, and "a good stock" of ammunition. The same day, eighty-nine RCASC trucks were unloaded from ships offshore. Although forty-three of these were given to the infantry brigades to relieve their transport shortage, the rest were used to bolster the supply movement system. Slowly the division was getting back its mechanized mobility, but the infantry would still be largely dependent on "shank's mare."[26]

ON THE MORNING of July 14, General Montgomery toured the division and spoke to the men. Because each brigade had scattered its battalions around either Giarratana or Ragusa, Montgomery could not carry out a single collective inspection. Brigadier Howard Graham met Montgomery at a pre-arranged map reference from which he intended to guide the Eighth Army commander to his respective battalions. It was a typical hot, dusty July day in Sicily. Montgomery arrived in a camouflaged touring car with its top cut off. When Graham said he would lead the way in his Jeep, Montgomery smiled and said he should instead just show on the map where they were to go. "The foxy old fellow wasn't going to eat the Brigadier's dust," Graham thought. Off they went, Montgomery's car throwing up billows of grit, Graham and his driver choking on it as they raced to keep up.[27]

The battalions had been given little warning of the inspection. It was already 0822 hours when Captain Galloway received orders to report with the other company commanders to RCR headquarters. Montgomery, Lieutenant Colonel Crowe told them, would inspect their men at 1100 hours. In a quick diary notation, Galloway seethed: "Even the order of dress is laid on. One would think we were still soldiering in Sussex! It will take about an hour to get down there, if not longer, and all of two hours to get back. Have just sent the order out to the platoons, one man per section is to be left in position, the rest have to shave, readjust their equipment and move off, so that we won't be late. The heat is going to be bloody. It is now, although not yet 9 o'clock."[28]

Monty's inspections were tightly scripted to boost troop morale. An essential component was not to keep the men waiting hours for his arrival. They were also only required to wear shorts, shirts, steel helmets, and web belts, so the individual preparation was relatively simple. Nobody had to polish boots; the dust would have rendered the effort pointless after the first step. In most cases the men barely reached their parade area before the open car arrived. They formed in open square and gave Montgomery the general salute. "After taking the salute, he just yelled to the men to group around his car," Lieutenant Jack Francis Wallace of the Three Rivers Tank Regiment wrote. "You never saw such a sudden rise of dust as the men sprinted to his car. He spoke to us very informally asking the men as to what part of Canada we came from." The tankers had been gathered together with the Loyal Edmonton Regiment, and Monty reflected that when the Eddies served under him in England, they had been barracked for awhile in an old brewery. Would they like some beer now? "There was one big yes. Monty said, 'In due time.'"[29]

At each inspection Montgomery had the men gather about the car. Brigadier Graham was struck by how deftly the general worked the crowd. His "relationship with the troops" made it "easy to see why he is a great commander."

"Sit down, boys, and take off your helmets. I want to see your good Canadian faces again…I hope you are enjoying it here. They tell me it looks just like Canada." The men guffawed. "I hope the Brigadier is getting the beer up to you every day." More roars of laughter. Montgomery smiled broadly, seeming to enjoy his jokes as much as the troops.

Then his voice softened; his expression turned serious. He was glad to have the Canadians in Eighth Army. They had done "a splendid job" so far and he was sure they would continue doing so. But he wanted to warn them "that we are going to be faced with difficult country and soon you will be running up against the Germans. So far you have met only the Italians, and they don't want to fight; but the Germans are tough, very tough opponents. But I am confident that you can master them. I will make good plans. I wouldn't be here today if I didn't make good plans. But good plans need good soldiers to carry them out. I have confidence in you. You have confidence in me, and all will be well."[30]

As he was making these speeches, Montgomery was also taking the measure of the Canadians. "They are a grand Division," he confided to his diary, "and when we get them tough and hard and some of the fat off them, they will be absolutely first class."[31]

When Montgomery spoke to the Seaforth Highlanders, Private Richard Latimer considered his remarks "the usual bag of clichés…

yet somehow that wiry, ordinary looking little guy in his baggy pants...and the famous black beret with the two cap badges [General's and Armoured Corps] exuded confidence and it could not help rubbing off on us." On the march back to their rest area, Latimer confided this thought to Private Jim Carney. Normally, he would have kept such sentiments to himself because "even the faintest praise of the army and its officers was just not done." But Carney was someone he could discuss emotions with. "I had that feeling too," Carney replied. Same old hash, but "I was amazed to find that I got a little lift out of it. Of course, I've also heard that Monty simply will not rush into anything until he's completely ready and I think that's bound to help you feel you have a chance at least."[32]

Galloway was less impressed and made the mistake of loosing his thoughts on the rest of the RCR officers later that afternoon. He told them it was "rather ridiculous, making the men march and counter-march throughout the heat of the day and relegating the tactical situation to second place in order to create an audience for Monty's speechmaking...[It was] hard enough to make the men realize the seriousness of the situation when there was apparently no enemy around, without causing them to lose the proper perspective by listening to a general talk nonsense for fifteen minutes." Galloway's comments earned him "a sharp ticking off" from Lieutenant Colonel Crowe.

But the captain was unrepentant, for Crowe immediately turned to discussing a march that was to begin before the day was out. Instead of spending the first part of the day resting and preparing their battle kit, the men had been forced to trudge cross-country to hear a general talk. Actions, Galloway thought, not words, would win the day.[33]

10

Wranglings

G ENERAL BERNARD MONTGOMERY had warned the Canadians
they would henceforth be fighting only Germans, for by July 14,
the Italian forces in Sicily had effectively been eliminated. The 206th
Coastal Division had disintegrated, its general surrendering to the
Canadians on July 13 at Modica. As for 54th Napoli Division, Generale
di Divisione Count Giulio Cesare Gotti-Porcinari had spent July 12
trying to pull his shattered command together. The division's artillery regiments had largely been overrun or had deserted. One
infantry regiment ended the day encircled by the British near Siracusa and the entire divisional line was riddled with gaps and holes. A
British patrol slipping through one hole the morning of July 13 surprised Gotti-Porcinari and his entire divisional headquarters, taking
virtually everyone prisoner. Napoli Division ceased to exist, the surviving remnants being attached to the Hermann Göring Division.
The 4th Livorno Division had been similarly shredded by the Americans. The sailors and troops defending Fortress Augusta, commanded
by Admiral Ugo Leonardi, had mostly deserted their posts—leaving
the naval officer to surrender the city on the morning of July 12 to a
British naval party. Even the Italian high command was left in disarray after a July 13 air raid on Sixth Army headquarters in Enna almost
killed Generale d'Armata Alfredo Guzzoni, shattered the building,

destroyed most of its signal equipment, and forced a move to somewhere safer.[1]

Hermann Göring Division's commander, Generalmajor Paul Conrath, had been disgusted to see that many Italian units, "either led by their officers or on their own, marched off without firing a single shot. Valuable equipment fell into the hands of the enemy in undamaged condition. The good intentions of some commanders and the good appearance of some officers and non-commissioned officers must not lead one to overlook the fact that 90% of the Italian Army are cowards and do not want to fight...Future actions to be planned as if there were no Italians at all in the area...Italians must see as little as possible of our own positions, intentions, strength and formation."[2]

"In consequence of the defection of the Italian defence forces in the southeastern part of the island," concluded one German summary, "operations against the mounting British-American attacking forces [falls] almost entirely to the German formations. The important thing now was to prevent the enemy from thrusting forward to Catania from the Syracuse or the Gela areas, and then with united forces pushing through to the Straits of Messina. At the same time, the strong enemy force that was advancing from Licata toward the north must be prevented from breaking through in the direction of Palermo, thereby making it impossible to bring up those troops still in the western part of the island, and the evacuation of important supplies."[3]

While the Italians crumbled, the Germans reinforced their two divisions. First to arrive on July 12 were II Battalion, 382nd Panzer Grenadier Regiment and the Panzer Grenadier Battalion Reggio. These two regiments had been waiting in reserve in southern Italy. The former was attached to Hermann Göring Division and the latter to Battle Group Schmalz, the element of 15th Panzer Division facing the British Eighth Army. More important, however, was the arrival of 1st Parachute Division's 3rd Parachute Regiment. The 1,817 paratroops jumped from more than one hundred HE-111 transports at 1900 hours onto the Catania plain to join Battle Group Schmalz. The following day, 1st Parachute Division airlifted 1st Parachute Machine Gun Battalion, 1st Parachute Engineer Battalion, 4th Parachute Regiment, and part of 1st Parachute Artillery Regiment to Sicily. All came under Colonel Wilhelm Schmalz's command.[4]

Generalfeldmarschall Albert Kesselring and General der Panzertruppen Fridolin von Senger und Etterlin had been on the ground with Schmalz to see 3rd Parachute Regiment's jump. Kesselring had flown into Enna earlier that day. By the evening, the Commander-in-Chief South had concluded that coming to Sicily had "yielded nothing but a headache. I had seen for myself the total breakdown of the Italian divisions and the tactical chaos resulting from their disregard for the agreed defence plan."[5] Ever optimistic, however, Kesselring believed the situation could be saved if the entire 29th Panzer Grenadier Division was immediately ferried across the Straits of Messina and 1st Parachute Regiment also committed. Even Hitler's immediate prevarication that forestalled 29th Division being sent to Sicily in whole did little to whittle down Kesselring's confidence, although having informed Mussolini this division was on the way caused considerable personal embarrassment when it was held back. Kesselring's spirits were further buoyed when Hitler approved giving overall command for German troops in Sicily to xiv Panzer Corps General der Panzertruppen Hans Valentin Hube.

Nicknamed *"Der Mensch"* ("the Man"), the fifty-two-year-old Hube had been soldiering since his eighteenth birthday. A wound at the Battle of Verdun had cost him his right arm. At the head of 16th Panzer Division, Hube had carved out a reputation as a brilliant tactician during the German drive across Russia in 1941, which garnered him the Knight's Cross and Oak Leaves to the Knight's Cross. Given command of xiv Panzer Corps, Hube was caught in the Soviet encirclement of Generalfeldmarschall Friedrich Paulus's Sixth Army at Stalingrad. On January 16, 1943, Hube—who had said he would stay and die with his men—was forced at gunpoint by Waffen ss, under Hitler's orders, to fly out of the rapidly shrinking cauldron. Hube was given the job of rebuilding xiv Panzer Corps, which was transferred in mid-June to Italy. His chief of staff, Oberst Bogislaw von Bonin, considered Hube "a brave soldier, calm, well-balanced, equal to any situation, never in doubt and always ready to take over responsibility."[6]

Disinclined to accept Kesselring's assertion that part of Sicily could be held indefinitely, Hube still did not consider the situation hopeless. For once, Hitler's direct orders had been clear and concise. Issued on July 13, they simply read: "After the bulk of the Italian forces are eliminated the Germans alone will be insufficient to push the enemy into the sea. It will therefore be the objective of the Germans to delay the enemy advance, and bring it to a halt west of Mount Etna." The final defensive line was to run southward from Santo Stéfano di Camastra on the northern coast to Adrano, immediately southwest of Mount Etna, and then cut across the southern flank of the volcano to Catania. In the meantime, Hube would establish a series of *Hauptkampflinie* (main defensive lines) and force the Allies to fight through each in turn at heavy costs in men and matériel.

Augmenting Hitler's orders came typically precise and cynical instructions from Oberkommando der Wehrmacht (Armed Forces High Command) operations chief Generaloberst Alfred Jodl. While maintaining the pretence that Guzzoni retained command of Axis troops in Sicily, Hube was to "take over the overall leadership in the bridgehead of Sicily itself, while unobtrusively excluding the Italian headquarters. The remaining Italian formations are to be divided up and placed under the command of the various German headquarters." Jodl added that Hube was to "fight a delaying action and gain further time for stabilizing the situation on the mainland." Henceforth, the campaign in Sicily was intended to pin down the Allies on the island for as long as possible, while ensuring that German forces survived to fight again on mainland Italy.[7]

Denying Catania to Eighth Army was a vital component of the new German strategy. This had less to do with the city's port facilities than with Sicily's geography and limited transportation network. About seven miles south of Catania, the muddy Simeto River descended from Mount Etna to cut a sluggish, winding course across the Catania plain before spreading out into a broad marshy estuary on the coast. A single bridge—Ponte Primosole—spanned the Simeto a mile and a half west of the marsh and provided Highway 114's link between Lentini to the south and Catania. Ponte Primosole was no wonder of engineering. It was a 400-foot-long structure of steel girders standing eight feet above the river. The land north of the bridge was thickly forested by olive and almond groves, which provided excellent cover for defending troops. To the south, the ground was flat and devoid of vegetation.

Both the Germans and British recognized possession of the bridge was vital. On the morning of July 13, 1st Parachute Machine Gun Battalion had landed at Catania airfield. Although British fighters managed to intercept and shoot down several aircraft bearing most of the battalion's anti-tank guns, the paratroops were soon dug in about two thousand yards south of the bridge on the edge of an orange grove, which provided a rare spot of cover this side of the river. The battalion's commander, Major Werner Schmidt, had been warned by 3rd Parachute Regiment's Oberstleutnant Ludwig Heilmann to expect the British to attack the bridge either by air or by sea landing. Schmidt was to hold the bridge at all costs.[8]

HEILMANN HAD DIVINED British intention perfectly. For that very night, Montgomery had ordered an air assault on the bridge by 1st Parachute Brigade, with gliders scheduled to land two troops of light artillery three hours later. No. 3 Commando would simultaneously land from the sea three miles north of Lentini and seize a small bridge at Malati. The commandos and paratroops were to hold their bridges until XIII Corps advanced from Sortino. As the crow flies, it was about fifteen miles from Sortino to Primosole Bridge, but the winding roads doubled the distance. Montgomery realized the paratroops could only be expected to hold the bridge for a short time, so the division was ordered to reach them within twenty-four hours. By the evening of July 14, Montgomery wanted the paratroops relieved and a bridgehead established north of the bridge.[9]

It was an audacious plan rendered even more so by Montgomery's decision to split his army into two forces advancing *away* from each other. Encouraged by the rapidity of the invasion's initial gains, Montgomery thought that if he acted decisively, the entire island could be won in a matter of days. There was time neither for hesitation nor for appropriate consultation with superiors. Consequently, at 2200 hours on July 12, Montgomery sent a terse signal to General

Harold Alexander suggesting a decisive change in the boundaries between Eighth Army and the U.S. Seventh Army. "My battle situation very good," the signal read. "Have captured Augusta and my line now runs through Sortino–Palazzolo–Ragusa–Scicli. Intend now to operate on two axes. 13 Corps on Catania and northwards. 30 Corps on Caltagirone–Enna–Leonforte. Suggest American division at Comiso [45th Division] might now move westwards to Niscemi and Gela. The maintenance and transport and road situation will not allow of two armies both carrying out extensive offensive operations. Suggest my army operate offensively northwards to cut the island in two and that the American Army hold defensively on line Catlanisetta–Canicatti–Licata facing West. The available maintenance to be allocated accordingly. Once my left Corps reaches area Leonforte–Enna the enemy opposing the Americans will never get away."[10]

In his diary the same evening, Montgomery complained that Alexander and his staff at 15th Army Group were no longer coordinating the invasion. The Americans were fighting one battle, he another. If this continued, "the enemy might well escape[;] given a real grip on the battle I felt convinced we could inflict a disaster on the enemy and capture all his troops in Sicily." Leaving Alexander no real time to respond to his signal, Montgomery ordered xxx Corps's 51st Highland Division and 23rd Armoured Brigade to immediately drive up the Vizzini–Enna highway and outflank the Germans facing the Americans. At the same time, he set into motion the airborne and seaborne operation against the bridges south of Catania. "I intended to make a great effort to reach Catania by nightfall on July 14; given some luck I felt it could be done; but I must have the luck."[11]

By the evening of July 13, the 51st Highland Division was pushing for Vizzini, but so too was the 157th Regiment of the U.S. 45th Division. Colonel Charles Ankcorn could only stand by helplessly as he watched British troops marching up Highway 124 ahead of his troops. The highway was clearly in the American operational zone. Ankcorn had no idea what was going on, but his road north had been pre-empted.[12]

Montgomery was again running ahead of things while sending signals to Alexander to clean up after him. "My troops are now advancing between Vizzini and Caltagirone and unless something is done there will be a scene of intense military confusion [on the road]." He suggested 45th Division be redirected to the Gela area and the entire American effort shifted westward forty miles along the coast to Agrigento.[13]

At 2116 hours, Alexander played catch-up with a signal to both army commanders. "Operations for the immediate future will be Eighth Army to advance on two axes, one to capture port of Catania and the group of airfields there and the other to secure the network of road communications within the area Leonforte–Enna. Seventh Army will conform by pivoting" to face west. The boundary between each army was Highway 124, "all inclusive to Eighth Army."[14]

"This will raise hell for us," American II Corps commander General Omar Bradley fumed when Seventh Army's General George Patton gave him the news. "I had counted heavily on that road." But Patton, strangely quiescent for the moment, told him the order stuck. The Americans were left with no alternative but to carry out a time-consuming withdrawal of 45th Division from II Corps's right flank to its far left.[15] Bradley also had to shift his 1st Infantry Division west from Highway 117 to prevent running into XXX Corps where this highway intersected its route through San Michele and Piazza Armerina.[16] Effectively, XXX Corps was cutting across the entire front of the American II Corps, forcing Bradley to halt his advance and assume a defensive posture—which meant all the Americans were doing was guarding Eighth Army's flank.

This was hardly a role either Patton or Bradley had envisioned their army playing. Bradley was seething. Seventh Army, he believed, was poised for a breakout from the Gela beachhead. "Our troops were in marvelously aggressive spirits, all having performed far beyond my wildest expectations. We had reached the main road north [Highway 124]. With our superior trucks and self-propelled artillery, we could move much faster than the British. The enemy front before us was soft from his withdrawals; he was concentrating in the main before XIII Corps at Catania, not us. We were in ideal position for a fast run to the north coast—before the enemy could organize his defensive perimeter—and an encircling right turn toward Messina."

Troops unloading a Landing Craft, Mechanized, on Bark West on the afternoon of
July 10. Frank Royal, IAC PA-141663

above · A Princess Patricia's Canadian Light Infantry platoon warily advances out of an orchard into open ground. Jack H. Smith, LAC-130214

top centre · Royal Canadian Regiment captain Strome Galloway was one of few Canadians in Sicily who had previous combat experience. Courtesy of Strome Galloway

top right · Brigadier Chris Vokes (front, right) in discussion with Major P.R. Bingham of the Royal Canadian Regiment. Note the soldier in the back of the truck is wearing a captured Italian pith helmet. Jack H. Smith, LAC PA-114510

bottom right · Having lost much of their transport at sea, the Canadians often commandeered peasant carts, mules, and donkeys to carry supplies forward. Here troops of the Princess Patricia's Canadian Light Infantry are advancing towards Modica on July 12. Frank Royal, LAC PA-163669

top left · Seaforth Highlanders medics treat a Sicilian girl whose insect bites have become infected. Terry F. Rowe, LAC PA-132780

bottom left · Royal Canadian Regiment commander Lieutenant Colonel Ralph Crowe (right) and Major Billy Pope died within four days of each other. Frank Royal, LAC PA-132777

above · On shank's mare. The Canadian infantry advanced across Sicily almost entirely on foot. Jack H. Smith, LAC PA-163671

above · German prisoners being escorted back from the front. Jack H. Smith, LAC PA-130254

top right · During a whirlwind tour on July 14, General Bernard Law Montgomery managed to personally address gatherings of 1st Canadian Infantry Division troops, such as this group on the sand of Bark West. Monty is standing on a DUKW (amphibious truck). Frank Royal, LAC PA-130249

bottom right · The rough, winding Sicilian roads, generally overlooked by higher ground that could hide German antitank guns or armour, greatly limited the effectiveness of the Shermans of the 1st Canadian Tank Brigade. Dwight E. Dolan, LAC PA-141304

Canadian Press reporter Ross Munro wrote the story that gave 1st Division its "Red Devils" nickname. Here he types a story near Leonforte. Frank Royal, LAC PA-136201

Bradley was certain the Americans could have pulled off the breakout and relieved the pressure on Montgomery so he could win Catania. But it was all fruitless speculation, for the British were now trudging up the route he would have barrelled along.[17]

Meanwhile, there was little luck to be found for Montgomery the night of July 13 as the paratroops and commandos went for their respective bridges south of Catania. The nearly four hundred men of No. 3 Commando landed at about 2130 hours and won a stiff fight for control of Malati Bridge against a company of Italian troops, only to be counterattacked by an Italian anti-tank battalion and company of motorcyclists. After fierce fighting, the commandos grudgingly broke off the action by splitting into small sections and escaping southward. At a cost of twenty-eight dead, sixty-six wounded, and fifty-nine missing, they prevented the Italians from destroying the bridge.

The jump by 1st Parachute Brigade played out as disastrously as most other airborne operations over Sicily. As they neared the coast, anti-aircraft gunners aboard the Allied ships savaged the planes with streams of fire. Twenty-six planes turned about because of damage suffered from the all-too-common friendly fire incidents or mechanical failures. Eleven were shot down and another three crashed for unexplained reasons. Most of the remaining 107 planes scattered to avoid the flak and dropped their paratroops up to twenty miles away from Primosole Bridge. Only twelve officers and 283 men out of 1,856 were dropped close enough to fight for and win the bridge. But not for long. Throughout the course of July 14 they met ever more determined resistance and at 1930 hours the men remaining were forced to abandon the bridge and withdraw to a height of ground south of it. Soon after, tanks from XIII Corps's 4th Armoured Brigade broke through to them. The Germans pulled back to positions just north of the bridge. With neither side possessing the bridge, all Montgomery could claim for the sacrifice of the paratroops was that the Germans had been prevented from blowing it up. But Eighth Army's route to Catania remained blocked, and the British now faced a costly battle of attrition to gain the city. The paratroop casualties at Primosole Bridge numbered 115 out of 292 men.[18]

Things had also gone badly on the xxx Corps axis, with the 51st Highland Division only managing to capture Vizzini late on July 14 after an assist of artillery fire by the American 45th Division. Clearly, Montgomery's bold left hook had also failed.[19] The Hermann Göring Division had disengaged from the Americans in time to get in front of xxx Corps, which now faced fighting its way forward against an enemy intent on blocking it at every turn.

The 51st Highland Division was so exhausted that Montgomery ordered it into reserve, with instructions to clear up outstanding Italian garrisons in the Scordia–Francofonte–Militello area; 1st Canadian Infantry Division would take over the advance.[20] Having finally caught up with Montgomery, Alexander decided that xxx Corps would "split the island in half." This would be accomplished by first seizing Enna, where almost all the major roads on the island intersected. From Enna, the corps would take Nicosia. That would leave the Axis forces controlling only the northern coastal road running from Messina to Palermo. If he could cut that highway at Santo Stéfano, roughly midway between the two cities, "the interruption of communications would be complete."[21]

In a subsequent July 14 signal to the chief of the imperial general staff, General Sir Alan Brooke, Alexander summarized his intentions. "Future operations envisage thrust towards Messina through Catania by xiii Corps. xxx Corps will drive to the north coast at San Stéfano, then turn east to join up with xiii Corps at Messina. When the island is split in two from north to south, American Seventh Army will be directed towards Palermo and Trapani. Meanwhile they will hold Caltanissetta–Canicatti."[22] The first step along this path required the Canadians to capture Grammichele and Caltagirone.

ON THE NIGHT of July 14–15, 1st Canadian Infantry Division advanced towards Vizzini, with 1st Canadian Infantry Brigade approaching the town in a long motorized column via a secondary road running out of Giarratana, where it had spent the thirty-six-hour rest period. To the west, 2nd Canadian Infantry Brigade was also moving along a secondary road leading to Highway 124. The Loyal Edmonton Regiment's 'C' Company, mounted aboard Shermans of the Three Rivers Tank Regiment's 'C' Squadron, acted as this column's advance guard. Passing through Ragusa, 'C' Company suffered the first Loyal Edmonton casualties of the war when it came under heavy machine-gun fire.[23]

Lieutenant Jack Wallace's tank troop was in the lead with a platoon of Edmontons aboard. Wallace was sitting up in the turret chatting with the platoon commander "when suddenly a burst of machine-gun fire whistled across in front of us. [Trooper] Ace Elliot my driver halted so as to give the infantry time to clear off. Everything was quiet for a minute and then in the pitch black a couple more bursts float across. I got out of the tank and asked where the firing was coming from and the men pointed out a house about two hundred yards up the hill. I gave [Trooper] Jim Trueman the orders as to where to fire and he let blast with the 75-millimetre gun. That put an end to the nuisance."[24]

The platoon commander told him that he had six men wounded and three dead—twenty-five-year-old Private Leslie Brimacombe, twenty-eight-year-old Private James Nelson Rasmussen, and thirty-seven-year-old Private Laurence Robinson.[25] Whether the machine gun was manned by diehard Italian soldiers or Fascist civilians was never determined, but the incident prompted Lieutenant General Oliver Leese to send an officer to Ragusa with instructions to "mark down 6 or 12 hostages who will be shot if this happens again." A plan was put into action whereby as the corps passed through each town, several residents were taken hostage until it became clear there would be no guerrilla activity.[26] In a letter to his wife, Leese wrote that night: "In one town they threw bombs and shot at our troops. I'm now going to take hostages, and I shall shoot them if we have any more nonsense." When the Ragusa shooting proved to be an isolated case, however, the hostage-taking policy was quietly abandoned and nobody was ever shot.[27]

The short firefight in Ragusa also led to orders for the Loyal Edmonton Regiment to leave 'D' Company behind to ensure the town was secure for other units passing through. This denied the battalion a quarter of its strength.[28]

As the Canadians moved towards Enna, Leese was far from happy about his orders. He wondered if the Americans, with their greater mobility provided by a large fleet of vehicles that were almost all equipped with four-wheel drive, perhaps should have been allowed the pursuit rather than his footslogging Canadians. Having only recently met Bradley, Leese had been impressed by the man's dash. He worried that Montgomery and Alexander underestimated the Americans. It was a problem born of the North Africa campaign, in which the Americans had fumbled badly at Kasserine Pass and elsewhere while learning the trade of war. But in Sicily, the Americans had so far performed credibly. Perhaps, he brooded, Montgomery was "a bit impatient and hasty with others," while Alexander "simply does not step in and control the issue at critical moments." Leese fretted that by "treating the Seventh Army as a poor relation Monty might well irk the Americans to moving in the opposite direction—westwards—and thus lose the chance of the Americans" guarding his flank.[29]

The Canadians were oblivious to the high-level controversies. All Major General Guy Simonds knew was that the main drive by XIII Corps had faltered on the Catania plain and his orders were to "press towards Enna as quickly as possible."[30] Of course, it was not as simple as that. At the head of I CIB, the RCR arrived at Vizzini at 0300 hours to find the 51st Highland Division still clearing the town. RCR commander Lieutenant Colonel Ralph Crowe pushed through once he had word that the British troops had moved to the northeast. Crowe set his battalion on the western outskirts and advised Brigadier Howard Graham that the way was clear for the next battalion to pass into the lead. Standing by his Jeep on the roadside, Graham and Lieutenant Colonel Bruce Sutcliffe of the Hastings and Prince Edward Regiment watched that battalion push into the town with orders to make for Grammichele ten miles west. It was about 0600 hours and Graham was feeling grimy and unshaven. He had been on the move throughout the night and, with his driver and radio signaller as company in the Jeep, planned to follow the self-propelled battery of Royal Devon Yeomanry supporting the advance.

Suddenly a Jeep pulled alongside with Major General Simonds aboard. It was the first time since the landings that the divisional commander had come to see Graham at the front. "Why hasn't your brigade moved forward before this?" Simonds snapped.

"They have moved forward. The RCR are in Vizzini and the Hastings are through or going through."

"What is all the delay? My orders were for you to move through Vizzini as soon as the 51st Division had cleared it." Simonds ground on with one accusation after another until Graham finally cut him off. "I assure you we haven't wasted any time, but I want to get forward now and we can continue this discussion at your 'O' Group [Orders Group] this evening." Although furious, Graham kept his tone level, the words crisp and to the point. "Drive on," he instructed his Jeep driver and was away. "That's terrible," the driver commented. "Jesus, he was mad," the signaller offered from the rear.

The brigade was grinding along the paved state Highway 124, which tended to parallel a narrow-gauge railway that also ran to Enna. 'B' Company of the Hasty Ps was mounted on Shermans from the Three Rivers' 'A' Squadron. Close behind was the battalion's 'A' Company with one platoon aboard Bren carriers and the rest on tanks. Behind this leading force, which could quickly dismount to join battle, followed 'D' and 'C' companies in a variety of trucks and commandeered Italian vehicles. By 0730, the Hasty Ps were two miles beyond Vizzini, moving through a long, narrow valley, and had yet to see any enemy.[31]

July 15 had developed into a typical Sicilian summer day— sizzling hot with not a cloud to be seen. Yet for men who had spent most of the past five days on this island marching endless miles, the novelty of riding to war made it almost pleasant. Major John Tweedsmuir, the Hasty Ps' second-in-command, thought it "a beautiful day and the Sicilians harvesting in the fields made it hard to believe that we were in enemy country headed for the enemy and [were] in fact the spearhead of the whole Eighth Army." Three carriers from a Three Rivers reconnaissance section, under command of Lieutenant Pete Ryckman, and a scout car with the tank regiment's second-in-command, Major C.B. van Straubenzee, slipped past them on the road shoulder and moved ahead of the column. Soon Tweedsmuir saw the carriers and scout car stopped under some trees at a road junction. Ryckman told him that his men had "seen a Hun running from the spot at high speed." Scattered under the trees were crates of Italian grenades and dozens of their box mines. The mines were deadly things—small wooden boxes packed with explosives that were detonated, depending on how they were primed, either by shutting or opening the lid. Normally, they were buried with the lid slightly ajar, so the weight of a vehicle or person would force it closed and cause the mine to explode. Because of their wood construction mine detectors were incapable of discovering them. Tweedsmuir figured the German had been booby trapping the mines, and the men were told to stay away from them.[32]

Before the column started moving again, a truck suddenly roared around a corner and almost collided with the lead tank. Out jumped two German privates with hands held high. Seemingly embarrassed, one of them confessed to misreading the map. The Hasty Ps standing around the two men sympathized. They were finding the maps inaccurate and confusing, while the countryside itself was such a patchwork of interconnecting valleys cutting through networks of rugged hills and ridges that keeping a sense of direction was increasingly difficult. In the distance there always seemed to be another dun-coloured hilltop town or village that looked much like the others, and each could as easily be the objective as not. The Canadians dumped the ammunition that the German truck had aboard, turned the truck around, and added it to the column's transport.[33]

Once they were moving again, Tweedsmuir noticed something on a hillside reflecting sunlight. Soon he made out the shape of a wrecked airplane bearing American markings. "The atmosphere grew more and more electric with every mile we went," everyone expecting something to happen. But it was hard not to wonder if they were in for nothing more than a pleasant drive in the country and the peaceful occupation of yet another town. They had been warned the Germans were ahead, but the Hasty Ps knew nothing of fighting them. They knew Italians, who either surrendered or ran away.

"Suddenly," Tweedsmuir later wrote, "the narrow valley gave way to a broad open plateau with the town of Grammichele perched like all Sicilian towns on a hill top. The road ran, a straight white ribbon, slightly raised above the cornfields to the foot of the hill three miles farther on, and we could see our carriers far ahead approaching the town."[34]

Grammichele had a population of about thirteen thousand. Rebuilt after being destroyed by an earthquake in 1693, the town had a curious spider-web layout that gave it a hexagonal shape with six roads radiating outward from its central plaza. It stood on a ridge about 250 feet above the valley floor, with its outskirts descending down the eastern slope. Nothing could approach unseen across the open plain. As the carriers and scout car disappeared into its outskirts with three tanks carrying part of 'B' Company following close behind, the rest of the column was still two miles back.[35] Tweedsmuir had lost sight of the carriers and tanks at about the time the main column came to a road crossing with a great crater blown in the middle of it. While the tanks might work around it, wheeled vehicles could not. Tweedsmuir had just got the men out of their trucks and busy filling in the hole when "the shooting started." Machine guns and small artillery pieces opened fire from some high ground left of the battalion's position. "We got under cover and shifted as many of the trucks as we could off the road. Mortars opened up, accurately ranged on the road, and those trucks that couldn't be shifted were soon burning, popping and banging as ammunition exploded."[36]

In the outskirts of Grammichele, the lead formation had driven into the middle of an ambush launched by the 4th Hermann Göring Flak Regiment and attached infantry. Several 20-millimetre *Flakvierling*— self-propelled four-barrelled guns (spgs) that could be used against either aircraft or tanks—slashed into sthe carriers and tanks. The scout car was hit, and Major van Straubenzee took a bullet in the shoulder. Aboard one of the carriers, Lieutenant Ryckman used its 50-calibre Browning machine gun to spray tracer rounds at the various German guns or to mark their position for the tankers. In short order, however, all three carriers were burning. The Shermans jockeyed for position, returning the German fire with 75-millimetre high-explosive rounds.[37] When a chance hit from one of the flak guns penetrated the tank commanded by Lieutenant P.E. Sheppard, it exploded. Twenty-year-old Ellis James Lloyd, the tank's loader-operator, died. The rest of the crew suffered burns and other injuries while bailing out.[38]

As the rest of 'B' Company fought its way into the streets around the beleaguered advance guard, Hasty Ps' Corporal Ernie Madden arrived aboard a carrier just in time to spot the crew of an 88-millimetre gun in the process of reloading. Madden floored the carrier and rushed the gun head-on. The carrier crashed into the gun's square protective shield, sending the gunners flying. Several were crushed under the carrier's tracks.[39]

A crazy, wild fight had developed that was less controlled by officers than by men just going for the enemy. The Hasty Ps had trained for fighting through ambushes such as this, so the companies reacted instinctively. 'B' Company had gone straight into the face of the main German fire. Caught in the open at the base of the hill, 'A' Company slipped left of the road into whatever cover it could find and started throwing fire out in aid of 'B' Company, while 'A' Squadron weighed in with a barrage of 75-millimetre rounds.

This spontaneous action gave Lieutenant Colonel Bruce Sutcliffe the precious minutes needed to cobble together a hurried plan of attack. Telling 'A' Company to continue providing fire support, he directed 'C' and 'D' companies with a battery of self-propelled guns (SPGs) from the Royal Devon Yeomanry to "make a wide left sweep into the town." Brigadier Graham was present and approved Sutcliffe's plan, but just as the battalion commander readied to issue the necessary orders, Simonds showed up again. "I want this battle stopped," he declared after Sutcliffe explained his intentions. "I don't like the plan." Regimental Sergeant Major Angus Duffy, hovering close by, slipped away in embarrassment at hearing two senior officers he respected being so bluntly reprimanded.[40] Graham and Sutcliffe stood their ground and Simonds backed off, but it was plain the bad blood between him and the brigadier was worsening. Sutcliffe had his men quickly on the move, supported also by several Shermans, which "succeeded in scoring direct hits on one enemy tank and on the flak position which had been shelling the road."[41]

Tweedsmuir had set up a headquarters section in the ditch by the road next to 'A' Company. With him was a forward observation officer, who seemed to be terrifically slow getting any shelling of the town under way. Whenever Tweedsmuir popped his head out of the ditch, Germans started sniping at him.[42]

By 1130 hours, the tanks, SPGs of the Devons, and artillery fire finally called in by the FOO were starting to tell on the German positions, many of their guns having been knocked out. But 'A' Company had started taking "extremely heavy, observed mortar fire from the right and front." There was also one of the deadly rapid-fire 20-millimetre guns ripping off bursts from somewhere on the left and three machine guns tearing away from both its flank and front. Realizing somebody needed to do something about the mortars, Private I.J. Gunter—who was part of the battalion's intelligence section—ventured out and located their positions. Returning to one of the tanks, he directed its fire against the mortars and soon silenced them. Meanwhile, Private H.E. Brant attacked one of the strongest German positions single-handedly. Firing his Bren gun from the hip, Brant advanced on about thirty enemy troops. Those who were not killed surrendered. Both Gunter and Brant were awarded Military Medals for their actions.[43]

As soon as 'B' Company reorganized around the burning carriers and tank to begin pushing deeper into the town, the Germans started withdrawing out the opposite side. By 1200 hours the fight was over, and the Hasty Ps left to take an accounting of their situation. For having walked straight into the maw of an ambush, the infantry had got off surprisingly lightly. Of the total twenty-five casualties, fifteen were Hasty Ps and none of these were killed.[44] The Three Rivers Tank Regiment suffered the other ten casualties, with Lloyd being the only fatality.

Tweedsmuir walked over to where the "wounded lay in the shadow of a wall, propped up and bandaged with the flies buzzing round them, stoically smoking." Considering the incredible volume of fire the flak battalion had thrown at them, he recognized they had been lucky.[45] How many Germans had been killed or wounded was never tallied, but the Hasty Ps counted two of the flak guns, two Panzer Mark ivs, and two Panzer Mark iiis knocked out. There were also a number of German trucks and a great deal of supplies that had been abandoned.[46] Included in the captured booty were cases of tinned fruit. Tweedsmuir made sure that the wounded were given all the fruit they desired.[47] Orders came from Brigadier Graham for the Hasty Ps to bivouac around Grammichele, while the 48th Highlanders passed through to continue the advance towards the town of Caltagirone—about eight miles farther west on Highway 124.

The Hasty Ps were well pleased with how they had performed. After the fact, so was Simonds. He went around the companies congratulating the battalion on "extricating itself from a dangerous trap and then driving the enemy from his superior position."[48] The fight for Grammichele was the first time the Canadian division had met German troops. While they had walked into the ambush, they could console themselves with the rapidity of their recovery. And speed was certainly of the essence. That evening Simonds received a signal from Montgomery advising that as xiii Corps was "held temporarily on the right, it is now all the more important to swing hard with our left; so push on with all speed to Caltagirone, and then to Valguarnera–Enna–Leonforte. Drive the Canadians hard."[49]

11

Hazards and Hardships

WHILE 1ST CANADIAN Infantry Brigade had been winning Grammichele, 2nd Canadian Infantry Brigade had marched from near Ragusa through rough country to gain Highway 124. Only the Loyal Edmonton Regiment, mounted on the tanks of the Three Rivers Regiment's 'C' Squadron, and the brigade headquarters had transport. Left far behind this leading column, which also included 3rd Canadian Field Regiment, the Seaforth Highlanders and Princess Patricia's Canadian Light Infantry were forced to make the passage of thirty miles on foot. This distance came as a rude shock to the brigade, for an inaccurate road trace on their maps had showed it as being only about seventeen miles. Exemplifying the worst of Sicilian construction practices, the unpaved and narrow track snaked treacherously up and down steep hills and through narrow valleys. Switchbacks were so tight the Shermans had to back and fill to execute turns. At one point, the head of the armoured column was directly across from its tail with the middle out of sight behind an intervening hill. Because of the ubiquitous dust boiling up around each Sherman, the tank commanders at the front and back mistook each other for German armour. Several 75-millimetre rounds were exchanged before the error was discovered.[1]

"An infernal Devil's stairway," the Seaforth's war diarist declared the road. Each hill climbed only revealed another higher one beyond.

With nightfall, word was passed that the march must continue. The brigade was not to pause until it reached Grammichele.[2]

In his Sherman, named "Commodore," Lieutenant Jack Wallace realized the column was not only plagued by inaccurate maps but had actually driven completely off the one provided. The squadron commander, Major F.L. "Fern" Caron, passed instructions that the tanker at the front was to guide the column forward by means of the North Star. "I never saw so many mountain roads in all my life," Wallace complained later. At midnight, his driver, Trooper Ace Elliot, "became violently sick" because of the twisting road. The bow-gunner, Trooper Vic Harvey, took over the controls. "He gave me some awful moments as he tried to negotiate some of those turns in one swoop. Once he had to jam on the brakes or else we would have been hurled over the cliff...He never tried that kind of stuff again after the blast he got from me over the intercom," Wallace recalled. At about 0300 hours, the mechanized column passed through Chiaramonte Gulfi. Dawn of July 16 found it approaching the little village of Licodia—a short distance south of Highway 124—where the brigade halted. For the last mile of the journey, Wallace's tank had to be towed by another because it had run out of fuel. The other Shermans had almost dry tanks.[3]

Licodia was teeming with Americans from the U.S. 45th Infantry Division's 157th Regiment. Lieutenant Colonel Charles Anckorn told Brigadier Chris Vokes his troops "had been ordered back from Grammichele in order to conform with the move of the Canadian Division."[4] While Anckorn and Vokes discussed impending moves, their soldiers set to trading. Lieutenant Wallace cadged twenty gallons of fuel from an artillery officer after learning that the fuel trucks would not arrive for hours. The men in his troop, meanwhile, "practically traded all their food for American food. The yanks were glad to see our stew and tea whereas our lads were glad to see some coffee and beans."[5]

Although the tankers, Loyal Edmonton Regiment, and other units in the mechanized column were able to spend a leisurely morning resting in Licodia, the brigade's other two battalions were still marching. Finally, at about noon, some trucks from the Royal Canadian Armoured Service Corps established a shuttle service to carry the

Seaforths and PPCLI forward in lifts.[6] This transport was provided only on a temporary basis. Despite orders from divisional headquarters that 2 CIB was to take over the advance from 1 CIB, which had closed on Caltagirone late on July 15, it remained desperately short of vehicles. As the Eddies had enjoyed some time to rest, this battalion was again mounted on 'C' Squadron's tanks and sent forward with the 3rd Field Regiment and brigade headquarters in trail. The Seaforths and PPCLI would follow by foot. From Caltagirone, the brigade was to head directly for Enna.[7]

During its counterattacks on the American beaches, the Hermann Göring Division had used Caltagirone—another town with a population of about thirty thousand—as a headquarters. When the 48th Highlanders started moving towards the town on the evening of July 15, expectations were that the ten-mile journey from Grammichele would be carried out quickly because the battalion was riding on carriers provided by the Saskatoon Light Infantry—the division's support battalion—and Shermans of the Three Rivers Regiment's 'B' Squadron. After a mile and a half, however, the lead vehicle carrying Lieutenant Edward MacLachlan "came across a burned-out enemy vehicle which it by-passed, thereby touching the soft shoulder at the side of the road, passed over an enemy mine and blew up."[8] MacLachlan and the carrier's SLI driver were killed, and 48th Highlander wireless signaller Private Douglas May was badly wounded. MacLachlan was the battalion's first fatality.[9] Engineers then came forward and "started the laborious process of clearing the whole road to Caltagirone of mines."[10]

The Highlanders fell out on the side of the road, expecting a long wait. But when Lieutenant Colonel Ian Johnston reported the situation, Brigadier Howard Graham came forward. Leave the vehicles, he said, and advance alongside the road on foot. "I'll buy you the best bottle of Málaga in Sicily if you take Caltagirone before daylight," he told Johnston.[11]

Once the battalion had departed, Graham had his Jeep parked behind a hedge of cactus. Firing up his Sterno stove, the brigadier treated himself to a wash and shave while ruminating over what to do about Simonds. The clash could not go unaddressed. At every turn,

Simonds was "cold and critical." Every gesture or word from the major general seemed intended to drive home the message that Graham did not measure up. Sitting in the shade of the cactus, the brigadier "decided that this morning's tongue-lashing was the last straw." He was fed up with Simonds, who was six years younger and had less experience commanding troops. Clearly, Simonds was waiting for an excuse to fire Graham, so why let him choose the moment?

Graham drove to the divisional 'O' Group, which was held in a field outside Grammichele. After Simonds issued his orders for the following day, Graham called him aside. "This morning you scolded me and bawled me out and humiliated me in the presence of my driver and signaller. I feel the time has come for us to part company, and therefore I request release from my command at once." The RCR's Lieutenant Colonel Ralph Crowe, Graham said, was competent to take over the brigade.

"You'll get a bad report for this," was Simonds's only response.

Returning to his brigade headquarters truck, Graham typed up a short note confirming his request to be relieved of command and recommending Crowe for it. This was the hardest decision of Graham's life. He cared about the brigade and felt his handling had been competent. It seemed a particular shame that he should suffer such a personal and career setback on this day, which was his forty-fifth birthday.

Graham was packing his kit when a signal from Lieutenant General Oliver Leese instructed him to report immediately to XXX Corps headquarters. Telling his brigade major that Simonds would soon send someone to take over the brigade, Graham started the long journey to the rear.[12]

At about 0200 hours on July 16, Crowe took over "temporary command of the brigade." In his absence, Major Billy Pope assumed command of the RCR. This battalion was already on the march, advancing with two companies well out on either side of Highway 124 to protect the flanks of the 48th Highlanders.[13]

When Graham reported to Leese, the XXX Corps commander told him to bed down somewhere and that General Montgomery was coming to see him. The Eighth Army commander showed up first thing in the morning. "Now, what is this trouble between you and Guy Simonds?"

Graham briefly explained. Montgomery interrupted once to ask if he had ever refused to obey an order. Never, Graham responded. Montgomery told him he was to go back and resume commanding his brigade. When Graham said that would be difficult because of the words passed between himself and Simonds, Montgomery said not to worry. The army commander then had a private conversation with Leese, who soon informed Graham that he would accompany the brigadier back to 1st Canadian Infantry Division's headquarters.

Pacing back and forth under some olive trees, Simonds and Leese had a long conversation, after which the xxx Corps commander departed while the divisional commander retired to his caravan. Eventually he emerged and walked over to Graham. "Howard, let's just forget about this whole business; you go back to your brigade and I'll tear up this note." Tugging the resignation note from his shirt pocket, Simonds ripped it up.[14] Divisional general staff officer Lieutenant Colonel George Kitching, who knew Simonds had wanted to sack Graham, was relieved to see the matter blow over. He also thought it showed that Simonds "could forgive, forget and be generous as well."[15]

In a letter to Leese, Montgomery wrote immediately after the incident, "This is a great pity. Graham is an excellent fellow and much beloved in his [brigade]. I expect Simonds lost his temper. Simonds is a young and very inexperienced Divisional general, and has much to learn about command. He will upset his Division if he starts sacking Brigadiers like this." Simonds would, he added, "be well advised to consult his superiors before he takes violent action in which he may not be backed up."[16]

About the time Brigadier Graham was bunking down at xxx Corps headquarters in the early morning hours of July 16, the 48th Highlanders had reached the outskirts of Caltagirone. They waited outside the town until the engineers cleared the roads to enable the Three Rivers 'A' Squadron to come up. At about 0400 hours, the battalion "marched into town" with the tanks trundling behind. "There was no opposition," the 48th Highlanders war diarist noted, as "the Germans had left 6 hours previous."[17] Because it had been a German divisional headquarters, the town had been subjected to heavy Allied bombing. The Canadians "found the place a veritable shambles, with the streets badly blocked by rubble and many fires burning. In the very inadequate local hospital, the Highlanders' medical section did what it could for the civilian casualties, and the 4th Field Ambulance gave assistance when it arrived. Despite all their troubles, the nuns who operated the hospital insisted on serving the Canadians coffee—made of crushed acorns."[18]

IN THE LATE afternoon of July 16, General Harold Alexander had sent signals to both General George Patton and General Bernard Montgomery reiterating that Eighth Army was to "drive the enemy into the Messina Peninsula." Seventh Army's role was "to protect the rear" of Eighth Army. Only when Montgomery's troops were well beyond Enna would Patton be released to occupy Agrigento and adjacent Porto Empedocle on the southern coast.[19]

Although Patton had accepted without protest the order on July 13 to cease the northward advance of his II Corps and to surrender use of Highway 124 to 1st Canadian Infantry Division, he was increasingly chafing at playing second fiddle to Montgomery. But he did not make his dissatisfaction known to Alexander—exposing a serious misunderstanding by both men over military protocol. In the British and Canadian armies, broad-based directives, such as those Alexander had issued, were considered open for discussion with regards to details of execution. Montgomery never hesitated to protest and propose alternatives to any order he believed wrong. It had been precisely such intervention that had allowed Montgomery, more than anyone else, to lay the framework for Operation Husky and subsequently win the case for Eighth Army making the drive on Messina while Seventh Army was relegated to covering his left flank.

The American military was not so flexible. Orders from above were precisely that. To stand about debating the rights and wrongs of an order from a superior ran counter to the whole American expectation of decisive command.[20]

If not prepared to challenge Alexander's orders, Patton was willing to resort to subterfuge. On July 14, he quietly assembled a plan to carry out an end run north across the western part of the island and seize Palermo. "Monty is trying to steal the show...and may do so," he wrote his wife. "It is my opinion that when the present line of the combined armies is secured, which will probably be around the 19th, it will be feasible to advance rapidly with the 3rd Division and 2nd Armored Division and take Palermo."[21]

"There's plenty of room for both of us to fight," Patton assured General Omar Bradley.[22] In a July 17 diary notation, Patton charged that Alexander was "putting the Americans in a secondary role, which is a continuation of such roles for the whole campaign and may find the war ending with us being overlooked. I am flying to Tunis to see General Alexander.

"I am sure that neither he nor any of his British staff has any conception of the power or mobility of the Seventh Army, nor are they aware of the political implications latent in such a course of action.

"I shall explain the situation to General Alexander on the basis that it would be inexpedient politically for the Seventh Army not to have equal glory in the final stage of the campaign."[23]

Later that morning, Patton met with Alexander at his headquarters in Tunis. Patton proposed splitting his forces by creating a second corps composed of the majority of Seventh Army's armour and mobile infantry—named the Provisional Corps—which would race for Palermo, rather than support operations aimed at Messina. He would leave a smaller covering force to protect Montgomery's left flank. Alexander, who was overly conciliatory by nature, agreed. "He gave me permission to carry out my plan if I would assure him that the road net near Caltanis[s]etta would be held...If I do what I am going to do, there is no need of holding anything, but it's a mean man who won't promise, so I did," Patton wrote.[24]

The fact that the Axis forces were slowly withdrawing into the northeastern corner of Sicily in order to position themselves for an evacuation across the Straits of Messina seemed of little importance to Patton. He wanted Palermo, just as he had during the early planning for the invasion. Even the American official historians ultimately concluded that Patton's "preoccupation with Palermo amounted to an obsession" and could find no strategic purpose for its capture. While

Porto Empedocle at Agrigento had been a logical objective, giving as it did additional port facilities to the minor ones available at Gela and Licata, Palermo's additional capacity exceeded Seventh Army's needs. General Lucien Truscott, commander of the U.S. 3rd Division, believed Palermo drew Patton "like a lode star" and had done so since Operation Husky's inception. "General Patton," he later said, "made no secret of the fact that he was not only desirous of emulating Rommel's reputation as a leader of armor, he wanted to exceed it. General Patton was also anxious for the U.S. armor to achieve some notice... The capture of Palermo by an armored sweep through western Sicily appeared to suit his purpose."[25]

After his meeting with Alexander, Patton believed he had his endorsement to go for Palermo to demonstrate American armoured power, to prove his masterful generalship, and to provide a visible prize of war. For the foreseeable future, then, the Allied campaign in Sicily would be fought by two armies heading in different directions, neither able to offer the other meaningful support.

THE CANADIANS ADVANCING out of the ruins of Caltagirone had no inkling of this brinkmanship. Their sights were set on Enna, with the intermediary objective for July 16 being Piazza Armerina. In the early morning, the Loyal Edmonton Regiment passed through 1 CIB's lines as the vanguard of 2 CIB. 'C' Company was at the head of the convoy, once again riding on Three Rivers 'C' Squadron tanks. Trucks had been provided to carry the rest of the battalion forward. Following behind the tanks and infantry was a battery of self-propelled guns from the Royal Devon Yeomanry and the entire 3rd Canadian Field Regiment.

While 2 CIB moved towards Piazza Armerina, 1 CIB's battalions sent patrols north from Caltagirone to check out some secondary roads and ensure that several villages were clear of the enemy. The 3rd Canadian Infantry Brigade, still in divisional reserve, was instructed "to be ready at an hour's notice to follow [2 CIB] and 'secure communications in the area of Leonforte,' with one reconnaissance squadron [from the Princess Louise Dragoon Guards] and one field regiment under command." When 3 CIB moved through 2 CIB it would split its strength in two—one group clearing the way through Valguarnera and the other driving to Enna and then swinging eastward to take Leonforte. This program laid down on 3 CIB by Major General Simonds was ambitious, but he believed it practical as the distance to be covered was no more than what 2 CIB had travelled during the preceding twenty-four hours in its move from Ragusa to Caltagirone.[26]

As 'C' Squadron clattered along the well-paved road, Lieutenant Jack Wallace was a happy tanker. Although at the back of the column, he did not have to swallow dust kicked up by the Shermans ahead. The pace was good, and there was not a sign of opposition other than the demolition of a little bridge, which happened moments after Wallace's tank rolled off it. The explosion was chalked up to the Germans having sown a time-delayed mine under the bridge. After five miles, they rolled into San Michele di Ganzeria and were greeted by "a bevy of sheets hanging from every conceivable place."[27] Crowding the streets of the town and standing along the side of the road on its outskirts were large numbers of Italian troops trying to surrender. Lieutenant Colonel Jim Jefferson was in a hurry and issued orders for the column to ignore them, leaving it to the other battalions behind to take them prisoner.[28]

Just beyond San Michele, the column came to the point where Highway 124 intersected the highway running from Gela to Enna. Making a hard right onto the northward-trending Highway 117, the advance continued towards Piazza Armerina. By noon, from a distance of three miles, the town of about 22,000 was clearly visible in the distance atop a 2,366-foot-high summit. This was the highest Sicilian community the Canadians had so far encountered, and beyond it the terrain looked to be increasingly mountainous.

As the column descended a long, level ridge into a steep, narrow gully at about noon, it approached a sharp bend in the road. Suddenly, from positions all over the heights south of the town, the enemy opened up with machine guns, mortars, and artillery.[29] The Edmontons of Major W.T. Cromb's 'C' Company spilled off the tanks, while the other two companies piled out of the lorries with equal haste. The battalion adjutant, Captain C.H. Pritchard, spotted tracers coming from three different machine-gun positions just as a mine exploded in the road ahead of the column and created a large crater. Except for the three machine-gun positions, nobody could see any sign of the well-concealed Germans. One truck burned in the middle of the road, but the others had pulled to one side where there was some cover.[30] The lead tanks of 'C' Squadron destroyed a German machine-gun position in a house near the road, but thereafter the tankers were unable to elevate their guns high enough to fire on the enemy holding the high upper slopes.[31] Helpless, the tanks of 'C' Squadron swung off the left side of the road while 'A' Squadron came up and rumbled into covered positions to the right.[32]

Mortar and artillery rounds were exploding along the length of the road. The two most forward companies had deployed to either side of it and were trying to work towards the enemy positions. Jefferson ran forward, found Cromb, and ordered a halt while he assessed the situation. It was going to be an infantry fight, he realized, because the tanks were unable to raise their gun barrels and the artillery would need time to deploy. Shorthanded because of the decision to leave 'D' Company back in Ragusa, he decided to hold Cromb's men as his reserve and send 'A' and 'B' companies to seize the high ground on either side of the road. The only fire support he could offer was the battalion's 3-inch mortars and two 6-pound anti-tank guns, which were close enough to be brought to bear. The anti-tank guns had to be unhooked from the trucks towing them and dragged off the road. As one of the guns was being moved forward, it was knocked out by German fire. The other soon went into action against a machine-gun position in another nearby house "which it blew to pieces, scattering snipers in all directions." To dodge counterbattery fire from the Germans, the mortar teams kept moving after firing a few rounds. One team delayed too long in making its hop and was caught by a German mortar round, which wounded four men.

'A' Company went straight up the heights on its side of the road, despite heavy fire, and quickly cleared the Germans out. Jefferson sent 'C' Company up to reinforce the position. On the other side of the road, 'B' Company ran into trouble when its commander, Captain A.A. Gilchrist, along with one platoon, was pinned down in an orchard by machine-gun and mortar fire. When his wireless set failed, the company was cut off from battalion headquarters. Having lost contact with his company commander, Captain A.F. Newton decided to work his way back to the battalion to restore communications. Accompanied by Private A.E. McCormack, he set off cross-country, only to be ambushed and taken prisoner by some Germans.

With Newton missing and Gilchrist separated from the majority of his company, Lieutenant K.J. Rootes took command and led most of 'B' Company forward in a running fight to finally clear the high ground.[33] With these hills in hand, the Eddies were overlooking Piazza Armerina. But the Germans were still tight in the town. They were also throwing a great weight of 75-millimetre shells towards the column on the road, despite countering fire by the Royal Devon Yeomanry and the powerful 5.5-inch guns of 7th Medium Regiment.[34]

Lieutenant Wallace realized they were "right in the centre of the arc of fire with shells from both directions flying overhead. They sound nice when they go overhead like that." Running towards their Shermans after conducting a reconnaissance of the perimeter, he and another tanker heard "one coming ever so close, so we hit the dirt but fast. The shell lands about 10 yards away and really shakes us up, but we did not get a nick. Pretty lucky. Everything seems to be alright with the way that we have dispersed our tanks so I detail Jim Trueman and Ed Lawrence (Gunner and Operator) to make some orangeade. The shelling continues but we must have our orangeade. Only the occasional one lands close." But it was a different matter for 'A' and 'B' squadrons, Wallace saw, for shells and mortar rounds were exploding constantly in their positions. With a chuckle, Trueman, who had started monitoring the tank's wireless, caught Wallace's attention. The two men listened with grim amusement to Lieutenant Colonel Leslie Booth, the regiment's commander, ordering his driver to move the tank away from the shelling. In his excitement, Booth was broadcasting over the regimental net, rather than switching his radio key to engage the tank's intercom. "It really sounds funny hearing him getting frantic, probably wondering why the driver doesn't obey his orders. Jim gets disgusted and tells him to get the hell off the air. Every man in the regiment was listening to the C.O. screaming, it was amusing while it lasted."[35]

Things took a more serious turn when No. 4 Troop of 'B' Squadron moved out left of the road in an attempt to close on a mortar position. Finding the ground impassable, the three tanks halted in the open and were subjected to concentrated shellfire. One shell exploded in front of the tank on the far left and broke a track. As the crew bailed out to head towards the cover of the closest other tank, another shell landed in their midst—Corporal William Hulse and Troopers George Karcameron and James Harold MacTavish were killed.[36]

The Loyal Edmonton Regiment's battalion headquarters was also taking a pounding from the German guns, and Captain Pritchard was aghast when "one of our men came up to me...with one side of him covered from head to foot with what appeared to be blood and since he appeared dazed and spoke incoherently I immediately concluded that a shell had exploded in the midst of a group of men and rushed to the scene of the disaster. There I found nothing but the remnants of what had been a mulberry bush. Apparently the mortar bomb had exploded near this mulberry bush, blowing away all its fruit which had spattered on the soldier."[37]

Finally at about 2100 hours, fully nine hours since the battle had broken out, the German fire slackened and it soon became clear that a withdrawal to Piazza Armerina was under way. Knowing that his men, who had been almost constantly on the move for two nights and a day, were exhausted by the action, Jefferson decided to wait until morning before testing whether the town had been evacuated. The Edmontons had suffered twenty-seven casualties.[38] Surprisingly hard hit, since tanker casualties were normally expected to be far lighter than those suffered by infantry, the Three Rivers Regiment added another eleven men killed or wounded.[39]

AT 2230 HOURS, Simonds convened an 'O' Group with his brigadiers and set out a new plan. Rather than the Eddies clearing Piazza Armerina, Simonds told Brigadier Chris Vokes to give that task to the Seaforths and PPCLI. They were to keep pressure on the Germans to push them out of the town during the night and also secure the heights to its north and northeast. Simonds stressed that 2 CIB was to "maintain contact with the enemy regardless of the situation," so the Germans could not break and run. While 2 CIB cleared Piazza Armerina, 3rd Canadian Infantry Brigade would muster south of the town in readiness to take over the advance on Enna at 0500 hours. If 2 CIB had not by then finished opening the way for 3 CIB, Vokes was to put in a hard attack on Piazza Armerina supported by the entirety of the division's artillery.[40]

The division's final objective remained Enna, which Simonds emphasized "controls the four main roads running from east to west in Sicily and acts as a sort of clearing centre for traffic in the northern part of the island. It is felt that once Enna is taken the Italian forces on the island will pack up. The Germans are attempting to reach the Straits of Messina intact and it is our job to knock out as many of them as we can before their main body attempts the evacuation to Calabria."[41]

In the early morning hours of July 17, the Seaforths and PPCLI sent patrols into Piazza Armerina and found that the Germans had pulled out. Progress by the Seaforths was hampered not by the enemy but by civilians, who the moment the Germans departed began "to pick up everything in sight, beds, and boxes out of the barracks, water pails, anything they can lay their hands on."

Piazza Armerina was discovered to have been a headquarters for the Italian XVI Corps "and a great deal of signal equipment as well as a large quantity of petrol, reported to be 52,000 gallons, were taken as booty." The Seaforths' war diarist noted that many Italian army vehicles were also seized and pressed into service, which gave the division almost full mobility. This, however, also resulted in major congestion on the single highway "due to 1 and 3 [CIB] passing through 2 [CIB]," which contributed to 3 CIB's delayed start.[42]

As the day progressed, the division's intelligence officers determined that the Germans the Edmontons had engaged were from 2nd Battalion, 104th Panzer Grenadier Regiment of the 15th Panzer Grenadier Division—meaning this division was shifting from its earlier positions in the western part of Sicily to hold the centre.[43] The PPCLI's Lieutenant Colin McDougall's platoon from 'C' Company had taken a few Panzer Grenadiers prisoner. They struck him as being "lean, sun-tanned professionals, superbly arrogant," and realized that such "soldiers always would take some beating."[44]

From Piazza Armerina to Enna was a mere twenty-two miles by Highway 117, and Simonds fully expected 3 CIB to reach the city before sunset on July 17. The Carleton and York Regiment was at the head of the brigade, with one company mounted on Three Rivers 'B' Squadron tanks and the rest following in trucks. Behind this New Brunswick infantry regiment were all three field regiments of the division's artillery stretched out in a long line. Then came the Royal 22e Régiment and West Nova Scotia Regiment, as well as the other two Three Rivers Tank squadrons. This extended column rumbled into Piazza Armerina at about 0600 hours to find the main street clogged with vehicles of the other two brigades, all moving in the same direction with no instruction from division as to which brigade had priority.[45] The result was a "mammoth traffic jam in the narrow, winding streets...which took several hours to sort out."[46]

Just four miles north of the town, the column came to a blown bridge over a dry streambed whose banks were too steep for either tanks or trucks to negotiate. No. 1 Platoon of the 4th Canadian Field Regiment, RCE brought a bulldozer up and began carving out a diversion.[47] While this work was under way, the Carletons sent foot patrols ahead to scout for enemy positions.

They were soon observing a road junction four miles beyond the blown bridge, where a side road branched to the right off Highway 117 and ran six miles to Valguarnera. This town overlooked the Dittaino River valley and western Catania plain from a high summit and had been identified as an important objective for the Canadian division. Not surprisingly, the Germans had realized that holding the junction blocked any advance along Highway 117 to Enna and also up the side road to Valguarnera. Topography encouraged this strategy. Immediately before the road forked, Highway 117 climbed "through a narrow gap in a long ridge which broke from the backbone of the Erei Mountains to bend around to the north-east and cover Valguarnera from the south and east sides." This pass was called Portella Grottacalda and on its west flank stood 2,700-foot-high Monte della Forma. Manning this mountain and other heights on either side of the pass were troops of the 2nd Battalion, 104th Panzer Grenadier Regiment—who had withdrawn from Piazza Armerina the previous night—reinforced by part of the regiment's 1st Battalion. On the north slope of Monte della Forma, the Germans had several heavy mortars hidden from Canadian view. The scouts, however, observed much enemy movement around the junction. Returning to the blown bridge, they warned brigade headquarters to expect resistance once the column entered the pass.[48]

It took until 1630 hours for the engineers to open a crossing for 3 CIB and Brigadier Howard Penhale ordered the advance resumed. Little more than a mile beyond the blown bridge, the column came under heavy machine-gun and mortar fire. 'B' Squadron "dumped" the Carletons it had aboard and "took hull down positions along the crest overlooking the valley towards Enna." While the tankers began firing 75-millimetre rounds towards any German positions spotted, the infantry deployed hard by either side of the road and started creeping forward.[49]

The rest of the Three Rivers Regiment soon joined 'B' Squadron on the crest and added the weight of their guns to the attempt to blast the way open for the infantry, something the tankers were convinced they were achieving, even though much of the fire was aimed towards targets 2,500 yards or more away.[50] A mile short of the pass, however, Lieutenant Colonel F.D. "Dodd" Tweedie signalled that his Carletons "were pinned down by long range mortars and machine-guns" and that the tanks "were of no help to our infantry."[51]

As soon as the Carletons had run into trouble, the West Nova Scotia Regiment's Lieutenant Colonel M. "Pat" Bogert had thrown his 'B' Company out in a right-hand flanking move that pushed the Germans off one hill from which Tweedie had indicated he was taking fire. Captain J.R. Cameron started leading his men towards Monte del Forma but was forced to ground by heavy volumes of machine-gun and mortar fire from its summit. Bogert was sending more West Novas to reinforce Cameron's company when Penhale signalled that he should pull back and issue the troops dinner, while division put together a more calculated plan for taking the pass. Simonds had abandoned hope of the Canadians gaining Enna before the day was out.[52]

At 1900 hours, the division's chief staff officer (11), Major Dick Danby, wrote a quick situational report explaining that 3 CIB was "in touch with the enemy," who were "making use of delaying action. We are now coming into mountainous country and the fighting is becoming more and more difficult. The Boche is a tough fighter at all times and add to that the hazards and hardships of mountain warfare and one can see that the days ahead of us will be difficult ones."[53]

BATTLE FOR
THE SICILIAN HILLS

12

Long and Savage Minutes

A T 1700 HOURS on July 17, during an 'O' Group with his brigade commanders, Major General Guy Simonds announced for the first time in Sicily that 1st Canadian Infantry Division would launch a two-brigade attack with all six battalions committed. The Three Rivers Tank Regiment and the divisional artillery would support the infantry. Simonds ordered Brigadier Howard Penhale, a portly Great War veteran artilleryman turned infantry commander, to punch 3rd Canadian Infantry Brigade through Portella Grottacalda and continue along Highway 117 to Enna. Simultaneously, Brigadier Howard Graham would outflank the Germans blocking the pass and road junction by striking cross-country towards Valguarnera with 1st Canadian Infantry Brigade.[1] The two brigades, Simonds said, would carry out "a well supported attack in strength."[2]

Although the divisional plan described the attack as committing two brigades, they did not go together at the same time. Instead, 3 CIB advanced at 2000 hours when Penhale passed the Royal 22e Régiment through the Carleton and York Regiment's position a mile short of the entrance to the pass.[3] The French-Canadian Permanent Force regiment moved towards combat well before 1 CIB's battalions even cleared Piazza Armerina. In this brigade's van was the Hastings and

Prince Edward Regiment, and its troops would not be positioned to begin their attack until 2130 hours.[4]

In his instructions to Lieutenant Colonel Paul Bernatchez, Penhale emphasized the need for a rapid advance to keep the Van Doos in contact with the Germans. To that end, the battalion would go forward aboard Bren carriers and trucks. During his 'O' Group with the battalion company and platoon commanders, Bernatchez made no attempt to hide the fact he "did not much like this idea of going to meet the enemy in trucks." But as Lieutenant Pierre-Ferdinand Potvin noted with a Gallic shrug, "Those are the orders."

Bernatchez put Major Gilles Turcot's 'B' Company out front with one section of Potvin's No. 11 Platoon loaded on carriers, under command of Lieutenant Guy Vaugeois. All the other men in Turcot's company would be in trucks, as would those of the other three rifle companies. The formation behind 'B' Company consisted of 'A' Company, the battalion headquarters with its support platoons, 'C' Company, and finally 'D' Company.[5] It was a risky move, for the vehicles would be driving without headlights, relying on moonlight to illuminate the way. That same moonlight would also light them up for the Germans, while the sounds of the carriers and trucks must carry well ahead of their advance.[6]

The Van Doos had stripped the tarpaulins off the trucks before setting off. Kneeling in the truck beds, the men scanned the darkness. Bren gunners trained their automatic weapons towards either side of the road. Advancing at six or seven miles per hour, the column crept warily towards the pass.

At 2200 hours, still well short of it, Vaugeois signalled a halt and reported that a large crater blocked the road. On one side of the road was a steep mountainside and on the other, a sheer cliff fell into a narrow ravine. Potvin and his platoon clawed their way up the mountainside and established a covering position beyond the crater, to cover the engineers called forward to repair the road. A platoon from the 4th Canadian Field Regiment, RCE was soon led to the scene by Lieutenant Henri Chassé. The Van Doo officer insisted on inspecting the ground for booby traps or mines before giving permission for the engineers to begin work. As engineers and infantry worked shoulder to shoulder filling in the crater, the Germans blasted the area with a continuous bombardment that clearly indicated they were alert to the Canadian mechanized advance. A half-hour later the job was finished, but the enemy shelling had taken its toll on the engineers. Both the platoon commander, Lieutenant Hugh Carey, and the regimental commander, Major Jim Blair, were hit by shrapnel, along with several other engineers. Blair was evacuated to the nearest casualty clearing station with severe wounds, but Carey died on the spot.[7]

The convoy carried on along the road, which was still bordered by the mountain to the right and the ravine to the left as it snaked towards the valley bottom, where a bridge crossed a dry streambed before climbing towards the pass. Beyond the bridge, several half-constructed houses stood alongside the road. While the road remained above ground for the ascent into the pass, a paralleling railway track bored through the facing mountain via a narrow tunnel. In the moonlight, the Van Doos could see Monte della Forma looming over the valley to their right. They felt dangerously exposed.[8] At the column's head, the carriers had just crossed the bridge and started climbing when several machine guns erupted with heavy bursts of fire from either side of the road. Frantically, the carrier drivers tried to turn about, only to find the road too narrow and the houses hemming them in. At first the men in the carriers remained aboard, firing their Bren guns and rifles point-blank at the Germans. But the incoming fire was so intense that Vaugeois soon shouted for everyone to bail out and find cover.

In the trucks behind, the other Van Doos had already tumbled out to gain the roadside ditches. Seconds later, one truck was hit by an anti-tank shell and exploded in a fireball. There was little cover, and some men dove behind rocks or isolated clumps of low shrubbery, while others hunkered as low as they could in the ditches. Unable to get into the houses, the men who had jumped off the carriers squeezed up against the sides of the vehicles or underneath them for protection. From these exposed positions, the Van Doos began throwing a fierce rate of fire back at the Germans.

Up by the carriers, 'B' Company's Potvin realized his No. 11 Platoon either got on the offensive or died. The rifle section with the carriers was pinned down, the men there unable to crawl out of the German trap. That left him with two sections of six men, his seven-man platoon command post, and a three-man Bren gun team. Potvin ordered one rifle section to work their way up onto a low shoulder of ground and provide covering fire, while he led the other section directly up a near-vertical slope to attack the nearest machine-gun position, which was about 150 feet above the road and firing directly down on his men.[9]

While Potvin had been casting together his hurried plan, 'B' Company commander Major Turcot had directed Nos. 10 and 12 platoons far enough out on either side of the road that they were able to support Potvin's move with covering fire. Farther back, 'A' Company's Captain Léo Bouchard led his men up the steep slope to the right in order to close on 'B' Company's exposed flank.

Potvin's little team cautiously climbed towards the German machine-gun position. As they closed in, Potvin made out four men manning the machine gun. They were intent on firing at the Van Doos by the road, obviously thinking their position impervious to attack. At his signal, the riflemen struck the Germans with a volley of fire that killed two of them. When the other two broke and ran, a couple of Van Doos went after them in close pursuit and cut both down. Quickly establishing themselves in and around the machine-gun nest, Potvin and his men began bringing German positions lower down under fire. This took the worst of the pressure off 'B' Company and allowed some men in the carrier section to jump back into their vehicles to bring the mounted machine guns into action.

Looking towards the houses, Potvin spotted a German self-propelled gun jockeying to fire on the carriers and pointed it out to his 2-inch mortar team. Private Cloutier, who his mates boasted could "put a mortar bomb into a jam jar from a thousand feet," started pumping out the 2.5-pound bombs at a rate of four rounds a minute. Using the mortar fire to cover his movement, Potvin led three men in an attack on the house where the SPG had been sighted. Finding the German armoured vehicle had fled, the men threw a No. 36 fragmentation grenade into the building and killed the German infantrymen inside with a fierce volley of gunfire. When the firing abated, Potvin discovered he and his men had only a single Bren gun magazine and two fifty-round belts of ammunition left. It was time to fall back on the mortar position.

As Potvin went up the hill, he could see more Panzer Grenadiers forming up next to the house they had just cleared. The lieutenant ordered Cloutier to bring them under fire, and after a few rounds the Germans withdrew. Having eliminated most of the German positions immediately threatening the front of the column, Potvin was able to consolidate his platoon around the carriers. They dug in, ready to meet any renewed attacks. For his actions in leading his platoon's fight out of the ambush, Potvin was awarded the Military Cross.[10] Four other Van Doos would also earn decorations this night, with Lieutenants Bouchard and Maurice Trudeau receiving Military Crosses and Lance Sergeant René Beauregard and Corporal Georges-Edmond Patenaude receiving Military Medals.[11]

While Potvin had been creating havoc on the right, Major Turcot had regrouped the rest of 'B' Company. He sent Lieutenant Roger des Rivières's No. 10 Platoon out to the right and had Lieutenant Joseph Laliberté dig in his No. 12 Platoon immediately south of the bridge. With both platoons having the road at their back, they were able to fend off attempts by German infantry to overrun their positions.

At the same time 'A' Company, which had moved to protect 'B' Company's right flank, got into a tight spot when Captain Bouchard realized a group of Germans were trying to get behind his men to cut them off from the rest of the battalion. Bouchard ordered everyone into a defensive circle, and they opened fire on the enemy. With the situation now reversed, the Germans broke off the action and withdrew. Several Panzer Grenadiers were cut down before the rest "vanished into the night."[12]

Although the Van Doos had managed to stabilize their situation, they were still in serious trouble, unable to either advance or pull back from their extended position along the road. Lieutenant Colonel Bernatchez had managed to organize the companies so they were each clustered on ground that provided relatively good cover and from which each could support the other with fire. But his wireless set had been knocked out, so he had no means to call in artillery fire.

What he did have, however, was a 2nd Light Anti-Aircraft Battery team with its 40-millimetre Bofors anti-aircraft gun. Setting up on a low hill, the gun crew opened fire on the buildings still occupied by the Germans. Seconds later, a covey of Panzer Grenadiers were observed scrambling out of two houses "while tracer shells were coming in the doors and windows."[13] The gunners were credited with knocking out four machine-gun positions.[14]

The companies, meanwhile, were sending men out to try to rescue the battalion's anti-tank guns, which had been left tethered to their trucks when the troops went to ground. Sergeant F. McMahon was in the process of dragging one of the guns into his company perimeter when a German shell exploded nearby and shrapnel fractured his right ankle. Despite the wound, McMahon continued helping three of his men until they safely extracted the gun.

At the same time, Corporal Georges-Edmond Patenaude was accomplishing a feat that won him a Military Medal. Seeing stranded on the road several men who had been wounded by fire coming from a concrete blockhouse, he jumped into a carrier and provided covering fire with its mounted machine gun until they crawled to safety. Picking up a PIAT gun, Patenaude then charged the blockhouse and killed the Germans inside with several anti-tank bombs.

Other soldiers, including Major Turcot, exposed themselves to the shelling and machine-gun fire that continued to rake the road in order to move trucks into covered positions. As the night wore on, the Germans abandoned trying to overrun the Van Doos and confined themselves to harassing fire. "From time to time, a bullet would hit its target, a mortar bomb would destroy a vehicle. Ammunition, rations, emergency rations, weapons, and baggage went up in flames. Lieutenant Potvin's men, who had left all their gear behind to move more freely, had to eat with fingers for two long weeks and borrow razors from their friends," the regimental historian later wrote.[15]

At sunrise the "Battle of the Horseshoe," as the Van Doos dubbed this action, was still under way. The Germans remained ensconced around Portella Grottacalda, and the French Canadians lacked the firepower to force their passage. All they could do was hold in place until divisional and brigade headquarters decided what to do next.

ABOUT THIRTY MINUTES before the Van Doos had tripped the ambush at 2200 hours on July 17, 1st Canadian Infantry Brigade's Hastings and Prince Edward Regiment had started cross-country towards Valguarnera. Departing Highway 117 two miles north of Piazza Armerina, the battalion had 'A' Company leading, followed in order by 'C' Company, Lieutenant Colonel Bruce Sutcliffe and his headquarters, 'B' Company, 'D' Company, and then the carrier, anti-tank, and mortar platoons. Carrying sixty- to one-hundred-pound packs jammed with ammunition, grenades, and emergency rations, the infantry moved in a long single file into the mountainous country-side "interspersed with deep ravines and dried up water courses."[16]

Initially, the battalion followed a sandy track wide enough for the carriers and towed 6-pounder anti-tank guns. Having got a later start, a Three Rivers tank, carrying an artillery FOO, also ground up the track. Major John Tweedsmuir had stationed himself on the tank's front fender to serve as a guide, and the FOO was similarly mounted opposite. "The trail continued to climb through a pinewood that gave way to open sandy uplands. The moon came up clear and bright, and from our perch...we could follow the tracks of the carriers in the sand. We lost sight of them on some hard ground but picked them up further on. Somehow they didn't look quite familiar and we stopped to examine them. It was lucky that we did; they were the tracks of a German Tiger tank. We scouted about until we found the tracks of the carriers and followed them until we found our anti-tank guns halted beside some scrub. Two hundred yards further on we came to the edge of the escarpment. No tank or carrier could hope to get on. It fell away in a steep rocky slope to vineyards below. The moon silvered the leaves in the great bowl below us and shone on two long ridges of hills running across the landscape. The tracks of the marching infan-try were lost on the hard-baked side of the escarpment.

"There was no sound except the distant barking of dogs, where we knew the battalion was pushing forward on foot through the vines. There was nothing for it but to return to our vehicles."[17] Tweedsmuir decided that the carriers and tank would continue along Highway 117 to a side road the Royal Canadian Regiment was going to try using to reach Valguarnera. It was a worrisome situation, because if the

Hasty Ps tumbled the Germans, they would not be able to call on artillery support.[18]

At the head of the infantry column, Captain Alex Campbell had realized that the mazelike countryside rendered the maps useless. Resorting to dead reckoning and a great deal of guesswork, Campbell led 'A' Company along a series of goat tracks. Sometime after midnight, word came up the line that the rest of the battalion was no longer behind it. The Hasty Ps had become broken into three groups, with 'C' Company having strayed off on a different goat track, and the rest of the battalion losing its way on yet another. Whether any were headed towards Valguarnera, nobody knew.[19]

Sometime later, 'A' Company, groping its way along a track, turned a corner and bumped head-on into 'C' Company. Campbell and 'C' Company's Captain "Rolly" Cleworth spent several minutes sorting the men into a single formation, and then they descended a steep slope in the pre-dawn light. At the bottom of the hill lay a paved road, but Campbell and Cleworth were unable to orient it with anything similar on their maps. On the opposite side of the road was a dome-shaped hill with stone-terraced slopes that would provide good fighting positions. The two companies darted by platoons across the road and scrambled up the hill, only to find it occupied by about a hundred Sicilian refugees. Travelling with 'A' Company was Lieutenant Pat D'Amore, an Italian-speaking British intelligence officer. He learned that the Hasty Ps were only a mile from Valguarnera but were unable to see it because of an intervening ridge. The refugees also said the town was teeming with Germans. The road below was the main lateral highway running from Valguarnera to Catania and a major route for German traffic.[20]

Campbell and Cleworth kicked this information around for a few minutes. On one hand, they were within striking distance of the objective. On the other, they had lost contact with the rest of the battalion and the small-pack wireless sets were proving useless in this mountainous country. Unable to contact anyone, the two companies were effectively cut off inside enemy territory. Without supporting arms, the two officers decided an attack on Valguarnera would be "unwise." If they heard the rest of the battalion engaged in a fight, the two companies would then move towards the sounds. In the meantime, they decided to dig in on the hill and await developments.[21]

The plan to passively wait on events did not sit well with either company commander, and at about 0600 hours they asked for volunteers to go back and report their situation to the battalion's rear headquarters. Regimental Sergeant Major (RSM) Angus Duffy, who had ended up attached to 'C' Company during the night's wanderings, and Company Sergeant Major (CSM) George Ponsford volunteered to make the eight-mile return trek. Armed with one of the questionable maps, they headed off. Pushing hard, the two men made the journey in just three hours and found Tweedsmuir there with all the battalion's motorized vehicles—the track they had been going to use having also proved impassable. After learning that Tweedsmuir knew nothing of the other companies and, in the absence of wireless communication, could not support the infantry, Duffy and Ponsford loaded packs with all the ammunition they could carry and headed back.[22]

On the hill, 'A' and 'C' companies had still been digging in when six trucks, each loaded with about twenty to thirty Panzer Grenadiers, came along the road below their position. The Hasty Ps could see that most of the Germans were literally napping and from a range of about one hundred yards unleashed a torrent of rifle and Bren-gun fire. Captain Campbell—considered odd at the time by the rest of the Hasty Ps because he expressed an intense hatred for anything and anybody German—grabbed a Bren gun and powered his large body down the slope, firing from the hip. Clenched in his teeth was a spare Bren magazine, around which he roared incomprehensible demands at the Germans.[23] One truck still had most of its complement in the back and Campbell raked it with fire, personally killing eighteen Panzer Grenadiers.[24]

The carnage was unlike anything the Hasty Ps had ever witnessed. Lieutenant Farley Mowat was horrified to see badly wounded Germans sprawled around the trucks or hanging out of open doors and off the sides. A German medical orderly wandered about in plain view checking the men, but he seemed to lack any first-aid supplies and could do nothing for them. Neither could the Canadians, for they had little in the way of medical kits beyond what was needed to treat their own wounded.

One German's plight particularly haunted Mowat: a truck driver, draped over his steering wheel, coughing up foaming blood from a lung shot that gushed through the splintered cracks in the windshield his face pressed against. Each bloody cough was accompanied by a sucking heave and then a hissing expulsion, as the man tried desperately to clear his lungs of the blood relentlessly drowning him.[25]

The ambush had stirred up a hornet's nest. Although the convoy was decimated, with between eighty and ninety Germans killed and eighteen taken prisoner, what soon appeared to be an entire battalion of Panzer Grenadiers stormed towards their hill from Valguarnera. Heavy mortars behind the intervening ridge supported the attack, relentlessly hammering the exposed hilltop. The first German rush was thrown back with heavy casualties inflicted, but there was nothing that could be done about the mortar fire. At 1400 hours, with ammunition draining rapidly away, Campbell and Cleworth decided it was fight their way out or be overrun. Some of the more seriously wounded men were secreted away in a Sicilian peasant's nearby shack, while litters were prepared for several others deemed strong enough to survive being carried eight miles or more cross-country.[26]

'A' Company left first, Cleworth's men putting out a heavy fire to prevent the Germans realizing a withdrawal was under way. When 'A' Company was established in a position from which it could provide covering fire, 'C' Company leapfrogged through to where it could set up a similar position. The process was then repeated until the two companies broke contact with the Germans. Wearily the men marched back towards Highway 117.[27]

During the withdrawal, Captain N.R. Waugh of 'C' Company had spotted a wounded Canadian down the side of a ravine. Accompanied by a private, Waugh scrambled down the slope under fire, and the two soldiers carried the man back to safety. Waugh's valour in this and other incidents during the course of July 18 earned a Military Cross.[28]

Some hours after the two companies had made their getaway, RSM Duffy and CSM Ponsford slipped up to the hilltop and found it abandoned. The refugees offered the two men a little food, but seeing how little they had the sergeants refused. Ponsford saw some Germans approaching and shouted at Duffy that he was going to engage them. A bloody mad idea, Duffy realized, and ordered a fast withdrawal into the cover of a large cactus stand. From there the two men headed back to Highway 117—their fifth trip in one or the other direction, for a total of forty miles of hiking clocked in less than twenty-four hours.[29]

Dawn on July 18 had meanwhile found the rest of the battalion on a hill about a mile south of Valguarnera, looking down on the main road running to the village from the junction that 3 CIB's Van Doos had been trying to win. Lieutenant Colonel Sutcliffe and the commanders of 'B' and 'D' companies faced the same frustration of lacking supporting arms to back an attack on the village. When Sutcliffe decided to test the waters by sending 'B' Company forward, immediate strong resistance forced a quick retreat up a hill to the left of 'D' Company. From this position, it could provide covering fire for 'D' Company, which Sutcliffe positioned alongside the road to ambush any vehicles using it.[30]

They had been lying in wait only a short time when a dozen-strong convoy approached from Valguarnera. The lead vehicle was a half-track armoured personnel carrier towing an 88-millimetre anti-tank gun. A well-placed PIAT bomb ignited 88-millimetre munitions aboard and the half-track exploded, killing all the Germans aboard and consuming the towed gun. The rest of the convoy frantically turned about and withdrew under heavy small-arms fire from 'D' Company. Hoping to confuse the Germans into thinking his was a larger, better armed force than was the case, Sutcliffe led one platoon in a push towards Valguarnera, but was soon driven back by a hail of fire from the village. It also became clear that the convoy, rather than being in full flight, had only withdrawn a safe distance to unload a full company of Panzer Grenadiers. Methodically, these troops began closing on the 'D' Company platoon on the left flank. Although 'D' Company was deployed in a half-moon arc to face potential attacks from any of three fronts, the advancing Germans enjoyed numerical superiority, and 'B' Company was unable to bring fire onto them from its hilltop position. At noon, Sutcliffe realized the game was up. Ammunition was running low and the Germans were almost on top of the left-hand platoon. He and 'D' Company's Major Bert Kennedy

222 / OPERATION HUSKY

decided to "withdraw into the hills." Because extracting the platoons as a unit was impossible due to the closeness of the enemy, Sutcliffe ordered each platoon commander to break clear independently and return by whatever route he wanted to the battalion's cross-country start point on Highway 117.[31] Sutcliffe had displayed cool-headed leadership and taken a "very active part in the fighting through the day," also pausing at one point while under heavy fire to dress the wounds of a seriously wounded soldier and carry him to safety. His conduct garnered a Distinguished Service Order.[32]

'D' Company's breakout was anything but smoothly executed. Platoons ended up fragmented into small groups, each out of touch with the rest. One section found itself on the wrong side of the road when the Germans moved into the abandoned position. Their ammunition exhausted, the men scrabbled into a culvert. Here they remained for twelve hours with German trucks and tanks rumbling overhead at regular intervals. With nightfall, they managed to get clear.

Lieutenant Manley Yearwood ended up alone, except for a German officer he had taken prisoner. Suddenly the German jumped him, and the two men struggled desperately for control of Yearwood's revolver for "long and savage minutes...The German lost, and died where he had fought."[33]

After it had seen 'D' Company off, 'B' Company disengaged. Less hard-pressed by the Germans, the company was able to stick together and moved southwestward towards the supposed line of advance that the Royal Canadian Regiment was to have followed to Valguarnera. It would be fully twenty-four hours before the entire battalion emerged from the hills by dribs and drabs onto Highway 117. During this time, speculation ran that casualties were extreme, and it was feared up to sixty men—including Lieutenant Colonel Sutcliffe— had been lost. But by the end of the day on July 19, the majority straggled into the lines. Sutcliffe was among the last to appear. Total casualties were finally determined at four men killed, three captured, and fifteen wounded. In exchange, the Hasty Ps confirmed they had killed about one hundred enemy and more likely twice that number, wounded at least another hundred, destroyed fourteen vehicles and guns, and brought back twenty prisoners. More importantly, they seriously disrupted attempts by 15th Panzer Grenadier Division to reinforce the Germans engaging 3 CIB at Portella Grottacalda.[34]

THE ROYAL CANADIAN Regiment had also played a part in 1 CIB's blocking of enemy reinforcements. Carried on trucks from Piazza Armerina to a rough side road running north from a position just behind the embattled Royal 22e Régiment, the RCR companies had dismounted at 0100 hours on July 18. As had been the case for the Hastings and Prince Edward Regiment to their right, the track proved too rough for use by carriers or the tank carrying their artillery FOO. An attempt to bring up the carrier with the battalion's 3-inch mortars resulted in its overturning into a gully. The wireless sets failed to raise a signal in the mountainous countryside, and Lieutenant Colonel Ralph Crowe led the troops forward with no more support than Sutcliffe had enjoyed.[35]

Hearing intense gunfire from the Van Doos' position, Crowe thought it likely the Germans were putting their main effort into holding the Highway 117–Valguarnera road junction. If true, his battalion stood a good chance of slipping through to Valguarnera by following a ridgeline that paralleled the road. Crowe also hoped to link up with the Hasty Ps to the south of the town around dawn, so the two battalions could attack together. He could not, however, hear any sounds of fighting from the direction where the "Plough Jockeys," as they were nicknamed, were supposedly located. Nor was he able to establish any wireless contact with Sutcliffe.[36]

Like most plans in war, Crowe's fell into trouble a few yards beyond the start line. Germans there were in plenty, and the RCR worked its way through the wild country in a pitch blackness cut only by the darting flash of tracer rounds, which helped the German machine guns range on the Canadians from their positions on rocky outcrops. Snipers also worked from the flanks, firing a couple of shots before slipping away to another hide. This resistance inflicted only a few minor casualties, but each position had to be assailed in turn by platoons closing on it with fire and manoeuvre tactics that ate away the minutes. Invariably, when the platoon gained the position, they found nothing but spent cartridges. Soon another MG 42 machine gun, or just as likely the same one, started firing on the column from another position and the process started anew.

Still, the RCR were able to keep pushing forward against this harassing fire and by 0800 hours were on a ridge a mile and a half southwest of, and overlooking, Valguarnera. Just before reaching the overlook, Crowe had passed 'A' and 'B' companies through to the front. At the head of 'B' Company, Captain Strome Galloway was crawling along the crest of the ridge to gain a vantage within some scrubby undergrowth from which he could examine the town. His batman, Private Harry Armitage, was right behind. Since landing on the beach, Galloway had realized the awkwardness a company commander faced trying to pack a Thompson submachine gun and its ammunition plus his map case and binoculars. So he had Armitage dump his rifle and gave him the Thompson. Over the ensuing days, the captain had trained Armitage to be his bodyguard—there to protect him from the enemy and leave Galloway free to study his maps or the ground ahead. It seemed a good arrangement, the batman taking to his protective duties with a keen interest. As was his wont, Galloway wore his army cap that morning rather than a helmet. When he had put it on before the RCR started its move forward, Galloway had noted with satisfaction how Armitage had shone his "cap badge until it glittered like the Star of the East." That was typical Armitage, meticulous about spit and polish even when the battalion was operating in the dust of Sicily.

Parting some brush, Galloway peered into the valley towards the town. He could feel Armitage's breath on the back of his head as the man pressed close to also get a look. Suddenly the batman jerked, let out a loud gurgle, and began gasping for breath. Galloway spun around to see blood spewing from Armitage's throat and realized a sniper round had struck him. The battalion's medical officer, Captain Jake Heller, came running up. He "dropped beside the wounded Armitage and applied his skilled fingers to the gushing throat. He bound it with a first field dressing, but it was only his skill and speedy response, despite the bullets now whizzing about, that saved Armitage's life. My poor batman, unable to speak, looked at me with the eyes of a dying stag." Some weeks later, Galloway received a letter from Armitage advising that he had indeed survived.[37]

Galloway had no time to dwell on Armitage's fate, for within ten minutes he had completed organizing Company 'B' and was leading it into the attack behind 'A' Company. As he moved into position, Galloway caught the eye of Major Billy Pope, the battalion second-in-command. Pope "was wearing a beret and had a tommy-gun slung over his shoulder. With his flashing smile and his bare knees he looked awfully young."[38]

Captain Slim Liddell was at the head of 'A' Company, which "deployed like an exercise in section leading, walking down the forward slope...with the enemy M.G.s supplemented by a couple mortars, kicking up the dirt around them. A few yards in their rear came the leading platoons of 'B' [Company], and in between, eager to keep the action rolling, walked Lieutenant Colonel Crowe, his signaler [Private A.J.] Wiper, and Lieutenant J.B. Hunt [battalion intelligence officer]."[39]

Galloway watched with admiration as Liddell and his men maintained perfect battle formation while pushing through tall grass and over rocky obstructions, even as mortar rounds hunted them. Then Liddell drew his men over to the right, creating a preplanned space for 'B' Company to come up on his left so that they would move towards the enemy side by side. Galloway lunged out ahead of his men, realizing as he did so that by carrying a walking stick and wearing a forage cap with a gleaming badge—which, he suspected, had reflected sunlight and drawn the sniper's attention to him back where Armitage had been shot—he presented not only a romanticized figure of an officer from the Great War but also a perfect target. Yet the fusillade of small-arms fire that tore into the company missed Galloway entirely, cutting down four of his platoon section commanders instead. One took a bullet in the foot, another a round through the shoulder, and the other two went down with bullet wounds Galloway was unable to see. Private W.J. Huff also fell, a bullet having drilled directly into an eye. Although none were fatal wounds, the fact that all five men had been knocked down in seconds was shocking.

Yet the company never faltered—instead, the men charged forward. Private H.R. Dolson, who looked to Galloway to be all of fourteen despite having been overseas since 1939, "tore down the slope swearing and wrestling with his Bren gun which had suddenly had a stoppage. So fast did we sweep across the low valley, now burning as a result of the Jerry mortar bombs, that in no time we were up on 'A' Company's right flank and engaging the enemy with rifle and Bren. Pte. Kamalznuck lay a burst from his Bren into a group of the enemy dispersing those who remained standing. Cuthbertson, my company-quartermaster-sergeant, got in some rapid fire with his rifle, for Company HQ dashed forward in the same assault wave as the fighting platoons. Leaping into tracked vehicles, the Germans drove off in speedy retreat. We had driven them from the field, but as our reward had only the prospect of further pursuit."[40]

The RCR was now within a half-mile of the town and had gained two small knolls that provided good cover and firing positions. They started digging in, Crowe expecting to be counterattacked at any moment. During the advance, the RCR had come upon a section of men from the Hasty Ps in 'D' Company that had been hiding out after wandering lost for several hours. The platoon officer commanding this party reported to Crowe that the Plough Jockeys had broken into groups to withdraw to the highway. It was disappointing news, as Crowe had still expected them to come up on his flank for a two-battalion attack. Still unable to establish wireless communication with brigade, he was unable to tee up any reinforcement. Crowe decided that taking the town would have to be entirely an infantry operation and that his task was to gain control of the ground in front of the outskirts. Once this was accomplished, he would somehow establish contact with brigade headquarters to get the other battalions forward in support.

As 'A' and 'B' companies had carried out their charge, which the RCR's war diarist dubbed "a truly amazing sight to see,"[41] Major Billy Pope had spotted a section from the Hasty Ps in 'D' Company pinned down in a draw to the right. With Crowe forward, Pope was chafing at standing idly by in his role as battalion second-in-command—a sort of "always the bridesmaid, never the bride" problem. Here was the perfect opportunity for action. Gathering a section of men from 'C' Company, he led them in a scramble down a virtual cliff to the Hasty Ps' position. Leading the rescued men back to the battalion lines, Pope spotted an enemy blockhouse about three hundred yards away on the southern outskirts of Valguarnera.

Back on the ridge, Pope grabbed a PIAT gun and several bombs. Gesturing for the 'C' Company section to follow, Pope headed for the blockhouse. Crawling to within one hundred feet of the position, Pope struck the blockhouse with two bombs that killed its occupants and severely damaged the structure. While Pope was attacking the block-house, three Mark IV tanks grinded up onto a nearby roadway and started blasting 'A' Company's position with their 75-millimetre main guns and machine guns. Pope went for the tanks, dashing around some houses on the town's southeast edge to get into firing range. He had three PIAT bombs left. Either because in his excitement he forgot to prime the bombs or because the detonators failed (quite common until the PIAT bombs were modified in early 1944), none of the bombs exploded. Out of options, Pope headed towards 'A' Company's position on the knoll. As he led the section across a slightly exposed rise, one of the tanks caught him with a machine-gun burst. The thirty-year-old officer from Victoria fell dead—the RCR's first officer fatality.[42]

By now it was 1400 hours. From Valguarnera came the racket of trucks and tanks on the move, and the RCR observed a long mecha-nized column streaming out of the town's northern exits. It appeared the Germans might be giving the place up, but Crowe was still wary. He scribbled a note explaining that due to a lack of supporting arms, he intended to wait until nightfall before sending a patrol into Val-guarnera. Crowe handed the note solemnly to Rusty Wilkes. The RCR padre had volunteered to carry it back to brigade headquarters with a request for reinforcement. Wilkes made the journey on foot, alone, almost constantly being sniped at by hidden German riflemen try-ing to isolate the RCR. Upon receiving the report, Brigadier Howard Graham quickly ordered his reserve battalion, the 48th Highlanders of Canada, towards Valguarnera from their holding position about two miles south of the town.[43]

The Highlanders had not had an entirely easy time themselves during the morning of July 18, having arrived at the hill to find it occupied by Germans. But they were fortunate to have been able to maintain wireless contact with the artillery regiments and so had the feature shelled. They then charged and took the hill, killing thirty-five Germans and wounding another twenty in the process, at a cost of four dead and six wounded. During this action, Corporal William Frederick Kay led his section of five men from 'D' Company's No. 17 Platoon in a charge against a strong position containing three machine guns manned by seventeen Germans. Although shot in the arm, Kay threw two grenades into the position and then rushed it with his Thompson submachine gun blazing. When the smoke cleared, eight Germans were dead and the others severely wounded prisoners. Kay was awarded the Distinguished Conduct Medal.[44] After nightfall, the Highlanders moved to enter Valguarnera from the right flank and found its streets and buildings abandoned.[45]

About the same time, Lieutenant Colonel Ralph Crowe—with tears in his eyes—was admonishing his RCR officers that Major Billy Pope's death "should never have been; that it was an object lesson for all of us. We were not to expose ourselves needlessly. The Second-in-Command had no business stalking enemy armour and we, the company commanders, had even less business putting ourselves in positions of great danger when our men were supposed to be properly led by the sound application of our tactical training and by accepted techniques of command and control." As he summed up Crowe's comments, Captain Strome Galloway had to acknowledge their sense.[46]

It also occurred to Galloway that the regiment now had only one major, meaning two such ranking slots were open. Crowe had previously held off promoting either Galloway or Captain Slim Liddell to the third opening until he could compare their combat performance. Now there was opportunity for both men to be promoted, and the awkward competition between two friends to be put to an end. But Crowe said nothing about this, which failed to surprise Galloway. To do so immediately after Pope's death would have been poor form. Instead, Crowe drew hard on a cigarette and told Major Pappy Powers that he was now the battalion's second-in-command. Captain Charles "Chuck" Lithgow would take over 'D' company. "Stay well back," Crowe cautioned Powers. "I can't afford to lose you too."[47]

13

Mountain Boys

WHILE IST CANADIAN Infantry Brigade had been striving to take pressure off 3rd Canadian Infantry Brigade's Royal 22e Régiment by seizing Valguarnera in a cross-country flanking movement, Major General Guy Simonds had set in motion a major set-piece attack to break the German grip on Portella Grottacalda and the Highway 117 junction. Just after dawn on July 18, 3 CIB's Brigadier Howard Penhale ordered Lieutenant Colonel Paul Bernatchez to hold his Van Doos at the entrance to Portella Grottacalda so the Germans would continue concentrating on blocking their advance. Penhale hoped this would distract attention away from the Carleton and York Regiment, which he had Lieutenant Colonel Dodd Tweedie send over the hills right of the pass to cut the road running to Valguarnera, just north of its junction with Highway 117.[1] Given the German ferocity to this point and reports that I CIB was meeting stiff resistance north of his brigade, Penhale's plan seemed unlikely to succeed. But as the action had been unfolding, Penhale demonstrated growing uncertainty over what to do, and his orders became less articulate. Without guidance from above, Penhale was floundering.[2]

On the move shortly after 0700 hours, the Carletons reported that Germans were right of their line of advance, and about twenty-five minutes later, that they could hear tank engines nearby.[3] The advance slowed, before stalling entirely at 0900 due to "fierce enemy fire."[4]

Almost precisely to the minute that Tweedie was reporting to Penhale that his troops were blocked, Simonds and Brigadier Bruce Matthews, the division's artillery commander, walked into 3 CIB headquarters. After Penhale briefed them, Simonds improved on his plan. Rather then keep any battalion in reserve as per conventional tactical wisdom, Simonds ordered the West Nova Scotia Regiment moved out from its position on the road behind the Van Doos in a wide left hook around the western flank of Monte della Forma to cut Highway 117 behind the Germans. With 1 CIB driving towards Valguarnera, Simonds hoped to trap the enemy defending Portella Grottacalda by preventing their retreat either to the north or west to Enna.[5]

While Penhale set the West Novas in motion, Simonds and Matthews worked up an artillery program to support 3 CIB's assault with every divisional gun other than those of the Royal Devon Yeomanry, whose self-propelled guns were standing by to support 1 CIB if and when communication with its two advancing battalions was restored. By 0930 hours, Matthews had two fire plans, with the first to begin at 1200 hours and the second at 1305.[6] The fire plans would saturate four selected targets around the pass with concentrated fire from four artillery regiments—the 1st Canadian Field Regiment (Royal Canadian Horse Artillery), 2nd Canadian Field Regiment, 3rd Canadian Field Regiment, and 7th Medium Regiment, Royal Artillery—at sixty-eight rounds per gun.[7] Three field regiments having a total of seventy-two 25-pound guns and the medium regiment's sixteen 5.5-inch guns meant the Canadian gunners would throw 5,984 shells out in the largest gunnery operation they had ever fired.

While Simonds and Matthews returned to divisional headquarters to ready the artillery, the West Novas started out with a one-and-a-half-mile withdrawal back along the road. From here, at 1030 hours, they advanced cross-country due west, heading for about two miles to where a small riverbed followed a northerly course between two high hills and then crossed Highway 117. Although the streambed was dry, the descent into it was too steep for the carriers to negotiate.[8] Dismounting, Lieutenant Reginald Warren Bullock had his 3-inch mortar section break the heavy, bulky tubes down and follow the rifle companies on foot.[9] Although the carriers were unable to negotiate the streambed, a troop of Shermans from Three Rivers Regiment's 'B' Squadron managed to keep pace.[10] The West Novas' commander, Lieutenant Colonel Pat Bogert, expected any moment to bump a German defensive line. But the only opposition met, as one hour ground into the next, was the blazing sun that transformed the hard-baked clay of the valley into a veritable oven. The men also had to hack their way through thick stands of bamboo.[11] At noon, the West Novas looked eastward as the Canadian guns thundered and shells began exploding on the imposing height of Monte della Forma.

Manning one of the Royal Canadian Horse Artillery guns was twenty-three-year-old Gunner Henry Worrell. Stripped to the waist like all the other gunners, he wore only shorts and boots. Each time the 25-pounder roared, it kicked up a blinding, suffocating cloud of dust. The gun shook violently with each shot because the searing heat interfered with the recoil mechanism. He worried that the gun was going to shake itself to pieces if they kept firing at such a rapid rate.[12]

A short way behind the Van Doos, Canadian Press war correspondent Ross Munro had been watching as the gunners fired occasional shots to range in on the concentration points selected for the bombardment. Then, suddenly, "they hit out furiously...[Monte della Forma] to the west of the fork was plastered with shell bursts...I see a grey forest of trees growing suddenly and magically before my eyes. As a shell hits the brown earth, the grey smoke billows up like a full-blown tree sprouting from the soil. There were half a dozen at first, well scattered, and then twenty, fifty, one hundred or more, crowding each other for space. The hillside was covered with the grey forest and then the smoke drifted and merged into a dirty, grey curtain over the brown hillside.

"You heard the grumble of the guns miles behind and the swish and whine of the shells overhead like a long train going through a tunnel. There wasn't much commotion on the hill-side target. Twenty-five-pounder shells dig only a shallow crater, usually just a scoop in the ground about five inches deep, with the blast spreading for fifty yards or more around.

"The smoky hill flickered with bursts of shells, but the bursts did not seem large. They just sparked and were followed by more sparks."[13] From his vantage, Munro could see the Carletons going up a shell-blasted hill towards the Germans—the battalion's 'B' and 'C' companies advancing side by side.[14] The riflemen had bayonets fixed, while those men with Thompson submachine guns or Bren guns snapped off bursts from the hip. Then the entire battalion disappeared into the smoke and dust thrown up by the artillery. He lay alongside the road listening to the sheet-ripping sound of the German MG 42 machine guns and the slower, harder thump of the Bren guns' return fire. It seemed to go on interminably, hours dragging by. Late in the afternoon, Munro recognized Canadians closing on German positions, "little clusters of men in khaki moving cautiously forward and then running and falling flat as they took cover. Some men were hit and fell and didn't move.

"The others couldn't stop, and kept going, firing, dodging, creeping, sweating forward. Stretcher-bearers, with their Red Cross arm-bands standing out clearly, reached the falling men and bound them up or left them dead on the brown, scorched earth."[15] One of the men charging up the hill was Private Maurice Brisson of 'D' Company. With two other Carletons, he stormed a machine gun. When the other two were killed by a long burst of fire, Brisson worked around the position to attack it from the rear. Shooting two of the gun crew dead, he battered the life from the third with his rifle butt. Brisson was awarded the Distinguished Conduct Medal.[16]

As he gained the crest of the hill, twenty-five-year-old Lieutenant Joseph Beverley Starr of Wolfville, Nova Scotia, was killed while throwing a grenade at a German position. Nearby, Captain Thomas Southall raised binoculars to his eyes only to have a bullet split them in two and penetrate his forehead. The twenty-nine-year-old Ottawa native fell dead.[17]

By 1600 hours it was over. The West Novas, having encountered en route only a single machine-gun position, which was easily eliminated, ensconced themselves on a hilltop dominating Highway 117 west of Portella Grottacalda and the junction. In their drive north of the pass, the Carletons had cut the road to Valguarnera and won a hill to the west. As the Carletons closed in on the road, the Panzer

Grenadiers flooded up it to escape the closing trap. The battalion suffered forty-six casualties in the sharp battle, with two officers and nine other ranks killed.[18]

After fourteen hours of continuous action, the Van Doos were surprised when the enemy broke off the engagement. They moved through the pass unobstructed and reported the junction in hand at 1700 hours. During the artillery barrage, some rounds had fallen short, but only two or three men had been wounded. In the protracted fight, however, they had suffered thirty-one casualties, seven of which were fatal.[19]

The battles waged around Valguarnera and Portella Grottacalda between the night of July 17–18 and the following evening had largely involved battalions fighting individually with little or no artillery or tank support. Yet the Canadians had prevailed and inflicted heavy losses on the Germans, who fought from well-camouflaged and strong defensive positions. While the two battalions of 104th Panzer Grenadier Regiment had managed to hold up two Canadian brigades for twenty-four hours, they did so at the cost of about five hundred officers and men either taken prisoner or killed. Total Canadian casualties were set at 145, of which forty were fatal.[20]

"At Valguarnera I succeeded in enveloping and cutting off their rearguard," Simonds boasted to First Canadian Army's commander Lieutenant General Andrew McNaughton on July 30. "The slaughter was terrific and only remnants got away."[21] While overstating results, Simonds could draw satisfaction from his division's performance.

In his daily report to Berlin, Generalfeldmarschall Albert Kesselring wrote on July 20: "Near Valguarnera troops trained for fighting in the mountains have been mentioned. They are called 'Mountain Boys' [by the Panzer Grenadiers] and probably belong to the 1st Canadian Division."[22] It was high praise for the Canadians, whose only real mountain warfare training had consisted of about eight days climbing cliffs at Sussex by the Sea.

MAJOR GENERAL GUY Simonds knew his Canadians were now entering Sicily's mountainous heart. General Harold Alexander had once again adjusted Eighth Army's boundary with that of the U.S. Seventh Army. "It was now clear," he wrote, "that Eighth Army would not have the strength to encircle Etna on both sides against the stout resistance of the Germans. The Canadians were therefore ordered to advance on Leonforte and then turn east to Adrano."[23] This meant the division was to immediately dogleg north at the Highway 117 junction onto the road leading to Valguarnera and abandon the drive towards Enna, despite his earlier July 13 decision to shift the capture of this town from the Americans to the Canadians.[24] Although intending that responsibility for securing Enna was now being returned to the Americans, these instructions reached neither General George Patton nor General Omar Bradley. This may well have been an oversight on Alexander's part, or some nefarious sleight of hand on the part of Patton's chief of staff, Brigadier Hobart R. Gay.

On the morning of July 19, Alexander cabled Patton with clarifying instructions for Seventh Army's northward advance. Instead of driving for Palermo—as Patton understood he had been authorized to do during the July 17 meeting in Tunis—Seventh Army would first advance directly north from its current positions in the centre of the island to cut Sicily in half and cover the left flank of Eighth Army. Only when it had gained the northern coast about thirty miles east of Palermo should Patton move against the city. Realizing the cable would scupper Patton's intentions, Gay passed only the first part of the message—which ordered the 1st Division of II Corps to lead the push to the north coast—to Bradley and hid the rest in his desk. Next, Gay signalled Alexander's headquarters that the message had been garbled and would need to be retransmitted.[25]

Bradley, already unhappy that his corps was to carry out the task Alexander had previously assigned the entire Seventh Army, exploded into fury when he learned that Eighth Army was constricting its line of advance east of Enna. In a signal to xxx Corps commander Lieutenant General Oliver Leese, Bradley growled: "I have just learned that you have side-slipped Enna, leaving my flank exposed. Accordingly we are taking Enna at once, even though it is in your sector. I assume we have the right to use any of your roads for this attack."[26] The claim on roads was a belated retort against Alexander's earlier decision to give exclusive use of Highway 124 to the Canadians.

Anxious to prevent the divide between the American and British commands from widening further, Leese hurriedly apologized and sent Bradley a peace offering of two bottles of Scotch. He felt shame-faced that, no matter what instructions had emanated from Alexander regarding this, his corps staff had neglected to ensure that the Americans realized Enna was being bypassed.[27]

In reality, it was of little import. Although Enna had served as Sixth Army headquarters and was an ancient fortress that would challenge any besieger, 15th Panzer Grenadier Division commander Generalmajor Eberhard Rodt had decided against making a stand. With Valguarnera lost and the Canadians set to advance on Leon-forte, any German forces in Enna risked being cut off. To prevent this, Rodt shifted his division northeastward to the area extending from Leonforte to the south and north to Nicosia. Rodt's intention was to delay xxx Corps as long as possible, without risking serious casualties.[28] On the night of July 18–19, the Canadians heard a mas-sive explosion from Enna, and intelligence officers surmised correctly that the Germans were destroying munition dumps as part of a withdrawal.[29]

On July 19, realizing that Enna no longer posed a threat and that the Germans were falling back across his front in an eastward with-drawal, Major General Guy Simonds decided to concentrate his strength to the north. The only force assigned to cover his left flank was the division's reconnaissance regiment—the Princess Louise Dragoon Guards—which he directed to take up watching positions a few miles east of the town.[30]

By hooking hard right while still short of Enna, Simonds was able to use two roads that cut through the Dittaino River valley to the north of Valguarnera for the next advance. One ran almost due north of Val-guarnera to intersect Highway 121—the main Palermo–Catania highway—next to the Dittaino River. From the valley floor, this high-way wound through the hills to Leonforte. Simonds assigned this route to 2nd Canadian Infantry Brigade, ordering it to move on the night of July 18–19 via the just-opened Portella Grottacalda to the Highway 117 junction, then north to Valguarnera and on to Leonforte. The other road, which would be used by 1st Canadian Infantry Brigade, angled in a northeasterly descent into the valley to Dittaino Station, a railway stop on the Catania–Enna line that bordered the river. From the station, the road turned northward and climbed to the town of Assoro, which lay a short distance to the east of Leonforte. Just beyond the latter town, the road converged with Highway 121. Here Simonds envisioned the two brigades would link up. Having gained the highway, the division would then advance in line with one brigade forward through Nissoria to Agira. At Agira, the Canadians would be met by the 231st (Malta) Brigade.

On July 17, this British brigade had moved independently between 1st Canadian Infantry Division and the 51st Highland Division. The brigade had made good progress, capturing Raddusa—eight miles east of Valguarnera—the following day and gaining the Dittaino River early on July 19. They had then quickly advanced to within three miles of Agira. In the course of their two-day drive, the brigade had rounded up more than one thousand prisoners—mostly Italians from the collapsed Livorno Division—and faced only relatively light resistance. As the brigade was headed for a juncture with the Canadians, General Bernard Montgomery placed it under Simonds's command on the morning of July 19. Simonds immediately ordered Brigadier Robert Urquhart to hold his troops in place until Leonforte and Assoro were won. Intelligence reports indicated that the Germans had transformed Agira into a stronghold, so Simonds planned to attack it simultaneously from two flanks. His expectation was that his two-brigade advance on Leonforte and Assoro would quickly gain these two towns and that Agira's capture would rapidly follow.[31]

In making his plans, Simonds was conforming to those set out by Montgomery just a few hours earlier. Forced to admit that 50th Division's advance towards Catania had been blocked, Montgomery decided he must focus on the western flank. The 5th Division from XIII Corps was instructed to advance towards Misterbianco, while XXX Corps's 51st Division drove towards Paterno. Both these towns lay on Highway 121, close to the southern flank of Mount Etna, with Paterno situated roughly midway between Adrano to the west and Catania to the east. Once Eighth Army had virtually all of Highway 121 in hand, it would be poised to send divisions around the western flank of the volcano to threaten the rear of the Germans holding Catania, while simultaneously advancing directly east towards the city via the highway.[32]

NEAR PIAZZA ARMERINA, Brigadier Chris Vokes started 2 CIB marching at 2230 hours on July 18. The Seaforth Highlanders led with the brigade's support group immediately behind and brigade headquarters in trail. A little farther back were the Princess Patricia's Canadian Light Infantry and the Loyal Edmonton Regiment.[33] All went well until, in the early morning hours of July 19, the brigade came to a bridge a half-mile south of Valguarnera and found it blown. Leaving their motorized transport behind, the infantry yet again marched forward, while a call went back for engineers to bring up a bulldozer and create a crossing.

Carriers stranded, the Seaforth's 3-inch mortar platoon watched forlornly as the infantry disappeared. The march assumed the all-too-familiar character of past Sicilian advances. While the temperature was less than the 100 degrees Fahrenheit normal for July days, the heat remained oppressive. Weary men quickly lost whatever renewal of energy the brief interlude in reserve had yielded. They slogged through the thick, white dust that lay several inches deep upon the roads. Private Richard Latimer noted that nobody spoke. All seemed focussed purely on putting one foot before the other. Each company adhered to a set ritual whereby the heavier weapons—the 23-pound Bren, 35.3-pound PIAT, and 23.7-pound 2-inch mortar—were passed around, so that every man had a turn. This was in addition to the weight of the almost 9-pound Lee-Enfield most carried and the rest of their battle gear. Each fifty minutes of marching was followed by a ten-minute break. Latimer and the others just flopped down in their tracks on the road. A few lucky men could instantly slip into a deep sleep, but most lay panting. Dysentery was rife, so there was a steady procession of soldiers scurrying a few feet away from the road to drop their pants and relieve themselves before the order came to start marching.[34] More than a few of the afflicted soiled their pants before a halt was called. Anyone who broke ranks, no matter the cause, had to run to catch up with his platoon. Already exhausted, such a sprint could finish a man. Consequently, they tried to resist until the next rest.

At 0430 hours on July 19, the Seaforths trudged into the bleak, dark streets of Valguarnera. 'A' Company was out front, followed by Lieutenant Colonel Bert Hoffmeister and his battalion headquarters, with the other three companies in line behind. The men marched in single file with good spacing between, so that if fired on they would be less hard hit than if they bunched together. Scattered through the town were abandoned German vehicles and corpses that were already putrefying.[35] Padre Roy Durnford was so struck by the town's condition that he could not "believe that squalor was the direct result of war. It bore unmistakable signs of having been there for generations."[36] On the northern outskirts, the Seaforths halted for a rest that lasted until dawn.

With first light the battalion had its inaugural view of the new battleground. Forty miles to the northeast hulked Mount Etna. About six miles northwest, Enna stood on a 3,300-square-foot crag. Between Etna and Enna stretched a chain of hills and low mountains ranging from five hundred feet to three thousand feet. Those closest to Etna were higher, rising in steps until the last shouldered against the volcano. Two rivers—the Dittaino and the Salso—pierced through this rugged country, both coursing roughly west to east within paralleling valleys. Descending from the north, the Troina intersected the Salso to the west of Adrano shortly before that river discharged into the larger Simeto River. None of these rivers—reduced by summer drought to mere trickles connecting shallow pools scattered along their broad, boulder-strewn beds—posed any obstacle to the infantry. But it required engineers to construct crossings for either wheeled or tracked vehicles. On either side of the rivers, their valleys stretched to a width of about a mile.[37] Here Sicilian farmers had planted orchards and grew wheat in small fields, while parched vineyards were scattered across the rocky slopes. Few people lived on the valley floors; instead they dwelt in the mountaintop towns—descending each day to tend their farms and trudging back up the steep hillsides after sunset.[38]

Before them, the Seaforths could see Leonforte atop a nearly two-thousand-foot summit. With its rows of houses set out in ever-narrowing layers as the town closed on the narrow summit, 'B' Company's Corporal Johnnie Cromb thought it resembled "a big wedding cake."[39] Rising like a giant broken tooth to the right of Leonforte was the summit of Assoro, higher by about one thousand feet. The western slope of this mountain was its least precipitous and Assoro village clung to this side, houses bordering steep, narrow streets that switchbacked to within a few hundred feet of the summit. On the summit stood "the fragmentary ruins of a castle built in the twelfth century by Roger ii. The Norman king had chosen his site well, planting his stronghold in what seemed a well nigh impregnable position on the edge of the eastern cliff, which towered a thousand feet above the valley."[40]

Between Leonforte and Assoro, a saddlelike ridge linked the two summits and formed the northern flank of the Dittaino valley. From the two mountaintops and the crest of the ridge, the Germans could fire on the Canadians wherever they tried to cross the valley floor.[41] But before they reached the Dittaino River, 2 CIB had to first descend from Valguarnera by way of a broad saucer-shaped valley through which the road ran to a three-way junction, which was the Seaforth's immediate objective. Although everything seemed peaceful enough, Lieutenant Colonel Hoffmeister looked at the high ground on either side of the road closing on the junction and decided the site was "a natural for an ambush."[42] Instinctively, he ordered the battalion onto the high ground right of the road. Unable to establish wireless communication with 'A' Company's Captain F.W.I. "Bill" Merritt, Hoffmeister sent the battalion's second-in-command, Major Douglas Forin, and his batman ahead to deliver the message on foot. Forin had just reached the tail of the company and sent the message forward by verbal relay when the Germans opened up with heavy machine-gun, mortar, and artillery fire from a ridge on the far side of the valley commanding the road.[43] 'A' Company was pinned down on the slope. Every time Merritt attempted to send men forward, they were driven to ground by machine-gun volleys.

Company Sergeant Major D.R. Penman ordered the men to dig in, but eighteen inches down they hit bedrock. The German mortar rounds lit the stubbly grass on fire. Bursts of machine-gun fire kicked up puffs of dry earth, while the mortar bombs exploded on impact, mixing rocks and other debris in with the deadly shrapnel spray. Most of the men hit at the outset were farthest down the hill and could only be dragged to safer positions by men dangerously exposing themselves.[44] Private J.G. McBride and Lance Corporal R.R. Story never hesitated. A medical orderly, McBride was wounded three times while helping other struck men. Suffering painful burns from phosphorous loosed by an incendiary bomb, Story ignored his own injuries in order to render first aid and drag the wounded to covered positions. Both men were awarded Military Medals.[45]

Penman realized 'A' Company was "actually in it" as they had never been before and he saw no way out. It was about two hundred yards back up the hill to the rest of the battalion, which appeared to have gone to ground on the opposite slope. Later the Seaforths would learn that the best way out of an ambush like this was to charge forward rather than retreat, but "we were green," Penman recalled. "We couldn't tell noises to be such and such a thing, self-propelled or stationary guns... it was a baptism to us. The main thing was self-preservation," and the only hope of that was to hunker down in the shallow slit trench and hope for the storm of fire to pass by.[46]

Although 'A' Company was caught in the open, the entire battalion could have been slaughtered had Hoffmeister not ordered the shift to the right of the road. In doing so, he forced the Germans to trigger their ambush prematurely.[47] "If we'd had the whole battalion stretched out on the road, even moving at tactical intervals, we would have been massacred," he said later.[48] With battalion headquarters, Padre Roy Durnford was struck by the accuracy and fury of the German fire. "Vicious bursts of flame and clouds of dust, dirt and rock flew into the air to the left and right of us... In the not too distant hills we could hear the enemy guns fire and we could count the seconds which elapsed before the shell landed in our gulley. It was an anxious time for us all." With the medical officer, Captain Ken McDonald, Durnford descended into 'A' Company's position to oversee the casualties. "But to the dying [the shellfire] meant nothing. They were calm and bravely faced the end. Some were unconscious, having received morphine earlier from our first aid men. We dug graves out of sun-baked rock and rock-like soil and for hours we sweated over this before the last man was laid down in his blanket."[49]

McDonald was seen running back and forth from 'A' Company's exposed position with medical supplies and tending the wounded on both sides of the ridge. He seemed to be continually "where the fire was hottest to offer immediate aid to the wounded." Although such bravery was typical of the man, for this day's action he was awarded a Military Cross.[50]

While Durnford buried the dead and helped tend the wounded, Hoffmeister frantically tried to extract those still in the fight. The problem was their inability to strike back at the Germans. His 3-inch mortars were well back, the carriers just waddling across the stream-bed via the diversion. Repeated calls for artillery support yielded only the news that all the division's field regiments were out of range and it would be some time before the 7th Medium Regiment's heavier guns could be brought to bear.[51]

In this action, Hoffmeister established a reputation for leading from the front. Dodging through flying shrapnel, he seemed to be everywhere and anywhere—his presence and apparent disregard for the enemy fire helping to steady the Seaforths and prevent a panic that could have resulted in a rout.[52] In an effort to establish personal contact with 'A' Company, Hoffmeister "went forward to see... through the smoke. I was going up one side of a cactus hedge, and could hear tanks not far away, when all of a sudden I came face to face with a German Mark IV tank right out of the smoke. The tank commander was riding with his head out of the turret and he saw me as soon as I saw him. Fortunately the gunner let go with a 75-millimetre round instead of his machinegun...and this...went whizzing past my head. That was all the encouragement I needed to go straight through the cactus hedge, which I did and didn't get a scratch... When I landed on the other side, I was all right, but running in high gear. I nipped up the other side of the hedge and the tank figured he was getting a little too far into our position and turned around and went back again."[53]

Shortly before noon, the 3-inch mortar platoon finally arrived, and its commander, Lieutenant Don Harley, deployed behind battalion headquarters. The men were quickly pumping out rounds. A few minutes later the Saskatoon Light Infantry section ground up aboard its carriers and brought its 4.2-inch mortars into action.[54] When the FOO from 2nd Canadian Field Regiment, who was accompanying the Seaforths, established contact with the gunners of 7th Medium Regiment, they dropped two rounds from each of the sixteen 5.5-inch guns on selected targets in a shoot lasting just a minute.[55] The explosive weight of these shells was seventy-nine pounds, more than three times a field regiment's 25-pounder, and the effect was instantaneous. Within an hour, the Germans broke off the action, and Hoffmeister called for ambulances to come forward to evacuate the casualties. Eighteen 'A' Company men had been killed or wounded, most in the first minutes after the ambush was sprung.[56]

While the Seaforths licked their wounds, the PPCLI passed through their lines after sunset and continued 2 CIB's advance towards Leonforte. But they were not the first Canadians to venture beyond the battalion's lines. At 1730 hours, 2 CIB's Brigade Major Richard S. Malone had gone forward in a carrier to personally reconnoitre the approach to Leonforte. Malone had felt cocky as hell, for at last he was loose on the battlefield rather than stuck back in brigade headquarters while Brigadier Vokes was upfront with the brigade's tactical headquarters team. Earlier that afternoon Vokes had come back for a brief rest and Malone had pleaded to be sent forward. "All right," Vokes said. "Be careful. Take the carrier I got from Howard Graham."[57]

Earlier, 1 CIB's Brigadier Graham had lent Vokes a carrier tricked out with brigade-level wireless sets to stand in for the one 2 CIB had lost at sea. When Malone reached the Seaforths, he never paused to check in with Hoffmeister. Instead, he pressed on to where he looked down upon the Dittaino valley floor and up at Leonforte. Malone saw that a small bridge crossing the river was still intact. A few German shells were landing nearby, otherwise all seemed quiet. If that bridge was taken, Malone realized, the attack on Leonforte could be supported by the anti-tank and mortar platoons of whichever infantry battalion drew the assignment. Realizing he had what the infantry did not—mobility—Malone ordered the carrier driver to run for the bridge. Once he was in control of it, Malone could use the wireless to call for support. At top speed, the carrier lunged forward. About two hundred yards short of the bridge, the carrier rolled over two Teller mines planted in the road and was hurled into the air, as the metal disks, each loaded with about twelve pounds of explosive, erupted under a track. Before Malone lost consciousness he was "aware of hurtling through the air, realizing what had happened and then hitting the ground again with a great force."[58]

Coming to a few minutes later, Malone stared in confusion at "a round object about the size of a football. It was red and wet. With horror, I slowly recognized that it was [a] head...with the scalp and flesh torn off." When Malone tried to move, he found he was unable to do so and wondered sickeningly if his legs were gone. A gingerly probe with one hand "grabbed something wet and sticky. I brought my hand back to look and found I was grasping what looked like raw liver." Confused, Malone thought everyone else aboard had been killed. But the driver had escaped injury because the carrier's floor had been lined with sandbags to dampen the blast of mines. These same bags saved Malone's life, while the wireless operator, forty-three-year-old Corporal Ralph William Devlin of the Royal Canadian Corps of Signals, had been killed outright.[59]

Using his arms, Malone dragged himself into the ditch by the road and fell into a half-conscious stupor. Eventually, a section of Canadians slipped down to the position and rescued the two men. Malone's legs were fine, but his spine had suffered a severe battering and several ribs had been cracked. Evacuated to Tunis, Malone would be sidelined for months. He was grateful to have survived, and took away from the ill-conceived charge on the bridge "confidence in the knowledge that in action I did not panic or become paralysed with fear and was able to handle my job with some intelligence."[60]

While Malone had been lying next to the destroyed carrier, the PPCLI had launched an attack on the hilltop positions from which the Germans had ambushed the Seaforths. 'B' Company had come under light fire as it moved forward along the hill left of the road. Halting in some ground that offered good cover, the company was able to provide supporting fire as the rest of the battalion advanced. 'D' Company led, followed by 'C' Company, and finally 'A' Company.

The expected fight never materialized. The Germans had already melted into the gathering darkness. Posing a graver danger than the Germans were the blazing fires that had spread into the grain fields through which the infantry had advanced. Several men suffered serious burns, including the battalion's intelligence officer, Lieutenant Gordon Smith.[61] "In their hasty withdrawal," the PPCLI war diarist recorded, "the enemy had been forced to leave behind considerable weapons, ammunition and equipment."[62] The battalion dug in on the heights they had won, looking down upon the Dittaino valley and the bridge where Malone had been blown up.

Neither the PPCLI nor the Seaforths recorded their casualties for the day, but the totals returned to brigade headquarters by each led to an overall report of four officers and fifty-nine other ranks either killed or wounded. Most of these were Seaforths. Although 2 CIB had managed to secure the road from Valguarnera to the three-way junction on the southern flank of the Dittaino valley, Simonds was disappointed by the day's gains. He had hoped a quick advance to the outskirts of Leonforte and Assoro would be concluded by the following day, July 20. The fact that the Germans had been able to pin a battalion in place, then pull back at leisure and without significant casualties, was sobering. Possession of the junction—which cut a road running from Enna to Dittaino Station and also closed German use of the Valguarnera–Leonforte road—provided little comfort. Looking across the valley at the threatening heights of Leonforte and Assoro, it was clear the Canadians would face harder fighting ahead.[63]

14

Private Miracles

J UST BEFORE MIDNIGHT on the night of July 19–20, the Loyal
Edmonton Regiment took point on the 2nd Canadian Infantry
Brigade's front and descended into the Dittaino valley. Because of
Brigade Major Malone's encounter with the road mine and other
intelligence reports that "elaborate minefields might be found along
the axis of advance," the battalion went forward with its companies
spread out in an extended line across a wide front. As it happened,
no mines were encountered, and the Edmontons were closing on the
virtually dry streambed by 0445 hours. When 'D' Company slipped
across, they triggered machine-gun fire from four German posts to
the east. While the rest of the battalion moved into cover south of the
streambed, Lieutenant Colonel Jim Jefferson called for artillery fire
on the enemy guns. This was quickly brought to bear and "proved to
be very effective," according to the regiment's war diarist. Once the
German machine guns were silenced, 'B' Company crossed into the
bridgehead and the Eddies settled in with two companies on either
side of the river.[1] They also gained control of the bridge that Malone
had failed to reach.

Dawn found all of 2 CIB dangerously exposed to German artillery
and mortars positioned on the heights of Assoro and neighbouring
hills. While the Edmontons were hidden somewhat in the valley, the

Seaforth Highlanders were stuck in plain view and subjected to intense shelling throughout the morning from these positions. The Princess Patricia's Canadian Light Infantry and brigade headquarters, which had moved up into their area, were "also worried by enemy harassing fire."[2]

Of more concern to Brigadier Chris Vokes was the presence of a mountain, about two miles behind the Edmontons' position, that commanded the forthcoming line of advance. Monte Desira Rossi, as the summit was identified on topographical maps, had not been noticed previously, but now Vokes realized that before he could advance the brigade the five miles from the river to Leonforte, it had to be taken.[3]

Vokes gave the job to the PPCLI, whose scouts returned from a reconnaissance to report that the mountain appeared to be held in strength by the enemy. This news prompted Vokes to postpone any attack to the late afternoon, so that he could put together a set-piece assault with "divisional artillery, a troop of tanks, medium machine guns and mortar detachments in support of the infantry."[4] The division's historical officer, Captain Gus Sesia, was present for the 'O' Group at which Vokes outlined his attack plan to the officers from the various supporting arms and the PPCLI. Off to the right, 1st Canadian Infantry Brigade was already putting in an attack towards Assoro and being "held up by sticky mortar fire. We could see the mortar bombs bursting everywhere in their area from our position and there were numerous grass fires. It must have been proper hell for the men to be lying about in that stuff under the scorching sun."

Turning his attention to Vokes, Sesia was "impressed by the manner in which [he operated.] It was certainly the most informal giving of orders that I have ever witnessed. To begin with, we were all smoking cigarettes and standing on the sky-line and certainly in full view of the enemy's [observation posts]. Vokes would point out to the officer to whom he was giving the orders the target or area which was to be attacked and describe it something like this: 'Now do you see that ridge over there, Bill? Well, that's where I want you to bring up your troops and capture the farmhouse just to the side of it.' Then he would say to the gunner officer: 'Do you see that line of trees there, Joe? Well, just plunk a few on this side of it and then put a few more into that farmhouse over there, and you might as well stick a couple in the left of that clump of bushes for good measure.' I am sure that all his officers were as clear in their instructions as though they had been formally written out. In no case to date has it been the policy of this [Division] to issue written orders and this, I believe, has been General Montgomery's policy since the day he took over at El Alamein."[5]

As the PPCLI was forming on the start line for the attack, it was delayed in pushing off by enemy artillery fire. Soon enough, however, the battalion was on the move, with 'B' and 'D' companies leading and 'A' and 'C' companies close behind in reserve. Commanding 'D' Company, Captain R.W. "Sam" Potts was surprised that apart "from a difficult climb in the heat of the day, the attack was uneventful. We took up positions on the top of the hill and dug in for the night."[6]

The ground was now set for 2 CIB to concentrate on seizing Leonforte, which Vokes planned to do the following day.

About the time Vokes had begun planning the set-piece attack on Monte Desira Rossi, Major General Guy Simonds learned that General Omar Bradley had ordered Major General Terry Allen's U.S. 1st Infantry Division to seize Enna. Allen had sent his 18th Infantry Regiment with tanks from the 70th Light Tank Brigade in support.[7] The Americans were expecting fierce resistance and were anxious to cover the exposed flank created when 1st Canadian Infantry Division had been redirected northward through Valguarnera and towards Leonforte and Assoro.

Seeing the concentration of force the Americans were bringing to bear on Enna, Simonds decided it was time for a little rivalry. Despite Enna being now in the Seventh Army's operational zone, he would see if the Canadians could get there ahead of Allen's troops. Confident that the Germans had already abandoned the town and this move was pure gamesmanship, Simonds merely ordered 'A' Squadron of the Princess Louise Dragoon Guards to "push out patrols toward Enna to endeavour to enter the town before the Americans."[8]

This squadron was the only part of the division's reconnaissance regiment to have been landed in Sicily. The rest of the regiment was not due to deploy until July 27. 'A' Squadron consisted of five officers

and 159 other ranks equipped with mostly Bren carriers and a few
light armoured cars.[9] The squadron commander, Major Duck, decided
his No. 3 Troop would suffice for the task, and its men and four carriers were duly dispatched. The troop's Lieutenant Burkham was
warier than his superiors, so the little party "made its way cautiously
along the road and attained a point about [five and a half] miles from
Enna." Here they bumped into some Sicilians, armed with rifles and
grenades, who started firing at them. Whether these were Fascist
fanatics or merely civilians angry at the Allies for having half-
destroyed Enna during numerous heavy bomber raids, the "Plugs"—as
the Dragoons were nicknamed—had no idea. Wheeling about, the
troop headed back for reinforcements.

En route, one of the carriers threw a track. Back at squadron headquarters, Major Duck ordered Burkham to get on with the assignment.
Crowding into the remaining carriers, the troop went back up the
road. By now the civilians had withdrawn, and the troop advanced to
about four miles from Enna, only to find the road so badly cratered by
demolitions that it was impossible to carry on in the carriers.

When Burkham contacted Duck by wireless, he was told to advance
a small foot patrol to Enna. Four men, Sergeant Taylor, Corporal Jackson, Corporal Murphy, and Trooper McAllister, were detailed to the
task. It was uphill all the way, following a road with one hairpin turn
after another. After about a mile and a half of trudging along in the
sweltering heat, the dragoons—used to riding in carriers or armoured
cars—"got browned off and commandeered a donkey to carry them
in turns. A pretty sight they were, a patrol led by a man on a donkey
to capture Enna for the Canadians."

Ninety minutes later, the little party "came to the outskirts of the
town and lo and behold, saw two truckloads of troops just going [in].
Were they Yanks or Germans? That was the question. They were a
very, very thankful patrol indeed when the Germans turned out to
be Yanks who had just arrived at the edge of the town." Releasing the
donkey, the patrol hitched a ride in a Jeep and in this manner rode
triumphant into Enna as part of the American vanguard. "Who took
the town?" one dragoon asked in a report. "Who knows? Actually I
think Corporal Jackson was the first out of the Jeep when it arrived at

the town square and to him should go the honour of the capture of Enna by Canadians...The hard work of the patrol was rewarded by some vino par excellence which made the 4-1/2 mile walk back to the squadron much easier."[10]

When word of Enna's liberation reached BBC correspondents, they broadcast reports that the Canadians alone had taken the town, although it was unclear whether they knew anything about the role the four dragoons had played or were inventing details. The reports incensed the Americans right up the entire command chain to Supreme Commander, Allied Expeditionary Force, General Dwight D. Eisenhower, who fired off an angry letter to Prime Minister Winston Churchill demanding the record be set straight.[11]

"We took Enna," Patton wrote in his diary. "The Canadians came in from the east eight minutes later...I sent a dispatch to General Alexander saying that we [both] arrived at the same time. I will bet they claim to have got there first."[12] Bradley saw the BBC reports as part of a British media pattern that "credited Monty with all the hard fighting while we were depicted as 'eating grapes' and 'swimming.' Since BBC broadcasts were our main source of outside news on Sicily, our men were naturally infuriated."[13]

The Canadian division's general staff war diarist summarized with a trace of amusement the major plan that Allen's 1st U.S. Division had put together, which he believed entailed two infantry regiments attacking on two flanks. "From what could be observed it was a tie with perhaps our patrol getting the edge," he observed. "In any case the credit went to the Americans."[14]

WHILE THE CONQUEST of Enna had been under way and 2 CIB had been simultaneously dealing with Monte Desira Rossi, 1st Canadian Infantry Brigade had moved into the valley on the road that descended to Dittaino Station and then hooked northwestward to Assoro. The 48th Highlanders of Canada led. As the Loyal Eddies had done, the Highlanders descended in an extended line because of the danger of mines. But again none were encountered, and the battalion was soon enjoying nothing more than a fast walk under a hot sun. "Met with no opposition whatever for ten miles," the regiment's war diarist gloated as the Highlanders held up at Dittaino Station and let the Royal Canadian Regiment take the lead.[15]

It was high noon when Captain Slim Liddell's 'A' Company and Captain Strome Galloway's 'B' Company crossed the Dittaino next to the train station. Their orders were to seize two low foothills either side of the road leading to Assoro.[16] Coming up the road behind the infantry were the Shermans of the Three Rivers Regiment's 'C' Squadron. Shortly before the Highlanders had reached the railway station, Allied fighter bombers had attacked a line of boxcars standing on the tracks. As his Sherman rolled past the station, Lieutenant Jack Wallace realized the boxcars had been loaded with ammunition.[17] There was also some kind of factory beside the tracks that had been bombed and was still smouldering. Burning grass added to the pungent smoke emanating from the boxcars and factory. The entire valley floor seemed to have burned off or was still being licked by flames.[18] The boxcars were on "fire and making a hell of a racket." Clanking along behind the infantry, Wallace had to constantly warn the driver of obstacles because the terrain was "all hills, ditches, and rocks...terrible stuff for tanks to cross." Every few minutes an artillery shell exploded near one of the Shermans. From somewhere on the ridgeline between Leonforte and Assoro, a single German gun was taking potshots at them. For the first time since landing in Sicily, Wallace decided the situation warranted exchanging his black tanker's beret for a tin helmet. The shelling worried 'C' Squadron commander Major Pat Mills enough that he ordered the tanks to spread out in the relatively open and level ground behind 'A' Company's line of advance to avoid presenting a bunched target.

As the tanks jockeyed to assume the new formation, Liddell tried to warn them off because his men had just discovered an anti-tank minefield. He was too late. Wallace had gone no more than twenty yards when a "terrific explosion...lifted the front...off the ground. I thought that we had received a direct hit on the tracks from a shell...The force of the concussion sat me right down on the floor of the tank. I had been standing up. I knew that I had been hit on the head because blood was pouring from a gash in my forehead. My helmet was knocked off and my gunner and operator both looked at me and the gunner wrapped a dirty gun cleaning rag on my head." Although dazed, Wallace jammed his wireless headset back on and reported that his tank had been hit. Over the wireless net he heard one tanker after another saying the same thing and realized what had happened. Rather than being shelled, they had "run smack onto a minefield. I picked up my helmet and there was a gash about two inches long and about an inch wide in it. It was a lucky thing that I wore it or else instead of getting a gash on the noggin I would have had my brains perforated."[19]

Each tank squadron consisted of four troops equipped with three Shermans and a three-tank headquarters section, for a total of fifteen tanks.[20] In a matter of seconds, 'C' Squadron had nine Shermans disabled by mines and the other six frozen on the spot. Moving an inch in any direction might well detonate a mine.[21]

"As we could not move we shelled the ridge onto which the infantry were advancing. We were so mad that we shelled any place that looked...a likely spot for the enemy to hole up in." After about thirty minutes of this, Wallace climbed out to inspect the damage his Sherman had suffered. "We were getting shelled pretty regularly now as we were sitting ducks. I got out through the escape hatch in the bottom of the tank." Including his, Wallace confirmed nine tanks disabled. One had detonated two mines at once, causing such a terrific explosion that the torn-off track had ended up draped over the main gun barrel. Wallace's Commodore "had two bogie wheels and the front right drive sprocket smashed. The track was laying off to the side of the tank...What a beautiful mess." Word came that no engineers were immediately available to clear the mines, so the tankers started the work themselves. They had lifted between 150 and 200 mines before the engineers showed up in the midafternoon to finish the job. Shortly after the engineers declared the field clear, the squadron's mechanics drove up in their truck to begin making repairs on the tanks, only to trigger a mine that wrecked the vehicle. The sergeant commanding the mechanic section was badly wounded.[22]

While the mine clearing had been going on, the Germans had sporadically shelled the area with artillery and mortars. But shortly after most of the mines had been lifted, the firing intensified and the tankers were forced to take shelter inside their Shermans. For five hours the bombardment raged, and the "danger was increased when the stubble was set afire and...ammunition and petrol dumps in the immediate vicinity went up in flames." The shelling, fires, exploding ordnance, and loss of the truck carrying mechanical repairs forced Major Mills to decide that the squadron would have to spend the night out in the open. He hoped that under cover of darkness the tankers could repair the disabled tanks and carefully extract them from the minefield.[23]

HAVING CARRIED ON alone, the RCR met no opposition during its advance. Both 'A' and 'B' companies slogged up their respective grass-covered hills to find them abandoned. Captain Strome Galloway was suitably impressed by the defensive works that had been carefully dug on the top of 'B' Company's objective. The slit trenches were deep, and several well-protected magazines had been stuffed full of mortar bombs and grenades. Scattered about the area were bits and pieces of Italian uniforms, boxes of rations, and other paraphernalia that looked as if they had been abandoned in a hurry. Galloway figured that the position could not have been vacated more than twelve hours before.

When the battalion's intelligence officer came up, he surmised that the Italians had been ordered to hold the hills as a screen to cover the German withdrawal from Valguarnera. Undoubtedly they had been expected to make a stand, but the moment the Germans were out of sight had instead fled and hidden in the caves of the nearby higher hills. This theory would be borne out three days later when 'D' Company's second-in-command, Captain R.A. "Dick" Couche, was "heeding the call of nature" and looked up to find a platoon of Italian soldiers watching him. "They had been hiding in a cave and were surrendering to Dick. It was an embarrassing moment. He was certainly caught with his pants down!" Galloway wrote in his diary that evening. The Italians confessed they had been ordered to hold the hills, but had run away and waited until the fighting was well past before coming down from the caves to give up.[24]

Having gained their objective, 'B' Company had just started to settle into the defensive positions prepared by the Italians when a strong wind came up, spreading a grass fire, which had been burning about two hundred yards away, in their direction. Galloway and his men were thrown into a panic as the flames raced through the short, dry grass around the magazines containing the mortar rounds and grenades. But the fires passed by so quickly the ordnance failed to explode. The men "avoided being burned by standing up and hopping over the wall of flame as it approached us...[to land in] the blackened and smoking grass over which it had passed a second before."[25]

After spending several uneventful hours on the scorched hilltops, the two companies were called down to the battalion's position by the road between the two heights. Galloway headed for Lieutenant Colonel Ralph Crowe's battalion headquarters to attend an 'O' Group. He found Crowe and his headquarters group "eating a greasy supper of stew off an improvised table in the barnyard of a dilapidated farm. Seated around the table on broken chairs, a wooden box and a long bench they looked grubby and unkempt. Piles of manure lay all around." About fifty yards to one side a body "lay under a blanket, stiff and still."

Captain Slim Liddell arrived just after Galloway. He had "sweat streaming in rivulets down his flame-fanned body" and was "naked to the waist, carrying his sooty, damp bush shirt over his arm. He looked exhausted from the long walk back from the hill. He saluted and then almost collapsed on an old box near one end of the table, content that he had done a good day's work. I felt the same way, but being a few years younger than Slim, I was not quite so near to a state of collapse. Besides, I still had my shirt on.

"Slim had hardly found time to open his lips and exhale the journey's fug from his lungs when Crowe barked out: 'Captain Liddell, what do you mean, coming into an officers' mess improperly dressed?'

"There were times," Galloway thought, "when the enemy was the least of our worries," as Liddell hurriedly donned his grimy shirt to achieve some semblance of the propriety demanded of a peacetime officers' mess.[26] A few minutes later, Galloway and Liddell learned that the nearby corpse was that of the Hastings and Prince Edward Regiment's commander, Lieutenant Colonel Bruce Sutcliffe.

The officer had been killed while conducting a reconnaissance to confirm a plan that he and 1 CIB's Brigadier Howard Graham had decided for the capture of the heights of Assoro. Both men had reckoned Assoro would be virtually impregnable and that the Hasty Ps, who were to pass through the Royal Canadian Regiment that night to carry out the assault, would be lucky not to be decimated in the attempt. Graham looked up at the ruined Norman castle high on the summit and followed the switchback course of the road winding up to it. He could easily imagine that the road would be mined and blown up in parts to prevent its use by tanks. Bordering houses and adjacent clusters of brush and trees provided countless concealed positions for machine guns and snipers, while from the summit the road would be exposed to artillery and mortar fire. "To hope for success by moving up the torturous road was out of the question," Graham said. "The regiment would be slaughtered."[27]

So what to do? With binoculars, the two officers studied the summit. Right upon the highest point were the "stark ruins" of the castle, "and to the left of this, clear against the sky, was a row of cypress trees that I knew marked a burying ground. The southeast face of the cliff was almost sheer, but there was a considerable amount of scrub, and we could discern what appeared to be goat tracks in some places." Holding the map and standing beside Sutcliffe and Graham was the Hasty Ps' intelligence officer, Captain Maurice Herbert Battle Cockin. He had graduated from Cambridge University and had experience mountaineering in the Andes before the war.

A right hook up that sheer side of the mountain was the only hope the Hasty Ps had, the three men agreed. Use the goat paths or scale the bloody thing if they had to in order to get on top of the escarpment above the town. It was unlikely the Germans would consider an attack from that side possible, so they would have their defences covering the road and concentrated in the town rather than on the summit. The assault companies would strip down to minimal gear— weapons, ammunition, water bottles. And they would go up in darkness.

Gamble agreed upon, Graham headed to divisional headquarters to work up an artillery-support plan. He wanted to knock out the artillery that was firing from the summit so it could not swing around to slaughter the Hasty Ps as they crawled up the cliff.[28]

Sutcliffe and Cockin went to the RCR battalion headquarters for a closer look at possible routes up the cliff face. They arrived to find the area being shelled intermittently by the German 88-millimetre guns on the summit. Lieutenant Colonel Ralph Crowe guided Sutcliffe and Cockin to a position beside a clump of trees in which the RCR's anti-tank platoon had its guns concealed. From the gun position, Lieutenant Sherry Atkinson watched the battalion commanders discuss the situation. Crowe signalled Atkinson over and told him to fire at the German guns with a high explosive tracer-fitted round, so they could see where it fell. Atkinson passed the order to his gun sergeant, who adamantly protested that firing a tracer would expose their position and undoubtedly draw return fire "right up the spout." Mustering his arguments, Atkinson went back to Crowe and set them out, only to be told to get on with firing the round. Standing beside Crowe, Sutcliffe remained silent, while Atkinson pleaded to be allowed to drag one gun out of the concealed position with ropes to another firing position. This would prevent betraying the hiding place of the other guns. When he said this would take only fifteen minutes, Crowe agreed.

The gun was soon set up, with Crowe, Sutcliffe, and Cockin standing behind it to observe the fall of the tracer. Moments after the shot was fired, a reply round from an 88-millimetre slammed down. Sutcliffe was killed outright and Cockin gravely wounded. Atkinson was amazed that he, Crowe, and all the gun crew were unharmed. The anti-tank gunner shot Crowe a look that "told it all," though he was not sure whether it had been the RCR commander or Sutcliffe who had wanted the round fired or what purpose it was to have served. Crowe ordered that Sutcliffe's body be covered and a message sent to the Hasty Ps to see if they wanted the RCR to bury him or hold the body for pickup.[29]

BACK AT THE Hasty Ps' battalion headquarters, Major John Tweedsmuir could hear the "distant crump of shells ahead where the enemy were ranging on the road" that Sutcliffe and Cockin had gone up earlier on their reconnaissance. Then suddenly the news "came through quite bluntly" at 1530 hours that Sutcliffe "had been killed by a shell." A Jeep with Cockin loaded on board in a stretcher came in soon after. Someone told Tweedsmuir that the intelligence officer wanted to speak with him. The major hurried over and crouched down to where Cockin lay face down on the stretcher. In a feeble voice, he said, "For God's sake don't go up that road." As the intelligence officer was carried towards the Regimental Aid Post, Tweedsmuir headed for a briefing at brigade headquarters.[30] Cockin died of his wounds.

The briefing was held in a deserted barn by lamplight. Although shocked by Sutcliffe's death, Graham did not let his emotions show as he outlined the plan that he and the two dead officers had agreed on. He also confirmed Tweedsmuir's immediate promotion to command of the Hasty Ps. Thinking it would be unfair to the new battalion commander to directly order him to carry out such a risky attack if he opposed it, Graham asked Tweedsmuir if he was prepared to carry it out. Graham was pleased that "he not only agreed but seemed enthusiastic."[31]

When the meeting broke up, Tweedsmuir went to the RCR battalion headquarters for his own look at things. He saw Sutcliffe lying face down. "He was a grand fellow, a good soldier, and a great friend," Tweedsmuir thought. But there was a battle to be fought and no time for grief. Directly north stood Assoro. "The broad valley ended abruptly in a mass of high hills, showing blue in the early dusk. A twisting ribbon of white road wound up the slopes in the direction of the town which was out of our sight on the heights. Above the town was the highest hill of all. It rose straight and steep from the valley dominating the hills beyond. The map showed a Norman castle on the top and gave the height at 906 metres. I realized fully what Cockin had meant by not going down the road."

At dusk, the bodies of Sutcliffe and Cockin were wrapped in blankets and buried in a field by the road near brigade headquarters. The Hasty Ps' pioneers marked the graves with a couple of crudely made wooden crosses.[32]

When the quick burial service ended, Tweedsmuir hurried back to his battalion and soon had it on the move. They were carried by truck to Dittaino Station, and from there the infantry went forward on foot. The fire had spread from the boxcars to the station itself. In single file the men marched up the road, a column more than a mile long. About a quarter mile from the station, the Hasty Ps left the road on a path running to the northeast. "The moon was high now and very bright. It shone on rolling pasture land through which dry stream beds cut deep gullies. The path ended and we entered a narrow rocky stream bed. It was very narrow and we stumbled on loose rocks. Every now and then we halted to rest. Once out of the stream bed the land rose and we found a sheep track."[33]

The troops could hear the division's medium artillery laying down an intense barrage on the crossroads at the western base of the mountain and walking shells up the slope to pound the town and summit. Soon all the division's artillery joined in with fire on the town and approaches. From 2100 hours to 0100 hours on the morning of July 21 the guns thundered, serving to cover any sounds the Hasty Ps might make and to convince the Germans that the assault would come up the road.[34]

Before the Hasty Ps had moved out for the attack at 2130 hours, Tweedsmuir had decided to create a special assault company composed of hand-picked men from the entire battalion. All were volunteers. Captain Alex Campbell commanded, Lieutenant George Baldwin acted as company second-in-command, Lieutenants Farley Mowat, Fred Burt, and Cliff Broad were the platoon leaders.[35] Each platoon commander had charge over "twenty of the fittest men."[36] They "were stripped of all their gear except for essential arms and ammunition, for it was to be their task to lead the Regiment; to scale the cliffs, and before dawn broke clearly, to occupy the mountain crest."[37]

Tweedsmuir was close to the head of the single-file column as it wound carefully overland towards the "loom of the big mountain [that] showed faintly in the blue black distance." Whenever a farm was spotted or a dog barked, the Hasty Ps gave each a wide berth. Soon they were climbing a gentle slope that led to the cliff. Coming to a rocky ridge, Tweedsmuir realized they had ascended to one side of a ravine that separated them from the mountainside. Before him, the mountain "looked vast in the paling darkness and the ravine that girdled the bottom looked formidable."[38]

It was 0400 hours, and the Hasty Ps had penetrated three miles into enemy territory to reach their start point for the climb. Tweedsmuir directed Campbell's assault company to climb directly up what looked to be a virtually sheer thousand-foot cliff on the left, with 'A' Company following in support. Meanwhile, he would take 'B' and 'C' companies by a gentler, but still formidably steep, route up the right-hand side of the eastern face. 'D' Company would remain at the mountain base to protect their rear.[39]

The immediate problem was the ravine. It was about forty feet deep "with absolutely smooth sides forming a natural moat to the stronghold which they were going to assault. It looked impossible but they went ahead, discovered a goat track down the ravine and clambered up the other side."[40] Traversing the ravine had eaten up precious time. To the east the sky was brightening with a false dawn.

Campbell led the assault company up the cliff, while Tweedsmuir guided the majority of the battalion along the route to the right. Both groups were soon engaged in what many later said was the most strenuous and terrifying experience of their war. Farley Mowat believed "each of us performed his own private miracle."[41]

Centuries before, the mountain had been sculpted into forty-seven steep, badly overgrown terraces. "From ledge to ledge the dark figures of [the assault company] made their way, hauling each other up, passing along weapons and ammunition from hand to hand. A signaller made that climb with a heavy wireless set strapped on his back—a thing that in daylight was seen to be impossible. Yet no man slipped, no man dropped so much as a clip of ammunition. It was just as well, for any sound by one would have been fatal to all."[42]

To the right, Tweedsmuir marvelled at the stamina of the men. Rightly exhausted by the approach march to the mountain itself, they dug deep into some inner core of will and overcame the desire to declare it "impossible to continue."[43] Not easy, "when always above was a tantalizing false crest, which unfolded to another crest when one approached it." Tweedsmuir and Regimental Sergeant Major Angus Duffy were right at the front of the rightward column, silently enduring "the forty sweating...minutes before we stood on the top beside the shell of the great Norman castle and realized that we had achieved complete surprise."[44]

Campbell's company had gained the summit moments earlier. The two men in the lead "dragged themselves up over a stone wall and for one stark moment stared into the eyes of three sleepy Germans manning an observation post. Private [Alfred Keith] Long cut down one of the Germans who tried to flee. The remaining enemy soldiers stood motionless, staring as children might at an inexplicable apparition," as the rest of the Hasty Ps streamed over the wall.[45]

Looking around a corner of the castle, Tweedsmuir was astonished to see not a single German soldier. The summit, with parched dry grass growing under widely interspersed clusters of wild oaks, was deserted. Only the sharp retort of a Bren gun told him that Campbell's men had encountered something, but it cut off so quickly that he knew any opposition on that front had been silenced.[46]

Quickly the leading Hasty Ps rushed to the summit's western edge and took up firing positions directed down on the town and road. With each passing minute another man at the head of "the two long columns of climbing men" arrived to add his firepower.[47] About ten minutes after the first men gained the summit, "as the sun cleared the eastern hills," they were all assembled and looking down upon a convoy of German trucks winding up the road towards the town. The Hasty Ps could hear the drivers grinding gears and the roar of the overworked engines straining under the weight of the ammunition, rations, and water they carried.[48] As the dozen or so trucks swung around a hairpin turn before the entrance to the town, they passed immediately below the Hasty Ps. Without waiting for an order, one Bren gunner fired a long burst. A dozen other Bren guns immediately began spitting bullets, while several 2-inch mortars chunked out bombs and the other men weighed in with their rifles. Eight of the trucks were immediately knocked out, two or three bursting into flames.[49]

Although taken by surprise, the 15th Panzer Grenadiers in the convoy and manning the positions on the west side of the mountain responded rapidly. "From the ditches beside the burning trucks German drivers returned the Regiment's machine-gun fire with rifle shots. The crews of four light anti-aircraft pieces, sited beside the road, cranked down their guns to fire point-blank at the Canadians upon the crest. Machine-gun detachments, hurriedly withdrawn from the front, scrambled up the road, flung themselves down behind stone fences and engaged the Brens in a staccato duel. With commendable, but frightening efficiency, the enemy's batteries, which had been concentrating their fire on Second Brigade in front of Leonforte, slewed their guns around to bear upon Assoro. Within an hour after dawn the crest of the hill was almost hidden in the dust of volleying explosions."[50]

About five hundred Canadians clung to Assoro's summit, which was so rocky that digging in was virtually impossible. For the next three hours the Hasty Ps endured a fierce bombardment as the Germans hurled between two and three hundred shells down upon the small circle of ground they held. At regular intervals, the shelling would cease and Panzer Grenadiers would press up the hill, to be immediately thrown back by bursts of fire. The only ammunition the Plough Jockeys had was what they had carried up the cliff face, and they were burning through it at a terrific rate. Water was disappearing equally fast, and there were no wells on the summit. Down the slope towards the town there was a well, but when one man tried to reach it, he was driven back by a shower of German grenades. Out of the inevitable bright, blue sky, the searing sun baked down on the hard Sicilian ground, and the Hasty Ps fought a battle with their backs against a wall.[51]

15

Faces to the Foe

DOWN IN DITTAINO valley, the Hastings and Prince Edward Regiment officers of the battalion's support units had anxiously watched the summit of Assoro. They looked for a pre-arranged signal, two green flares that the rifle companies were to fire when they knew the road to the town was clear and safe for the battalion's vehicles to ascend. In the pre-dawn light, Major C.S. Nickle and the others saw the flares, precisely as planned. Within minutes, about thirty trucks and carriers hauling supplies and the support platoons were on the move—not one of the men aboard aware that, by coincidence, the Germans "used this same signal in calling for mortar fire."[1]

The Canadian convoy made its way undisturbed to where the road began winding up to Assoro before coming upon a minefield. From nearby, "spasmodic rifle fire was opened on them but it appeared to be from small isolated positions and it was decided to try and advance. Almost immediately the enemy opened up with [medium machine guns] and mortars." The Hasty Ps jumped out of their vehicles and took up defensive positions, desperately returning the enemy fire. Yanking one of the 3-inch mortars out of a carrier, the mortar platoon managed to get it into action. Quickly enough, Nickle and his group realized they were seriously outgunned. Drivers rushed back to their vehicles and madly jockeyed them about. With its three

6-pounder guns hitched to the rear carriers, the anti-tank platoon was unable to turn around and had to abandon the weapons and vehicles. Several heavyweight trucks were also unable to turn about and were left behind. When all the vehicles that could be were pointed back the way they had come, everyone loaded up. With the Germans still bringing down a terrific rate of fire, the convoy retreated.[2] Although four vehicles and the three anti-tank guns were destroyed in this debacle, only four men were wounded and none killed.[3]

Now 1st Canadian Infantry Brigade knew that the Hasty Ps on the summit were cut off and in serious danger, but Brigadier Howard Graham realized no attempt to push a relief force through in daylight could succeed. Summoning the 48th Highlanders of Canada commander, Lieutenant Colonel Ian Johnston, Graham told him to make an attack that night up the south and southwest flanks of the mountain to gain the town.[4]

Meanwhile, Major John Tweedsmuir and his men had decided the key to survival lay in taking the battle to the enemy. The German artillery fire was growing ever more accurate, the castle serving as a perfect marking point, and the gunners had switched to timed fuses so the shells exploded overhead to spray great swaths of area with shrapnel. More than twenty men had been wounded. They were crowded into a shallow cave and laid out on straw that the stretcher-bearers had gathered. "The narrow space looked and stank like a slaughterhouse. Blood was everywhere, glaring from torn, dust-whitened clothing, naked grey flesh and yellow straw." The medical officer, Captain Krakauer, had nothing but a few first-aid kits that had been carried up the cliff and so was unable to staunch the flow of blood from the more gaping wounds.[5] "They suffered terribly though we managed to keep them dosed with morphia," Tweedsmuir later wrote.

The newly minted battalion commander was under no illusions. If the artillery fire "wasn't stopped soon we were plainly going to take serious casualties."[6] That was when someone remembered there had been an artillery spotter's telescope in the observation post the assault company had overrun. A soldier dashed across open ground flayed by shrapnel from the airbursts, retrieved the telescope, and delivered it into the hands of the battalion's second-in-command, Major Bert Kennedy.[7] It was a beautifully precise, 20-power, scissor-type instrument.

Before the war, Kennedy had trained with a militia artillery regiment in his hometown of Owen Sound. The battalion had but a single wireless set—but it was perfect for the job. Having seen the poor performance of the battalion No. 18 and company No. 38 models in the mountain country of Sicily's interior, Tweedsmuir had insisted on having a signaller from the Royal Corps of Signals accompany the battalion. This lance corporal had lugged a 24-pound No. 46 wireless set up the cliff. He now "netted his set to the artillery frequency, and within minutes," Kennedy was able to go to work.[8]

Through the glasses, Kennedy "caught the wink of one of the guns as it fired and sent an urgent call on the radio for artillery support. It was not long in coming, and on the third correction our shells lit squarely on it. We ordered three rounds 'gunfire' and the shelling ceased. It was none too soon."[9]

For an hour Kennedy "gave the distant Canadian artillery a series of dream targets. As each German gun fired up at Assoro, its position was radioed to the rear and within minutes salvos of Canadian shells fell upon it. There was no escape, for every movement of the German gunners could be seen. Methodically, carefully, [Kennedy] directed the counter-battery fire, until by noon well over half the enemy's artillery was out of action, and the rest was hurriedly withdrawing to safer sites."[10]

The Hasty Ps' long siege of July 21 ground on. Worried they were going to run out of ammunition before any relief reached them, Captain W.K. "Bill" Stockloser and RSM Angus Duffy volunteered to climb down the cliff to organize a party to come back up with rations and ammunition. It was a journey, at several points under enemy fire, that took six hours. Arriving at the battalion headquarters of the Royal Canadian Regiment, the two men reported to Lieutenant Colonel Ralph Crowe. Brigadier Graham was with Crowe. The RCR battalion commander immediately offered to organize a company to carry supplies up the cliff to the Hasty Ps.[11]

Back on the embattled summit, things were looking up at 1700 hours as the "enemy fire had become spasmodic and ineffective."[12] The Hasty Ps were exhausted; men kept nodding off to sleep despite the incoming fire and risk of snipers that kept picking away at them from hides within the town. Suddenly, at 2000 hours, the Germans

opened up with heavy mortars, and two Panzer Grenadier companies came out of the town directly towards where the summit group
was holding. The men there were down to counting rounds, but they
opened up with carefully aimed fire that started knocking down the
Germans climbing up the slope.

Kennedy was instantly on the wireless, knowing they had to stop
this counterattack in its tracks. He called for an immediate bombardment of the town. "The first salvo hit the castle and we gave the
correction of 300 yards west. The next was dead on the edge of the
town, on the slope below: as the shells shrieked into the tightly packed
houses it occurred to me to wonder whether this was the origin of
the phrase, 'to paint the town red,'" Tweedsmuir wrote. "Our guns
pounded the town intermittently and a long night began." The counterattack melted away, the slope leading up from the town littered
with German dead.[13]

At midnight, the RCR's 'D' Company, under Captain Charles Lithgow, prepared to carry a full day's ration and ammunition supply
sufficient for a battalion up to the Hasty Ps. They put the supplies
"in their small packs, which they had emptied of all their personal
possessions, in some Everest packs and in bandoliers around their
necks," and headed for the eastern cliff face. Stockloser and Duffy
served as guides.[14]

To make the trip there and back before daybreak required taking
a shorter route than the two Hasty P sergeants had followed on their
way back from the mountain. The supply party found itself literally
creeping "under the nose of...enemy positions" to gain the cliff. Then
it was a long, back-breaking slog up the hill to reach the summit and
hand over the supplies. Few words were exchanged. The RCR troops
thankfully dropped their burdens and set off back down the mountain. They reached battalion headquarters at 0600 hours on July 22,
having suffered no casualties.[15] Tweedsmuir was elated. "We were
now well fed and well enough armed to deal with anything."[16]

THE HASTY PS on Assoro posed a grave threat to the overall defensive front that 15th Panzer Grenadier Division had established to
block the Canadians' northward advance. Assoro to the east and

Leonforte to the west were like bookends to the defensive line that stretched along the ridge linking these two summits. Generalmajor Eberhard Rodt's dilemma was simple. His division must hold both summits and the ridge or abandon the front in its entirety, because losing any part of it exposed the troops holding the rest to the danger of being outflanked and cut off from their line of retreat eastward to Messina. With the Hasty Ps solid on the summit by the night of July 21–22, the Panzer Grenadiers could only hope to keep them penned in while trying to stave off Canadian efforts to both break through to Assoro with a relief force and gain ground elsewhere along the ridge and at Leonforte.[17]

During the course of the day on July 21, the RCR had sent a platoon from 'B' Company "to probe the high ground between Leonforte and Assoro, and determine if the enemy was holding it in any strength." With 2nd Canadian Infantry Brigade beginning a push towards Leonforte and the Hasty Ps atop Assoro, Major General Guy Simonds had wanted to know whether "the intermediate ground might, or might not, be held. The only way to find out was to go in and 'trouble shoot.'" Captain Strome Galloway selected Lieutenant Harry Keene to lead the patrol, which consisted of a volunteer composite platoon drawn from the entire company. Although Keene would command, Galloway was not going to be left out of the excitement and went along as an observer.

As the ground in front of the ridge was open and flat, no amount of fieldcraft could prevent the Germans from spotting the patrol. The patrol tried to keep hidden by following shallow gullies that led towards the ridge or tucking in close to the smoke from the persistent grass fires smouldering throughout the valley. By noon, Galloway and his men were working their way up the slope towards the ridgeline—sweating, gasping from the exertion, and feeling on the edge of exhaustion—when a shot rang out.[18] Private Alvin Cameron, the company's lead scout, who was well ahead of the rest of the platoon, slumped to the ground and lay still. Three other men were shot and wounded moments later. Bren gunner Private D.H. Robinson was struck in the arm by one slug, while a second punched through his water bottle with such force it spun him around and knocked him down. For a terrifying moment the man thought the wetness on one side of his body was blood gushing from a mortal wound, but then he saw the hole through the water bottle.

The patrol dodged back to the cover of a gully. Flames from the grass fires licked across the open ground they had just vacated, and Galloway realized that Cameron was still out there somewhere. If he was alive, the man would be burned to death. Lieutenant Harry Keene and stretcher-bearer Private J.A. Bancroft volunteered to go with Galloway to rescue Cameron. The three men crept out, ducking around the edge of the fire, until they found the scout. Confirming the man was dead, they started back but immediately came under dangerously close sniper fire. As the three sprinted for the gully, Corporal Joseph Ernest Norton got up on the slope to provide covering fire and was shot in the stomach. Bancroft rushed to Norton, grabbed an arm and slung it over his shoulder, and dragged him to the cover of a large boulder. Although the stretcher-bearer was able to bandage the wound and staunch the bleeding, it was obvious that Norton was in bad shape. "I'm finished, sir," Norton responded when Galloway said they would quickly get him back to the Regimental Aid Post. Norton succumbed to his wound five days later.

Galloway considered the patrol a "disaster." But it had confirmed that the ridge was held in strength. During the five hours that the patrol was out, Galloway had been able to spot several German positions on the ridge. He told Lieutenant Colonel Ralph Crowe that none of these could be attacked frontally in daylight.[19] The only way to effectively break the German defensive wall between Assoro and Leonforte would be to secure both summits and the towns set upon them. Doing so would give the Canadians control of the roads behind the ridge, which the enemy required for their eventual withdrawal.

Early on July 21, the Seaforth Highlanders of Canada were established on a ridgeline facing Leonforte from the south. A deep ravine lay between their position and the town, which ascended the western slope of a mountain in a series of terraced rows stretching up to the top. At the bottom of the ravine was a dry streambed. Highway 121 crossed this obstacle by a bridge, which the Germans had blown, and then it climbed through Leonforte via a long central thoroughfare.[20]

From their position on the ridgeline, the Seaforths were unable at first to determine whether Leonforte was occupied by the enemy. To find out, Lieutenant Colonel Bert Hoffmeister had Major Budge Bell-Irving take a patrol of about thirty men down into the ravine directly in front of the town. In command of the leading section, Corporal Johnnie Cromb was well down the slope when the patrol came under machine-gun fire from positions all along the escarpment in front of Leonforte. Cromb and his section dived into a nearby ditch and started throwing out covering fire to give the rest of the patrol time to find shelter or withdraw. In those first chaotic seconds, however, all cohesion had been lost.[21]

Bell-Irving, accompanied only by Lance Corporal Gordie Tupper, "ran all the way down the hill into the river and into the dead ground under the town." Realizing the rest of the platoon had failed to follow this charge, Bell-Irving and the man with him had little choice but to start working their way back up the hill by following a series of gullies that concealed them from the Germans.[22]

One section, meanwhile, had retreated up the ridge, while the other had deployed in the ditch immediately to the left of Cromb's men. The men here were in a poor position, badly exposed to German fire from positions in among houses that looked down upon the ditch. Several machine guns were firing on them and soon a couple of mortars joined in. To Cromb, the Germans seemed to be everywhere. "They were shooting from windows, from doors, from streets and there was on our right an armoured car...[It] would make its appearance, fire a few shots and then back away." Some of the Germans in the buildings were so close they were within range of the Thompson submachine gun Cromb was carrying. He ripped off one burst after another that shattered glass in windows and punched holes in doors.

Casualties mounted alarmingly as men were hit by bullets and shrapnel. As Cromb looked at the carnage around him, a stanza from William Edmondstoune Aytoun's *Lays of the Scottish Cavaliers* played repeatedly through his mind: "One by one they fell around it, / As the archers laid them low, / Grimly dying, still unconquered, With their faces to the foe." Struck in the thigh by two bullets, Cromb was using a rifle for a crutch. He was dimly aware that his twenty-four-year-old brother, Charles Alexander Cromb, lay dead in the ditch. The patrol's dwindling ranks were pinned down. Cromb knew that going up the slope would be suicide, but staying where they were also meant dying. Their situation seemed hopeless.[23]

At the Seaforths' battalion headquarters, the whereabouts and dire predicament of the patrol were unknown. Hoffmeister and his staff had only a tentative grasp of what was going on with their rifle companies, some of which were attempting to carry Leonforte with a direct attack in broad daylight and with no artillery support. At a hurried 'O's Group, the battalion's second-in-command, Major Douglas Forin, had, on his own initiative, ordered 'C' Company's Major Jim Blair and his two platoon commanders to push two platoons into Leonforte. This attack quickly faltered. With casualties mounting, the company drifted westward in the face of drenching German machine-gun fire and finally ended up atop a hill overlooking the town. Here 'C' Company would remain until nightfall enabled it to slip back to the battalion lines.[24]

Captain E.W. "June" Thomas's 'D' Company, meanwhile, had been directed by Hoffmeister to work around by what appeared to be a route screened from German observation and gain the high ground north of Leonforte. If successful, this action would cut off the Germans holding the town. With 'A' and 'B' companies providing covering fire from the southern ridge, the company headed into the ravine and came under immediate heavy fire just as Lieutenant Arthur Vernon French's lead platoon reached the streambed. French's men were pinned down in the bottom of the gully, while Thomas's headquarters section and another platoon were similarly trapped on the slope above. Several wounded men were stranded in such exposed positions that it was impossible for anyone to go to their aid until nightfall. Among these was the thirty-three-year-old French, who would succumb to his wounds on July 28. By noon, the battalion's heavy mortars and an anti-tank gun were able to provide sufficient covering fire to enable most of 'D' Company to escape up the ridge. But Thomas and a number of other men remained trapped on the slope.[25]

Thomas had gone into the attack thinking the orders to see "how far we could get" were pretty vague. "We didn't get very far...We just got slaughtered. [The Germans] had a clear view. Every time we moved we were fired on. I was pinned down there the whole day."[26]

AFTER REORGANIZING FROM this poorly planned initial attempt to bounce Leonforte in broad daylight, Brigadier Chris Vokes and Hoffmeister put together a plan for the Seaforths to attack the town under cover of an artillery bombardment at 1630 hours. With 'C' Company cut off from the rest of the battalion, 'D' Company badly cut up, and part of Bell-Irving's patrol still pinned down in the ravine, the battalion would go into the attack disorganized and badly depleted.

At 1530 hours, Hoffmeister convened an 'O' Group in a farmyard behind the ridge. All the company commanders, save Captain June Thomas, were present, as were the battalion staff officers. Most of the men were standing on a concrete platform, "which every Sicilian farm seemed to have and which was built and used for the purpose of thrashing grain thereon by driving mules in a circle over it."[27] As Hoffmeister gave the briefing, the opening salvos of artillery fire began falling on Leonforte. When he finished, the party began breaking up, the company commanders heading back to their men. Hoffmeister was standing next to his adjutant, Captain Douglas Haig Strain, "discussing the finer details of the battle" when suddenly the farmyard exploded in flames. Two shells from the medium artillery regiment had struck the edge of the platform, and these were followed almost immediately by two more rounds. Hoffmeister was blown flat on his face, unharmed, "the only person in that whole group who was not killed or seriously wounded."[28] Strain died instantly. Lieutenant James Harry Budd, the pioneer platoon's commander, succumbed to his injuries within minutes of the medical officer reaching his side.[29] Captain Bill Merritt had "his leg practically blown off. He was lying there bleeding badly."[30] (Merritt was the younger brother of Lieutenant Colonel Cecil Merritt, who had won a Victoria Cross for gallantry at the head of the South Saskatchewan Regiment during the Dieppe raid.) Two signallers, Corporal Garth Johnson Carmichael and Private Thomas Fowler Simpson, were killed. Several other men were badly wounded.

Both a Canadian and a British artillery officer, who were nearby, rushed to their wireless sets and called for an immediate ceasefire to prevent more rounds falling short onto the Seaforth positions. Major Forin, who had moments before been standing close to Hoffmeister, had been knocked flat on his rump by the first blast. He had rolled down a nearby bank into the cover of a sunken roadway and come to his feet facing a Seaforth company advancing along this route towards the ravine. Fearing the men were marching into a zone the artillery had designated as a target, he ordered the company to turn about and return to its forming-up position. Forin then walked back up through the smoke to the farmyard.[31]

Captain Howard Mitchell of the Saskatoon Light Infantry was one of the first men on the scene. He looked down upon a "fine young Canadian man, alive, lying on his side on the ground, shocked into immobility for the moment, his hands near his face, his legs and feet together, the only thing that was wrong was that his legs from below his knees to above his ankles were completely gone. Just as clean as could be. His clothes were not damaged and there was very little blood. His boots were even polished."[32]

"It was just an awful schemozzle," Hoffmeister realized, "so I got Chris Vokes and told him precisely what had happened. There was no way we could carry on with the plan. We would have to delay the action until such time as we could get replacements and get radio sets up and generally reorganize because it was a terrible blow."

Vokes came forward to make a personal assessment. When he saw the broken state of the battalion headquarters, the brigadier said to Hoffmeister, "Forget about it. I'll send the Edmontons."[33]

Standing nearby, Padre Roy Durnford saw that Hoffmeister was "feeling dazed" and "could not feel equal to the attack, for he had lost his Adjutant, and his senior officers also were too badly shaken to lead men with any degree of confidence. The Brigadier called us together and spoke encouragingly of our share in the action up-to-date; he urged us not to lose confidence in our artillery because of faulty shells or a rare mistake. It was essential that we, as officers, should retain at all costs an unswerving loyalty to and a complete trust in our artillery. The demoralization effects upon infantrymen who feared their own artillery could be easily understood." Durnford agreed with Vokes.[34]

Hoffmeister remained badly shaken. "From an emotional point of view, it was a terrible thing for me to have to absorb," he admitted later. Had the gunners responsible walked up to him at that moment, the lieutenant colonel feared he would have done something violent. "I was so mad. I just wouldn't have trusted myself."[35]

In one respect, the opening of the bombardment had benefited the Seaforths. Only one battery had been responsible for the friendly fire—the rest had dropped their shot on the German positions in and around Leonforte. With the shells forcing the Germans to ground, Captain Thomas and Corporal Johnnie Cromb both seized the opportunity to lead their men to safety. Cromb brought out two wounded men by having each sit on two Bren guns with arms around the shoulders of the soldiers carrying them.[36]

"The men are feeling very blue this evening," the Seaforth's war diarist wrote on the evening of July 21. "Many good officers and men were lost. Bloody Hill the men call [the ridge.]"[37]

VOKES WASTED NO time ordering the Loyal Edmonton Regiment to take over and attack at 2130 hours. As the battalion had moved during the day to a position a mile southeast of the Seaforths, it was able to go into action on short notice. Lieutenant Colonel Jim Jefferson started getting the Eddies ready, while Vokes arranged for divisional headquarters to back up the infantry with massed artillery support. Simonds pulled out the stops, directing all divisional field regiments along with the 7th Medium Artillery Regiment to drench Leonforte with shells for thirty minutes of fire in what was the heaviest Canadian bombardment since the landing.

The moment the guns fell silent, the 4.2-inch mortars and heavy Vickers Mark I machine guns of the Saskatoon Light Infantry opened up. With an accuracy range of eleven hundred yards, the Vickers were capable of flinging .303-calibre slugs more than twice that distance if the gunners simply intended to pound an area with indirect fire. Alternatively, the gunners could fire from 60 to 250 rounds a minute, depending on whether a slow or fast rate of fire was wanted.

In the final minutes of the sli's thirty-minute fire program, the mortars switched to smoke rounds that created a screen to conceal the advance of the infantry. "The artillery and mortar concentrations were terrific and accurate," the 2 cib war diarist recorded with satisfaction.[38] Divisional intelligence reports estimated that the Germans had side-slipped many Panzer Grenadiers from the east into Leonforte and that there were now at least five hundred ready to make a stand. They predicted that the Edmontons would have to make a determined effort "to dislodge them."[39]

The presence of so many Germans in Leonforte offered a tempting opportunity to cut off their line of retreat. So despite the battered state of the Seaforths, Simonds ordered Lieutenant Colonel Hoffmeister "to send a rifle company to get astride the road north of the town to act as a stop."[40] Once the Edmontons had pushed into the town, sappers from 3rd Field Company, rce were to bridge the ravine to open the route to tanks and infantry support vehicles.[41]

Major Budge Bell-Irving led a strong patrol composed mostly of men from the Seaforths' 'B' Company out to the left of Leonforte to set up the blocking position. As he led the men forward, Bell-Irving realized many were so exhausted they were stumbling on their feet. It quickly became evident that this was going to be "a very unsuccessful sortie" when "a very large proportion of the company... fell sound asleep on the way, climbing the hill. They were very tired indeed." The major, the lone lieutenant with him, and a handful of men pressed on to the road and tried to seal the German line of escape. Soon they could hear the sounds of fierce fighting inside Leonforte and kept watching for the Edmontons to break through to their position. Instead, several hours later, they heard the grinding sounds of German tanks approaching from the north. A short, uneven firefight ensued between tanks and infantry lacking any piat guns, which culminated in the Seaforths finally scattering. Bell-Irving, thinking most of his men had been killed, wandered alone cross-country for a long time—before coming upon an equally lost corporal from the Edmontons. The two men passed into the Seaforth lines just before dawn. "I was so ashamed of my performance," Bell-Irving later wrote, "that I was more or less ready to be killed myself at that moment."

However, as the day wore on, almost every one from the unlucky patrol turned up unharmed.[42]

At 2100 hours on July 21, the Edmontons had begun their descent from the ridge under the covering fire of the Saskatoon Light Infantry's heavy weapons. 'A' Company had led on the right with 'D' Company to the left. 'B' Company was behind the latter company with orders to "mop up the lower [southwestern] portion of the town." 'C' Company "followed in reserve, prepared to form a firm base within the town." Lieutenant Colonel Jim Jefferson had his battalion headquarters section moving with Major W.T. Cromb's 'C' Company. Once they crossed the streambed on either side of the blown bridge, the two leading companies began working into the town by following the highway up the steep mountain.[43]

The artillery and sli fire had done its job, causing most of the Panzer Grenadiers to fall back to the northern part of the town. Consequently, the battalion met only light resistance during the initial advance. Coming to a fork in the road, 'A' Company, under Captain H.D.P. "Pat" Tighe, continued up the highway and slipped deep into the heart of Leonforte. 'D' Company followed the other road to the left and was making good progress when, accidentally, its commander, Major Bill Bury, fired a green Very light that was supposed to signal the battalion's having gained control of the town.[44]

This brought an immediate response, as German machine guns mounted on the rooftops of buildings up ahead "raked the streets." Bury's company was quickly locked in a desperate fight for survival. Tighe's 'A' Company, meanwhile, slogged right through Leonforte to seize the summit. Along the way it wiped out several strongpoints and killed twenty-four Panzer Grenadiers in exchange for three men killed and another four wounded. Skirting the western edge of the built-up part of Leonforte, 'B' Company emerged on the height of ground beyond the town without meeting significant opposition. Behind it, however, a battle raged in the streets. The company commander had no idea where the rest of the battalion was and could not raise anyone on the wireless set.[45] With the roar of German tanks warming up their engines audible to the immediate north, he decided his men should fight their way back to the starting point for the attack.[46]

Inside Leonforte, fierce "fighting ensued in the dark streets and houses, illuminated only by the lurid lights of battle." The battalion had quickly become broken up as the companies tried to find routes up the winding streets that would take them to the summit. Some platoons were out of touch with the rest of their companies, and, due to the failure of the wireless sets, Jefferson could exert little influence over anybody but the men within shouting distance.

When the Panzer Grenadiers counterattacked in strength with the support of tanks and more machine-gun positions established on the rooftops, the Edmontons were thrown into complete disarray. Jefferson's headquarters section linked up with two platoons from 'C' Company and some odds and sods from 'D' Company. As the tanks ground towards this group, 'C' Company's Major Cromb "ordered his [men] to break into houses on either side of the lateral street and form a defensive position...Their PIAT was useless as the man who had the fuses was either wounded or dead. They were therefore unable to engage the German tanks which they saw patrolling the main street."[47] Hoping to call the anti-tank platoon forward to counter the tanks, Jefferson had his signallers climb up on the roofs of several high buildings and attempt to get a wireless transmission through to brigade headquarters. But each foray resulted in nothing more than their picking up bursts of static.[48]

By midnight, the Edmontons were in dire straits. 'B' Company had fought its way clear and was headed back to where it had started. 'D' company was badly scattered, most of its men making their way back to the start point. A few soldiers from this company were among the force of about one hundred, composed mainly of Cromb's 'C' Company and Jefferson's battalion headquarters section, that was holding in the town centre.

Tighe's 'A' Company was still slugging its way up the highway towards its exit from the northern outskirts of Leonforte. When several German machine-gun posts in fortified houses halted their advance, a team of PIAT gunners brought the buildings under fire with such devastating effect that "some...were split from top to bottom." Fighting on, 'A' Company broke out of Leonforte and tried to establish a roadblock on the northern edge of the town. Tighe was hoping the rest of the battalion would come up in support, but in the early morning hours of July 22, he realized the remnants of 'A' Company were cut off. Ammunition all but spent, Tighe ordered his men to break out along a ridge leading to some high ground south of the town. In that advance, 'A' Company overran several German positions and killed about thirty Panzer Grenadiers before digging in on the heights. Their assault greatly disorganized the enemy forces operating on the right side of Leonforte. For his leadership that day, Tighe earned a Military Cross.[49]

From his position on the heights, Tighe could see the engineers of 3rd Field Company working methodically under enemy fire to get a bridge across the streambed. Because the span was forty feet wide, the engineers were forced to install a collapsible steel Bailey bridge of the same length. The division's chief engineer, Lieutenant Colonel Geoff Walsh, considered the undertaking so important and dangerous he personally supervised the installation. To his knowledge, this was the first time Allied troops had erected a Bailey bridge under enemy fire. He was determined the effort would not fail.[50] Initial preparation work had begun at 2130 hours. Lieutenant H.W. Dickson's platoon worked under constant mortar and machine-gun fire, which the engineers later described as "slightly high."[51]

In response, 3rd Field Company's commander, Major Ken Southern, led a small party of two engineers and some Loyal Edmonton infantry into the outskirts of Leonforte with a mind to eliminating some of the German positions firing on his work crew. Southern and the others were soon engaged by a machine-gun position that was covering an advance towards the bridging party by a group of Panzer Grenadiers and two tanks. Despite being seriously outgunned, Southern and his men opened up with such intense small-arms fire that the tanks and infantry pulled back. Southern decided his team would have to hold their ground to prevent a renewed attack, which could easily end up wiping out his engineers and the bridge to boot.

Fortuitously, the commander of the 90th Canadian Anti-Tank Battery, Major G.A. "Tiger" Welsh, had come forward to assess when it might be possible to get a couple of 6-pound anti-tank guns across the bridge and into Leonforte. Under constant fire, Welsh dashed up the southern slope of the ravine, leading two of his gun teams into the action. His men manhandled the guns across the streambed and up to Southern's position. Opening fire, they destroyed the German machine-gun position and managed to knock out one of the tanks. For so courageously protecting the engineers, Welsh and Southern were each awarded the Distinguished Service Order (DSO).[52]

Chief engineer Walsh, who also received a DSO for this night's work, went back at 0200 hours to brigade headquarters and told Vokes the bridge was ready for use. "What's the use of a bridge?" the brigadier retorted. "The poor Edmontons are decimated!"[53] For hours, the only news Vokes had been getting of the fighting in Leonforte was from Edmonton stragglers. "By midnight I felt the despair of failure. I considered that I had lost a fine battalion."[54] Walsh had nothing to offer the disconsolate brigadier, so he shrugged and returned to divisional headquarters. The engineers had done their duty, and it was up to Vokes to either find a way to rescue the Edmontons or not. A total of six officers and other ranks in 3rd Field Company would receive medals for their bravery under fire during the construction of the Bailey bridge.[55]

After the engineer left, Vokes drove to divisional headquarters to personally report to Major General Simonds his belief that the Edmontons were lost. General staff officer Lieutenant Colonel George Kitching led him to the divisional commander's caravan. Simonds "listened as Chris told the story; and then to my surprise and delight," Kitching recorded, he "spoke very quietly to Chris and told him that in his opinion the battalion was probably holed up somewhere in the town and conserving its ammunition as they assumed there would be no re-supply until daylight. He encouraged Chris to think on the bright side and make a plan to get support across the ravine as soon as the bridge across it was completed."[56]

Daring and Spectacular Actions

THE EDMONTONS INSIDE Leonforte were, in fact, in a bad way, but they were not yet destroyed. Although the rest of the battalion had by dribs and drabs left the town and were either holding positions outside it or had returned to the start point on the south side of the ravine, Jefferson's one hundred men were "dodging about from building to building."[1] Surrounded, they fought for survival, giving no thought to surrender. An erroneous report had reached 2 CIB headquarters to the effect that Jefferson had ordered the Edmontons to withdraw, but he had done no such thing. Jefferson had told 'C' Company's Major Cromb emphatically that the embattled group must hold until reinforced.[2] He was giving no thought to trying to break out and considered the battalion had established "a firm base" inside Leonforte.[3]

But that base, Jefferson knew, could not be held indefinitely without help. As the night progressed, the Edmontons were being systematically pushed out of one house after another. It was clear that the Panzer Grenadiers were intent on tightening the ring until they had nowhere left to run. In a command post set up in a wine cellar under one building, Jefferson was trying to come up with a way to notify the brigade of his situation when ten-year-old Sicilian Antonio Giuseppi walked in. Realizing the boy would know his way around the town and surrounding countryside, Jefferson "gave young Tony whatever I had in my pockets at the time. It must have been an adequate amount of money as [his] eyes bulged at the sight of it."[4] Using an apple barrel for a table, Jefferson scribbled a note on a scrap of paper and addressed it to "any British or Canadian officer."[5] Jefferson wrote that he was "prepared to hang on, and urged that tanks be sent up."[6] The boy dashed into the bullet-torn darkness, and the Edmontons returned to the fight with the faint hope that he might actually get through.

Young Antonio found his way directly to 2 CIB headquarters and personally delivered the note to Vokes. Reading it, Vokes felt a "great ray of hope."[7] He knew then he had a chance of rescuing Jefferson and his men "if they could hold out until morning. At the time I bet that he would hold out. Jefferson was a very determined man who never flapped when the going got rough." (Thirty years later, Vokes would attempt to personally thank Antonio during a visit to Leonforte, but he discovered that the Canadians had only learned his given names. These were so common as to be of no use. He regretted not being able to have "spoken to him about his heroism as a lad.")

Vokes decided to assemble "a flying column," consisting of one Princess Patricia's Canadian Light Infantry company, four Three Rivers Regiment tanks, and some 90th Anti-Tank Battery guns. "The infantry would ride on the tanks and the anti-tank gun tractors. The column would roar down our side of the ravine, cross the bridge and charge up the road to the other side and into the town."[8]

When Vokes set out his plan to Lieutenant Colonel Bob Lindsay, the PPCLI commander worried that the column "seemed rather small." But he thought that mounting the entire company on the tanks and anti-tank guns might enable it to break through before the Germans could react. Success would depend on speed.[9] Fortunately, Lindsay had already moved 'C' Company to a position overlooking the bridge, so he had a ready number of men for the column. In fact, when the four tanks arrived along with four 6-pounder guns and their tractors, the company commander, Captain R.C. "Rowan" Coleman, realized there was no way he could get a hundred men aboard the vehicles. Instead, No. 15 Platoon and his company headquarters would provide the motorized infantry element. The rest of the company would run behind, under the command of Lieutenant Colin McDougall.

At 0645 hours, the column was forming up when it came under such heavy mortar and machine-gun fire that the "attack was postponed indefinitely."[10] Vokes, increasingly anxious about the fate of Jefferson's men in Leonforte, ordered another attempt at 0900. This time there was no hesitation. "The Shermans, followed by the anti-tank troop, thundered down the road, the infantry-men riding on the tanks and in the tractors and clinging to the guns, some even astride the barrels themselves. At breakneck speed the column swept across the bridge and raced up the long hill into Leonforte. Such was the speed of the assault that it sustained only one casualty as it passed through the enemy fire. It fell like a whirlwind upon the German posts at the entrance to the town and won their immediate surrender," the army's official historian wrote of the charge.[11]

Coleman and the troops aboard the vehicles never bothered to take the surrender of the Panzer Grenadiers at the town's entrance. They just kept going into its heart and left it to McDougall's men to mop up behind them. A short way into the town, the enemy fire grew too heated and Coleman ordered the infantry to dismount. They "immediately engaged in house to house fighting, working their way right into the centre of the town."[12]

McDougall's group soon caught up to the mobile column and after an hour of intense fighting, the combined force reached Jefferson's headquarters in the nick of time. With tanks closing on the building, Jefferson and about thirty men inside it "had been lying low for fear of attracting" their attention. It was a relieved battalion commander who stepped out of the wine cellar to welcome the Sherman leading the way up the street. Coleman was right behind to offer Jefferson a salute and a handshake.[13]

The troop of Shermans from 'A' Squadron, commanded by Lieutenant Lou Maraskas, continued up the main street. Taking a wrong turn, Maraskas manoeuvred along a perilously narrow lane, with the sides of the Sherman almost brushing the buildings on either side, and emerged back on the main thoroughfare about fifty yards from where a Mark III Panzer was poking its main gun barrel tentatively out from a corner. Catching the German by surprise, Maraskas ordered his gunner to fire, and the first shot set the enemy tank alight.[14]

As the Mark III's ammunition began cooking off, flames engulfed the tank, creating a fiery hulk that completely blocked the street to Coleman's supporting tanks and anti-tank guns. With no alternative, he and the rest of 'C' Company edged warily past the sizzling wreck and started alone towards the northern end of Leonforte.[15] Things went well for a few minutes as they moved up the mile-long main streets, then 'C' Company came under fire from three machine-gun posts hidden in houses overlooking the northern outskirts. Unable to continue in the face of this fire, Coleman ordered Lieutenant McDougall to veer to the right with No. 14 Platoon towards a railway station. Although the Panzer Grenadiers tried to stop the platoon, it pushed through to the station, even though several men were wounded or killed. Once the station was lost, the Germans slunk back about three hundred yards along the railway tracks into previously prepared dugouts. By this time, 'C' Company had shot its bolt and needed reinforcement.[16]

Lindsay was on top of that situation. "Not liking [only] one company for such a task" as clearing Leonforte, he had received permission from Vokes to bring two more companies into the town to carry on the fight.[17] 'A' Company arrived first aboard the rest of 'A' Squadron's Shermans and paused at the southern end of the town while its commander, Major J.R.G. Sutherland, ran up to Coleman's position to find out where he could best situate his men. While the two officers were conferring, Captain Donald Brain's 'B' Company passed by, only to be brought up short by a machine gun firing from "a large house dominating the main street." The anti-tank gunners quickly came to the aid of the infantrymen. Dragging a gun up a side lane to get around the burning German tank, a crew was able to silence the German position with a single shot.

To pass through the town, the highway cut across the summit's westerly flank. Looking up to the houses above it, Brain saw a cluster of Panzer Grenadiers and yelled for his No. 11 Platoon to go for the summit. No sooner did the men set out than they came under heavy mortar fire, and Brain realized it would take the entire company to win the feature. No. 12 Platoon, under Lieutenant W.L. Smith, "worked to the forward edge of the hill. Here they were fired on from a tank and dual purpose gun [88-millimetre] directly in front of them and from the high grounds on their left, which overlooked the main street and...suffered 17 casualties including Lieutenant Smith," Coleman reported.

The PPCLI were hamstrung by the lack of wireless communication, and the fight for Leonforte hung in the balance. Coleman, Brain, and Sutherland, communicating by runners, realized they urgently needed to put together a coherent plan or face the same fragmentation that had befallen the Edmontons. Lindsay was somewhere farther back, out of touch with the three officers, who decided 'C' Company would "hold the ground it had gained, B [Company] should continue to attack the high ground at right, and 'A' [Company], with whatever support it could muster, would attack the high ground to the left." They were going for total control of Leonforte.[18]

Nothing the PPCLI had experienced before matched the nature and intensity of the fighting in Leonforte, which foreshadowed the street battles their brother battalions of 2 CIB would face in less than six months in Ortona. "It was the first time we really bumped into what was a very strong defence of a town by the Germans," Corporal Felix Carriere said. Before Leonforte, contact with the Germans had always been of short duration and had involved only a portion of the battalion. "All of a sudden, zap, this wasn't the case anymore. Everyone was involved. You're in the centre of a street and there's nothing but fire flies running by and these are tracer bullets flying by." Carriere discovered that "it doesn't take long to know whether you can handle this or not. Some people, sadly, can't handle it. Their makeup is such that their mind will not function, accept this and try to do the best they [can] with it...these are exceptions...The soldier finds a way to accept this and finds a way to be careful and in no time at all he is considered a battle veteran. All you have to do is go through one good strong battle...All the kid stuff is gone. This is serious business and you die unless you follow a set pattern of precautions while still doing your job."[19]

The PPCLI learned the job on July 22. So, too, did the Three Rivers Regiment tankers (who would also be embroiled in the thick of

Ortona come December). By 1330 hours, the wrecked Mark III had been shoved aside by Shermans, and the leading tank came under fire from the 88-millimetre gun that had been firing on Brain's 'B' Company. It suffered two direct hits and began to burn. In the tank behind, Lieutenant Maraskas "jumped out...and went to drag the driver out, who was wounded. He stood on the front of the tank in view of the enemy and successfully got the driver out. The enemy must have been poor shots because they hit the tank with machine gun fire but they did not hit the little Greek," his friend Lieutenant Jack Wallace recorded.[20]

'A' Company's Major Sutherland had the battalion's 3-inch mortars with him and directed their fire onto the 88-millimetre gun. With the mortar crews pumping out round after round, 'A' Company put in an attack on the summit at 1520 hours.[21] In the midst of the rush, Sutherland fell wounded. Commanding No. 7 Platoon, Lieutenant Rex Carey led his men across some ground that the German machine guns covering the artillery piece were unable to bear on. With grenades and bayonets, Carey's men silenced one after another of the three machine-gun positions. Seeing another position in the ruins of a house, Private W. Reilly rushed it and killed the crew single-handedly. Carey was awarded a Military Cross and Reilly, the Military Medal.[22]

At the same time, No. 8 Platoon had been on the move. A sergeant accompanied by two men, including twenty-three-year-old Private Sidney John Cousins of Bagot, Manitoba, moved under covering fire of a Bren gunner to take out an enemy machine-gun position. The three men closed within twenty-five feet of the gun, but found they had no angle of fire on the Germans manning it, which was not the case for the enemy. A burst of fire wounded the sergeant and killed the man crouched beside Cousins. Snatching up the fallen soldier's Bren gun, Cousins "rushed this post, firing from the hip. He knocked it out and killed 5 of the enemy therein. He then went to ground, changed magazines, and repeated his performance on another post, again knocking out 5 of its occupants. As a result of his gallant action, the whole of the enemy line collapsed, and the [company] successfully gained and held the ridge."[23] Later that evening, Cousins was killed.

Lindsay put him in for a Victoria Cross, but the recommendation was denied. Because neither the Military Medal nor the Distinguished Conduct Medal (the other commendations designated for other ranks) could be awarded posthumously, he ended only Mentioned in Despatches.[24]

With the summit of Leonforte lost, the Germans withdrew rapidly from the town. The PPCLI's 'D' Company helped them on their way by clearing the snipers who tried to stay behind. With a population of about twenty thousand, Leonforte was blessed with a small hospital. The PPCLI took over some of this sanitary space for its Regimental Aid Post. There was plenty of work for the medical personnel, as casualties from all of 2 CIB "poured in" throughout the night.[25] Stretcher-bearer Jock Mackie would never forget this day in Leonforte. His first casualty was a man who had both legs torn off. "There's nothing but a mess. You can't tourniquet or anything like that. You can bleed to death in a minute with both the main arteries gone. And it's just as well because what man wants to live with no legs?"[26]

The PPCLI had suffered twenty-one killed and forty wounded. Despite the desperateness of their situation during the night of July 21–22, the Edmontons emerged with only seven dead, seventeen wounded, and one lost as a prisoner. The Seaforths, meanwhile, had come off worst of all with twenty-eight dead and forty-eight wounded. Total 2 CIB casualties came to 275.[27] Not counted in this tally were casualties suffered by the Three Rivers Tank Regiment, which had one officer fatally wounded and several other ranks injured. Lieutenant Douglas Neil McIntyre was mortally wounded by shrapnel while standing on the southern ridgeline behind his Sherman searching for targets to be fired on by his tank troop. Although his troop corporal carried him immediately to the Seaforths' Regimental Aid Post, McIntyre died soon after.[28]

A significant number of decorations for bravery were awarded for actions carried out during the Leonforte battle. In all, twenty-one medals were presented. These included DSOs for Chris Vokes and Jim Jefferson, the latter's commending his "aggressive leadership in this action." Coleman received a Military Cross for his demonstration of "leadership and skill." He was also shortly promoted to major.[29]

THE DISPROPORTIONATE RATIO of medals handed out to 2 CIB versus the 1st Canadian Infantry Brigade would remain a bone of contention for the Hastings and Prince Edward Regiment because of their decisive seizure of the summit of Assoro and its subsequent defence. Not a single member of the Hasty Ps was awarded a decoration, although its acting commander, Major John Tweedsmuir, put in ten men for citations. There was no explaining the oversight; it was just the inefficient nature of the army beast, which declared that the recommendations had been received after a self-imposed deadline had passed. Only one officer from 1 CIB, Captain Dick Dillon of the Royal Canadian Regiment, received a decoration. Dillon garnered a Military Cross while leading his Bren carrier platoon up to the vicinity of Assoro.[30]

While the Loyal Edmonton Regiment had been carrying out its assault on Leonforte, the Hasty Ps had continued grimly defending their position atop Monte Assoro. Although resupplied by the RCR, they had received no indication that an attempt was under way to break through by following the main road. 'B' and 'D' companies of the 48th Highlanders of Canada led this effort. Their objective was a T-shaped junction where the road executed a hard left to become the main street leading into the town, while a secondary track wound off to the east along the southern flank of the mountain for a short distance before coming to a dead end. Brigadier Howard Graham's hope was that, in seizing the junction, the Highlanders would cut the only road that provided a line of retreat for the Panzer Grenadiers. While the infantry could get away by scrambling cross-country, they would be forced to abandon any tanks, guns, and vehicles.

Given the way the road switchbacked up the mountain and was probably covered by German machine-gun and mortar positions, the Highlanders had rejected following it directly.[31] Close to the base of the mountain, the road was badly cratered and also blocked farther along by the still-smouldering wreckages of the Hasty Ps' motorized column that had been ambushed on July 21. These obstacles made it impossible for the infantry attack to be accompanied by tanks, although a troop of tanks from the Three Rivers Regiment's 'C' Squadron was going to attempt to gain a ridge next to the destroyed vehicles in order to provide covering fire.[32]

The Highlanders hoped to carry off the same kind of stealthy climb the Hasty Ps had executed the previous night, despite the fact the Germans would likely be watching for such an attempt. Because of the way the road zigzagged up the mountain's face, both companies would be forced to cut across each leg of its twisting ascent. Captain Bob Lyon's 'B' Company would go up about a half-mile west of Assoro, while Major D.W. Banton's 'D' Company would be farther to the right and aimed directly at the junction. As the two companies started climbing a little after midnight, the moon had set and they were left with only starlight for illumination. The road followed no natural course. It had been carved out of the face of the mountain with its outside edge braced by stone walls that were virtual cliff faces about thirty to forty feet high. Climbing these, soundlessly and in darkness, was no mean feat. Yet that was what the Highlanders did. Like the Hasty Ps, they had stripped down to essential gear—guns, ammunition, grenades, and a precious water bottle. Both companies had a No. 18 wireless set, but these proved nothing more than a worthless burden to the signallers carrying them. When the two companies reached their assigned forming-up positions on a comparatively level shelf a little short of the junction, they waited for the dawn and a pre-arranged artillery bombardment of the town.[33]

While the Highlanders had been scaling the mountain, No. 1 Troop from 'C' Squadron—aided by engineers—had managed to navigate over and around the craters and vehicle obstacles to gain a low rise next to where the road started its winding ascent up the mountain. Lieutenant Slim Waldron led his tanks off the road and up a "boulder-strewn cutting" to a position that, when the day dawned, should provide a good line of fire on the junction. Waldron knew it was a hellish position, for they would be exposed to the Germans above who must have heard their engines and tracks grinding away during the climb. They were also right "amid a ghastly mess of burned and shot up vehicles, with burned bodies strewn about them and breathing the unforgettable stench of burned human flesh."[34]

As dawn broke, a series of multicoloured flares shot into the sky from a position in the valley bottom, where Lieutenant Colonel Ian Johnston had set up his advance battalion headquarters. All but the red one were decoys intended to confuse the Germans as to their purpose. The red flare told the two companies to start moving. Seconds later, the artillery began pounding the town and road junction. Lyon and Banton's men advanced, catching the few Germans in the area by surprise and quickly overrunning their positions.[35] No. 1 Troop also swung into action and "with steady blasts of 75-[millimetre high-explosive], succeeded in clearing the enemy from their positions in the many coves in the mountainside."[36] By 1100 hours, the Highlanders were inside the town and engaging Panzer Grenadiers, who were clearly offering only a fighting withdrawal. The junction's capture denied the Germans their only viable route to receive supplies and evacuate casualties. Having realized their grip on Assoro was loosening, the Panzer Grenadiers had slipped most of their mechanized weapons and vehicles out during the night before the Highlanders had concluded their climb. At 1400 hours, the last German infantry ran down the northern slope to gain the road that led up to a junction with Highway 121, northeast of Leonforte. They left behind four trucks, a single 88-millimetre gun, a large number of mortars and machine guns, and two crates of excellent marmalade, which was a welcome addition to the Highlanders' rations.[37] The Highlanders had lost only one man killed and seven wounded.[38]

Contact was quickly established with the Hasty Ps. The rivalry between these two battalions was legendary. So it was little surprise that the "Glamour Boys" of Toronto crowed about having to rescue the Plough Jockeys, who affected puzzlement over why it had taken them so long to arrive. Setting aside the competition for another day, the two battalions got busy. The Highlanders pitched in to help evacuate twelve stretcher cases off the summit.[39] During their stand on the summit, the Hasty Ps had lost only eight men killed and failed to record the number of wounded. It was probably surprisingly low, for divisional headquarters estimated its entire casualties during the July 19–22 period at about 300, and Leonforte accounted for 276 of these.[40] For their part, the Highlanders counted two men dead and fifteen wounded.[41]

While Canadian casualties in this battle were significant, 15th Panzer Grenadier Division's 1st Panzer Grenadier Regiment had taken a harder beating. From captured documents, Canadian intelligence officers estimated its 2nd Battalion had lost seven officers and 230 other ranks as of July 21. The 1st Battalion, meanwhile, had reported 385 casualties. Although the division's 3rd Battalion had just come into contact with the Canadians on July 22, more than one hundred of its troops had been taken prisoner, and the battalion's No. 10 Company had been "all but wiped out." They predicted this regiment would soon have to pull back to reorganize.[42]

"The seizure of the Assoro pinnacle by the Hastings and Prince Edward Regiment," the army's official historian concluded, "was as significant to the Canadian Division's advance as it was dramatic, for it upset the whole German plan of defence on that front, and thus hastened the fall of Leonforte."[43]

Canadian Press war correspondent Ross Munro joined the Hasty Ps on the summit. Looking down the cliff the soldiers had climbed made him dizzy. The padre, Captain Reg Lane, was having graves dug by the wall of a shattered church. He found Major John Tweedsmuir and some other officer in their outpost. They were using the captured telescope to direct artillery fire on a machine-gun post set in an olive grove about a mile away. As the shells fell upon the position, Munro "could see Germans running through the grove for shelter in a valley behind. The Hastings grinned. They had taken a pounding like that the day before and stuck it out." Munro later reflected that of "all the actions in Sicily, I look back on this exploit of the Hastings at Assoro as the most daring and spectacular."[44]

WHILE THE CANADIANS had been winning Assoro and Leonforte, General George Patton's highly mobile Provisional Corps had carried out a literal romp through the western part of Sicily. With the Germans having withdrawn eastward to a line running approximately through the centre of the island, there remained only four Italian divisions between the Americans and Palermo. These surrendered by the thousands, usually without offering any resistance. On July 22, Palermo followed suit as three U.S. divisions converged on the city. The remaining western ports—Trapani, Marsala, and Castellammare—were captured the next day, and western Sicily was declared conquered.[45] Patton got his triumphal parade through the streets of Palermo, and the Allies inherited thousands of prisoners they then had to care for, as well as gaining the dubious advantage of an excess of ports. The Germans, meanwhile, concentrated their defensive lines on the northeastern corner of Sicily and its all-important port of Messina—their exit point whenever the campaign on the island became too costly.

Eighth Army, meanwhile, had achieved little anywhere but in the Canadian sector. The "Germans were still in possession of the Catania Plain and had successfully defeated every effort of the [XIII] British Corps to move forward. On the [XXX] Corps front, the [51st] Highland Division had run into heavy opposition at the inland end of the Plain. The Canadian division, and the 231st British Infantry Brigade, which was advancing on its right toward Agira under its command, were considerably in advance of the rest of the British forces. In these circumstances, the Army Commander [General Bernard Montgomery] decided to hold on the [XIII] Corps front, while the Canadians were to swing eastward along the main Leonforte–Catania road (Highway No. 121), pushing on towards Aderno (also called Adrano) as rapidly as possible. They were, in fact, to deliver a 'left hook' against the inner hinge of the enemy's line. At the same time, the Army Commander gave orders for the 78th British Infantry Division to be brought over from North Africa with a view to strengthening this left wing which had suddenly acquired such unforeseen importance."[46]

This left hook had become Montgomery's last hope for preventing the deadlock that the Germans threatened to impose on his army. As General Harold Alexander's 15th Army Group headquarters assessed the situation, it "was plain now that the enemy had concentrated his main forces in the Catania plain opposite [XIII] Corps and intended to retain possession of Catania as long as possible. The terrain was admirably suited to defence, being cut by numerous rivers, drainage ditches and canals, rendering the employment of armour extremely difficult. The enemy's positions in the plain were backed by the foothills of the Mt. Etna mass, giving the enemy superior observation. In the plain lay the largest group of airfields in Sicily.

Although our advance to the Simeto [River] had rendered these air-fields virtually unserviceable to the enemy, they were strategically the most important and vital objectives which the enemy sought to deny us the use of by his prolonged defence in Sicily."

Recognizing that Eighth Army was losing the initiative had prompted Montgomery on July 21 to suggest that the Americans—Patton's business in western Sicily largely concluded—should "thrust eastwards along [the] north coast road towards Messina." He further asked that all Allied air power in North Africa, and at the few air-fields that had been brought into operation in Sicily, be directed against "the enemy army now hemmed in to the northeast corner." With the Canadian victory at Leonforte, Montgomery reported that this "important centre of road communication is being firmly held and the thrust of Canadian [Division] eastwards from Leonforte toward Agira and Aderno has now begun. 231 [Brigade] moving against Agira from the south is now within two miles of that place. When 78 [Division] has arrived I shall put in a blitz attack supported by all possible air power on thrust line Adrano-Bronte-Randazzo. Date for this will be about 1 August. This attack, if successful, should almost finish the business provided American thrust eastwards along northern coast road is heavy and sustained."[47]

xiv Panzer Corps's General der Panzertruppen Hans Valentin Hube, responsible for Sicily's defence, was keenly aware of the threat that the Canadian and likely American advances towards the north-east posed to his vital need to keep the Straits of Messina open. Should he have forgotten for even a moment, the Oberkommando der Wehrmacht operations chief, Generaloberst Alfred Jodl, was quick to send reminders from Berlin. Jodl had one fear about the campaign. "The vital factor," he warned repeatedly, "is under no cir-cumstances to suffer the loss of our three German divisions. At the very minimum, our valuable human material must be saved."[48]

Knowing that once Palermo fell, the Americans would surely do precisely what Montgomery had suggested to Alexander, Hube had been forced to seek permission to reinforce his current three divisions in Sicily with another that had been standing in reserve across the strait at Reggio. Reluctantly, okw consented to this move on July 21.

Over the next couple of days, much of the 29th Panzer Grenadier Division was ferried across the strait. In the week prior to this reinforcement, some parts of the division had already been brought into Sicily to strengthen Hube's defences. The 1st Battalion of 15th Panzer Grenadier Regiment had arrived on July 14 and been attached to 15th Panzer Grenadier Division. On July 18, Hube had added the other two battalions from this regiment, the IIIrd (Heavy) Battalion of 29th Motorized Artillery Regiment, and 1st Company of the 29th Engineer Battalion. These troops were commanded by 15th Panzer Grenadier Regiment's Colonel Max Ulich. Group Ulich, as it was called, was brought forward on July 22 to defend the coastal highway by setting up a blocking position at Cefalù. This became Hube's anchor point for the line facing westward from north of Mount Etna. By July 25, Hube would push the majority of this division into the line to create a continuous, although in places thinly held, frontage.[49]

Although the disposition of divisions and battle groups looked strong on a map, the Germans were hamstrung by a lack of numbers and the total loss of air superiority to the Allies. In the move to Cefalù, for example, Ulich's troops were constantly harried by Allied aircraft and "lost fifty vehicles and a battery of artillery before they even saw an American infantryman."[50] On July 22, American and British fighter bombers, operating out of airfields at Pachino, had struck in support of the Canadians. Ranging westward from Randazzo at the northwestern corner of Mount Etna along the road running to Troina, the planes ambushed a long convoy of about three hundred German vehicles and guns moving towards the Canadians. Repeatedly the planes strafed and bombed the column, flying 156 sorties against it over the course of the day. By evening, they reported sixty-five "flamers" and claimed many more vehicles and guns damaged.[51]

AGAINST THIS STRATEGIC backdrop, there could be no respite for 1st Canadian Infantry Division. On the afternoon of July 22, Major General Guy Simonds issued detailed instructions to the four brigades under his command. The 231st (Malta) Brigade was to continue threatening Agira from the south, while 3rd Canadian Infantry Brigade moved in behind the British troops and took up positions in the

Dittaino valley around the Raddusa–Agira railway station. Simonds was getting these two brigades into position to take over the division's advance once Agira was carried. Until this town fell, however, the main thrust would continue to be delivered by 1st Canadian Infantry Brigade and 2nd Canadian Infantry Brigade. The attack on Agira would be put in by one of 1 CIB's battalions, and another would guard the division's left flank by straddling Highway 117, which led north off Highway 121 to Nicosia. Remaining in Leonforte and Assoro to provide a firm base for 1 CIB's operations, 2 CIB would get a short breather.

The distance by road from Leonforte to Agira was only eight miles. The medieval town "perched high on its mountain cone overlooking the Salso and Dittaino valleys. In this sector of its course the main Palermo–Catania highway (Highway 121) followed what was for Sicily a comparatively direct route along the rugged plateau which separated the two river systems. The road was generally free from very steep gradients, but at least four times between Leonforte and Agira it curved over low hill barriers which crossed the plateau from north to south. Four miles west of Agira, in the relatively flat ground between two of these ridges, lay the village of Nissoria, a small community of less than one thousand inhabitants. Because it was overlooked from the high ground to west and east, Nissoria itself was not expected to present a serious obstacle to the 1st Brigade's advance," one army assessment concluded.[52]

Upon receiving his instructions, Brigadier Howard Graham ordered the 48th Highlanders to march from Assoro to occupy the junction of Highway 121 and Highway 117—a mile east of Leonforte. Once the junction was in hand, the Royal Canadian Regiment would pass through and lead the way to Agira. Despite the fact that they had carried the weight of the fight for Assoro that day, 'B' and 'D' companies were to be on point. The two companies began forming up at about 2300 hours on some open ground north of Assoro. Suddenly, several powerful German artillery shells exploded in their midst. Four men were killed and ten wounded in this deadly salvo. Among the dead were two stretcher-bearers, Privates William James Thompson and Jim Cameron. They had run forward from the cover of slit trenches at the first cries of the wounded, only to be cut down by the last shell.

After sorting themselves out from this calamity, the Highlanders began marching shortly after midnight. It was the morning of July 23, and 'B' and 'D' companies had been constantly on the go for more than twenty-four hours. They had five miles to cover. There had been no time for any reconnaissance. They had no idea whether Germans waited to bar their path. The companies moved in single file, one behind the other, the men maintaining five-yard intervals. One and a half miles from the junction, a pause was called while the company commanders finalized the plan for the last leg to the junction. Although they had encountered no opposition, nobody expected the Germans would have left such an important junction undefended. From somewhere, the Germans obviously enjoyed excellent observation of the route, for no sooner had the halt been called than another salvo bracketed the line of troops. Two men were killed and another four wounded. The casualties had been so low only because the Highlanders had maintained their single-file formation and spacing.[53]

Increasingly sensing their every move was observed, the Highlanders warily approached the junction with 'B' Company leading. When Captain Bob Lyon's advance platoon entered the crossroads, the sudden eruption of machine-gun fire from a rise that overlooked it from a range of only twenty-five yards ended the growing suspense. As Lyon yelled at his men to spread out on either side of the road, the only thing that prevented their being butchered was the fact the German fire was passing overhead. Firing high was a common mistake during nighttime actions, and the German error gave Lyon's men precious seconds needed to find cover. With mortars adding to the weight of incoming fire, 'B' Company was pinned down. Hoping to get men up on the Germans' left flank, Lyon shouted for Lieutenant Bob Moncur to take his platoon in that direction. Moncur never heard the order. He had been wounded in the leg and was bleeding profusely. Sergeant Charlie Fraser heard Lyon, but there was no way anyone could move forward. Although doing so exposed him to the German fire, Fraser kept dodging back and forth between two Bren gunners to point out targets. When one of the men was wounded, Fraser took over the gun himself. Realizing their two companies were badly outgunned, Lyon and 'D' Company's Major D.W. Banton directed their men to wriggle back out of the ambush zone.

As the rest of the men went back, Sergeant Fraser carefully scoured the open ground around the junction to make sure none of the wounded had inadvertently been left behind. Satisfied everyone was clear, Fraser rejoined his company. His bravery during this action resulted in the war's first Military Medal award to a 48th Highlander.[54]

When the two companies fell back on the rest of the battalion, Lieutenant Colonel Ian Johnston ordered 'D' Company to set up a defensive position facing the road while he organized a dawn attack. At first light, 'A' and 'C' companies went forward but found the Germans gone. Johnston brought the rest of the battalion up to a position immediately east of the junction. Setting battalion headquarters in the centre, he surrounded it with the rifle companies to create an all-round defence. A few German stragglers were rounded up. They seemed "to be mostly very young men, including a number from the occupied countries who were forced in." Shortly after the Highlanders got dug in, they were attacked by long-range mortar and 88-millimetre fire that was so eerily accurate that Johnston suspected the gunners were homing in on their wireless transmissions to brigade with some kind of directional finder. Although the Highlanders possessed the junction, which was to have served as the start line for the Royal Canadian Regiment's advance to Agira, the heavy shelling convinced Major General Simonds to delay that move for a day while he organized a staged attack.[55]

PART FOUR

THE EASTWARD ADVANCE

Follow the Band

I N AN ATTEMPT to gather information on German strength to the north and east of the junction of Highways 121 and 117 outside Leonforte, Major General Guy Simonds ordered 'A' Squadron of the Princess Louise Dragoon Guards (PLDG) to push patrols up both roads. No. 2 Troop, under Lieutenant W.C. Stuart, moved along Highway 121 with the intention of going as far as Nissoria. They were just approaching "the flat white cluster" of buildings composing this village when the men in the lead carrier spotted either a tracked personnel carrier or tank in the village. At the same time, a small enemy tank was sighted to the right of the highway and brought under heavy machine-gun fire by another carrier crew. The Germans lashed back with a deluge of mortar fire that convinced Stuart to disengage. As No. 2 Troop began withdrawing, one carrier broke down and had to be abandoned. Once the other carriers were safely behind the high ground west of Nissoria, Stuart returned with several men to see if the carrier could be retrieved. They arrived in time to see the Germans towing it away.

The PLDG patrol up Highway 117 fared no better. Three miles beyond the junction, it came under heavy German fire that forced it to fall back to a hilltop. Here, the men remained through the day, trying to observe suspected German positions. By nightfall on July 23,

'A' Squadron had regrouped between Leonforte and the junction. The nine officers and 195 other ranks were settling down to dinner when the area came under heavy mortar fire. While nobody was injured, one round scored a direct hit on a light armoured car. The turret was blown cleanly off and hurled thirty yards through the air.[1]

Little intelligence had been garnered by the PLDG patrols, particularly the one towards Nissoria. The fighting at Leonforte and Assoro had revealed a change in German tactics that concerned intelligence officers. "Hitherto the German rearguard has pulled stakes cleanly and retired some 8 or 10 miles to a new position," they pointed out in a written summary. "The fact that they are not voluntarily retiring from their latest strongpoint but are fighting for every yard of ground indicates that we are nearing something like a serious defence zone. Beyond doubt they would have held Leonforte had they not been driven out of it."[2]

What did this mean for Agira? Perched on its mountain cone 2,700 feet above sea level, the ancient dun-coloured town dominated both the Dittaino and Salso valleys and the high plateau—along which Highway 121 ran—that separated the two rivers. This intervening ground was hardly what most Canadians would consider a plateau. It was rugged, undulating, "treed, and covered with orchards, vineyards, and olive groves."[3] Such country provided a multitude of potential fighting positions, but the intelligence officers considered it unlikely the Germans would put up more than token resistance in front of Agira. Surely the Germans would recognize that the Canadians could bring "overwhelming artillery and aerial support" to bear. Observers positioned next to the Norman castle on the summit of Assoro, which the Canadians now called "Castle Hill," would be able to direct the artillery onto any pockets of German resistance with deadly effect. Also, they believed the Germans were too few in number to do anything but make a stand inside Agira itself.[4]

Generally, the mood at divisional headquarters was optimistic. A good, solid artillery and aerial bombardment plan would be put together. The Royal Canadian Regiment, followed by the rest of 1st Canadian Infantry Brigade, would march behind this covering fire across the six or so miles of plateau, climb the mountain to gain Agira, and clear out what should be thoroughly dazed, battered, and demoralized Germans. The whole business would be concluded by nightfall on July 24.

General Bernard Montgomery had visited Major General Guy Simonds on July 22 and guaranteed the Canadians priority call on Eighth Army's artillery. Because the shells were still being brought across the beaches, there were some shortages. To ensure that the Canadians were untouched by this, the rest of the army faced a daily restriction of thirty rounds per gun.[5]

At about 1800 hours on July 23, divisional artillery commander Brigadier Bruce Matthews and Simonds sat down with their staffs and spent the evening setting out the support plan in minute detail.[6] There would be a "timed program of artillery concentrations on successive targets along the route; a creeping smoke barrage 1,000 yards ahead of the forward troops would conceal them by a screen 2,000 yards long; and in front of this curtain Kittyhawk fighter bombers of the Desert Air Force would bomb and strafe targets along the road while six squadrons of medium bombers attacked Agira and its immediate vicinity."[7]

As the plan developed, the division's general staff officer, Lieutenant Colonel George Kitching, felt a growing sense of unease. Simonds "appeared to be wedded to the barrage type of support of The Great War vintage." Known as a "creeping barrage," the guns dropped shells a specified distance ahead of the advancing soldiers, shifting their fire forward to each successive point of concentration according to a precise schedule timed to match the pace of the infantry. It was "designed to pulverize the enemy in their defensive positions just before our infantry reached them," Kitching wrote. But there was one flaw with this strategy that he had observed during the past two weeks. The 25-pounder, which was the backbone of the divisional artillery, "did not fire a shell that was effective against strong defences or deep trenches, although it was a very potent killer when engaging enemy in the open." The Germans were countering the creeping barrage by taking shelter when the artillery began firing and emerging quickly after the guns passed by to engage the infantry, just as they were about twenty-five or fifty yards from the position.

Having been in Simonds's service long enough to take the general's measure, Kitching knew better than to express his concerns. Once

Simonds made his mind up, there was little likelihood of getting him to reconsider. And this plan seemed quintessential Simonds in action. A trained gunner, Simonds "believed artillery was essential to the success of any battle." Several times during the campaign, he had delayed an attack to deploy the artillery and bring it to bear in support—even when the infantry brigade and battalion commanders had wanted to strike without a bombardment in order to capitalize on surprise and speed. Trained as an infantryman, Kitching had generally thought the brigade and battalion commanders correct, while artilleryman Simonds let the allure of guns "unduly influence some of his tactical decisions."[8]

Besides being convinced that he might more easily move a mountain than talk Simonds out of the artillery plan, Kitching held his tongue for another reason. His would be the lone voice of dissent. The permeating sentiment that night, Kitching noted, was "that nothing could stop troops that were going to be supported by 5 field regiments and 2 medium regiments. Over 150 guns in support of *one* battalion!"[9] In addition to the division's inherent three field artillery regiments, the Royal Devon Yeomanry would once again be in support, as would another British field regiment, the 165th. The British 7th Medium and 64th Medium regiments would also be firing.[10]

As was his custom, Simonds went to bed at 2300 hours and was not to be awakened until 0600 unless there was a dire emergency. During the night, Kitching maintained divisional command.[11] By 0630 hours, the general was always ready for a briefing prior to breakfast on anything of import that had occurred in the night. After breakfast, Simonds would either hold a conference with his brigade commanders or personally visit their brigade headquarters and perhaps also drop in on some of the battalion commanders.[12]

THE MORNING OF July 24, Simonds convened a conference and the plan was explained in detail to the brigadiers. Brigadier Howard Graham was appalled.[13] The RCR was expected to cover about one hundred yards every two minutes to keep pace with the lifts of artillery providing the creeping barrage. There would be nearly a two-thousand-yard-wide smokescreen created by lifting the guns firing the smoke a thousand yards every twenty minutes. Together, "guns and aircraft [would] carpet an area about eight miles long and three miles wide with fire, behind which the RCR from the west... would march in to occupy Agira."[14]

"My God! The man must be crazy," Graham thought. The brigadier was all for artillery support. He loved to see forward observation officers with the battalions, ready to call guns down on identified targets. That was eminently useful to infantry. But to "shoot around the country in the hope of hitting something, and to time this shooting on the assumption that the people you want to support will be within one hundred yards of the shells when they hit the ground, is nonsense." The elaborate smokescreen struck Graham as more dangerous to his men than useful. It was entirely likely that a strong wind or change in wind direction would blow it away or even send it drifting into the German positions, so that they were covered while his men were left exposed.[15]

Graham knew he was skating on thin ice with Simonds already so never considered objecting. Besides, the plan was too far advanced. Already, ground crews on airfields around Pachino and in North Africa would be fuelling and loading ordnance into hundreds of bombers and fighter bombers while the flight crews were briefed on targets. Closer by, the gunners would be stacking shells next to the guns, as their commanders worked out firing angles and ranges to deliver the rounds precisely where they were required.

Returning to his brigade headquarters, Graham summoned the battalion commanders and explained the plan. Lieutenant Colonel Ralph Crowe assembled the RCR's company commanders on a treed ridge from which they were able to see Agira. Crowe said he was pleased the battalion "had been selected to put on this ambitious attack." His dispositions were that 'C' and 'D' companies would advance astride the highway with the former on the right, the latter the left. Crowe set out several specific positions where the leading companies would halt and then be leapfrogged by the two following behind. In this manner, 'A' and 'B' companies would be out front when Nissoria was reached. They would clear the village and then move up to the top of the high ground east of it, whereupon the original two leading companies would pass again to the fore. Just before Agira, 'A' and 'B' companies would again leapfrog into the lead and seize the town.[16]

Hearing all these tidily set-out details, 'C' Company's Captain Ian Hodson noted how "little flexibility there was in the plan, and no options for company commanders." Crowe emphasized that the report lines were sacrosanct and not to be crossed early because that would put the infantry in the way of their own shells. Checking his watch, Crowe told the officers they were to immediately get off the ridge because very shortly the artillery plan called for it to be the first targeted area. Hodson and the other company commanders exchanged puzzled expressions. "Why was it necessary to fire on ground we held, why waste ammunition?" Hodson wondered.[17]

The RCR's war diarist pondered the same question. "The feature is so important to gain that the [battalion]...will be supported by the complete [divisional artillery], plus ninety bombers, plus more than a hundred fighter-bombers in close support. It is a set piece attack, with a timed [artillery] program, report lines, bells, train whistles and all the trimmings." He worried about the fact that the 48th Highlanders, in securing the highway junction, had "been fairly vague as to the enemy dispositions, but it is felt that the support will be so overwhelming that resistance before Agira will be slight."[18]

'B' Company's Captain Strome Galloway recalled the old military adage that "time spent in reconnaissance is seldom wasted" and believed that the senior divisional commanders had twisted it into "No time for reconnaissance, get going!" So far in this campaign, Galloway had seen them hustle the infantry into "many minor disasters, which when added up, [resulted] not only in too many unnecessary casualties, but in a loss of faith in much of our leadership."

This creeping barrage chilled his blood. In the Great War this tactic had been used successfully to "shoot the infantry onto the objective." But that objective was generally no more than a few hundred or a thousand yards from where the infantry went over the top and into No Man's Land. Simonds expected the RCR to march two miles to its start line in the afternoon heat of Sicily and then advance

behind the barrage for another seven miles to Agira. "As any infantry officer knows," he fretted, "controlling advancing infantry behind
a succession of linear barrages over such a distance, especially when
the ground is rough, undulating and scattered with orchards and
farm buildings is next to impossible. The advancing troops lose the
barrage as it moves on with mathematical precision and they move
on as the ground allows." But Simonds had "never fought as a foot
soldier, or any other kind of a soldier for that matter, [and] appeared
to have no appreciation of the physical limitations of even the best
trained soldiers."[19]

Nearby, the tank officers of the Three Rivers Regiment's 'A' Squadron had been similarly briefed for their role in supporting the RCR
advance. The intelligence summary given was optimistic. It stressed
the fact that the PLDG had met no opposition before reaching Nissoria
and mentioned only one known German strongpoint, which was
about one thousand yards southwest of Agira. "The enemy troops are
the same as we have previously engaged," the briefing officer assured
the men, "namely one Panzer Regiment, Italian troops and some reinforcements of paratroops." 'A' Squadron was to assist the RCR in the
attack and once Agira was taken, 'C' Squadron would "exploit to the
east as far as a bridge on the river Salso... and hold the position" with
the Hastings and Prince Edward Regiment at its side.[20]

By early afternoon, Simonds and most of his senior divisional
officers were assembled on Castle Hill to observe the attack. A good
number of British officers from XXX Corps were also in attendance.
The division's historical officer, Captain Gus Sesia, lay on his stomach on the cliff edge, and nearby the war artist, Will Ogilvie, busily
sketched the scene. There was also a gaggle of war correspondents,
including Lionel Shapiro of the Montreal *Gazette*. Although the correspondent found Simonds "colourless," he thought him a "tactical
genius." At 1500 hours precisely, the guns roared and the attack went
in. "As I looked over the side of precipitous Assoro, I could see the
battle developing," Shapiro wrote. "Tanks... were crawling along the
single road; from this height they looked like undersized snails. The
smoke of shell explosions rolled lazily over the valley. Now and again
I could see the minute figures of infantry parties scurrying from

shrubbery to shrubbery. The confused rumble of artillery and automatic fire filled the valley. It was suddenly cut through by the shriek of planes...Here was a panorama for the gods of war."[21]

While Shapiro thought all was unfolding as it should, the division's officers soon realized there were serious problems. "A lot of the shells passed over our heads," Sesia wrote. "We could see the target quite plainly below us. It was a large field surrounded on three sides by a heavy wood. The artillery fire was fairly accurate, and from the bursts one could easily determine its concentrated nature." Someone came up to stand next to where he lay and remarked that the concentration was quite good. "Yeah," Sesia responded before turning and seeing he was addressing Simonds. The major general said "he was not satisfied with the smoke, though, and with reason. There was a fresh breeze blowing across the field at the time and the smoke concentration did not seem effective in spite of the number of shells dropped."[22] Simonds ordered the guns firing smoke rounds to increase their rate of fire from one to three shells per minute, but the crosswind continued to dissipate the smoke too rapidly for the screen to be effective.[23]

The valley was soon enveloped in a haze of smoke and dust from the exploding shells, making "visibility poor," Sesia noted, "particularly for the Air Force." One Kittyhawk after another peeled off to drop its bombs as close to the road as possible, but the historical officer realized that the five squadrons of medium bombers never showed up. He thought perhaps the poor visibility had resulted in their being warned off the target area.[24] The true cause was a foul-up by the RAF signals arm, which had failed to notify the bomber squadrons of their task.[25]

Advancing along either side of Highway 121, the RCR enjoyed no such bird's-eye view of the battleground. The battalion had begun marching at 1400 hours to gain its start line on a rise just east of the highway junction. 'D' Company's Captain Charles Lithgow saw ahead the "undulating ground covered with olive groves and grapevines while Nissoria looked white and deceptively clean in the burning sun. On the far side of the town, our intermediate objectives were two hills north and south of the white, winding road. On the northernmost of these was a red building, the only splash of colour in an otherwise drab picture.

"Everyone was in good spirits as the artillery barrage began its solid pounding and the troops plunged forward over the terraced hillsides toward Nissoria. The companies moved easily at first but with ever increasing difficulty over some of the steep slopes, and the barrage, lifting a hundred yards in two minutes began to draw ahead leaving an increasing gap between it and the forward troops. About one mile from the start line, 'D' and 'B' companies crossed to the north side of the road and the advance continued with the inner flanks of the companies moving on the road."[26]

Captain Strome Galloway, like the other RCR commanders, had his platoons deployed in an arrowhead formation with one forward and two following close behind and out on either flank. The troops were arrayed in single file. As each platoon's line wound through the orchards, many of the men "plucked apples, figs, and plums from the trees...Just as we were emerging from the treed area and coming out below Nissoria, CSM Goodridge ran forward and handed me a beautiful apple. I was munching this as we came out into the open."[27]

Just behind the two leading companies, Lieutenant Colonel Ralph Crowe's battalion headquarters section was coming up the road with the Three Rivers tanks of 'A' Squadron following in line. "As the ground leveled out near Nissoria," Lithgow looked over his shoulder and saw the Shermans deploying "to either side of the road." Everything seemed to be going perfectly, he thought, the expectation that Nissoria would not "prove much of an obstacle" bearing out. "In fact, the enemy had shown no reaction to this point. It was almost a training picture...the irregular line of troops moving steadily forward... shouts and hand signals from officers and NCOS controlling the advance...the 'clank' and whine of the Shermans as they lifted great clouds of dust...and in the distance the artillery laying a smoky, metal pall over the hills.

"All at once, with a shriek and a 'crump'...enemy mortar fire fell upon the reserve platoons of the leading companies. Fortunately it was behind the forward troops and only became truly effective as they broke into the western section of the town. House cleaning was begun automatically, but with a difference...all the doors were locked and neither LMG [Bren light machine gun] nor Tommy gun fire would open them. This took everyone aback momentarily but it was decided to move on and assume the buildings empty, which indeed they were, for the inhabitants had fled."[28]

The mortar fire that had fallen on Lithgow's reserve platoons had also caught 'B' Company. Sergeant Lloyd Oakley, who was commanding the lead platoon, "had just gone over a slight crest when the barrage came down. Over to the right of us, near a cemetery, which stands on a hill, 'A' Company caught its full weight also," Galloway observed. "My rear platoons kept advancing and closing up on the forward platoon, so I gave Oakley a shout and signalling with my cane, got the whole platoon to rush over the ridge and down into a depression ahead. They dashed forward although the whole area was smothered in clouds of dust and smoke."[29]

Inside Nissoria, 'D' Company had come under increasingly heavy fire and then discovered that the village's eastern exit was "a natural defile...well covered" by German fire. "Rather than attempt to break out of the town at this point," Lithgow "swung his troops to the left and ordered the advance to continue out the north side of the town. An order to 'Push on' given by Colonel Crowe over the wireless failed to reach 'D' Company and as a result, 'A', 'B' and 'C' companies moved to the right and bypassing the German positions sped through the hills toward Agira. It was at this time that the battle broke into two distinct phases. It was almost impossible to shout now for the rattle of machine guns and the constant 'crump' of mortar fire and the high pitched 'crack' of the 75[-millimetre] guns erased all other sounds.

"The move of 'D' Company was carried out, but not without confusion, for changes of plan in the middle of a battle are difficult of execution. By about 1630...a small party of 'D' Company personnel were gathered in the valley just east of the town and about two hundred yards north of the axis. On the road were several burning Shermans...all victims of an enemy gun apparently situated near the red building."

Lithgow led his men up the hill and "in extended line they clambered up the terraces to the crest and then moved southward towards the road. A silence had dropped around the battle as they crept forward...Suddenly a shout. [Corporal F.R. Hawke] had spotted Germans behind a waist high rock wall about thirty feet from the party. They had lain 'doggo' until now, when a hail of 'potato mashers' [stick grenades] and Schmeisser fire...opened" up. "A battle erupted at once with grenades, rifles and Tommy guns being used freely. [Corporal] Hawke distinguished himself in this action and was awarded the Military Medal. All at once, off to the right near the road, with a labouring whine, a [Mark] III tank appeared, machine-gunning the grape vines in which our men were crouched. Armed only with rifles and Tommy guns, the party was forced to withdraw to the bottom of the hill and there the seven men gathered."

Lithgow had no idea where the rest of his company had got to, but from all around there were sounds of Canadian and German weapons being fired. So he knew the company was still in the fight.[30]

THE FEARS OF Kitching, Graham, Galloway, and other infantry officers had been fully realized. Having pulled well ahead of the infantry, the barrage had rolled over the Germans dug in to the east of Nissoria, and once it passed they tumbled out of shelters and brought weapons to bear. It was a strong, well-positioned force, concentrated on the very objectives that the RCR was to have won—two hills either side of the road to the east of the village, one of which had a red house on top of it. The force consisted of two companies from 2nd Battalion of the 15th Panzer Grenadier Division's 104th Panzer Grenadier Regiment and smaller units from the 1st and 3rd battalions. There were also a number of the division's artillery subunits and several tanks.[31] As always, the Panzer Grenadiers were amply equipped with the deadly MG 34 and newer-version MG 42 machine guns, Schmeisser submachine guns, and numerous light and heavy mortars. The artillery units had positioned a mix of 75-millimetre and 88-millimetre guns so that they were able to bring deadly fire onto the road from a variety of angles.

'A' Squadron had approached Nissoria with No. 1 Troop to the right and No. 5 Troop to the left of the road. Just before the village, heavy mortar fire had bracketed the tankers. Then No. 1 Troop literally "ran into a brick wall which blocked the way. This was due to poor reconnaissance beforehand," Sergeant J.A. "Les" Allen wrote later. Both tank troops were forced to advance "down the main street of the town which was a bottleneck." As the tanks waddled out of the village in single file, they drove into the middle of the German's designated killing ground about a mile east of Nissoria and entered into a sharp exchange with the enemy guns. Allen's tank, in the lead, was hit by a 75-millimetre shell. He spotted a gun firing "through a gap between two houses." His gunner replied with a high-explosive shell that destroyed the German anti-tank gun. Coming to a corner in the road with stone walls on either side blocking any possibility of heading cross-country, Allen hesitated to make the turn without knowing what might be lurking beyond it.

Behind him, a Sherman burst into flames after being hit by an 88-millimetre round. Allen had his gunner shoot high-explosive rounds at the hill on the left in an attempt to neutralize the fire coming from there. When the tanks behind also directed their fire against that front, he swung the turret frontward again so its main gun was covering that direction. Realizing something had to be done to get the tanks moving, Allen called 'A' Squadron commander Major J.D. "Jack" Pearson on the wireless and secured permission to venture out on foot to see what lay beyond the corner. Dashing up a small hill on the right, he spotted two anti-tank guns and marked their position. Back in his Sherman, Allen provided Pearson with the map references pinpointing the enemy guns and asked for artillery to fire on them. Pearson made the request, but no artillery support was ever provided.

With no room to manoeuvre, 'A' Squadron was taking a beating. The Sherman just ahead of Pearson's took a hit that killed both the driver and co-driver and wounded the rest of the crew. As the three injured survivors abandoned the tank, a sniper opened fire and the crew commander was wounded a second time. Then an exploding shell tore Trooper Frank Henry Granite's leg off. Pearson had his Sherman crowd up alongside where Granite had fallen. The major jumped out of the tank to try to stop the blood gushing out of the stump and give Granite a morphine injection. A machine gun shrieked out a burst, and Pearson was thrown to the ground by the impact of two bullets. One pierced his thigh, the other his hip.

Inside Pearsons's tank "Ajax," his co-driver had opened the escape hatch in the floor while the driver backed up the Sherman and then drove forward so it straddled the wounded major. The co-driver then reached out and dragged him through the hatch. While this rescue was going on, the tank's gunner had been firing smoke rounds and his machine gun simultaneously to provide cover for the two wounded men from the other tank who were capable of walking. When the rescue was complete, Ajax kept backing up, the wounded keeping its armoured bulk between them and the German snipers and machine gunners. As the tank was working its way past Captain Bilodeau's Sherman, an 88-millimetre round struck the turret and shattered the gunner's periscope. Unable to see to aim, his guns were rendered useless. Trying to crowd by Bilodeau's tank, Ajax's one track crumbled the soft road shoulder and the tank half-slid into a ditch. When the driver tried to regain the road, Ajax overbalanced and rolled onto its side. The gunner, co-driver, and driver managed to drag Pearson out of the Sherman while the loader-operator ran into Nissoria to look for medical help for the wounded major.

Unable to find any medical personnel, the loader-operator came back empty-handed and found the other men had taken cover near Bilodeau's tank. When the fire eased slightly they carried Pearson into Nissoria and eventually found the tank regiment's newly established Regimental Aid Post. Pearson would survive his wounds, but Trooper Granite perished.

With Pearson wounded, Bilodeau assumed command of the squadron. Soon after, his tank was targeted by an 88-millimetre gun. A first shell struck the left side of the turret, breaking loose the ready-ammunition rack and its fittings. The concussion also slightly injured the loader-operator, driver, and co-driver. The latter two were in the process of climbing out of their respective hatches when a second shell penetrated the top corner of the driver compartment. Both men escaped safely, but the shell set the tank on fire. Five more shells hit the tank in quick succession. Bilodeau was wounded and bailed out, thinking he was the last man to leave. Realizing the loader-operator, Trooper H.R. Betts, was still inside, the driver—Sergeant Cushing—went back inside to help the more seriously injured man escape. As Cushing re-emerged, a machine-gun burst ripped the Thompson submachine gun he was holding from his hands. Once everyone was clear of the tank, the men worked their way towards Nissoria under cover of the continuing "dust and smoke from exploding [high-explosive] shells."[32]

Command now devolved to Lieutenant Lou Maraskas, who yelled over the wireless net for everyone who could to "fall in and follow the band." Maraskas then began jockeying his Sherman about in order to lead the rest of the squadron in a withdrawal to the western side of Nissoria.[33]

The battalion's intelligence officer, Lieutenant O.L. Roberts, had gone forward in his tank with 'A' Squadron to provide a wireless link back to where Lieutenant Colonel Leslie Booth's headquarters section had established itself on Nissoria's western edge. In the ensuing shootout with the German anti-tank guns, his tank was hit and began to burn fiercely. After going back on foot to report what he knew of the situation, Roberts made three trips from the village into the battle zone to bring out wounded tankers. His bravery garnered a Military Cross.

Sergeant Allen, meanwhile, had lost touch with his own tank troop and ended up assembling an ad hoc one consisting of his tank and two from No. 5 Troop. Just as the three tank commanders finished netting their wireless sets in with each other, Allen spotted a German truck pulling out of a farmyard and heading past the corner he had been wary to turn. Aiming to knock out the truck, Allen rolled around the bend and into a vicious mêlée, with fire coming at him from all angles. The other two Canadian tanks came up on either side of his, and together the three Shermans blasted away at the virtual banquet of targets presented. Allen destroyed the truck and knocked out two light tanks with precision shooting. To the right, Sergeant Stewart destroyed a carrier and a half-track, while Corporal Ceasarine knocked out another half-track. That decided the matter, as suddenly the only fire coming their way was a few ineffectual bursts from light machine guns that pinged harmlessly off the armour.

Ordering the other two tanks to cover him, Allen led the way to the next bend in the road. "On rounding the corner, I saw an enemy tank and self-propelled gun which fired on me, but I managed to get one shot in before retiring. It was then decided to outflank that obstacle and we proceeded along a steep road to the right. My tank was fired on by an anti-tank gun from an unknown position and I replied with several shots in the general direction of his position. On finding that only nine rounds of H.E. remained in the tank, I ordered the crew to evacuate. Sgt. Stewart's position seemed hopeless, although he was still firing, so I told him to evacuate. Cpl. Ceasarine's tank had stalled and he also evacuated."

The three non-commissioned officers told their crews to link up with the infantry and let them know they were staying near the tanks in hopes of recovering them once night fell. Soon after the twelve men headed off, however, they encountered some German Panzer Grenadiers and beat a hurried retreat to Nissoria. Allen, Stewart, and Ceasarine remained hidden near the tanks until darkness descended. They then crawled into their respective tanks, fired them up, and drove them to the battalion harbour area. Allen's actions during this protracted fight earned a Military Medal.[34]

'A' Squadron's fight cost it dearly. Ten Shermans had been knocked out, four men were dead, and another thirteen were wounded. Both its commander and second-in-command were among the casualties. It had also been a fight waged in isolation from the infantry, which had spent the afternoon and evening of July 24 locked in their own brutal struggle with the Panzer Grenadiers east of Nissoria.

[18]

Red Patch Devils

WHEN THE GERMANS had slashed into the Royal Canadian Regiment as it approached Nissoria, the battalion had effectively split into three groups. 'D' Company had passed through the village and out to the left towards the hill topped by the red house. The other three rifle companies had broken to the right, rounded Nissoria, and were south of the road leading to Agira. Lieutenant Colonel Ralph Crowe, meanwhile, had brought his battalion headquarters into Nissoria and paused among some buildings in the southeastern corner to establish wireless contact with the companies that were nowhere to be seen.

Having received confused reports that led him to believe 'C' Company had taken the hill to the right of the highway, which was its objective, Crowe ordered 'A' and 'B' companies to leapfrog past the hill positions and "push on."[1] The commanders of these two companies, Captain Slim Liddell and Captain Strome Galloway, had taken their men to ground when the heavy German mortar and artillery fire started falling. Liddell's 'A' Company was to the south of Galloway's men and the two officers had come together to figure out their next move when Crowe's order came over the wireless. Seeing a heavily wooded gully running out in front of their position that seemed to trend south of the German strongpoints on the hills, they decided to follow it in hopes of outflanking the enemy.[2]

The two companies "streaked up" the gully and had soon reached the point where the battalion plan called for 'C' and 'D' companies to leapfrog them and lead the advance to Agira, which could be plainly seen a mile to the east.[3] When Liddell and Galloway tried to report their success to Crowe, however, they were unable to establish wireless contact with battalion headquarters. Finally, they raised Captain Ian Hodson, who said he and 'C' Company had entered the same gully about an hour behind them and would be on their position soon.[4]

Back in Nissoria, Crowe was desperate to know what had happened to his missing rifle companies, which were out of wireless contact. Still convinced that 'C' Company had seized its objective hill, Crowe decided to go there and establish personal contact with Hodson. Assembling a party consisting of the battalion's five signallers, the pioneer platoon commander, and two pioneers, he set out. The small group, heavily burdened by the wireless sets, climbed the hill only to find no sign of 'C' Company. No longer able to establish wireless contact with anyone, Crowe decided to push on to the position where 'C' and 'D' companies were to have passed through the other two. Undoubtedly that was where his lost companies would be found. As the party moved forward, it encountered the bodies of several dead Canadians, and Crowe took their presence on the hill as confirmation that the advance had proceeded according to plan. Nearing the top of a rise about three hundred yards south of the road, the party came under heavy rifle fire. Shouting "R-C-R!" to identify who they were, Crowe kept going until a machine gun suddenly opened up. Crowe was hit and wounded. Grabbing a rifle out of the hands of one of his signallers, Crowe charged the gun alone and was immediately shot dead. The signaller, Private Frederick Arthur Turner, was killed crawling forward to retrieve Crowe's body. Private Douglas Melvin Cummings was also shot down and killed. The remainder of the group reeled back to Nissoria.[5]

On the other side of the road, 'D' Company's situation had rapidly deteriorated as Captain Charles Lithgow lost contact with most of his platoons when they moved in extended line up the hill and directly into an intense firefight. Forced to withdraw, Lithgow had ended up at the base of the hill with only seven men. Deciding to link up with 'C'

Company, which according to the plan should have captured the hill on the opposite side of the road, Lithgow headed in that direction. Along the way he gathered in a few more men, bringing his strength to fifteen. "In the gathering dusk, and by flickering light cast by the burning tanks the men crossed the road and commenced to climb the other hill." They quickly came under machine-gun fire from the same positions that had engaged Crowe's party, but carried the German position with "a spirited charge" and took seventeen prisoners. Expecting to soon be contacted by men from 'C' Company, Lithgow had his men set up a defensive perimeter to await their arrival. As the night drew on, however, and no Canadians appeared, Lithgow decided their position was too vulnerable and led his men to the village. Here, they were met by officers of battalion headquarters. "Voices normally quiet seemed more subdued than usual and the reason for this was readily discovered." Lithgow considered Crowe's death "a bitter blow for [he] had lived for the Regiment and his place would not easily be filled."[6]

UNDER A NIGHT sky sparkling with stars, three company commanders, all vying for promotion to major, stood next to an olive grove and weighed their options. Captain Ian Hodson was the senior officer, though only by a midge, and Galloway had more combat experience, having led a British company in North Africa. Liddell, too, was in the running. But Crowe had made it a competition. How they performed in combat would dictate who got the major's crowns. In this operation, he had emphasized that, due to the risk of moving into the fire zone of the artillery barrage, they were not to advance beyond the current line until authorized by battalion headquarters. Ahead of them was a sunken road that seemed to lead right to Agira, and they knew that for the moment the Germans were unaware of their presence. A hard drive by what amounted to about three hundred men and they might well have the damned place. But they had their orders, sent down from division to brigade to battalion: only proceed if the plan played out according to the script, which had gone into the shredder within minutes of their crossing the start line. Although the complex and rigid artillery and aerial bombardment seemed to have largely fizzled out, the three captains could not be sure that another phase might not kick in at any moment. Nobody had seen any sign of the medium bombers that should have turned Agira into a cauldron of fire, so they could only assume the planes were still to come.

Time and again their wireless signallers tried to raise someone, anyone, but without success. They needed guidance, Hodson decided, and sent 'C' Company's Sergeant Major D.M. "Danny" Stillwell to find out why battalion headquarters would not respond to any of their wireless transmissions.[7] Meanwhile, the three company commanders agreed to send forth cautious patrols to test the defences before Agira. Hodson instinctively believed that not going for Agira with the force at hand was wrong, but they were all just captains and throwing their three companies into the face of the Germans likely defending the hilltop town might doom them to destruction. And should they survive, such a screw-up would put paid to any dreams of promotion. So the captains waited for CSM Stillwell to return with orders, the sensible decision under the circumstances.[8]

From ahead, they were continuously harassed by three machine-gun and two mortar positions. Galloway decided something needed to be done about them and told Lieutenant Harry Keene to wipe them out. As Keene warily led his platoon forward, he heard the sounds of tracked vehicles hurriedly withdrawing. They found the Germans gone.[9] Encouraged, Keene pressed on and actually pushed into the outskirts of Agira, capturing the Italian district commandant's driver.[10]

Damn the communications. The three captains were within a short, one-mile charge of Agira. But they had no orders, no link to battalion. Their men had no food. As always, water was desperately short. They were exhausted by the hard marches under the searing Sicilian sun and the ensuing fighting. You can only ask so much of even the best soldiers. Galloway, Hodson, and Liddell decided they must stay put until CSM Stillwell returned. There would be no bold dash for Agira.

THE FOG OF war had completely descended upon 1st Canadian Infantry Division. At both divisional headquarters in Valguarnera and 1st Canadian Infantry Brigade headquarters on the western outskirts of Assoro, all contact with the Royal Canadian Regiment had been lost since late afternoon. This prompted Major General Simonds to signal Brigadier Howard Graham at 1540 hours on July 24 that he should "consider using [Hasting and Prince Edward Regiment] on final attack on town if RCR used up."[11]

In an attempt to clarify the RCR's situation, Graham commandeered a Three Rivers tank to take him into Nissoria. There he met with Major Thomas "Pappy" Powers, who had just come forward from the RCR's rear headquarters to assume command after Crowe's death. Powers told him he had one decimated company in the town with his battalion headquarters and three others lost somewhere between Nissoria and Agira. Effectively, Powers had no control over the RCR. Powers pointed out the known German positions on the two hills covering Highway 121 east of Nissoria. The brigadier decided that because of the clear German strength, he should delay any further attacks until morning and then hit the hills with concentrated artillery fire.[12]

Back at his headquarters, Graham called divisional headquarters and spoke to Lieutenant Colonel George Kitching. Not wanting to awaken Simonds, who had already gone to bed for the night, Kitching instructed Graham to proceed with the original plan. With the RCR obviously "used up," the Hasty Ps should go forward immediately and put in a night attack. "Perhaps the enemy would retire," Kitching offered weakly.[13]

Major John Tweedsmuir had just been going to bed when a message from Graham said he would meet the Hasty Ps' acting commander at a specific location on Highway 121. "It was about midnight and very dark," Tweedsmuir wrote. "My Jeep driver took a great deal of waking." They found Graham standing in the road. "Trouble was in the air and the [brigadier] didn't waste time in preliminaries. The RCR were scattered ... and it was our job to try and reach Agira ... and capture it. The only thing was to get as far as possible in darkness and hope for the best."

The major quickly sent orders to his second-in-command, Major Bert Kennedy, to get the battalion marching. He and Graham then went into Nissoria to talk with Powers. "We went into a stable to study the map by torchlight."[14] What information Powers could offer seemed pretty slight.

Kennedy, meanwhile, had rousted up the Hasty Ps at 0030 hours on July 25 with news they were going into an immediate attack. Thirty minutes later, the men marched towards Nissoria.[15] When the battalion reached the village, Tweedsmuir stepped forward to greet Kennedy. An RCR platoon guided the Hasty Ps to a hill that part of Captain Charles Lithgow's 'D' Company was holding. This would serve as the battalion's start line. "We formed our familiar single file with the leading company patrolling ahead and made our way across country. We moved thus for about a mile when we met the enemy. They were emerging from a bivouac and had we been certain that they were Germans we could have wiped them out, but they had no helmets on and could possibly have been the missing companies of the RCR. The leading company set out to encircle them. The Germans moved over to what we later learned was their alternative positions and began to dig. They were silhouetted against the pale light of the coming dawn. The leading company could have surprised them completely had not an unfortunate accident occurred. Two men who had got left behind, and were hurrying to catch up their company, missed their way and blundered into the Huns. Next moment streams of golden tracer bullets were flying at random, and the fight was on. We were on the highest point of an undulating ridge, sparsely covered with trees and surrounded by a low stone wall."

Tweedsmuir could see German machine-gun positions firing from a ridge north of their position. In fact, there seemed to be fire coming at the battalion "from a confusing number of points." He formed the battalion into a "rough square on the hilltop." When the sun came up, the Hasty Ps were presented with many targets to shoot at because there were so many Germans dashing about on the slopes around their position. But it was equally clear that the battalion was badly outnumbered and virtually pinned down, as mortars added their weight of fire to that of the machine guns. The mortars, Tweedsmuir realized, were working "to fill in the gaps in the geometrical patterns made by the machine-gun fire and with extraordinary accuracy they did it."[16] Also kicking into the fray were three Mark III tanks that the Germans had "dug in on commanding points."[17]

The number of dead and wounded on the hill was mounting alarmingly. Captain Alex Campbell was with 'A' Company dug in behind a stone wall on the left-hand side of the hill. He "had a bullet through his tin hat and a bullet graze on his cheek. Beside him a wounded man was repeating over and over again, 'Give 'em hell, Tweedsmuir, give 'em hell,' as we called the artillery on the radio. We could not pick good targets or get a good position to observe from, which was a terrible handicap. The steady rate of fire we were maintaining was telling on the ammunition supply.

"I was just moving to the right hand company when four mortar bombs fell beside me. I passed command to Captain [Bill] Stockloser and came-to twenty minutes later, some hundred yards further back, with my head pillowed on a steel helmet in 'D' Company's position."[18] Tweedsmuir had suffered a bad leg wound. Before a couple of men carried him to the rear, he ordered the battalion to withdraw.

There was little choice. No amount of bravery could reverse the fact that the Hasty Ps would die if they stayed on the hill. Among those who had already died trying to save the situation was Lance Sergeant Ernest Johnson. The twenty-three-year-old had single-handedly charged an anti-tank gun and killed its crew with grenades before being shot down.

Corporal Freddy Punchard, "a rangy, taciturn lad, was caught completely out in the open. Punchard ordered his men to break away while he gave them cover, and they crawled through the appalling weight of machine-gun and mortar fire, most of them to reach safety in the end. The Germans moved in on Punchard and called on him to surrender, but there were still two wounded men of his section in danger and Punchard cried out, 'Not bloody likely!' and fired the last of his Bren magazines. When that was done he picked up a [Thompson] and waited for the ultimate attack. It came in a few moments. Punchard did not die alone, for when the position was cleared several days later, his body was found with those of seven grenadiers to bear him company."

As the battalion pulled back, Private Alfred Keith Long—who had been the first man to gain the mountaintop at Assoro—was badly wounded by a mortar round. A couple of men moved to drag him along with them during the retreat, but he warned them off. They last saw the thirty-year-old from Port Hope, Ontario, "sitting with his body braced against the shattered remnant of an olive tree, sucking on an empty pipe, and leafing through a pocket edition of *Macbeth*."[19]

By early morning, the Hasty Ps had fallen back to a position just west of Nissoria and were sorting themselves out. They discovered that one platoon section from 'B' Company was missing. Corporal F.R. Bullier and his men had been forty yards from a strong German position when the order to withdraw came. Going to ground in some brush, they hid until night fell to conceal their withdrawal.

Lying on a stretcher, Tweedsmuir reported the battalion's failure to Graham and then passed out. He woke again in a Casualty Clearing Station in Valguarnera that had been a nunnery. All around him lay men from the Hasty Ps. "A statue of the Virgin and Child looked down on the several rows of stretchers, and the men, dirty, torn khaki blotched with rust-coloured stains of blood. No one complained. The badly wounded men smoked stoically, others talked or slept. We were all so dog tired that few can have felt pain. There were about fifty of us and in a few days time we were evacuated and scattered to Malta and all over North Africa."[20]

The Hasty Ps lost five officers, and seventy-five other ranks were dead, wounded, or missing. This would be the highest casualty count that a Canadian battalion suffered during a single day of the Sicily campaign.[21]

DURING THE NIGHT, while the Hasty Ps had been fighting to retain their hold on the hilltop south of the highway, Company Sergeant Major Danny Stillwell of the Royal Canadian Regiment carried out a dangerous cross-country trek back to Nissoria from the three lost companies' position near Agira. The danger came mostly from friendly artillery fire being called down by Major Tweedsmuir—who miraculously had been able to maintain a wireless link back to brigade. Stillwell reached the RCR battalion headquarters shortly before dawn and, based on his directions, the carrier platoon commander set off with a small patrol to bring the companies in. At about 0900 hours on July 25, a sentry looking out over a gully to the west of where the lost companies were holding spotted a carrier with a man standing on it waving semaphore flags. "D-I-L-L-O-N," the flags signalled. The signal was quickly answered, and thirty minutes later Captain Dick Dillon rolled into the RCR perimeter aboard the carrier.

Captains Ian Hodson, Strome Galloway, and Slim Liddell had been expecting instructions to push on to Agira. Instead, Dillon told them they were ordered back to Nissoria. They learned also that Lieutenant Colonel Ralph Crowe had been killed, the wireless sets lost, and that this was the reason the three companies had been unable to communicate with battalion headquarters. Because the Germans were in control of the two hills dominating Highway 121 east of Nissoria, the troops followed "a devious route" back to avoid being detected. For about a mile this entailed following "a low, stone stairway, surely a relic of Roman days. The steps were about four feet square and with a rise of six inches. They looked worn with the traffic of the centuries."

By 1100 hours, the RCR had regrouped west of the village. The men from the lost companies broke open crates of compo rations—each containing enough tinned and packaged food, tea, cigarettes and other sundries to meet the daily needs of a platoon section—and filled their bottles with water. Galloway "ate a tin of cold Irish stew with a skewer made from a twig, my first food for thirty hours!"[22] The RCR's casualties, in addition to the death of Crowe, totalled three officers and forty-three men with sixteen of the other rank losses being fatal.[23]

During the late morning of July 25, Simonds directed Graham to try again to take the heights between Nissoria and Agira. Graham worried that doing so would simply expose his remaining battalion—the 48th Highlanders of Canada—to the same kind of mauling the other two had suffered. But the orders were firm.[24] There was also a report floating around divisional and brigade headquarters that a small patrol sent out by the Princess Louise Dragoon Guards reconnaissance squadron had gained a ridge that ran from a summit identified as Monte di Nissoria, about 750 yards north of Highway 121, to the red house on the hill—without contacting any enemy troops.[25] The report was erroneous. In fact, the PLDG's 'A' Squadron had spent the day moving into a forming-up position well west of Nissoria. From there it was to bound ahead on its carriers, as soon as 1st Canadian Infantry Brigade seized Agira, and make contact with the 231st (Malta) Brigade.[26] This brigade's 1st Hampshire Regiment had managed to advance from the south to cut Highway 121 east of Agira on the night of July 24–25, but was soon forced back by German fire from the heights around the town.[27]

However, on the basis of this faulty intelligence report, Graham decided that the 48th Highlanders should try to get around the hill with the red house—which had by now been nicknamed "the Schoolhouse" because it resembled the small country schools so commonly painted red back in Canada—by seizing Monte di Nissoria and advancing across the ridge immediately below it. Wary of the whole scheme, 48th Highlanders commander Lieutenant Colonel Ian Johnston decided to send a couple of patrols to first test the situation.

'C' Company's Captain Ian Wallace led one ten-man patrol forward with Lieutenant George Fraser commanding a second patrol of the same strength. Fraser and his men headed for the Schoolhouse. When the patrol got close to it, the lieutenant sent four men towards a low knoll north of the building while he took up position on the roof of a small shed to watch its advance. As Corporal Joe Lapp led the men up onto the knoll, he spotted a dug-in Mark IV tank on the ridge to the north slowly depressing its gun barrel to bring his men under fire. Fraser also saw the tank and yelled at Lapp to get out of there. As Lapp and his group fled the knoll, the tank slammed them with a high-explosive shell. Dodging around a boulder, Lapp suddenly found himself in the middle of a group of Panzer Grenadiers. They were all lying on the ground, either sleeping or sunbathing. The corporal ducked back behind the boulder and with the other three men ran to safety before the surprised Germans could grab their weapons and bring them to bear.

Captain Wallace's patrol managed to gain the summit of the ridge and was soon looking down on another Mark IV Panzer. Its crew and some other soldiers were sitting beside it playing cards. Wallace's ten-man force opened fire on the Germans. Within seconds four of the Germans were dead and several were wounded. Having thrown the larger enemy force into confusion, Wallace and his men beat a hasty retreat back to Nissoria.[28]

Johnston had his answer when the patrols returned at about 1300 hours. The ridge was held in strength by Panzer Grenadiers supported by tanks and undoubtedly the ubiquitous 88-millimetre guns. Because of the earlier faulty intelligence, only a modest artillery support plan had been arranged and the lieutenant colonel realized it "was too late at this time to lay on" something more elaborate and powerful. As both the RCR and Hasty Ps had reported that the Germans were using caves on the face of the ridge for shelters, Johnston had the medium machine guns of the Saskatoon Light Infantry positioned so they could spray the ridge with fire as his battalion went forward.

Graham had ordered Johnston to take a cautious approach to ensure the 48th Highlanders were not shredded like his other two battalions. Just one company would advance on Monte di Nissoria. If it attained success, the other three companies would be fed into the attack and, one after the other, strike positions on the ridge that were progressively farther to the south. In this way, should the Germans counterattack at any point in the operation, at least one company would still be on the start line and able to provide a firm base that the others could fall back on. That such a careful approach might be seen as ensuring the attack's failure was something Graham was willing to accept.

A defile that cut around the base of the mountain's northern flank appeared to offer a good route forward. At 1800 hours, 'D' Company's Major D.W. Banton led his men up the defile, while the SLI slashed the ridge with machine-gun fire and some 25-pounder guns also provided supporting fire onto the rocky hillside. All seemed to go well at first and in short order Banton came up on the wireless to tell Johnston that his men were on the objective, having made the climb in rapid order. 'B' Company was sent forward, climbing up the ridge by surmounting a series of the now-familiar terraces covered in vineyards, olive groves, and brush.

Suddenly 'D' Company reported it was being subjected to enfilading fire from mortars positioned on a ridge that fingered out to the left of Monte di Nissoria. Banton also realized that the crest his men had gained was in fact a false summit and Monte di Nissoria still loomed ahead. The true summit bristled with German machine-gun positions that now opened up on the company. All along the ridge running over to the Schoolhouse, Germans were springing into action. Rather than being positioned in caves on the front of the ridge, as the Highlanders had been led to expect, the Panzer Grenadiers in fact had shelters on the reverse slope, which completely protected them from the Canadian support fire.[29]

Both companies were driven to ground, forced to take cover "on the narrow ledges below the German positions." Back at battalion headquarters, Johnston was attempting to tee up artillery against the positions on the reverse slope, but the reduction of transmission distances caused by intervening hills suddenly put him out of communication with the artillery regiment supporting the Highlanders. The sets 'D' and 'B' companies were carrying also stopped being able to reach Johnston.

'D' Company was fighting on, but every attempt to push towards the summit was quickly beaten down. When Lieutenant Robert Free "Bob" Osler moved into the open to set up a new Bren gun position, he was shot in the head and killed. Four men managed to gain the crest in a wild dash, but twenty-year-old Private Daniel James Murray was killed "on the lip of the first slit trench." Lying dead just three feet away was also Private Ronald Macgregor Warrener. The other two men fell back down the slope.[30]

The situation facing the two companies was clearly hopeless, and both began pulling back towards the start line.[31] Between them the companies had about thirty-six wounded men to evacuate across rough terrain. Except for a few soldiers serving as rear guard, almost every fit man was required for the job—some stronger men carrying the lighter wounded men on their backs, while other injured were bundled into blankets with a man holding each corner. The companies had gone into the attack understrength, and 'D' Company had only forty-two men who were not wounded. 'B' Company was little better off.

At battalion headquarters, meanwhile, Johnston had been debating what to do next. In the distance, he could hear the sounds of fighting, which indicated that 'D' and 'B' companies were still hotly engaged. But were they advancing, stalled, or being beaten back? Lacking a wireless link to either, he had no idea. Deciding to bet that the attack was still going forward, he ordered 'C' Company to advance on the Schoolhouse. If the other two companies had gained the ridge, they would be positioned to support its attack with flanking fire.

Captain Ian Wallace led his men slowly and quietly into the darkness that had descended on the battleground. They were well along when the sounds of fighting to the left ceased. By 2300 hours, his men were a little down the slope from the crest upon which the Schoolhouse stood and getting ready for a final charge. Suddenly, a pair of German tanks opened fire from a position directly above, and within seconds several machine guns weighed in. Then, as abruptly, the enemy fire ceased. The Highlanders could hear tank tracks grinding into the distance. Cautiously probing forward, the lead platoon gained the summit and reported back to Wallace that the Germans had withdrawn. The Schoolhouse and possibly the entire ridge was theirs for the taking. Their casualties attested to the truth of this—just two wounded and one man missing.[32]

But it was too late. For within a short while a runner from Johnston arrived with orders for 'C' Company to fall back from wherever it was, because the withdrawal of the two other companies had left it with "exposed flanks."[33] Before dawn on July 26, the Highlanders were back west of Nissoria. The battalion had suffered forty-four casualties, including thirteen dead.[34]

The failed attack by the Highlanders on the night of July 25–26 shot the bolt for 1 CIB and Simonds ordered it into reserve for regrouping. Early the following morning, he issued orders for 2nd Canadian Infantry Brigade to pass through 1 CIB's lines at 1800 hours the same day to begin operations to capture Agira.[35]

WHILE IST CANADIAN Infantry Division's attempt to seize Agira had been an abject failure that left Simonds deeply frustrated, it was hard for anyone at divisional headquarters to be in anything but good spirits. As most of the staff officers and a group of war correspondents had been eating breakfast that morning, they heard on the BBC's eight o'clock report that Mussolini had resigned as head of Italy's government. Tending to the needs of the Canadians was a young Italian soldier the officers had adopted as their mess orderly by giving him a Canadian cap and badge to wear with his soldier's uniform. Hearing the news, the boy shouted: "Look at our people. Look at their boots and their clothes. He has starved and ruined our fine country." Seemingly embarrassed at his outburst, the boy then set about pouring tea.

Details remained sketchy, but it appeared a coup the day before within the Grand Fascist Council had led to a demand that Mussolini step aside. Bowing to the inevitable, Il Duce had tendered his resignation, and King Vittorio Emmanuel III had accepted it. Mussolini had been placed in protective custody, and the government was now headed by Maresciallo d'Italia Pietro Badoglio, who had immediately dissolved the Fascist Party.

Anxious to get some reading of the Italian—or, at least, Sicilian—reaction to this news, Canadian Press war correspondent Ross Munro jumped into a Jeep and raced into Leonforte with a Canadian signaller of Italian ethnicity. The signaller told a group of "old men, boys in their 'teens and wrinkled old women the news of Mussolini's downfall." Munro was astonished by the depth of the "spontaneous outburst of emotion" that followed. "'Bravo, bravo,' they shouted, and clapped their hands and grabbed our arms and embraced us. The news flashed from group to group until the main street of Leonforte, with the two hulks of German tanks still lying at the corner, was filled with their cheers and the clamour of these excited, joyous folk.

"They shrieked in shrill Italian, 'Death to Mussolini!' and tore posters from the walls of the stores and defaced pictures of the grimacing dictator. A carabiniere ran off to get a bottle of wine and we had a dozen invitations to imbibe as Leonforte celebrated...The shadows of two-score years of Fascism slipped away from those people's lives that morning and I felt I was seeing happy Italians for the first time since we had landed. Even the smiles of the old women sparkled.

"They believed this would now bring peace to Sicily and Italy and prophetically the men told me that Marshal Badoglio would aid the Allies now that he was in charge in Rome. The Marshal would bring peace to this country and there would be no more fighting.

"And as they spoke these hopeful words, our guns were rolling through the streets, and along the road the western infantry regiments [of 2 CIB] were moving to the starting-line for another crack at the Nissoria slopes."[36]

Munro was soon hammering out a story about Mussolini's fall and the response to it for Canadian readers at home, but for 1st Canadian Infantry Division, the journalist scribed another tale of greater import. The Germans, he wrote, were calling the division "the Red Patch Devils" because the "battle patch worn by the Canadian troops here is a bright red rectangle carried near the shoulder.

"One prisoner told a Canadian officer today: 'We see the Red Devils coming and we fire our mortars hard. But the Red Patches just keep running through the fire.

"'I can't understand it. Other troops we fought lay down and took shelter when the mortars fired right on top of them. The Red Patches are devils. They keep on coming.'"[37]

Whether Munro's story was apocryphal would never be discerned, but it sparked the imagination of the division and was quickly picked up by the media in Canada. The division would thereafter be nicknamed "the Red Patch Devils," and Munro would title his Canadian Press account of Canada's role in the Sicily campaign, which was published in late 1943: *Red Patch in Sicily: The Story of the 1st Canadian Division in Action.*

ALTHOUGH THE TROOPS in 1st Division generally liked being thought of as devils, most remained painfully aware that they were made of mortal flesh that was all too vulnerable to the German fire. Yet if Agira was to be won, the blood of fresh men would have to be sent into harm's way. In the words of the Princess Patricia's Canadian Light Infantry's regimental historian, "It was time to get out the whips and to spare neither men nor machines."[38]

At 0900 hours on July 26, Brigadier Chris Vokes convened a preliminary 'O' Group with his staff and battalion commanders on the heights of Assoro to examine the ground 2nd Canadian Infantry Brigade must cross. In his possession was a message from 1 CIB's Brigadier Howard Graham that offered some good advice. The 48th

A section of the Princess Patricia's Canadian Light Infantry in action during a fight for a typical open Sicilian valley. The fires up ahead are from burning German vehicles struck by Canadian artillery rounds. Frank Royal, LAC PA-163670

above · Princess Patricia's Canadian Light Infantry Bren gunner Private Stephen Wallace rests near Valguarnera. The Canadians were ill prepared for the scorching Sicilian heat. Jack H. Smith, LAC PA-130217

top right · A crew from 7th Battery, 2nd Field Regiment, RCA feed rounds into their 25-pounder during one of the increasingly heavy bombardments Canadians fired during the advance on Agira. Jack H. Smith, LAC PA-151748

right · Medical personnel work in the field on wounded Canadian infantrymen. Jack H. Smith, LAC PA-116846

far right · Unshaven and bronzed by the sun, despite the cloth used to protect his neck, 48th Highlanders sergeant H.E. Cooper was a seasoned combat veteran by the time the Sicilian campaign neared its end. Jack H. Smith, LAC PA-130215

top · A Canadian Sherman tank grinds past piles of rubble in one Sicilian village. Frank Royal, LAC PA-116849

above · Agira was spared a heavy artillery and aerial bombardment after a general German withdrawal was detected. Still, Princess Patricia's Canadian Light Infantry troops—such as this patrol moving up the main street—faced some stiff fighting against rearguard units to win the town. Jack H. Smith, LAC PA-138269

top· Left to right: Private Wilfred Reilly, Major Ron Coleman, Lieutenant
Rex Carey, and Corporal Bob Middleton were all Princess Patricia's Canadian
Light Infantry personnel who won awards for valour during the Sicilian campaign.
Terry F. Rowe, LAC PA-162142

above · Major C.W. Abell, Lieutenant Colonel F.D. "Dodd" Tweedie, Captain J.D. Augh-
erton, Lieutenant W.W. Wilson, and Private V.W. Richard (seated next to a wireless set)
of the Carleton and York Regiment confer before an attack. Frank Royal, LAC PA-169997

above · Trucks carrying personnel from the West Nova Scotia Regiment and Royal 22e Régiment (Van Doos) roll past a knocked-out German carrier. Frank Royal, LAC PA-143902

top centre · A bulldozer of 1st Field Company, RCE at work on the road the engineers created in the Salso River valley. Jack H. Smith, LAC PA-168706

top right · Men of the Loyal Edmonton Regiment loading equipment onto a mule train to take supplies up to where the battalion was fighting in the Salso River valley on August 2. Jack H. Smith, LAC PA-166498

bottom right · The sounds of victory. The Seaforth Highlanders pipe band plays "Retreat" in Agira's main square. A CBC recording of the event was broadcast around the world. Photographer unknown, LAC PA-193886

Van Doo lieutenant Pierre-Ferdinand Potvin receives the Military Cross from General Montgomery in recognition of his valour during the battle at Portella Grottacalda. Frank Royal, LAC PA-151170

Highlanders, he reported, had tried to take Monte di Nissoria and the area of ridge south of it and to the north of Highway 121, only to be "mortared off." Rather than being dug in on the forward slope of the ridge, as intelligence reports had indicated, the Germans "were in positions on reverse slopes and the [artillery concentrations] on the [forward] slopes & top did not damage the enemy too much." The Germans also had several tanks buttoned down in well-hidden firing positions, and Graham cautioned that the difficult ground made it rough going for the Three Rivers Regiment's Shermans. Having succinctly summed up his brigade's experience, Graham then offered Vokes the key to Agira. Lieutenant Colonel Ian Johnston, he said, believed "that a wide right flanking move toward the rear of the enemy [positions] with *deep* [concentrations; emphasis in the original] from right & left would give best chance of success."[39]

The advice was sound, but Vokes was unable to immediately act upon it because Simonds was once again assembling a set-piece attack intended to allow his battalions to advance by weight of artillery. Although his plan did not call for a protracted advance of six miles over rugged terrain, it still had the infantry moving forward more than three miles—mostly in darkness. A series of phased objective lines had been marked out between Nissoria and Agira, each given the code name of a large predatory mammal. "Lion," the ridge that had so bedevilled 1 CIB's battalions—lying about one thousand yards east of Nissoria—was the first. Next was "Tiger," a ridge that stood about fifteen hundred yards farther along. After this, a fresh battalion would pass through and drive three thousand yards to gain "Grizzly," a stretch of high ground less than a half-mile from Agira that rose at either end to well-defined crests—Monte Crapuzza to the north of the highway and Monte Fronte to the south.[40]

Simonds was going to throw into the barrage all the guns under his command—three field regiments, two medium regiments, and the Saskatoon Light Infantry's 4.2-inch mortars. Each gun was to fire 139 rounds, but Simonds had ordered 400 rounds delivered to the gun pits in case extra firepower was required.[41] This was not a simple supply order for the Royal Canadian Armoured Service Corps to fulfill on short notice. By this time, the Canadians were dependent on a supply line running 150 miles—mostly along inadequate roads—back to the beaches at Pachino. "This trip took between two and three days, including time spent issuing and loading," noted the official history of the Royal Canadian Ordnance Corps. Having lost almost five hundred trucks when the ships carrying them had been sunk, the truckers were desperately short of necessary transportation. While Eighth Army had provided substitutes for most of the trucks lost, they were smaller, clapped-out vehicles—and Dodges to boot— for which the Canadians had no spare parts.[42] Despite the handicaps, using 150 trucks including a number borrowed from xxx Corps the truckers managed to deliver the shells on time.[43]

While the trucks ground towards the battlefront throughout the day on July 26, Vokes set his plans in place. The PPCLI would push past Lion and seize Tiger. Leapfrogging through, the Seaforth Highlanders of Canada would then punch on to Grizzly.[44] Taking Agira thereafter fell to the Loyal Edmonton Regiment. To confuse the Germans and disrupt their ability to either reinforce or withdraw troops from the area, the Edmontons were ordered to send a company-strength patrol north from Nissoria to cut the highway running northwest from Agira. The 231st (Malta) Brigade would also be at work behind the German front, coming down from the hills southeast of Agira to cut Highway 121 and take positions atop the high ground north of it. If the Canadians succeeded in the main assault, the British troops were under orders to remain in place. Should the attack fail, however, they would withdraw in the morning to their fortified positions in the hills to the south.[45]

By 1300 hours, the division's chief gunner, Brigadier Bruce Matthews, had set out the "details of barrage." Traces showing the lines of fire were soon marked on maps, which were reproduced and hurried to the gun regiments.[46] "The initial artillery plan consisted of two minutes intense followed by fifteen minutes normal fire on the opening line just west of Nissoria, by the guns of the [three] field regiments less two batteries. This was to be followed in turn by sixteen 100-yard lifts at three-minute intervals with a further five minutes on the last line. The barrage was to pause for 20 or 30 minutes after the first objective to permit the reserve infantry companies to come up and prepare to advance on the second objective. Then it was to continue five minutes on a new start line followed by twelve 100-yard lifts at three-minute intervals."[47]

At 1500 hours, Vokes held a final briefing on Castle Hill. Then the battalion commanders moved to the various points around Nissoria where each had his unit waiting for the attack. The brigade commander returned to his newly established headquarters, which had been set up in a rock quarry that seemed to be "the home for all the fleas in Sicily." Along with everyone else there, Vokes was soon scratching furiously and worrying the fleas were a sign "that all was not to go well."[48]

Lion, Tiger, and Grizzly

<hr>

AT 2000 HOURS on July 26, the Canadian barrage began. Because the "very narrow front" gave "a density unrivalled in any of the great battles of the desert, the effect was terrific."[1] "The artillery frontage is only about five hundred yards," noted Three Rivers' 'C' Squadron tanker, Lieutenant Jack Wallace, whose troop was supporting the Princess Patricia's Canadian Light Infantry attack. "Must have been over two thousand shells fell in that small area in five minutes and the barrage kept up for at least fifteen minutes. You could hear the shells whistle overhead and was that ever a comforting sound."[2]

The PPCLI advanced towards the ridge hard on the heels of the artillery, which moved about one hundred yards ahead at three-minute intervals, adhering to the set pattern. Captain Rowan Coleman's 'C' Company was on the right, Major A.E.T. Paquet's 'D' Company the left. The other two companies would pass to the front at Lion and lead the way to Tiger. Covering the distance between the start line and Lion was to take forty minutes. The moment it crossed the start line, 'D' Company was struck by heavy fire from three machine-gun positions covering Highway 121 from around the Schoolhouse. On the company's extreme right by the road, Lieutenant V.O. Auger's No. 17 Platoon immediately charged one enemy gun position, and its Bren gun section quickly killed the Panzer Grenadiers manning the weapon. "By dint of keeping extremely close to the barrage," Auger's men broke through to the objective right on schedule. Meanwhile, No. 18 Platoon—the farthest platoon to the left—managed to get around the machine guns blocking its path and married up with Auger's men on the objective.

Pushing forward "to continue the clearing of the hill," the two platoons came under heavy mortar fire from several positions while also being shot at by an anti-tank gun stationed near the road. No. 16 Platoon, accompanied by the company headquarters section, was initially checked by the machine guns. Soon, however, the German guns fell silent and they carried on to the objective. Lieutenant Auger's No. 17 Platoon, meanwhile, had "endeavoured to get to grips with the enemy but were pinned down by heavy fire." As Major Paquet and the rest of the company joined the two forward platoons on the ridge, he was shot in the right elbow. Refusing to be evacuated until the fight was concluded, Paquet remained with his headquarters until daybreak. Having attained the objective, 'D' Company stood its ground while the Germans withdrew to a position about three hundred yards distant. Sporadic exchanges of fire continued through the night. Despite the stiff firefight gaining the hill, the company suffered only two men killed and seven wounded.

Captain Coleman's 'C' Company had a comparatively easy advance. Crossing the start line "at 2017 [hours] and keeping close under the terrific barrage [they] got right on to their objective. The enemy was so demoralized by the shelling that about 15 of them surrendered immediately and others were pursued with bayonet and caught. However, opposition now appeared and a spirited grenade and Tommy-gun fight ensued," Coleman wrote afterward. The Canadians won the shootout. Taking stock, Coleman found that No. 13 Platoon on the right side of the advance had lost two sections during the fast night advance. No. 14 Platoon, in the centre, also had a section missing. "In their enthusiasm [these men had] continued forward for another thousand yards" beyond the objective. Realizing they had outrun their company, the seven men took up a defensive position for the night and only returned to Lion just after dawn.[3]

On Lion itself, the men there had immediately started digging in to find shelter from the intensifying fire coming at them from Tiger and German positions on the ground between. Two troops from 'C' Squadron had also ground up the hill and set up alongside the infantry, but it had been too dark for them to see any targets. Lieutenant Wallace and the other tank commanders decided they were going to be in for an uncomfortable night sleeping inside the tanks unless ordered back to the start line. Standard doctrine being that tanks were not to be left in exposed, forward positions during hours of darkness made a recall order likely.[4]

The intensity of the barrage and the PPCLI's success in keeping pace with its advance had left the Germans "dazed by the audacity of our attack," Lieutenant Colonel Bob Lindsay reported enthusiastically. At dawn, 'C' and 'D' Company counted its prisoner toll at seventy and the German dead strewn around at between seventy and eighty.[5] Captured German reports later revealed that most of the Panzer Grenadiers who escaped from the hills had been nursing wounds.[6] One dazed soldier, who had fought in Poland, France, Russia, and North Africa, told the Canadians "he never saw the likes of our chaps for their tenacious fighting spirit in the face of [heavy] concentrated fire."[7] To the delight of the gunners, one German officer—now that he was a prisoner and out of the war—asked to "see the automatic field gun that had such an amazing rate of fire."[8]

But much of this stunningly effective artillery fire had been for naught. As the gunners had opened with the second phase of the barrage and started advancing in lifts from Lion towards Tiger, the two reserve PPCLI companies failed to appear. As Lindsay defensively put it, "Unfortunately, the other two [companies] lost their way, thereby losing the advantage of the barrage. During the cessation of the barrage the enemy's heads came up again and they offered stiff opposition to both [companies,] a bitter fight then taking place. Neither of the [companies] gained their objectives."[9]

Back in the quarry pit that served as 2 CIB's headquarters, Brigadier Chris Vokes learned of the calamity "at midnight." "I was furious at this disobedience," he declared later. "I determined to houseclean the Patricias as soon as the battle was over." But the damage was done. Tiger remained in German hands and the Panzer Grenadiers were lashing Lion with everything they had. Tanks prowled in the brush below, and a terrific rate of mortar and machine-gun fire saturated the ridge. Having no idea where half of the PPCLI had got to, and Lindsay also having no inkling, Vokes decided to push the Seaforths forward immediately to take both Tiger and Grizzly.

It was poor timing for the tankers when Lieutenant Colonel Leslie Booth, who was on the wireless near where Vokes stood glowering at a map, received a wireless request from 'C' Squadron's Major Pat Mills to withdraw the armoured troops. "'Wait one,' Booth said. 'I have to ask 'Grandfather.'"

"Booth left the wireless and moved the few feet to where I was busily scratching at my fleas," Vokes wrote later. "I was already in a bad temper, vexed at the errant Patricias, choleric on account of the fleas." Booth explained that Mills was worried he might lose some tanks in the night. Vokes demanded if any had so far been knocked out, and Booth admitted none had. "'Then hell, no!' [Vokes] exploded in total exasperation. 'If the infantry can stick it up there tonight, so can Mills and his tanks. It will give the infantry confidence to have the tanks with them.'"

When Booth broke the news to Mills, Vokes heard the tanker reply, "Tell the old bastard to come up here himself and have a dose of the crap that is flying around!" Vokes "had to smile...I ignored the outburst. That moment was no time for 'rabbit ears.'"[10]

THE SEAFORTHS RESPONDED rapidly to the change in plan. Lieutenant Colonel Bert Hoffmeister simply put into play the plan for the advance from Tiger to Grizzly, with Lion becoming the start line. 'A' Company, now commanded by Major Budge Bell-Irving, would be left of the road and Major Jim Blair's 'C' Company on the right. The rest of the battalion would follow close behind.[11]

By 0330 hours on July 27, Bell-Irving and 'A' Company ventured out from Lion in single file and moved alongside Highway 121 without meeting any initial resistance. The moment 'C' Company started off the ridge, however, it came under accurate machine-gun and mortar fire that pinned the men down. In front of Leonforte, Major

Bell-Irving had demonstrated little ability to keep his men together and properly oriented in a night move. Success for this outing depended on his getting both things right. Still hugging the highway, 'A' Company spotted a German tank only a short distance from the PPCLI positions. Its turret hatch was open and Bell-Irving realized the crew was asleep inside. When a couple of men tried tossing grenades into the hatch, both missed. As the grenades exploded, Bell-Irving and his men scampered into the darkness to get clear of what was likely to be an angry bunch of tankers. By wireless, the major provided Hoffmeister with the tank's map-referenced location and suggested the 90th Anti-Tank Battery supporting the operation come forward and knock it out. Realizing any Germans guarding the road would have been alerted by the grenade explosions and 'C' Company's ongoing fight back at the start line, Bell-Irving headed cross-country on a donkey trail winding through a wood.

As the company moved in a long extended line, the major grew "more and more worried, because I didn't know where I was...It began to look as if it might be first light pretty soon. I knew I had Germans well behind me, and I was trying to figure out what to do when all of a sudden a Nebelwerfer went off right in my face."[12] One after another, the six large rounds from this multibarrelled mortar, nicknamed "Moaning Minnie" because of the shriek its firing made, blasted directly over Bell-Irving's head from a position only yards away. Sensing the German gunners had failed to spot him, the major wheeled sharply to the right and up a hill.[13]

Get his men on top of the hill and wait for daylight, Bell-Irving decided. Blundering around in the dark was only going to result in 'A' Company walking right into an enemy position. Sure enough, just before the crest they bumped into some Panzer Grenadiers and a sharp firefight ensued. But the surprised Germans were quickly put to flight. Captain F.H. Bonnell, however, was wounded in this action. "I remember looking at the hole in him and suggesting that it was time he went back, but he didn't seem interested in that proposition," Bell-Irving wrote.[14]

Coming onto the summit, they found Highway 121 running across it and then bending southeastward towards Agira. The centre of the hilltop was a saucerlike bowl and on its opposing lip, about seventy-five yards away from Bell-Irving's company, stood a tank. "It was light now...and there was no sign of enemy except this tank. Purely by good luck...'A' Company had arrived on the very centre of the Tiger objective."[15]

So far the tankers seemed unaware they had company, so Bell-Irving told Lieutenant Jim Harling to take a PIAT team, work "around to the left below the ridge, and come up close to the tank and knock it out. Good idea, but they discovered they didn't have any PIAT bombs. [These] had been strapped on a donkey, which had decided to go home" during the march.[16]

From their position on Lion, however, a 'C' Squadron tanker spotted the German tank and opened fire. This prompted the German crew commander to stand up in his turret, exposing his head and chest. Bell-Irving raised his rifle and shot the man. As the tank started backing off, a round from the Three Rivers' tank blew a track off. The tank managed to keep moving into some cover that Harling reported concealed a second tank. The Shermans on Lion started indiscriminately shelling the hill. As the Seaforths hugged the ground, Lieutenant Marriott Wilson was killed and several other men were wounded.[17]

Back on Lion, dawn had kicked the battle into full gear. Lieutenant Jack Wallace poked his head out of Commodore's turret and saw "an awful flash, then another and about two hundred yards away something burst into flame. It was Ted Smith's tank which was doing all the shooting. He had spotted a German tank through the haze and let loose before the Boche could get his own gun trained on Ted. Ted told us after that he was never so surprised in all his life...That bit of shooting started the fireworks, for machine guns all around opened up."[18]

In the morning light of July 27, even while ducking incoming German fire, the men from the two PPCLI companies and the Seaforth's 'C' Company that were on Lion were able to see signs "of the terrific battle which had been fought in the past three days" for control of the ridge. "German anti-tank guns and tanks dotted the area together with Sherman tanks. Some had their turrets blown right off, a few had careened into ditches and one or two had been 'flamers.' German equipment—rifles, unopened rations, ammunition, etc.— was scattered about, and so too were the dead." And from cleverly concealed positions in the vineyards and olive groves between Lion and Tiger, Panzer Grenadiers were throwing out a fierce rate of fire.[19]

Just before dawn, Lieutenant Colonel Lindsay had finally found his lost companies. Now that it was light, he put 'A' Company on the left-hand side of the road and 'B' on the right and told their commanders "to take objective 'Tiger' at all cost."[20] The Seaforth's 'C' Company was advancing with the battalion's anti-tank platoon, led by Captain Gordon Money, pushing their guns along behind the riflemen to bring fire on any tanks or anti-tank guns encountered. Several Shermans crawled forward, guns banging out rounds. Within ninety minutes, this loosely organized force gained the summit of Tiger and found Bell-Irving's men waiting.[21] The major had watched in frustration as a "large number of [Germans were] retiring, going past where we had come up" towards Agira. When the tanks arrived, he pointed to the retreating enemy "and they had a great shoot from on top of this hill."[22]

Atop Lion, Wallace could see "all the ground for miles around." He opened fire on a German convoy of trucks "about four miles off. We scatter them and put three out of action. We shoot up numerous haystacks in the valley below us in hope that there may be a Boche tank hidden in one of them. No such luck. We get an awful pasting from some Jerry mortars for about half an hour. They caught me outside of my tank and for a few moments my life was not worth a plugged nickel. During this time the Seaforths were moving into position for the attack on the ridge immediately in front of Agira. The shelling didn't bother them for they just walked straight through it." A wireless signal from Major Pat Mills instructed Wallace's troop to support the Seaforth advance.[23]

Lieutenant Colonel Bert Hoffmeister wanted to keep going for Grizzly, but a signal from division instructed the battalion to hold in place because the town was scheduled for a noon aerial bombardment. In frustration, Hoffmeister called 'C' Company, which was already on the move, at 0730 hours and told them to hold up. Taking

a couple of artillery FOOS and the battalion's mortar platoon commander along, Hoffmeister hurried to Tiger to examine the highway's
route into Agira and begin shelling any German positions they
could spot.[24]

ABOUT THREE MILES northwest of Tiger, the men in a Loyal Edmonton Regiment platoon from 'D' Company were also examining the
ground before them that morning. During the night, twenty-year-old
Lieutenant John Alpine Dougan and his platoon had set out from
Nissoria to carry out a raid behind enemy lines. Only a couple of days
earlier, Dougan and his friend Lieutenant John Earl Christie had
come up from the battalion's reinforcement pool near Pachino to fill
slots created when their predecessors had been either killed or
wounded at Leonforte. Dougan and Christie were two of four Canadian Officers Training Corps cadets from the University of Alberta,
who had all enlisted on March 25, 1942, after being exempted from
taking their final exams leading to undergraduate degrees. The other
two young officers, Lieutenants Alon Johnson and Keith McGregor,
had also been posted to the Edmontons but remained in the reinforcement pool.

Dougan commanded 'D' Company's No. 17 Platoon, while Christie
had drawn its No. 15 Platoon. Shortly before midnight, company
commander Major Bill Bury had ordered Dougan to take the lead in
a cross-country move of about two miles to come astride the road
running from Agira to Nicosia.[25]

Dougan was eager to prove himself. Orienting himself by compass and map-reading, he set off at a good pace. His platoon had been
on the move only a few minutes when the man at the rear sent word
forward that the rest of the company had disappeared. Calling a halt,
Dougan waited until it was obvious that Bury and the other platoons
had gone astray somehow. Assuming they would make for the spot
on the road that had been set as the rally point, Dougan started moving again. "Sicily is a terrible place to manoeuvre," he later commented.
"We were never quite sure where we were, as the ground was terribly
rough and badly broken. It's very desolate, rocky, dry and mountainous. Water was always a problem. You would be terribly thirsty. Had

to be careful of the water you did find. Not that it was poisoned, but because of whether it was drinkable or not. Had to be careful of mosquitoes, which was hard to do when you were on the move in the darkness and wearing shorts and short sleeves. There was a lot of malaria, jaundice, and dysentery."

Despite the difficulties, when dawn broke on July 27, No. 17 Platoon was looking up at the road winding along the side of a steep mountain. Dougan and his men scrambled up the slope and into the Agira–Nicosia road's intersection with a rough track that snaked back to Nissoria. This was the spot Bury had selected for the company to set up a roadblock. Dougan saw no sign of the rest of the company, but just as they came up on the road, "three or four German trucks came in from the north. There was a firefight. When they fired the first burst of fire, I thought it was some type of insect because I hadn't heard bullets before. Heard this crackle around my ears and thought it might be a bee and then suddenly realized what the hell it was." On foot, the Edmontons had the advantage and were able to rip into the Germans before most could bring their guns to bear. No. 17 Platoon kept firing until there was no more sign of movement from around the trucks.

As their guns fell silent, Dougan spotted another long convoy approaching from Agira. He was thinking "we should carry out some redeployment, but before we were able to do that a German tank came around the corner. There was some infantry on it. He saw us and, I suppose, the range wasn't more than twenty-five yards and the PIAT man fired and missed. This was pretty awkward, because we had nowhere to go. And that damned big gun was swinging around and the PIAT man reloaded and fired standing—an act of tremendous fortitude—and he hit the tank just at the turret ring and jammed the gun. The blast dispensed with the infantry riding on the tank. And then we tried to drop grenades in the open hatch but our aim wasn't too good and the tank pulled back and just went around the corner and blew up."

So far the platoon had suffered not a single casualty while wreaking significant havoc, but Dougan figured he was pushing luck. "We were several miles behind the line and the whole countryside was swarming with, as far as I could see, uniforms of the wrong shade." Having carried several "Hawkins" grenades—small anti-tank mines that weighed 2.25 pounds each and could either be shallowly buried or thrown at a vehicle—Dougan and his men planted these in the gravel on either side of the road "and carried out a tactical withdrawal to a little better position."

Even moving cross-country, the platoon kept coming within about one hundred yards or less of long formations of German infantry marching away from Agira. "But they thought we were Germans, too, and we didn't do anything to dispel that thought. We ran into some people and couldn't avoid them, so we took them prisoner." One group they captured had three Canadian prisoners with them—an artillery captain, a gunnery sergeant, and a wireless signaller—who were immediately liberated and added to the strength of the little band. The platoon had withdrawn about a quarter mile when it was intercepted by a runner sent from the battalion. The platoon, he said, was "to hold the road at all costs, if I was on the road." The message added that the rest of the company had failed to get through, but 'C' Company was being sent to reinforce the position.

"So we turned and trudged back, taking more prisoners on the road. Got to the intersection and...there was another tank knocked out, the track had been blown. A couple halftracks and a truck were also knocked out. One halftrack was loaded with cherry brandy and plum jam. So we helped ourselves to that and also took quite a few prisoners. By this stage, we were getting so damned many prisoners they were becoming a real problem." Dougan positioned the platoon on the side of the mountain above the road and they dug in. Sporadic groups of Germans kept sallying towards their position in what Dougan considered less attacks than confused attempts to determine "who we were and where we were and what we were. A few rounds of Bren-gun fire and they seemed to scatter a bit."[26]

Late in the afternoon, 'C' Company arrived and Major W.T. Cromb's men dug in alongside the platoon. By this time, all attempts to push traffic up the road had ceased, and the Germans were only occasionally probing the Edmonton position with section-sized units. These were easily chased off, and the men enjoyed a relatively quiet night.

On the morning of July 28, the Germans launched a series of weak counterattacks that came in alternately from the north and south. These were easily repelled.[27] Late that afternoon, the battalion's carrier platoon trundled brashly up the road and its commander told Dougan he had come to take them home.

This sustained action of more than thirty-six hours had been Dougan's battle christening. Later, when he understood better the nature of combat, Dougan would regret not putting the PIAT man up for a medal. "At the time, I thought that kind of bravery was just normal. I didn't know any better. I thought this was just a normal operation. It wasn't normal at all. It was quite admirable." The Edmontons suffered not a casualty. "We were just so lucky. We took all sorts of booty and prisoners and had tanks knocked out. The Company commander [Bury] got the DSO for the operation, although he wasn't within miles of it."[28]

Bury's citation, which was submitted by the Edmontons' Lieutenant Colonel Jim Jefferson, claimed that by "map and compass, on this dark and moonless night, this officer unerringly led his men, cross country over the six mile stretch of rugged precipitous rock. Reaching the post at dawn Major Bury personally led the bayonet charge which captured the post, then the company dug in."[29] This was possibly one of the most blatant examples of the relatively common practice of senior officers falsifying reports in order to secure a fellow officer a coveted medal of valour. After the war, when an army historical officer interviewed Major Cromb about the patrol, he "expressed surprise" that the DSO citation "gave the work of the Edmonton platoon as the basis for his award."[30] Confronted on the matter, Jefferson defended his citation report on the basis that Bury had "organized" the feat.[31]

DURING THE MORNING of July 27, meanwhile, the Seaforth Highlanders had been gearing up on Tiger to attack Grizzly, the last defensible ground that barred the western approach to Agira. Lieutenant Colonel Bert Hoffmeister carefully studied the complex obstacle that Grizzly presented. It consisted really of two features. South of Highway 121 stood Monte Fronte, a square-topped hill, while on the road's opposite flank a wooded ridge extended a short distance to the north and tied in with the heights of Monte Crapuzza. On the southern end of the ridge, a cemetery sat on ground slightly higher than the rest. The Canadians dubbed this high point "Cemetery Hill." Together, these heights on either side of the road composed Grizzly. Behind them, Agira hugged the western slope of "a still higher cone-shaped hill lying astride the highway."

At noon, as scheduled, all these features were subjected to a heavy battering by Allied medium bombers and strafing fire from fighter bombers. The Seaforths could "observe the bursts of the big bombs as they fell in the northern and western sections of the town." At 1400 hours, 'A' and 'D' companies went forward on either side of the road behind a heavy divisional-scale artillery barrage with each also supported by a troop of 'C' Squadron tanks. In both cases, the Shermans—unable to keep pace with the infantry in such rough ground—were left far behind and played no role in the forthcoming fight.[32] Also on the move was the Seaforth's 'C' Company, which was driving south from Tiger in an attempt to outflank Grizzly. If the direct attack failed, Captain Jim Blair's company might manage to get behind the feature and loosen the German defences there.

Major Budge Bell-Irving had 'A' Company deployed in arrowhead formation, with No. 8 Platoon forming the tip, his company headquarters section directly behind, and the other two platoons flared out on either flank a little farther back. As his men reached the base of Monte Fronte, the Germans struck them with a withering rate of fire. What followed next was a "classic battle-drill attack" carried out to perfection. With no orders from Bell-Irving, No. 8 Platoon's commander led his men directly into the face of the enemy fire with two sections covering the advance of the third. Once this section gained some protected ground, it began laying down fire to enable those behind to jump past its position. In this manner, one section was able to reach the steep face of Monte Fronte and climb a short distance up to overrun an MG 42 position. When the Germans counterattacked, the section slithered back down the slope, taking the gun with them.[33]

The moment the company had been struck by the drenching fire from ahead, Bell-Irving had assumed No. 8 Platoon would do the right thing and had signalled No. 9 Platoon on the right flank to begin a wide flanking movement. He tucked the company headquarters section onto No. 9 Platoon's tail, as No. 7 Platoon cut across from the left to follow the formation southward. Hooking around to the southern flank of Monte Fronte, this element of 'A' Company stared up an "almost perpendicular," nearly three-hundred-foot slope that led to a narrow and apparently undefended summit. Bell-Irving realized the Germans must have thought the slope impossible to climb. The men from British Columbia set about proving the Panzer Grenadiers wrong. Weapons slung and burdened by the rest of their fighting packs, they went up like monkeys from one handhold to another and gained the summit within minutes.

Corporal F.W. Terry was at the head of his section when it clambered over the lip. Seeing a nearby machine-gun position whose crew were firing westward at No. 8 Platoon, Terry charged and captured the gun. His action earned a Military Medal.[34] The ground 'A' Company found itself on consisted of "very rocky, narrow steps, with a cliff behind." Bell-Irving advanced his men quickly so that the company's forward platoon, under Lieutenant Jim Harling, had the "protection of...a stone wall about two feet high." Before them the summit levelled off and was only lightly vegetated. Having taken the Germans by surprise, the Seaforths were well positioned when the Panzer Grenadiers realized their presence and rounded on them with machine guns they had been firing at No. 8 Platoon.[35] The shifting of this fire enabled the platoon holding on the mountain's eastern slope to disengage and begin moving to join the rest of 'A' Company on the summit.

But that move would take an hour or more to complete. Meanwhile, the men on the summit attracted the full fury of the Germans. 'A' Company, like all the other Seaforth companies, had gone into the attack badly understrength. There were barely more than fifty men on the summit. "It was hot, the men were exhausted, ammunition was running short, water was scarce...A terrific firefight went on, with the Germans using rifle and machine-gun fire as well as rifle grenades, but the various platoons, well tucked into the rocky crevices and using the protection afforded by terraces, suffered few casualties and not only held on to their positions but slowly improved them," the Seaforth's regimental historian recorded.[36]

On the north side of the road, 'D' Company had earlier gone for Cemetery Hill. Like most cemeteries in Sicily, this one was surrounded by a high wall braced by family tombs and bordered on the outside by "tall, sombre cypress trees."[37] Captain June Thomas and his men never even got close. Raked by machine guns hidden in and around the cemetery and heavily mortared, 'D' Company kept reeling forward despite growing casualties. The wireless signaller next to Thomas was killed and his set destroyed. Forced to ground, Thomas sent a runner back to Tiger to request reinforcements and a new wireless set.[38] Hoffmeister instead "decided that the northern end of Grizzly was too strongly held to be captured by one company, so he ordered 'D' Company to withdraw into Battalion reserve." He would concentrate the Seaforth's effort on winning the battle for Monte Fronte.[39]

South of this objective, Major Jim Blair's 'C' Company became mired in a hellish maze of "vine-terraced hills and valleys" that had his men constantly either climbing or descending through rugged terrain. Blair had no wireless link to battalion and was so disoriented that even deciding which high point was Grizzly proved impossible. One platoon, under Lieutenant John F. McLean, became separated. At about 1700 hours, McLean and his men charged up what they thought was Grizzly, only to find the summit they won was three-quarters of a mile too far south. Dispirited, the platoon surrendered their undisputed hold on the worthless feature and headed for Monte Fronte. With nightfall, McLean decided if he kept pushing his exhausted men they would be useless, so they settled in for a night of sleeping rough. The rest of 'C' Company, meanwhile, had fared little better. It ended the day having stormed a summit that was almost the correct one, but still too far south. Blair, too, opted to hold where he was until morning.

Hoffmeister had spent much of the afternoon going forward through machine-gun and mortar fire in an attempt to establish contact with 'C' Company and direct it onto Monte Fronte. Unable to find the lost company, he returned to Tiger and sent 'B' Company to 'A' Company's support. Trying to approach the summit from the north flank, the company ran into such strong mortar fire from Agira and Cemetery Hill at 1830 hours that it was driven to ground. 'A' Company would have to hold the hill through the night on its own.[40]

WHEN HOFFMEISTER TOLD Brigadier Chris Vokes that he had shifted the entire weight of his battalion against the Grizzly objective south of the highway, the 2 CIB commander decided to commit another battalion to carrying Cemetery Hill. At 2000 hours on July 27, the Loyal Edmonton Regiment advanced with three companies in line abreast. 'A' Company was on the left, 'B' Company in the centre, and 'D' Company (less Lieutenant John Dougan's platoon) on the right. With a skeleton battalion headquarters, Lieutenant Colonel Jim Jefferson stationed himself behind the centre company. The Edmonton commander was throwing everything he had at the objective, for 'C' Company had gone to the aid of Dougan's patrol.[41]

With night falling, the Edmontons moved into "country broken by hills and ravines." Their maps next to useless, they blundered forward as blindly as the Seaforth's 'C' Company had during its right hook towards Monte Fronte. By the time they reached the assigned forming-up position for the final assault, the supporting artillery had finished firing several hours before.[42]

'A' Company was more fortunate than the others. Its objective was Monte Crapuzza, which stuck out prominently on the left-hand flank of the ridge. Captain Pat Tighe and his men swarmed up the mountain to find it undefended. To the south, they could see tracers spitting through the darkness and the flash of explosions. But there were no obvious targets that were clearly Germans and might not prove to be Edmontons. So they settled in and watched the fireworks.

A half mile to the south, the other two companies reached the slope leading up Cemetery Hill shortly after midnight on July 28. In some places the slope proved to be "an absolute cliff." The Germans above "poured heavy concentrations of mortar fire and threw 'potato mashers'" down at them.[43] Stalled in front of the cliffs, 'B' Company was pinned by this fire and racking up casualties. Its commander, Captain A.A. Gilchrist, was wounded, as was one of the platoon commanders, Lieutenant H.M. Turner. To the right, 'D' Company's Major Bury sent a section from one platoon to hook around to the south next to the road and get in behind the Germans. Moments after these men headed out, Bury was killed by a mortar bomb. The attack was beginning to crumble when 'D' Company's second-in-command,

Captain H.W. Smith, "came forward and rallied the remainder of the company." Hearing gunfire to the rear of the Germans defending the cemetery, Smith "deduced the section had been successful in getting into position; he then led the greatly reduced company in an assault up the cliffs and by the use of 2-inch mortars, hand grenades, and [Bren guns] carried the hill against a…numerically superior opposition estimated at 150 of the enemy as against his own total strength of about 40 all ranks. The section behind the hill was particularly effective in distracting the enemy and contributed in no small measure to the success of the engagement. The enemy had, in fact broken their lines under this assault and their flight into the town was nothing more…than a disorganized retreat."

Realizing the fight for Agira had tipped far in favour of the Canadians, 'A' Company's Major Tighe sent a patrol under Lieutenant L.T. Swan towards the town. Coming upon a house on the outskirts, Swan observed it was full of heavily armed German and Italian troops that had probably just fallen back from Cemetery Hill. Taking a Thompson submachine gun, he crept up alone and demanded their surrender. The seventeen Germans and four Italians meekly complied. As the platoon led their prisoners back towards Monte Crapuzza, the party was caught by German mortars, and several of the prisoners were killed or wounded. At dawn on July 28, Tighe was further encouraged to send a couple more fighting patrols to the north to cut the Agira–Nicosia road. The Edmontons were solidly in control of Grizzly on the north side of the highway.[44]

They had suffered relatively light casualties in this protracted night action—three men killed and thirty-one wounded.[45] Bury, of course, was among the dead. The forty-five-year-old veteran of the Great War had been a popular officer—the probable motive for Jefferson's fudging of the facts about Dougan's patrol. He wanted to ensure the major received a DSO citation as a tribute. Dougan never minded that Jefferson misspoke, for he had found Bury "a very brave, good man."[46]

DURING THE NIGHT, while the Edmontons had been assaulting the northern portion of Grizzly, the Seaforth's 'A' Company had staved off several fierce counterattacks. It was a terrific fight, but the Seaforths clung grimly to their summit lodgement on the southern edge of Monte Fronte. Shortly after midnight on July 28, the Panzer Grenadiers came at them with a bayonet charge. "This attack," Bell-Irving wrote, "was concentrated and heavily supported by point blank small arms fire by plastic rifle grenades." Lieutenant Jim Harling and his platoon were behind the two-foot stone wall and he "stood up to his full height and threw grenades at the oncoming enemy—one after the other—while singing [a Hawaiian song] at the top of his lungs. He, more than any other, was responsible for the successful holding of Grizzly Hill."[47]

Just before first light, Lieutenant McLean's platoon from 'C' Company climbed up the cliff and came in behind 'A' Company. The lieutenant had got his men moving as soon as he thought they were rested sufficiently, and they had moved towards the sounds of the fighting. McLean seemed as delighted to see Bell-Irving as the major was to see him. Bell-Irving was ecstatic—less because of the added manpower than because the men carried a good supply of ammunition and 2-inch mortar bombs.

This booty was quickly shared around and then Bell-Irving decided it was time for offensive action. For one thing, his fifty-man force was desperately short of water and the only well stood next to a small German-held house. Bell-Irving worked out a plan whereby McLean and three men would "crawl towards the enemy occupied house under the cover of smoke grenades and the fire" from Harling's platoons. Once McLean's party was close enough, "they would rush the building with the two platoons close on their heels."

In a fine display of fieldcraft, the four men crawled to within charging range of the house. "Close behind them, Harling, a big man, threw grenades over their heads as if [they] were softballs, inspiring his men as he had for the past two days. Then McLean and his men, followed by the two platoons, got up and raced towards the enemy strongpoint and such was the force of their charge that they kept going beyond it to the far end of the feature, clearing it of the enemy."[48]

Soon Bell-Irving was able to report back to Hoffmeister that Monte Fronte was in Seaforth's hands. Despite the fierce and extended nature of the fight, 'A' Company had only two men killed and five wounded. Lieutenant McLean's platoon lost nobody. Seventy-five German dead were counted on the summit, fifteen prisoners were taken, and numerous blood trails indicated a high number of Panzer Grenadiers had been wounded and carried from the field. For their brave handling of this action, Bell-Irving and Hoffmeister were both awarded Distinguished Service Orders. Bell-Irving put Harling in for a decoration as well, but it was refused. He later admitted his inexperienced citation writing was the probable reason.[49]

At 0855 hours on July 28, Brigadier Chris Vokes sent an exultant message to Major General Guy Simonds. "Whole of Grizzly in our hands. Nearly all enemy killed. Survivors retreating northwards. We have lost contact. All approaches safe." The door to Agira had been kicked open, and the town was his for the taking.[50]

[20]

Hard Fighting

ROM PRISONERS AND captured documents, 1st Canadian Infantry Division intelligence officers gleaned that the Germans who had defended Grizzly had consisted of the entire 1st Battalion, 15th Panzer Grenadier Regiment of the 29th Panzer Grenadier Division. This unit, attached early in the campaign to the 15th Panzer Grenadier Division, had taken over the position on July 27 from the battalions of 104th Panzer Grenadier Regiment, which in the fighting for Leonforte and the ridges to the west of Agira had lost more than two hundred men killed and had a far greater number wounded. The estimated dead for 1st Battalion, 15th Panzer Grenadier Regiment was conservatively set at 125 with the wounded total far surpassing that. All German units had lost many men as prisoners.

By July 28, the 15th Panzer Grenadier Division was fast withdrawing to a new position running from Regalbuto through Gagliano to a point just east of Nicosia.[1]

For their part, the Canadians were not yet thinking about breaking the new German line. There remained still the matter of taking Agira itself. After the street battle for Leonforte, it was feared this medieval town with its narrow, winding streets, barely wide enough to allow passage of a burdened donkey, would be similarly defended.

Taking no chances, Vokes ordered Agira bombarded at 1545 by all divisional artillery and mortars. The Princess Patricia's Canadian Light Infantry would then advance on either side of the highway from a point just west of Grizzly.[2]

Once again the trucks rolled through the morning to deliver about four hundred rounds to each gun pit. While these preparations were under way, a 1st Field Regiment (Royal Canadian Horse Artillery) FOO and his signaller walked cautiously towards Agira in search of an observation point from which to support the PPCLI with directed artillery fire after the bombardment ceased. Seeing no enemy activity, Captain G.E. Baxter kept moving closer until the two gunners walked right into the town and decided the Germans had withdrawn. Quickly reporting the news by wireless, Baxter was able to stop the bombardment—an act that undoubtedly saved many civilian lives, as well as sparing many of Agira's ancient buildings from destruction.[3]

'A' and 'B' companies were already marching to the forming-up position when Lieutenant Colonel Bob Lindsay advised Captains W. "Bucko" Watson and R.F.S. Robertson that the shoot had been cancelled "to conserve ammunition."[4] The three officers decided Watson's 'A' Company would send a fighting patrol in to confirm the report. If Agira proved clear, both would go up and occupy it. But if any "enemy were encountered the supporting fire would be laid on again." As these plans were being cut the weather took an unusual turn, as the thin layer of cloud that had been building all morning released a drizzle of rain.

In this cooler, damper weather, the patrol moved along Highway 121 until it was adjacent to a large open plaza that stood at the town's entrance. Working around the edge of the plaza, hugging the shops and houses for cover, the patrol gained and started up the steep, narrow main street that led into the heart of the mountaintop town. All went well until it came to a second, smaller plaza set on a level shelf, where the main road branched into several narrower lanes all tightly flanked by two- and three-storey buildings. From the plaza to the upper level of the town, the slope became ever steeper until it reached the summit. On the right-hand side, just below the summit, the tower of a large church was visible. The lanes ahead looked dark and threatening, not a soul to be seen. Cautiously, the patrol edged into the plaza and immediately came under fire from what appeared to be only a small party of Germans. A hasty withdrawal was made, and the patrol reported its findings back to Watson and Robertson.

Deciding the slight resistance met was insufficient to justify unleashing the artillery, the two captains agreed to "divide the town in half between them, 'B' Company right and 'A' Company left and proceed to a first objective, a line parallel to our front joining two easily distinguishable churches about three quarters of the way up the hill." At 1430 hours, the PPCLI entered the outskirts and were greeted by "quite an ovation from the local population."[5] Holding at the entrance to the town, in case they were needed, was No. 3 Troop from the Three Rivers Regiment's 'C' Squadron, under command of Lieutenant "Beez" Gordon.

About three hundred yards into the town, however, all signs of civilian activity ceased, and 'A' Company's leading platoon was attacked by fire from a machine-gun position and was forced to take cover. Hearing the gunfire, No. 3 Troop rumbled through the ever-narrowing streets until it came up behind 'A' Company. Gordon dismounted and went to find Watson, but a burst from the machine gun knocked the tanker down with a serious wound. Realizing they were next to useless and badly exposed in the tight confines of Agira's streets, the tankers withdrew.[6] Watson, meanwhile, had stationed a Bren-gun section on the roof of a building overlooking the enemy position. From here the Bren gunner was able to kill the machine-gun team with some well-aimed bursts.

After having progressed halfway through the town without incident, 'B' Company had also become hotly engaged. No. 10 Platoon, under Corporal S.C. Butterick, had been leading the advance up a rain-slicked cobblestone street when it came under fire "from about ten men" armed either with Schmeissers or MG 42 machine guns. A two-hour firefight followed that required "house to house fighting" to roust out the enemy. "Fighting was made all the more difficult because of narrow alleyways paved with slippery cobblestones which the enemy could cover with his automatics." Only by working around the flanks of the Germans was the platoon able to close in and kill them all. During the shootout, Butterick was wounded in both legs. Propped against a wall, he continued to direct his men until the fight was concluded—garnering a Military Medal for his conduct.

While No. 10 Platoon had been eliminating resistance, the rest of 'B' Company had moved unchallenged up a different lane and gained the line next to one of the churches. Here, at 1630 hours, No. 10 Platoon caught up.

'A' Company's fight lasted longer. After clearing the first machine-gun position, it ran into another, firing from a house fifty yards farther up the slope. Watson sent a platoon around the left flank of the building and their PIAT man hammered it with several bombs, which the Canadians judged must have "shook the enemy up inside considerably." One section, after chucking about ten grenades through windows and doors, rushed inside and took ten prisoners. The advance continued, with the company having to root out several more machine-gun positions while dodging sporadic sniper fire. Lieutenant John Stewart Carnegie de Balinhard, the son of a PPCLI officer from the Great War, climbed onto a rooftop to try sighting an enemy position and was hit by a sniper round. Watson, who had come forward to consult him, found the thirty-three-year-old sprawled dead where he had been struck. Not until 1900 hours did 'A' Company reach its objective alongside 'B' Company, and Agira was declared clear of enemy. The battalion's casualties were one officer killed and another officer and ten other ranks wounded. German losses "amounted to eighty killed, wounded or prisoners."[7] Three anti-tank guns, about thirty MG 42s, 100,000 rounds of machine-gun ammunition, and many mortar bombs were also captured.[8]

In fact, the 29th Division's 1st Battalion, 15th Panzer Grenadier had about 125 men taken prisoner and an equal number killed in this action. The estimated 250 remaining members of this battalion joined the mauled 1st Panzer Grenadier Regiment of 15th Division's withdrawal to the vicinity of Gagliano, where it faced the American advance.[9] Extending its flank northward, the Hermann Göring Division assumed responsibility for blocking further advances by the Canadians.[10]

"So Agira fell, after five days of hard fighting in which practically the whole of the Canadian Division, with the exception of the 3rd

Brigade...had been engaged," wrote the army's official historian. "It was the Division's biggest battle of the Sicilian campaign and it cost 438 Canadian casualties." The 231st (Malta) Brigade added about three hundred casualties from its battalions in this protracted engagement.[11]

AS THE BATTLE for Agira had raged, 3rd Canadian Infantry Brigade had been advancing within the Dittaino valley towards a major three-way junction at the town of Catenanuova. On July 23, the brigade had been arrayed on either side of the Dittaino River, about eight miles south of Agira. The Royal 22e Régiment stood close to the Raddusa–Agira Station, the West Nova Scotia Regiment was about three miles southeast at the hamlet of Libertinia, and the Carleton and York Regiment straddled the river's northern flank guarding the road that led to Agira. With the rest of the division beginning the advance from Leonforte to Agira, 3 CIB was ordered to remain in place to provide a pivot point for the forward-wheeling movement going north of it and also to await the 51st Highland Division coming up on its right-hand flank.[12]

On the ridges overlooking the valley from both north and south, German troops could be regularly seen moving about. Throughout the day, the West Novas—holding a more easterly position than the other two battalions—were intermittently shelled. Four other ranks were killed and another three wounded by this fire. At 1600 hours, two corporals from the Hermann Göring Division approached under protection of a white flag and informed battalion adjutant Captain C.B. "Clary" Higgins that the West Novas had one hour to surrender or "they would loose the whole force of the Wehrmacht upon us." Telling them to "go to hell," Higgins had the two escorted to division for questioning. No attack developed.[13]

July 23, however, proved disastrous for the Carleton and York Regiment. At 1100 hours, a twenty-eight man patrol from 'A' Company set out to check whether a pink house on a nearby hill was occupied. Sergeant Arthur Wallace Eatman's instructions were to be back by dusk, but the patrol failed to return. The following day a company-strength patrol went out and found five bodies. These were identified as Eatman and Privates Walter James Lapointe, Omar B. Gallagher,

William Joseph McCauley, and William Henry Morris. The rest of the patrol was presumed lost as prisoners. Except for one, all were later confirmed as having been captured. Private Arlie William Hanson was designated as missing, presumed dead.

What happened to the patrol was never determined, but it caused great dissension within the regiment. Lieutenant Colonel Dodd Tweedie blamed the company commander, Captain Glen Foster, for giving inadequate orders to the sergeant. Others set the fault with Tweedie for sending a large patrol out under a sergeant's command, but the lieutenant colonel defended his action on the basis that no officer was available and that Eatman was so experienced he was under consideration for a battlefield commission. Even the patrol's purpose became subject to debate. Tweedie said it was to check the pink house, but 3 CIB's Brigade Major G.F.C. Pangman contended it acted on his orders to reconnoitre the area around Monte Scalpello, which lay about six miles east of the Carleton's position. It also emerged that battalion headquarters had sent an uncoded wireless signal telling the patrol to follow a set path along a height within sight of 'A' Company. Many a Carleton believed this breach of security had been intercepted and the patrol walked into a resulting ambush.[14]

Late on July 24, realizing that the rest of the division was entangled in a protracted struggle for Agira, the Carletons and Van Doos moved eastward along the valley floor to come abreast of the West Novas at Libertinia. The brigade was to begin an eastward advance without waiting for the rest of the division and would draw its artillery and other fire support from the 51st Highland Division. The routes taken had been heavily mined by the Germans, so progress was slow. A Carleton carrier driven by Private Graydon Alexander Taylor blew up on a mine. Taylor was killed and Lance Sergeant T.W. Harrison was seriously wounded.[15]

Because of the mines, the brigade's further advance was delayed until July 26. With the 51st Highlanders already well ahead, xxx Corps declared it was now urgent that Brigadier Howard Penhale push his battalions through to Catenanuova—about seven miles to the east. The Van Doos led, Penhale ordering them to cut around the north flank of Monte Scalpello to gain its eastern slope.[16]

As with the Grizzly position before Agira, the full brigade objective required capturing two mountains—one on either side of the Dittaino valley railway track. Monte Scalpello, a massive "feature whose rocky ridge towered in a long razor-back nearly 3,000 feet above the road," was on the valley's southern flank while the nearly eight-hundred-foot Monte Santa Maria lay about two miles to the northeast of the first summit. The Van Doos would have to secure both heights in order to open the way to Catenanuova, which was about a mile beyond Santa Maria.[17]

'B' Company, under Major Gilles Turcot, took point. Its men were using mules to carry water, rations, and ammunition. The company advanced along the right side of the dried-up riverbed, while a short distance farther back Captain Léo Bouchard's 'A' Company trudged up the left side. By nightfall, the two companies were digging in on the slopes in front of the mountains on their respective sides of the riverbed. 'A' Company was to attack Monte Santa Maria in the morning and 'B' Company, Monte Scalpello.[18]

By the afternoon of July 26, 'A' Company was within 550 yards of Monte Santa Maria. Seeing movement on the round and treeless summit, Bouchard called on the wireless for an artillery concentration on it. The bombardment lasted fifteen minutes. At the end, the artillery laid a smokescreen to cover the Van Doos, who charged up the slope with fixed bayonets. Two platoons, commanded by Lieutenants Guy Robitaille and Côme Simard, led, with Lieutenant François LaFleche's platoon following in reserve. "Lightning fast and under perfect control, the [company], under heavy machine-gun fire crossed a tilled field about 500 yards across. Once past that field, there remained only a few yards before beginning the climb. The platoons were rapidly reorganized. While one section advanced, the other gave covering fire."

'A' Company was under "intense fire" from infantry dug in on the summit and was also being heavily mortared with deadly accuracy. Bouchard was killed by a fragment from a mortar round. Seconds later Robitaille was hit in the leg, but continued leading his men forward. Hit again in the stomach and then a third time in his arm, the lieutenant finally collapsed. His actions this day earned a Military

Cross. Lieutenant LaFleche was also wounded in the hand. Simard's platoon, meanwhile, had been pinned down by the fierce fire. Learning Bouchard was dead and Robitaille critically wounded, Simard took command of the company. Slowly the platoons fought their way up the slopes, the sections advancing by bounds, with one moving as the other two covered with supporting fire.[19] When Corporal Jean Baptiste Montminy's Bren gunner was killed, he grabbed the weapon, single-handedly outflanked three enemy positions, and "routed the enemy who were holding up the advance of the entire platoon." He was awarded the Military Medal for this action.[20]

Simard led two platoons onto the summit, but saw that No. 9 Platoon had been forced to ground in front of a pillbox bristling with machine guns. Taking No. 8 Platoon—the second one under his command—Simard swung around the right flank of the pillbox and broke through the rear entrance. The ten Germans inside surrendered. Simard reported that 'A' Company controlled Monte Santa Maria. He also requested ammunition and water be immediately sent up, but the road was so heavily mined that the battalion quartermaster was unable to get anything to the Van Doos, who were hungry, thirsty, and badly short of ammunition. When the Germans counterattacked in strength at about 2000 hours, Simard had no option but to surrender the hard-won mountain by withdrawing.

'B' Company, meanwhile, had attacked at 1500 hours but come under intense 88-millimetre fire when only six hundred yards east of Libertinia. Resorting to fieldcraft, the company slipped forward by way of various gullies and dense thickets to a little hill called Nicolella, northwest of Monte Scalpello. Here they encountered a Sicilian woman who spoke fluent French and gave them good information on the nature of the ground and numbers of German troops ahead. Pressing on through the night, the company easily gained the summit.

Dawn of July 27 found the Van Doos with 'A' Company dug in at the base of Monte Santa Maria and 'B' Company sitting solid atop Monte Scalpello. When 'C' Company joined the latter, the two companies were able to clear the entire feature in a bout of heavy fighting. Major Turcot was wounded in the right foot but continued to command the two companies until the battle ended later in the day.[21]

Taking advantage of the German fixation on the Van Doos, the West Novas had slipped unobserved around the southern flank of Monte Scalpello to take up a position about two miles southwest of Catenanuova. Although they were well placed to push on to the town, the battalion was ordered to hold in place and await further orders from XXX Corps. Eighth Army was developing a new operational plan and further advances by the Canadians would have to be "woven into the wider design." For the Van Doos, the past thirty-six hours had proved costly. The three companies committed were entirely exhausted from the constant action. They had also suffered seventy-four casualties including the deaths of one officer and seventeen other ranks.[22]

CODE-NAMED "HARDGATE," EIGHTH Army's wider design had developed during a meeting between General Harold Alexander and his two army commanders at Cassibile on July 21. The plan laid out details for a dual offensive directed on Messina scheduled to begin August 1. Seventh U.S. Army was to advance from the San Stéfano–Nicosia road along two axes—the coastal Highway 113 and a parallel inland route, Highway 120, that ran from Nicosia to Randazzo. Eighth Army, meanwhile, would commit XXX Corps to a main attack directed at breaking the so-called German Etna Line by capturing Adrano, while XIII Corps launched a feint on the Catania plain to hold the enemy there in place.

As part of Hardgate, the rest of 1st Canadian Army Tank Brigade was to be committed to active operations for the first time. This brigade, less the Three Rivers Regiment, had landed at Siracusa on July 13–14 and become part of the Eighth Army's armoured reserve. The fighting teeth of this brigade were provided by its two remaining tank regiments—the Ontario Tank Regiment and Calgary Tank Regiment. On July 23, the brigade had moved to positions four miles northeast of Scordia and just south of the Gornalunga River. Its role, which was set out in instructions issued on July 26, was to patrol a ten-mile gap between XIII Corps and XXX Corps and "destroy all enemy attempting to attack between" their respective flanks.[23] The tankers were not alone in this duty. Also closing the gap was the 5th British Infantry Division's reconnaissance regiment and its 105th Anti-Tank Regiment. The Canadians were expected to become engaged with the enemy only if it became necessary to "fight an armoured battle."[24]

Two divisions would be aimed at Adrano—the newly arrived 78th British Infantry Division and 1st Canadian Infantry Division. The former division would advance from Catenanuova northeastward via a road that passed through Centuripe to Adrano, while the Canadians would drive through Regalbuto and then hook northward into the Salso valley for the final approach directly from the west into the town.

As a preliminary to Hardgate, 3rd Brigade came under 78th Division command on July 29 and was given the task of capturing Catenanuova for the British to use as their starting point. Hardgate's timetable called for 1st Canadian Division to begin its drive towards Regalbuto on the night of July 30–31, with the 78th Division entering operations on the night of August 1–2.

At 2336 hours on July 29, the gunners of the 78th Division fired a heavy artillery barrage in support of 3 CIB's attack. The Van Doos had two tasks, recapturing Monte Santa Maria and carrying Hill 204 about one thousand yards northeast of it. From their position southeast of Monte Scalpello, the West Novas would drive into Catenanuova after which the Carletons would send a company-sized patrol through to seize a junction of roads running alternately northwest and northeast to Regalbuto and Centuripe, respectively.[25]

At midnight, the West Novas advanced behind the barrage, which crept forward at the normal bound rate of about one hundred yards every three minutes. 'A' and 'B' companies were leading, both trying to keep at least two hundred yards back from the exploding shells. Just as the men swept into the Dittaino riverbed, several shells fell short and 'A' Company's Captain S.D. Smith and seven men from 'B' Company were wounded. Lieutenant Ross Guy took over 'A' Company, and the troops kept moving without missing a beat. The riverbank was extremely wide and overgrown by a sour-smelling coarse grass, so the entire battalion advanced within it for about one hundred yards because of the steep banks on either side. Although this forced them to bunch up dangerously, there was hardly any German fire and no casualties resulted. According to the plan, the two lead companies were to cut through the outskirts of Catenanuova to gain the heights north of the town, while the following companies peeled off to clear the place itself.

Coming to a bend in the river, the West Novas scrambled up the bank facing the town. Beyond was the raised bed of the railway track and behind that a long eight-foot-high concrete wall, which 'A' Company headed directly towards. As the company reached the wall, several potato-mashers came over from the opposite side. These grenades had a metal-cased explosive charge attached to a hollow wooden handle. They had a blast radius of twelve to fourteen yards but tended to generate more concussive force than body-slashing shrapnel. True to type, the grenades caused no injuries, and 'A' Company was more delayed by the problem of trying to boost men over the wall. Discovering a gap created by the shellfire, the company poured through the opening and entered the railway yard. Having been heavily bombed by Allied aircraft over the preceding couple of days and then singled out for particularly intense shelling, the rail yard was a shambles. Dozens of smashed boxcars, many of which were on fire, had been thrown far off the tracks. Severed high-voltage power lines hung from leaning poles and others sparked and sizzled on the ground. The troops carefully avoided touching them with their bodies and weapons as they passed.

Moving into the town's outskirts, 'A' Company dodged forward in the face of sporadic bursts of small-arms fire loosed by pockets of Germans who appeared to be withdrawing rather than seeking a fight. Avoiding the narrow streets with walls or houses pressing close on either side, the platoons climbed over walls to gain one backyard after another.[26] Reaching its objective at sunrise on the high ground north of Catenanuova, 'A' Company was just starting to hack at the hard-baked ground with picks and shovels when two companies of infantry supported by a self-propelled gun began a counterattack. Caught in the open, the company scattered for the nearby cover of several cactus hedges. Lieutenant Ross Guy and his signaller ended up in a shell hole with the No. 18 wireless set, Guy's pistol, and four grenades. The Germans were shelling the entire area, while their infantry sprayed it with small-arms fire. From somewhere Guy was unable to see, the SPG was banging away with its 75-millimetre gun. With signaller in tow, Guy moved into this fire. Managing to round up about nineteen of his men, he set up a position behind the cover of a stone wall. Fifty yards from the wall was a cactus grove in which the Germans had concentrated. Facing each other, the two sides traded gunfire.

Suddenly there was a flurry of gunfire from within the grove, and the Germans bolted into the open. Guy and his men ripped into them with deadly fire, and from the grove more guns joined in. When there were no more targets to fire at, Guy spotted some West Novas signalling from the grove. They were his two platoon commanders, Lieutenants E.N. Doane and C.C. Reeves, who had gathered their men and attacked the grove from the rear. Enemy casualties in this action were estimated at about thirty-five in exchange for twelve 'A' Company men killed or wounded.

Guy got on the wireless and asked Lieutenant Colonel Pat Bogert to immediately send reinforcements, ammunition, and artillery support to break up the counterattacks. Bogert told him the heavy artillery fire the Germans were directing at the brigade area was hampering efforts by the engineers of 4th Field Company to clear mines and create a crossing over the riverbed that would allow transport trucks to reach the forward positions. There would be no ammunition or reinforcement likely for the rest of the day. But he had artillery on call if Guy could provide target references. Like most junior officers, however, Guy had received no training in directing artillery fire. Bogert proceeded to calmly talk the lieutenant through the process, and after a few shots were fired and corrections made, he was soon ranging the guns onto various targets, which convinced the Germans to keep their distance. Guy's work earned a Military Cross.[27]

'B' Company had been more fortunate in its advance, encountering only a machine gun on the edge of the town, which was quickly silenced. By 0230 hours, it was on the objective astride the Catenanuova–Regalbuto Road. The Germans appeared unaware that this company had cut the road, for a truck soon came roaring out of town towards it. A Bren gunner from No. 12 Platoon ripped a burst through the windshield that severely wounded the two Germans aboard, and the truck was quickly moved to the side of the road. Over the next hour, two more trucks met the same fate.[28]

As planned, the battalion's other two companies had entered Catenanuova proper to clear any German forces there. 'C' Company met no opposition and was soon dug in on the heights, while 'D' Company eliminated two machine-gun positions in its assigned sector before joining the rest of the battalion on the town's northern edge. The company from the Carleton and York Regiment also met no opposition and easily reached its objective. It soon became clear that the 923rd Fortress Battalion, tasked with Catenanuova's defence, had largely bolted to escape the barrage. A German report on the failure to defend the town stated that the "battalion fled in the direction of Centuripe in a shameful manner without enemy pressure. The immediate dissolution of the battalion has been ordered. [Generalfeldmarschall Wilhelm] Keitel has initiated Court Martial proceedings against the Officer Commanding and the guilty officers."[29]

Troops from 3rd Paratroop Regiment, attached to the Hermann Göring Division, had attempted to repair the damage by mounting the counterattack against 'A' Company. More such attacks followed as July 30 wore on. "The nature of the landscape, all hills and folds, slashed by gullies and studded with cactus and olive groves, made it possible for their assault groups to approach and appear without warning, but it also confused their direction and the result was a queer disjointed battle which raged for several hours," observed the West Nova Scotia's regimental historian.[30]

On the battalion's left flank, 'C' Company faced Monte Santa Maria and Hill 204, which the Royal 22e Régiment was attacking. The company was approached by a two-platoon-strong force that shouted, "Van Doos, Van Doos." Bad accents betrayed them as Germans, who quickly melted away under heavy fire. Sounds of digging indicated that the Germans were setting up a position in a gully next to the West Novas, so Captain G.L.F. McNeil led his men in "a spirited bayonet charge." Several Germans were killed and the remaining twenty-one taken prisoner in this action, which earned the captain a Military Cross.[31]

At times, small packets of paratroops tried to infiltrate Catenanuova but were driven out by West Nova patrols. By day's end, the situation was stabilized. The entire Carleton and York Regiment had arrived, and the engineers had cleared a route of mines and then constructed a rough road along it so that supplies could be brought forward. The West Novas counted eight men wounded in this action and the Carletons, six men wounded. It had been a costly task for 4th Field Company, as the work was carried out under intensive mortar and artillery fire. One platoon commander, Lieutenant G.E. Atkinson, had both arms mutilated when an exploding shell sprayed him with shrapnel. He continued directing his men until the work was completed, earning a Military Cross. At 1900 hours, the track was declared open, at a cost of one officer and seven other ranks wounded.[32]

In an attempt to provide covering fire for the engineers, a troop of tanks from the Three Rivers Regiment's 'B' Squadron had worked its way past Regalbuto and along the road to within a mile of Catenanuova. As the tankers had gained a ridge overlooking the town, "they found that they were, upon any movement, immediately subjected to terrific mortar and [high-explosive] barrages from the enemy." An 88-millimetre shell scored a direct hit on the cupola of the Sherman commanded by Corporal Charles Willoughby, who was killed instantly. A few seconds after the rest of the crew evacuated the tank, a German mortar round "landed dead centre through the turret hatch...and exploded inside." The blast blew off the turret and tossed it more than twenty feet from the hull. Realizing their mission was hopeless, the troop returned to 'B' Squadron's harbour area near Agira.[33]

THE COUP DE GRÂCE that finally ended German attempts to regain Catenanuova was the Royal 22e Régiment's successful attacks on Monte Santa Maria and Hill 204. Their attack had gone in later than that of the West Nova Scotia Regiment because the forming-up position in the riverbed was found to be riddled with mines, which had to be lifted by the engineers. Consequently, it was not until 0300 hours on July 30 that 'C' Company, under Major Charles Bellavance, assaulted Monte Santa Maria. Once Bellavance reported success, 'D' Company would slip around the flank of the mountain and strike northward to Hill 204.

'C' Company went forward with its Nos. 13 and 14 platoons out front. Having been thrown off this summit previously, the Van Doos expected a hard fight. But they reached the top without meeting resistance and found it occupied "only by the dead." German artillery and mortar fire, however, was unrelenting. Bellavance had his ankle broken by a shell fragment while trying to send a wireless transmission reporting the objective taken. He found he was unable to raise 'D' Company.

Captain Bernard Guimond was meanwhile standing in the riverbed staring impotently at his company's No. 18 wireless, which had broken down. Finally deciding he could wait no longer for some sign that 'C' Company had taken Monte Santa Maria, Guimond led 'D' Company forward. The company was still marching along the riverbed with No. 17 Platoon under Lieutenant André Langlais out front when day broke and they were fired on by two machine guns. Quick work with a PIAT gun and the 2-inch mortar dispersed the paratroops manning the gun positions. The advance resumed.[34] Reaching the base of the hill at 0745 hours, 'D' Company came under heavy small-arms fire and also shelling by a couple of 88-millimetre guns firing from positions left of the hill. Detailing Langlais to attack the enemy position, Guimond led the other two platoons up the slope and quickly secured the objective.

Working its way forward, No. 17 Platoon identified one position inside a stone house, which the Germans had knocked a wall out of to get the gun inside. With one section providing covering fire, a second under Sergeant René Drapeau closed to within fifteen feet of the house and showered it with grenades. Inside they found a single dead German, the rest having abandoned the gun. Looking southward, Drapeau and Lance Corporal Gérard Gagnon spotted a 105-millimetre gun also concealed in a stone house about one hundred yards away. For a few minutes they tried wrestling the 88-millimetre around to bring the other gun under fire, but the task proved impossible. Despite heavy fire, the two men advanced to within fifty yards of the 105-millimetre gun and attempted to kill the crew with grenades, only to be forced to flee when they were fired on by friendly artillery.

When the British guns ceased firing, Lance Corporal Gagnon and Privates Lachance and Grégoire returned to the stone house and decided to try for the 105-millimetre gun one more time. With Grégoire providing covering fire, the other two men went forward by bounds from one abandoned German entrenchment to another. They were within one hundred feet of the gun position when a paratrooper emerged waving a white flag. When Gagnon stepped into the open to accept the surrender, the paratrooper dropped the flag, and the other Germans in the building shot the French Canadian down. Lachance ran to Gagnon but saw he was dead. The private spotted the Germans fleeing in the opposite direction.

The silencing of this gun concluded the Royal 22e Régiment's fight for Monte Santa Maria and Hill 204. For his part in No. 17 Platoon's assault on the two guns, Drapeau was awarded the Distinguished Conduct Medal. Gagnon, whose brother, Private Jules Alphonse, had been killed while serving with the South Saskatchewan Regiment at Dieppe, was unsuccessfully put in for a Victoria Cross and received not even a Mention in Despatches. The Van Doos suffered surprisingly few casualties despite heated fighting—five killed and eight wounded.[35]

With the successful seizure of these summits, 3rd Canadian Infantry Brigade concluded its task to secure the start point for the 78th British Infantry Division's role in Hardgate. That night, two battalions of the division's 11th Brigade passed through the West Novas and advanced about two miles northeastward from Catenanuova along the road to Centuripe. To enable the British to concentrate on their advance, however, 3 CIB would remain in the area for three more days to guard the division's flank. With a series of cross-country moves north of the Catenanuova–Centuripe–Adrano road, they would secure several hills that might provide observation or gun positions for the Germans.

Monte Peloso, a rocky summit halfway between Catenanuova and Regalbuto, was taken without incident by the West Novas on July 31. The next day, the battalion marched three miles northeast to seize the nearly two-thousand-foot crag of Monte Criscina, midway between Centuripe and Regalbuto. Halfway to the objective, the battalion was ordered to halt and take up position on a ridge next to the tiny hamlet of Rosamarina. Here the Carleton and York Regiment came up on the right flank, while the Van Doos moved forward on the left. As the first two battalions sent out patrols to test the strength of the enemy's hold on Monte Criscina, the Van Doos prepared to advance up the road towards Regalbuto to link up with the rest of 1st Canadian Infantry Division, which was advancing eastward from Agira.[36]

At first light on August 2, a West Nova patrol reported no signs of the enemy on Monte Criscina. Captain A.W. Rogers immediately led 'D' Company towards the mountain. They were about halfway there when Germans on the lower slopes opened up with heavy machine-gun fire. 'A' Company advanced on the right to try and strengthen the attack, but Lieutenant Ross Guy and his men were pinned on the foot of the slope "by the German bullet storm." The British artillery officer moving with 'A' Company vanished, leaving behind his plotting board, and the No. 18 wireless set was irreparably damaged. Guy lost contact with battalion headquarters. 'D' Company was also unable to communicate with the rear.[37]

The fighting became terribly confused, and platoon commanders were able to maintain little control over their sections. This meant that often individual gallantry dictated whether men lived or died. When all the Bren gunners in one section were killed or wounded, Private Thomas Martell retrieved the weapon and all the ammunition the crew had carried. He then dashed back across a hundred yards of ground, through a continuous hail of fire, "to his section, who were in an advanced position and isolated without an automatic weapon," read his Distinguished Conduct Medal citation.[38]

Private Gerald Joseph Doucette also scooped up a fallen Bren gun and charged, firing from the hip, towards German positions up the hill. Pausing to reload, the twenty-year-old from Belliveau Cove, Nova Scotia, was shot down and killed. While trying to carry a message to Lieutenant Charles Reeves, Private Frederick William Keyes was also shot dead. Reeves died soon after while trying to organize his platoon for a charge.

From the ridge behind, the other company commanders could see the predicament the two companies were in and began directing artillery fire against the enemy positions. This enabled the two embattled companies to disengage and fall back some distance to reorganize.[39] With nightfall, the attack was broken off. In the morning it was found that, with Centuripe and Regalbuto both threatened, the Germans had abandoned the hill. The abortive assault on Monte Criscina yielded the most costly day the West Novas faced in Sicily. One officer and eighteen other ranks were killed and another officer and twenty-six other ranks wounded.[40]

After this, 3 CIB ended its time of exile from the rest of 1st Canadian Infantry Division by moving north on August 4 to return to the fold.

21

Roughest Country Yet

WHILE 3RD CANADIAN Infantry Brigade had been concluding its Dittaino valley operations, 1st Canadian Infantry Division had kicked off Hardgate with the 231st (Malta) Brigade advancing on Highway 121 from Agira towards Adrano. Both 1st Canadian Infantry Brigade and 2nd Canadian Infantry Brigade were exhausted from their five-day drive from Leonforte to Agira. Accordingly, they were stood down for a brief rest, while the British brigade was tasked with pushing through to Regalbuto.

"The order of the day," wrote the Hastings and Prince Edward Regiment's war diarist on July 29, "consisted of cleaning up, eating large quantities of food and resting, an order which was conscientiously adhered to by the troops."[1] There was also time for pomp and ceremony. On the evening of July 30, the Seaforth Highlanders of Canada's band formed in Agira's main plaza to play the retreat. CBC reporter Peter Stursberg and his sound engineer Paul Johnson had reached the front the day before with recording equipment loaded aboard an ammunition truck.

Hearing what the Seaforths planned, Stursberg determined to record the performance. Transferring the equipment to a Jeep, the two drove to the town square and set up beside the steps of Agira's main cathedral. The recording was to be done directly to a vinyl disk via a turntable and Johnson had only one disk, so there could be no retakes. Everyone had to perform flawlessly the first time. Stursberg explained this to the pipe major, who promised his band could be relied upon to give a flawless performance. The situation was then explained to the priests "in their shabby black robes who were going to ring the church bells...when I gave the signal."

With the pipers waiting their cue to begin lustily playing, Stursberg recorded a broadcast that was soon transmitted around the world on the BBC. "I am standing on the steps of the ancient church in the main square of Agira," the reporter intoned. "Directly in front of me is the pipe band of the Seaforth Highlanders which is going to give a concert...Besides hundreds of townspeople there are scores of Canadian soldiers perched on the top of carriers and trucks parked near the church...At the end of the street, over there, you can look across the yellow sunburned valley and see the hills where the Germans are. You can see the smoke of battle as well, and hear the rumble of the guns. The bells of the old church are going to ring out before the pipers begin playing...And there they are ringing now, the church bells of Agira...And now the band under Pipe Major Edmund Essen of Vancouver" began playing. The recording was perfect, and Stursberg made radio history—providing the first recorded broadcast from inside conquered territory. Stursberg would later write, a bit smugly but truthfully, "This was the first sound of liberation, and the poor, government-financed CBC had bested the wealthy U.S. networks."[2]

The night before the Seaforths' performance in Agira, the British brigade's 1st Hampshire and 1st Dorsetshire battalions had advanced, with the Three Rivers 'A' Squadron providing tank support. The brigade was also backed by the 25-pounders of 3rd Canadian Field Regiment and the British 165th Field Regiment. As the Canadians had learned during the advance on Agira, the country bordering Highway 121 favoured the German defenders in every way. "There was the same succession of rocky ridges crossing the road at right angles, each one a potential site for a German rearguard action. In this broken and mountainous terrain, much of it covered by thick olive and almond groves, it was practically impossible for reconnaissance to detect the enemy's whereabouts, and frequently an advancing body of company strength or less might suddenly find itself committed against a defensive force too firmly entrenched to be successfully engaged by anything less than a battalion with supporting arms," the Canadian Army's official historian observed.

Initially, despite the terrain, the advance went well for the Hampshires—they gained about six miles without meeting serious resistance. With night falling, Brigadier Robert Urquhart ordered them to attack a long parallel-trending ridge south of the highway. As the battalion formed for the assault, it came under heavy *Nebelwerfer* fire from the ridge. The multibarrelled mortars had such a rapid rate of fire that dozens of rounds exploded among the British troops before they could seek cover. Almost every man in one platoon was killed or wounded. Quickly reorganizing, the Hampshires pressed bravely up the slope, only to be caught in a vicious machine-gun crossfire. It became clear that the ridge was strongly held by the Hermann Göring Armoured Engineer Battalion, and with casualties mounting rapidly, the Hampshires broke off the attack.[3]

The engineer battalion had been ordered to defend Regalbuto and not to retire until 15th Panzer Grenadier Division to its north was first forced back to the east of the town. Backing up the battalion was at least a company of tanks, the 4th Battery of the Hermann Göring Artillery Regiment, and a company of 3rd Parachute Regiment paratroops. In a general order to his troops, the battalion commander made it "absolutely clear that the present position must be held at all costs. Any instructions for withdrawal are preparatory. There must be no doubt about this point. The abandonment of the present position and a fighting withdrawal to the bridgehead position will only be carried out on express orders from division."[4] These instructions accorded with those given to the Hermann Göring Division's commander, Generalmajor Paul Conrath, by XIV Panzer Corps's General der Panzertruppen Hans Valentin Hube, who feared that Regalbuto's fall would force a premature withdrawal to the Adrano–Randazzo line. The engineers must prevent this from happening.[5]

Dawn fully revealed what a tough nut 231st Brigade was trying to crack. Anchoring the ridge's eastern flank was the nearly two-thousand-foot summit of Monte Santa Lucia. From its lofty heights the Germans completely dominated the eastern and southern approaches to Regalbuto, which itself stood about sixteen hundred feet above sea level. The town, in fact, was stationed in a saddle where three large features converged. Running to the southwest was mile-long Regalbuto Ridge. To the northwest, a spur named Monte Serione thrust a mile north into the Salso valley. East of Regalbuto, and separated by a deep ravine from Monte Santa Lucia, was the westernmost extremity of a mass of hills and mountains that extended over to Centuripe. It was via the ravine that the road from Catenanuova entered Regalbuto.

On the morning of July 30, Major General Guy Simonds and Urquhart together studied this complex natural system of fortifications and decided that gaining the town would require a major attack with heavy artillery support. By 1000 hours, Simonds had returned to divisional headquarters and begun assembling the artillery plan.[6] Despite his past reliance on firepower to blast a path through German defences, Simonds realized this time that a frontal attack would surely fail. The plan therefore called for 2nd Battalion, the Devonshire Regiment, to approach Regalbuto Ridge from the northwest in a night move. Only at the last minute would the battalion cut across Highway 121 to drive up the ridge's western flank.[7]

While the attack was being organized, those units tasked with carrying it out were subjected to unrelenting mortar and *Nebelwerfer* fire regularly reinforced by German artillery. At 1330 hours, the Three Rivers 'A' Squadron was badly mortared in its concentration area. One round scored a direct hit on a truck loaded with high-explosive shells, and it "went up in the manner that ammunition trucks usually go up when hit," the regiment's war diarist noted. The explosion killed twenty-year-old Trooper Norman Wright, and the regiment's second-in-command, Major Fern Caron, was wounded in the right knee by flying shrapnel. En route to an 'O' Group at Urquhart's headquarters about an hour later, Lieutenant Colonel Leslie Booth and his intelligence officer were caught in a mortar concentration just east of Agira. Bailing out of their Jeep, the two officers huddled in a stone culvert until the fire slackened slightly. Returning to the Jeep, they careened along the road with mortar rounds exploding around them.

After attending the 'O' Group, the two men "again ran the gauntlet of fire" back to their headquarters without the Jeep taking a single hit. Another Three Rivers vehicle was not so lucky. Late in the afternoon, a water truck approaching 'A' Squadron's position was struck by a mortar round. Lance Corporal Donald Forrest and Trooper John Frederick Marsh were mortally wounded by shrapnel.[8]

In the afternoon, 3rd Canadian Field Regiment's headquarters received news that Major G.A. "Gordy" Rutherford of the 77th Battery, who had been serving as Urquhart's artillery officer, had been wounded by mortar fire. With the artillery program in support of the Devons about to begin, Lieutenant Colonel J.S. Ross rushed forward to take over Rutherford's duties.[9]

At 2300 hours on July 30, the Devons went forward behind a creeping barrage fired by 144 guns from four field and three medium regiments. Coming as they did from an unlikely angle and behind such heavy shelling, the Devons gained the crest of Regalbuto Ridge thirty-five minutes later and fired a flare signalling that the ridge was in their hands. But the battalion was desperately weak, having suffered the loss of about two hundred of its nearly seven hundred men since landing in Sicily. When the Germans counterattacked at dawn with infantry directly supported by three tanks, the Devons were thrown back from the easternmost corner of the ridge. Standing firm on the western portion, the Devons repelled repeated attacks before committing their reserve company to a last-gasp counterattack that proved successful. By midmorning, the entire ridge was regained, but at a heavy cost in casualties of eight officers and 101 other ranks.

While the fight for the ridge had been seesawing back and forth, Urquhart had sent three companies of 1st Battalion, Dorsetshire Regiment, up Monte Serione, to the north of the highway. One company became embroiled in a bloody fight with a group of Germans dug into a walled cemetery, but by midafternoon the Dorsets had won the length of this ridge and were on Regalbuto's outskirts.

The intensity of the fighting, combined with its earlier losses, left 231st Brigade's battalions spent. Recognizing this and hoping to retain the momentum won, Major General Simonds rushed 1st Canadian Infantry Brigade's 48th Highlanders of Canada forward on the morning of July 31. To avoid a loss of impetus while the rest of the brigade came forward to take over the advance, the Highlanders temporarily came under Urquhart's command.[10]

At noon the battalion left for the front on trucks from their rest area west of Agira.[11] About four miles along Highway 121, the troops unloaded and marched hard cross-country to gain the ridge held by the Dorsets before dusk. There being no road into the area, the 48th Highlanders left all their carrier-borne support platoons behind—the rifle companies would be entirely dependent on the weapons they carried.[12]

Once the Canadians took over the front lines held by the Dorsets, that battalion sent its reserve company on an eastward patrol to "Tower Hill"—named after a stone lookout perched on its summit. The Dorsets attempted to reach the hill by cutting around Regalbuto's western flank and then coming up from the ravine. But the moment the company entered the low ground, it came under fire from tanks stationed on a rise to the south and was forced to retire.[13]

SIMONDS, MEANWHILE, HAD decided Tower Hill held the key to Regalbuto. From its heights, the Canadians would be able to cut the German line of escape to Adrano. Accordingly, at 1630 hours, he ordered the Royal Canadian Regiment to seize it in a night attack. In a hurried Orders Group, Major Tom "Pappy" Powers—who had just been confirmed as the RCR commander the previous day—told the officer that 231st Brigade had "made a balls-up of their attack on Regalbuto and lost heavily...we are to go in and show the Limeys how it's done." 'B' Company's Captain Strome Galloway scribbled in his diary: "That ought to be good. Pappy is going to take the company commanders on a recce [reconnaissance] in about half an hour. It's damned near dark now and we won't see a bloody thing. But we have to push off at ten o'clock...We are to seize the hogsback that runs along the right of the town and thus dominate it in such a way that the Boche will have to pull out before daylight...Well, Pappy is saying 'Let's go.' Slim [Liddell], Chuck Lithgow and Gerry Nelson are teed up so I'd better get a move on. By the time we get to the forward positions it will be so dark a recce by a blind man would be just as good. Then we have to walk all the way back, put our platoon commanders in the picture and trudge ahead of our companies into God knows what!"[14]

The reconnaissance played out to Galloway's expectations. Night fell before they arrived, so there was nothing to see. Worse, to give the artillery specific targets to fire at, a Dorset company had been sent forward to draw enemy fire for marking by the watching FOOs. The Dorsets sent on this mission had become disoriented and had wandered far to the north without contacting any Germans, before finally returning to their lines. Lacking targets, the artillery support was cancelled. The RCR would instead take Tower Hill by stealthy manoeuvre.[15]

From Agira, the RCR marched along Highway 121 for six miles and then swung south on a rough track to gain the southern flank of Regalbuto Ridge. The march was "hellish. The road was inches thick in white dust and the hundreds of boots churned it up in clouds. Everybody was choking, sweating and cursing as they stumbled along under their heavy loads. There were numerous halts along the way and everybody just slumped down and fell asleep. Then when we started to move again I had to go around and waken them," Galloway wrote.[16]

Their forming-up position proved to be on the edge of a thin line of houses curving around the eastern flank of the ridge in a rough horseshoe pattern that marked the town's southern extremity.[17] 'C' Company, under Major Gerry Nelson, and the battalion headquarters section set up among these buildings. Their job would be to provide covering fire and tactical support while the other three companies attacked Tower Hill, which rose dramatically ahead of their position. Set between the hill and the row of houses, the troops could see the dim outline of the ravine. This feature was not indicated on their maps, but the Dorsets had thought it was only about ten feet deep and easily crossed.[18]

At 0200 hours on August 1, 'D' Company descended into the ravine. 'A' and 'B' companies would follow at thirty-minute intervals. "The object was for the first company to draw fire to pin point the enemy positions and then capture a knoll overlooking the remainder of the feature. The second company was to advance on their right if the first company succeeded, proceed to the top of the ridge, swing east and followed closely by the third company clear out whatever enemy would be encountered," Powers later explained in a report on the action.[19]

The ravine Captain Chuck Lithgow led 'D' Company into turned out to be about one hundred feet deep with its banks carved into terraced steps separated by four-foot sheer drops. Loose shale clattered noisily underfoot and skittered out beneath the men's boots. The racket of their descent brought an immediate response of heavy fire, which forced Lithgow and his men to take cover deep in the ravine.[20]

Thirty minutes after 'D' Company disappeared into the gloom and the Germans began firing into the ravine, 'A' Company slipped over the lip. Captain Slim Liddell had no idea what had happened to 'D' Company, for wireless contact had been lost the moment Lithgow departed. Seeing no sign of the missing company, Liddell's men picked their way down the slope. The going was so rough that it took thirty minutes to reach the bottom and the same amount of time to scrabble up the other side. As the company emerged from the ravine, it found itself among another cluster of buildings, and Liddell realized "the town extended much farther...than indicated by map." Passing a building, No. 8 Platoon stepped into the street beyond and drew immediate fire from a nearby tank.[21]

Liddell signalled Lieutenant M.C.D. "Buck" Bowman to outflank the tank with No. 9 Platoon from the left. Getting behind the tank, they headed up Tower Hill and after a short, hard climb gained the battalion's final objective. But the rest of the company was still pinned down by the tank below. Bowman told Sergeant E.F. Carron that "something had to be done quickly." Leaving the sergeant with one section to clear the hilltop, Bowman went back to attack the tank with the rest of the platoon.[22]

By now the RCR assault was in disarray. On schedule, 'B' Company had headed into the ravine and found Lithgow and his men still hunkered on the eastern slope, taking fire from another tank and several machine guns stationed on the lip above. Hoping to break the impasse, Galloway sent a platoon to flank the tank on the right and knock it out with a PIAT, but the platoon was forced back by a hail of fire. Finally, just before daybreak, Lithgow got one of his platoons up the slope and established a link with Liddell's 'A' Company.

With the three companies now in contact, it was decided they would dig in on the eastern slope of the ravine and hope for reinforcement or for an easing of German pressure sufficient to allow a renewal of the battalion's advance on Tower Hill.[23]

Lieutenant Bowman's platoon, meanwhile, was cut off from the rest of 'A' Company, and stiffening German resistance also prevented it from fighting its way back to the section left on Tower Hill. A runner, who tried to get through to Sergeant Carron with instructions to fall back on Bowman's position, was captured.

Up on Tower Hill, in the first light of dawn, Carron "saw that the town was occupied in strength" and on the right "were dug in tanks hull down on the reverse slope." To the left of their position, an MG 42 machine gun began searching for them with bursts of fire. Carron dashed into the tower and climbed its circular staircase to the top to try to catch a glimpse of other RCR units. An armour-piercing round "coming through the tower from a dug-in tank, however, made it not the ideal spot to tarry."

Running back to his men, Carron learned that the Bren-gun team had been overrun and either killed or captured. The amount of fire coming in was intensifying rapidly. For two hours, Carron's remaining five-man group endured the enemy fire and occasional poundings by Canadian artillery before the sergeant conceded the situation was hopeless and surrendered. Three of his men were wounded, and the Germans immediately evacuated them to a hospital. One of the wounded men, Private Joe Grigas, shortly managed to escape and reach British lines. The rest of the section was moved to a prisoner-of-war cage at Messina and then ferried to the mainland. Carron and a couple of others escaped from a freight train en route to Germany and were interned in Switzerland. After the invasion of Normandy, the sergeant and several other Canadians made their way to France to be eventually picked up by American troops near Marseilles.[24]

Lieutenant Bowman, meanwhile, had realized that what remained of No. 9 Platoon would never be able to rejoin the RCR on the edge of the ravine. Instead, he led the men north through the heart of Regalbuto—carefully avoiding the many German positions— and by late morning reached the lines of the 48th Highlanders on

Monte Serione.[25] Liddell would later write of this feat that "the move was done without casualties and apparently without discovery, reflecting most favourably on Lt. Bowman's ability to move his men unseen through difficult country."[26] For this action, Bowman was awarded a Military Cross.

While the rest of the RCR spent a day on the eastern flank of the ravine, 'C' Company and battalion headquarters were pinned down among the buildings on the western edge. "It was a very helpless feeling because there was very little we could do and we were continually being sniped at, shelled, and mortared," Major Gerry Nelson later confessed.[27] When the anti-tank platoon manhandled a 6-pounder into 'C' Company's position in hopes of taking on the German tanks, it immediately drew fire from a dug-in Tiger and was destroyed by a direct hit. Private Kenneth John Earnshaw was killed, and the anti-tank officer, Lieutenant E.H. "Ted" Shuter, was wounded along with the rest of the gun crew.

At 1800 hours, Major Powers received a wireless signal from 1 CIB headquarters that the RCR should retire as soon as night fell.[28] 'A' and 'D' companies slipped back across the ravine, while 'B' Company covered their withdrawal. Then Galloway sent his men back by platoons, with the company headquarters section last to leave. They were under enemy mortar, tank, and artillery fire the entire way—rounds striking all around them—while machine guns searched through the darkness with measured bursts. Yet not a single 'B' Company man was even nicked. During the course of the earlier fighting, however, two men had been wounded, and Private Thomas Francis Mason was killed by a sniper round. By about 0100 hours on August 2, the entire battalion was a couple of miles west of Regalbuto and bedding down.[29] The RCR's last action in Sicily had ended in defeat.

AS THE RCR'S frontal attack had clearly failed, Major General Simonds cut a new plan in the early afternoon of August 1. The enemy on the heights east of the town, he explained, would not withdraw "unless ordered to do so by his own higher command. He is well sited and possesses about eight tanks. It is probable that he will fight hard to hold his present position." Simonds therefore decided that 1st

Canadian Infantry Brigade would carry out a wide right-flanking movement to seize first Monte Tiglio, then Monte San Giorgio, and then strike directly northward to carry Tower Hill.[30] Meanwhile, on the left, 2nd Canadian Infantry Brigade would "cut across country north of the [Salso] River toward Adrano."[31] At the same time, 231st (Malta) Brigade—retaining the 48th Highlanders under command—would provide a firm base in front of Regalbuto and, when the time was right, surge forward and carry the town.[32]

Once again it fell to the Hastings and Prince Edward Regiment to undertake a long trek in darkness over mountainous terrain. Major Bert Kennedy distrusted the maps, and there was no intelligence about the possible dispositions of German forces south of Regalbuto. Twice before, the Hasty Ps had gone forward into this kind of situation with a "buccaneering rush into the unknown." At Assoro, such daring had yielded stunning success, but before Nissoria it had brought disaster. Kennedy was fed up with the battalion going in blind. From a hilltop, the battalion commander, his company commanders, and the assigned artillery FOO spent the afternoon studying the ground and developing a detailed battle plan.[33] Yet they all knew that observation of such rugged country from a distance could only yield a limited appreciation of possible obstacles and next to nothing about German strength.

So Kennedy sent a patrol of twenty-seven men from 'C' Company, under Lieutenant George Baldwin, to check the planned line of advance. The men stripped down to the lightest weapons and ammunition kit possible so they could take along several No. 18 wireless sets. Kennedy had devised a novel idea whereby the patrol would drop these sets off at regular intervals to create a signal chain, which would enable it to maintain communications with battalion headquarters. This system worked flawlessly at first, but at 1500 hours contact with the patrol was lost. Two hours later, Company Sergeant Major George Ponsford—who had accompanied the patrol and was a veteran solo marcher across Sicilian countryside—arrived. When he left the patrol, Ponsford said, it had not yet bumped into any enemy and had been closing on Monte Tiglio.[34]

This intelligence would have to suffice, because there was no time to wait for the patrol's return. At 2000 hours, the battalion started marching. Moving with the company headquarters was an artillery FOO team, burdened by their 48.5 pound No. 21 wireless set. The mortar platoon was also manhandling its heavy weapons and ammunition, for once again vehicles could not possibly operate in the mountains.[35]

Kennedy led his men "through some of the roughest country yet encountered." 'A' Company led, followed in line by 'B', 'C', and 'D' companies. By midnight, the battalion was halfway to Monte Tiglio and able to make good time because a bright moon lit their path. They followed a mule track that "went twice as far up and down as it went along."[36] At 0300 hours on August 2, the battalion stood at the mountain's base. Hoping to catch the Germans on the summit literally napping, 'A' and 'B' scaled it in a mad scramble that brought them to the top in just fifteen minutes. "There were no enemy on the hill," the battalion's war diarist noted, "but from equipment captured it appeared that they had moved out shortly before the arrival of our troops."[37]

For once, the wireless set worked, and Kennedy reported the first objective taken. Brigadier Howard Graham told him "to rest for a few hours while the final details of the second part of the plan for the attack northwards were worked out."[38] Lieutenant George Baldwin's patrol turned up on the hill just after first light. Baldwin told Kennedy that Monte Tiglio had still been occupied by Germans when he had probed the position during the night, and the patrol had also determined that Monte San Giorgio had enemy paratroops on its summit. At 1000 hours, to the consternation of all on the mountain position, two Bren carriers ground up to its base. Regimental Sergeant Major Angus Duffy and a couple of drivers had somehow managed to pick their way cross-country with a heavy load of rations and water. "With several hours' rest and a good meal, the battalion was ready to go again," the war diarist recorded.[39]

While the Hasty Ps rested and ate, the artillery supporting the division spent the entire morning and afternoon pounding Regalbuto and the highway east of it. Twenty-five fighter bombers also bombed and strafed a position that the artillery marked for the planes with smoke shells. When the Hasty Ps moved off, they were to go forward behind a barrage laid down by the three Canadian field regiments. Fighter bombers would be circling overhead in readiness to attack the German transport, tanks, and towed guns expected to be flushed from Regalbuto.[40] Divisional headquarters was certain "that the enemy would withdraw when the assault developed and it was hoped that the air attack would pin him down to the ground and prevent this."[41]

Zero hour for the Hasty Ps' assault kept getting pushed back through the afternoon because of persistent trouble maintaining wireless communications in "such extremely rough ground" between the various headquarters involved in the full-scale attack. Just before the latest start time of 1600 hours, the 48th Highlanders reported that one of the many patrols they had sent forward to harass the Germans had managed to enter Regalbuto and found it abandoned. On the basis of this intelligence, Simonds cancelled the artillery plan and ordered Kennedy to move immediately on his two remaining objectives.[42]

The battalion went forward, with 'D' Company leading, followed by 'A,' 'B,' and 'C' companies. As 'D' Company started across the Catenanuova–Regalbuto road, it came under fire from the direction of Regalbuto and the southern slope of Tower Hill. Carrying on without pause, the company clambered up Monte San Giorgio and found it recently vacated. Kennedy had the 3-inch mortars deployed on the summit so they could support the northward advance to Tower Hill. 'D' Company descended from the summit alone to test the German reaction, which was immediate and consisted of heavy machine-gun and mortar fire from Tower Hill. The bombardment struck just as the Hasty Ps reached the bottom of the intervening valley. There was little vegetation or folds in the ground to provide cover, and the company would have undoubtedly suffered heavy casualties had the 3-inch mortars not suddenly opened up "with such an effective barrage that the enemy's fire became very inaccurate and considerably reduced." 'D' Company withdrew to the summit of Monte San Giorgio, and Kennedy decided on a new plan.

This time, he sent 'B' and 'C' companies down the slope with the mortars and the other two companies throwing out all the weight of fire they could. Enjoying a sustained period of wireless communication, the 2nd Canadian Field Regiment officer with the battalion called in accurate artillery fire. As Kennedy's battalion headquarters was also in wireless contact with the two advancing companies throughout the attack, the FOO was able to shift the guns to any targets their commanders identified. 'B' Company reached the base of Tower Hill first and quickly drove off the few Germans who had hung around to meet the Canadians. Leapfrogging past, 'C' Company pushed to the summit in time to see the last of the two estimated companies of paratroops that had fought to stem their assault legging it down the other side. "The outflanking movement, by the battalion, succeeded in smashing this strongpoint and opening the way for the advance on Adrano," the Hasty Ps' war diarist rightly concluded.[43]

Regalbuto, which had been the last bastion barring a Canadian advance on Adrano, was now taken. From Tower Hill, the Hasty Ps could see a line of German vehicles fleeing eastward. Allied fighter bombers were diving down and dropping bombs or shooting up vehicles with their guns. The flyers would report destroying forty vehicles caught on the open road between Regalbuto and Adrano. To the north, Troina was being attacked by the 1st U.S. Division and another general withdrawal had begun there, which put heavy traffic onto Highway 120 paralleling Highway 121. Allied flyers claimed that fifty vehicles were turned into wrecks by their bombs and bullets along that route.[44]

Regalbuto's fall did not mean an end of the fighting for 1st Canadian Infantry Division, but it did conclude 1st Canadian Infantry Brigade's part in hostilities. The brigade's three battalions moved into reserve positions south of Highway 121. Regalbuto was a ruin. "Attacked several times by aircraft and heavily shelled by artillery, hardly a building remained intact. One section of the main road through the town was completely blocked with rubble, though the engineers, with the aid of bulldozers had forced a one-way route through a side street. The town was deserted; most of the inhabitants had fled to the hills or the railway tunnels, but with the entry of the Allied troops they were beginning to return. They were a pitiful sight, dirty, ragged, frightened and apparently half-fed," one divisional staff officer observed.[45]

"When the folks around Belleville, Trenton, Picton and Madoc are preparing their welcome for the Hasty Petes, they'll do well to note that the town hall steps are strictly out," Toronto's *Globe and Mail* correspondent Ralph Allen wrote in a story blazed across the paper's front page on August 18. "The Hasty Petes have already done enough climbing to put a mountain goat on full retirement pension. They've done a lot of fighting too. While the brigade and divisional staff officers sort out the triumphs and lessons of the Canadians' first major campaign in this war, no single group earns higher marks than the hard young warriors from the farms, hills and factories of Eastern Ontario...There's a story for every mile of the Hastings' grim journey."[46]

22

Such a Party

AFTER REGALBUTO'S CAPTURE, 1st Canadian Infantry Division shifted its line of advance about a mile north of Highway 121 to the point inside the Salso valley where the river exited a deep gorge and entered a wide plain. Forming the valley's northern flank was "a tangle of peaks and ridges extending eastward to the base of Etna [that] was virtually trackless," while low hills composed its southern boundary. Although the railway from Regalbuto to Adrano snaked alongside the Salso's winding course, the valley was devoid of roads. The Canadians, well-versed in fighting their way "across territory so rugged that the passage of a body of troops seemed a virtual impossibility," must carry out such a task yet again.[1]

During a meeting held at 1100 hours on July 31, Major General Guy Simonds had warned 2nd Canadian Infantry Brigade's Brigadier Chris Vokes that his troops would carry the advance through the valley. Following the Salso, he added, was necessary because 79th British Infantry Division was rapidly closing on Highway 121 from the southwest and the two formations would soon be rubbing shoulders. The Canadians slipping northward a little would give both divisions room to manoeuvre.[2] Vokes spent several hours with the division's photographic interpretation officer getting a sense of the ground.[3] As far as the two men could determine, the area "appeared to be unoccupied, but the route along the Salso Valley was strewn with boulders and therefore impassable for wheeled vehicles, or even tanks."[4]

Knowing this, Simonds had promised Vokes every mule and donkey the division possessed to ensure that each battalion could carry a forty-eight-hour allotment of rations, the 3-inch mortars and their ammunition, and the heavy Vickers machine guns of the Saskatoon Light Infantry. While 2 CIB was advancing, the engineers of 3rd Field Company would construct a road in its wake to enable vehicle traffic into the area as soon as possible.[5]

Intelligence officers reported the valley defended by 382nd Panzer Grenadier Regiment, which fielded two battalions. Its soldiers were either veterans of the Russian front or had served with the 164th Light Africa Division in North Africa. Stationed behind this regiment to defend the Simeto River—a tributary that flowed into the Salso from the north about a mile west of Adrano—were the 1st and 3rd battalions of the 3rd Parachute Regiment. The strength of this regiment had been bolstered by absorbing the officers and men of the 923rd Fortress Battalion, dissolved after its disgrace in the July 30 rout from Catenanuova.[6]

On the night of July 31–August 1, the Loyal Edmonton Regiment made the Canadians' opening gambit by sending two patrols to determine if the Germans were occupying Hill 736. This promontory, identified by its height in metres, stood on the eastern flank of a string of mountains overlooking the gap through which the Troina River met the Salso. One patrol was commanded by Lieutenant C.F. Swan and the other by Sergeant J.W. Robertson, both of 'C' Company.[7]

When one patrol reached the base of Hill 736, it fired several Bren-gun bursts towards the summit without drawing any response. Both patrols returned on the morning of August 1 and reported seeing no sign of German troops. They cautioned that the trails shown on aerial photographs were only "dried up stream beds filled with rocks and the going would be difficult even for personnel and mules."[8]

Vokes ordered Lieutenant Colonel Jim Jefferson to quite literally saddle up the Edmontons and take Hill 736 that night. It was afternoon before the mule train was delivered to the battalion area. Each animal had a pack saddle, and the men started loading these with ammunition, mortars, wireless sets, water, and food. Although many of the Edmontons had experience working with livestock, they found the mules cantankerous and difficult to handle. The hours trailed away, and soon the loading was slowed even more by nightfall. Finally, an exasperated Jefferson ordered the rifle companies to move out without the mules. These would be brought up by the rear-area units. Jefferson had been "hoping to...take at least some signal sets with him when he joined the battalion but he had to go on without anything, thus being out of communication for many hours."[9]

The march turned into a terrific ordeal, which Lieutenant John Dougan thought "seemed to go on for miles and miles and miles." It was hot and terribly dusty. What they could see of the valley in the moonlight seemed "bleak, forbidding."[10] The terrain was so difficult to negotiate that the battalion progressed at a mere one mile per hour. Several times unidentified aircraft dropped flares, and the troops quickly threw themselves to the ground to avoid being spotted by any Germans who might be on Hill 736. August 2 dawned with the Edmontons still a mile short of the hill.

At 0600 hours, the battalion paused on a low rise to reorganize for the assault and immediately came under fire from machine guns and mortars stationed on the summit. From the hills on the valley's southern flank, several German self-propelled guns also opened up.[11] Despite the intensity of fire, Jefferson ordered three companies into the assault. While 'A' and 'B' companies went straight for Hill 736, 'D' Company tried to work around the eastern flank. Jefferson held 'C' Company back as a reserve alongside his battalion headquarters section, their position continually hammered by artillery and mortar rounds.

Captain Pat Tighe's 'A' Company along with 'B' Company managed to gain a foothold on the lower slopes before being driven to ground by sheer weight of fire. The platoons scattered into cover provided by boulders or pressed up against cliff faces to avoid the German machine-gun fire. Captain Jim Stone, who had only recently returned to the regiment from duties as a beach master, had finally realized his ambition of commanding a rifle company. He led 'D' Company through thickening fire that finally stopped it cold on a shelf next to the hill's eastern flank.[12] The ground was so rocky that digging in proved impossible, so the men found whatever shelter they could behind rocks and in a couple of shallow gullies.

All three companies repeatedly tried to renew the advance, only to be driven to ground again. 'B' Company took several casualties, and a call went out for stretcher-bearers. Private John Low and Private Colback, both from 'D' Company, crawled "from boulder to boulder up the fire-swept slope" for 150 yards. Colback was knocked down by a bullet wound, but Low pressed on. "To his comrades, the further advance of this soldier could only end in death, but to their amazement he continued on towards the wounded men. German fire appeared to centre around him. Bullets were seen kicking up the dust along the line of his path, but [Private] Low, showing intense devotion to duty and conspicuous bravery, successfully crawled the remaining 300 yards and reached the wounded men. In the open, and under... murderous fire, he dressed the wounds of each of the three in turn, found cover for them, and carried and aided them to it." Low would be decorated with a Distinguished Conduct Medal for this courageous and selfless act.[13]

Late in the morning, a leading element of the mule train arrived. Its twenty-eight mules were laden with the heavy machine guns of the SLI group. The animals and handlers drew the attention of the machine guns and mortars on the hill. Breaking free of the men holding their reins, the mules scattered and three of the Vickers guns were lost. Weaponless, the SLI trudged back to their starting point. Only Corporal M.J. Taje stayed behind to search for the strayed mules and missing guns that were strapped to their backs.[14] Taje's efforts eventually resulted in the retrieval of two guns and sufficient ammunition to bring them into action—an achievement that won the corporal a Military Medal.[15]

As morning gave way to afternoon, the German fire continued relentlessly. Jefferson ordered the Edmontons to disengage, and the three companies fell back to a sheltered area near the riverbed. From here reconnaissance patrols were sent out to find a better line of approach.

Meanwhile, back at 2 CIB headquarters, the day was "one of grave uncertainty...About noon reports began to trickle back to the effect that the unit had bumped opposition, and could not gain their objective without hard fighting, into which they had entered with their usual eagerness to set about the enemy," wrote brigade intelligence officer Captain Norman Pope. That evening Jefferson clarified the situation by coming back to personally brief Vokes and Pope. He described the fighting as heavy, but said the Edmontons could soon have things in hand if the mule train got forward with the needed supplies. Until then, the rifle companies were too low on ammunition to renew the attack.[16]

Jefferson headed back into the Salso valley, and the remainder of the mule train was finally assembled during the night of August 2–3. Setting off in the morning, the train moved into the valley. Soon muleteers and mules alike were struggling across the rough terrain. Not until the evening of August 3 did the train reach an orchard behind the Edmonton position, where a patrol from 'C' Company made contact and led them forward.[17] By this time, the men in 'D' Company's No. 16 Platoon had been out of rations and water for more than a day. Lieutenant Dougan had come across a potato patch and was able to hand out raw potatoes to his men. Someone else found a number of eggs. Dougan cracked one open and swallowed its contents raw because they had no means of boiling water.[18] The arrival of the mules was greeted with relief. Loaded onto them was not only food and water but, more importantly, a No. 22 wireless set and the battalion's 3-inch mortars. There was also a good supply of ammunition. The Edmontons were back in action.[19]

During the course of August 3, patrols had also identified a better path for carrying Hill 736. Instead of striking at it frontally, the battalion would move that night against a spur that lay about a mile south of the main objective. This was Point 344, which lay midway between Hill 736 and the Troina River. From here they would advance from one ever-higher point to another until they reached Hill 736 itself. While this plan would undoubtedly take a couple of days to complete, its prospects for success seemed good.[20]

REGALBUTO HAD FALLEN on August 3, and with this obstacle finally clear, Major General Guy Simonds directed Brigadier Vokes to push the Seaforth Highlanders of Canada northeast from the town that night to gain a railway bridge that crossed the Troina River. From the bridge, patrols would then "tap out" the high ground east of the river to reconnoitre a route for an ensuing advance on the night of August 4–5 to the eastern flank of Monte Revisotto. This mountain loomed over the junction of the Salso and Troina rivers from a position immediately to the northeast. On the night of August 5–6, a squadron of Three Rivers Regiment's tanks and a 3.7-inch howitzer battery would be attached for the brigade's final leg to the Simeto River.[21] Thereafter, the division's other two brigades would pass through to cover the three remaining miles to Adrano.[22]

At 2300 hours on August 3, 'C' Company of the Loyal Edmonton Regiment started towards Point 344. The company was under the command of thirty-six-year-old Major A.S. "Archie" Donald whose prematurely grey hair made him look far older. Donald had taken over the company a few days earlier when Major W.T. Cromb had contracted sandfly fever. 'C' Company fought its way forward against considerable resistance. By 0430 the next morning, Donald reported that his men controlled the heights and were patrolling towards Hill 736 but were taking heavy fire from its summit.[23]

Vokes decided that the Edmontons could easily take Hill 736 after nightfall in a two-company attack and therefore ordered Lieutenant Colonel Jim Jefferson to send 'A' and 'B' companies eastward to carry Monte Revisotto. After loading up with ammunition, rations, and water from the mule train, the two companies moved "eastward along the valley of the Salso in the shelter of the northern bank" to a forming-up position about one hundred yards east of the base of Revisotto.[24]

For the Seaforth Highlanders, the advance on the night of August 3–4 had started out easily enough with a welcome truck ride from their rest area near Agira through Regalbuto and up a dirt road that petered out about a mile and a half north of the town. Here they unloaded and started marching—as they had done for most of the miles put behind them in Sicily.[25]

The terminus of this road had been the starting point for No. 3 Field Company's road-construction project, which the engineers had wasted no time in launching into once Regalbuto fell. Early in the morning, Lieutenant D.D. Love and a small reconnaissance party had gone forward on foot to the Salso River. Although pinned down for some time by mortar fire, Love was able to examine the railway bridge crossing the streambed and also figure out a crossing point for the road. Love reported that the railway bridge was in good enough condition to take the weight of vehicles, but ramps would have to be built at either end to provide access.

When night fell, the engineering platoons went forward to carry out the work under cover of darkness. No. 2 Platoon erected the ramps to make the bridge usable. At the same time, No. 1 Platoon used bull-dozers to develop "a crossing across the dry river bottom. This [was a] difficult task due to [the] huge number of very large boulders" that had to be pushed aside so that the riverbed could be levelled. The crossing would allow for uninterrupted two-way traffic across the Salso—vehicles going one way using the bridge and those travelling the other taking the crossing. No. 3 Platoon, meanwhile, staked out a route for the road from the Salso to the Troina River, where another crossing would need to be constructed.[26] While the sounds of machinery working in the valley drew some German fire, this was not the hazard the engineers feared most. A number of men were thrown into a panic when their labours unearthed snakes, which the valley seemed to support by the thousands. Some were known to be venomous, but it was impossible for the Canadians to identify which ones they were. However, by noon on August 4 the engineers reported that the bridge and river crossing were ready to handle traffic.[27]

The Seaforths had passed by the engineers during the night, marched a mile east along the riverbed, and then "swung north into the range of craggy hills." They were pushing hard, hoping to reach their objective northeast of Regalbuto and immediately west of the Troina River before dawn. Resistance was scant, nothing more than an occasional sniper who popped off a couple of rounds and then melted into the darkness. Daybreak found the battalion three-quarters of the way to its objective, and at 0630 hours Major Budge Bell-Irving led 'A' Company halfway up its slope before coming under heavy fire from the summit. 'B' and 'C' companies leapfrogged into the lead and, despite having no mortars or heavy machine guns to support their attack, gained the summit at 0900 hours.[28] The Germans made a half-hearted attempt to cling to the hill's north slope, but withdrew after Captain W.G. Harris's 'B' Company fired a few Bren-gun bursts in their direction.[29]

From their north-facing position, the Seaforths could see Monte Revisotto to the northeast and on the opposite bank of the Troina River. It was "topped on the left by a rocky crag jutting straight up to the clouds. On the right flank of the hill the slope became more gentle, studded here and there with olive trees," noted the Seaforth's war diarist. The entire battalion quickly concentrated in this position, with Lieutenant Colonel Bert Hoffmeister setting up his forward headquarters in a small ravine a few hundred yards to the right. In order to maintain wireless contact with the brigade, Hoffmeister's signallers had dragged a heavy No. 22 wireless set forward on a handcart. 'D' Company, which was in reserve, was stationed within a line of trees that ran from the ravine to a small red-stone house where the Regimental Aid Post was established.[30]

The valley was an eerie place, the horizon on all sides consisting of dense ranges of rocky hills. To the west, the Seaforths "saw the river bed of the Salso winding up through the hills till it passed out of sight north of Agira. In places they could see the track from Regalbuto to the river, and far away they could hear the bulldozers working on the river crossing. Throughout the day the enemy mortars continued to shell this point, trying to prevent the supporting arms coming forward. To the southeast...they could see the river winding on down to the Catania Plain, while to the east and northeast other rugged hills were visible, and beyond them the massive outline of Mount Etna. To their rear, on the south side of the valley they could see still more hills with the town of Centuripe crowning the highest one. Closer at hand patches of corn and orange trees dotted the valley, which was furrowed by irrigation ditches but away from any water the ground was as bare as a desert." There was no shade to be had on the hill or in the ravine, and the men dripped sweat under a blistering sun.[31]

Once Hoffmeister considered the battalion's position consolidated, he decided the situation was sufficiently fluid to accelerate the rigid timetable that called for forcing a crossing of the Troina during the coming night. At 1800 hours, he sent 'A' Company to seize a height of ground about one and a half miles to the east. Besides gaining a bridgehead across the Troina, this move would put the company in position to dominate the road running from Adrano north to the town of Troina—where the Americans were locked in a fierce battle. As a Saskatoon Light Infantry platoon had arrived with its Vickers machine guns, Hoffmeister placed it on a small knoll in front of his headquarters to support the attack.

Major Budge Bell-Irving was counting more on stealth than fire support to win his objective, so the guns remained silent while his platoons advanced warily along a series of gullies. Gaining the base of the hill undetected, Bell-Irving decided to replicate the stunt used at Grizzly and led his men on a right-flanking manoeuvre. Once again the trick worked perfectly. 'A' Company came up on the southern tip of the hill and was immediately entangled in a sharp firefight with a sizable force of Panzer Grenadiers. "The sections had a field day, working sometimes independently, throwing Jerry from his M.G. posts and sniper posts. Many sections rounded rocky crags and came face to face with German sections—slowly the enemy posts were knocked out one by one."

Back on their knoll, the SLI gunners manning the Vickers found the range too great to provide effective support, and in any case, "they could not distinguish friend from foe."[32] It took 'A' Company two hours to drive the Germans off the feature. They did so at a loss of only one man killed and another wounded.[33]

Hoffmeister's independent move had jump-started a general advance. After 'A' Company's success, Vokes committed the Princess Patricia's Canadian Light Infantry—which had been waiting in the wings on the north side of the Salso next to the railway bridge—to leapfrog the Seaforths and establish a bridgehead astride the Adrano–Troina road. This would provide protection for the engineers to construct a crossing over the Troina River. Because the PPCLI would take some time to reach the river, Captain June Thomas's 'D' Company was ordered to precede its advance. Supporting this move were two troops of the Three Rivers Regiment's 'C' Squadron, which had cautiously used the railway-bridge crossing to gain the north side of the river.

As Thomas and his men started forward, they were fired on by several machine-gun positions and snipers stationed on top of the high crags to the north, but the six Shermans opened up with their 75-millimetre main guns and in short order the German resistance collapsed.[34] At 1930 hours, the PPCLI's 'A' and 'C' companies pushed across the Troina and solidified the bridgehead as assigned. The other two companies and battalion headquarters joined them at 2045 hours. A patrol sent out by Captain Rowan Coleman's 'C' Company soon bumped into 'A' and 'B' companies of the Loyal Edmonton Regiment, who were facing Monte Revisotto. Wireless having failed, the Edmontons were no longer in contact with their battalion headquarters. The PPCLI's Lieutenant Colonel Bob Lindsay "through force of circumstances" took them under his command.[35]

ON AUGUST 4, as events were unfolding rapidly in the Salso valley, the enemy's Sicilian campaign was simultaneously entering its final phase. The earlier losses of Agira and Catenanuova, combined with the fall of both Regalbuto and Centuripe on August 3, forced German Tenth Army's Generalfeldmarschall Albert Kesselring to accept that the time for a general evacuation of the island was rapidly approaching. This meant withdrawal from the Catania plain, the first signs of which were reported by forward divisions of Eighth Army's XIII Corps that evening. In their haste, the Germans blew up ammunition dumps and other supplies that could not be taken with them.

XIV Panzer Corps General der Panzertruppen Hans Valentin Hube and General d'Armata Alfredo Guzzoni also agreed on a new defensive line. In the north, the 15th Panzer Grenadier and 29th Panzer Grenadier divisions would fall back to a line running from behind the Zapulla River's confluence with the Tyrrhenian Sea to Randazzo, on the northwestern corner of Mount Etna. The formations of the Hermann Göring Division, currently fighting in front of Catania, would abandon continued defence of this city and withdraw to a line running from the volcano across to the town of Riposto on the eastern coast. In both cases, the withdrawals would dramatically narrow the frontages the Germans had to defend, while putting the most forward units within close range of Messina in preparation for evacuation across the strait. The German strategy henceforth was focussed on "delay, disengagement, evacuation."[36]

The British immediately recognized that a major withdrawal was under way, and on the afternoon of August 4, General Bernard Montgomery issued new orders to capitalize on the situation. XIII Corps was to push forward on Eighth Army's right flank, but "without incurring heavy casualties." It fell instead to XXX Corps "to do the punching" with a move around the western and northern flanks of Mount Etna. The U.S. Seventh Army, meanwhile, would push straight eastward, with one division following the coastal highway and another advancing from Troina (which fell during the day) towards Randazzo.[37] Montgomery conceded that the Americans would enjoy a positional advantage when they reached Randazzo, effectively pinching off the XXX Corps line of advance. Consequently, General George Patton would have the honour of liberating not only Palermo but also Messina.

Before Lieutenant General Oliver Leese convened a meeting at XXX Corps headquarters to inform his divisional commanders of their role in Montgomery's new plan, he accompanied Major General Guy Simonds, the division's chief artillerist Brigadier Bruce Matthews, and 78th British Infantry Division's Major General Vyvyan Evelegh to the top of the steep Centuripe hill. From this commanding height, the entire battleground lay before Simonds and the others like "a miniature model on a sand table," and the Canadian general examined it with his usual eye for meticulous detail.

"On his right, half a dozen miles to the north-east, the bleached tiled roofs of Adrano, the Corps objective, stood out clearly in the... sun against the vast background of Mount Etna. In front of him the ground swept upward from the far bank of the Salso in rolling foothills to the peaks of Hill 736, Revisotto and Seggio, outposts of the great rampart of heights which filled the northern horizon. Below and to his left, a widening of the rocky bed of the Salso marked the entry of the Troina from its ravinelike valley west of Mount Revisotto. Along the floor of the valley at his feet the dry course of the Salso meandered eastward in wide loops to meet the fast-flowing Simeto River, which made its appearance from the north behind a

long, outlying spur of Mount Seggio. Near the point where this spur
flattened into the level plain the tiny hamlet of Carcaci stood on a
slight mound among irrigated plantations of lemon and orange trees.
Once a thriving community of more than one thousand inhabitants,
Carcaci had been reduced by successive epidemics of malaria to a population of less than one hundred living in a mere handful of houses.
Through these ran the road from Troina, to join Highway No. 121 a
mile to the south-east, just before the latter crossed the Simetto and
began its long zig-zag climb to Adrano."[38]

Back at xxx Corps headquarters, Leese explained that "the punching" meant Adrano must fall more quickly than originally thought.
Accordingly, 78th Division would establish a bridgehead over the
Salso immediately north of Centuripe that night. The following night
it was to push across the Simeto River north of its juncture with the
Salso. Simonds's division would secure Monte Seggio on the night of
August 5–6 and also force a crossing of the Simeto River. On the
third night, 78th Division would take Adrano. Should that attack fail,
a joint venture would be mounted twenty-four hours later by both
divisions. The 51st Highland Division would continue guarding the
right flank of the corps and seize Biancavilla—Adrano's neighbouring town—in concert with the 78th Division's attack.

With no time to waste, Simonds rushed back to his headquarters
and then on to Brigadier Vokes's command post. Once the PPCLI had
established its bridgehead across the Troina River that evening and
the engineers had created crossings, he believed, "a quick blow can
be struck in the undulating country north of the river which will
carry you right up to the western bank of River Simeto." To guard
the division's left flank, Vokes would still have to seize the heights of
Hill 736, Revisotto, and Seggio. But at the same time Simonds
wanted him to organize a mobile force under command of Three
Rivers Regiment's Lieutenant Colonel Leslie Booth. It would be composed of Booth's tank regiment, one self-propelled artillery battery,
one or two troops of anti-tank guns, one infantry battalion, and 'A'
Squadron of the Princess Louise Dragoon Guards reconnaissance
regiment. The force's objective would be the eastern bank of the Simeto River. "I think that such a move will startle the enemy and will

probably result in a good mix up in the open country where the tanks will really be able to manoeuvre. I think Booth will handle such a party well."

Simonds had already put much of this force on standby and also requested that the 11th Royal Horse Artillery provide the self-propelled artillery battery. Its arrival had been promised for 0830 hours on August 5. Because the division's artillery was in the process of repositioning to bring the guns within firing range of Adrano, Simonds could only offer Vokes support from 3rd Field Regiment, the 165th Field Regiment, Royal Artillery (which remained under Canadian command), and the 7th Medium Regiment to about noon. After that, the column should be so far forward it would have to rely entirely on inherent firepower.

Back at his headquarters, Simonds detailed these instructions in a formal letter. He concluded by saying: "You must be the final judge as to whether or not the local situation presents an opportunity for the blow I envisage, but indications today are that enemy resistance is crumbling, and I think we can afford to take bigger chances than we have been able to in the last few days."[39]

Vokes agreed and had already done much to pull together "Booth Force," as it was named in honour of its commander. Booth had received instructions from the brigadier at 2100 hours and been told the attack must begin at 0600 the following morning. The Seaforths would provide the mobile force's infantry. With his 'C' Squadron committed to supporting the Edmontons and PPCLI in their operations against the three mountains, Booth would have only two squadrons available. But he judged that more than sufficient.[40]

After getting the mobile arm of the force organized, Booth went forward to Hoffmeister's headquarters in the Salso valley. The Seaforth commander was up with 'A' Company when a battalion runner arrived with a message summoning him back for the meeting. Sick and weak from an onset of dysentery, Hoffmeister "struggled down from 'A' Company's exposed position" at about 0200 hours on August 5.[41] The meeting was held by a candle's flickering light in the empty farmhouse the Seaforths were using for their Regimental Aid Post. German mortar rounds exploded regularly nearby, and overhead their flares regularly lit up the valley floor. Once Booth finished briefing Hoff-meister, he returned to his headquarters to give a final briefing at 0300 hours to the other officers involved.[42]

The mobile force was to join the Seaforths at the Troina River crossing that the engineers would create during the night. Leading the column would be the carriers and armoured cars of the Princess Louise Dragoon Guards. Immediately behind would be a section of engineers to lift any mines encountered. The main body of the force would be organized so that a Seaforth company riding on 'B' Squad-ron's tanks would lead. Next would come a troop of the 90th Anti-Tank Battery and then 'A' Squadron with the second Seaforth company aboard. The rest of the force would be in trail.

TO REACH THE start line, Booth Force's vehicles and tanks had to negotiate the railway bridge across the Salso.[43] The PLDG found that driving along the railway line and then over the bridge caused "vicious difficulties for both tracks and wheels. It called for the greatest driv-ing skill to negotiate them in darkness."[44] One delay compounded another, and it was daylight before the mobile elements arrived at the start line. During their wait, the Seaforths—in their khaki shorts and shirts—had been driven nearly insane by the thousands of mos-quitoes lurking in the dry riverbed. Not until 0800 hours was Booth Force assembled and able to push off. The engineers had opened the crossing over the Troina and cleared the mines on both banks. Hav-ing gained the eastern bank without mishap, the column soon reached the Troina–Adrano road and started rolling at a brisk rate toward Carcaci. The little hamlet was the objective for the reconnais-sance squadron, which was to link up there with the 78th Division's 2nd Battalion, London Irish Rifles, while the rest of Booth Force hooked off the road and headed eastward for the Simeto River.

Major Jim Blair's 'C' Company was riding on the tanks of 'B' Squadron, and Major Budge Bell-Irving's 'A' Company was aboard 'A' Squadron's Shermans. Just before the advance began, Blair had told Company Sergeant Major R.M. Black "that he had a feeling that something was going to happen...and that he wasn't going to come out of it okay."[45] But everything seemed to be going extraordinarily well. The infantry clinging to the tanks were even getting some shade cover as the Shermans rolled through the orange groves. Bell-Irving's company was short a platoon because he had left it behind to hold the hill won the day before. That had worried him initially, but now he wondered if its absence mattered.[46]

The reconnaissance squadron had just reached the point where the rest of the column would break left for the objective ridge north of the road, when troops of the 3rd Parachute Regiment opened fire with machine guns and mortars from a string of rocky nests scattered along the front of the ridge. Having held their fire in hopes of catching the infantry still aboard the tanks when these came within range, the Germans were disappointed, because Hoffmeister—riding inside Booth's headquarters tank—had expected an attack from the ridge and had ordered his men off moments earlier. It was 1030 hours when the infantry-cum-tank action that Simonds had hoped for broke out.

Major Blair's company advanced with 'B' Squadron providing fire support from directly behind. Blair, CSM Black, and the seven men in his headquarters section were pinned down by machine-gun fire and lost touch with the leading platoons. "I'll have a look see," Blair told Black. He "moved off to our left to try to make contact."[47]

Blair caught up to the leading two platoons when they were about halfway up the slope and moving past a little group of farm buildings. About 150 yards farther up, the paratroops tore into them with heavy fire from a strong position behind a stone wall, driving the Seaforths to ground. Blair sent the leading platoon to flank the wall by going up a gully on the left. The platoon was commanded by a corporal because the Seaforths were so thin on the ground from casualties suffered during the overall campaign. The following platoon, under Lieutenant John F. McLean, was directed to the right. No sooner were both platoons on the move than the paratroops drenched the farm position with heavy fire, and several dashed forward to take Blair, who had remained there alone, prisoner.

McLean's platoon ran into trouble straight away, suffering several casualties. Platoon Sergeant James Clifford Poole was killed. A bullet struck McLean in the shoulder, "and as he lay in a rocky crevice he was hit again by tracer bullets which burned off part of his clothes." Evacuated by a Jeep ambulance to the RAP at the farmhouse, McLean told the medical officer, Captain Ken MacDonald, that there were still wounded lying exposed on the hill. MacDonald rushed forward to help the men, only to be killed by a sniper while tending to Private W.T. Broad of 'C' Company.

Hoping to get the advance moving again, Hoffmeister ordered 'A' Company to push past 'C' Company and continue up to the ridge's summit. Major Bell-Irving led the way through a cactus hedge to start the climb. Suddenly, "I was met by a burst of machine-gun fire which sprayed my face with cactus thorn, so that I attacked this bat-tle in a very bad temper," he wrote later. He was also going into battle short a platoon, something he momentarily forgot, and without knowing that one of the two platoons that were with him had not received his orders to go forward. But it mattered little, because the Shermans were providing such excellent fire support. "We were shot on to the objective by the 75-millimetre guns... It was a magnificent piece of support—the tanks acting in their best possible role. They fired over open sights—right close over our heads—until we got within grenade distance of the summit. A number of Germans were still on top and they were either killed by grenades or small arms fire and a few ran away down the other side—most of them did not get too far. It was only then...that I discovered that my company consisted of a very small handful of men...My batman apologized to me for being stupid enough to get his arm practically shot off, which touched me very much indeed. We had a Company Sergeant Major and one man carrying a radio set and one or two odds and sods, and that's about all."[48]

Despite their weakness in numbers, the Seaforths carried the day largely through sheer grit. At about 1130 hours, Corporal G.L. McPar-lon was leading his section up the hill to the right of 'A' Company when machine-gun fire hit him in the leg and back. McParlon ordered his men to provide covering fire and, armed with a Thomp-son submachine gun, headed for the gun alone. Off to the left, Corporal R.J.P. Donahue saw him going forward. Turning his sec-tion over to another man, Donahue grabbed a Bren gun and a couple of ammunition pouches filled with ten magazines apiece. Joining McParlon in "his lonely advance," Donahue crawled alongside him across about five hundred yards of bullet-swept ground. When the two men were within point-blank range, they sprayed the paratroops manning the gun with bursts of fire until all were killed. Both corporals were awarded the Military Medal.

The section under Corporal D. Hadden also came under withering machine-gun fire short of the crest and two men fell wounded onto the rocky, bare slope. Ordering his men to scatter to cover, Hadden took the Bren and kept going. About seven hundred yards of naked ground stood between him and the German machine gun, but each time the paratroops raised their heads to sight on him, Hadden loosed a burst that forced them to duck. When he was within grenade range, the corporal chucked five grenades one after the other into the position and lunged forward waving his bayonet. Those paratroops still alive fled. Hadden received a Distinguished Conduct Medal for his bravery.

Courage often carries a terrible price. During the advance, Lieutenant Frank Constant Hall fell badly wounded. When his men hesitated and several moved to treat his wounds, Hall shouted at them to keep going and assured them he would be fine. After they gained the ridge, several men went back and discovered Hall had bled to death.[49] Company Sergeant Major Black counted seventeen men left when 'C' Company finally stood triumphant on the ridge. The little group dug in alongside 'A' Company's handful. Looking back down the slope Black saw "Padre [Roy] Durnford making his way up the hill, using a shepherd's hook to propel himself. When he got to us, he gave us two very wizened up lemons, half a bottle of water, and eight cigarettes."[50]

By midafternoon it was all over. "The operation by Booth Force had been completely successful," the army's official historian noted. It had been watched from the lofty heights of Centuripe by Simonds, Montgomery, and even Prime Minister Winston Churchill, who had travelled to Sicily for a personal briefing. All these luminary souls agreed "that it was a model infantry-cum-tank" operation.[51] Simonds declared it "the most successful of the First Canadian Division's campaign."[52] Booth was awarded the Distinguished Service Order for coordinating the operation.

Good communication among all the arms of service involved was a key factor in this success. Riding in the same tank, Booth and Hoffmeister were able to ensure that the infantry and tanks worked closely together. They were also fortunate that wireless communication with the Seaforth company and Three Rivers squadron commanders remained mostly good throughout. Riding in the headquarters section tank behind Booth's had been the 3rd Field Regiment's forward observation officer, directing the artillery support for the time it was available over a No. 22 wireless netted into the Three Rivers frequency. "He afterwards claimed that he had never before had such a 'field day' and never before had the advantage of such excellent wireless communications with which to carry out his tasks. The whole operation...went according to plan, with every arm carrying out its role perfectly," the Three Rivers war diarist wrote.[53]

Canadian casualties were relatively light considering the strength of the opposition in both numbers and position. Although no tally was taken, the ridge was strewn with German dead and a dozen paratroops were taken prisoner. But it was noticed that most fought to the death rather than surrender. The Seaforths—typical of what the British tellingly called the "PBI" or "Poor Bloody Infantry"—paid the worst. Their losses were eleven killed and thirty-two wounded. The PLDG had come through unscathed, while the tankers had two men killed by sniper fire.[54]

That evening, despite being terribly weak from dysentery, Hoffmeister came up onto the ridge. The battalion commander stood on the hill chatting with the men that meant so much to him. Although they could not know it yet, the Seaforths had fought their last battle in Sicily.

23

On a Barren Sicilian Mountainside

O N THE MORNING of August 5, the Loyal Edmonton Regiment's 'C' Company, behind Booth Force, had fought their way up the ever-rising heights until they were within a half-mile of the base of Hill 736—towering to 2,400 feet ahead. Major Archie Donald realized his men were spent. They had been under almost constant fire "for four days in a blazing sun and with practically no sleep," the Edmontons' adjutant noted. Donald asked for reinforcements, and Lieutenant Colonel Jim Jefferson sent two platoons from 'D' Company to lead the attack.[1] It took a couple of hours for Nos. 15 and 16 platoons to reach 'C' Company's position. Lieutenant John Dougan, who had shown such resourcefulness during his combat debut at the roadblock on the Agira–Nicosia road, still commanded No. 16 Platoon. His friend and former University of Alberta classmate, Lieutenant Earl John Christie, had No. 15 Platoon.[2] Although these two platoons were in better condition than those of 'C' Company, they were hardly strong. Christie and Dougan had just forty-three men between them, instead of what should have been seventy-two.

Donald told the two lieutenants he believed there were about one hundred well-entrenched Germans on the hill, so the platoons would be badly outnumbered and attacking a well-prepared position. Hill 736 was so steep and fronted by such rugged ground that tank support was out of the question. Donald had resorted to planning a creeping barrage by one field regiment, a detachment of mortars, and two Saskatoon Light Infantry Vickers machine guns. Wireless reception was troublesome on this flank of the Salso valley, so the "supporting fire involved a very elaborate chain of shouted commands and No. 18 wireless sets in order to relay the fire orders from the observation post to the gun positions." Effectively this entailed Donald shouting target information from where he crouched in a relatively exposed position to Lieutenant J.H. Snell, the battalion's mortar platoon commander. Snell relayed these to the 3rd Field Regiment's Captain D.J. Watson at battalion headquarters, who passed the coordinates to the artillery regiment for laying of guns on the target.

"Registration proved slower with this form of communication," the battalion adjutant acknowledged, but it did work. At 0430 hours, the two 'D' Company platoons ran towards Hill 736 as the artillery, mortars, and machine guns blazed away.[3] Dougan wished he had insisted on smoke rounds being mixed into the plan—it seemed an oversight. Despite the heavy supporting fire, the forty-five men were terribly exposed. Christie and his platoon were out on the right, Dougan going up on the left. "Keep close to the barrage," Dougan shouted at his men. Shells were exploding less than two hundred yards ahead with a flash of flame and boil of smoke. Bits of stone, clods of soil, and slivers of shrapnel spattered around the men as they scrambled upward. "No rounds will fall short," Dougan told himself. "Have faith. Keep going."

Suddenly, the barrage rolled on to the crest and lifted. Dougan could see Germans in their coal-scuttle–style helmets and hear them yelling. They sounded mad as hell. Everyone seemed to open fire at once and the air was thick with lead as "a very, very sharp gunfight" broke out. Dougan was ripping off bursts with his Thompson submachine gun. Behind him, No. 16 Platoon's Sergeant James Shannon Hammell, a forty-one-year-old Great War veteran whom Dougan had come to rely on heavily during his short stint as a platoon commander, was shot dead. To the right, Lieutenant Christie lay dying not far from the corpse of No. 15 Platoon's Sergeant Robert McEwan. Yet the attack kept going, the section leaders exerting control over the rapidly diminishing number of men under their command.

Something struck Dougan a tremendous blow. The next thing he knew, he was flat on his back. A slug had gone through the front of his helmet, buzzed around the circumference, and punched its way out the back. Another bullet had pierced his left arm, while a third had struck the Thompson, sending splinters of steel and wood into both arms and hands. All over the slope, men were down, wounded or dead. Screams rent the air only to be drowned out by the sheet-ripping shriek of the MG 42s raking them.

Dougan staggered to his feet. They were still short of the crest, well short of the German positions. His Thompson was gone. Reaching behind him, Dougan drew his officer's revolver from its hiding place in the waistband of his shorts. (Nobody used holsters because a visible revolver would surely draw the fire of a sniper wanting to bag an officer.) His hands were so cut up and his arms in such a bad way it was impossible to hold the revolver one-handed. Blood was showering from a cut on Dougan's scalp, across his face and into his eyes. More blood was spurting in rhythm to his heartbeat from the bullet wound in his left arm. Gripping the revolver in both hands, arms held straight out, Dougan went towards the Germans. Those men still in the fight followed, except for Dougan's batman, who ducked hard to the left flank and worked his way up behind the machine gun that was mauling the platoon. He silenced it with a grenade, buying the precious seconds Dougan and the others needed to gain the summit. After that Dougan was aware of very little. There was more gunfire and then it was over, the Germans having melted away, leaving many dead scattered in their gun pits.[4]

"So this is what battle is like," Dougan thought with a sense of dread and awe. If "this was ordinary platoon fare," he wondered how anybody could survive. The platoon stretcher-bearer ripped Dougan's shirt off and bound his wounds as best he could. Dougan walked down the hill, passing Major Donald and 'C' Company as they came forward to consolidate the Edmonton hold on Hill 736. He was soon in a clearing station. Shirtless, covered in dried blood, and swathed in bandages, Dougan noticed the attendants were carrying him towards a holding area crammed with wounded other ranks. "Just a moment, I'm an officer," Dougan said.

"You're an officer?" the man at the head of the stretcher asked skeptically.

"May not look it, but I am." A check of his identity disk proved the point and he was taken to where officers were treated. Those mad minutes on Hill 736 kept running through Dougan's mind, a chaotic collage that was becoming ever more difficult to keep in clear focus. "We took the objective," he thought, "but, my God, we did lose a lot of good people doing it."[5]

Just how many Edmontons fell on Hill 736 was never recorded. Dougan was awarded a Military Cross, and Major Donald received a Distinguished Service Order for his handling of 'C' Company in its four days of fighting. After several months' hospitalization, Dougan returned to the Loyal Edmonton Regiment. During the course of those months he had forgotten the name of his batman, who apparently was no longer with the regiment. Dougan thought he quite likely owed his life to the batman's knocking the machine gun out, but there was no way to thank him for the act.[6] Sometime later, war artist Will Ogilvie and an unnamed officer ascended Hill 736. "We had to stop four times, just walking. You can imagine how steep the hill was. Our rifle company boys were simply marvelous and fearless. Words are inadequate to describe them," the officer wrote.[7]

WHILE THE ATTACK on Hill 736 had been drawing to its bloody conclusion, the Edmontons' 'A' and 'B' companies had attempted to carry Monte Revisotto on the eastern flank of the Troina River. Although getting almost to the base of the mountain, the two companies suffered the same fate as 'C' Company had earlier in front of Hill 736—heavy fire from the summit driving the men to ground. By this time, Hill 736 had fallen, and it was decided that the successful support provided by artillery in that venture should be emulated. The attack was postponed until 0930 hours on August 6 to gear up a gunnery plan.[8]

Brigadier Chris Vokes was increasingly frustrated by how long it was taking the Edmontons and Princess Patricia's Canadian Light Infantry to carry Hill 736, Monte Revisotto, and Monte Seggio. All these features were to have been taken on August 5, but the shadows were already growing long, and from the latter two objectives the Germans still threatened movement in the Salso valley. To make matters worse, Vokes had been informed by Major General Guy Simonds that the 3rd Canadian Infantry Brigade was to pass through the valley the next morning and exploit out of the bridgehead across the Simeto River that Booth Force had won that afternoon.

Summoned to an Eighth Army meeting at Catenanuova, Vokes headed off in the early evening while his brigade major, Major P.R. Bingham, passed tersely worded instructions to the Edmontons, the PPCLI, and the supporting tank and artillery commands that "come what may," Revisotto and Seggio were to "be taken by tomorrow morning."[9]

Vokes would have gone into a foaming lather had he been aware that at the time this order was issued, the PPCLI had not begun moving towards Monte Seggio from a holding position south of Monte Revisotto. Only at 2030 hours did Lieutenant Colonel Bob Lindsay send 'A' and 'B' companies towards the mountain. Curiously, despite the fact that the two Edmonton companies assaulting Monte Revisotto were to be heavily supported by artillery and tanks while the PPCLI attack was unsupported, Lindsay held the rest of the battalion in place "to provide a firm base" for the Edmontons.[10]

Just thirty minutes before the two companies pushed off, Lieutenant Syd Frost had jumped out of a truck outside battalion headquarters. He had landed in Sicily on July 12 as part of the PPCLI reinforcement pool, spent a curious time from July 16 to August 3 serving as the town mayor of Ispica, and then been ordered forward with a draft of replacements. Frost no sooner checked in with headquarters than he was told to report to 'A' Company. Grabbing his battle kit, the young officer dashed into the night. "Silent forms began to glide past in the darkness, broken only by flashes from our guns and fires in the valley ahead and on the surrounding hills. I had not the slightest idea where I was, much less where our troops, the enemy or the objective were." Spotting what he took for an officer, Frost said, "I've just arrived...and been posted to 'A' Company. Any idea what platoon I'm supposed to join?"

"Take the first one that goes by without an officer," a voice growled from the darkness. Frost intercepted No. 8 Platoon. Falling in alongside the sergeant who had been commanding it, Frost headed towards his first battle.[11]

Captain W. "Bucko" Watson was commanding 'A' Company, Major Donald Brain 'B' Company. Both had already seen their share of fighting in Sicily. They expected the fight for Monte Seggio would be a hard one. A more immediate problem was simply finding the forming-up position. Their maps bore little resemblance to the terrain illuminated by "burning straw stacks and houses and in one spot an ammunition dump which flared up every now and then. There were flashes of gun fire and shell explosions in the darkness on either side."

At 2300 hours, the PPCLI column was challenged by a Seaforth sentry. He guided them to battalion headquarters in a farmhouse to speak with Lieutenant Colonel Bert Hoffmeister. "The old room at the back of the house presented a strange sight," Brain wrote. "A very dirty oil lamp, 'scrounged' from somewhere was burning on a ledge. The C.O. was sitting on a dilapidated straw chair munching away at some hardtack spread with jam and looking very tired. In another corner [Captain J.H.] Gowan was supervising a can of hot tea, from which we were given a welcome drink; while against the wall, on a pile of straw, lay a couple of wounded officers waiting to be evacuated.

"We were given the story of the hard fight the Seaforths had had in gaining their ground that afternoon. They also told us about Monte Seggio. To the best of their knowledge the hill still was held in some strength, although no mortaring or shelling of their area had occurred since nightfall. In our experience of the Germans, this had little significance.

"Our plan was discussed with Colonel Hoffmeister before we pushed off. On reaching the road again we encountered a squadron of tanks on their way forward to relieve another squadron which had expended its ammunition and petrol. We accepted the offer of a lift and loaded two companies on the tanks. Unfortunately a wrong turning was made and we finally offloaded on the edge of an irrigation ditch which the tanks could not cross.

"Then began our search for the forward companies of the Seaforths. A patrol was sent out which returned after twenty minutes. A second patrol was dispatched and it, too, returned after a short time but with the good news that contact had been made with Major Bell-

Irving's company. We moved forward once more and at 0230 hours we were inside the Seaforth area."

The two PPCLI company commanders and Major Budge Bell-Irving discussed the attack, worrying about the likelihood of succeeding without any fire support from artillery or tanks. They finally decided to wait until first light to make the assault, hoping in the meantime to arrange support from the tanks that had given them the earlier lift and also to find a FOO, who could call in some artillery "to deal with the enemy posts which had been engaging the Seaforths the previous evening."[12]

While the PPCLI companies sacked out on the ground within the Seaforth's 'A' Company position, at 2 CIB headquarters Vokes and Brigade Major Bingham awaited word that the attacks had begun, but the news from the front was "as per usual vague...With first light it was learnt that neither of the two features had been taken."[13]

Neither the Edmonton nor the PPCLI attack got off at first light, due to problems tying in the supporting arms. The Edmontons were ready first and started up Monte Revisotto at 0930 hours on August 6 behind "a very heavy artillery barrage from the Divisional Artillery as well as fire from 17 pounders, a troop of tanks and a platoon of medium machineguns."[14] Either the artillery "was too much for them or the attack by 'D' [Company] on [Hill] 736 was still too fresh in their minds, but the enemy in any event offered no opposition and the infantry encountered no enemy except for one forlorn PW [prisoner of war]," the battalion's adjutant recorded.[15]

Ninety minutes later, a FOO having been found who arranged some artillery, the PPCLI went forward. Although the tanks had never shown up, the artillery, medium machine guns, and 4.2-inch mortars laid down a massive bombardment behind which the men struggled up the rugged slopes of Monte Seggio and assaulted. "Luck was with us," Frost wrote. "The enemy had decamped in haste, leaving behind a damaged heavy machine gun, tools, 'potato mashers,' ammunition belts and a dead officer—a paratroop lieutenant.

"It was my first view of a dead German soldier. He had been caught in our barrage and his lower body was a horrible mess of bone, flesh, guts and torn uniform. I reached inside his camouflaged jacket and pulled out a wallet. Papers, postcards and pictures fell to the ground. I picked up a blood-stained postcard he had apparently written home but never posted. On the front was a picture of his idol—Adolph Hitler.

"'The poor misguided bastard,' I mumbled to myself. 'Thousands of miles from home, his shattered body lies abandoned by his comrades on a barren Sicilian mountainside. Soon the peasants will steal his boots; the follow-up troops will take his watch and iron cross.'"

Frost turned to his men and, summoning his best commanding officer tone, shouted, "Come on, platoon. He's just another dead Kraut. Let's get moving." Soon they dug in on the highest part of the summit of Monte Seggio, facing no other enemy but the searing Sicilian sun that pushed the temperature that day to 110 Fahrenheit.[16]

The fighting in the Salso valley from August 2 to August 6 had cost 2 CIB more than 150 casualties.[17] No estimate of German losses in the battle was ever determined. But three paratroops taken prisoner on August 6 told divisional intelligence officers that the units fighting there had become badly disorganized and "broken into groups of two or three, with instructions to make their way back as best they could to rejoin the main body of troops."[18]

The Salso valley remained a dangerous place, subject throughout the course of August 6 to shelling from the heights east of Adrano. While moving towards Monte Seggio, the PPCLI were subjected to particularly heavy bombardment. Lieutenant John D'Arcy Horn, a popular officer, was mortally wounded when a shell landed in the midst of his platoon.[19]

Brigadier Vokes was furious at the PPCLI for delaying their attack— believing, rightly or wrongly, that if the entire battalion had struck Monte Seggio during the night, "they might have carried their objective with disastrous results to the enemy withdrawal," as he wrote in an August 6 memo.[20] It baffled him why Lieutenant Colonel Bob Lindsay had sent only two companies to carry out the attack while providing a "firm base" for the Edmontons. In doing so, and by remaining back with those companies, it fell to two company commanders to execute the assault. This had led to what appeared to be an independent decision on their part—possibly reached as a result of conversations with Lieutenant Colonel Hoffmeister and Major Bell-Irving of the Seaforths—to delay to first light. If Lindsay had countenanced this decision or even been aware of it, Vokes thought he should have notified the brigade. But Lindsay had not done so, and as far as Vokes was concerned, this failure was tantamount to direct disobedience of an order, and either the battalion commander or the two company commanders involved must shoulder the blame. The final nail in the coffin that Vokes was building, and into which he was about to consign Lindsay's military career, was that the PPCLI had gone into the attack on Monte Seggio fresher than the rest of the battalion, for it had seen no fighting in the Salso prior to this attack.[21]

WHILE 2 CIB had been finishing up the Salso valley operation, 3 CIB had passed through its lines to continue the drive to Adrano. Royal 22e Régiment led the brigade advance and arrived in the Simeto River bridgehead in the early morning of August 6. Lieutenant Colonel Paul Bernatchez immediately ordered 'C' Company to occupy the hills northeast of the river while 'D' Company came up on its right. The former company had just come under command of Captain Paul Triquet—who in December of that year would win a Victoria Cross in the legendary battle for Casa Berardi outside Ortona. His men made the advance quickly and without meeting opposition. While clearing some houses, they found an abandoned 88-millimetre gun, about two hundred mortar rounds, and two machine guns. These objectives in hand, Bernatchez ordered the companies to send fighting patrols forward to Adrano itself.

'C' Company's Lieutenant Yves Dubé led one patrol to a road junction in front of the town and rounded up three German prisoners lurking about, two of whom were wounded. Having lost wireless contact with the rest of the battalion and believing his patrol was followed by the rest of the Van Doos, Dubé marched his men into town.

Meanwhile, however, Bernatchez had been warned by 1st Canadian Infantry Division headquarters to withdraw back to the Simeto River, because the 78th British Infantry Division was going "to take the town which is in their new axis of advance." All the other patrols were hurriedly recalled, but Bernatchez was unable to reach Dubé. Oblivious to the changed plans, Dubé and his men marched through Adrano's battered streets without seeing any enemy. Adrano had been reduced to a ruin by relentless artillery and aerial bombardment. Until well into the night, when it became obvious the rest of the battalion was not coming forward, the platoon remained among the shattered buildings and torn-up streets. Throughout this time, Dubé was puzzled by the fact the Canadian artillery continued relentlessly shelling Adrano, despite the fact it had obviously been abandoned. Were he and his men the only ones to realize this? Deciding the answer to this question was probably affirmative, the lieutenant withdrew from Adrano and returned to the battalion lines in the early morning hours of August 7.

Lieutenant Dubé had led his men through 1st Canadian Infantry Division's last combat action in Sicily. They had fired no shots and suffered not a single casualty. Brigadier Howard Penhale had quickly notified divisional headquarters that the Germans had evacuated Adrano. At 1100 hours on August 7, Penhale sent a message to the Van Doos: "General [Simonds] and myself are very pleased of your exploit of last night and this morning...your initiative in patrolling which produced first information of enemy withdrawal...enabled us to score one up on our friends on our right [78th Division]."[22]

Although Dubé's patrol closed the division's active role in Operation Husky, a small number of Canadian troops were still engaged. Having deployed in late July to close the gap between Eighth Army's two corps, 1st Canadian Army Tank Brigade had encountered no enemy. By July 31, it was clear the Germans were not going to attempt to push into this gap. While the Calgary Tank Regiment and the rest of the brigade remained in place, the Ontario Tank Regiment was detached to support an advance by the 5th British Infantry Division's 13th Brigade northeast from the Dittaino River towards Paterno, which lay about three miles southeast of Adrano. Their initial task was to guard the Sferro bridgehead across the river that provided the base for the British advance.[23]

At 1240 hours on August 1, the Ontarios were warned that a German armoured counterattack was driving towards the bridgehead.

At first the number of tanks headed towards them was given as eight but was soon increased to twenty-five. The Canadian tankers jockeyed their Shermans into positions sited on several hillsides in front of the river valley and braced for what promised to be Eighth Army's largest tank battle of the campaign. When the German tanks were about six thousand yards distant, however, the divisional artillery struck with a deadly accurate barrage. One tank exploded in flames and the others scattered, quickly retreating towards Paterno.

The following day, 'B' Squadron sent a troop under command of Captain L.I. Knowle from Sferro to support the advancing infantry. In this action, Knowle's tank fired the regiment's first shots in Sicily against a couple of German mortar positions that were giving the infantry grief. Knowle's gunner, Corporal M. Corrigan, opened fire from a range of 2,500 yards. Ten high-explosive shells eliminated the mortar positions, as well as firing up a haystack that had concealed the observation post directing their fire.[24]

On August 3, a troop from 'A' Squadron accompanied an advance by 2nd Battalion, Wiltshire Regiment, towards Gerbini aerodrome. Lieutenant D.S. Barlow joined the Wiltshire's commander in a Jeep and together the two men looked for a suitable crossing over the Simeto River. As they approached the riverbed, two 37-millimetre anti-tank guns on the opposite shore opened fire. By wireless, Barlow directed the fire of his tanks against these guns and they were both destroyed.[25]

During the night, 2nd Battalion, the Royal Inniskilling Fusiliers, crossed the Simeto River. 'B' Squadron was to have accompanied the infantry, but no serviceable bridge could be found. So the tankers consoled themselves with setting up on hills overlooking the line of advance and taking potshots at any likely targets. In the morning, engineers created a crossing, and two troops from 'C' Squadron joined the advance on Paterno while the rest of the squadron provided fire support for a set-piece attack on Monte Prefalci. Actually a low hill, it lay about fifteen hundred yards southeast of Paterno. The only real obstacle to the infantry advance was a large house near the summit that sheltered several German machine-gun and mortar positions. The tankers found it "deeply satisfying...to test the destructive ability of their guns" on the house, and it was soon "battered into a ragged shell."

On the morning of August 6, 'A' and 'C' squadrons supported two infantry battalions in an assault on Paterno, but arrived to find the town had been abandoned during the night. With the Germans now conducting a general withdrawal, the tankers were hard-pressed to catch up. They were also often found outdistanced by the infantry, because the advance had entered the southeastern foothills of Mount Etna and at times required moving along the lower slope of the volcano itself. August 9 saw 'A' Squadron struggling along a mountain road that clung to Etna's eastern slope. They were about two thousand feet above sea level and nearing Safferana Etnea when the Germans launched a sharp counterattack, which infantry and tankers fought off together. When the counterattack was broken, the Ontario Regiment received orders to return to a rest area near Monte del Casale, where all other elements of the 1st Canadian Army Tank Brigade were concentrating.

At 2300 hours on August 11, the tankers had just climbed out of their Shermans at Monte del Casale when several German bombers swept in and bombed the area. A nearby ammunition bunker was set on fire. Men scattered as hundreds of shells and bullets began exploding. One Ontario tanker was killed and two others wounded.[26] Twenty-six-year-old Trooper Richard Arthur Burry had the misfortune of being not just the Ontario Regiment's only fatality in the Sicily campaign but the last Canadian to die on the island due to enemy action.[27]

ON THE DAY Burry died, 1st Canadian Infantry Division began moving to a rest area in a valley west of Militello. "We moved south," the Seaforth's Padre Roy Durnford wrote, "passing through the debris which once was Regalbuto and on to Agira and south to the Catania plains. At 7:30 p.m. we arrived at our Happy Valley by means of a winding road corkscrewing down precipitous slopes for 3 1/2 miles to a river and broad green valley. Here I settled down in solid comfort— that is to say, with a camp bed and a canvas sheet for shade and my tea kettle going all day long. This was heaven. Peace and the absence of mortars, machine guns and shell fire."[28]

"Happy Valley," as the Canadians would forever remember this area, was only relatively heavenly. Despite its many olive and orange groves there was little shade to be had, flies were a "scourge," and the camps had to be set on the higher ground to avoid the valley bottom, which had been declared a "malarial area." However, the troops supplemented rations with bountiful harvests of figs, grapes, lemons, and oranges—most of the latter still green. There was also an abundance of local wine, the purchase of which was officially forbidden to all but the messes. This rule was widely ignored.

Most of the hundreds of wounded Canadians did not spend time in Happy Valley. The majority were evacuated to hospitals in North Africa. Among them was Seaforth Lieutenant Robert L. McDougall, who had been wounded in the fighting for Grizzly on July 27. From 95th General Hospital in Tripoli, McDougall wrote his mother on August 8. "First and foremost I'm doing very nicely, thank you, though still rather washed out from loss of blood. I have two wounds on exhibit—both from Heine bullets. One of them passed through my left thigh and down, coming out between my legs. There was an artery injured but otherwise a complete miss on vital stuff so a month or so should see everything O.K. The other bullet nicked my right leg at the back about six inches above the ankle—the fibula and the Achilles tendon took a spot of rough treatment, but again nothing that will not mend in fairly short order. Well, these are the gory details, dear mother!... Being wounded, is, of course, a new experience! One imagines what it will be like, and then one finds it is quite different—that's the way it is with most experience. I do not ask for a repetition. The wound itself on the battlefield is nothing because you are a bit dazed; it's the long trip back in an ambulance over Sicilian roads, lying on a stretcher on the crowded floors of rooms and corridors. Just between you and me...there were times when I felt I'd hit a new high in human suffering—and mine was one of the less serious cases!"[29]

For the Canadians in Happy Valley the forthcoming weeks were dedicated to achieving three official purposes. First, there was "rest and recreation," second, "resumption of normal training and discipline," and third, "planning for the next operation."[30] The troops cared more about the first object than the others. Brigadier Chris Vokes was designated president of a divisional sports committee that organized sports days, interunit softball games, and brigade sports meets. When the fighting on the island drew to a close with completion of the German evacuation on August 16, swimming excursions were organized to Mediterranean beaches.

Outside of physical activity, few other recreational pursuits were on offer. All towns were strictly off limits, and patrols were in place to round up anybody who decided to disobey the prohibition. So the men drank bootlegged wine, gambled, wrote and read letters, fought with mates, fantasized about sex, and grew bored. Despite strenuous efforts to keep the men away from Sicilian women, Vokes was alarmed that the number of men contracting venereal diseases was on the rise. He proposed an unorthodox solution—setting up brigade brothels where the prostitutes would be vetted. The planning process for this was well along when a group of padres got wind of the plan and nixed it.[31]

Vokes was a man of strong opinion. He made good on his decision to relieve PPCLI commander Lieutenant Colonel Bob Lindsay. Cameron Ware, who had managed to talk his way to Sicily just in time to see the campaign's end, took command—realizing a boyhood dream.

Lindsay was not the only Canadian officer to be punished for perceived failures during the campaign. The Carleton and York Regiment's Lieutenant Colonel Dodd Tweedie was relieved by 3rd Canadian Infantry Brigade's Brigadier Howard Penhale, who told Major General Guy Simonds that he had "lost all confidence in this officer." John Pangman, the brother of 3 CIB's Brigade Major G.F.C. Pangman, took over the Carletons.[32]

Penhale, too, was for the chop. The division's senior brigadier, he would normally have been in line to succeed Simonds. But Simonds believed Penhale's "over caution and hesitation in making operations decisions in face of apparent risks may well result in creating even greater risks." Given sufficient time to make decisions, the brigadier reached the right conclusions, but he was not able to think quickly enough for the pace of modern combat. Penhale was shuffled off to a staff position at Canadian Military Headquarters in London.[33]

More career reputations were made, however, than broken by the campaign. Simonds told Vokes he was in line to succeed him, and Lieutenant Colonel Bert Hoffmeister would be first choice for 2 CIB's command in that eventuality. Lieutenant Colonels George Kitching, Geoff Walsh, Paul Bernatchez, and Pat Bogert all performed well in their respective duties and were tipped for future brigade command. Each would rise to such commands during the division's forthcoming campaign.

That campaign would open on September 3 with Eighth Army's amphibious crossing of the Straits of Messina and the beginning of the invasion of Italy. The final decision to use Sicily as a springboard into Italy had been reached on August 16. This was the same day that the Germans concluded their stunningly successful evacuation from the island. Over the course of the previous fifteen days, 39,569 German troops, 9,605 vehicles, 47 tanks, 94 guns, and 17,000 tons of vital supplies had been ferried out of Sicily. Allied naval and air force attempts to disrupt the transfers were dismal. How this escape was achieved quickly became the subject of an intense debate that continues still, with fingers pointing at numerous Allied senior officers or arms of service. It also gave the Germans fodder for claiming the Sicily campaign more a victory than a defeat.

This was hardly the case. German forces in Sicily lost 6,663 soldiers captured and about 5,000 killed. They also lost 78 tanks, 287 guns, and 3,500 vehicles, as well as vast amounts of matériel. German high-command claims that the divisions evacuated from Sicily arrived on the mainland "ready for immediate service" were far from truthful. The Hermann Göring Division reported its mobility levels at about 50 per cent, and the 29th Panzer Grenadier Division stated its fighting power also at only 50 per cent of normal.

Operation Husky basically knocked Italy out of the war. Although 59,000 Italian soldiers and 3,000 sailors were evacuated, 137,000 remained as prisoners. Another 2,000 had been killed and about 5,000 wounded. Mussolini was deposed, and the Italian government engaged in secret talks with the Allies to secure a peace accord. On July 30, Hitler ordered German formations lurking on the northern border of the mainland to occupy the nation and put to an end the sham that Italy was still a trusted Axis partner.

As Churchill and his Chief of Imperial General Staff, General Sir Alan Brooke, had predicted at the outset, Sicily forced the Germans to divert strength away from the Russian front and, because they could not know for certain where in the Mediterranean the Allies would strike next, to strengthen garrisons in southern France and the Balkans. Sardinia and Corsica were rendered untenable, and German troops evacuated these islands in September.

Allied casualties were substantial, but far below what Operation Husky planners had feared. The U.S. Seventh Army suffered 7,402 casualties and Eighth Army, 11,843. About a quarter of the latter were Canadians—2,310. Including those men who died at sea, 40 officers and 522 other ranks were killed, 124 officers and 1,540 other ranks were wounded, and 8 officers and 76 men were taken prisoner. Among the wounded were 12 nursing sisters injured when an anti-aircraft shell struck No. 5 Canadian General Hospital in Catania on September 2.[34]

The soldiers of 1st Canadian Infantry Division had marched 120 miles through Sicily's difficult heartland mountains "in continuous and extreme heat, and in contact for most of the way with a stubborn foe." They marched farther than any other Eighth Army Division and, due to the problems with transport, covered most of that distance with their boots. Originally, Eighth Army had ascribed the division only a minor role in Operation Husky. Blocked from advancing on the Catania plain, however, Montgomery was forced in the last two weeks of the invasion to call upon the Canadians to bear "the brunt of the fighting...No other division in the Allied force made a larger contribution to the victory," concluded one Canadian army historical report on the campaign.[35]

While in Happy Valley, Captain Strome Galloway put on the major's crowns that he had carried in anticipation throughout the course of the fighting. Having led a British company in North Africa and seen hard fighting there, he thought the Canadians got off lightly in Sicily in terms of casualties. "It was, however, a hard campaign from the standpoint of discomfort, long gruelling marches, the stench of burning grass, and unburied dead, including soldiers, civilians and mules, and the incredible heat, with thirst, hunger and painful sunburn our constant scourges. Lack of sleep, caused by the continuous movement, and bowel trouble caused by contaminated fruit and water helped to wear down some troops. Fortunately, the training in Britain had turned us into the right material from which to make hardy campaigners. Besides, we were young."[36]

Padre Durnford would have argued against Galloway's dismissal of Canadian casualties as light. "As I look back over this great episode, I am filled with admiration for my fellow officers, my [commanding officer], and the men of my battalion. They proved to be men of sterling worth in the face of great odds. I look back, too, and see in my mind's eye many dead faces—unforgettably imprinted on my mind. They were the faces of brave men who were ready to pour out their lives to the last full measure of devotion."[37] Although he spoke of the Seaforths, his words could have applied to any and all of the Canadians in Sicily.

Operation Husky in Memory

I STAND IN THE Agira Canadian War Cemetery next to the headstone of Lieutenant Earl John Christie. A group of Canadians are gathered before me. Behind them is the entrance to the cemetery and then the Sicilian countryside—a mix of grain fields, olive orchards, and vineyards—spreads across the narrow valley and up the steep slopes of surrounding mountains. To the east, Agira is perched atop its mountaintop.

It is late afternoon, the sun a hard brightness to the west. Although it is September rather than July or August, the heat is withering. Our clothes are damp with sweat. When I was in this place some years earlier it had been late fall, and rosemary dotted with purplish blue flowers had twined around the cool white marble headstones that stretch out in precisely straight lines from one side of the cemetery to the other. But this is a summer of drought, and there are few flowers, what rosemary there is lies shrivelled, and the grass is coarse and brown underfoot.

The people with me are participants in a battlefield tour. For the past few days, we have been driving in vans along the route that 1st Canadian Infantry Division followed from Pachino to Adrano. This day has seen visits to Leonforte, Assoro, and Agira, before ending at the cemetery. For some, this stop at Agira cemetery is their first expe-

416

rience of a Commonwealth war cemetery, while others are old hands at such visits. No matter, all are moved. Basil Libby is one of two World War II veterans present. He was navy, not army—an Able Bodied Seaman whose last war-time posting was aboard the HMCS *Antigonish*. With his son, Ross, he has made a couple of rubbings on paper of the headstones of men buried here who came from the South Porcupine–Timmins area of Ontario. The rubbings will be displayed, along with others they have gathered from earlier visits to Commonwealth cemeteries in Europe, in Libby's local Royal Canadian Legion.

Others in the group have collected similar rubbings of specific headstones or photographed them for use in various acts of remembrance. In front of some headstones, one or the other of us has pushed a little paper maple leaf flag into the hard soil as a personal tribute to the man lying in the earth below.

Now we are gathered about Lieutenant John Earl Christie's headstone, and I tell the story of how a young man from Medicine Hat, Alberta, came to die on August 5 while leading his platoon of Loyal Eddies up Hill 736 into deadly fire. Beyond the facts of his death, there is another story I relate here—told me by John Dougan, the other officer on that hillside, who, though badly wounded, walked away at the end of that bloody day. It is a story that Dougan told once while we sat on the patio of his home outside Victoria, sipping iced tea on a warm summer day. The volcanic cone of Mount Baker had been visible across Haro Strait, just as Etna had been within his view on August 5, 1943.

I had interviewed Dougan on several occasions and considered him a friend now, rather than just an interview subject. He always chose words carefully, which was fitting, for after the war he had been a Rhodes Scholar in 1946 and then had a distinguished career with the Department of External Affairs, where he represented Canada in various overseas postings. This day, our conversation had turned to the matter of Christie's death. Johnnie reminded me that he and Christie had been two of four young officers all from the same year at the University of Alberta and posted together to the Loyal Edmonton Regiment. Christie had died in his first action, while the others survived the war. Who lived and who died seemed mere chance in

Dougan's estimation. But some deaths were more tragic than others. Christie had been studying medicine before he enlisted. Dougan and his friends all agreed that before him waited a brilliant medical career. Christie would make some great discovery or become a leading surgeon. Instead he bled out his life on Hill 736. All that potential lost to the whims of war. The four had known the odds were that one or all might die. But it had seemed particularly cruel fate that it should be Christie—who the others had agreed was the best and brightest of them.

Christie was but one of 562 Canadians who perished in Operation Husky. Some were lost at sea, but most died in the bare, sun-baked landscape of Sicily. Almost four hundred of them lie in Agira Canadian Cemetery. While some Commonwealth cemeteries annually draw thousands of visitors engaged in remembrance tours, the visitor book at Agira has many days that are blank between visits by small groups or even a single person. Isolated, difficult to get to without a vehicle, this Canadian cemetery is seldom a place of active remembrance.

Perhaps this should not be surprising, for Canada's participation in the Sicily invasion is not well remembered. Even those who are aware that Canadians fought in Italy are often oblivious to the Sicilian part of the story. Twenty-eight grinding days of combat have been easily forgotten. But consider the historical record. This book is the first Canadian work dedicated solely to Canada's role in the campaign. Outside Canada, most histories of Operation Husky give our participation less attention than seems warranted by 1st Canadian Infantry Division's exploits.

Canada could, of course, have stayed out of Operation Husky. But we sent men there, and they fought well in the nation's first test of sustained combat on a divisional scale. For the Canadian officers and soldiers involved, Sicily was a proving ground and a place where many lessons were learned that would serve the army well over the course of the rest of the war.

This was true for the Allies as a whole. Initially, the Americans had not wanted an invasion in the Mediterranean. They had wanted to get on immediately with the cross-channel invasion of France. In grudgingly conceding to the Sicily invasion, they unwittingly avoided likely disaster. The amphibious invasion of Sicily was complex, and the planning that went into it tried to meet every contingency. Yet so many things went wrong—landings on wrong beaches, friendly fire slaughtering airborne troops, problems in maintaining the follow-up flow of supplies and reinforcements, to cite just a few calamities. Had the beaches been guarded by veteran German troops rather than ill-trained and war-weary Italians, the invaders may not have got ashore at all. When Allied planners began work on the invasion of Normandy, which would be launched on June 6, 1944, they drew well on the lessons learned in Operation Husky. Thousands of lives, and quite likely the success of the invasion itself, were saved because of this prior experience.

If the Sicily invasion is not much remembered in Canada, that is not the case on the island itself. On the same day we visited Agira Cemetery, our group paused in a pullout below the towering heights of Assoro. As we got out and I started speaking about the Hastings and Prince Edward Regiment's heroic scaling of the back slope on the night of July 22, a farmer strode towards us from where he had been working in his driveway. He looked angry, ready to send us packing. *"Il canadese, il guerra,"* I said—as if that might explain why these strangers were milling about on the edge of his property. His Sicilian dialect was rapid as a machine-gun burst, but suddenly he was smiling and gesturing towards the farmhouse. When everyone crowded inside, wine was broken out, glasses handed around. A cellphone was chattered into and soon a little black car roared into the yard and a young man who spoke a little English arrived. Assoro loomed over us. The farmer spoke of a time when he had been young, the war had come to this place, and there had been Canadian soldiers. Beyond this it was hard to comprehend much because the young man's English was barely more serviceable than my crude Italian, but gratitude was mentioned repeatedly.

He reminded us of the monument recently erected on the summit by the Canadian Battlefields Foundation. It is the first of what is promised to be several set up to mark key events in the course of the 120-mile march across Sicily. In the future, these will serve as waypoints for tours.

There is another monument in Sicily of import to Canadians. It sits on the side of a road between Bark West beach and Ispica and was largely funded by one Canadian, Syd Frost. A lieutenant in the Princess Patricia's Canadian Light Infantry, Frost had landed in the unlikely role of temporary mayor of Ispica. His experiences during what was only about two weeks left an indelible impression and forged a longstanding relationship between him and the people of this Sicilian town. The monument was unveiled on July 10, 1991, to commemorate the 48th Anniversary of the landings and 1st Canadian Infantry Division.

But Frost and the people of Ispica were not done. In 2000—in a joint effort—additional panels were unveiled that honoured the Italian troops and civilians of Ispica who had fallen during the invasion. Due to health problems, Frost was unable to attend that ceremony and could only send a heartfelt letter to be read to the crowd. The three-panel monument, as it stands today, formally honours the bond between Canada and Sicily that is the result of mutual sacrifice and loss during Operation Husky. It symbolizes a desire by the Sicilian people never to forget the experiences of war nor their dead or the dead of their Canadian liberators.

APPENDIX A:
PRINCIPAL UNITS AND COMMANDERS
IN OPERATION HUSKY

BRITISH

Chief of Imperial General Staff—Gen. Sir Alexander Brooke

Deputy Supreme Commander Mediterranean—Gen. Harold
Alexander

Eighth Army—Gen. Bernard Law Montgomery

XIII Corps—Lt. Gen. Miles Dempsey

XXX Corps—Lt. Gen. Oliver Leese

Air Chief Marshal Arthur Tedder

Admiral of the Fleet Andrew Cunningham

78th Division—Maj. Gen. Vyvyan Evelegh

231st Malta Brigade—Brig. Robert Urquhart

AMERICAN

Chief of Staff, United States Army—Gen. George Marshall

Commander-in-Chief Mediterranean—Gen. Dwight D. Eisenhower

U.S. Seventh Army—Gen. George S. Patton

II Corps—Gen. Omar Bradley

1st Infantry Division—Maj. Gen. Terry Allen

CANADIAN

First Canadian Army—Lt. Gen. Andrew McNaughton

1st Canadian Infantry Division—Maj. Gen. Harry Salmon,
then Maj. Gen. Guy Simonds

    1st Canadian Infantry Brigade (1 CIB)—Brig. Howard Graham

        Royal Canadian Regiment (RCR)—Lt. Col. Ralph Crowe,
then Maj. Tom Powers

421

Hastings and Prince Edward (Hasty Ps)—Lt. Col. Bruce
Sutcliffe; then Maj. John Buchan, 2nd Baron
Tweedsmuir; then Maj. Bert Kennedy
48th Highlanders of Canada—Lt. Col. Ian Johnston
2nd Canadian Infantry Brigade (2 CIB)—Brig. Chris Vokes
Princess Patricia's Canadian Light Infantry (PPCLI)—
Lt. Col. Bob Lindsay
Seaforth Highlanders of Canada (Seaforths)—
Lt. Col. Bert Hoffmeister
Loyal Edmonton Regiment (Edmontons, Eddies)—
Lt. Col. Jim Jefferson
3rd Canadian Infantry Brigade (3 CIB)—Brig. Howard Penhale
Royal 22e Régiment (Van Doos)—Lt. Col. Paul
Bernatchez
West Nova Scotia Regiment (West Novas)—Lt. Col. Pat
Bogert
Carleton and York Regiment (Carletons)—Lt. Col. Dodd
Tweedie
1st Canadian Army Tank Brigade
Three Rivers Tank Regiment—Lt. Col. Leslie Booth

GERMAN
OKW Commander—Generaloberst Alfred Jodl
Commander-in-Chief South—Generalfeldmarschall Albert Kesselring
XIV Panzer Corps—General der Panzertruppen Hans Valentin Hube
Herman Göring Division—Generalmajor Paul Conrath
15th Panzer Grenadier Division—Generalmajor Eberhard Rodt

ITALIAN
Sixth Army—Generale di Corpo Mario Roatta, then Generale
d'Armata Alfredo Guzzoni
XVI Corps—Generale di Corpo Carlo Rossi
206th Coastal Defence Division—Generale di Divisione Achille d'Havet
54th Napoli Division—Generale di Divisione Count Giulio Cesare
Gotti-Porcinari

APPENDIX B:
THE CANADIAN ARMY IN OPERATION HUSKY
(COMBAT UNITS ONLY)

IST CANADIAN INFANTRY DIVISION
4th Reconnaissance Regiment
(Princess Louise Dragoon Guards)

The Royal Canadian Artillery
1st Field Regiment
(Royal Canadian Horse Artillery)
2nd Field Regiment
3rd Field Regiment
1st Anti-Tank Regiment
2nd Light Anti-Aircraft Regiment

Corps of Royal Canadian Engineers
1st Field Company
3rd Field Company
4th Field Company
2nd Field Park Company

Brigade Support Group
The Saskatoon Light Infantry

1st Canadian Infantry Brigade
The Royal Canadian Regiment (Permanent Force)
The Hastings and Prince Edward Regiment
48th Highlanders of Canada Regiment

2nd Canadian Infantry Brigade
Princess Patricia's Canadian Light Infantry Regiment (Permanent
    Force)
Seaforth Highlanders of Canada Regiment
Loyal Edmonton Regiment

3rd Canadian Infantry Brigade
Royal 22e Régiment (Permanent Force)
Carleton and York Regiment
West Nova Scotia Regiment

1st Canadian Army Tank Brigade
11th Canadian Armoured Regiment (Ontario Tanks)
12th Canadian Armoured Regiment (Three Rivers Tanks)
14th Canadian Armoured Regiment (Calgary Tanks)

HQ COMPANY

No. 1 Signals Platoon

No. 2 Administrative Platoon

SUPPORT COMPANY

No. 3 Mortar Platoon (3-inch)

No. 4 Bren Carrier Platoon

No. 5 Assault Pioneer Platoon

No. 6 Anti-Tank Platoon (6-pounder)

A COMPANY

No. 7 Platoon

No. 8 Platoon

No. 9 Platoon

B COMPANY

No. 10 Platoon

No. 11 Platoon

No. 12 Platoon

C COMPANY

No. 13 Platoon

No. 14 Platoon

No. 15 Platoon

D COMPANY

No. 16 Platoon

No. 17 Platoon

No. 18 Platoon

Private (Pte.)
Gunner (artillery equivalent of private)
Trooper (armoured equivalent of private)
Lance Corporal (L/Cpl.)
Corporal (Cpl.)
Lance Sergeant (L/Sgt.)
Sergeant (Sgt.)
Company Sergeant Major (CSM)
Regimental Sergeant Major (RSM)
Lieutenant (Lt. or Lieut.)
Captain (Capt.)
Major (Maj.)
Lieutenant Colonel (Lt. Col.)
Colonel (Col.)
Brigadier (Brig.)
Major General (Maj. Gen.)
Lieutenant General (Lt. Gen.)
General (Gen.)

AXIS MILITARY ORDER OF RANK

Because the German Army and the Luftwaffe ground forces had a ranking system where rank also usually indicated the specific type of unit in which one served, only basic ranks are given here. The translations are roughly based on the Canadian ranking system, although there is no Canadian equivalent for many German ranks. Italian ranks more closely mirror those used by the Canadian Army.

GERMAN	ITALIAN	CANADIAN
Schütze	Soldato	Private, infantry
Grenadier	Granatiere	Private, infantry
Kanonier	Cannoniere	Gunner
Panzerschütze	Personale del carro armato	Tank crew member
Pionier	Pioniere	Sapper
Funker	Segnalatore	Signaller
Gefreiter	Caporale scelto	Lance Corporal
Obergefreiter	Caporale	Corporal
Unteroffizier	Sergente scelto	Lance Sergeant

GERMAN	ITALIAN	CANADIAN
Unterfeldwebel	Sergente	Sergeant
Feldwebel	Sergente maggiore	Company Sergeant Major
Oberfeldwebel	Maresciallo	Regimental Sergeant Major
Leutnant	Scottotenente	Second Lieutenant
Oberleutnant	Tenente	Lieutenant
Hauptmann	Capitano	Captain
Major	Maggiore	Major
Oberstleutnant	Tenente Colonnello	Lieutenant Colonel
Oberst	Colonnello	Colonel
Generalmajor	Generale di Brigata	Brigadier
Generalleutnant	Generale di Divisione Generale di Corpo	Major General
General der Artillerie	Generale di artiglieria	General of Artillery
General der Infanterie	Generale di fanteria	General of Infantry
General der Kavallerie	Generale di cavalleria	General of Cavalry
General der Pioniere	Generale del pionieri	General of Engineers
General der Panzertruppen	Generale delle truppe armate	General of Armoured Troops
Generaloberst	Generale d'Armata	Colonel General
Generalfeldmarschall	Maresciallo d'Italia	General Field Marshal

APPENDIX F:
THE DECORATIONS

Many military decorations were won by soldiers in the invasion of Sicily. The decoration system that Canada used in World War II, like most other aspects of its military organization and tradition, derived from Britain. A class-based system, most military decorations can be awarded either to officers or to "other ranks," but not both. The exception is the highest award, the Victoria Cross, which can be won by a soldier of any rank.

The decorations and qualifying ranks are:

VICTORIA CROSS (VC): Awarded for gallantry in the presence of the enemy. Instituted in 1856. Open to all ranks. The only award that can be granted for action in which the recipient was killed, other than Mentioned in Despatches—a less formal honour whereby an act of bravery was given specific credit in a formal report.

DISTINGUISHED SERVICE ORDER (DSO): Officers of all ranks, but more commonly awarded to officers with ranks of major or higher.

MILITARY CROSS (MC): Officers with a rank below major and, rarely, warrant officers.

DISTINGUISHED CONDUCT MEDAL: Warrant officers and all lower ranks.

MILITARY MEDAL: Warrant officers and all lower ranks.

NOTES

INTRODUCTION: THE SUPREME TRAGEDY

1 C.P. Stacey, *The Canadian Army, 1939–1945: An Official Historical Summary* (Ottawa: King's Printer, 1948), 47.

2 J.L. Granatstein, *Canada's Army: Waging War and Keeping the Peace* (Toronto: University of Toronto Press, 2002), 213.

3 G.W.L. Nicholson, *The Canadians in Italy, 1939–1945*, vol. 2 (Ottawa: Queen's Printer, 1956), 23.

4 Ibid.

5 R.H. Roy, *The Seaforth Highlanders of Canada, 1919–1965* (Vancouver: Evergreen Press, 1969), 137.

6 Richard Victor Latimer, "The Gibblers: Or Balmorals and Bully Beef," unpublished memoir in possession of author, 245.

7 Roy, 137.

8 C. Sydney Frost, *Once a Patricia: Memoirs of a Junior Infantry Officer in World War II* (Ottawa: Borealis Press, 2004), 86.

9 Strome Galloway, *Sicily to the Siegfried Line: Being Some Random Memories and a Diary of 1944–1945* (Kitchener, ON: Arnold Press, n.d.), 1–3.

10 Farley Mowat, *And No Birds Sang* (Toronto: McClelland & Stewart, 1979), 35.

11 Nicholson, *Canadians in Italy*, 20–21.

12 Ibid., 24–26.

13 Historical Officer, Canadian Military Headquarters, "Report No. 126: Canadian Operations in Sicily, July–August 1943, Part I: The Preliminaries of Operation 'Husky' (The Assault on Sicily)," Directorate of Heritage and History, Department of National Defence, 6.

1: IF THE ARMY CAN'T AGREE

1 G.W.L. Nicholson, *The Canadians in Italy, 1939–1945*, vol. 2 (Ottawa: Queen's Printer, 1956), 26.

2 J.L. Granatstein, *Canada's Army: Waging War and Keeping the Peace* (Toronto: University of Toronto Press, 2002), 202–05.

3 George Kitching, *Mud and Green Fields: The Memoirs of Major General George Kitching* (Langley, BC: Battleline Books, 1986), 140.

4   Ibid., 148–49.

5   "Appreciation by Comd 1 CDN DIV at Norfolk House 27 Apr 43," RG24, vol. 10878, Library and Archives Canada, 7–8.

6   Howard Graham, *Citizen and Soldier: The Memoirs of Lieutenant-General Howard Graham* (Toronto: McClelland & Stewart, 1987), 138.

7   Historical Officer, Canadian Military Headquarters, "Report No. 126: Canadian Operations in Sicily, July–August 1943, Part 1: The Preliminaries of Operation 'Husky' (The Assault on Sicily)," Directorate of Heritage and History, Department of National Defence, 74–76.

8   Nicholson, *Canadians in Italy*, 4.

9   Ralph Bennett, *Ultra and Mediterranean Strategy, 1944–1945* (London: Hamish Hamilton, 1989), 220.

10 Turnbull Higgins, *Soft Underbelly: The Anglo-American Controversy Over The Italian Campaign, 1939–1945* (New York: Macmillan, 1968), 45.

11 C.J.C. Molony, *The Mediterranean and Middle East: The Campaign in Sicily 1943 and The Campaign in Italy 3rd September 1943 to 31st March 1944* (London: Her Majesty's Stationery Office, 1973), 2.

12 Ibid., 4.

13 Ibid., 3.

14 Arthur Bryant, *The Turn of the Tide: A History of the War Years Based on the Diaries of Field-Marshal Lord Alanbrooke, Chief of the Imperial General Staff* (Garden City, NY: Doubleday, 1957), 556.

15 Molony, 7.

16 Winston S. Churchill, *The Second World War*, vol. 5, *Closing the Ring* (London: Cassell, 1952), 25.

17 Viscount Alexander of Tunis, "The Conquest of Sicily," MG27, vol. III A1, Library and Archives Canada, 1.

18 Molony, 6.

19 Ibid., 7–10.

20 Carlo D'Este, *Patton: A Genius for War* (New York: Harper Collins, 1995), 492.

21 Carlo D'Este, *Bitter Victory: The Battle for Sicily, 1943* (New York: Harper Perennial, 1988), 74–75.

22 Molony, 2–10.

23 Viscount Alexander, 4–5.

24 Molony, 10.

25 Nigel Hamilton, *Monty: Master of the Battlefield, 1942–1944* (London: Hamish Hamilton, 1983), 245.

26 Viscount Alexander, 7.

27 Hamilton, 246.

28 Bernard Law Montgomery, *The Memoirs of Field Marshal The Viscount Montgomery of Alamein, K.G.* (London: Collins, 1958), 170–72.

29 Hamilton, 252.

30 Eric Morris, *Circles of Hell: The War in Italy, 1943–1945* (New York: Crown Publishers, 1993), 14–15.

31 D'Este, *Bitter Victory*, 92.

32 Montgomery, *Memoirs*, 34–35.

33 Thomas Parrish, ed., *The Simon and Schuster Encyclopedia of World War II* (New York: Simon and Schuster, 1978), 13.

34 Rick Atkinson, *The Day of Battle: The War in Sicily and Italy, 1943–1944* (New York: Henry Holt and Company, 2007), 131.

35 Hamilton, 257.

36 D'Este, *Bitter Victory*, 116.

37 Martin Blumenson, *The Patton Papers: 1940–1945* (Boston: Houghton Mifflin, 1974), 236–37.

38 Viscount Alexander, 8–10.

39 Blumenson, 241.

2: FINALLY, THE FINAL PLAN

1 "Appreciation by Comd 1 CDN DIV at Norfolk House 27 Apr 43," RG24, vol. 10878, Library and Archives Canada, 7.

2 Ibid., 9–10.

3 George Kitching, *Mud and Green Fields: The Memoirs of Major General George Kitching* (Langley, BC: Battleline Books, 1986), 149–51.

4 Kitching, 150–52.

5 Historical Officer, Canadian Military Headquarters, "Report No. 126: Canadian Operations in Sicily, July–August 1943, Part I: The Preliminaries of Operation 'Husky' (The Assault on Sicily)," Directorate of Heritage and History, Department of National Defence, 28–29.

6 Dominick Graham, *The Price of Command: A Biography of General Guy Simonds* (Toronto: Stoddart Publishing, 1993), 71.

7 Richard S. Malone, *A Portrait of War, 1939–1943* (Toronto: Collins Publishers, 1983), 41.

8 J.L. Granatstein, *The Generals: The Canadian Army's Senior Commanders in the Second World War* (Toronto: Stoddart Publishing, 1993), 156.

9 Chris Vokes, *My Story* (Ottawa: Gallery Press, 1985), 88.

10 Dominick Graham, 70.

11 Howard Graham, *Citizen and Soldier: The Memoirs of Lieutenant-General Howard Graham* (Toronto: McClelland & Stewart, 1987), 140.

12 Kitching, 152–53.

13 Historical Officer, "Report No. 126," 34.

14 Ibid., 35.

15 Kitching, 134.

16 Historical Officer, "Report No. 126," 35–36.

17 Kitching, 154.

18 Dominick Graham, 73.

19 Historical Officer, "Report No. 126," 36.

20 Vokes, 89.

21 G.W.L. Nicholson, *The Canadians in Italy, 1939–1945*, vol. 2 (Ottawa: Queen's Printer, 1956), 32.

22 Bert Hoffmeister, interview by B. Greenhouse and W. McAndrew, transcript, 2001/26, Directorate of Heritage and History, n.d., 41.

23 Nicholson, *Canadians in Italy*, 32.

24 Thomas de Faye, interview by author, Victoria, 3 November 1998.

25 Nicholson, *Canadians in Italy*, 35–36.

26 Howard Mitchell, *My War With the Saskatoon Light Infantry (M.G.) 1939–1945* (n.p., n.d.), 70.

27 Robert Kingstone, "Transcription of Interview Number 31D 1 Kingstone," interview by D.W. Edgecombe, 6 October 2000, Canadian War Museum, 4–5.

28 Nicholson, *Canadians in Italy*, 41.

29 James Riley Stone, interview by William Thackray, 13, 20 May and 3, 10, 17 June 1980, University of Victoria Special Collections.

30 Historical Officer, "Report No. 126," 44.

31 Dr. John Haley, interview by author, Victoria, 30 October 1998.

32 Historical Officer, "Report No. 126," 45.

33 Nicholson, *Canadians in Italy*, 42.

34 Reginald H. Roy, *The Seaforth Highlanders of Canada, 1919–1965* (Vancouver: Evergreen Press, 1969), 145–46.

35 Captain A.T. Sesia, "Personal Notes and Observations: Part 1—Sicily, 24 Apr. 43– 2 Sep. 43," RG24, vol. 10878, Library and Archives Canada, 13.

3: EVERYONE KNOWING HIS JOB

1 Bert Hoffmeister, interview by B. Greenhouse and W. McAndrew, transcript, n.d., 2001/26, Directorate of Heritage and History, 42.

2 Frederick Norman Pope, interview by Chris Bell, 31 May and 7, 10, 15, 22 June 1982, University of Victoria Special Collections.

3 George Kitching, *Mud and Green Fields: The Memoirs of Major General George Kitching* (Langley, BC: Battleline Books, 1986), 158–59.

4 Carlo D'Este, *Bitter Victory: The Battle for Sicily, 1943* (New York: Harper Perennial, 1988), 184.

5 Ibid., 185–86.

6 Walter Warlimont, *Inside Hitler's Headquarters, 1939–1945*, trans. R.H. Barry (New York: Frederick A. Praeger, 1964), 318.

7 G.A. Shepperd, *The Italian Campaign, 1943–45: A Political and Military Re-assessment* (London: Arthur Baker Limited, 1968), 22.

8 Historical Section (GS), Army Headquarters, "Report No. 14: The Sicilian Campaign (July–August 1943), Information from German Sources," University of Victoria Special Collections, 3–4.

9 Albert Kesselring, *The Memoirs of Field-Marshal Kesselring*, trans. Lynton Hudson (London: William Kimber, 1953), 158–61.

10 Samuel W. Mitcham Jr. and Friedrich von Stauffenberg, *The Battle of Sicily* (New York: Orion Books, 1991), 18–20.

11 Ibid., 30.

12 Ibid., 31.

13 C.J.C. Molony, *The Mediterranean and Middle East: The Campaign in Sicily 1943 and The Campaign in Italy 3rd September 1943 to 31st March 1944* (London: Her Majesty's Stationery Office, 1973), 40–41.

14 Warlimont, 321–22.

15 Molony, 41.

16 Mitcham and von Stauffenberg, 33.

17 Molony, 41.

18 Mitcham and von Stauffenberg, 33.

19 Ibid., 34–35.

20 D'Este, *Bitter Victory*, 207.

21 Mitcham and von Stauffenberg, 43.

22 Ibid., 36.

23 Molony, 42.

24 D'Este, *Bitter Victory*, 207.

25 Mitcham and von Stauffenberg, 52.

26 Douglas Orgill, *The Gothic Line: The Italian Campaign, Autumn 1944* (New York: W.W. Norton, 1967), 12.

27 Warlimont, 322.

28 Mitcham and von Stauffenberg, 53–54.

29 Kesselring, 161.

30 1st Canadian Infantry Division, General Staff War Diary, July 1943, Library and Archives Canada, 1.

31 Historical Officer, Canadian Military Headquarters, "Report No. 126: Canadian Operations in Sicily, July–August 1943, Part 1: The Preliminaries of Operation 'Husky' (The Assault on Sicily)," Directorate of Heritage and History, Department of National Defence, 77.

32 Ibid., 78.

33 Pope, interview.

34 Kitching, 157.

35 Historical Officer, "Report No. 126," 78.

36 Ibid.

37 Ibid., 53–54.

38 Strome Galloway, *Some Died at Ortona* (n.p., n.d.), 123–24.

39 Historical Officer, "Report No. 126," 56–58.

40 Ibid., 58.

41 Ibid., 59.

42 Hoffmeister interview.

43 Historical Officer, "Report No. 126," 79–80.

44 Felix Carriere, interview by Tom Torrie, 4 June 1987, University of Victoria Special Collections.

45 Robert Law McDougall, "Letter to Mother," July 1943, Robert Law McDougall Fonds, R-10755, Library and Archives Canada, 1–2.

4: GOING TO BE SOME PARTY

1 George Kitching, *Mud and Green Fields: The Memoirs of Major General George Kitching* (Langley, BC: Battleline Books, 1986), 160.

2 Cameron Ware, interview by Dr. Reginald Roy, 23, 25 June, and 10 July 1979, University of Victoria Special Collections.

3 http://www.uboat.net/allies/merchants/ship.html?shipID=2977 (accessed 26 June 2008).

4 Ware interview.

5 1st Canadian Infantry Division, General Staff War Diary, July 1943, Library and Archives Canada, 4.

6 http://www.uboat.net/allies/merchants/2978.html (accessed 26 June 2008).

7 Ware interview.

8 http://www.uboat.net/allies/merchants/2978.html (accessed 26 June 2008).

9 G.W.L. Nicholson, *The Canadians in Italy, 1939–1945*, vol. 2 (Ottawa: Queen's Printer, 1956), 46.

10 Daniel G. Dancocks, *The D-Day Dodgers: The Canadians in Italy, 1943–1945* (Toronto: McClelland & Stewart, 1991), 27.

11 http://www.uboat.net/allies/merchants/2981.html (accessed 26 June 2008).

12 Historical Officer, Canadian Military Headquarters, "Report No. 126: Canadian Operations in Sicily, July–August 1943, Part 1: The Preliminaries of Operation 'Husky' (The Assault on Sicily)," Directorate of Heritage and History, Department of National Defence, 79.

13 Captain A.T. Sesia, "Personal Notes and Observations: Part 1—Sicily, 24 Apr. 43–2 Sep. 43," RG24, vol. 10878, Library and Archives Canada, 17.

14 ADMS, 1st Canadian Infantry Division War Diary, July 1943, Library and Archives Canada, 1.

15 9th Canadian Field Ambulance War Diary, July 1943, Library and Archives Canada, n.p.

16 W.R. Freasby, ed., *Official History of the Canadian Medical Services, 1939–1945*, vol. 1., *Organization and Campaigns* (Ottawa: Queen's Printer, 1956), 134.

17 ADMS, 1st Canadian Infantry Division War Diary, July 1943, 1.

18 Sesia, 17.

19 ADMS, 1st Canadian Infantry Division War Diary, July 1943, 9.

20 "An Account given by Lt-Col. D.G.J. Farquharson, R.C.O.C., ADOS 1 Cdn Div, at Rear Div HQ nr Regalbuto, 7 Aug 43," RG24, vol. 10878, Library and Archives Canada, 1.

21 ADMS, 1st Canadian Infantry Division War Diary, July 1943, 6.

22 Sesia, 18.

23 ADMS, 1st Canadian Infantry Division War Diary, July 1943, 6–7.

24 Ibid., 9–10.

25 Nicholson, *Canadians in Italy*, 47.

26 Ibid.

27 C.J.C. Molony, *The Mediterranean and Middle East: The Campaign in Sicily 1943 and the Campaign in Italy 3rd September 1943 to 31st March 1944* (London: Her Majesty's Stationery Office, 1973), 32–33.

28 http://www.vac-acc.gc.ca/general/sub.cfm?source=feature/italy99/ithistory/armynavy (accessed 26 June 2008).

29 Molony, 46–50.

30 Samuel W. Mitcham Jr. and Friedrich von Stauffenberg, *The Battle of Sicily* (New York: Orion Books, 1991), 61.

31 Sesia, 22.

32 Molony, 52.

33 http://www.junobeach.org/e/4/can-tac-lca-e.htm (accessed 9 July 2008).

34 W.A.B. Douglas, et al., *A Blue Water Navy: The Official Operational History of the Royal Canadian Navy in the Second World War*, vol. 2, pt. 2 (St. Catharines, ON: Vanwell Publishing, 2007), 125–27.

35 Nicholson, *Canadians in Italy*, 48–49.

36 Molony, map opp. 29.

37 Sesia, 22–23.

38 Kitching, 162–63.

39 Sesia, 22–23.

5: THE ACTUALITY OF WAR

1   Princess Patricia's Canadian Light Infantry War Diary, July 1943, Library and Archives Canada, 5.

2   Thomas de Faye, interview by author, Victoria, 3 November. 1998.

3   Chris Vokes, "Some Reflections on Operational Command," *Canadian Army Journal*, vol. 2, no. 10 (January 1949), 9.

4   Bert Hoffmeister, interview by author, Vancouver, 23 November 1998.

5   R.H. Roy, *The Seaforth Highlanders of Canada, 1919–1965* (Vancouver: Evergreen Press, 1969), 150.

6   Diary of Major Durnford, RG24, vol. 20405, Library and Archives Canada, 4.

7   Loyal Edmonton Regiment War Diary, July 1943, Appendix 1, Library and Archives Canada, n.p.

8   Howard Graham, *Citizen and Soldier: The Memoirs of Lieutenant-General Howard Graham* (Toronto: McClelland & Stewart, 1987), 147–48.

9   Major D. Brain, "The initial landing in Sicily," in "Accounts of Actions during the Sicilian campaign as prepared by various officers of the Princess Patricia's Canadian Light Infantry," RG24, vol. 10982, Library and Archives Canada, 38–39.

10 Felix Carriere, interview by Tom Torrie, 4 June 1987, University of Victoria Special Collections.

11 Brain, 38.

12 Historical Officer, Canadian Military Headquarters, "Report No. 126: Canadian Operations in Sicily, July–August 1943, PART I: The Preliminaries of Operation 'Husky' (The Assault on Sicily)," Directorate of Heritage and History, Department of National Defence, 80.

13 "1 Canadian Division Operation Order No. 1, 7 Jun, 43," RG24, vol. 10879, Library and Archives Canada, 1–4.

14 Ibid., 10.

15 Strome Galloway, *Some Died at Ortona* (n.p., n.d.), 132.

16 Strome Galloway, *Bravely Into Battle: The Autobiography of a Canadian Soldier in World War II* (Toronto: Stoddart Publishing, 1988), 21–23.

17 Galloway, *Some Died at Ortona*, 120–21.

18 Galloway, *Bravely Into Battle*, 23–25.

19 Durnford Diary, 11–12.

20 Ibid., 16–17.

21 Ibid., 17.

22 Jock Gibson, interview by Ken MacLeod, Vancouver, n.d.

23 Carriere interview.

24 G.W.L. Nicholson, *The Canadians in Italy, 1939–1945*, vol. 2 (Ottawa: Queen's Printer, 1956), 68.

25 Farley Mowat, *And No Birds Sang* (Toronto: McClelland and Stewart, 1979), 74.

26 Nicholson, *Canadians in Italy*, 68.

27 "1 Canadian Division Operation Order No. 1," 4.

28 Roy, 158.

29 Princess Patricia's Canadian Light Infantry War Diary, July 1943, Library and Archives Canada, 6.

30 G.R. Stevens, *Princess Patricia's Canadian Light Infantry, 1919–1957*, vol. 3 (Griesbach, AB: Historical Committee of the Regiment, n.d.), 72.

31 Hastings and Prince Edward Regiment War Diary, July 1943, Library and Archives Canada, n.p.

32 Farley Mowat, *The Regiment*, 2nd ed. (Toronto: McClelland & Stewart, 1973), 56–57.

33 Galloway, *Bravely Into Battle*, 25–26.

34 Graham, 150–51.

35 Roy, 159.

36 Robert L. McDougall, *A Narrative of War: From the Beaches of Sicily to the Hitler Line with the Seaforth Highlanders of Canada, 1943–1944* (Ottawa: Golden Dog Press, 1996), 4.

37 Stevens, *Princess Patricia's Canadian Light Infantry*, 73.

38 Brain, 38.

39 Stevens, *Princess Patricia's Canadian Light Infantry*, 73.

40 Carriere interview.

41 Brain, 39.

42 David Bercuson, *The Patricia's: The Proud History of a Fighting Regiment* (Toronto: Stoddart Publishing, 2001), 176.

43 Brain, 39.

44 Stevens, *Princess Patricia's Canadian Light Infantry*, 73.

45 Roy, 159–160.

46 Gibson interview.

47 George A. Reid, *Speed's War: A Canadian Soldier's Memoirs of World War II* (Royston, BC: Madrona Books & Publishing, 2007), 7–8.

48 Harry Rankin, interview by author, Vancouver, 15 October 1998.

49 Gibson interview.

50 Col. S.W. Thomson, "Wounded in Sicily: 12 July 1943," *Canadian Military History*, vol. 2, no. 2 (Autumn 1993), 109.

51 Seaforth Highlanders of Canada War Diary, July 1943, Library and Archives Canada, n.p.

6: WHICH DIRECTION DO WE TAKE?

1 L. Col. Ian Hodson, "'D' Day Sicily, 10 July 43," http://thercr.ca/history/1939-1945/d-day_sicily_10jul43.htm (accessed 26 June 2008).

2 Historical Officer, Canadian Military Headquarters, "Report No. 127: Canadian Operations in Sicily, July–August 1943, Part II: The Execution of the Operation by 1 Cdn Inf Div, Section 1: The Assault and Initial Penetration Inland," Directorate of Heritage and History, Department of National Defence, 3.

3 Farley Mowat, *And No Birds Sang* (Toronto: McClelland & Stewart, 1979), 74.

4 "Comments by Seaforth Veterans on Chapter VI," Reginald H. Roy Collection, University of Victoria Special Collections, 1–2.

5 Hastings and Prince Edward War Diary, July 1943, Library and Archives Canada, n.p.

6 Maj. R.G. Liddell, "The Assault on the Beaches of Pachino, Sicily; July 1943," http://thercr.ca/history/1939-1945/pachino_1943_liddell.htm (accessed 26 June 2008).

7 Historical Officer, "Report No. 127," 3.

8 Hodson.

9 Mowat, *And No Birds Sang*, 74–78.

10 Farley Mowat, *The Regiment*, 2nd ed. (Toronto: McClelland & Stewart, 1973), 59.

11 Ibid., 59.

12 Mowat, *And No Birds Sang*, 78.

13 Hastings and Prince Edward Regiment War Diary, n.p.

14 Mowat, *And No Birds Sang*, 79–80.

15 Hastings and Prince Edward Regiment War Diary, n.p.

16 Historical Officer, "Report No. 127," 2.

17 Mowat, *The Regiment*, 60.

18 Sam Lenko, interview by author, Edmonton, 4 October 1998.

19 Strome Galloway, *Bravely Into Battle: The Autobiography of a Canadian Soldier in World War II* (Toronto: Stoddart Publishing, 1988), 26–27.

20 Bert Hoffmeister, interview by B. Greenhouse and W. McAndrew, transcript, n.d., 2001/26, Directorate of Heritage and History, 46.

21 Bob Hackett letter, n.d., possession of the author.

22 Bill Worton written summary, n.d., possession of the author.

23 R.H. Roy, *The Seaforth Highlanders of Canada, 1919–1965* (Vancouver: Evergreen Press, 1969), 161–62.

24 "Account by Lieutenant-Colonel I.S. Johnston, Officer Commanding 48 Highlanders given on 14 August 1943 at the Battalion Rest Area near Scordia," RG24, vol. 10880, Library and Archives Canada, n.p.

25 Kim Beattie, *Dileas: History of the 48th Highlanders of Canada: 1929–1956* (Toronto: 48th Highlanders of Canada, 1957), 221.

26 Johnston, n.p.

27 G.W.L. Nicholson, *The Canadians in Italy, 1939–1945*, vol. 2 (Ottawa: Queen's Printer, 1956), 70.

28 Historical Officer, "Report No. 127," 4.

29 Howard Graham, *Citizen and Soldier: The Memoirs of Lieutenant-General Howard Graham* (Toronto: McClelland & Stewart, 1987), 151–52.

30 Robert Kingstone, "Transcription of Interview No. 31D 1," interview by D.W. Edgecombe, 6 October 2000, Ottawa, Canadian War Museum Oral History Project Collection.

31 Frederick Norman Pope, interview by Chris Bell, 31 May and 7, 10, 15, 22 June 1982, University of Victoria Special Collections.

32 Rennie Harry Heggie, *The History of the Three Rivers Regiment (12 Canadian Armoured Regiment), 1943–1945* (n.p., n.d.), 24.

33 Historical Officer, "Report No. 127," 5.

34 Dominick Graham, *The Price of Command: A Biography of General Guy Simonds* (Toronto: Stoddart Publishing, 1993), 85.

35 C.J.C. Molony, *The Mediterranean and Middle East: The Campaign in Sicily 1943 and the Campaign in Italy 3rd September 1943 to 31st March 1944* (London: Her Majesty's Stationery Office, 1973), 59–60.

36 Norm Bowen, interview by A.E. "Tony" Delamere, 28 September 2000, Ottawa, Canadian War Museum Oral History Project Collection.

37 W.A.B. Douglas, et al., *A Blue Water Navy: The Official Operational History of the Royal Canadian Navy in the Second World War,* vol. 2, pt. 2 (St. Catharines, ON: Vanwell Publishing Limited, 2007), 129–30.

38 Molony, 59–64.

39 Ibid., 80–81.

40 Nicholson, *Canadians in Italy,* 75–76.

41 Molony, 68.

7: CALL THIS A FIGHT?

1 Strome Galloway, *Bravely Into Battle: The Autobiography of a Canadian Soldier in World War II* (Toronto: Stoddart Publishing, 1988), 27.

2 Maj. R.G. Liddell, "The Assault on the Beaches of Pachino, Sicily; July 1943," http://thercr.ca/history/1939-1945/pachino_1943_liddell.htm (accessed 26 June 2008).

3 Galloway, *Bravely Into Battle,* 27–28.

4 Royal Canadian Regiment War Diary, July 1943, Library and Archives Canada, n.p.

5 Galloway, *Bravely Into Battle,* 29.

6 L. Col. Ian Hodson, "'D' Day Sicily, 10 July 43," http://thercr.ca/history/1939-1945/d-day_sicily_10jul43.htm (accessed 26 June 2008).

7 Royal Canadian Regiment War Diary, July 1943, n.p.

8 Liddell.

9 Hastings and Prince Edward War Diary, July 1943, Library and Archives Canada, n.p.

10 Liddell.

11 Hastings and Prince Edward War Diary, July 1943, n.p.

12 Galloway, *Bravely Into Battle,* 29.

13 Liddell.

14 Royal Canadian Regiment War Diary, July 1943, n.p.

15 Liddell.

16 Ibid.

17 Hodson.

18 Ibid.

19 Liddell.

20 Royal Canadian Regiment War Diary, July 1943, n.p.

21 Hodson.

22 Historical Officer, Canadian Military Headquarters, "Report No. 127: Canadian Operations in Sicily, July–August 1943, Part II: The Execution of the Operation by 1 Cdn Inf Div, Section 1: The Assault and Initial Penetration Inland," Directorate of Heritage and History, Department of National Defence, 6.

23 Farley Mowat, *The Regiment*, 2nd ed. (Toronto: McClelland & Stewart, 1973), 60–61.

24 Farley Mowat, *And No Birds Sang* (Toronto: McClelland & Stewart, 1979), 84–86.

25 Howard Graham, *Citizen and Soldier: The Memoirs of Lieutenant-General Howard Graham* (Toronto: McClelland & Stewart, 1987), 168–69.

26 Daniel G. Dancocks, *The D-Day Dodgers: The Canadians in Italy, 1943–1945* (Toronto: McClelland & Stewart, 1991), 62.

27 "Personal Account by Lt.-Col. The Lord Tweedsmuir of the Sicilian Campaign," 145.241011(D31), Directorate of Heritage and History, Department of National Defence, 1.

28 Kim Beattie, *Dileas: History of the 48th Highlanders of Canada: 1929–1956* (Toronto: 48th Highlanders of Canada, 1957), 222–23.

29 Historical Officer, "Report No. 127," 6.

30 48th Highlanders of Canada War Diary, July 1943, Library and Archives Canada, n.p.

31 Howard Graham, 153.

32 Seaforth Highlanders War Diary, n.p.

33 Hoffmeister, interview.

34 R.H. Roy, *The Seaforth Highlanders of Canada, 1919–1965* (Vancouver: Evergreen Press, 1969), 162.

35 Hoffmeister interview.

36 Roy, 163.

37 Hoffmeister interview.

38 Roy, 163.

39 G.R. Stevens, *Princess Patricia's Canadian Light Infantry, 1919–1957*, vol. 3 (Griesbach, AB: Historical Committee of the Regiment, n.d.), 74.

40 Princess Patricia's Canadian Light Infantry War Diary, July 1943, Library and Archives Canada, 6.

41 Stevens, *Princess Patricia's Canadian Light Infantry*, 74–75.

42 Ibid., 75.

43 Princess Patricia's Canadian Light Infantry War Diary, 7.

44 Historical Officer, "Report No. 127," 11.

45 Ibid., 8.

46 Ibid.

47 Nicholson, *Canadians in Italy*, 72.

48 Historical Officer, "Report No. 127," 12.

49 Princess Patricia's Canadian Light Infantry War Diary, 7.

50 Mowat, *The Regiment*, 62.

8: THESE MEN HAVE SURRENDERED

1 Historical Section (GS) Army Headquarters, "Report No. 14, The Sicilian Campaign (July–August 1943), Information from German Sources," University of Victoria Special Collections, 5–6.

2 Walter Warlimont, *Inside Hitler's Headquarters, 1939–1945*, trans. R.H. Barry (New York: Frederick A. Praeger, 1964), 335.

3 Albert Kesselring, *The Memoirs of Field-Marshal Kesselring*, trans. Lynton Hudson (London: William Kimber, 1953), 162.

4 Jochen Mahnke, "Assault on Sicily, 1943," *Military History Journal*, vol. 7, no. 2 (December 1986), the South African Military History Society, http://rapidttp.com/milhist/vol072jm.html (accessed 26 June 2008), 16.

5 Kesselring, 162.

6 Historical Section, "Report No. 14," 6.

7 Historical Officer, Canadian Military Headquarters, "Report No. 127: Canadian Operations in Sicily, July–August 1943, Part II: The Execution of the Operation by 1 Cdn Inf Div, Section 1: The Assault and Initial Penetration Inland," Directorate of Heritage and History, Department of National Defence, 27.

8 G.W.L. Nicholson, *The Canadians in Italy, 1939–1945*, vol. 2 (Ottawa: Queen's Printer, 1956), 78.

9 Historical Officer, "Report No. 127," 27.

10 Hugh Pond, *Sicily* (London: William Kimber, 1962), 71.

11 Carlo D'Este, *Bitter Victory: The Battle for Sicily, 1943* (New York: Harper Perennial, 1988), 282–88.

12 Kesselring, 163.

13 Nicholson, *Canadians in Italy*, 78.

14 Kesselring, 163.

15 Warlimont, 335.

16 "Account given by Major A.R. Campbell Officer Commanding 'A' Company and Captain N.R. Waugh, MC, Officer Commanding 'D' Company, Hastings and Prince Edward Regiment, on 18 August 1943, at Battalion Rest Area near Militello in val di Catania, Sicily," RG24, vol. 10880, Library and Archives Canada, n.p.

17 Nicholson, *Canadians in Italy*, 79.

18 G.W.L. Nicholson, *The Gunners of Canada*, vol. 2 (Toronto: McClelland & Stewart, 1972), 143.

19 *History of the 3rd Canadian Field Regiment, Royal Canadian Artillery—September, 1939 to July, 1945* (n.p., 1945), Canadian War Museum, 33.

20 Ibid.

21 1st Canadian Field Company, RCE War Diary, July 1943, Library and Archives Canada, 23-N-3.

22 Historical Officer, "Report No. 127," 13.

23 Ibid., 15.

24 Ibid., 14.

25 Nicholson, *Canadians in Italy*, 79.

26 Historical Officer "Report No. 127," 14–15.

27 Seaforth Highlanders of Canada War Diary, July 1943, Library and Archives Canada, n.p.

28 Princess Patricia's Canadian Light Infantry War Diary, July 1943, Library and Archives Canada, 8.

29 Seaforth Highlanders of Canada War Diary, July 1943, n.p.

30 R.H. Roy, *The Seaforth Highlanders of Canada, 1919–1965* (Vancouver: Evergreen Press, 1969), 164.

31 Historical Officer, "Report No. 127," 15–16.

32 Princess Patricia's Canadian Light Infantry War Diary, July 1943, 8.

33 Nicholson, *Gunners of Canada*, 145.

34 *History of the 3rd Canadian Field Regiment*, 33–34.

35 Princess Patricia's Canadian Light Infantry War Diary, 8.

36 G.R. Stevens, *Princess Patricia's Canadian Light Infantry, 1919–1957*, vol. 3 (Griesbach, AB: Historical Committee of the Regiment, n.d.), 76.

37 Kim Beattie, *Dileas: History of the 48th Highlanders of Canada: 1929–1956* (Toronto: 48th Highlanders of Canada, 1957), 228–29.

38 48th Highlanders of Canada War Diary, July 1943, Library and Archives Canada, n.p.

39 Beattie, 229.

40 "Personal Account by Lt.-Col. The Lord Tweedsmuir of the Sicilian Campaign," 145.241011(D31), Directorate of Heritage and History, Department of National Defence, 2.

41 Strome Galloway, *Bravely Into Battle: The Autobiography of a Canadian Soldier in World War II* (Toronto: Stoddart Publishing, 1988), 34.

42 "The Historical Account of the Fighting Operations of the 12th Canadian Tank Regiment (Three Rivers Regiment of Quebec) from the Time of Their Landing in Sicily Up to and Including Their Last Action Fought West of Adrano on August the 5th, 1943," RG24, vol. 10990, Library and Archives Canada, 1.

43 48th Highlanders of Canada War Diary, n.p.

44 "Account by Lieutenant-Colonel I.S. Johnston, Officer Commanding 48 Highlanders Given on 14 August 1943 at the Battalion Rest Area near Scordia," RG24, vol. 10880, Library and Archives Canada, n.p.

45 Galloway, *Bravely Into Battle*, 36–37.

46 Sheridan Atkinson and Harold Ghent, "The 'Liberation' of Modica, Sicily," unpublished manuscript in possession of author, 1–3.

9: ON SHANK'S MARE

1 G.W.L. Nicholson, *The Canadians in Italy, 1939–1945*, vol. 2 (Ottawa: Queen's Printer, 1956), 81.

2 G.R. Stevens, *Princess Patricia's Canadian Light Infantry, 1919–1957*, vol. 3 (Griesbach, AB: Historical Committee of the Regiment, n.d.), 76.

3 Princess Patricia's Canadian Light Infantry War Diary, July 1943, Library and Archives Canada, 9.

4 Sheridan Atkinson and Harold Ghent, "The 'Liberation' of Modica, Sicily," unpublished manuscript in possession of author, 4–6.

5 Richard S. Malone, *A Portrait of War, 1939–1943* (Toronto: Collins Publishers, 1983), 157–58.

6 Peter Stursberg, *The Sound of War: Memoirs of a CBC Correspondent* (Toronto: University of Toronto Press, 1993), 100.

7 Malone, 159–60.

8 Stursberg, 100–01.

9 G.R. Stevens, *The Royal Canadian Regiment*, vol. 2 (London, ON: London Print & Lithography, 1967), 72.
10 Strome Galloway, *Bravely Into Battle: The Autobiography of a Canadian Soldier in World War II* (Toronto: Stoddart Publishing, 1988), 40–41.
11 Stevens, *Royal Canadian Regiment*, 72.
12 Col. S.W. Thomson, "Wounded in Sicily: 12 July 1943," vol. 2, no. 2 (Autumn 1993), *Canadian Military History*, 109.
13 Seaforth Highlanders of Canada War Diary, July 1943, Library and Archives Canada, n.p.
14 R.H. Roy, *The Seaforth Highlanders of Canada, 1919–1965* (Vancouver: Evergreen Press, 1969), 167.
15 "Diary of Major Durnford," RG24, vol. 20405, Library and Archives Canada, 31–32.
16 Kim Beattie, *Dileas: History of the 48th Highlanders of Canada: 1929–1956* (Toronto: 48th Highlanders of Canada, 1957), 232.
17 48th Highlanders of Canada War Diary, July 1943, Library and Archives Canada, n.p.
18 Hastings and Prince Edward Regiment War Diary, July 1943, Library and Archives Canada, n.p.
19 Farley Mowat, *The Regiment*, 2nd ed. (Toronto: McClelland & Stewart, 1973), 64.
20 Mowat, *The Regiment*, 64–65.
21 Nicholson, *Canadians in Italy*, 83.
22 Hastings and Prince Edward War Diary, July 1943, n.p.
23 G.W.L. Nicholson, *The Gunners of Canada*, vol. 2 (Toronto: McClelland & Stewart, 1972), 143–44.
24 *History of the 3rd Canadian Field Regiment, Royal Canadian Artillery–September, 1939 to July, 1945* (n.p., 1945), 34–35.
25 Norm Bowen, interview by A.E. "Tony" Delamere, 28 September 2000, Canadian War Museum Oral History Project Collection.
26 Historical Officer, Canadian Military Headquarters, "Report No. 127: Canadian Operations in Sicily, July–August 1943, Part II: The Execution of the Operation by 1 Cdn Inf Div, Section 1: The Assault and Initial Penetration Inland," Directorate of Heritage and History, Department of National Defence, 23.
27 Howard Graham, *Citizen and Soldier: The Memoirs of Lieutenant-General Howard Graham* (Toronto: McClelland & Stewart, 1987), 156.
28 Galloway, *Bravely Into Battle*, 41.
29 "Diary of Lt. J.F. Wallace," MG30, vol. 1, Library and Archives Canada, 9.
30 Graham, 156.
31 Nigel Hamilton, *Monty: Master of the Battlefield, 1942–1944* (London: Hamish Hamilton, 1983), 309.
32 Richard Victor Latimer, "The Gibblers: Or Balmorals and Bully Beef," unpublished memoir in possession of author, 255.
33 Galloway, *Bravely Into Battle*, 43.

10: WRANGLINGS

1 Samuel W. Mitcham Jr. and Friedrich von Stauffenberg, *The Battle of Sicily* (New York: Orion Books, 1991), 138–46.

2 "Report of Panzer Division 'Hermann Goering' (Operation section–1a) On the Sicilian Campaign," RG24, vol. 20509, Library and Archives Canada, 3–4.

3 "Report on the Fighting in Sicily from 10 Jul–17 Aug 43," OB SW: Ops, RG24, vol. 20959, Library and Archives Canada, 7–8.

4 Mitcham and von Stauffenberg, 141–58.

5 Albert Kesselring, *The Memoirs of Field-Marshal Kesselring*, trans. Lynton Hudson (London: William Kimber, 1953), 163.

6 Mitcham and von Stauffenberg, 168–76.

7 Ibid., 176–79.

8 Ibid., 148–49.

9 Carlo D'Este, *Bitter Victory: The Battle for Sicily, 1943* (New York: Harper Perennial, 1988), 349–51.

10 Nigel Hamilton, *Monty: Master of the Battlefield, 1942–1944* (London: Hamish Hamilton, 1983), 303–04.

11 Ibid., 304–05.

12 Flint Whitlock, *The Rock of Anzio: From Sicily to Dachau, a History of the 45th Infantry Division* (Boulder, CO: Westview Press, 1998), 49.

13 C.J.C. Molony, *The Mediterranean and Middle East: The Campaign in Sicily 1943 and the Campaign in Italy 3rd September 1943 to 31st March 1944* (London: Her Majesty's Stationery Office, 1973), 88.

14 "Message Form, 15 Army Group to 7 Army & 8 Army," July 1943, RG24, Vol. 10994, Library and Archives Canada, n.p.

15 Whitlock, 49.

16 Historical Officer, Canadian Military Headquarters, "Report No. 135: Canadian Operations in Sicily, July–August 1943, Part II: The Execution of the Operation by 1 Cdn Inf Div, Section 2: The Pursuit of the Germans from Vizzini to Adrano 15 Jul–6 Aug," Directorate of Heritage and History, Department of National Defence, 3.

17 Omar N. Bradley and Clay Blair, *A General's Life: An Autobiography* (New York: Simon and Schuster, 1983), 189.

18 Molony, 95–96.

19 Field Marshal Alexander, *The Conquest of Sicily*, MG 27, vol. III A1, Library and Archives Canada, 22.

20 Bernard Law Montgomery, *El Alamein to the River Sangro* (New York: St. Martin's Press, 1948), 101.

21 G.W.L. Nicholson, *The Canadians in Italy, 1939–1945*, vol. 2 (Ottawa: Queen's Printer, 1956), 86.

22 Nigel Nicolson, *Alex: The Life of Field Marshal Alexander of Tunis* (London: Weidenfeld and Nicolson, 1973), 201.

23 Loyal Edmonton Regiment War Diary, July 1943, Library and Archives Canada, n.p.

24 "Diary of Lt. J.F. Wallace," MG30, vol. 1, Library and Archives Canada, 10.

25 G.R. Stevens, *A City Goes to War* (Brampton, ON: Charters Publishing, 1964), 234.

26 Historical Officer, "Report No. 135," 7.

27 Rowland Ryder, *Oliver Leese* (London: Hamish Hamilton, 1987), 140.

28 Loyal Edmonton Regiment War Diary, July 1943, n.p.

29 Ryder, 141.

30 Historical Officer, "Report No. 135," 4.

31 Hastings and Prince Edward Regiment War Diary, July 1943, Library and Archives Canada, n.p.

32 "Personal Account by Lt.-Col The Lord Tweedsmuir of the Sicilian Campaign," 145.241011(D31), Directorate of Heritage and History, Department of National Defence, 5.

33 Farley Mowat, *The Regiment*, 2nd ed. (Toronto: McClelland & Stewart, 1973), 69–70.

34 Tweedsmuir, 6.

35 Nicholson, *Canadians in Italy*, 89.

36 Tweedsmuir, 6.

37 "The Historical Account of the Fighting Operations of the 12th Canadian Tank Regiment (Three Rivers Regiment of Quebec) from the Time of Their Landing in Sicily Up to and Including Their Last Action Fought West of Adrano on August the 5th, 1943," RG24, vol. 10990, Library and Archives Canada, 3–4.

38 Wallace, 11.

39 Mowat, *The Regiment*, 71.

40 Kenneth B. Smith, *Duffy's Regiment: A History of the Hastings and Prince Edward Regiment* (Toronto: Dundurn, 1987), 87.

41 Hastings and Prince Edward Regiment War Diary, July 1943, n.p.

42 Tweedsmuir, 6.

43 Historical Officer, "Report No. 135," 5.

44 Nicholson, *Canadians in Italy*, 90.

45 Tweedsmuir, 6.

46 Hastings and Prince Edward Regiment War Diary, July 1943, n.p.

47 Tweedsmuir, 6.

48 Hastings and Prince Edward Regiment War Diary, July 1943, n.p.

49 Historical Officer, "Report No. 135," 6.

II: HAZARDS AND HARDSHIPS

1 Historical Officer, Canadian Military Headquarters, "Report No. 135: Canadian Operations in Sicily, July–August 1943, Part II: The Execution of the Operation by 1 Cdn Inf Div, Section 2: The Pursuit of the Germans from Vizzini to Adrano 15 Jul–6 Aug," Directorate of Heritage and History, Department of National Defence, 7.

2 Seaforth Highlanders of Canada War Diary, July 1943, Library and Archives Canada, n.p.

3 "Diary of Lt. J.F. Wallace," MG30, vol. 1, Library and Archives Canada, 10.

4 2nd Canadian Infantry Brigade War Diary, July 1943, Library and Archives Canada, n.p.

5 Wallace, 11.

6 Seaforth Highlanders of Canada War Diary, n.p.

7 2nd Canadian Infantry Brigade War Diary, n.p.

8 "Account by Lieutenant-Colonel I.S. Johnston, Officer Commanding 48 Highlanders given on 14 August 1943 at the Battalion Rest Area near Scordia," RG24, vol. 10880, Library and Archives Canada, n.p.

9 Kim Beattie, *Dileas: History of the 48th Highlanders of Canada: 1929–1956* (Toronto: 48th Highlanders of Canada, 1957), 241.

10 The 48th Highlanders of Canada War Diary, July 1943, Library and Archives Canada, n.p.

11 Beattie, 242.

12 Howard Graham, *Citizen and Soldier: The Memoirs of Lieutenant-General Howard Graham* (Toronto: McClelland & Stewart, 1987), 160–62.

13 Royal Canadian Regiment War Diary, July 1943, Library and Archives Canada, n.p.

14 Graham, 161–62.

15 George Kitching, *Mud and Green Fields: The Memoirs of Major General George Kitching* (Langley, BC: Battleline Books, 1986), 169.

16 J.L. Granatstein, *The Generals: The Canadian Army's Senior Commanders in the Second World War* (Toronto: Stoddart Publishing, 1993), 158.

17 48th Highlanders War Diary, n.p.

18 G.W.L. Nicholson, *The Canadians in Italy, 1939–1945*, vol. 2 (Ottawa: Queen's Printer, 1956), 90.

19 "Message Form, 15 Army Group to 7 Army & 8 Army," July 1943, RG24, vol. 10994, Library and Archives Canada, n.p.

20 W.G.F. Jackson, *Alexander of Tunis: As Military Commander* (London: B.T. Batsford Ltd., 1971), 221.

21 Martin Blumenson, *The Patton Papers: 1940–1945* (Boston: Houghton Mifflin, 1974), 287–89.

22 Nigel Hamilton, *Monty: Master of the Battlefield, 1942–1944* (London: Hamish Hamilton, 1983), 314.

23 Blumenson, 289–90.

24 Hamilton, 319.

25 Albert N. Garland and Howard McGaw Smyth, *United States in World War II: The Mediterranean Theatre of Operations, Sicily and the Surrender of Italy* (Washington, D.C.: Center of Military History United States Army, 1993), 226.

26 Historical Officer, "Report No. 135," 8.

27 Wallace, 12.

28 "Account by Capt. C.H. Pritchard, Edmn R., formerly Adjutant and now carrier pl. comd. Given in bn rest area, 18 Aug 43, near Militello in Val di Catania," RG24, Vol. 10982, Library and Archives Canada, 28.

29 Nicholson, 93.

30 Pritchard, 28.

31 Historical Officer, "Report No. 135," 9.

32 Wallace, 12.

33 Loyal Edmonton Regiment War Diary, July 1943, n.p.

34 Nicholson, *Canadians in Italy*, 93.

35 Wallace, 12–13.

36 Rennie Harry Heggie, *The History of the Three Rivers Regiment (12 Canadian Armoured Regiment), 1943–1945* (n.p., n.d.), 25–26.

37 Pritchard, 28–29.

38 Nicholson, *Canadians in Italy*, 94.

39 Three Rivers Tank Regiment War Diary, July 1943, Library and Archives Canada, 9.

40 Historical Officer, "Report No. 135," 10.

41 1st Canadian Infantry Division, General Staff War Diary, July 1943, Library and Archives Canada, 25.

42 Historical Officer, "Report No. 135,"10–11.

43 Nicholson, *Canadians in Italy*, 93.

44 G.R. Stevens, *A City Goes to War* (Brampton, ON.: Charters Publishing, 1964), 235.

45 Historical Officer, "Report No. 135," 11.

46 Robert Tooley, *Invicta: The Carleton and York Regiment in the Second World War* (Fredericton, NB: New Ireland Press, 1989), 126.

47 4th Canadian Field Regiment, RCE War Diary, July 1943, Library and Archives Canada, n.p.

48 Nicholson, *Canadians in Italy*, 95.

49 "The Historical Account of the Fighting Operations of the 12th Canadian Tank Regiment (Three Rivers Regiment of Quebec) from the Time of Their Landing in Sicily Up to and Including Their Last Action Fought West of Adrano on August the 5th, 1943," RG24, vol. 10990, Library and Archives Canada, 5.

50 Wallace, 14.

51 Carleton and York Regiment War Diary, July 1943, Library and Archives Canada, 2.

52 West Nova Scotia War Diary, July 1943, Library and Archives Canada, n.p.

53 1st Canadian Infantry Division, General Staff War Diary, July 1943, 26.

12: LONG AND SAVAGE MINUTES

1 Historical Officer, Canadian Military Headquarters, "Report No. 135: Canadian Operations in Sicily, July–August 1943, Part II: The Execution of the Operation by 1 Cdn Inf Div, Section 2: The Pursuit of the Germans from Vizzini to Adrano 15 Jul–6 Aug," Directorate of Heritage and History, Department of National Defence,13.

2 G.W.L. Nicholson, *The Canadians in Italy, 1939–1945*, vol. 2 (Ottawa: Queen's Printer, 1956), 96.

3 Historical Officer, "Report No. 135," 13.

4 "Account given by Major A.R. Campbell Officer Commanding 'A' Company and Captain N.R. Waugh, MC, Officer Commanding 'D' Company, Hastings and Prince Edward Regiment, on 18 August 1943, at Battalion Rest Area near Militello in val di Catania, Sicily," RG24, vol. 10880, Library and Archives Canada, n.p.

5 Appendix 6, "La March du 22e, Sur La Ville D'Enna (Sicile)," in Royal 22e Régiment War Diary, July 1943, Library and Archives Canada, 68.

6 Charles-Marie Boissonault, *Histoire du Royal 22e Régiment* (Quebec: Éditions du Pélican, 1964), 128.

7 Ibid., 129.

8 Appendix 6, "La March," 68.

9 Boissonault, 130–32.

10 Ibid., 130–31.

11 Historical Officer, "Report No. 135," 129–31.

12 Appendix 6, "La March," 69.

13 Boissonault, 132.

14 *2 CDN LAA Reg't RCA* (n.p., 1945), 18.

15 Boissonault, 131.

16 Historical Officer, "Report No. 135," 15.

17 "Personal Account by Lt.-Col The Lord Tweedsmuir of the Sicilian Campaign," 145.241011(D31), Directorate of Heritage and History, Department of National Defence, 8–9.

18 Historical Officer, "Report No. 135," 15.

19 Farley Mowat, *The Regiment*, 2nd ed. (Toronto: McClelland & Stewart, 1973), 74.

20 Farley Mowat, *And No Birds Sang* (Toronto: McClelland & Stewart, 1979), 109–10.

21 "Account given by Major A.R. Campbell Officer Commanding 'A' Company and Captain N.R. Waugh, MC, Officer Commanding 'D' Company, Hastings and Prince Edward Regiment, on 18 August 1943, at Battalion Rest Area near Militello in val di Catania, Sicily," RG24, vol. 10880, Library and Archives Canada, n.p.

22 Kenneth B. Smith, *Duffy's Regiment: A History of the Hastings and Prince Edward Regiment* (Toronto: Dundurn, 1987), 88.

23 Mowat, *The Regiment*, 78.

24 Historical Officer, "Report No. 135," 17.

25 Mowat, *And No Birds Sang*, 112.

26 Historical Officer, "Report No. 135," 17.

27 Mowat, *The Regiment*, 80.

28 Campbell and Waugh, n.p.

29 Smith, 89.

30 Historical Officer, "Report No. 135," 16.

31 Hastings and Prince Edward War Diary, July 1943, Library and Archives Canada, n.p.

32 Historical Officer "Report No. 135," 16.

33 Mowat, *The Regiment*, 79.

34 Ibid., 80.

35 G.R. Stevens, *The Royal Canadian Regiment*, vol. 2 (London, ON: London Print & Lithography, 1967), 74.

36 Royal Canadian Regiment War Diary, July 1943, Library and Archives Canada, n.p.

37 Strome Galloway, *Some Died at Ortona* (n.p., n.d.), 138.

38 Strome Galloway, *Bravely Into Battle: The Autobiography of a Canadian Soldier in World War II* (Toronto: Stoddart Publishing, 1988), 55.

39 Royal Canadian Regiment War Diary, July 1943, n.p.

40 Galloway, *Bravely Into Battle*, 54.

41 Royal Canadian Regiment War Diary, n.p.

42 Ibid.

43 Nicholson, *Canadians in Italy*, 99.

44 Historical Officer, "Report No. 135," 18.

45 Nicholson, *Canadians in Italy*, 99.

46 Strome Galloway, *Some Died at Ortona*, 132–33.

47 Strome Galloway, *Bravely Into Battle*, 56.

13: MOUNTAIN BOYS

1 3rd Canadian Infantry Brigade War Diary, July 1943, Library and Archives Canada, 4.

2 Michael Pearson Cessford, *"Hard in the Attack: The Canadian Army in Sicily and Italy, July 1943–June 1944,"* PhD thesis, Carleton University, September 1996, 171.

3 3rd Canadian Infantry Brigade War Diary, July 1943, 4.

4   Robert Tooley, *Invicta: The Carleton and York Regiment in the Second World War* (Fredericton, NB: New Ireland Press, 1989), 127.

5   G.W.L. Nicholson, *The Canadians in Italy, 1939–1945*, vol. 2 (Ottawa: Queen's Printer, 1956), 96.

6   Headquarters, 1st Divisional Artillery, RCA War Diary, July 1943, Library and Archives Canada, 10.

7   Nicholson, *Canadians in Italy*, 96.

8   Historical Officer, Canadian Military Headquarters, "Report No. 135: Canadian Operations in Sicily, July–August 1943, Part II: The Execution of the Operation by 1 Cdn Inf Div, Section 2: The Pursuit of the Germans from Vizzini to Adrano 15 Jul–6 Aug," Directorate of Heritage and History, Department of National Defence, 15.

9   Thomas H. Raddall, *West Novas: A History of the West Nova Scotia Regiment* (n.p., 1947), 90.

10 West Nova Scotia Regiment War Diary, July 1943, Library and Archives Canada, n.p.

11 Nicholson, *Canadians in Italy*, 96–97.

12 Daniel G. Dancocks, *The D-Day Dodgers: The Canadians in Italy, 1943–1945* (Toronto: McClelland & Stewart, 1991), 57.

13 Ross Munro, *Gauntlet to Overlord: The Story of the Canadian Army* (Toronto: Macmillan Company of Canada, 1945), 392–93.

14 Tooley, 128.

15 Munro, 392–93.

16 Nicholson, *Canadians in Italy*, 97.

17 Tooley, 129.

18 Historical Officer, "Report No. 135," 15.

19 Charles-Marie Boissonnault, *Histoire du Royal 22e Régiment* (Quebec: Éditions du Pélican, 1964), 134.

20 Nicholson, 99.

21 "Letter Major-General Simonds to Lieutenant-General McNaughton, 30 July 1943," MG30, vol. 202, McNaughton Papers.

22 Nicholson, *Canadians in Italy*, 100.

23 Ibid., 102.

24 Bill McAndrew, *Canadians and the Italian Campaign, 1943–1945* (Montreal: Éditions Art Global, 1996), 49.

25 Carlo D'Este, *Bitter Victory: The Battle for Sicily, 1943* (New York: Harper Perennial, 1988), 425.

26 Robin Neillands, *Eighth Army: From the Western Desert to the Alps, 1939–1945* (London: John Murray, 2004), 270–71.

27 Rowland Ryder, *Oliver Leese* (London: Hamish Hamilton, 1987), 141.

28 C.J.C. Molony, *The Mediterranean and Middle East: The Campaign in Sicily 1943 and The Campaign in Italy 3rd September 1943 to 31st March 1944* (London: Her Majesty's Stationery Office, 1973), 112–13.

29 Nicholson, *Canadians in Italy*, 103.

30 4th Reconnaissance Regiment (Princess Louise Dragoon Guards) War Diary, July 1943, Library and Archives Canada, n.p.

31 Historical Officer, "Report No. 135," 20–22.

32 Nicholson, *Canadians in Italy*, 102.

33 2nd Canadian Infantry Brigade War Diary, July 1943, Library and Archives Canada, n.p.

34 Richard Victor Latimer, "The Gibblers: Or Balmorals and Bully Beef," unpublished memoir in possession of author, 299–300.

35 R.H. Roy, *The Seaforth Highlanders of Canada, 1919–1965* (Vancouver: Evergreen Press, 1969), 171.

36 "Diary of Major Durnford," RG24, vol. 20405, Library and Archives Canada, 34.

37 Nicholson, *Canadians in Italy*, 102.

38 Historical Officer, "Report No. 135," 19–20.

39 "Comments by Seaforth Veterans," Dr. Reginald Roy Collection, University of Victoria Special Collections, 4.

40 Nicholson, *Canadians in Italy*, 104.

41 Ibid., 102.

42 Bert Hoffmeister, interview by B. Greenhouse and W. McAndrew, n.d., transcript, 2001/26, Directorate of Heritage and History, 51.

43 Roy, 172.

44 "Comments by Seaforth Veterans," 3–4.

45 Roy, 173.

46 "Comments by Seaforth Veterans," 3–4.

47 Roy, 172–73.

48 Hoffmeister interview, 51.

49 Durnford, 35.

50 Roy, 173.

51 Headquarters, 1st Divisional Artillery, RCA War Diary, July 1943, 10.

52 Douglas E. Delaney, *The Soldier's General: Bert Hoffmeister at War* (Vancouver: UBC Press, 2005), 58–59.

53 Hoffmeister interview, 50–51.

54 Seaforth Highlanders of Canada War Diary, July 1943, Library and Archives Canada, n.p.

55 Headquarters, 1st Divisional Artillery, RCA War Diary, July 1943, 10.

56 Roy, 173–74.

57 Chris Vokes, *Vokes: My Story* (Ottawa: Gallery, 1985), 109.

58 Richard S. Malone, *A Portrait of War, 1939–1943* (Toronto: Collins Publishers, 1983), 162–63.

59 2nd Canadian Infantry Brigade War Diary, July 1943, n.p.

60 Malone, 163.

61 G.R. Stevens, *Princess Patricia's Canadian Light Infantry, 1919–1957*, vol. 3 (Griesbach, AB: Historical Committee of the Regiment, n.d.), 80.

62 Princess Patricia's Canadian Light Infantry War Diary, July 1943, Library and Archives Canada, 12.

63 Historical Officer, "Report No. 135," 21.

14: PRIVATE MIRACLES

1 Loyal Edmonton Regiment War Diary, July 1943, Library and Archives Canada, n.p.

2 "Account by Capt F.N. Pope, 10, 2 Cdn Inf Bde on the battles of Leonforte and Aderno," RG24, vol. 10982, Library and Archives Canada, 16.

3 G.W.L. Nicholson, *The Canadians in Italy, 1939–1945*, vol. 2 (Ottawa: Queen's Printer, 1956), 102–03.

4 G.R. Stevens, *Princess Patricia's Canadian Light Infantry, 1919–1957*, vol. 3 (Griesbach, AB: Historical Committee of the Regiment, n.d.), 80.

5 Captain A.T. Sesia, "Personal Notes and Observations: PART I—Sicily, 24 Apr. 43– 2 Sep. 43," RG24, vol. 10878, Library and Archives Canada, 42.

6 Captain R.W. Potts, "The Regiment's First Contact With the Germans" in "Accounts of Actions during the Sicilian campaign as prepared by various officers of the Princess Patricia's Canadian Light Infantry," RG24, vol. 10982, Library and Archives Canada, 42.

7 Gerald Astor, *Terrible Terry Allen: Combat General of World War II—The Life of an American Soldier* (New York: Ballantine Books, 2003), 210.

8 4th Reconnaissance Regiment (Princess Louise Dragoon Guards) War Diary, July 1943, Library and Archives Canada, n.p.

9 H.M. Jackson, *The Princess Louise Dragoon Guards: A History* (Ottawa: The Regiment, 1952), 119.

10 "A Squadron, 4 Cdn Recce Regt (4 PLDG)," 141.4A4011(D5), Directorate of Heritage and History, Department of National Defence, 77–78.

11 Astor, 211.

12 Martin Blumenson, *The Patton Papers: 1940–1945* (Boston: Houghton Mifflin, 1974), 298.

13 Omar N. Bradley and Clay Blair, *A General's Life: An Autobiography* (New York: Simon and Schuster, 1983), 193.

14 Historical Officer, Canadian Military Headquarters, "Report No. 135: Canadian Operations in Sicily, July–August 1943, Part II: The Execution of the Operation by 1 Cdn Inf Div, Section 2: The Pursuit of the Germans from Vizzini to Adrano 15 Jul–6 Aug," Directorate of Heritage and History, Department of National Defence, 24.

15 48th Highlanders of Canada War Diary, July 1943, Library and Archives Canada, n.p.

16 Strome Galloway, *A Regiment at War: The Story of the Royal Canadian Regiment, 1939–1945* (repr. Royal Canadian Regiment, 1979), 77.

17 "Diary of Lt. J.F. Wallace," MG30, vol. 1, Library and Archives Canada, 15.

18 Strome Galloway, *Bravely Into Battle: The Autobiography of a Canadian Soldier in World War II* (Toronto: Stoddart Publishing, 1988), 58.

19 Wallace, 15.

20 John Marteinson and Michael R. McNorgan, *The Royal Armoured Corps: An Illustrated History* (Toronto: Robin Brass Studio, 2000), 422.

21 Three Rivers Tank Regiment War Diary, July 1943, Library and Archives Canada, 13.

22 Wallace, 15.

23 "The Historical Account of the Fighting Operations of the 12th Canadian Tank Regiment (Three Rivers Regiment of Quebec) from the Time of Their Landing in Sicily Up to and Including Their Last Action Fought West of Adrano on August the 5th, 1943," RG24, vol. 10990, Library and Archives Canada, 6.

24 Galloway, *Bravely Into Battle*, 67–68.

25 Ibid., 59.

26 Galloway, *Some Died at Ortona,* 139–40.

27 Howard Graham, *Citizen and Soldier: The Memoirs of Lieutenant-General Howard Graham* (Toronto: McClelland & Stewart, 1987), 166–67.

28 Ibid., 167–68.

29 Sheridan Atkinson, correspondence with author, 17 November 2007.

30 "Personal Account by Lt.-Col The Lord Tweedsmuir of the Sicilian Campaign," 145.241011(D31), Directorate of Heritage and History, Department of National Defence, 12.

31 Graham, 169.

32 Ibid., 169.

33 Tweedsmuir, 12–13.

34 Historical Officer, "Report No. 135," 30.

35 Hastings and Prince Edward Regiment War Diary, July 1943, Library and Archives Canada, n.p.

36 "Account given by Major A.R. Campbell Officer Commanding 'A' Company and Captain N.R. Waugh, MC, Officer Commanding 'D' Company, Hastings and Prince Edward Regiment, on 18 August 1943, at Battalion Rest Area near Militello in val di Catania, Sicily," RG24, vol. 10880, Library and Archives Canada, n.p.

37 Farley Mowat, *The Regiment,* 2nd ed. (Toronto: McClelland & Stewart, 1973), 83–85.

38 Tweedsmuir, 13.

39 Hastings and Prince Edward War Diary, July 1943, n.p.

40 Historical Officer, "Report No. 135," 30–31.

41 Farley Mowat, *And No Birds Sang* (Toronto: McClelland & Stewart, 1979), 128.

42 Mowat, *The Regiment,* 84.

43 Historical Officer, "Report No. 135," 31.

44 Tweedsmuir, 14.

45 Mowat, *The Regiment,* 84.

46 Historical Officer, "Report No. 135," 31.

47 Tweedsmuir, 14.

48 Mowat, *The Regiment,* 85.

49 Mowat, *And No Birds Sang,* 130–31.

50 Mowat, *The Regiment,* 85.

51 Historical Officer, "Report No. 135," 31.

15: FACES TO THE FOE

1 Historical Officer, Canadian Military Headquarters, "Report No. 135: Canadian Operations in Sicily, July–August 1943, Part II: The Execution of the Operation by I Cdn Inf Div, Section 2: The Pursuit of the Germans from Vizzini to Adrano 15 Jul–6 Aug," Directorate of Heritage and History, Department of National Defence, 31.

2 Hastings and Prince Edward Regiment War Diary, July 1943, Library and Archives Canada, n.p.

3 Farley Mowat, *The Regiment,* 2nd ed. (Toronto: McClelland & Stewart, 1973), 86–88.

4 Historical Officer, "Report No. 135," 32.

5 Farley Mowat, *And No Birds Sang* (Toronto: McClelland & Stewart, 1979), 134.

6 "Personal Account by Lt.-Col The Lord Tweedsmuir of the Sicilian Campaign,"
145.241011(D31), Directorate of Heritage and History, Department of National
Defence, 14.

7 Mowat, *And No Birds Sang*, 133.

8 John S. Moir, ed. *History of the Royal Canadian Corps of Signals, 1903–1961* (Ottawa:
Corps Committee, Royal Canadian Corps of Signals, 1962), 129.

9 "Personal Account by Lt.-Col The Lord Tweedsmuir of the Sicilian Campaign,"
145.241011(D31), Directorate of Heritage and History, Department of National
Defence, 15.

10 Mowat, *The Regiment*, 89.

11 Kenneth B. Smith, *Duffy's Regiment: A History of the Hastings and Prince Edward
Regiment* (Toronto: Dundurn, 1987), 96.

12 Hastings and Prince Edward War Diary, July 1943, n.p.

13 Tweedsmuir, 15.

14 Historical Officer, "Report No. 135," 32.

15 Royal Canadian Regiment War Diary, July 1943, Library and Archives Canada, n.p.

16 Tweedsmuir, 16.

17 G.W.L. Nicholson, *The Canadians in Italy, 1939–1945*, vol. 2 (Ottawa: Queen's
Printer, 1956), 107.

18 Strome Galloway, *Bravely Into Battle: The Autobiography of a Canadian Soldier in
World War II* (Toronto: Stoddart Publishing, 1988), 60–61.

19 Strome Galloway, *Some Died at Ortona* (n.p., n.d.), 141–42.

20 Historical Officer "Report No. 135," 25.

21 "Comments by Seaforth Veterans," Dr. Reginald Roy Collection, University of
Victoria Special Collections, 4–5.

22 Henry "Budge" Bell-Irving correspondence, 3 May 1967, Dr. Reginald Roy Collection,
University of Victoria Special Collections, 2.

23 "Comments by Seaforth Veterans," 5.

24 R.H. Roy, *The Seaforth Highlanders of Canada, 1919–1965* (Vancouver: Evergreen
Press, 1969), 175–76.

25 Roy, 178–79.

26 E.W. "June" Thomas, interview by author, Victoria, 23 October 1998.

27 Roy, 178.

28 Bert Hoffmeister, interview by B. Greenhouse and W. McAndrew n.d., transcript,
2001/26, Directorate of Heritage and History, 59.

29 Roy, 178.

30 Hoffmeister interview, 59.

31 Roy, 178.

32 Howard Mitchell, *My War With the Saskatoon Light Infantry (M.G.) 1939–1945* (n.p.,
n.d.), 74.

33 Hoffmeister interview, 59.

34 "Diary of Major Durnford," RG24, vol. 20405, Library and Archives Canada, 42–43.

35 Hoffmeister interview, 59–60.

36 "Comments by Seaforth Veterans," 6.

37 Seaforth Highlanders of Canada War Diary, July 1943, Library and Archives Canada, n.p.

38 2nd Canadian Infantry Brigade War Diary, July 1943, Library and Archives Canada, n.p.

39 1st Canadian Infantry Division, General Staff War Diary, July 1943, Library and Archives Canada, 29.

40 2nd Canadian Infantry Brigade War Diary, July 1943, n.p.

41 Historical Officer, "Report No. 135," 25–26.

42 Henry "Budge" Bell-Irving correspondence, 20 February 1967, Dr. Reginald Roy Collection, University of Victoria Special Collections, 2.

43 Loyal Edmonton Regiment War Diary, July 1943, Library and Archives Canada, n.p.

44 "Further Discussion With Lt-Col Cromb," RG24, vol. 10981, Library and Archives Canada, 2.

45 G.R. Stevens, A City Goes to War (Brampton, ON: Charters Publishing, 1964), 237–38.

46 "Account by Capt. C.H. Pritchard, Edmn R., formerly Adjutant and now carrier pl. comd. Given in bn. rest area, 18 Aug 43, near Militello in Val di Catania," RG24, vol. 10982, Library and Archives Canada, 30.

47 "Further Discussion, 13 Dec 49," 2.

48 "Interview D.D.H.S. with Brigadier J.C. Jefferson," RG24, vol. 10982, Library and Archives Canada, n.p.

49 Pritchard, 30.

50 Daniel G. Dancocks, The D-Day Dodgers: The Canadians in Italy, 1943–1945 (Toronto: McClelland & Stewart, 1991), 69.

51 Col. A.J. Kerry and Maj. W.A. McDill, History of the Corps of Royal Canadian Engineers, vol. 2 (Ottawa: The Military Engineers Association of Canada, 1966), 141.

52 Nicholson, Canadians in Italy, 108–09.

53 Dancocks, 70.

54 Chris Vokes, My Story (Ottawa: Gallery Press, 1985), 111.

55 Historical Officer, "Report No. 135," 27.

56 Dominick Graham, The Price of Command: A Biography of General Guy Simonds (Toronto: Stoddart Publishing, 1993), 95.

16: DARING AND SPECTACULAR ACTIONS

1 G.R. Stevens, A City Goes to War (Brampton, ON: Charters Publishing, 1964), 238.

2 "Further Discussion With Lt-Col Cromb, 13 Dec 49," RG24, vol. 10981, Library and Archives Canada, 2–3.

3 Loyal Edmonton Regiment War Diary, July 1943, Library and Archives Canada, n.p.

4 Stevens, A City Goes to War, 238.

5 G.W.L. Nicholson, The Canadians in Italy, 1939–1945, vol. 2 (Ottawa: Queen's Printer, 1956), 108.

6 "Interview D.D.H.S. with Brigadier J.C. Jefferson," RG24, vol. 10982, Library and Archives Canada, n.p.

7 Nicholson, Canadians in Italy, 108.

8 Chris Vokes, My Story (Ottawa: Gallery Press, 1985), 111–13.

9 "Statement by Lt-Col. R.A. Lindsay on the Engagements of the PPCLI from battle at Piazza Armerina to the battle for Agira given on 30 Jul 43," RG24, vol. 10982, Library and Archives Canada, 3.

10 Major Coleman, MC, "Sicilian Campaign—Leonforte," in "Accounts of Actions during the Sicilian campaign as prepared by various officers of the Princess Patricia's Canadian Light Infantry," RG24, vol. 10982, Library and Archives Canada, 43.

11 Nicholson, *Canadians in Italy*, 109.

12 Lindsay, 4.

13 Jefferson, n.p.

14 "Diary of Lt. J.F. Wallace," MG30, vol. 1, Library and Archives Canada, 17.

15 G.R. Stevens, *Princess Patricia's Canadian Light Infantry, 1919–1957*, vol. 3 (Griesbach, AB: Historical Committee of the Regiment, n.d.), 82.

16 Coleman, 44.

17 Lindsay, 4.

18 Coleman, 44.

19 Felix Carriere, interview by Tom Torrie, 4 June 1987, University of Victoria Special Collections.

20 Wallace, 17.

21 Coleman, 44.

22 Stevens, *Princess Patricia's Canadian Light Infantry*, 83.

23 Historical Officer, Canadian Military Headquarters, "Report No. 135: Canadian Operations in Sicily, July–August 1943, Part II: The Execution of the Operation by 1 Cdn Inf Div, Section 2: The Pursuit of the Germans from Vizzini to Adrano 15 Jul–6 Aug," Directorate of Heritage and History, Department of National Defence, 28–29.

24 Nicholson, *Canadians in Italy*, 110.

25 Princess Patricia's Canadian Light Infantry War Diary, July 1943, Library and Archives Canada, 15.

26 David Bercuson, *The Patricia's: The Proud History of a Fighting Regiment* (Toronto: Stoddart Publishing, 2001), 190.

27 Nicholson, *Canadians in Italy*, 110.

28 Three Rivers Tank Regiment War Diary, July 1943, Library and Archives Canada, 14.

29 Historical Officer, "Report No. 135," 26–34.

30 Ibid., 34.

31 Kim Beattie, *Dileas: History of the 48th Highlanders of Canada: 1929–1956* (Toronto: 48th Highlanders of Canada, 1957), 263–64.

32 Three Rivers Tank War Diary, 13.

33 Beattie, 265–66.

34 Three Rivers Tank War Diary, 13.

35 Beattie, 266.

36 Three Rivers Tank War Diary, 13.

37 Beattie, 269.

38 48th Highlanders of Canada War Diary, July 1943, Library and Archives Canada, n.p.

39 Beattie, 269–70.

40 Historical Officer, "Report No. 135," 34–35.

41 Beattie, 271.

42 Ibid., 34.

43 Nicholson, *Canadians in Italy*, 107.

44 Ross Munro, *Gauntlet to Overlord: The Story of the Canadian Army* (Toronto: Macmillan Company of Canada, 1945), 400–04.

45 Historical Officer, "Report No. 135," 35.

46 Canada, Department of National Defence, *The Canadian Army at War*, vol. 2, *From Pachino to Ortona: The Canadian Campaign in Sicily and Italy, 1943*. 2nd ed. (Ottawa: King's Printer, 1946), 55–56.

47 Historical Officer, "Report No. 135," 35–38.

48 Nicholson, *Canadians in Italy*, 117.

49 Samuel W. Mitcham Jr. and Friedrich von Stauffenberg, *The Battle of Sicily* (New York: Orion Books, 1991), 224–26.

50 Ibid., 226.

51 Nicholson, *Canadians in Italy*, 110.

52 Ibid., 120–21.

53 Beattie, 271.

54 Ibid., 272–74.

55 48th Highlanders War Diary, n.p.

17: FOLLOW THE BAND

1 4th Reconnaissance Regiment (Princess Louise Dragoon Guards) War Diary, July 1943, Library and Archives Canada, n.p.

2 G.W.L. Nicholson, *The Canadians in Italy, 1939–1945*, vol. 2 (Ottawa: Queen's Printer, 1956), 112.

3 Bill McAndrew, "Fire or Movement?: Canadian Tactical Doctrine, Sicily—1943," *Military Affairs*, vol. 51, no. 3, 142.

4 Historical Officer, Canadian Military Headquarters, "Report No. 135: Canadian Operations in Sicily, July–August 1943, Part II: The Execution of the Operation by 1 Cdn Inf Div, Section 2: The Pursuit of the Germans from Vizzini to Adrano 15 Jul–6 Aug," 40–41, Directorate of Heritage and History, Department of National Defence,

5 McAndrew, 142.

6 Headquarters, 1st Divisional Artillery, RCA War Diary, July 1943, Library and Archives Canada, 12.

7 G.W.L. Nicholson, *The Gunners of Canada*, vol. 2 (Toronto: McClelland & Stewart, 1972), 149.

8 George Kitching, *Mud and Green Fields: The Memoirs of Major General George Kitching* (Langley, BC: Battleline Books, 1986), 167–68.

9 Daniel G. Dancocks, *The D-Day Dodgers: The Canadians in Italy, 1943–1945* (Toronto: McClelland & Stewart, 1991), 74.

10 Nicholson, *Gunners of Canada*, 149.

11 Dominick Graham, *The Price of Command: A Biography of General Guy Simonds* (Toronto: Stoddart Publishing, 1993), 95.

12 Kitching, 167.

13 Howard Graham, *Citizen and Soldier: The Memoirs of Lieutenant-General Howard Graham* (Toronto: McClelland & Stewart, 1987), 174.

14 McAndrew, 142.

15 Graham, 174.

16 Strome Galloway, *Bravely Into Battle: The Autobiography of a Canadian Soldier in World War II* (Toronto: Stoddart Publishing, 1988), 68–69.

17 Dancocks, 74.

18 Royal Canadian Regiment War Diary, July 1943, Library and Archives Canada, n.p.

19 Strome Galloway, *Sicily to the Siegfried Line: Being Some Random Memories and a Diary of 1944–1945* (Kitchener, ON: Arnold Press, n.d.), 5–8.

20 Three Rivers Tank Regiment War Diary, July 1943, Library and Archives Canada, 15–16.

21 L.S.B. Shapiro, *They Left the Back Door Open: A Chronicle of the Allied Campaign in Sicily and Italy* (Toronto: Ryerson Press, 1944), 59–61.

22 Captain A.T. Sesia, "Personal Notes and Observations: PART I–Sicily, 24 Apr. 43–2 Sep. 43," RG24, vol. 10878, Library and Archives Canada, 50.

23 Nicholson, *Gunners of Canada*, 149.

24 Sesia, 50.

25 Historical Officer, "Report No. 135," 41.

26 Major C.H. Lithgow, "The Battle of Nissoria; 24 July 1943, 'D' Day Sicily, 10 July 43," http://thercr.ca/history/1939-1945/nissoria_1943.htm (accessed 26 June 2008).

27 Galloway, *Bravely Into Battle*, 69.

28 Lithgow.

29 Galloway, *Bravely Into Battle*, 69–70.

30 Lithgow.

31 Historical Officer, "Report No. 135," 40.

32 Three Rivers Tank War Diary, 16–22.

33 "Diary of Lt. J.F. Wallace," MG30, vol. 1, Library and Archives Canada, 18.

34 Three Rivers Tank War Diary, 21–23.

18: RED PATCH DEVILS

1 "Account given by Major T.M. Powers, second-in-command, Royal Canadian Regiment, on 18 August 1943 in Battalion rest area near Scordia, Sicily," RG24, vol. 10880, Library and Archives Canada, n.p.

2 Strome Galloway, *Bravely Into Battle: The Autobiography of a Canadian Soldier in World War II* (Toronto: Stoddart Publishing, 1988), 70.

3 Major C.H. Lithgow, "The Battle of Nissoria; 24 July 1943, 'D' Day Sicily, 10 July 43," http://thercr.ca/history/1939-1945/nissoria_1943.htm (accessed 26 June 2008).

4 Galloway, *Bravely Into Battle*, 70–71.

5 Royal Canadian Regiment War Diary, July 1943, Library and Archives Canada, n.p.

6 Lithgow.

7 Galloway, *Bravely Into Battle*, 70–71.

8 Daniel G. Dancocks, *The D-Day Dodgers: The Canadians in Italy, 1943–1945* (Toronto: McClelland & Stewart, 1991), 76.

9 Galloway, *Bravely Into Battle*, 71.

10 Historical Officer, Canadian Military Headquarters, "Report No. 135: Canadian Operations in Sicily, July–August 1943, Part II: The Execution of the Operation by 1 Cdn Inf Div, Section 2: The Pursuit of the Germans from Vizzini to Adrano 15 Jul–6 Aug," Directorate of Heritage and History, Department of National Defence, 44–45.

11 1st Canadian Infantry Brigade War Diary, July 1943, Appendix: Situation Reports, July 43, Library and Archives Canada, 30-1-17.

12 Dancocks, 77.

13 Howard Graham, *Citizen and Soldier: The Memoirs of Lieutenant-General Howard Graham* (Toronto: McClelland & Stewart, 1987), 176.

14 "Personal Account by Lt.-Col The Lord Tweedsmuir of the Sicilian Campaign," 145.241011(D31), Directorate of Heritage and History, Department of National Defence, 17–18.

15 Hastings and Prince Edward Regiment War Diary, July 1943, Library and Archives Canada, n.p.

16 Tweedsmuir, 18–19.

17 Hastings and Prince Edward War Diary, n.p.

18 Tweedsmuir, 19.

19 Farley Mowat, *The Regiment*, 2nd ed. (Toronto: McClelland & Stewart, 1973), 95–96.

20 Tweedsmuir, 19–20.

21 G.W.L. Nicholson, *The Canadians in Italy, 1939–1945*, vol. 2 (Ottawa: Queen's Printer, 1956), 125–26.

22 Galloway, *Bravely Into Battle*, 72.

23 Nicholson, *Canadians in Italy*, 126.

24 Graham, 177.

25 1st Canadian Infantry Brigade War Diary, 30-1-18.

26 4th Reconnaissance Regiment (Princess Louise Dragoon Guards) War Diary, July 1943, Library and Archives Canada, n.p.

27 Historical Officer, "Report No. 135," 49.

28 Kim Beattie, *Dileas: History of the 48th Highlanders of Canada: 1929–1956* (Toronto: 48th Highlanders of Canada, 1957), 281–82.

29 Historical Officer, "Report No. 135," 50.

30 Beattie, 284–88.

31 48th Highlanders of Canada War Diary, July 1943, Library and Archives Canada, n.p.

32 Beattie, 291–93.

33 48th Highlanders War Diary, n.p.

34 Nicholson, *Canadians in Italy*, 126.

35 Historical Officer, "Report No. 135," 52.

36 Ross Munro, *Gauntlet to Overlord: The Story of the Canadian Army* (Toronto: Macmillan Company of Canada, 1945), 413–15.

37 Strome Galloway, *A Regiment at War: The Story of the Royal Canadian Regiment, 1939–1945* (repr. Royal Canadian Regiment, 1979), 83.

38 G.R. Stevens, *Princess Patricia's Canadian Light Infantry, 1919–1957*, vol. 3 (Griesbach, AB: Historical Committee of the Regiment, n.d.), 85.

39 Historical Officer, "Report No. 135," 53.

40 Ibid., 53.

41 G.W.L. Nicholson, *The Gunners of Canada*, vol. 2 (Toronto: McClelland & Stewart, 1972), 150.

42 William F. Rannie, ed., *To The Thunderer His Arms: The Royal Canadian Ordnance Corps* (Lincoln, ON: W.F. Rannie, 1984), 129.

43 Nicholson, *Gunners of Canada*, 150.
44 Historical Officer, "Report No. 135," 53.
45 Ibid., 56.
46 Headquarters, 1st Divisional Artillery, RCA War Diary, July 1943, Library and Archives Canada, 13.
47 Historical Officer, "Report No. 135," 53.
48 Chris Vokes, *My Story* (Ottawa: Gallery Press, 1985), 114.

19: LION, TIGER, AND GRIZZLY

1 *History of the 3rd Canadian Field Regiment, Royal Canadian Artillery–September, 1939 to July, 1945* (n.p., 1945), 37.
2 "Diary of Lt. J.F. Wallace," MG30, vol. 1, Library and Archives Canada, 19.
3 Major Coleman, MC, "Nissoria—Night July 26/27, 1943," in "Accounts of Actions during the Sicilian campaign as prepared by various officers of the Princess Patricia's Canadian Light Infantry," RG24, vol. 10982, Library and Archives Canada, 45–47.
4 Wallace, 19.
5 "Statement by Lt-Col. R.A. Lindsay on the Engagements of the PPCLI from battle at Piazza Armerina to the battle for Agira given on 30 Jul 43," RG24, vol. 10982, Library and Archives Canada, 5.
6 G.W.L. Nicholson, *The Canadians in Italy, 1939–1945*, vol. 2 (Ottawa: Queen's Printer, 1956), 129.
7 Lindsay, 5.
8 *History of the 3rd Canadian Field Regiment*, 5.
9 Lindsay, 5.
10 Vokes, 114–15.
11 Douglas E. Delaney, *The Soldier's General: Bert Hoffmeister at War* (Vancouver: UBC Press, 2005), 62.
12 R.H. Roy, *The Seaforth Highlanders of Canada, 1919–1965* (Vancouver: Evergreen Press, 1969), 181.
13 Henry "Budge" Bell-Irving, interview by Ken MacLeod, Vancouver, n.d.
14 Henry "Budge" Bell-Irving correspondence, 3 May 1967, Dr. Reginald Roy Collection, University of Victoria Special Collections, 3.
15 Roy, 182.
16 Bell-Irving interview.
17 Roy, 182.
18 Wallace, 19–20.
19 Roy, 182–83.
20 Lindsay, 5.
21 Roy, 183.
22 Bell-Irving interview.
23 Wallace, 20.
24 Roy, 183–84.
25 John Alpine Dougan, interview by author, Victoria, 30 October 1998.
26 John Alpine Dougan, interview by Tom Torrie, 27 July 1989, University of Victoria Special Collections.

27 Nicholson, 130.

28 Dougan interview by Torrie.

29 Historical Officer, Canadian Military Headquarters, "Report No. 135: Canadian Operations in Sicily, July–August 1943, Part II: The Execution of the Operation by 1 Cdn Inf Div, Section 2: The Pursuit of the Germans from Vizzini to Adrano 15 Jul–6 Aug," Directorate of Heritage and History, Department of National Defence, 56.

30 "Notes on Interview D.D.H.S. With Lt-Col W.T. Cromb, Edmonton, 10 December 1949," RG24, vol. 10981, Library and Archives Canada, 1.

31 "Interview D.D.H.S. with Brigadier J.C. Jefferson," RG24, vol. 10982, Library and Archives Canada, n.p.

32 Historical Officer, "Report No. 135," 56–57.

33 Roy, 185.

34 Ibid., 185.

35 Henry "Budge" Bell-Irving correspondence, 3 May 1967, Dr. Reginald Roy Collection, University of Victoria Special Collections, 4.

36 Roy, 186.

37 Nicholson, *Canadians in Italy,* 132.

38 E.W. "June" Thomas, interview by author, Victoria, 23 October 1998.

39 Historical Officer, "Report No. 135," 59.

40 Roy, 186–87.

41 "Account by Capt. C.H. Pritchard, Edmn R., formerly Adjutant and now carrier pl. comd. Given in bn. rest area, 18 Aug 43, near Militello in Val di Catania," RG24, vol. 10982, Library and Archives Canada, 31.

42 Nicholson, *Canadians in Italy,* 132.

43 Historical Officer, "Report No. 135," 59–60.

44 Ibid., 60.

45 G.R. Stevens, *A City Goes to War* (Brampton, ON: Charters Publishing, 1964), 242.

46 John Alpine Dougan, interview by Ken MacLeod, Vancouver, n.d.

47 Roy, 188.

48 Ibid., 188.

49 Ibid., 187–88.

50 Nicholson, *Canadians in Italy,* 133.

20: HARD FIGHTING

1 G.W.L. Nicholson, *The Canadians in Italy, 1939–1945,* vol. 2 (Ottawa: Queen's Printer, 1956), 131–34.

2 Historical Officer, Canadian Military Headquarters, "Report No. 135: Canadian Operations in Sicily, July–August 1943, Part II: The Execution of the Operation by 1 Cdn Inf Div, Section 2: The Pursuit of the Germans from Vizzini to Adrano 15 Jul–6 Aug," Directorate of Heritage and History, Department of National Defence, 61.

3 G.D. Mitchell, RCHA—*Right of the Line: An Anecdotal History of the Royal Canadian Horse Artillery from 1871* (Ottawa: RCHA History Committee, 1986), 98.

4 "Statement by Lt-Col. R.A. Lindsay on the Engagements of the PPCLI from battle at Piazza Armerina to the battle for Agira given on 30 Jul 43," RG24, vol. 10982, Library and Archives Canada, 6.

5 "Street Fighting in Agira," in "Accounts of Actions during the Sicilian campaign as prepared by various officers of the Princess Patricia's Canadian Light Infantry," RG24, vol. 10982, Library and Archives Canada, 48.

6 "The Historical Account of the Fighting Operations of the 12th Canadian Tank Regiment (Three Rivers Regiment of Quebec) from the Time of Their Landing in Sicily Up to and Including Their Last Action Fought West of Adrano on August the 5th, 1943," RG24, vol. 10990, Library and Archives Canada, 14.

7 "Street fighting in Agira," 48–49.

8 Lindsay, 6.

9 Historical Officer, "Report No. 135," 64.

10 Samuel W. Mitcham Jr. and Friedrich von Stauffenberg, *The Battle of Sicily* (New York: Orion Books, 1991), 239.

11 Nicholson, *Canadians in Italy*, 134.

12 Historical Officer, "Report No. 135," 71–72.

13 West Nova Scotia Regiment War Diary, July 1943, Library and Archives Canada, n.p.

14 Robert Tooley, *Invicta: The Carleton and York Regiment in the Second World War* (Fredericton, NB: New Ireland Press, 1989), 132.

15 Carleton and York Regiment War Diary, July 1943, Library and Archives Canada, n.p.

16 3rd Canadian Infantry Brigade War Diary, July 1943, Library and Archives Canada, 7.

17 Nicholson, 137.

18 Historical Officer, "Report No. 135," 72.

19 Appendix 6, "Bataille des Monts Scalpello Et Santa Maria En Sicilie," in Royal 22e Régiment War Diary, July 1943, Library and Archives Canada, 71–73.

20 Historical Officer, "Report No. 135," 72.

21 Appendix 6, "Bataille des Monts," 73–75.

22 Nicholson, *Canadians in Italy*, 138–39.

23 Historical Officer, Canadian Military Headquarters, "Report No. 132: Canadian Operations in Sicily, July–August 1943, Part III: The Story of 1 Cdn Army Tk Bde," Directorate of Heritage and History, Department of National Defence, paras. 21–28.

24 Nicholson, *Canadians in Italy*, 167.

25 Ibid., 139.

26 Thomas H. Raddall, *West Novas: A History of the West Nova Scotia Regiment* (n.p., 1947), 94–95.

27 Ibid., 96–97.

28 Appendix, "B Company in the Capture of Catenanuova," in West Nova Scotia Regiment War Diary, July 1943, n.p.

29 Nicholson, *Canadians in Italy*, 141.

30 Raddall, 96.

31 Historical Officer, "Report No. 135," 80.

32 Nicholson, *Canadians in Italy*, 141–43.

33 "The Historical Account of the Fighting Operations of the 12th Canadian Tank Regiment," 14–15.

34 Charles-Marie Boissonault, *Histoire du Royal 22e Régiment* (Quebec: Éditions du Pélican, 1964), 145–47.

35 Ibid., 147–49.

36 Nicholson, *Canadians in Italy*, 143–44.

37 Raddall, 103–05.

38 Historical Officer, "Report No. 135," 83.

39 Raddall, 103–05.

40 Nicholson, *Canadians in Italy*, 144.

21: ROUGHEST COUNTRY YET

1 Hastings and Prince Edward Regiment War Diary, July 1943, Library and Archives Canada, n.p.

2 Peter Stursberg, *The Sound of War: Memoirs of a CBC Correspondent* (Toronto: University of Toronto Press, 1993), 113–14.

3 G.W.L. Nicholson, *The Canadians in Italy, 1939–1945*, vol. 2 (Ottawa: Queen's Printer, 1956), 147.

4 C.J.C. Molony, *The Mediterranean and Middle East: The Campaign in Sicily 1943 and The Campaign in Italy 3rd September 1943 to 31st March 1944* (London: Her Majesty's Stationery Office, 1973), 160–61.

5 Carlo D'Este, *Bitter Victory: The Battle for Sicily, 1943* (New York: Harper Perennial, 1988), 459.

6 1st Canadian Infantry Division, General Staff War Diary, July 1943, Library and Archives Canada, 34–35.

7 Nicholson, *Canadians in Italy*, 148.

8 "The Historical Account of the Fighting Operations of the 12th Canadian Tank Regiment (Three Rivers Regiment of Quebec) from the Time of Their Landing in Sicily Up to and Including Their Last Action Fought West of Adrano on August the 5th, 1943," RG24, vol. 10990, Library and Archives Canada, 15.

9 *History of the 3rd Canadian Field Regiment, Royal Canadian Artillery–September, 1939 to July, 1945* (n.p., 1945), 37.

10 Nicholson, *Canadians in Italy*, 147–49.

11 48th Highlanders of Canada War Diary, July 1943, Library and Archives Canada, n.p.

12 Historical Officer, Canadian Military Headquarters, "Report No. 135: Canadian Operations in Sicily, July–August 1943, Part II: The Execution of the Operation by 1 Cdn Inf Div, Section 2: The Pursuit of the Germans from Vizzini to Adrano 15 Jul–6 Aug," Directorate of Heritage and History, Department of National Defence, 86.

13 Nicholson, *Canadians in Italy*, 149.

14 Strome Galloway, *Bravely Into Battle: The Autobiography of a Canadian Soldier in World War II* (Toronto: Stoddart Publishing, 1988), 83–84.

15 G.R. Stevens, *The Royal Canadian Regiment*, vol. 2 (London, ON: London Print & Lithography, 1967), 82–83.

16 Galloway, *Bravely Into Battle*, 85.

17 Nicholson, *Canadians in Italy*, 149.

18 Appendix, "'A' Coy The Royal Cdn Regt. Sicily 10 July/12 Aug 43," in Royal Canadian Regiment War Diary, July 1943, Library and Archives Canada, 4.

19 "Account given by Major T.M. Powers, second-in-command, Royal Canadian Regiment, on 18 August 1943 in Battalion rest area near Scordia, Sicily," RG24, vol. 10880, Library and Archives Canada, n.p.

20 Stevens, *Royal Canadian Regiment*, 83.

21 Appendix, "'A' Coy," 4.

22 Lieut. E.F. Carron, "Escape," http://thercr.ca/history/1939-1945/escape_1943.htm (accessed 26 June 2008).

23 Galloway, *Bravely Into Battle*, 86–87.

24 Carron.

25 Powers, n.p.

26 Appendix: "'A' Coy," 4.

27 Appendix, "Part Played by 'C' Coy in Sicilian Campaign," in Royal Canadian Regiment War Diary, July 1943, Library and Archives Canada, 3.

28 Stevens, *The Royal Canadian Regiment*, 84.

29 Galloway, *Bravely Into Battle*, 88.

30 Nicholson, *Canadians in Italy*, 150–51.

31 Seaforth Highlanders of Canada War Diary, August 1943, Library and Archives Canada, n.p.

32 Nicholson, *Canadians in Italy*, 151.

33 Farley Mowat, *The Regiment*, 2nd ed. (Toronto: McClelland & Stewart, 1973), 99.

34 Hastings and Prince Edward War Diary, Library and Archives Canada, n.p.

35 Mowat, *The Regiment*, 99.

36 Historical Officer, "Report No. 135," 92.

37 Hastings and Prince Edward War Diary, n.p.

38 Historical Officer, "Report No. 135," 92.

39 Hastings and Prince Edward War Diary, n.p.

40 Nicholson, *Canadians in Italy*, 151.

41 Historical Officer, "Report No. 135," 92.

42 Nicholson, *Canadians in Italy*, 151–52.

43 Hastings and Prince Edward War Diary, n.p.

44 Nicholson, *Canadians in Italy*, 152.

45 Historical Officer, "Report No. 135," 93–94.

46 Kenneth B. Smith, *Duffy's Regiment: A History of the Hastings and Prince Edward Regiment* (Toronto: Dundurn, 1987), 101–02.

22: SUCH A PARTY

1 G.W.L. Nicholson, *The Canadians in Italy, 1939–1945*, vol. 2 (Ottawa: Queen's Printer, 1956), 153.

2 Historical Officer, Canadian Military Headquarters, "Report No. 135: Canadian Operations in Sicily, July–August 1943, Part II: The Execution of the Operation by 1 Cdn Inf Div, Section 2: The Pursuit of the Germans from Vizzini to Adrano 15 Jul–6 Aug," Directorate of Heritage and History, Department of National Defence, 94.

3 2nd Canadian Infantry Brigade War Diary, July 1943, Library and Archives Canada, n.p.

4 Chris Vokes, *My Story* (Ottawa: Gallery Press, 1985), 118.

5 2nd Canadian Infantry Brigade War Diary, n.p.

6 Nicholson, *Canadians in Italy*, 154.

7 Loyal Edmonton War Diary, August 1943, Library and Archives Canada, n.p.

8 Ibid., n.p.

9 Ibid.

10 Ken MacLeod, *Born to Be a Soldier: Johnny Dougan in WW2 in His Own Words* (n.p., 2006), 7.

11 Nicholson, *Canadians in Italy*, 155.

12 "Account by Capt. C.H. Pritchard, Edmn R., formerly Adjutant and now carrier pl. comd. Given in bn. rest area, 18 Aug 43, near Militello in Val di Catania," RG24, vol. 10982, Library and Archives Canada, 32.

13 Nicholson, *Canadians in Italy*, 155.

14 Pritchard, 32.

15 Historical Officer, "Report No. 135," III.

16 "Accounts by Capt F.N. Pope, 10, 2 Cdn Inf Bde on the battles of Leonforte and Aderno," RG24, vol. 10982, Library and Archives Canada, 17.

17 Loyal Edmonton War Diary, n.p.

18 MacLeod, 7.

19 Historical Officer, "Report No. 135," 98.

20 Nicholson, *Canadians in Italy*, 156.

21 Historical Officer, "Report No. 135," 98.

22 2nd Canadian Infantry Brigade War Diary, n.p.

23 Pritchard, 33.

24 Loyal Edmonton War Diary, n.p.

25 R.H. Roy, *The Seaforth Highlanders of Canada, 1919–1965* (Vancouver: Evergreen Press, 1969), 192.

26 3rd Canadian Field Company, RCE War Diary, August 1943, Library and Archives Canada, n.p.

27 Col. A.J. Kerry and Maj. W.A. McDill, *History of the Corps of Royal Canadian Engineers*, vol. 2 (Ottawa: Military Engineers Association of Canada, 1966), 146.

28 Roy, 193.

29 Seaforth Highlanders of Canada War Diary, August 1943, Library and Archives Canada, n.p.

30 Ibid.

31 Historical Officer, "Report No. 135," 100–01.

32 Seaforth Highlanders War Diary, n.p.

33 Roy, 194.

34 Nicholson, *Canadians in Italy*, 157.

35 Princess Patricia's Canadian Light Infantry War Diary, August 1943, Library and Archives Canada, 5.

36 C.J.C. Molony, *The Mediterranean and Middle East: The Campaign in Sicily 1943 and The Campaign in Italy 3rd September 1943 to 31st March 1944* (London: Her Majesty's Stationery Office, 1973), 164.

37 Historical Officer, "Report No. 135," 102.

38 Nicholson, *Canadians in Italy*, 158.

39 Historical Officer, "Report No. 135," 104–05.

40 Three Rivers Tank Regiment War Diary, August 1943, Library and Archives Canada, 3.

41 Bert Hoffmeister correspondence, 27 April 1967, Dr. Reginald Roy Collection, University of Victoria Special Collections, 1.

42 Historical Officer, "Report No. 135," 106.

43 Nicholson, *Canadians in Italy*, 160.

44 "A Squadron, 4 Cdn Recce Regt (4 PLDG)," 141.4A4011(D5), Directorate of Heritage and History, Department of National Defence, 80.

45 R.M. Black correspondence, 3 June 1967, Dr. Reginald Roy Collection, University of Victoria, Special Collections, 1.

46 Henry "Budge" Bell-Irving correspondence, 24 April 1967, Dr. Reginald Roy Collection, University of Victoria Special Collections, 1–2.

47 Black correspondence, 2.

48 Bell-Irving correspondence.

49 Roy, 199–201.

50 Black correspondence, 3–4.

51 Nicholson, *Canadians in Italy*, 160–61.

52 Historical Officer, "Report No. 135," 110.

53 Three Rivers Tank War Diary, 5B.

54 Nicholson, *Canadians in Italy*, 161.

23: ON A BARREN SICILIAN MOUNTAINSIDE

1 "Account by Capt. C.H. Pritchard, Edmn R., formerly Adjutant and now carrier pl. comd. Given in bn. rest area, 18 Aug 43, near Militello in Val di Catania," RG24, vol. 10982, Library and Archives Canada, 17.

2 John Alpine Dougan, interview by author, Victoria, 30 October 1998.

3 Pritchard, 33.

4 Dougan interview.

5 John Alpine Dougan, interview by Tom Torrie, 27 July 1989, University of Victoria Special Collections.

6 Dougan interview by author.

7 G.R. Stevens, *A City Goes to War* (Brampton, ON: Charters Publishing, 1964).

8 Historical Officer, Canadian Military Headquarters, "Report No. 135: Canadian Operations in Sicily, July–August 1943, Part II: The Execution of the Operation by 1 Cdn Inf Div, Section 2: The Pursuit of the Germans from Vizzini to Adrano 15 Jul–6 Aug," Directorate of Heritage and History, Department of National Defence, 112.

9 2nd Canadian Infantry War Diary, August 1943, Library and Archives Canada, n.p.

10 Princess Patricia's Canadian Light Infantry War Diary, August 1943, Library and Archives Canada, 6.

11 C. Sydney Frost, *Once a Patricia: Memoirs of a Junior Infantry Officer in World War II* (Ottawa: Borealis Press, 2004), 122.

12 Major D. Brain, "Sicilian Campaign—The Advance to Monte Seggio," in "Accounts of Actions during the Sicilian campaign as prepared by various officers of the Princess Patricia's Canadian Light Infantry," RG24, vol. 10982, Library and Archives Canada, 49–50.

13 2nd Canadian Infantry Brigade War Diary, August 1943, n.p.

14 Historical Officer, "Report No. 135," 112.

15 Pritchard, 33.

16 Frost, 123–24.

17 G.W.L. Nicholson, *The Canadians in Italy, 1939–1945*, vol. 2 (Ottawa: Queen's Printer, 1956), 163.

18 Frost, 124.

19 Princess Patricia's Canadian Light Infantry War Diary, August 1943, 6.

20 Nicholson, *Canadians in Italy*, 163.

21 Chris Vokes, *My Story* (Ottawa: Gallery Press, 1985), 119–20.

22 Royal 22e Régiment War Diary, August 1943, Library and Archives Canada, 3–4.

23 Nicholson, *Canadians in Italy*, 166–67.

24 Lex Schragg, *History of the Ontario Regiment, 1866–1951* (n.p., n.d.), 117–18.

25 "Account by Lt-Col. M.F. Johnston, OC 11 C.T.R. (The Ontario Regt), given at the Regimental Rest Area nr Scordia, 25 Aug 43," RG24, vol. 10990, Library and Archives Canada, 19.

26 Schragg, 122.

27 11th Canadian Army Tank Regiment (Ontario Regiment) War Diary, August 1943, Library and Archives Canada, n.p.

28 "Diary of Major Durnford," RG24, vol. 20405, Library and Archives Canada, 63.

29 Robert Law McDougall, "Letter to Mother," 8 August 1943, Robert Law McDougall Fonds, R-10755, Library and Archives Canada, 1.

30 Historical Officer, "Report No. 135," 122.

31 Vokes, 122–29.

32 Robert Tooley, *Invicta: The Carleton and York Regiment in the Second World War* (Fredericton, NB: New Ireland Press, 1989), 141–42.

33 Dominick Graham, *The Price of Command: A Biography of General Guy Simonds* (Toronto: Stoddart Publishing, 1993), 101.

34 Nicholson, *Canadians in Italy*, 171–75.

35 Historical Officer, "Report No. 135," 128.

36 Strome Galloway, *Some Died at Ortona* (n.p., n.d.), 145.

37 Durnford, 63.

BIBLIOGRAPHY

BOOKS

Astor, Gerald. *Terrible Terry Allen: Combat General of World War II—The Life of an American Soldier.* New York: Ballantine Books, 2003.

Atkinson, Rick. *The Day of Battle: The War in Sicily and Italy, 1943–1944.* New York: Henry Holt and Company, 2007.

Beattie, Kim. *Dileas: History of the 48th Highlanders of Canada, 1929–1956.* Toronto: 48th Highlanders of Canada, 1957.

Bennett, Ralph. *Ultra and Mediterranean Strategy, 1944–1945.* London: Hamish Hamilton, 1989.

Bercuson, David. *The Patricias: The Proud History of a Fighting Regiment.* Toronto: Stoddart Publishing, 2001.

Blumenson, Martin. *The Patton Papers: 1940–1945.* Boston: Houghton Mifflin, 1974.

Boissonault, Charles-Marie. *Histoire du Royal 22e Régiment.* Québec: Éditions du Pélican, 1964.

Bradley, Omar N., and Clay Blair. *A General's Life: An Autobiography.* New York: Simon and Schuster, 1983.

Brodsky, Gabriel Wilfrid Stephen. *God's Dodger.* Sidney, BC: Elysium Publishing, 1993.

Bryant, Arthur. *The Turn of the Tide: A History of the War Years Based on the Diaries of Field-Marshal Lord Alanbrooke, Chief of the Imperial General Staff.* Garden City, NY: Doubleday, 1957.

Canada. Canadian Army. Royal Regiment of Canadian Artillery. *History of the 1st Anti-Tank Regiment, Royal Canadian Artillery: 5 Sep. 39–31 July 45.* Np., 1945. Canadian War Museum.

———. *History of the Second Field Regiment, RCA: Sep 1939–Jun 1945.* Utrect: Kemink, 1945. Canadian War Museum.

———. *History of the 3rd Canadian Field Regiment, Royal Canadian Artillery—September, 1939 to July, 1945.* N.p., 1945. Canadian War Museum.

Canada. Department of National Defence. *The Canadian Army at War. Vol. 2, From Pachino to Ortona: The Canadian Campaign in Sicily and Italy, 1943.* 2nd ed. Ottawa: King's Printer, 1946.

Churchill, Winston S. *The Second World War. Vol. 5, Closing the Ring.* London: Cassell, 1952.

Dancocks, Daniel G. *The D-Day Dodgers: The Canadians in Italy, 1943–1945.* Toronto: McClelland & Stewart, 1991.

Delaney, Douglas E. *The Soldier's General: Bert Hoffmeister at War.* Vancouver: UBC Press, 2005.

D'Este, Carlo. *Bitter Victory: The Battle for Sicily, 1943.* New York: Harper Perennial, 1988.

———. *Patton: A Genius for War.* New York: Harper Collins, 1995.

Douglas, W.A.B., et al. *A Blue Water Navy: The Official Operational History of the Royal Canadian Navy in the Second World War.* Vol. 2, pt. 2. St. Catharines, ON: Vanwell Publishing, 2007.

Eisenhower, Dwight D. *Crusade in Europe.* Garden City, NY: Doubleday, 1948.

Freasby, W.R., ed. *Official History of the Canadian Medical Services, 1939–1945.* Vol.1, *Organization and Campaigns.* Ottawa: Queen's Printer, 1956.

———. *Official History of the Canadian Medical Services, 1939–1945.* Vol. 2, *Clinical Subjects.* Ottawa: Queen's Printer, 1953.

Frost, C. Sydney. *Once a Patricia: Memoirs of a Junior Infantry Officer in World War II.* Ottawa: Borealis Press, 2004.

Galloway, Strome. *A Regiment at War: The Story of The Royal Canadian Regiment, 1939–1945.* Reprinted by Royal Canadian Regiment, 1979.

———. *Bravely Into Battle: The Autobiography of a Canadian Soldier in World War II.* Toronto: Stoddart Publishing, 1988.

———. *Sicily to the Siegfried Line: Being Some Random Memories and a Diary of 1944–1945.* Kitchener, ON: Arnold Press, n.d.

———. *Some Died at Ortona.* N.p., n.d.

Garland, Albert N., and Howard McGaw Smyth. *United States in World War II: The Mediterranean Theatre of Operations, Sicily and the Surrender of Italy.* Washington, DC: Center of Military History, United States Army, 1993.

Graham, Dominick. *The Price of Command: A Biography of General Guy Simonds.* Toronto: Stoddart Publishing, 1993.

Graham, Howard. *Citizen and Soldier: The Memoirs of Lieutenant-General Howard Graham.* Toronto: McClelland & Stewart, 1987.

Granatstein, J.L. *Canada's Army: Waging War and Keeping the Peace.* Toronto: University of Toronto Press, 2002.

———. *The Generals: The Canadian Army's Senior Commanders in the Second World War.* Toronto: Stoddart Publishing, 1993.

Hamilton, Nigel. *Monty: Master of the Battlefield, 1942–1944.* London: Hamish Hamilton, 1983.

Higgins, Turnbull. *Soft Underbelly: The Anglo-American Controversy Over the Italian Campaign, 1939–1945.* New York: Macmillan, 1968.

Hogg, Ian V., and John Weeks. *Military Small Arms of the 20th Century.* 6th ed. Northbrook, IL: DBI Books, n.d.

Jackson, Lt.-Col. H.M. *The Princess Louise Dragoon Guards: A History.* Ottawa: The Regiment, 1952.

———. *The Royal Regiment of Artillery, Ottawa, 1855–1952.* N.p., 1952.

Jackson, W.G.F. *Alexander of Tunis: As Military Commander.* London: B.T. Batsford, 1971.

Kerry, Col. A.J., and Maj. W.A. McDill. *History of the Corps of Royal Canadian Engineers.* Vol. 2. Ottawa: Military Engineers Association of Canada, 1966.

Kesselring, Albert. *The Memoirs of Field Marshal Kesselring.* Translated by Lynton Hudson. London: William Kimber, 1953.

Kitching, George. *Mud and Green Fields: The Memoirs of Major General George Kitching.* Langley, BC: Battleline Books, 1985.

MacLeod, Ken. *Born to Be a Soldier: Johnny Dougan in WW2 in His Own Words.* N.p., 2006.

Malone, Richard S. *A Portrait of War: 1939–1943.* Don Mills: Collins Publishers, 1983.

Marteinson, John, and Michael R. McNorgan. *The Royal Armoured Corps: An Illustrated History.* Toronto: Robin Brass Studio, 2000.

McAndrew, Bill. *Canadians and the Italian Campaign, 1943–1945.* Montreal: Éditions Art Global, 1996.

McDougall, Robert L. *A Narrative of War: From the Beaches of Sicily to the Hitler Line With the Seaforth Highlanders of Canada.* Ottawa: Golden Dog Press, 1996.

Mitcham, Samuel W., Jr., and Friedrich von Stauffenberg. *The Battle of Sicily.* New York: Orion Books, 1991.

Mitchell, Major G.D. RCHA—*Right of the Line: An Anecdotal History of the Royal Canadian Horse Artillery from 1871.* Ottawa: RCHA History Committee, 1986.

Mitchell, Howard. *My War with the Saskatoon Light Infantry (M.G.) 1939–1945.* N.p., n.d.

Moir, John S., ed. *History of the Royal Canadian Corps of Signals, 1903–1961.* Ottawa: Corps Committee, Royal Canadian Corps of Signals, 1962.

Molony, C.J.C. *The Mediterranean and Middle East: The Campaign in Sicily 1943 and The Campaign in Italy 3rd September 1943 to 31st March 1944.* London: Her Majesty's Stationery Office, 1973.

Montgomery, Bernard Law. *El Alamein to the River Sangro.* New York: St. Martin's Press, 1948.

———. *The Memoirs of Field Marshal The Viscount Montgomery of Alamein, K.G.* London: Collins, 1958.

Morris, Eric. *Circles of Hell: The War In Italy, 1943–1945.* New York: Crown Publishers, 1993.

Mowat, Farley. *And No Birds Sang.* Toronto: McClelland & Stewart, 1979.

———. *The Regiment.* 2nd ed. Toronto: McClelland & Stewart, 1973.

Munro, Ross. *Gauntlet to Overlord: The Story of the Canadian Army.* Toronto: Macmillan Company of Canada, 1945.

———. *Red Patch in Sicily: The Story of the 1st Canadian Division in Action.* Toronto: Canadian Press, 1943.

Neillands, Robin. *Eighth Army: From the Western Desert to the Alps, 1939–1945.* London: John Murray, 2004.

Nicholson, G.W.L. *The Canadians in Italy.* Vol. 2. Ottawa: Queen's Printer, 1956.

———. *The Gunners of Canada.* Vol. 2. Toronto: McClelland & Stewart, 1972.

Nicolson, Nigel. *Alex: The Life of Field Marshal Alexander of Tunis.* London: Weidenfeld and Nicolson, 1973.

Orgill, Douglas. *The Gothic Line: The Italian Campaign, Autumn 1944.* New York: W.W. Norton, 1967.

Parrish, Thomas, ed. *The Simon and Schuster Encyclopedia of World War II*. New York: Simon and Schuster, 1978.

Pond, Hugh. *Sicily*. London: William Kimber, 1962.

Quayle, J.T.B. *In Action: A Personal Account of the Italian and Netherlands Campaigns of WW II*. Abbotsford, BC: Blue Stone Publishers, 1997.

Raddall, Thomas H. *West Novas: A History of the West Nova Scotia Regiment*. N.p., 1947.

Rannie, William F., ed. *To the Thunderer His Arms: The Royal Canadian Ordnance Corps*. Lincoln, ON: W.F. Rannie, 1984.

Reid, George A. *Speed's War: A Canadian Soldier's Memoirs of World War II*. Royston, BC: Madrona Books & Publishing, 2007.

Roy, Reginald H. *The Seaforth Highlanders of Canada, 1919–1965*. Vancouver: Evergreen Press, 1969.

Ryder, Rowland. *Oliver Leese*. London: Hamish Hamilton, 1987.

Schragg, Lex. *History of the Ontario Regiment: 1866–1951*. N.p., n.d.

Shepperd, G.A. *The Italian Campaign, 1943–45: A Political and Military Re-assessment*. London: Arthur Baker, 1968.

Smith, Kenneth B. *Duffy's Regiment: A History of the Hastings and Prince Edward Regiment*. Toronto: Dundurn, 1987.

Smith, Waldo E.L. *What Time the Tempest: An Army Chaplain's Story*. Toronto: Ryerson Press, 1953.

Stacey, C.P. *The Canadian Army, 1939–1945: An Official Historical Summary*. Ottawa: King's Printer, 1948.

Stevens, G.R. *A City Goes to War*. Brampton, ON: Charters Publishing, 1964.

———. *The Royal Canadian Regiment*. Vol. 2. London, ON: London Print & Lithography, 1967.

———. *Princess Patricias Canadian Light Infantry: 1919–1957*. Vol. 3. Griesbach, AB: Historical Committee of the Regiment, n.d.

Stursberg, Peter. *The Sound of War*. Toronto: University of Toronto Press, 1993.

Tooley, Robert. *Invicta: The Carleton and York Regiment in the Second World War*. Fredericton, NB: New Ireland Press, 1989.

2 CDN LAA [Light Anti-Aircraft] *Reg't RCA*. N.p., 1945. Canadian War Museum.

Vokes, Chris. *Vokes: My Story*. Ottawa: Gallery, 1985.

Wallace, John F. *Dragons of Steel: Canadian Armour in Two World Wars*. Burstown, ON: General Store Publishing House, 1995.

Warlimont, Walter. *Inside Hitler's Headquarters, 1939–1945*. Translated by R.H. Barry. New York: Frederick A. Praeger, 1964.

Whitlock, Flint. *The Rock of Anzio: From Sicily to Dachau—A History of the 45th Infantry Division*. Boulder, CO: Westview Press, 1998.

JOURNALS

McAndrew, Bill. "Fire or Movement? Canadian Tactical Doctrine, Sicily—1943." *Military Affairs*. Vol. 51, no. 3 (July 1987).

Thomson, Col. S.W. "Wounded in Sicily: 12 July 1943." *Canadian Military History*. Vol. 2, no. 2 (Autumn 1993).

Vokes, Chris. "Some Reflections on Operational Command." *Canadian Army Journal*. Vol. 2, no. 10 (January 1949).

WEBSITES

Carron, Lt. E.F. "Escape." http://thercr.ca/history/1939-1945/escape_1943carron.htm (accessed June 18, 2008).

Hodson, Lt. Col. Ian. "'D' Day Sicily, 10 July 43." http://thercr.ca/history/1939-1945/d-day_sicily_10jul43.htm (accessed June 18, 2008).

"Fighting the U-boats: Ships hit by U-boats—Allied ships hit by U-boats": *City of Venice,* http://www.uboat.net/allies/merchants/2978.html; *Devis* http://www.uboat.net/allies/merchants/2981.html; *St. Essylt* http://www.uboat.net/allies/merchants/ship.html?shipID=2977 (all accessed June 18, 2008).

"Italian Campaign," http://www.vac-acc.gc.ca/general/sub.cfm?source=feature/italy99/ithistory/armynavy (accessed June 18, 2008). A feature in the Archives section of the Veterans' Affairs Canada Web site, commemorating the 55th anniversary in 1999.

http://www.junobeach.org/e/4/can-tac-lca-e.htm (accessed July 9, 2008).

Liddell, Maj. R.G. "The Assault on the Beaches of Pachino, Sicily; July 1943." http://thercr.ca/history/1939-1945/pachino_1943_liddell.htm (accessed June 18, 2008).

Lithgow, Maj. C.H. "The Battle of Nissoria; 24 July 1943." http://thercr.ca/history/1939-1945/nissoria_1943.htm (accessed June 18, 2008).

Mahnke, Jochen. "Assault on Sicily, 1943," *Military History Journal.* Vol. 7, no. 2 (December 1986). http://rapidttp.com/milhist/vol072jm.html (accessed June 18, 2008).

UNPUBLISHED MATERIALS

"ADMS 1st Canadian Infantry Division War Diary, July–August 1943." RG24, Library and Archives Canada.

"Appreciation by Comd 1 CDN DIV at Norfolk House 27 Apr 43." RG24, vol. 10878, Library and Archives Canada.

"A Squadron, 4 Cdn Recce Regt (4 PLDG)." 141.4A4011(D5), Directorate of Heritage and History, Department of National Defence.

Atkinson, Sheridan, and Harold Ghent. "The 'Liberation' of Modica, Sicily." Unpublished manuscript, possession of the author.

Brain, Major D. "The initial landing in Sicily," in "Accounts of Actions during the Sicilian campaign as prepared by various officers of the Princess Patricia's Canadian Light Infantry." RG24, vol. 10982, Library and Archives Canada.

Campbell, Major A.R., and Captain N.R. Waugh. "Account given by Major A.R. Campbell Officer Commanding 'A' Company and Captain N.R. Waugh, MC, Officer Commanding 'D' Company, Hastings and Prince Edward Regiment, on August 18, 1943, at Battalion Rest Area near Militello in val di Catania, Sicily." RG24, vol. 10880, Library and Archives Canada.

Carleton and York Regiment War Diary, July–August 1943. RG24, Library and Archives Canada.

Cessford, Michael Pearson. "Hard in the Attack: The Canadian Army in Sicily and Italy, July 1943–June 1944." PhD thesis, Carleton University, September 1996.

Coleman, Major R. "Major Coleman, MC, 'Sicilian Campaign—Leonforte,'" in "Accounts of Actions during the Sicilian campaign as prepared by various officers of the Princess Patricia's Canadian Light Infantry." RG24, vol. 10982, Library and Archives Canada.

"Comments by Seaforth Veterans on Chapter VI." Reginald H. Roy Collection, University of Victoria Special Collections.

Cromb, W.T. "Further Discussion With Lt-Col Cromb, 13 Dec 49," RG24, vol. 10981, Library and Archives Canada.

Durnford, Roy C.H. "Diary of Major Roy Durnford, Chaplain (Padre), the Seaforth Highlanders of Canada, June 1943–June 1945." RG24, vol. 20405, Library and Archives Canada.

11th Canadian Army Tank Regiment (Ontario Regiment) War Diary, August 1943. RG24, Library and Archives Canada.

"Employment of Snipers in Sicily and Italian Campaign." RG24, vol. 10883, Library and Archives Canada.

Farquharson, Lt. Col. D.G.J. "An Account given by Lt.-Col. D.G.J. Farquharson, R.C.O.C., ADOS 1 Cdn Div, at Rear Div HQ nr Regalbuto, 7 Aug 43." RG24, vol. 10878, Library and Archives Canada.

5th Canadian Field Ambulance War Diary, July–August 1943. RG24, Library and Archives Canada.

1 Canadian Division Operation Order No. 1, 7 Jun, 43. RG24, vol. 10879, Library and Archives Canada.

1st Canadian Field Company, RCE War Diary, July–August 1943. RG24, Library and Archives Canada.

1st Canadian Infantry Brigade War Diary, July–August 1943. RG24, Library and Archives Canada,

1st Canadian Infantry Division, General Staff War Diary, July–August 1943. RG24, Library and Archives Canada.

48th Highlanders of Canada War Diary, July–August 1943. RG24, Library and Archives Canada.

4th Canadian Field Ambulance War Diary, July–August 1943. RG24, Library and Archives Canada.

4th Canadian Field Regiment, RCE War Diary, July–August 1943. RG24, Library and Archives Canada.

4th Reconnaissance Regiment (Princess Louise Dragoon Guards) War Diary, July–August 1943. RG24, Library and Archives Canada.

Harris, A.K. "Account by A.K. Harris." Dr. Reginald Roy Papers. University of Victoria Special Collections.

Hastings and Prince Edward Regiment War Diary, July–August 1943. RG24, Library and Archives Canada.

Headquarters, 1st Divisional Artillery, RCA War Diary, July–August 1943. RG24, Library and Archives Canada.

Heggie, R.H. "Three Rivers Regiment History of WW II." Unpublished manuscript. Michael Boire Collection.

"The Historical Account of the Fighting Operations of the 12th Canadian Tank Regiment (Three Rivers Regiment of Quebec) from the Time of Their Landing in Sicily Up to and Including Their Last Action Fought West of Adrano on August the 5th, 1943." RG24, vol. 10990, Library and Archives Canada.

Historical Section (G.S), Army Headquarters. "Report No. 14, The Sicilian Campaign (July–August 1943), Information from German Sources." University of Victoria Special Collections.

Historical Officer, Canadian Military Headquarters. "Report No. 126, Canadian Operations in Sicily, July–August 1943, Part I: The Preliminaries of Operation 'Husky' (The Assault on Sicily)." Directorate of Heritage and History, Department of National Defence.

———. "Report No. 127, Canadian Operations in Sicily, July–August 1943, Part II: The Execution of the Operation by 1 Cdn Inf Div, Section 1: The Assault and Initial Penetration Inland." Directorate of Heritage and History, Department of National Defence.

———. "Report No. 132, Canadian Operations in Sicily, July–August 1943 Part III: The Story of 1 Cdn Army Tk Bde." Directorate of Heritage and History, Department of National Defence.

———. "Report No. 135, Canadian Operations in Sicily, July–August 1943, Part II: The Execution of the Operation by 1 Cdn Inf Div, Section 2: The Pursuit of the Germans from Vizzini to Adrano 15 Jul–6 Aug." Directorate of Heritage and History, Department of National Defence.

"Italian Campaign—Sicily and Southern Italy, July 1943–April 1945." Condensed from an Official Historical Sketch prepared by the Canadian Army Historical Section. N.a., n.d., n.p. Directorate of History, Department of National Defence.

Jefferson, Brigadier J.C. "Interview D.D.H.S. with Brigadier J.C. Jefferson," RG24, vol. 10982, Library and Archives Canada.

Johnston, Lt. Col. I.S. "Account by Lieutenant-Colonel I.S. Johnston, Officer Commanding 48 Highlanders given on 14 August 1943 at the Battalion Rest Area near Scordia." RG24, vol. 10880, Library and Archives Canada.

Johnston, Lt. Col. M.F. "Account by Lt-Col. M.F. Johnston, OC 11 C.T.R. (The Ontario Regt), given at the Regimental Rest Area nr Scordia, 25 Aug 43," RG24, vol. 10990, Library and Archives Canada.

Latimer, Richard Victor. "The Gibblers: Or Balmorals and Bully Beef." Unpublished manuscript. Possession of the author.

Lindsay, Lt. Col. R.A. "Statement by Lt-Col. R.A. Lindsay on the Engagements of the PPCLI from battle at Piazza Armerina to the battle for Agira given on 30 Jul 43." RG24, vol. 10982, Library and Archives Canada.

Loyal Edmonton Regiment War Diary, July 1943. RG24, Library and Archives Canada.

"Major-General C. Vokes, CB, CBE, DSO biography," Directorate of History, Department of National Defence.

"Message Form, 15 Army Group to 7 Army & 8 Army," July 1943. RG24, vol. 10994, Library and Archives Canada.

9th Canadian Field Ambulance War Diary, July–August 1943. RG24, Library and Archives Canada.

No. 1 Canadian Field Dressing Station War Diary, July–August 1943. RG24, Library and Archives Canada.

No. 1 Canadian Field Surgical Unit War Diary, July–August 1943. RG24, Library and Archives Canada.

No. 2 Canadian Field Surgical Unit War Diary, July–August 1943. RG24, Library and Archives Canada.

OB Southwest. "Report on the Fighting in Sicily from 10 Jul–17 Aug 43." RG24, vol. 20959, Library and Archives Canada.

Pope, Capt. F.N. "Account by Capt F.N. Pope, 10, 2 Cdn Inf Bde on the battles of Leonforte and Aderno," RG24, vol. 10982, Library and Archives Canada.

Potts, Captain R.W. "The Regiments First Contact With the Germans" in "Accounts of Actions during the Sicilian campaign as prepared by various officers of the Princess Patricia's Canadian Light Infantry." RG24, vol. 10982, Library and Archives Canada.

Powers, Maj. T.M. "Account given by Major T.M. Powers, second-in-command, Royal Canadian Regiment, on 18 August 1943 in Battalion rest area near Scordia, Sicily." RG24, vol. 10880, Library and Archives Canada.

Prieur, Charlie. "Chronicles of the Three Rivers Regiment (Tank) at War." Unpublished manuscript. Michael Boire Private Collection.

Princess Patricia's Canadian Light Infantry War Diary, July–August 1943. RG24, Library and Archives Canada.

Pritchard, Capt. C.H. "Account by Capt. C.H. Pritchard, Edmn R., formerly Adjutant and now carrier pl. comd. Given in bn rest area, 18 Aug 43, near Militello in Val di Catania," RG24, vol. 10982, Library and Archives Canada.

Royal Canadian Regiment War Diary, July–August 1943. RG24, Library and Archives Canada.

Royal 22e Régiment War Diary, July–August 1943. RG24, Library and Archives Canada.

Seaforth Highlanders of Canada War Diary, July–August 1943. RG24, Library and Archives Canada.

2nd Canadian Field Regiment (RCA) War Diary, July–August 1943. RG24, Library and Archives Canada.

2nd Canadian Infantry Brigade War Diary, July–August 1943. RG24, Library and Archives Canada.

2nd Field Park Company, RCE War Diary, July–August 1943. RG24, Library and Archives Canada.

Sesia, Captain A.T. Personal Notes and Observations: Part I–Sicily, 24 Apr. 43–2 Sep. 43. RG24, vol. 10878, Library and Archives Canada.

Smith, Basil. "Memoirs of a Quarterbloke: Hastings and Prince Edward Regiment Canadian Army Overseas." N.p., n.d. Directorate of History, Department of National Defence.

"Street Fighting in Agira." In "Accounts of Actions during the Sicilian campaign as prepared by various officers of the Princess Patricia's Canadian Light Infantry." RG24, vol. 10982, Library and Archives Canada.

3rd Canadian Field Company, RCE War Diary, July–August 1943. RG24, Library and Archives Canada.

3rd Canadian Infantry Brigade War Diary, July–August 1943. RG24, Library and Archives Canada.

Tweedsmuir, Lord. "Personal Account by Lt.-Col The Lord Tweedsmuir of the Sicilian Campaign." 145.241011(D31), Directorate of Heritage and History, Department of National Defence.

12th Canadian Tank Regiment (Three Rivers Tank Regiment) War Diary, July–August 1943. RG24, Library and Archives Canada.

Viscount Alexander of Tunis. "The Conquest of Sicily." MG27, vol. III AI, Library and Archives Canada.

Wallace, J.F. "Diary of Lt. J.F. Wallace." MG30, vol. 1, Library and Archives Canada.

West Nova Scotia War Diary, July–August 1943. RG24, Library and Archives Canada.

INTERVIEWS AND CORRESPONDENCE.

Atkinson, Sheridan. Correspondence with author. November 17, 2007.

Henry "Budge" Bell-Irving. Correspondence with Reginald Roy. February 20, April 24, and May 3, 1967. Reginald Roy Papers, University of Victoria Special Collections.

———. Interview by Ken MacLeod. Vancouver, n.d.

Black, R.M. Correspondence with Reginald Roy. June 3, 1967. Reginald Roy Papers, University of Victoria Special Collections.

Bowen, Norm. Interview by A.E. "Tony" Delamere. Ottawa, September 28, 2000. Canadian War Museum Oral History Project Collection.

Carriere, Felix. Interview by Tom Torrie. Victoria, June 4, 1987. University of Victoria Special Collections.

de Faye, Thomas. Interview by author. Victoria, November 3, 1998.

Dougan, John Alpine. Interview by author. Victoria, October 23, 1998.

———. Interview by Ken MacLeod. Victoria, n.d.

———. Interview by Tom Torrie. Victoria, July 17, 1987. University of Victoria Special Collections.

Fairweather, Dave. Correspondence with Reginald Roy. September 10, 1967. Reginald Roy Papers, University of Victoria Special Collections.

Forin, J. Douglas. Correspondence with Reginald Roy. January 19, 1968. Reginald Roy Papers, University of Victoria Special Collections.

———. Memo to Dr. Reginald Roy. N.d. Reginald Roy Papers, University of Victoria Special Collections.

Gibson, Jock. Interview by author. Vancouver, November 23, 1998.

———. Interview by Ken MacLeod. Vancouver, n.d.

Hackett, Bob. Letter. N.d. Possession of author.

Haley, Dr. John. Interview by author. Victoria, October 30, 1998.

Hoffmeister, Bert M. Correspondence with Reginald Roy. April 27, 1967. Reginald Roy Papers, University of Victoria Special Collections.

———. Interview by B. Greenhouse and W. McAndrew. N.d. Transcript 2001/26, Directorate of Heritage and History.

———. Interview by author. Vancouver, November 23, 1998.

Kingstone, Robert. Interview by D.W. Edgecombe. October 6, 2000. Canadian War Museum.

Lenko, Sam. Interview by author. Edmonton, October 4, 1998.

McDougall, Robert Law. "Letter to Mother." July 1943. Robert Law McDougall Fonds, R-10755, Library and Archives Canada.

Mitchell, G.D. Correspondence with author. August 30, 1998.

———. Interview with author. Ottawa, September 5, 1998.

Pope, Frederick Norman. Interview by Chris Bell. May 31, June 7, 10, 15, and 22, 1982. University of Victoria Special Collections.

Rankin, Harry. Interview by author. Vancouver, October 15, 1998.

Stone, James Riley. Interview by William S. Thackray. Victoria, May 13 and 20 and June 3, 10, and 17, 1980. University of Victoria Special Collections.

Thomas, E.W. "June." Interview by author. Victoria, October 23, 1998.

Ware, Cameron. Interview by Reginald Roy. Victoria, June 23 and 25, and July 10, 1979. University of Victoria Special Collections.

Worton, Bill. Written summary. N.d. Possession of author.

GENERAL INDEX

Ranks given for individuals are highest attained as of August 6, 1943

Adams, RSM Bill, 153
Aderno. *See* Adrano
Adrano, 179, 234, 236, 238, 288–89, 356–57, 363, 366, 368, 371, 376, 379, 381–82, 386, 389, 391–94, 406–08, 416
Agira, 7, 236, 288–91, 293, 298–99, 301–03, 306, 312–16, 319–21, 324, 326–28, 334, 336–41, 343, 345, 347, 348–54, 361, 364, 366–67, 369, 371–72, 386, 388, 390, 399, 410, 416, 418–19
Agrigento, 182, 198, 200
Alexander, Gen. Harold, 33–35, 37–43, 44, 55, 181–82, 184, 186, 198–200, 233–35, 249, 288–89, 353, 356
Algiers, 31, 34, 38, 41, 50, 53, 80–81, 84–86
Allen, Maj. Gen. Terry, 247, 249
Allen, Ralph, 380
Allen, Sgt. J.A. "Les," 308, 310–11
Anfa Camp, 31
Ankcorn, Col. Charles, 194
Antigonish, HMCS, 417
Antonio Giuseppi, 277
Armitage, Pte. Harry, 224–25
Assoro, 236, 239, 244, 245–47, 249–50, 254, 256, 260, 261, 263–66, 284–87, 291, 298, 303, 315, 318, 326, 376, 416, 419
Atkinson, Lt. G.E., 361

Atkinson, Lt. Sheridan "Sherry," 156–65, 255
Auger, Lt. V.O., 330
Augusta, 42, 181

Baade, Oberst Ernst-Günther, 70
Badoglio, Maresciallo d'Italia Pietro, 325
Baldwin, Lt. George, 257, 376–77
Bancroft, Pte. J.A., 266
Banton, Maj. D.W., 285–286, 292, 322
Bark West, 75–77, 101–02, 112, 113, 116, 118, 124, 140, 142–43, 420
Baxter, Capt. G.E., 349
Bay of Biscay, 62
Beament, Brig. Warwick, 49
Beauregard, Lance Sgt. René, 215
Beevor, Capt. T.L., 46
Bellavance, Maj. Charles, 361–62
Bell-Irving, Maj. Henry "Budge," 120, 267, 269, 272, 333–36, 341–42, 346–47, 387, 389, 394–96, 405, 407
Bennett, R.B., 21
Bernatchez, Lt. Col. Paul, 212, 215, 229, 407–08, 413
Betts, Tpr. H.R., 310
Biancavilla, 392
Bilodeau, Capt., 309
Birkenhead, 58
Biscari, 101
Bizerta, 87
Black, CSM R.M., 394–95, 397
Blair, Maj. Jim, 107, 151, 213, 268, 333, 341, 343, 394–95

477

Forin, Maj. Douglas, 239, 268, 270
Forrest, Lance Cpl. Donald, 370
Foster, Capt. Glen, 353
Francofonte, 184
Fraser, Lt. George, 321
Fraser, Sgt. Charlie, 292–93
French, Lt. Arthur Vernon, 268
Frost, Lt. Syd, 5, 19, 403, 405–06, 420

Gagliano, 348, 351
Gagnon, Lance Cpl. Gérard, 362–63
Gagnon, Pte. Jules Alphonse, 363
Gairdner, Maj. Gen. Charles H., 34–35, 37–38
Gallagher, Pte. Omar B., 352
Galloway, Capt. Strome, 5, 19–20, 75, 103–05, 108–09, 119, 129–31, 154–56, 173, 175, 224–25, 228, 250, 252–53, 263, 265–66, 302, 305, 307, 312–15, 320, 371–73, 375, 414–15
Gardner, Pte. Jack, 134
Gay, Brig. Hobart R., 234
Gela, 36, 41, 43, 101, 126, 146–47, 177, 181–82, 200–01
Gela Gulf, 44
Gerbini, 41, 409
Ghent, Lance Sgt. Harold, 156, 162
Giarratana, 165, 169, 172–73, 184
Gibraltar, 45, 50, 64, 87–88
Gibraltar, Straits of, 80
Gibson, Sgt. Jock, 106–07, 111–12
Gilbride, Lt. Col. Preston, 109
Gilchrist, Capt. A.A., 202–03, 344
Glengyle, HMS, 99, 108–09, 123
Gordon, Lt. "Beez," 350
Gornalunga River, 356
Gotti-Porcinari, Generale di Divisione Count Giulio Cesare, 176
Gourock, 61
Gowan, Capt. J.H., 404
Gozo Island, 92
Graham, Brig. Howard, 30, 46, 49, 77, 99–100, 109, 123–24, 137–38, 154–55, 173–74, 186–87, 190–91, 195–97, 211, 227, 242, 254, 256, 262–63, 284, 291, 300–01, 307, 316, 319–22, 326–27, 377

Grammichele, 184, 186, 188–89, 191–92, 193–96
Granite, Tpr. Frank Henry, 308–09
Gray, Capt. Andrew, 99, 109
Gray, Lt., 105
Greenoch, 15, 60–61
Grigas, Pte. Joe, 134, 374
"Grizzly" ridge, 327–28, 330, 333, 336, 340–41, 343–47, 348–49, 354, 389, 411
Guimond, Capt. Bernard, 362
Gunter, Pte. I.J., 191
Guy, Lt. Ross, 357–58, 364
Guzzoni, General d'Armata Alfredo, 146–47, 176, 179, 390

Hackett, Cpl. Bob, 120–21
Hadden, Cpl. D., 397
Hammell, Sgt. James Shannon, 400
Hanson, Pte. Arlie William, 353
Hanson, R.B., 21
Harkness, Maj. Douglas, 83
Harley, Lt. Don, 241
Harling, Lt. Jim, 335, 342, 346–47
Harris, Capt. W.G., 388
Harrison, Lance Sgt. T.W., 353
Harris, Pte. Angus, 121
Hawke, Cpl. F.R., 307
Headley Court, 15
Heilmann, Oberstleutnant Ludwig, 180
Hendon Airport, 45
Hendricks, Pte. Chester, 110
Higgins, Capt. C.B. "Clary," 352
Hilary, HMS, 60, 63, 72, 85–87, 91–92, 99–100, 109, 125, 143
Hill 204, 357, 360–61, 363
Hill 736, 382–83, 385–86, 391–92, 399–402, 405, 417–18
Hitler, Adolf, 16, 64–65, 67, 71, 145, 178–79, 406, 413
Hodson, Capt. Ian, 103, 113–15, 131–32, 134–36, 302, 313–15, 320
Hoffmeister, Lt. Col. Bert, 18–19, 54, 62, 77, 97, 119–20, 138–39, 238–42, 267–72, 333–34, 336–37, 340, 343–44, 346–47, 388–89, 393–96, 398, 404, 407, 412
Hong Kong, Battle of, 16

INDEX OF FORMATIONS,

UNITS, AND CORPS

BRITISH AND COMMONWEALTH

Air Force
Desert Air Force, 299
Northwest African Coast Air Force, 88
Northwest African Strategic Air Force, 89

Army
15th Army Group, 34, 143, 181, 288
Eighth Army, 27, 29–30, 34, 38–42,
44–45, 47, 51, 54, 68, 72, 74, 92, 101,
103, 125, 127, 140, 146, 148, 166, 173–
74, 177, 179, 181–83, 187, 196, 198,
233–34, 236, 288–89, 299, 328, 356,
390–91, 403, 408–09, 413–14

CORPS
XIII Corps, 101, 125, 180, 182–84, 186,
192, 236, 288, 356, 390–91
XXX Corps, 41, 50, 76–77, 99, 101–02,
123, 125–26, 148, 163, 181–82, 184,
196–97, 234–36, 303, 328, 353, 356,
391–92

DIVISIONS
1st Airborne, 101
1st Infantry, 37
3rd Infantry, 28, 34, 37, 45–46
4th Infantry, 37
5th Infantry, 37, 91, 125, 236, 356, 408
50th Infantry, 91, 125, 236
51st Highland, 51, 101–02, 126, 135, 140,
153–55, 165, 181, 184, 186–87, 236, 288,
352–53, 392
56th Infantry, 37
78th Infantry, 37, 288, 357, 391–92, 394,
407–08

ARMOURED BRIGADES/REGIMENTS
4th Armoured Brigade, 183
23rd Armoured Brigade, 181

INFANTRY BRIGADES
1st Airlanding, 101, 127
11th Infantry, 363
13th Infantry, 408
17th Infantry, 125

231st (Malta) Infantry, 91, 99, 101, 126,
236, 288, 290, 321, 328, 352, 361, 368,
370–71, 376
1st Parachute, 180, 183

REGIMENTS/ BATTALIONS
Black Watch, 7th Battalion, 154
Devonshire Regiment, 135, 369–70
Dorsetshire Regiment, 1st Battalion, 367,
370–72
Hampshire Regiment, 1st Battalion, 321,
367–68
London Irish Rifles, 2nd Battalion, 20, 394

ARTILLERY REGIMENTS
7th Medium, 203, 230, 241–42, 271, 300,
393
11th Royal Horse, 393
64th Medium, 300
105th Anti-Tank Regiment, 357
165th Field Regiment, 300, 367, 393
Royal Devon Yeomanry, 158, 165, 186,
190, 200, 203, 230, 300

ROYAL NAVY AND MARINES
Royal Navy. *See also* General Index, ships
by names

ROYAL MARINE COMMANDOS
special Service Brigade, 101, 107, 118, 139,
143
No. 3 Commando, 180, 183
No. 40 Commando, 101, 107, 118, 144
No. 41 Commando, 101, 107, 118, 144

UNITED STATES

Army
Seventh Army, 6, 29, 34–35, 41–42, 44,
51, 92, 101, 155, 165, 181–82, 184, 186,
198–200, 233–34, 247, 356, 391, 414

CORPS
Provisional Corps, 199, 287
II Corps, 35, 101, 126, 182, 198, 234

THIS IS THE seventh volume in Mark Zuehlke's Canadian Battle Series, which chronicles the major campaigns and battles Canada's army fought during World War II. These best-selling books cemented his reputation as the nation's leading writer of popular military history. Noted for their intense combat scenes and depth of research, the series prompted *Quill & Quire* to state that "Zuehlke's skill in writing battle narrative remains unsurpassed." In 2006, the Canadian Battle book *Holding Juno: Canada's Heroic Defence of Canada's D-Day Beaches, June 7–12* won the City of Victoria Butler Book Prize. His Italian Trilogy of *Ortona: Canada's Epic World War II Battle*, *The Liri Valley: Canada's World War II Breakthrough to Rome*, and *The Gothic Line: Canada's Month of Hell in World War II Italy* is considered the definitive narrative of the Canadian army's role in the Italian Campaign. *Operation Husky* can be seen as a prequel to that series.

Zuehlke's five other historical works include *For Honour's Sake: The War of 1812 and the Brokering of an Uneasy Peace*, which won the 2007 Canadian Authors Association Lela Common Award for Canadian History.

Also a novelist, he is the author of the popular Elias McCann crime series. The first in the series, *Hands Like Clouds*, won the Crime Writers of Canada Arthur Ellis Award for Best First Novel in 2000, and the later *Sweep Lotus* was a finalist for the 2004 Arthur Ellis Award for Best Novel. Zuehlke lives in Victoria, British Columbia, and is currently at work on his next Canadian Battle book, which will carry the story forward from where his best-selling 2007 release, *Terrible Victory: First Canadian Army and the Scheldt Estuary Campaign: September 13–November 6, 1944*, left off.

He can be found on the Web at www.zuehlke.ca.